The New Damascus Document

# Studies on the Texts of the Desert of Judah

*Edited by*

Florentino García Martínez

*Associate Editors*

Peter W. Flint
Eibert J.C. Tigchelaar

VOLUME 56

# The New Damascus Document

The Midrash on the Eschatological Torah
of the Dead Sea Scrolls: Reconstruction,
Translation and Commentary

*by*

Ben Zion Wacholder

BRILL

LEIDEN · BOSTON
2007

This book is printed on acid-free paper.

**Library of Congress Cataloging-in-Publication Data**

Wacholder, Ben Zion.
  The new Damascus Document : The midrash on the eschatological Torah of the
Dead Sea Scrolls : reconstruction, translation, and commentary / by
Ben Zion Wacholder.
     p. cm. — (Studies on the texts of the desert of Judah, ISSN 0169-9962 ; v. 56)
  Contains reconstructed text in Hebrew and English, with commentary in English.
  Includes the text of a document reconstructed from manuscripts found in the Cairo
Genizah and from fragments of the Dead Sea scrolls and given the presumed title
"Midrash on the eschatological Torah," taken from the final words of the text.
  Includes bibliographical references and indexes.
  ISBN 90-04-14108-1 (alk. paper)
     1. Zadokites. 2. Qumran community. 3. Eschatology, Jewish. 4. Midrash. 5.
Midrash—History and criticism. I. Dead Sea  scrolls. Selections. English & Hebrew.
2004. II. Title. III. Series.

BM175.Z3W33 2004
296.1'55—dc22

BM
175
.Z3
W33
2007

2004057064

ISSN      0169–9962
ISBN 10:  90 04 14108 1
ISBN 13:  978 90 04 14108 7

PRINTED IN THE NETHERLANDS

In memory of my parents

Pinchas Shelomoh Wacholder and
Tzipporah Faiga Lederman Wacholder
זצ"ל

# TABLE OF CONTENTS

List of Tables .......................................... xi
Acknowledgements ...................................... xiii
Select Abbreviations ................................... xv
Sigla................................................... xvii
Foreword............................................... xix
Midrash ha-Torah ha-Acharon Tables .................... xxiii

Chapter 1. Introduction................................. 1
1.1   Methodogy........................................ 1
      1.1.1   Approach................................. 1
      1.1.2   Restorations and Reconstructions......... 2
1.2   History of MTA .................................. 3
      1.2.1   Date of Composition...................... 3
      1.2.2   Evidence from Medievalists .............. 4
              1.2.2.1   Al-Qirqisani .................. 4
              1.2.2.2   Maimonides ................... 8
      1.2.3   Evidence from Others..................... 8
      1.2.4   Theologizing History..................... 8
1.3   Unification ..................................... 9
1.4   Law ............................................ 12
1.5   Organization, Format and Layout of the Book......14
      1.5.1   Pagination of the Hebrew Text ...........14
      1.5.2   Headers within the Hebrew Text...........14
      1.5.3   Hebrew Text..............................15
      1.5.4   Verb Usage and Time Issues in the Text...16
      1.5.5   Number and Gender Agreement in MTA ......17
      1.5.6   Translation .............................17
      1.5.7   Notes on the Text........................18
      1.5.8   Commentary...............................18
      1.5.9   Headings and Subheadings.................18
      1.5.10  Tables  .................................18
      1.5.11  Indices  ................................19

Chapter 2. Text and Translation ........................21
2.1   Preamble .......................................22
2.2.  Body ...........................................26
2.3   Finale .........................................104

Chapter 3.  Commentary .............................. 109
3.1  Preamble (4Q266 F1; F2i:1–6a / 4Q268 F1:1–8)...... 109
    3.1.1  Prologue .................................. 109
    3.1.2  The Downfall of the Opposition............. 119
    3.1.3  The Promise to Reveal the Mysteries of
           History  .............................. 122
    3.1.4  Supplication.............................. 129
    3.1.5  A Tribute to the "Divisions of Times":
           The Calendation of the Book Of Jubilees ..... 134
    3.1.6  Summary of What the Cave Manuscripts Add
           to CD  .............................. 138
3.2  Body (CD-A; CD-B; assorted Cave manuscripts ending
    with 4Q266 F11:3a)........................... 141
    3.2.1  An Introduction to the Eschatological Torah     141
        3.2.1.1  Announcing the Coming Eschatology  141
        3.2.1.2  A Review of History............... 173
        3.2.1.3  The Sons of Zadok and Their
                Adherents ....................... 176
        3.2.1.4  Israel's Decline: The Past and
                Impending Crisis.................. 184
        3.2.1.5  Israel's Rise: The Life of the New
                Covenant in Damascus............. 216
    3.2.2  The Elaboration of the Eschatological Torah     255
        3.2.2.1  Restoration of Land in the Jubilee
                Year .......................... 257
        3.2.2.2  Intermingling Male and Female
                Garments ....................... 259
        3.2.2.3  Honesty in Business .............. 259
        3.2.2.4  Marriage and Adultery............. 260
        3.2.2.5  Eschatology of the Return .......... 262
        3.2.2.6  The Leadership of the Sage ........ 263
        3.2.2.7  Qualifications for Public Recitation of
                the Torah ...................... 264
        3.2.2.8  Causes for Defrocking a Priest....... 266
        3.2.2.9  Procedures in Both Cities and Camps  268
        3.2.2.10 The Organizational Structure of the
                Community...................... 344
        3.2.2.11 Discipline within the Community..... 351

3.3 Finale (4Q266 F11:3b–21)......................... 365
    3.3.1 The Convocation of the Camps in the Third
         Month ............................... 366
    3.3.2 Epilogue ............................... 367

Chapter 4. Unincorporated Fragments................... 369
4.1 4Q266 ......................................... 369
4.2 4Q267 ......................................... 375
4.3 4Q268 ......................................... 376
4.4 4Q269 ......................................... 376
4.5 4Q270 ......................................... 376
4.6 4Q272 ......................................... 377
4.7 4Q273 ......................................... 377

Bibliography ......................................... 379

Indices ............................................. 393
  Author ............................................. 393
  Subject ............................................. 395
  Ancient Sources .................................... 403
    Hebrew Bible .................................... 403
    Qumran ........................................ 407
    Pseudepigrapha ................................. 424
    Mishnah ....................................... 424
    Talmud ........................................ 425
    Other .......................................... 425
    New Testament .................................. 425

# LIST OF TABLES

Table 1. "Midrash ha-Torah ha-Acharon Text Parallels" . . .   xxiii
Table 2. "Midrash ha-Torah ha-Acharon Texts Parallel to
       other Qumran scrolls: 5Q12, 6Q15 & 1QS" . . . . . .   xxix
Table 3. "List of Primary Text Divisions" . . . . . . . . . . . . . . .   xxx

# ACKNOWLEDGEMENTS

To compose a work such as this has required a tremendous amount of assistance. This is especially true on account of my virtual blindness. I am profoundly indebted to Tim Undheim for his dedication and diligence beyond the ordinary in assisting in all phases of preparation of the manuscript, from scholarship to final editing. The indices were prepared by Mike Apodaka under the supervision of Martin Abegg. Others to whom I am deeply indebted include Clark Brooking and David Maas.

My gratitude also extends to the faculty, students and administration of Hebrew Union College – Jewish Institute of Religion for 40 years of association; from them I learned what I could accomplish.

My daughter, Nina Wacholder, has contributed in important though invisible ways to the completion of this project.

I am thankful for the devoted love and guidance of my late wife Elizabeth Krukowski.

## SELECT ABBREVIATIONS

| | |
|---|---|
| 1QH$^a$ | *Hodayot*$^a$ or *Thanksgiving Hymns*$^a$ |
| 1QM | *Milḥamah* or *War Scroll* |
| 1QpHab | *Pesher Habakkuk* |
| 1QS | *Serek ha-Yaḥad* or *Rule of the Community* |
| 4Q266–273 | Qumran Fragments of the *Damascus Document*$^{a-h}$ |
| 4QMMT$^{a-f}$ | *Miqṣat Maʿaśê ha-Torah*$^{a-f}$ |
| 11QMelch | *Melchizedek* |
| 11QPs$^a$ | *Psalms Scroll*$^a$ |
| *ABD* | *Anchor Bible Dictionary* |
| *Catena* $^a$ | 4QCatena$^a$ (4Q177, also known as *Midrash on Escha-tology*$^b$) |
| CD | Cairo Genizah copy of the *Damascus  Document* (Mss A [cols. 1–8; 9–16] and B [cols. 19–20]) |
| DJD | Discoveries in the Judaean Desert |
| *DSD* | *Dead Sea Discoveries* |
| DSS | Dead Sea Scrolls |
| *EDSS* | *Encyclopedia of the Dead Sea Scrolls* |
| *EncJud* | *Encyclopaedia Judaica* |
| *HUCA* | *Hebrew Union College Annual* |
| *IEJ* | *Israel Exploration Journal* |
| *JBL* | *Journal of Biblical Literature* |
| *JE* | *The Jewish Encyclopedia* |
| *JJS* | *Journal of Jewish Studies* |
| *JQR* | *Jewish Quarterly Review* |
| *JSOT* | *Journal for the Study of the Old Testament* |
| MTA | *Midrash ha-Torah ha-Acharon* |
| NJPS | *Tanakh: The Holy Scriptures: The New JPS Translation according to the Traditional Hebrew Text* |
| *RevQ* | *Revue de Qumran* |
| RSV | Revised Standard Version |
| *VT* | *Vetus Testamentum* |
| *ZAW* | *Zeitschrift für die alttestamentliche Wissenschaft* |

# SIGLA

| | |
|---|---|
| {א} | – erasure |
| א̸ | – strike through |
| <א> | – modern addition |
| <<א>> | – modern deletion |
| (א) | – modern clarification or amplification |
| \א/ | – modern transposition |
| א̇ | – supralinear insertion |
| ° | – illegible traces of a letter |
| א̊ | – possible reading |
| א̣ | – probable reading |
| *vac / vacat* | – vacat (DSS and CD-mss A) |
| : | – vacat (CD-mss B) |
| [א] | – reconstructed text |
| xx / xx | – parallel texts |

Transcriptions and Reconstructions:

    <sup>b</sup>א  (or untagged 4Q Damascus Document readings) =
    Baumgarten

    <sup>h</sup>א  =Hempel

    <sup>m/t</sup>א =Martínez-Tigchelaar

    <sup>q</sup>א  =Qimron

    <sup>r</sup>א  (or untagged CD reading)=Rabin

    <sup>sch</sup>א  =Schwartz

    <sup>s</sup>א  =Stegemann

    <sup>w</sup>א  =Wacholder

# FOREWORD

The New Damascus Document consists of three parts: a) a composite edition of the twelve ancient and medieval manuscripts with notes; b) a new translation of the Hebrew text; and c) a commentary upon the composite text.

Of the twelve manuscripts that survive from this work, two of them, the so-called CD-A and CD-B transcribed in the 11th and 12th centuries and discovered a century ago, remain the most important documents attesting to the 2,200 or 2,300 year-old composition. Fortunately, ten more manuscripts survive among the DSS found in 1947 and thereafter in the caves of Qumran—specifically eight in Cave 4 (4Q266–273), one in Cave 5 (5Q12) and one in Cave 6 (6Q15). The CD texts found in the genizah of the Cairo Synagogue are too well known to need description here. Some of the cave manuscripts overlap the CD material, but much more is new.

The extant manuscripts not only tell what survives, but also reveal a great deal about what has perished. Up to 1947 when only the CD texts were known, the extent of the original was completely unknown. Many presumed that the first lines of CD, "and now, heed me all you who know righteousness and discern the acts of God," were its original beginning. The Qumran manuscripts have shown that the original work contained more than a page preceding the text of CD. It has always been clear that the two medieval manuscripts did not have the original's last lines. Now, some three of the Dead Sea texts preserve the work's ending. The last three words of these concluding lines reveal to us, presumably, the book's original title which (like the *Book of Jubilees* whose beginning and conclusion contain its name, "The Division of the Days") reproduces also the Hebrew name of the work: מדרש התורה האחרון "The Midrash on the Eschatological Torah" (MTA).

Although these Qumran texts of CD were discovered between 1947 and 1956, they were kept under lock and key for several decades until the appearance of the first fascicle of *A Preliminary Edition of the Unpublished Dead Sea Scrolls*.[1] In 1996 Baumgarten published the

---

[1] Ben Zion Wacholder and Martin G. Abegg, reconstructors and eds., *A Preliminary Edition of the Unpublished Dead Sea Scrolls: The Hebrew and Aramaic Texts from Cave Four*, (Fascicle 1; Washington, D.C.: Biblical Archaeology Society, 1991).

remains of the Cave 4 texts in volume 18 of the DJD series with an English translation and brief comments.[2]

MTA presents the first diplomatic text of what survives in all twelve manuscripts. Let us remember, however, that the surviving material, large as it is, does not give us the original composition. How much has perished is not known, but in my estimation between a fourth and a third of the original work has not survived. In his edition, Baumgarten sometimes restores missing words and clauses. The present composite edition follows a more liberal system. I have attempted to restore or reconstruct many of the lacunae, going far beyond what is found in his work as well as in previous editions of CD, manuscript A in particular.

Ever since Schechter, scrollists have taken for granted that CD originated as a composite of extracts from diverse sources and (so to speak) had no author, rather only segments haphazardly fused together. Baumgarten and Campbell[3] still subscribe to this supposition. This commentary, however, argues that CD did have a singular author. The Rabbinic and Karaite traditions ascribe the origin of the sectarian movement to Zadok and Boethus, the disciples of Antigonus of Socho. Al-Qirqisani, a tenth century Karaite encyclopedic writer, alludes to a unified text as revealing half of the truth while Anan, the founder of the Karaite movement, revealed the whole. Yet, modern scholarship ignores altogether this Talmudic and Karaite evidence, building its entire structure on the mute stones of Qumran.

The title מדרש התורה האחרון opens a new window into the understanding of the Jewish literary tradition during the period of the Second Temple. Much of rabbinic literature is characterized by midrashic writings, some of them independent and others diffused within the Talmud. For centuries, this rabbinic material was transmitted orally and did not assume its present form until late antiquity or early Middle Ages. Now that we have a midrashic literary tradition in the DSS, there is no longer a question that this genre goes back to the period of the Second Temple and that sectarian and rabbinic midrash have their origin in post-exilic times.

Let me say a word about the new translation. Since Schechter's

---

[2] Joseph M. Baumgarten, (DJD XVIII; *Qumran Cave 4 XIII: The Damascus Document (4Q266-273)*, (DJD XVIII; Oxford: Clarendon, 1996).

[3] J. Campbell, "Essene-Qumran Origins in the Exile: A Scriptural Basis?" *Journal of Jewish Studies* 46 (Cambridge: England, 1995): 143–156.

first edition in 1910, it has been presumed that the מורה צדק (Just Teacher) presented for the first time in MTA was the founder of the sect. I contend, however, that the Just Teacher and his nemesis known as the Scoffer or Liar, are presented as figures or personalities of the future, those who will appear at the End of Days.[4] Previous translators have rendered many of the verbs relating to these personalities in the past tense, which in this translation are mostly in the future.

A running commentary follows the Hebrew text, translation and accompanying notes.[5] It elucidates the MTA in light of the new evidence provided by the composite text and its retranslation. The CD manuscripts generated a mass of scholarship. Much of it retains its validity, but on the other hand, a great deal of the secondary work has lost its relevance since it rested on only half of the material that is now available. Moreover, as just noted, much of it misrepresented the underlying Hebrew original.

It is hoped that the present edition will add to the scope and understanding of the Dead Sea Scrolls.

---

[4] This opinion is reflected in the translation. See too the article, Ben Zion Wacholder, "The Teacher of Righteousness is Alive, Awaiting the Messiah: האסף in CD as Allusion to the Siniatic and Damascene Covenants," *HUCA* 70-71 (1999–2000): 75–93.

[5] These are described in greater detail in the introduction along with other elements of organization of this book.

# MIDRASH HA-TORAH HA-ACHARON TABLES

## Table Sigla

Table 1. "*Midrash ha-Torah ha-Acharon* Text Parallels" is broken into 6 sections on pages xxiv–xxviii.
Table 2. "*Midrash ha-Torah ha-Acharon* Texts Parallel to other Qumran scrolls: 5Q12, 6Q15 & 1QS" is one unit on page xxix.
Table 3. "List of Primary Text Divisions" listing all the primary texts and giving their page numbers, is one unit on page xxx.
Numbering (description here may be applied to any of the texts in the tables below, please substitute numbers as necessary):

   CD 1:1 = Cairo Damascus Document page 1 line 1.
   Qumran 4Q266 2ii:1–2

     4    = Number of the cave in which the scroll was found.
     Q    = Qumran, indicating that the scroll was found in the vicinity of Qumran.
     266 = Scroll number.
     2    = Fragment number, or the number assigned to that particular fragment of the specific scroll number.
     ii   = Column number of the text in that fragment.
     1-2 = lines 1–2.

  /   = Parallel to.
  {} = Corresponding page numbers where the text may be found in this volume.
Note that texts with material overlapping from one page to another are listed with the page where the text begins.
Note that the primary texts are listed first, followed by the parallel text.
Primary texts are found by row; parallel CD texts are placed by row; parallel Qumran texts are placed by column.
These tables are not exhaustive.

Table 1. *Midrash ha-Torah ha-Acharon* Text Parallels

|  | 4Q266 | 4Q267 | 4Q268 | 4Q269 | 4Q270 | 4Q271 | 4Q272 | 4Q273 |
|---|---|---|---|---|---|---|---|---|
| CD 1:1-2:1 | CD1:1–2:1/ 4Q266 F2i:6b– 25 {page 26}<br><br>CD1:1–2:1/ 4Q266 F2ii:1– 2a {page 26} |  | CD1:1–2:1/ 4Q268 F1:9–17 {page 26} |  |  |  |  |  |

Continued on next page

Table 1. *Midrash ha-Torah ha-Acharon* Text Parallels, continued

| | 4Q266 | 4Q267 | 4Q268 | 4Q269 | 4Q270 | 4Q271 | 4Q272 | 4Q273 |
|---|---|---|---|---|---|---|---|---|
| CD 2:2–4:18 | CD 2:2–4:18/ 4Q266 F2ii:2a–24 {page 28}<br><br>CD 2:2–4:18/ 4Q266 F2iii {page 28}<br><br>CD 2:2–4:8/ 4Q266 F3i {page 28}<br><br>CD 2:2–4:8/ 4Q266 unidentified F34 {page 28} | | | CD 2:2–4:18/ 4Q269 F1–2 {page 28} | CD 2:2–4:18/ 4Q270 F1i {page 28}<br><br>CD 2:2–4:18/ 4Q270 F1ii(a) {page 28}<br><br>CD 2:2–4:18/ 4Q270 F1ii(b) {page 28} | | | |
| CD 4:19-7:5 | CD 4:19–7:5/ 4Q266 F3ii {page 34}<br><br>CD 4:19–7:5/ 4Q266 F3iii:4–6 {page 34} | CD 4:19–7:5/ 4Q267 F2 {page 34} | | CD 4:19–7:5/ 4Q269 F3–4 {page 34} | | CD 4:19–7:5/ 4Q271 F1 {page 34} | | | |
| CD 7:6–8:21 | CD 7:6–8:21/ 4Q266 F3iii:18–25 {page 40}<br><br>CD 7:6–8:21/ 4Q 266 F3iv {page 40} | | | CD 7:6–8:21/ 4Q269 F5 {page 40}<br><br>CD 7:6–8:21/ 4Q269 F6 {page 40} | | | | |

Continued on next page

Table 1. *Midrash ha-Torah ha-Acharon* Text Parallels, continued

| | 4Q266 | 4Q267 | 4Q268 | 4Q269 | 4Q270 | 4Q271 | 4Q272 | 4Q273 |
|---|---|---|---|---|---|---|---|---|
| CD 9:1–11:2 | CD 9:1–11:2/ 4Q266 F8ii:8b–iii:10 {page 82} | CD 9:1–11:2/ 4Q267 F9i {page 82} | | | CD 9:1–11:2/ 4Q270 F6iii:16–21 {page 82}<br><br>CD 9:1–11:2/ 4Q270 F6iv {page 82}<br><br>CD 9:1–11:2/ 4Q270 F6v:1–4 {page 82} | | | |
| CD 11:3–11 | | CD 11:3–11/ 4Q267 F9ii:2–3 {page 88} | | | CD 11:3–11/ 4Q270 F6v:12–16a {page 88} | CD 11:3–11/ 4Q271 F5i:1–7a {page 88} | | |
| CD 11:12–18 | CD 11:12–18/ 4Q266 F9i:1–4 {page 90} | CD 11:12–18/ 4Q267 F9ii:8 {page 90} | | | CD 11:12–18/ 4Q270 F6v:16b–21 {page 90} | CD 11:12–18/ 4Q271 F5i:7b–12 {page 90} | | |
| CD 11:19–14:2 | CD 11:19–14:2/ 4Q266 F9i:16–17 {page 90}<br><br>CD 11:19–14:2/ 4Q266 F9ii {page 90}<br><br>CD 11:19–14:2/ 4Q266 F9iii {page 90}<br><br>CD 11:19–14:2/ 4Q266 F10i {page 90} | CD 11:19–14:2/ 4Q267 F9iii {page 90}<br><br>CD 11:19–14:2/ 4Q267 F9iv {page 90}<br><br>CD 11:19–14:2/ 4Q267 F9v:–6a {page 90} | | CD 11:19–14:2/ 4Q269 F10i–ii:8 {page 90} | | CD 11:19–14:2/ 4Q271 F5i:13–21 {page 90}<br><br>CD 11:19–14:2/ 4Q271 F5ii {page 90} | | |

Continued on next page

Table 1. *Midrash ha-Torah ha-Acharon* Text Parallels, continued

| | 4Q266 | 4Q267 | 4Q268 | 4Q269 | 4Q270 | 4Q271 | 4Q272 | 4Q273 |
|---|---|---|---|---|---|---|---|---|
| CD 14:3–21 | CD 14:3–21/ 4Q266 F10i {page 96} | CD 14:3–21/ 4Q267 F9v:6b–14 {page 96} | CD 14:3–21/ 4Q268 F2 {page 96} | CD 14:3–21/ 4Q269 F10ii 9–12; 11ii:1–7 {page 96} | | | | |
| CD 15 | CD 15/ 4Q266 F8i {page 78} | | | | CD 15/ 4Q270 F6i:20–ii:10 {page 78} | CD 15/ 4Q271 F4i:4–ii:3a {page 78} | | |
| CD 16 | CD 16/ 4Q266 F8iii:1b–8a {page 80} | | | | CD 16/ 4Q270 F6ii:17–21 {page 80} CD 16/ 4Q270 F6iii:13–15 {page 80} | CD 16/ 4Q271 F4ii:3b–17 {page 80} | | |
| CD 19:1–34a | See table for CD 7:6–8:21 | | | See table for CD 7:6–8:21 | | | | |
| CD 19:34b–20:34 | CD 19:34b–20:34/ 4Q266 F4 {page 46} | CD 19:34b–20:34/ 4Q267 F3:1–7 {page 46} | | | | | | |

Continued on next page

Table 1. *Midrash ha-Torah ha-Acharon* Text Parallels, continued

| | 4Q267 | 4Q268 | 4Q269 | 4Q270 | 4Q271 | 4Q272 | 4Q273 |
|---|---|---|---|---|---|---|---|
| 4Q266 | 4Q266 F1/ 4Q267 F1:1–8 {page 22}<br><br>4Q266 F2i:1a/ 4Q267 F1:1–8 {page 22}<br><br>4Q266 F5i/ 4Q267 F5iii {page 52}<br><br>4Q266 F5ii/ 4Q267 F5iii {page 54}<br><br>4Q266 F6iii/ 4Q267 F6:1–6 {page 64}<br><br>4266 F7i–iii/ 4Q267 F8 {page 70} | | 4Q266 F10ii/ 4Q269 F11i:8–ii:2 {page 100}<br><br>4Q266 F11/ 4Q269 F16 {page 104} | 4Q266 F6iii/ 4Q270 F3ii:12–16 {page 64}<br><br>4Q266 F10ii/ 4Q270 F7i:1–6a {page 100}<br><br>4Q266 F11/ 4Q270 F7:16b–21 {page 104}<br><br>4Q266 F11/ 4Q270 F7ii {page 104} | | | 4Q266 F5i/ 4Q273 F1 {page 52}<br><br>4Q266 F5ii/ 4Q273 F2 {page 56}<br><br>4Q266 F5ii/ 4Q273 F4i {page 56} |
| 4Q267 | | | | | | | |
| 4Q268 | 4Q268 F1:1–8/ 4Q266 F2i:1–6a {page 24} | | | | | | |
| 4Q269 | | | | | | | |

Continued on next page

Table 1. *Midrash ha-Torah ha-Acharon* Text Parallels, continued

| | 4Q266 | 4Q267 | 4Q268 | 4Q269 | 4Q270 | 4Q271 | 4Q272 | 4Q273 |
|---|---|---|---|---|---|---|---|---|
| 4Q270 | 4Q270 F3ii:17–21/ 4Q266 F6iii:10 {page 66}<br><br>4Q270 F4/ 4Q266 F12 {page 76} | 4Q270 F2i–ii/ 4Q267 F4:2–15 {page 72}<br><br>4Q270 F3ii:17–21/ 4Q267 F6:7 {page 66}<br><br>4Q270 F7i:6b–16a/ 4Q267 F9vi {page 102} | | | | | | |
| 4Q271 | | 4Q271 F3/ 4Q267 F7:4–14 {page 50} | | 4Q271 F2/ 4Q269 F8i–ii {page 68}<br><br>4Q271 F3/ 4Q269 F9 {page 50} | 4Q271 F2/4Q270 F3iii:13–21 {page 68}<br><br>4Q271 F3/ 4Q270 F5 {page 50} | | | |
| 4Q272 | 4Q272 F1i–ii/ 4Q266 F6i {page 58} | | | 4Q272 F1i–ii/ 4Q269 F7 {page 58} | | | | 4Q272 F1i–ii/ 4Q273 F4ii {page 58} |
| 4Q273 | | | | | | | | |

Continued on next page

Table 2. *Midrash ha-Torah ha-Acharon* Texts Parallel to other Qumran scrolls: 5Q12, 6Q15, 1QS

| | 4Q266 | 4Q270 | 5Q12 | 6Q15 | 1QS |
|---|---|---|---|---|---|
| CD 4:19–7:5 | | | | CD 4:19–7:5/ 6Q15 F1–4 {page 34} | |
| CD 9:1–11:2 | | | CD 9:1–11:2/ 5Q12 F1 {page 82} | | |
| CD 14:3–21 | | | | | CD 14:3–21/ 1QS F6:24b–25a {page 96} |
| 4Q266 | | | | | 4Q266 F10ii/ 1QS F7:8–16a {page 100} |
| 4Q270 | | | | 4Q270 F2i–ii/ 6Q15 F5 {page 72} | 4Q270 F7:6b–16a/ 1QS F7:16b–21 {page 102} |
| 5Q12 | | | | | |
| 6Q15 | | | | | |
| 1QS | | | | | |

Table 3. List of Primary Text Divisions
(See 1.5.10 for Tables of Parallels)

CD 1:1–2:1 . . . . . . . . . . . . . . . . . . . . . . . . . . . . . . . . . . . . . . . . . . . . . . 26
CD 2:2–4:18 . . . . . . . . . . . . . . . . . . . . . . . . . . . . . . . . . . . . . . . . . . . . . 28
CD 4:19–7:5 . . . . . . . . . . . . . . . . . . . . . . . . . . . . . . . . . . . . . . . . . . . . . 34
CD 7:6–8:21 (CD A) and CD 19:1–34a (CD B) . . . . . . . . . . . . . . . . . . . . . 40
CD 9:1–11:2 . . . . . . . . . . . . . . . . . . . . . . . . . . . . . . . . . . . . . . . . . . . . . 82
CD 11:3–11 . . . . . . . . . . . . . . . . . . . . . . . . . . . . . . . . . . . . . . . . . . . . . . 88
CD 11:12–18 . . . . . . . . . . . . . . . . . . . . . . . . . . . . . . . . . . . . . . . . . . . . . 90
CD 11:19–14:2 . . . . . . . . . . . . . . . . . . . . . . . . . . . . . . . . . . . . . . . . . . . 90
CD 14:3–21 . . . . . . . . . . . . . . . . . . . . . . . . . . . . . . . . . . . . . . . . . . . . . . 96
CD 15 . . . . . . . . . . . . . . . . . . . . . . . . . . . . . . . . . . . . . . . . . . . . . . . . . . 78
CD 16 . . . . . . . . . . . . . . . . . . . . . . . . . . . . . . . . . . . . . . . . . . . . . . . . . . 80
CD 19:34b–20:34 . . . . . . . . . . . . . . . . . . . . . . . . . . . . . . . . . . . . . . . . . 46
4Q266 F1; F2i:1a . . . . . . . . . . . . . . . . . . . . . . . . . . . . . . . . . . . . . . . . . . 22
4Q266 F4 . . . . . . . . . . . . . . . . . . . . . . . . . . . . . . . . . . . . . . . . . . . . . . . 50
4Q266 F5i . . . . . . . . . . . . . . . . . . . . . . . . . . . . . . . . . . . . . . . . . . . . . . . 52
4Q266 F5i(c–d) . . . . . . . . . . . . . . . . . . . . . . . . . . . . . . . . . . . . . . . . . . . 54
4Q266 F5ii . . . . . . . . . . . . . . . . . . . . . . . . . . . . . . . . . . . . . . . . . . . . . . 54
4Q267 F5iii:1–2 . . . . . . . . . . . . . . . . . . . . . . . . . . . . . . . . . . . . . . . . . . 54
4Q266 F6i(a–e) . . . . . . . . . . . . . . . . . . . . . . . . . . . . . . . . . . . . . . . . . . . 60
4Q266 F6ii . . . . . . . . . . . . . . . . . . . . . . . . . . . . . . . . . . . . . . . . . . . . . . 62
4Q266 F6iii . . . . . . . . . . . . . . . . . . . . . . . . . . . . . . . . . . . . . . . . . . . . . . 64
4Q266 F6iv . . . . . . . . . . . . . . . . . . . . . . . . . . . . . . . . . . . . . . . . . . . . . . 66
4Q266 F7i–iii . . . . . . . . . . . . . . . . . . . . . . . . . . . . . . . . . . . . . . . . . . . . 70
4Q266 F10ii . . . . . . . . . . . . . . . . . . . . . . . . . . . . . . . . . . . . . . . . . . . . . 100
4Q266 F11 . . . . . . . . . . . . . . . . . . . . . . . . . . . . . . . . . . . . . . . . . . . . . . 104
4Q267 F4 . . . . . . . . . . . . . . . . . . . . . . . . . . . . . . . . . . . . . . . . . . . . . . . 72
4Q267 F7:1–3 . . . . . . . . . . . . . . . . . . . . . . . . . . . . . . . . . . . . . . . . . . . . 50
4Q268 F1:1–8 . . . . . . . . . . . . . . . . . . . . . . . . . . . . . . . . . . . . . . . . . . . . 24
4Q270 F2i–ii . . . . . . . . . . . . . . . . . . . . . . . . . . . . . . . . . . . . . . . . . . . . . 72
4Q270 F3i:17–21 . . . . . . . . . . . . . . . . . . . . . . . . . . . . . . . . . . . . . . . . . . 64
4Q270 F3ii:17–21 . . . . . . . . . . . . . . . . . . . . . . . . . . . . . . . . . . . . . . . . . 66
4Q270 F3ii(a) . . . . . . . . . . . . . . . . . . . . . . . . . . . . . . . . . . . . . . . . . . . . 66
4Q270 F4 . . . . . . . . . . . . . . . . . . . . . . . . . . . . . . . . . . . . . . . . . . . . . . . 76
4Q270 F7i:6b–16a . . . . . . . . . . . . . . . . . . . . . . . . . . . . . . . . . . . . . . . . . 102
4Q271 F2 . . . . . . . . . . . . . . . . . . . . . . . . . . . . . . . . . . . . . . . . . . . . . . . 68
4Q271 F3 . . . . . . . . . . . . . . . . . . . . . . . . . . . . . . . . . . . . . . . . . . . . . . . 50
4Q272 F1i–ii . . . . . . . . . . . . . . . . . . . . . . . . . . . . . . . . . . . . . . . . . . . . . 58
4Q273 F5 . . . . . . . . . . . . . . . . . . . . . . . . . . . . . . . . . . . . . . . . . . . . . . . 76

CHAPTER ONE

# INTRODUCTION

## 1.1. *Methodology*

### 1.1.1. *Approach*

The major task confronting the reader of this composite edition is determining what it tells us that we had not known from the previous versions of the Genizah text. This work consists of a radical rereading of the known material, both the CD texts available since 1910 and the fragmentary additions of the ten manuscripts found in the caves of Qumran. As conventional scholarship has by now become a virtual dogma that needs revision, I propose to question elements of that dogma and how they apply to historical and systemic questions, including standardized linguistics and philology. It is precisely this area of modern scholarship that I believe needs revision as well. Without a new translation and reinterpretation of the entire body of texts of MTA and related DSS texts, this ancient body of literature cannot be opened anew for intellectual debate. Permit me to underline that this synoptic edition does not (by any stretch of the imagination) presume to be a complete substitute for the original composition.

Pivotal points in understanding MTA are approach and methodology. Because so many phrases and clauses clearly draw on the wordage of the Hebrew Scriptures, modern interpreters beginning with Schechter take it for granted that the DSS be read biblically, applying a biblical interpretation to terms in the DSS which have scriptural parallels. In fact however, modern renditions of the *Tanakh* are often of little value: marvelous for restoring lost passages, they are nevertheless of little merit for rendering the DSS, since the language of the scribes who flourished in the Second Temple period varied from that of the Hebrew Scriptures. In addition, the authors of the DSS appear to have had their own version of the Hebrew texts, differing in certain respects from those transmitted by the Masoretes. Their version of the holy writ was similar to the independent text used by the Greek translators of the Septuagint. Even when their wording is the same as that of the traditional text, many terms have assumed new or modified senses, this being true also for grammar. An awareness of this phenomenon is important, because it tells us that the texts of MTA and much of the DSS have a language of their own, resembling in many respects, but not identical to Mishnaic and Talmudic Hebrew. In other words, the Hebrew of the DSS may be defined as a language that hovers between that of Scripture and the Mishnah.

## 1.1.2. *Restorations and Reconstructions*

A major problem with the DSS texts is that there exist many lacunae and large stretches of material that have perished. Some of these gaps are remedied by what survives from CD and the overlapping manuscripts. Even so, the lost material frequently constitutes a larger portion than what survives. I have, therefore, often filled in portions of these areas in a process which may be classed into three groups: 1) utilizing citations from Scripture whose missing words may be filled with reasonable certainty from the Masoretic Text or a modification of it; 2) selecting formulaic language from other parts of MTA which closely fits paleographically and ideologically the surviving material around the textual gaps to assist in their probable restoration; 3) employing related material from other DSS documents to more speculatively reconstruct the text.

In general, I have attempted to differentiate between restorations and reconstructions. The former apply to phrases or clauses whose missing material can be repaired with much probability on the basis of categories one and two in the above paragraph. Reconstructions, however, go beyond what is attested in the biblical or pseudepigraphic texts, building on the broader text of the DSS, as described in category three. Particularly helpful in this respect has been the *Rule of the Community* (1QS), since I believe that it often drew from MTA. The author's tendency to repeat or restate his material two or more times helps to fill a great deal of the lost material. The measure of probability of these proposed reconstructions, however, I leave to future scholarship.

## 1.2 *History of MTA*

### 1.2.1. *Date of Composition*

MTA has a long history. As was noted in the foreword, CD-A and CD-B (discovered toward the end of the 19th century) generated a great deal of scholarship. Discovered among the Genizah texts, they date back to the 11th or 12th century. A main issue in the debate concerned whether they emanated from antiquity or were composed during the early Middle Ages. The discovery of ten additional manuscripts among the DSS resolved this question in favor of pre-Christian origin. Yet, the problem of when its author flourished remains open. Majority opinion now maintains that they date from the middle of the second century B.C.E. This opinion contains some intrinsic difficulties. It supposes that the author flourished during and perhaps after the Hasmonean epoch. If so, the question arises as to why MTA lacks any obvious reference to the Antiochan persecution. It is amazing that texts which deal at length with the conflict between the righteous and the sinners would not mention the struggle between the Hasmoneans and the Syrian government. About these conflicts the DSS say nothing. The fact that only *Pesher Nahum* contains a reference to Antiochus and Demetrius suggests that the DSS writers did not refrain from mentioning contemporary events on principle. *Pesher Nahum* then is apparently one of the latest compositions of the DSS, as are the calendar texts 4Q317–334. Therefore, it is necessary to presume that the DSS in general and MTA in particular were composed prior to the Syrian persecution, evidently going back to the third century B.C.E. It is true that the argument here is from near silence. Still, the lack of mention of Antiochus and Demetrius does not diminish the plausibility of my theory of early authorship. Furthermore, much of what is in MTA echoes Ezekiel, further strengthening an early date of authorship.

It seems that one reason many date the sect to 150 B.C.E. is to lend support to the idea that the sect immediately preceded the advent of Christianity. Scholars have long sought to understand the sect as a precursor to Christianity, which necessitates a late date for the sect and its writings. The attempt to link the two testaments with the writings of the sect lends support to the connection with this new religious movement. However, this position, as desirable as it is for some, is untenable. While everyone agrees that the Hebrew Bible supplied much of the wording for the New Testament, several centuries elapsed between the two. The writing of the DSS community could therefore be nearer to the early Second Temple period, rather than just before the composition of the New Testament.

Numerous scrollists suppose that Khirbet Qumran defines the locus of many of the DSS manuscripts. This view likewise is untenable. Qumran served as a place where texts composed throughout Judea were reproduced. The texts did not originate in Qumran. The DSS contain a variety of views and are not unified, contrary to, for example, the New Testament which is bound together by a single concept, Jesus. The DSS reflect a variety of locations and points of view. It is inconceivable that all these documents, with their varying views, were written in one place or at the same time. In fact, none of the manuscripts found in the Judean Desert possess characteristics of original compositions such as rewritings or corrections. That there are multiple manuscripts of MTA suggests they derive from an archetype composed decades earlier. Even if these manuscripts were produced in the Hasmonean era, the original was generated considerably earlier. It follows, therefore, that Khirbet Qumran might have functioned as a scriptorium whose scribes specialized in reproducing manuscripts composed elsewhere, whose orthography therefore has little bearing on the dates of composition.

There are, however, other factors that, while not giving the actual date of composition, may be helpful for determining when they were written. These function in a method that is termed relative dating, a technique that studies the content of manuscripts to determine how they are used by others. The investigator seeks to determine which writers used works by other authors or if their own manuscripts were utilized by subsequent writers. As will be shown in the commentary, it is apparent that the author of the *Damascus Document* made use of works such as the books of *Enoch* and *Jubilees*. The derived text was then used by the writers of *Rule of the Community* and the Pesher Commentaries. The composition of the *Damascus Document* antedates 1QS (1QS *Rule of the Community*) as well as the Pesherite works.

### 1.2.2. *Evidence from Medievalists*

#### 1.2.2.1. *Al-Qirqisani*
Early scholars of CD dealt with its history, especially the testimonia of Jacob al-Qirqisani (Abu Yusuf Yaqub ibn Ishaq ibn Sam'away al-Qirqisani). References to the existence of the *Damascus Document* appeared first in Russia in the 19th century through the scholarship

of Abraham Harkavy, a Jewish savant in charge of the Judaica of the Imperial Library of Saint Petersburg. He was the first to draw attention to the existence of CD while editing a Karaite encyclopedia, *Book of Lights and Watch-Towers*, composed by al-Qirqisani in 947. Harkavy called attention to al-Qirqisani's major work, noting in particular al-Qirqisani's introduction in which he sketched the Jewish sects, beginning with Jeroboam's schism and continuing to his own time. An English version of al-Qirqisani's account first appeared in the *Hebrew Union College Annual* by Leon Nemoy.[1]

Like *Avot d'Rabbi Natan* 5, al-Qirqisani ascribes the foundation of the Zadokites to Boethus and Zadok, disciples of Antigonus of Socho. In his work, al-Qirqisani describes Zadok as one who revealed important truth to the people. For him, Zadok's teachings contained only half of what needed to be revealed to the people. Anan, the 8th century founder of the Karaite movement, revealed the rest of it. Was the need of Anan's completion evidence of problems with CD? No, this is not a valid proof that al-Qirqisani was either mistaken or that his copy of CD diverged from that available to us. Neither would al-Qirqisani deny the existence of other polemical statements against the rabbinates, for he was dealing with disputations that concern legal practices.

A more intriguing question pertains to the basis upon which al-Qirqisani asserts that the author of the work which we call the *Damascus Document* was Zadok. Did he base his information solely on rabbinic sources, such as *Avot d'Rabbi Natan*, or did he have access to materials no longer available to us? On one point, however, al-Qirqisani claimed to know something unknown to the modern reader of the DSS. He ascribes the making of a sectarian calendar to Boethus, who together with Zadok, repudiated the teachings of the master Antigonus and who, like Zadok, founded an independent sect. The ascription of a calendar to Boethus probably refers to the schematic reckoning of a 364-day tropical year. Al-Qirqisani's claim that Boethus authored the sectarian schematic calendar finds no support in the available sources, which ascribe its origin to the mythical antediluvian Enoch. It is conceivable, however, that Boethus himself, like other ancient writers, ascribed his calendation to the antediluvian Enoch. The question arises whether al-Qirqisani was aware of such an ascription to the antediluvian fig-

---

[1] Leon Nemoy, "Al-Qirqisani's Account of the Jewish Sects and Christianity," *HUCA* 7 (1930): 317–97.

ure. And if he had such awareness, was his sophistication on a level to disregard such an attribution? At any rate, he had access to the *Damascus Document*, which is mostly available to us. However, we have no inkling as to al-Qirqisani's source for his attribution of the schematic calendar of the 365-day year. Nevertheless, al-Qirqisani's ascription, while uncertain, is possible if not probable. We have no evidence to suggest that he was ever suspected of manufacturing sources.

Nevertheless, as Harkavy remarked more than a century ago, it is certain that the Karaite sage still perused the *Damascus Document* in the middle of the 10th century, perhaps in its entirety. The fact that the Cairo Genizah preserved 11th and 12th century copies of the *Damascus Document* and that other scribes vocalized some of the words in these manuscripts shows that the Essene sect, said to have vanished during the Roman conquest of Judea in 68–73 c.e., continued to produce its literature during the Middle Ages. This provides crucial evidence that elements of the Essene sect thrived during the late Middle Ages. Evidence suggests, therefore, that sectarian material was available throughout the centuries after the destruction of the Second Temple.

Let us not forget, moreover, that the Genizah text also contained fragmentary remains of a Zadokite text not attested in the DSS. In 1911 Israel Lévi published the fragmentary remains of *pergCfr*[2] (parchment Cairo fragment) of which nine lines survive.[3] According to J. Fitzmyer, it is a text "which undoubtedly was related to the *Damascus Document* . . . it apparently belonged to some medieval copy of the same text."[4] Scholars dealing with the *Damascus Document* have ignored Fitzmyer's opinion as well as this passage. Here is a slightly reconstructed version of the text.

*pergCfr*—Only the Sons of Zadok Serve in the Temple

|כהן                                                     1

בכול ע[ת יורוני(ו) מבני] בני צדוק הכהנים                 2

---

[2] Israel. Lévi, "Document relatif a la 'Communaute des fils de Sadoc,'" *REJ* 65 (1913): 24–31.

[3] The rendition below is a slight modification of my presentation of this text in "Historiography of Qumran: the Sons of Zadok and their Enemies," *Qumran Between the Old and the New Testaments*, ed. Frederick H. Cryer and Thomas L. Thompson. Journal for the Study of the Old Testament: Supplement Series 290 (Sheffield: Sheffield Academic Press, 1998), 360.

עדת בני צדוק] הכהנים[ 3

על חוק טמא ומ]הור[ 4

משפטיי (ט יי) ישטפ (ישפטו)[ 5

את קדושיו י]קדישו וחול] וקודש יבדילו 6

ש[ם יסובו דוכני [המזבח 7

וב]שיר יהללו או]תו 8

יי עז לעמו יתן] יי יברך את עמו בשלום[ 9

1) . . . ]Priest       2) [ . . . at all ti]mes some of the Sons of [Zadok, the priests] will instruct me (us) 3) [ . . . ] the congregation of the Sons of Zadok[, the priests . . . ] 4) [ . . . ] regarding the rules of purity and im[purity . . .] 5) [ . . . ]the law(s) of the LORD (they will adjudicate) [ . . . ] 6) [ . . . His holy things] they [shall] sanctify, but the ordinary[ and the holy they shall differentiate between . . . ] 7) [ . . . the]re they will encircle the platforms of [the altar . . . ]  8) [ . . . and with] song they will chant the Hallel to H[im . . . ] 9) [ . . . ]The LORD will give strength to His people; [the LORD will bless His people with peace . . . ] (Ps 29:11a)

The question arises whether or not Fitzmyer is correct in ascribing this text to the *Damascus Document*. Certainly, the newly found fragments (not available at the time to Fitzmyer) show no traces of this passage. This of course does not preclude the possibility that these lines were part of the still lost MTA. A glance at the wording of these lines shows that the author refers to himself as finding enlightenment, יורוני(ו), from the congregation of the Sons of Zadok. Furthermore, the speaker suggests that the sect still existed in the author's day. Likewise, if our understanding is correct, line 7 speaks of the Sons of Zadok circling (i.e. dancing) around the altar. This may indicate that the time element points to the pre-70 C.E. era. On the other hand, the imperfect tense of the verbs יורוני(ו), (ישטפ) ישטפ, יסובו, יהללו used consistently may imply that the text is essentially futuristic. If so, the general sense of these lines envisages a kind of eschatological encirclement or dance around the altar of Messiah.[5]

[4] Joseph A. Fitzmyer, "Prolegomenon," page 14 in Joseph A. Fitzmyer, ed., *Documents of Jewish Sectaries* (New York: Ktav, 1970); rep. with "Prolegomenon," of Solomon Schechter, *Fragments of a Zadokite Work* (Cambridge: Cambridge University Press, 1910).

[5] I am indebted to Amy Greenbaum for the wording of this line.

### 1.2.2.2. *Maimonides*

Maimonides states that those who do not believe in the Torah will
not inherit a portion of it in the world to come, specifically listing:
a) those who stated that not all the words of the Torah emanated from
God; and b) those who deny its interpretations (i.e. the Oral Torah)
and the veracity of those who repeated it (their sages), for example
Zadok and Boethus.[6] Writing in 1176, Maimonides claims to have
access to the writings of Zadok and Boethus. Whether or not he had
access to the DSS we do not know. However, evidence indicates that
the work of Zadok and his calendar, noted by al-Qirqisani in 943,
was accessible to Maimonides. He knows that it attacks the sages in
that he calls them מסיגי הגבול (shifters of the boundry). Thus, elements of the sect continue to flourish deep into the Middle Ages.

These and other indices show that Anan and the Karaite movement
were strongly influenced by MTA well into the medieval era.[7]

### 1.2.3. *Evidence from Others*

More evidence exists in an apparently medieval line appended to
Ben Sira[8] which is not found in the Greek and Syriac texts: Ben Sira
51.12a–p (i shown):

כי לעולם חסדו            הודו לבוחר בבני צדוק לכהן (i

i) Give praise to (God) who has chosen the Sons of Zadok as priest(s)
... for His mercy is eternal.

All this evidence makes it virtually certain that hope in the Zadokite
Priesthood continued to be a favorite topic among the medieval vestiges of the Essene movement.

### 1.2.4. *Theologizing History*

History plays an important role in MTA's theology. CD 2:14 begins
with the wicked and continues ascribing the origin of evil to the
giants who enticed the daughters of man; it recounts the patriarchs,

---

[6] Maimonides, *Hilchot Teshuvah* 3,8.
[7] See A. Harkavy, "Anan Ben David, Founder of the Karaite Sect," *JE* 1:553–56.
For a dissenting view, see Leon Nemoy, "Anan Ben David," *EncJud* 2:919–22.
[8] Ben Sira dates ca. 190–170 B.C.E.

builds to the exodus from Egypt and recalls the demise of the ignoble in Kadesh Barnea (CD 3:7). Only a new generation born in the wilderness could enter the Holy Land.

The theological importance of history becomes clear in the role of the migration to Damascus. Damascus is construed as if the coming migration[9] to the north bears a resemblance to that of Jacob's descent to Egypt. Just as the ancients migrated to Egypt and became corrupted there, so too the Israelites will migrate to Damascus, go astray and be redeemed once again, a future redemption heralded by the coming of the Just Teacher. Metahistory was never far from the author of MTA, flavoring the events in the life of the sect with biblical allusions.[10] *Urzeit* and *Endzeit* are intermingled. Thus, for the author of MTA, history or chronomessianism is also Torah.

### 1.3. *Unification*

Ever since Schechter's publication in 1910,[11] it has been taken for granted that CD originated as composite citations from various sources combined by an editor. Baumgarten and others maintain this view even after the publication of the additional passages found among the Dead Sea Scrolls.

However, an analysis of MTA, especially of the newly found fragments, shows that the text goes back to a single author. Among such indications are the tendency to be redundant, as many passages repeat themselves (see for example the comments on Haguy in CD 10:6, 13:2 and 14:7–8). Similarly, attacks on the opposition as מסיגי (ה)גבול are mentioned three times, apparently referring to the Pharisees. Such literal redundancy is appropriate for a single author. Multiple writers would implement various styles. On the other hand, the *Damascus Document* with its precisely repetitive passages is unique and demonstrates a single author. Another significant indication of the

---

[9] The occurrence of the migration in the future, rather than in the past, is discussed below.

[10] Ben Zion Wacholder, "The Teacher of Righteousness is Alive, Awaiting the Messiah: האסף in CD as Allusion to the Siniatic and Damascene Covenants," *HUCA* 70–71 (1999–2000): 75–93.

[11] Solomon Schechter, *Fragments of a Zadokite Work* (Cambridge: Cambridge University Press, 1910).

unity of MTA are the words unique to MTA but not found in the
other DSS. In fact, an entire vocabulary could be collected which is
characteristic of MTA, but (as far as we know) absent from the other
documents. Examples include the phrases משיח מאהרן ומישראל and
בוני החיץ. There is, moreover, a vocabulary that belongs to the DSS
family of documents. By family, I am referring to texts that reflect
dependence on and use of MTA such as *Rule of the Community* (1QS)
and the Pesher Commentaries on the Hebrew Scriptures, works such
as *Pesher Habakkuk, Pesher Psalms, Pesher Isaiah* and others. A common
feature of these texts centers on the fact that only they address questions pertaining to the Just Teacher (מורה צדק or יורה צדק).

A distinction should be drawn between clauses containing the word
משיחי in the plural and משיח מאהרן ומישראל (the Messiah from Aaron
and Israel) occurring four times in MTA (CD 12:23–13:1; 14:19;
19:10–11; 20:1), wherein the term "messiah" is in the singular. The
plural refers to those that are sanctified with oil, whereas the singular
to the anticipated messiah of the future. As stated above, the clause
משיח מאהרן ומישראל is unique to MTA. It contains the author's
"signature," supporting the view that this composition constitutes a
unity, not a mere collection of extracts.

What describes the personality of MTA is the idea of migration to Damascus or the claim that the community migrated from
Judea to Damascus, היוצאים מארץ יהודה ויגורו בארץ דמשק meaning
that they left the area of Jerusalem toward Damascus (CD 6:5).
No other DSS text knows of such mobility. Many scholars pursue
the claim that Damascus is equivalent to Qumran and that any
references to Damascus in the Qumran scrolls refer to a migration
to the Judean desert. In my view, this has no basis, since CD 7:14
expressly says that they travel to the north, citing Amos 5:27. It
is incredible that the author of MTA would refer to Qumran as
located in the north. Moreover, within the hundreds of documents
emanating from Qumran, only those related to MTA mention the
movement to Damascus. With the vast literature we have, there is
always a possibility that by accident all the other references to a
massive communal migration north have perished. This, however,
is implausible. In my opinion moreover, the migration to the north
in MTA is not historical but a prediction that it would occur in the
future; hence, the near silence about this migration in the DSS.

Still another important piece of evidence for the unity or integrity
of MTA is its title, מדרש התורה האחרון (The Midrash on the Eschato-

logical Torah), cited at the conclusion, and presumably originally at
the beginning of line 1, text which has perished.

4Q266 F11:20b–21

| | |
|---|---|
| הנה הכו[ל נ]כתב ע[ל [מ]דר[ש] התורה | ] 20 |
| [12[     [האחרון | 21 |

[ . . . Behold every]thing has been [written up]on "the Mi[d]ra[sh] on
the [Eschatological] Torah."

4Q266 F1:1–2a

| | |
|---|---|
| [הנה מדרש התורה האחרון על ב]נ' אור להנז' מדר[כי בני] | 1 |
| [חושך . . . | 2 |

[Here is "The Midrash on the Eschatological Torah": It is incumbent
upon the so]ns of light to keep separate from the wa[ys of the sons of
darkness . . . ]

With this framework the author of MTA echoes the style of the book
of *Jubilees* which preceded it, likewise repeating the book's name at
the very end of the composition: "and God taught him the earlier
and the later history of the *division of the days* of the law . . ." (*Jub.*
1:4) and "Herewith is completed the account of the *division of the
days*" (*Jub.* 50:13).[13]

Finally, an analysis of the dozen ancient and medieval manuscripts
in which the remains of MTA survive, attests to its unity. As will be
shown below, in spite of occasional divergences of wording, what is
remarkable is how frequently the overlapping passages coincide with
each other word by word. If there existed other documents from which
CD had been constructed, none of them seem to have survived. In
my opinion, therefore, it makes no sense to suppose that MTA's original diversity is incomplete. It has a unified vocabulary, literary style,
theology, eschatology and messianism.

---

[12]  Restored in part from 4Q270 F7ii:14b–15.
[13]  R. H. Charles, trans, *The Book of Jubilees or the Little Genesis* (London: Adam
and Charles Black, 1902) 1, 261. The italics are mine.

## 1.4. *Law*

Ever since Schechter,[14] scholars have divided CD into two subjects: admonitions and law. Prior to the publication of the Qumran manuscripts, some scrollists argued that the law originated independently from the remaining material. As Baumgarten has noted, the newly published texts show that the legal material was an integral part of the composition. In fact, in line 1b of the document, ". . . It is incumbent upon the so]ns of light to keep separate from . . .," the word *separate* is להנזר, literally to act as a Nazirite—essentially a legal concept regulating behavior. Likewise, the terms *Torah* and *Torah of Moses* and the numerous allusions to the מצות (commandments) and חוקים (laws) throughout MTA reflect an understanding of law as integral to the author's theology of Judaism.[15] Let us remember that keeping the commandments is reiterated on almost every page of the work. MTA's preamble sets the tone: "[ . . . Neither shall we depart from all that God has ordained, turning away] in small or large matters pertaining to To[rah and Admonition . . . ]" (4Q266 F1:17b–18a). A parallel passage is found in 4Q266 F6iv(a):1b–3a: "[And on]e [shall not turn] to the right nor to [the left from what the priests will instruct at the end of days . . . ]"

Baumgarten goes out of his way to make the point that MTA is essentially a legal text, not admonitory. "Although the laws are for the most part not formulated in polemical fashion they must be regarded both quantitatively and qualitatively as the core of the *Damascus Document.*"[16] This composite edition, I believe, casts doubt upon the prevailing opinion of dividing MTA into admonitions and laws. It demonstrates that the two themes are constantly interwoven. It would have been inconceivable for the author to think of Torah as legal and non-legal. Both are Torah. In fact, another favorite word of the author, מדרש, which as argued above was the first word of the title of the book, likewise applies to both legal and non-legal material. What scholars divide into admonition and law emanates from

---

[14] Schechter, *Fragments.*

[15] Ben Zion Wacholder, "The 'Torah of Moses' in the Dead Sea Scrolls, An Allusion to the Book of Jubilees," *Proceedings of the 13th World Congress of Jewish Studies* (Jerusalem, 2001).

[16] Joseph M. Baumgarten, *Qumran Cave 4.XIII: The Damascus Document (4Q266–273)* (DJDXVIII; Oxford: Clarendon, 1996), 7.

the Pauline view of Scripture. In Judaism, there is no difference in weight between legal and admonitory language.

The division in the law between the laws of the Torah—the חוקים and מצות of God on the one hand and the משפטים (regulations) of the sect on the other hand—is interesting. Whereas the former refer to the commandments given to Moses and their interpretation in works like *Enoch*, *Jubilees* and the *Temple Scroll*, the משפטים are disciplinary rules originating within the sect. In addition, even some of the laws of the sect diverge from Scripture; for example, polygamy (or bigamy) presumed in the Pentateuch is strictly forbidden in the sect. Exodus 35:2 deems any labor on the Sabbath a capital offense, a view endorsed by *Jub.* 50:8 and the rabbis; however, CD 12:4 gives the more lenient policy of the sect, "anyone who strays by profaning the Sabbath and the festivals shall not be put to death." This departure from Scripture cannot, I believe, be explained by leniency or humanity. In general, stringency is the rule of MTA. For example, all biblical prohibitions where punishment is not prescribed are, according to rabbinic tradition, subject to thirty-nine lashes; whereas in MTA, offenses without specified punishment imply the death penalty. Offenses without such punishment may be ascribed to the stringent way of observing the Sabbath for the sect. The limits on speech and behavior described in CD 10:14–11:18 show the sect's strictness, severity, and the difficulty of observance of its משפטים. The sages of the Mishnah and Talmud ruled that the laws of the Sabbath can be overridden when life is in danger. However, MTA does not accept this opinion, declaring instead, "And as to a person who falls into a ditch of water or into a [pi]t: one may not raise him up with a ladder, a rope or a tool" (CD 11:16–17a).

MTA devotes a special pericope to the discipline within the camp. This discipline contains social legislation unprecedented until modern times. For example, CD 14:12b–17b states,

> And this is the procedure of the 'Many' to fill all their needs: (Let there be) a wage withholding of least two days per month; and let it be administered by the Supervisor and the judges. From it they shall provide for (the healing of) their [wo]unded. And from it they shall assist the poor and the destitute, the elderly man who is [bent do]wn, him who suffers from lep[ro]sy, him who is taken captive by a foreign nation, a maiden who [does no]t have a re[dee]mer, a lad [w]ho has no guardian, and all the services provided by the association, so that [the association] not [perish for lack of] their [support.] And this is the elaboration concerning the habitation of the c[amps.

Thus, a levy of a minimum of two days wages was taken for support of the sick, disabled and elderly. A penalty was continuously
maintained for spitting or speaking out of order. The Supervisor
controlled admission of new members and could expel violators. The
text prescribes the length of the expulsion from ten days to life.[17]
The sect also maintained strict discipline regarding personal conduct,
including an apparent abstention from wine. Josephus records, "They
shun pleasures as a vice and regard temperance and the control of
the passions as a special virtue."[18] Scholars have not found any passage in the DSS supporting the assertion that the Essenes abstained
from wine. However, it could be that Josephus took the word להנזר
literally, to act like a Nazirite who was forbidden from drinking wine
and grapes.[19] For more discussion of להנזר, see the commentary.

### 1.5. *Organization, Format and Layout of the Book*

#### 1.5.1. *Pagination of the Hebrew Text*

The composite text raises a problem of paginal referencing. The pagination of CD follows Schechter's *editio princeps*, while on the other
hand, the Qumran material follows the organizational convention of
cave, manuscript, fragment, column and line numbers. Combining
the two complicates the sequence and pagination of the unified text.
The complication arises from the fact that the material from CD is
no longer a single unit with its content sequenced according to the
early pagination scheme, but is now scattered in accordance with the
apparent consecution in the Cave 4 manuscripts. The reader therefore,
is advised to consult the tables clarifying the organization and parallels of this unified text.[20]

#### 1.5.2. *Headers within the Hebrew Text*

The Hebrew text of MTA is organized according to textual content
and flow. Within the text are divisions to show the parallels between

---

[17] See להנזר above.
[18] Flavius Josephus, *J.W.* 2:120 (Thackeray, LCL), 369.
[19] Cf. Num 6:3.
[20] See the tables on pages xxiii–xxx.

the Genizah and Cave texts as well as parallels within the various
DSS manuscripts themselves. These sections, while important for
demonstrating parallels and the ease of finding material within this
unitary work, are somewhat arbitrary due to diacritical limitations.
Thus, they do not necessarily indicate a demarcation in the content of the text. For units of content within MTA please see the
translation, commentary, textual parallel tables and the the list of
primary text divisions.

### 1.5.3. *Hebrew Text*

The unification of the CD and Qumran texts presents its own problems. Although the overlapping manuscripts are remarkably identical,
differences in spelling and wording do occur between and within the
texts. Specifically, the spelling in CD generally diverges from that of
the manuscripts emanating from the period of the Second Temple.
For example, the final ך is often lengthened in DSS texts to כה. In
general, our composite text follows the orthography and readings of
the more ancient manuscripts of Qumran, and commonly so where
the medieval and cave texts parallel each other. For example, my
version of CD 2:3 contains the clause [ומכול שבילי חט]אים אזירכם
not in the Genizah text, but found extant in its 4Q266 parallel.
Another example is the clause ולוא האזינו [ל] in CD 3:8 of the composite text, found in 4Q269 F2:2, but not in the medieval witness.
When divergences among the manuscripts occur, our text follows that
of the primary manuscript as exemplified by 4Q268 1:4 which reads
כי אי[ן] לקדם [ו]ל[א]חר ממועדיה[מה but which in 4Q266 F2i:2 reads כי
אין [להת]ק[ד]ם ולהתאחר ממועדיהם (my text follows 4Q268). The primary
text is determined by comparing the various parallels, designating
the fullest text or manuscript as primary and the less full text or
manuscript as secondary, tertiary or the like. In general, the primary
text is 4Q266, but sometimes the other manuscripts become the main
text and 4Q266 is subordinate. The orthography in CD often radically diverges from that of the Cave 4 manuscripts. In exceptional
cases, when the readings in the ancient manuscripts appear to be in
disorder, the orthography of CD attains primary status. In many of
these instances, notes call attention to the differences in readings.
These notes accompany the text and translation.

## 1.5.4. *Verb Usage and Time Issues in the Text*

It is important to say a word concerning the role of verbs and time in this work. The text frequently shifts from the perfect to the imperfect and vice versa, especially when it uses the so-called ו-ההיפוך (conversive *waw*), which in an unvocalized tradition may often refer to the consecutive past or the future. Nothing can be said definitively about time, except by context.

A primary question is the state of the Hebrew in the Dead Sea Scrolls, especially in MTA. How much are precedents in Biblical Hebrew narrative relevant to the understanding of the language preserved in the Judean desert? The verbal forms of the DSS and especially of MTA bear a close resemblance to chapter eleven of Daniel, whose conventional verbal patterns are either ambiguous or frequently ignored. This constitutes a serious problem in MTA, especially in the relationship to the Just Teacher, the exile in Damascus and eschatology in general. The medieval vocalization וַיָּגוּדוּ עַל נפש צדיק (CD 1:20) exemplifies the historicizing of the verbs in this work, since the Just Teacher apparently never arrived. An instructive case is the divergence between verbs in the A and B manuscripts. Ms A uses התהלכו (7:7) and מלטו (7:21) whereas Ms B has יתהלכו (19:4) and ימלטו (19:10). Furthermore Ms A employs הסגירו (8:1) whereas B has the synonym ימסרו (19:10). The former tends toward historicizing while the latter anticipates the action described. Content and context in MTA play the major role in recognizing the nature of the tenses of a verb—perfect, imperfect, participle or infinitive. Conventional scholarship, looking for the origin of the Essenes as well as for precedents of Christianity, has tended to note the perfect form since its customary use to portray past tenses would yield the necessary information for the historian.

This work departs from this tradition, proposing a new understanding of what is past and what is future. Note that, as stressed before, most of these verbs are under the rubric of ראישונים[21] and אחרונים, the patriarchal past and later, that is to say the current time for the author of MTA. Frequently these rubrics serve to determine the time element of verbs. They will be analyzed on their own in a

---

[21] The spelling of citations of CD in this work follows that of the 4Q manuscripts when available. Thus, ראישונים is spelled with the י after the א as it is in 4Q268 1:12, not as in the Genizah text 1:4 ראשונים.

strictly contextual sense whether they refer to the past or the future. It is fallacious to read these texts as a precedent to Christianity, since these authors knew nothing of what would occur in the future. The language of the Dead Sea Scrolls in my view bears a resemblance to that of psalmic and wisdom literature where verbal forms often assume a general present and futuristic sense. The verbal conjugations in Ps 1 for example may serve as a model for the grammar of MTA.

### 1.5.5. *Number and Gender Agreement in MTA*

Another problem in the reading of MTA lies in the text's inconsistencies in number and gender, especially for suffixes. The DSS do not follow our modern understanding of Hebrew grammar. Grammatical inconsistencies are a functional element of the Hebrew language of the MTA and are reflected in the English translation.

### 1.5.6. *Translation*

Note that the translation provided often diverges from the standard renditions. This is true in particular with verbs which have been customarily translated as if they were in the past tense, here rendered either in the future or present perfect. Thus, concepts in the DSS tradition which have been entrenched to be part of DSS history are turned to futuristic material. For example, the Just Teacher is no longer a personality of the past, but a man of the future.[22] So too his future nemesis, the Scoffer or Wicked Priest.

The English rendition of the Hebrew text may be found on the facing page in line to line correspondence. Due to idiomatic and word order differences between Hebrew and English, in some instances the correspondence is not exact. In a few cases, the best English rendition is made by a radical departure from the sequencing, resulting in lines being grouped together.[23]

Our translation rarely mentions other renditions; however, divergences in the Hebrew text are found in the accompanying notes as detailed below. Comments on the translation of the Hebrew text are in the commentary section of the work as described below.

---

[22] Wacholder, "The Teacher of Righteousness is Alive," 75–92.
[23] For example, CD 15:5–6, 13–14; 16:16–18; 10:2–3.

### 1.5.7. *Notes on the Text*

Divergences in texts are discussed in the notes accompanying the
text and translation in chapter 2. These notes occur in numerical
order, the majority of which I have included with the Hebrew text. A
smaller number accompany the translation.

### 1.5.8. *Commentary*

I have also provided the first running commentary of the text on the
newly available material. I place it after the text and translation with
accompanying notes. It follows the order of MTA. Therefore, issues
raised by the text will be addressed in their textual order rather than
in a topical format. Topics will be addressed as they develop through
MTA, section by section. It should be helpful to the reader in terms
of the book's enigmatic wording and relations between MTA and
the DSS. Sometimes the commentary adumbrates general problems
such as the nature of the polemics and the divergences with Talmudic
tradition. However, it is not intended to be exhaustive.

### 1.5.9. *Headings and Subheadings*

For greater simplicity I have organized the majority of the contents
of the book into numerical divisions with headings and successive
subheadings arranged according to the following rubric: 1, 1.1, 1.2,
1.2.1, etc. Because of the complexity of the material, the numeration
sequencing in chapter three, the commentary, is rather extensive.
An abbreviated listing of these divisions is included in the Table
of Contents.

### 1.5.10. *Tables*

A series of tables (Tables 1.1–1.6, 2, 3) demarcate parallel texts within
MTA, especially the parallels between the Qumran manuscripts and
the Genizah fragments. The tables give the listing of the primary
text followed by a slash and then the appropriate designation for the
parallel text. The page number for the primary text and parallel is
also given, providing the reader with a means to locate specific texts
within the work. The tables should be read noting the organization
of the primary text in the intersection of the horizontal row with the
column. Therefore, readers using the tables to find specific texts should
begin in the appropriate horizontal row. The primary text rows are

organized in numerical order, beginning with the CD designations followed by the Qumran manuscript listings. The secondary text (or parallel text) columns are likewise in numerical order, with appropriate columns listed for each table from left to right. If certain CD pages or Qumran manuscripts do not appear as parallels in MTA for the specific rows given in a table, then the texts are not listed in the columns.

Table 2 lists the parallels within MTA to other Qumran manuscripts, 5Q12, 6Q15 & 1QS. The same organizational structure applies to table 2 as to tables 1.1–1.6.

### 1.5.11. *Indices*

Indices of modern authors, subjects and ancient sources are available at the back of the book.

TEXT AND TRANSLATION

## 2.1. *Preamble*

4Q266 F1; F2i:1a
Parallels: 4Q267 F1:1–8 (underline)

1:1 [הנה<sup>w</sup> מדרש התורה האחרון<sup>s/w</sup> על<sup>w</sup> ב]נٔי אור להنזר מדך[כי בני<sup>w</sup>]

1:2 [חושך<sup>s/w</sup> ולהתהלך על פי התורה<sup>s</sup>]<sup>2</sup> עד תום מועד /הٜ\פקודה<sup>3</sup> ב[קץ<sup>s</sup>]<sup>4</sup>

1:3 [הרשעה כי בחרון אפוٗ<sup>s</sup> יפק]וٓד<sup>w 5</sup> אל את כול מעש{יٔ}הٔ<sup>6</sup> להבי כל[ה]

1:4 בت[בל לאין שירית ופליטה<sup>s</sup>]<sup>7</sup> למסיגי גבול וכלה יעשה [לעוזרי<sup>w</sup>]<sup>8</sup>

1:5 רשעה̇ [ ועתה̇<sup>b</sup> בנים<sup>s</sup> שמעוٔ]<sup>9</sup> לי ואודיעה לכם במ[עשי<sup>s/w</sup> אל]<sup>10</sup>

1:6 הנורא[ים<sup>s/w</sup> בגבורות]<sup>11</sup> פלאו וٕאٜסٜפٜרٜ⟨⟨ר⟩⟩ה<sup>12</sup> לכ[ם נהיות עולם הנסתרות[<sup>w</sup>]<sup>13</sup>

1:7 מאנוש [מעמו<sup>w</sup> הי]מٕים<sup>14</sup> אשר חי כ[ו]ל [אדם אין אחר זולתו להביט<sup>w</sup>]

1:8 בעמקתٜ] רזיו והוא<sup>w</sup>] חكֵ[ק<sup>15</sup> נהיות עולם בלב אבן ויודיע עוز ידו<sup>w</sup>]

1:9 תֵם [רזים ויגלה נסתרות וירים כושלים ונופליהם<sup>w</sup> [

1:10 [ ]

1:11 [ ]

1:12 [ ]

1:13 ]° והמחזיקים<sup>w</sup>[

---

[1] Stegemann reconstructs [מדך[כי חושך. See Hartmut Stegemann, "Towards Physical Reconstructions of the Qumran Damascus Document Scrolls," in *The Damascus Document A Centennial of Discovery: Proceedings of the Third International Symposium of the Orion Center for the Study of the Dead Sea Scrolls and Associated Literature, 4–8 February, 1998* (ed. Joseph M. Baumgarten, Esther G. Chazon, and Avital Pinnick; Leiden: Brill, 2000); Vol. XXXIV in *Studies on the Texts of the Desert of Judah* (ed. F. García Martínez and A. S. van der Woude; Leiden: Brill), 193–94.

[2] Stegemann reconstructs ולהתהלך תמים על פי התורה ("Physical Reconstructions," 193–94).

[3] The supralinear ה is adjacent to the מ of מועד in the manuscript. However, as Baumgarten comments, it belongs with פקודה; hence our reading הפקודה. Cf. the phrase עד מועד פקודתו in 1QS 3:18.

[4] Baumgarten in his editio princeps restores [ב.רוח עולה]. See Joseph M. Baumgarten, *Qumran Cave 4.XIII: The Damascus Document* (4Q266–273) (DJD XVIII; Oxford: Clarendon, 1996), 31–32. My rendition [קץ הרשעה] (cf. also Stegemann) replaces [ב.אחרית הימים] of the preliminary edition. See Ben Zion Wacholder and Martin G. Abegg, Jr., reconstructors and eds., *A Preliminary Edition of the Unpublished Dead Sea Scrolls. The Hebrew and Aramaic Texts from Cave Four. Fascicle One* (Washington, D.C.: Biblical Archaeology Society, 1991), 3.

[5] Baumgarten restores ישמיֹ[ל ] (DJD XVIII, 31–32). My reconstruction finds support from CD 5:15–16.

[6] Baumgarten transcribes מעשיה (DJD XVIII, 31–32). My reading reflects the erasure dot above the *yod*, and replaces the transcription מעשה in Wacholder, "Preamble," 33.

## 2.1. *Preamble*

*Prologue; Downfall of the Opposition; Promise to Reveal the Mysteries of History; Supplication*

**4Q266 F1–2i:1a** 1:1[Here is "The Midrash on the Eschatological Torah." It is incumbent upon the so]ns of light to keep separate from the wa[ys of the sons] 1:2[of darkness and to walk in accordance with the Torah] until the completion of the period of remembrance at [the end of the epoch] 1:3[of wickedness, for in His burning anger] God [will remem]ber each and every deed, wreaking hav[oc] 1:4against the e[arth until] the Shifters of the Boundary [are without remnant or survivors]. Furthermore He will bring destruction [against those who act as accomplices in doing] 1:5evil. [But now O children, hear] me and I will make known to you 1:6the awesome ac[ts of God] along with His [miraculous] powers. And I will relate to yo[u the events of eternity hidden] 1:7from man. [The li]fespan of ev[er]y [man has been shortened. There is no one but He who can fathom] 1:8the profundities of [His mysteries. But He] has etc[hed the events of eternity into a stony heart, and makes known the strength of His hand.] 1:9He has sealed [mysteries, reveals the hidden, and raises those who stumble and fall . . . 1:13[ . . . those who cling] 1:14to the commandment[s . . .

---

<sup>7</sup> Stegemann reconstructs [בת]בל ואין שרית ופליטה] (Stegemann, "Physical Reconstructions," 193). My variation supplants בת] ובקן חרבן הארץ עמדו כו]ל מסיני גבול in Wacholder-Abegg, *Fascicle One*, 3, and בת]וך עדת בוגדים ובכו]ל מסיני גבול in Wacholder, "The Preamble to the Damascus Document," *HUCA* 69 (1998): 33.

<sup>8</sup> [לעוזרי] replaces [בקן] in Wacholder, "Preamble," 33; Baumgarten reconstructs [לפועלי] and Stegemann [לכול] (DJD XVIII, 31–32; Stegemann, "Physical Reconstructions," 193).

<sup>9</sup> Replaces [עד בוא משיח הצדק ועתה שמעו] in Wacholder, "Preamble," 33.

<sup>10</sup> Baumgarten reconstructs [מח]שבות אל] (DJD XVIII, 31).

<sup>11</sup> Baumgarten restores הנורא]ות (DJD XVIII, 31). My adoption of Baumgarten's reading גבורות preceded by ב rather than ו reflects a change from ברזי in Wacholder, "Preamble," 33.

<sup>12</sup> Baumgarten transcribes אספר>>ר<<ה, omitting ו (DJD XVIII, 31).

<sup>13</sup> Baumgarten restores [לב]ם אשר נסתרו] (DJD XVIII, 31)

<sup>14</sup> Baumgarten reads מאנוש י[מים] מספר (DJD XVIII, 31) and Stegemann מאנוש] חכמת ש[מים ("Physical Reconstructions," 193). Our reconstruction supplants כי מעטו מספר הי]מים in Wacholder, "Preamble," 33.

<sup>15</sup> Supplants הק]רוש [אל] בעמקת in Wacholder, "Preamble," 33. Stegemann transcribes בעמקת] כול רזו]י הק]וד]ש ("Physical Reconstructions," 193).

1:14    במצו[ת                                    ואנחנו לזכרון במועדינו[ᵂ]

1:15    בתרומ[ת]ᵇ שפתים נברכנו כחוק חרות לעד ברושי שנים ונשמע[ᵂ16]

1:16    לקו̇ל מושה[ ]                              ולא נלך[ᵂ17]

1:17    רכיל בחוס[י בני[ᵂ18] ומצ̇ות אל[ ובבריתו ולא נסור מכול אשר צוה אל לנטות[ᵂ19]

1:18    קטנה וגדולה לת̇[ורה ולתעודה ועתה אם נא מצאנו חן בעיניכה[ᵂ]

1:19    הודיענו נא א̇[ת דרככה ונדעכהᵂ                 מה אהבנו[ᵂ]

1:20    שיחתך א̇ם [נהללך ארך אפים עמך̇ᵂ ורוב סל[י̇חות ה[ל̇וא אתה[ᵂ20]

1:21    עמדתה ותתבונן [במחשבותינוᵂ 21 כאשר ת̇[צ̇וה ביד מוש̇[ה ᵂ ו̇ו̇ת̇י שו̇ב̇]

1:22    אפר ישיבו את א̇[שר22 צוהᵂ [מ̇[ו̇[שה?23 ]        [ל̇ ה̇ן̇ הו̇ם̇ᵉ 24 ] ונחנוᵂ מה̇ עפר̇]

1:23    ואפר ומי קד̇ו̇[ש25 ᵂ כמוכ[ה להבי [כלה אשרᵂ י̇[מ̇חה את מע̇[שי רשעה[ᵂ]

1:24    התבונ[ו[נתה̇ ᵂ[ה>לוא הבינותה אל̇ᵂ ᵂמשכל̇[י̇ם לדבר ד̇>כ̇<ר אל נב[י̇אים[ᵂ26]

1:25    ו̇ב̇פ̇[ו̇תכה27 נודך כי תסלח את̇ᵂ ח[ט̇את?ᵂ אשמתם [ולא תשמיד̇ כול̇[ᵂ]

2:1a    [בשר ובריאה[28


## 4Q268 F1:1–8
## Parallels: 4Q266 F2i:1–6a (underlined)

1    [מחלקות העתיםᵂ 29 ה[א̇ח̇רונות הלוא כן תבואינה] ככול ימ̇י̇ᵂ וכ[ᵂ30

2    [תקופות מועד̇י[ᵂ 31 איזה תחלתו ואיזה סופו ות̇[ג̇יד את הראישו[נ̇י̇ם̇ᵂ 32

[16] Baumgarten reconstructs [לא שמעו                     בתרומ[ה (DJD XVIII,
31).

[17] See DJD XVIII, 33.

[18] Baumgarten transcribes [בחוק[י] (DJD XVIII, 31). I thank David Maas for
suggesting the reading בחוס[י. The extant letters are written above the word ומצות.
Presumably it is additional, not a correction of מצות.

[19] Baumgarten reconstructs [לעשות     . See DJD XVIII, 31.

[20] Replaces ארך אפים עמו ורוב סל[י̇חות ת̇[נון ורחום of Wacholder, "Preamble," 33.

[21] Supplants במעשינו in Wacholder, "Preamble," 33.

[22] Baumgarten transcribes [אפר ישיבו את ◦] (DJD XVIII, 31).

[23] Replaces י̇[עשה in Wacholder, "Preamble," 33; Baumgarten transcribes שה◦[
(DJD XVIII, 33).

[24] Baumgarten transcribes לי◦◦הא̇ל̇ם (DJD XVIII, 33).

[25] Baumgarten transcribes [ומ̇י     ]ק[ (DJD XVIII, 31). Our reading supplants
ומי קד̇[ש ונורא כמוכה of Wacholder, "Preamble," 33.

[26] Replaces [י̇ם לדבר [ול̇[דר[ש] אל נב[ונים in Wacholder, "Preamble," 33.

Now as for us, in celebratory remembrance during our festivals [1:15]we will bless Him] with the offerin[g of lips as a statute engraved forever (to celebrate) at the beginning of each year. And we will hearken] [1:16]to the voice of Moses, [ . . . and we will not go around] [1:17]slandering [those] who seek refuge [in Him (God)], God's commandments [and in His covenant. Neither shall we depart from all that God has ordained, turning away] [1:18]in small or large matters pertaining to To[rah and Admonition. So now, if we have found favor in Your eyes] [1:19]please let us know [Your way that we may know You (Exod 33:13) . . . How much we love] [1:20]meditating about You when [we praise You. You are long-suffering and abundant in for]giveness. Sure[ly You] [1:21]have attended to and analyzed [our thoughts in accordance with what You] have commanded through Mose[s. And be it that] [1:22]they completely return to w[hat Mo]ses [commanded . . . ] . . . that day. [And what are we but dust] [1:23]and ashes and who is [as] sacr[ed as Yo]u, bringing [destruction, who] blots out ac[ts of wickedness.] [1:24]You have anal[yzed, and surely You have imparted understanding to the sage]s, speaking (about it) to pro[phets.] [1:25]And with [Your] word[s we extol You, for You forgive the s]in of their guilt [and do not destroy all] [2:1][flesh and creation.]

*The Divisions of the Times*

**4Q268 F1** [1:1][As for the Divisions of the] Eschatological [Epochs]: Surely they will occur (as was presaged) [according to all (the number of) its days and a]ll [1:2][(the number of) the cycles of] i[ts festivals,] when its beginning (was) and ending (will occur); for [(God)] has

---

[27] Baumgarten transcribes ]ّ∘َוٰ (DJD XVIII, 32). 4Q267 F1:7 reads וּבפֿויתכה. A metathesis of י and ו is probable.

[28] The reconstructed text on this line plausibly continues the next column of 4Q266. Line 1 of 4Q266 F2i may have read [בשר ובריאה והגיד את הראישונים ואת האחרוני]ٰפ ואת. [עד אשר This differs from Baumgarten's reconstruction: [בשר ובריאה איזה עד אשר]ٰפ[     ]ٰפ[ תחלתו ואיזה סופו (DJD XVIII, 34). See comments on the apparently greater length of 4Q268 at this point and the rationale for my reconstruction.

[29] Supplants [אֿחרונות דורות of Wacholder-Abegg, *Fascicle One*, 1.

[30] Replaces [כ]וֹל תבואינה of Wacholder, "Preamble," 34; Baumgarten restores כ[     ] (DJD XVIII, 119).

[31] Replaces [מועדיה]ٰפ of Wacholder, "Preamble," 34; Baumgarten transcribes ה[     ] (DJD XVIII, 119).

[32] Baumgarten transcribes ∘י[     ]וٰה (DJD XVIII, 119).

3  [ואת האחרונים ואת עֵֽד] אֲשֶׁר יבוא במה כי הֿ[כין שבתות ומוע]דֵֽ[w³ 33

4  [בריתו לעולםw 34 כי אֵי]ַֿן לֶקְדֵם [וֹ]לֹ[אַ]חֵר ממועדריהֿ[מה35 ומחורשיהמה[w]

5  [ומ]שׁבֵֿ[תות]פֵֿ 36 vacat וֹֿתֵֿ[וא] חקק 37 קֵצֵי הֵֿ[רון לעם לא ידעהו]

6  וֹֿהֿוא הֿכֿין [מועדי] רצון לדורשׁי מצוותיו ולֹ[הולכים בתמים]

7  דרך ויגל עֵֽ[יניה]מֿה בנסתרות ואוזנמה פתחוֹ [וישמעו עמוקות]

8  וֹיבינו בכול נהיות עד מה יבוא במה vacat [

## 2.2 Body

CD 1:1–2:1
Parallels: 4Q268 F1:9–17 (underline)
    4Q266 F2i:6b–25; ii:1–2a (overbar)
    extant and restored text unique to DSS (outline)
    paleo script is in DSS only

1:1  vacat ועתה שמעו ⅃ⅼ כֹוֹל יודעי צדק ובינו במעשׁי

1:2  ⅃ₓ כי ריב לו עם כֹול בשר ומשפט יעשה בכֹול מנאציו

1:3  כי במועלם אשר עזבוהו הסתיר פניו מישראל וממקדשׁ

1:4  וֹיתֵנם לחרב ובזכרו ברית ראִֿישֿוֿנים השאיר שאירית

1:5  לישראל ולֹֿוֹא נתנם לכלה ובקץ חרון שנים שלוש מאות

1:6  ותשעים לתיתו אוֹתם ביד נבוכדנאצר מלך בבל

1:7  פקדֿם ויצמח מישראל ומאהרֿ[וֹ]ן שֿורֿש מטעת לירוש

1:8  אֵת אֵרֿצו ולדשן בטוב אדמתו ויבינו בֵעוֹֿנֿם וידעו כי

1:9  ⟨⟨אנשים⟩⟩9 אֵשֿֿימים הסֿהֿ ויהיו כעורים וכימגשׁשׁים דרך

1:10  שנים עשרים ויבן אל אל מעשיהם כי בלב שׁלם דרשׁוהֿוֹ

1:11  ויקם להם מורה צדק להדריכם בדרך לבֿוֹ vacat ויודע

1:12  לדורות אחרונים את אשר עשה בדֿור אחרון בעדת בוגדים

---

33 Baumgarten transcribes דֵֿ[        ]הֿ (DJD XVIII, 119).
34 Supplants ואת קציהם לכול שני עולם of Wacholder, "Preamble," 34.
35 כי אין [להת]ק[ד]ֿם ולהֿתאחר מֿמֿוֹֿעֿריהם 4Q266 F2i:2.
36 Baumgarten transcribes בֿ[   ]ٚשׁ[ ] (DJD XVIII, 119).
37 חקוק 4Q266 F2i:3.

fore[told the firs]t [1:3][as well as the latter things and] what will transpire thereafter in them (the Divisions of the Eschatological Epochs), since H[e has set up Sabbaths and His covenantal festi]vals [1:4][for eternity (and) since one may neith]er advance [nor post]pone th[eir] festivals, [their months or] [1:5]their Sabb[aths]. And H[e] decreed epochs of a[nger for a people who knew Him not,] [1:6]but proclaimed agreeable [festivals] for those who observe His commandments faithfully and for [those who keep to the straight] [1:7]path. And He will (yet) open their e[ye]s to the hidden mysteries and they will open their ears [so that they will hear profound matters.] [1:8]And they will perceive all events to eternity (before) they occur to them. . .

## 2.2 *Body*

### *The Introduction to The Eschatological Torah*

### *Announcing the Coming Eschatology*

CD [1:1]And now, heed me all you who know righteousness and discern the acts [1:2]of God. For He is in contention with all flesh and will execute justice upon all those who vex Him. [1:3]For in their treachery, having deserted Him, God hid His face from Israel and His temple [1:4]and put them (Israel) to the sword.

But, when He remembers the covenant of the ancestral generations, He will leave a remnant [1:5]for Israel and will not hand them over to complete destruction. And towards the end of the epoch of anger—three hundred and [1:6]ninety years following God's handing them over to Nebuchadnezzar, king of Babylon—[1:7]He will remember them. And He will cause to sprout forth from Israel and from Aaron roots of a plant to inherit [1:8]His land and to grow fat in the fertility of His soil. And the people will become aware of their sin and they will know that [1:9]they are guilty. And they will be like the blind and like those groping for a way [1:10]for twenty years.

And God, noting their (righteous) deeds that they will have searched for Him with a perfect heart, [1:11]will raise up for them a Just Teacher so as to lead them in the way that will please Him. And He will make known [1:12]to the eschatological generations (of the righteous) what He will have done to the final generation, to the cabal of traitors.

1:13    הם סרי דרך היא העת היה אשר היה כתוב עליה [בספר הושע]ᵂ כפרה סוררה

1:14    כן סרר ישראל בעמוד איש הלצון אשר הטיף לישראל

1:15    מימי כזב ויתעם בתוהו ולוא דרך להשח גבהות עולם ולסור

1:16    מנתיבות צדק ולהסיע גבול אשר גבלו רישונים³⁸ בנחלתם למען

1:17    הדבק בהם את אלות בריתו להסגירם לחרב נקמת נקם

1:18    ברית בעבור אשר דרשו בחלקות ויבחרו במהתלות ויצפו

1:19    לפרצות ויבחרו בטוב הצואר³⁹ ויצדיקו רשע וירשיעו צדיק

1:20    ויעבירו ברית ויפירו חוק ויגודו על נפש צדיק [ובמחזיקי בבריתו]ᵂ ובכל הולכי

1:21    תמים תעבה נפשמה [רשת שמו גם ללכדם]ᵂ וירדפום לחרב ויסיסו לריב

      עם ויחר אף

2:1    אל בעדתם להשם את כל המונם ומעשיהם לנדה לפניו

---

CD 2:2–4:18

Parallels: 4Q266 F2ii:2a–24, iii; 3i; unidentified F34 (underline)
            4Q269 F1–2 (dotted underline)
            4Q270 F1i, ii(a), ii(b) (overbar)
                extant or restored text unique to DSS; DSS text whose
                sequencing evidently differs from that of CD (outline)

2:2    *vac* ועתה שמעו אלי כל באי ברית ואגלה אזנכם בדרכי

2:3    רשעים ומכל שבילי חט[אים אזיר אתכם]⁴⁰ *vac* אל אהב דעת חוכמה ותושייה

      הציב לפניו⁴¹

2:4    וערמה ודעת הם ישרתוהו ארך אפים עמו ורוב סליחות

2:5    לכפר בעד כל שבי פשע וכוח וגבורה וחמה גדולה בלהבי אש

2:6    בי<ד>ᵂ ⁴² כל מלאכי חבל לאין שאירית⁴³ ופליטה לסרי דרך

2:7    ומאהבי חק כי לא בחר אל בהם מקדם עולם ובטרם נוסדו ידע

2:8    את מעשיהם ויתעב את דורות מדם ויסתר את פניו מן הארץ

---

³⁸ ראשנים CD 1:16.

³⁹ צור 4Q266 F2i:22.

⁴⁰ Baumgarten restores ומכול שבילי חט[אים אזיר אתכם] (DJD XVIII, 119). Another
possibility is אבדילכם.

⁴¹ לפנו 4Q266 F2ii:4.

⁴² Cf. 1QS 4:12.

⁴³ 4Q266 F2ii:6 elides the guttural א and omits the י. As noted by Baumgarten, the
extant wording of 4Q266 F2ii:5–6 suggests a somewhat different sequence from that
of CD 2:6–7:

1:13They are the ones who have abandoned the (righteous) path. That will be the time concerning which has been written [in the book of Hosea]: "Like a belligerent heifer 1:14so Israel will have rebelled" (Hos 4:16), when the Scoffer arises, who will have dripped on Israel 1:15lying waters. 'Thus, He will lead them astray into a landless wilderness without an escape route' (Ps 107:40; Job 12:24), both lowering the heights of the world by turning away 1:16from the paths of justice and by removing the boundary that the ancestral generations had set in their inheritance, so that 1:17the curses of His covenant cling to them, resulting in them being handed over to 'a sword which will fiercely avenge 1:18(the violation of) the covenant' (Lev 26:25). For they will have interpreted (Him) with flattering words, choosing farce and looking 1:19for loopholes favoring the fine neck, that will result in declaring the wicked as righteous and the righteous as wicked. 1:20And they will transgress the covenant, abrogate the statute, 'and conspire against the pious person' (Ps 94:21) and despise [those who keep His covenant] and all those who are 1:21perfect. [They have set a snare to seize them], pursuing them even to the sword and will rejoice over the civil war of the people[1] so that God's anger will be provoked CD 2:1against their assembly to destroy all their legions, their acts being defiling to Him.

*A Review of History*

2:2And now, heed me all who are entering the covenant and I will reveal to you the ways 2:3of the wicked. And [I will keep you apart] from all the paths of sin[ners.] God loves knowledge. Wisdom and salvation He has placed before Himself. 2:4Prudence and knowledge minister to Him. He is patient and very forgiving, 2:5atoning for all penitent sinners. But (there will be) much power and great wrath with flames of fire 2:6–7by all the messengers of destruction, resulting in neither a remnant nor survivors for those who turn away from the way and despise the statute. For God did not choose them from the beginning of time. And even before they were established He knew 2:8their deeds, despising those generations on account of (their) bloody

---

[1] An alternative translation is "they will rejoice over Jeroboam."

---

6  בי⟨ד⟩ כל מלאכי חבל על סרדי דרך ומתעבי חק לאין שאידית

7  ופליטה למו כי לא בחר אל בהם מקדם עולם ובטרם נוסדו ידע

We follow Baumgarten's restoration of the DSS parallel (DJD XVIII, 36).

2:9 ‹‹מי››ʷ עד תומם וידע את שני מעמד ומספר ופרוש קציהם לכל

2:10 הוי עולמים ונהיית⁴⁴ עד מה יבוא בקציהם לכל שני עולם

2:11 ובכולם הקים לו קריאיֵ֯ם שם למען התיר פליטה לארץ ולמלא

2:12 פני תבל מזרעם vacat ויודיעם ביד משיחו⁴⁵ רוח קדשו וחוזי

2:13 אמת⁴⁶ ובפרוש ‹‹שמוס››ʷ שמותיהם ואת אשר שנא התעה

2:14 vacat ועתה בנים שמעו [א]לי⁴⁷ ואגלה עיניכם לראות ולהבין במעשי

2:15 אל ולבחור את אשר רצה ולמאוס ʷ ‹‹כ››‹‹אשר››⁴⁸ שנא [לֶלֶכֶת תָּמִ֯ים אל בברית הסר]⁴⁹ ʷ להתהלך תמים

2:16 בכ֯ו֯ל דרכיו ולא לתור במחשבות יצר אשמה ועני⁵⁰ זנות כי רבים

2:17 תעו בם וגבורי חיל נכשלו בם מלפנים ועד הנה בלכתם בשרירות

2:18 לבם נפלו עירי⁵¹ השמים בה נאחזו אשר לא שמרו מצות אל

2:19 ובניהם אשר כרום ארזים גבהם וכהרים גויותיהם כי נפלו

2:20 כל בשר אשר היה בחרבה כי גוע ויהיו כלא⁵² היו בעשותם את

2:21 רצונם ולא שמרו את מצות עשיהם עד אשר חרה אפו⁵³ בם

3:1 vacat בה תעי⁵⁴ בני נח ומשפחותיהם בה הם נכרתים

3:2 אברהם לא הלך בה ויעל אֹוהב בשמרו מצות אל ולא בחר

3:3 ברצון רוחו וימסור וישמרו מצות אל ולא בחר לישחק וליעקב וישמרו ויכתבו אוהבים

3:4 לאל ובעלי ברית לעולם vacat בני יעקב תעו בם ויענשו לפני

3:5 משגותם ובניהם במצרים הלכו בשרירות לבם להיעץ על

3:6 מצות אל ולעשות איש הישר בעיניו ויאכלו את הדם ויכרת

---

⁴⁴ Or ונהיות (cf. 4Q268 F1:8). For the meaning of נהיה, compare רז נהיה, a ubiquitous phrase in the מוסר texts.

⁴⁵ Read משיחי.

⁴⁶ Read שמותיהם בפרוש אמתו. Cf. 4Q266 F2ii:13 which begins with בפרוש שמותי[הם].

⁴⁷ The reading [א]לʼ is probable in 4Q266 F2ii:14. CD has לי.

⁴⁸ Qimron suggests reading באשר. See Elisha Qimron, "The Text of CDC," in *The Damascus Document Reconsidered* (Ed. Magen Broshi; Jerusalem: The Israel Exploration Society, 1992), 13. Cf. באשר in 1QHa 7:19.

⁴⁹ According to Baumgarten, Milik would have inserted this clause from 1QS 1:8 to fill up line 15 of 4Q266 F2ii (DJD XVIII, 39). Other possible clauses from the same text might be ולעשות אמת וצדקה ומשפט בארץ (lines 4–5) or לרחוק מכול רע ולדבוק בטוב (lines 5–6).

⁵⁰ Read ועיני.

⁵¹ עירי CD. 4Q270 F1i:2–3 seems to have been shorter here than the corresponding medieval text. בלכתם בשרירות לבם נפלו does not fit into what remains of this Qumran parallel.

⁵² כלו 4Q266 F2ii:20.

⁵³ אפה 4Q266 F2ii:21.

⁵⁴ Read תעו.

acts.[2] And He hid His face from the earth 2:9until they were destroyed. And He knows the years of (their) existence and the number and the details of their epochs for all 2:10beings of eternity including what will occur in the future during their eras forever. 2:11And during all (these epochs) He has raised up for Himself well known people in order to preserve a remnant in the earth and to fill 2:12the world with their descendants. And He has informed them through those who were anointed by His Holy Spirit and (through) the seers 2:13of His truth by elaborating on their names. But those whom He hated He has led astray.

2:14And now, hear me O children that I may open your eyes to see and to understand the acts of 2:15God, to choose what He desires, and to despise what He hates, [to observe the statutes of God with the loving covenant], to walk perfectly 2:16in all His ways and not to wander into thoughts inclining towards transgression with eyes of whoredom, since many 2:17have gone astray in these matters. Mighty armies have stumbled into them from the time of old until now. While walking in the stubbornness of 2:18their heart the Watchers of Heaven fell. In it (whoredom) were seized those who have not obeyed the commandments of God 2:19along with their children, whose height was like that of the cedars. And, their bodies were piled up like mountains, because 2:20all flesh which was on the dry land fell, for they died and were as if they had never been, because they were following 2:21their passions. And, they did not observe the commandments of their Maker until His anger was ignited against them. CD 3:1The children of Noah went astray in it and their families were cut off through it. 3:2(But) Abraham did not follow it. Rather he rose up to be beloved on account of his observing the commandments of God and did not choose to follow 3:3the passions of his spirit. And he handed it over to Isaac and Jacob, and they observed (them) and were recorded in writing as beloved 3:4of God and covenanters for eternity. But the sons of Jacob went astray in them and were punished on account of 3:5their folly, and their sons in Egypt followed the stubbornness of their heart to plot against 3:6the commandments of God, each doing as his eyes

---

[2] This is perhaps an allusion to the Flood.

3:7   זכורם במדבר להם בקדש[55] (לאמר)[w] עלו ורשו את [הָאָרֶץ וְלֹם אֹחֵז][b] רוחם[56] ולא שמעו

3:8   לקול עשיהם [וְלֹא הֶאֱזִינוּ לְ]מצות יוריהם וירגנו באהליהם ויחר אף אל בעדתם

3:9   וּבְנֵיהֶם בֶּן אבדו ומלכיהם בו נכרתו וגיבוריהם בן

3:10  אבדו וארצם בו שממה [בְּיַד כָּל אוֹיְבֵיהֶמָה וְגַם][w] [57] בו הבו[58] באֵי הַבְּרִית הַרִאשֹׁנִים ויסגרו

3:11  לחרב בעזבם את ברית אל ויבחרו בְּרְצוֹנָם וַיְתוֹרוּ אַחֲרֵי שרירות

3:12  לבם לעשות איש את רצונו vacat ובמחזיקים במצות אל

3:13  אשר נותרו מהם הקים אל את בריתו לישראל עד עולם לגלות

3:14  להם נסתרות אשר תעו בם כל ישראל vacat שבתות קדשו ומועדי

3:15  כבודו עידות צדקו ודרכי אמתו וחפצי רצונו אשר יעשה

3:16  האדם וחיה בהם vacat פתח לפניהם ויחפרו באר למים רבים

3:17  ומואסיהם לא יחיה והם התגוללו בפשע אנוש ובדרכי נדה

3:18  ויאמרו כי לנו היא ואל ברזי פלאו כפר בעד עונם וישא ויסא לפשעם

3:19  ויבן להם בית נאמן בישראל אשר לא עמד כמהו למלפנים ועד

3:20  הנה המחזיקים בו לחיי נצח וכל כבוד אדם להם הוא כאשר

3:21  הקים אל להם ביד יחזקאל הנביא לאמר הכהנים והלוים ובני

4:1   צדוק אשר שמרו את משמרת מקדשי בתעות בני יִשְׂרָאֵל

4:2   מעלי הם יגישׁו לי חלב ודם vacat הכהנים הם שבי ישראל

4:3   היוצאים מֵאֶרֶץ יהודה והנלוים עמהם vacat ובני צדוק הם בחירי

---

[55] Cf. Num 13:26.

[56] Deuteronomy 9:23 and Ezek 13:3 serve as the basis for the reconstruction of the preceding lacuna transcribed from 4Q269 F2:1–2.

[57] Cf. 4Q504 F1–2 recto v:4.

[58] Read חבו.

pleased. And they consumed blood and He cut off ³:⁷their males in
the wilderness in Kadesh, saying, "Go up and inherit [the land" (Deut
9:23). But they followed] their (evil) inclination, not listening ³:⁸to the
voice of their Maker. Neither did they heed the commandments of
their teachers, but murmured in their tents so that God became angry
³:⁹with their assembly. And their children perished on account of it,
and their kings were cut off because of it, and their mighty warriors
³:¹⁰perished as a result of it, and their land became desolate through
it [by all their enemies. Furthermore] the ancient covenanters became
culpable on account of it and were handed over ³:¹¹to the sword
because they forsook God's covenant. And they preferred their own
passion and they wandered away after the stubbornness ³:¹²of their
heart to do each one his own will.

*The Sons of Zadok*

But with those who are clinging to God's commandments, ³:¹³the
remnant, He will set His covenant with Israel forever, to reveal ³:¹⁴to
them hidden things in which all Israel has strayed away: His holy
Sabbaths and ³:¹⁵His glorious festivals, His righteous testimony and
His true paths and the things He desires, 'by which ³:¹⁶man shall
perform and live' (Neh 9:27)³ (for a thousand generations). (Each of
these) He has opened to them. And they will excavate the well for
living waters. ³:¹⁷But He will not let those who despise them live,
since they have wallowed in man's transgression and in the ways of
impurity, ³:¹⁸saying, "It (אמה, 'truth') belongs to us." But the Lord
in His wondrous mysteries has atoned for their sins (of the righteous)
and will forgo their transgressions. ³:¹⁹And He will erect for them
a faithful temple in Israel, the like of which has never existed from
earliest time until ³:²⁰now. The people who cling to Him are destined
for eternal life and all human glory will be accorded to them, just
as the Lord ³:²¹has established them by Ezekiel the prophet saying,
"As for the priests and the Levites and the sons ᶜᴰ ⁴:¹of Zadok who
have kept the courses of My sanctuary when the children of Israel
strayed ⁴:²from Me, they shall offer Me fat and blood" (Ezek 44:15).
The "priests" are the "penitent of Israel" ⁴:³who will depart from the
land of Judah, and those who will accompany them. And the "sons of

---

³ A paraphrase of Lev 18:5.

4:4    ישראל קריאי השם העמדים באחרית הימים הנה פרוש

4:5    שמותיהם לתולדותם וקץ מעמדם ומספר צרותיהם ושני

4:6    התגוררם ופירוש מעשיהם ⟨אנשי⟩ᵂ הקודש ᵂ⟨הרי⟩שונים אשר כפר

4:7    אל בעדם ויצדיקו צדיק וירשיעו רשע וכל הבאים אחריהם

4:8    לעשות כפרוש התורה אשר התוסרו בו הרי׳שנים⁵⁹ עד שלים

4:9    הקץ [כמספר]ᵇ לשנים האלה כברית אשר הקים אל לראשנים לכפר

4:10    על עונותיהם כן יכפר אל בעדם ובשלום הקץ למספר השנים

4:11    האלה אין עוד להשתפח לבית יהודה כי אם לעמוד איש על

4:12    מצודו נבנתה הגדר רחק החוק ובכל השנים האלה יהיה

4:13    בליעל משלח בישראל כאשר דבר אל ביד ישעיה הנביא בן

4:14    אמוץ לאמר פחד ופחת ופח עליך יושב הארץ *vacat* פשרו

4:15    שלושת מצודות בליעל אשר אמר עליהם לוי בן יעקב

4:16    אשר הוא תפש בהם בישראל ויתנם פניהם לשלושת מיני

4:17    הצדק הראשונה היא הזנות השנית⁶⁰ ההון⁶¹ השלישית

4:18    טמא המקדש העולה מזה יתפש בזה והניצל מזה יתפש

CD 4:19–7:5
Parallels: 4Q266 F3ii; iii:4–6 (underline)
            4Q267 F2 (overbar)
            4Q269 F3–4 (dotted underline)
            4Q271 F1 (italics)
            6Q15 F1–4 (lower underline)
            extant and restored text unique to DSS (outline)

4:19    בזה *vacat* בוני החיׄיׄ⁹ אשר הלכו אחרי צו הצו הוא מטיף

4:20    אשר אמר הטף יטיפון הם ניתפשים בשתים בזנות.לקחת

4:21    שתי נשים בחייהם ויסוד הבריאה זכר ונקבה ברא אותם

5:1    ובאי התבה שנים שנים באו אל התבה *vacat* ועל הנשיא כתוב

5:2    לא ירבה לו נשים ודויד לא קרא בספר התורה החתום אשר

---

⁵⁹ הראשונים CD.

⁶⁰ ות הש׳ and the second ל of line 18 may correspond to the unidentified 4Q266
F34.

⁶¹ Read ההון.

Zadok" are the chosen $^{4:4}$of Israel, called by name, who will arise in the end of days. Here is a listing $^{4:5}$of their names by their ancestry and the time of their officiating and the number of their troubles and the years $^{4:6}$of their sojourn and the elaboration of the deeds of their holy <anc>estors whose (sins) $^{4:7}$God has atoned for. And they will declare the just righteous and the sinful wicked.

Now as for all who succeed them, $^{4:8}$continuing to act in accordance with the elaboration of the Torah by which the forefathers were disciplined until the completion $^{4:9}$of the epoch [according to the number] of these years, in accordance with the covenant which God had established for the ancestors to atone $^{4:10}$for their sins, so God will atone for them.

*Israel's Decline: The Past and Impending Crisis*

And at the end of the epoch by the reckoning of these years $^{4:11}$one may no longer join the (new) house of Judah, but instead every person shall remain at $^{4:12}$his post (literally "stand upon his fortress").

The fence has been built, the statute is distant (Mic 7:11). And during all these years $^{4:13}$Belial will be let loose against Israel as God has spoken through Isaiah the prophet, son $^{4:14}$of Amoz, saying, "Fear and the pit and the snare are upon you, inhabitant of the land" (Isa 24:17). Its eschatological meaning is $^{4:15}$the three nets of Belial concerning which Levi son of Jacob said $^{4:16}$"with which he (Belial) trapped Israel and paraded them as if they were fronts for three classes $^{4:17}$of (un)righteous deeds": the first is whoredom, the second wealth (and) the third $^{4:18}$the defiling of the sanctuary. He who escapes from one will be trapped in the next; and whoever is saved from that will be trapped $^{4:19}$in the other.

As to the builders of the wall who went after "precept": Precept is a spewer $^{4:20}$of whom it says, "They shall surely spew" (Mic 2:6). They are ensnared by two (abominations): (the first) by whoredom through marrying $^{4:21}$two wives while (the first wife) is still alive. But the (divine) principle of creation is, "as a male and female He created them" (Gen 1:27). CD $^{5:1}$Moreover, those who entered the ark came in pairs to the ark. And concerning the leader (of the tribes and the head of the priests) it is written, $^{5:2}$"He shall not multiply wives for himself" (Deut 17:17). As to David, he could not read in the book

5:3   היה בארון כי לא {נפתֹת}[62]w נפתח בישראל מיום מות אלעזר

5:4   ויהושע ‹‹ויושֵעַ››[w] והזקנים אשר עבדו את העשתרת ויטמון

5:5   נגלה עד עמוד צדוק ויעלו מעשי דויד מלבד דם אוריה

5:6   ויעזבם לו אל וגם מטמאים הם את המקדש אשר אין הם

5:7   מבדיל כתורה ושוכבים עם הרואה את דם זובה ולוקחים

5:8   איש את בת אחיהֶם ואת בת אחותו vacat ומשה אמר אל

5:9   אחות אמך לא תקרב שאר אמך היא ומשפט העריות לזכרים

5:10   הוא כתוב וכהם הנשים ואם תגלה בת האח את ערות אחי

5:11   אביה והיא שאר vacat וגם את רוח קדשיהם טמאו ובלשון

5:12   גדופים פתחו פה על חוקי ברית אל לאמר לא נכונו ותועבה

5:13   הם מדברים בם כֻלם קדֹחי אש וֹמבערי זיקות קורי

5:14   עכביש קוריהם וביצי צפעונים ביציהֶם הקרוב אליהם

5:15   לא ינקה כהר ביתו[63] יאשם כי אם נלחֵץ כי למילפֿנים[64] פקד

5:16   אל אֵת מעֲשיהם ויחר אפו בעלילותיהם כי [אֵם] בֹלא בינות הוא[65]

5:17   הם גוי אבד עצות מאשר אין בהם בינה כי מלפניֹם עמד

5:18   משה ואהרוֹן ביד שר האורים ויקם בליעל את יחנה ואֵת

5:19   אֲחֹיהו במזמתֹו ‹‹בבהושע›› [w] ‹‹בהרשע›› ישֻראל את הראשונה vacat

5:20   vac ובקץ חרבן הארץ עמדו מסֹיֹגֹי הגבֹול[66] ויתעו את ישראל

5:21   ותישם הֹאֹרֹץ כי דברו סֶרֹה סרה על מצוֹת[67] אל ביד משה וגם

6:1   במשיחֹיֹ[68] הקודש וֹינֹבֹאֹו שקר להשיב את ישראל מאחֹרֹיֹ

6:2   אל ויזכר אל ברית ריאשונים[69] vacat ויקֹם מאהרוֹן נבונים ומישראל

---

[62] Rabin transcribed נפהתה and Qimron {נפֹ}. See Chaim Rabin, *The Zadokite Documents* (2d rev. ed.; Oxford: Clarendon, 1958), 19; Qimron, "The Text of CDC," 19.

[63] Read כהרבותו as proposed by Qimron in "The Text of CDC," 19.

[64] כי אם למילפנים CD. כי למ{ל}פנֹים 4Q266 F3ii:3.

[65] כי לא עם בינות הוא CD 5:16.

[66] מסגי גבול 4Q266 F3ii:7. The same phrase in 4Q271 F1:2 may be reconstructed as לֹ[מ]שֹכֹיֹגֹי הגבֹ[ו]ל.

[67] מצוות 4Q266 F3ii:8.

[68] במשיחו CD.

[69] ראשנים CD.

of the Torah which had been sealed since 5:3it was in the ark, for it (the ark) had not been opened in Israel since the day of the death of Eleazar and 5:4Joshua and the elders who worshipped the Ashtaroth. And he (Eleazar) hid 5:5the Niglah until Zadok arose. And the acts of David became acceptable (before God) aside from (the king's guilt pertaining to) the blood of Uriah, 5:6as God made him responsible for that.[4] They also defile the Temple, not 5:7separating (between clean and unclean) according to the Torah. And they lie with a menstruating woman and marry 5:8the daughter of one's brother or sister. However, Moses said, "You shall not 5:9come near the sister of your mother; she is a relation of your mother" (Lev 18:13). And the rules of incest are in male language, 5:10but they apply to women as well. Hence, if the brother's daughter uncovers the nakedness of her father's brother, 5:11she is a (forbidden) relation. And they (the opponents) also have defiled their holy spirit, and 5:12have opened (their) mouth with blasphemous language against the statutes of God's covenant, saying, "They are not right," and 5:13speak of them as an "abomination." All of them (the opponents) 'kindle fire' and burn 'firebrands' (Isa 50:11). 'Webs of 5:14a spider' are their webs and 'eggs of vipers' (Isa 59:5) are their eggs. Anyone who comes near to them 5:15will not be innocent. As he increases (his transgressions) he will be declared guilty, unless under duress. For formerly God recalled 5:16their (Israel's) deeds and God was angry with their misdeeds,[5] since they are [a people] without understanding (Isa 27:11). 5:17'They are a nation that has lost proper counsel' since 'they lack understanding' (Deut 32:28). For formally 5:18Moses and Aaron were guided by the Prince of the Urim (and Thummim), and Belial raised up Yahneh and 5:19his companion by his plot when Israel became wicked[6] the first time.

5:20Now during the epoch of the desolation of the land (concluding in 586 B.C.E.) the Shifters of the Boundary arose and misled Israel. 5:21And the earth has turned into wilderness because they spoke deviant counsel against the ordinances of God through Moses, and even CD 6:1through the anointed holy ones. And they have prophesied falsehood to make Israel turn away from 6:2God.

---

[4] Literally "them."

[5] Cf. Ps 99:8, וְנֹקֵם עַל־עֲלִילוֹתָם (and takes vengeance for their misdeeds).

[6] CD reads בהושע ישראל (when Israel was saved).

חכמים וישמיעם ויחפורו את הבאר אֲשֶׁר אָמַ֯ר מֹשֶׁ֯ה באר חפריה שרים כרוה 6:3

נדיבי העם במחוקק הבאר היאה התורה וחופריה המה 6:4

שבי ישראל היוצאים מארץ יהודה ויגורו בארץ[70] דמשק 6:5

אשר קרא אל את כולם שרים כי כֻ֯לָ֯ם[ ] דרשוהו ולֹא הושבה 6:6

פארתם בפי אחד vacat והמחוקק הוא דורש התורה אשר 6:7

אמר ישעיה מוציא כלי למעשיהו vacat ונדיבי העם הם 6:8

הבאים לכרות את הבאר במחוקקות אשר חקק המחוקק 6:9

להתהלך בם בכל קץ הרשיע וזולתם לא ישיגו עד עמד 6:10

יורה הצדק באחרית הימים vacat וכֻ֯ל אשר הובא[71] בברית 6:11

לבלתי בוא אל המקדש להאיר מזבחו [הֻ֯ ]א מסגרי[72] 6:12

הדלת אשר אמר אל מי בכם יסגור דלתיֿ ולא תאירו מזבחי 6:13

חנם אם לֹא ישמרו לעשות כפרוש התורה לקץ הרשע לֻהַבָדֵלֿ[73] 6:14

מבני [הַשַ֯]ֿל[74] ולהנזר מהון הרשעה הטמא בנדר ובחרם 6:15

ובהון המקדש ולגזול את עניי עמו להיות אלמנו[ ]ת שללם 6:16

ואת יתומים ירצחו לֻהַבְדֵיֿל[75] בין הטמא לטהור ולהודיע בין 6:17

הקודש לחול ולשמור אֵת יום השבת כפרושה ואת המוערות 6:18

ואת יום התענית כמצאֵת באי הברית הֲחֲדשה בארץ דמשק 6:19

להרים את הקדשים כפֵֿירֻ֯וֻ֯שֵ֯יֻ֯הֶֿם לֻ֯אֲהֻֿוב איש את אחיהו 6:20

כמהו ולֻֿהַחֲזִ֯יֻק. בְיֻד[76] עני ואביון וגר vacat ולדרוש אֻ֯יֻש בְשֻׁ֯לֻ֯וֻם[77] 6:21

אחיהו ולא ימעל איש בשאר בְשֻׁ֯רֻֿו להזיר מן הזונות 7:1

---

[70] Baumgarten reconstructs 4Q267 F2:12b as [ויֿ]גֿורו במגו]לֿ[י] [דמשק אשר קרא] ". . . and [dwell in the dwe]llings of [Damascus whom (God) called] . . ." (DJD XVIII, 97). The translation is mine.

[71] הובאו CD.

[72] CD 6:11b–13a has וכל אשר הובאו בברית לבלתי בוא אל המקדש להאיר מזבחו חנם ויהיו מסגירי הדלת. The spelling of the second to the last word is obscure in 4Q266 F3ii:18. Baumgarten transcribes it as מסֻגֻֿר• (DJD XVIII, 41). It is difficult to determine whether the supralinear mark actually appearing above the *samek* is a portion of a *yod*, *waw* or merely a mark on the parchment. Although the phrasing in the biblical text diverges from that of both CD and 4Q266, the use of the Qal stem of סגר in the biblical parallel מִי גַם־בָּכֶם וְיִסְגֹּר דְּלָתַיִם וְלֹא־תָאִירוּ מִזְבְּחִי חִנָּם (Mal 1:10), may support reading a Qal participle either as a short form as transcribed, or the full form סֻגֵֿרֿ in 4Q266 F3ii:18.

[73] ולהבדיל CD 6:14.

[74] השחת CD.

[75] ולהבדיל CD.

[76] 4Q269 F4ii:3 could be reconstructed as בֻֿ[ד. 

[77] איש את שלום CD.

*Israel's Rise: The Life of the New Covenant in Damascus*

But God will remember the covenant of the ancestors and will raise up from Aaron men of understanding and from Israel [6:3]wise men. And He will inform them. And they will dig the well, of which Moses had said, "The well which the princes have excavated [6:4]the nobles of the people dug by the direction of the Lawgiver" (Num 21:18). The well is the Torah and its excavators are [6:5]the penitent of Israel who will exit from the land of Judah and dwell in the land of Damascus, [6:6]all of whom God has called "princes," for [they] all will have interpreted it (the words of Moses) and [6:7]their glorious (interpretation) cannot be challenged by anyone. And the Lawgiver is the interpreter of the Torah about whom [6:8]Isaiah said, "One who brings forth an instrument for his works" (Isa 54:16). And the nobles of the people are [6:9]the ones who will come to excavate the well (Torah) with legislative mastery which the Lawgiver has etched [6:10]so that they will walk by them during the entire epoch of wickedness; and those who are apart from them will not attain (understanding) until [6:11]the True Lawgiver arises at the end of days.

And anyone who has been brought into the covenant [6:12](with the stipulation) not to enter into the sanctuary to kindle His altar is among those who close [6:13]the door, concerning whom God had said, "Who among you will close my door so as not to kindle my altar [6:14]in vain" (Mal 1:10), if they will not take heed to do according to the explanation of the Torah during the epoch of wickedness.

It is imperative to separate [6:15]from the sons of [injus]tice and to "nazirite" by means of a vow and ban from the defiling wealth of wickedness [6:16]as well as from the property of the sanctuary; and (neither) to rob the poor of his (God's) people, (nor) to make widows their booty, [6:17](nor) should they murder the fatherless (Isa 10:2). It is necessary to differentiate between what is defiling and pure and to make known between [6:18]what is sacred and what is ordinary; and to observe the day of the Sabbath including its elaborations and the festive seasons [6:19]and the day of fasting (atonement) in accordance with the practice of those who will enter the new covenant in the land of Damascus, [6:20]to set apart the holy (or priestly) tithings in accordance with their proper elaborations; that each love his companion [6:21]as himself and support the poor, destitute and proselyte, and that each be concerned with the welfare [CD 7:1]of his neighbor and that no one should adulterate his near kin, keeping apart from prostitutes

כמשפט להוכיח אִיש.אֶת אחיהו כמצוה ולא לנטור　7:2

מיום ליום וּלְהַבְדֵּל מכל הטמאות כמשפטם ולא ישקץ　7:3

אִיש אֶת רוח קדשיו כאשר הבדיל אל להם כל המתהלכים　7:4

באלה בתמים קדש על פי כל יסורו[78] ברית אל נאמנות[79] להם　7:5

Text Common to CD 7:6–8:21 (CD-A) and CD 19 (CD-B) (plain
text)
Text Unique to CD 7:6–8:21 (underline)
Text Unique to CD 19:1–34a (dotted underline)
Parallels: 4Q266 F3iii:18–25, iv (overbar)
　　　　　　4Q269 F5; 6 (lower underline)
　　　　　　　extant and restored text unique to DSS (outline)

לחיותם לְאַלְפֵי דֹרוֹת : כְּכָ[80] שׁוֹמֵר הַבְּרִית וְהַחֶסֶד לְאַהֲבֵי[81] וּלְשֹׁמְרֵי　7:6a

מִצְוֹתַי[82] לְאֶלֶף דֹר ָ:

vacat ואם מחנות ישבו כסרך[83] הארץ אֲשֶׁר הָיָה מִקֶּדֶם וְלָקְחוּ　7:6b

נשים כְּמִנְהַג הַתּוֹרָה והולידו בנים וְיִתְהַלְּכוּ[84] על פי התורה[85] וכמשפט　7:7

היסורים[86] כסרך התורה כאשר אמר בין איש לאשתו ובין אב　7:8

לבנו וכל המואסים במצות ובחקים[87] להשיב גמול רשעים　7:9

עליהם בפקדת אל את הארץ בבוא הדבר אשר כתוב בְּיַד[88] זְכַרְיָה הַנָּבִיא　7:10a

חֶרֶב עוּרִי עַל רֹעִי וְעַל גֶּבֶר עֲמִיתִי נְאֻם אֵל הַךְ אֶת הָרֹעֶה וּתְפוּצֶינָה הַצֹּאן

וַהֲשִׁבוֹתִי יָדִי עַל הַצֹּעֲרִים[89] : וְהַשֹּׁמְרִים אוֹתוֹ הֵם עֲנִיֵּי הַצֹּאן

(בבוא הדבר אשר כתוב)ʷ בְּדִבְרֵי יְשַׁעְיָה בֶּן אָמוֹץ הַנָּבִיא　7:10b

אֲשֶׁר אָמַר יָבוֹא[90] עָלֶיךָ וְעַל עַמְּךָ וְעַל בֵּית אָבִיךָ יָמִים אֲשֶׁר <לֹא>ʷ　7:11

---

[78] Read וסוריו.

[79] Read נאמנת after 4Q267 F9v:4 which parallels CD 14:2, a related passage
containing content and syntax similar to that of CD 7:5b–6a.

[80] ככתוב.

[81] Read לאהביו.

[82] Read מצותיו.

[83] כסרך CD-A 7:6.

[84] והתהלכו CD-A 7:5.

[85] A vacat follows התורה in CD-B 19:4.

[86] היסורים CD-B 19:4. Rabin emends the text to האסרום (binding vows). See Rabin,
*The Zadokite Documents*, 26–27.

[87] Following לבנו, A-7:9–10a reads וכל המואסים בפקד אל את הארץ להשיב גמול
רשעים עליהם בבוא הדבר אשר כתוב בדברי ישעיה .... Note that this edition unless otherwise
noted, unlike that of Rabin, prints the B text before the A. This is also true of variant
readings, sequences of words or English translations.

7:2in accordance with the rules; to reprove each his neighbor in accordance with the commandment and not to bear a grudge 7:3from day to day and to keep away from all kinds of defilement in accordance with their rule and that no one abominate 7:4His Holy Spirit as God has kept them apart. As for all who walk 7:5in these rules in perfect holiness, in accordance with all His chastisements, the divine covenant will remain faithful to them, 7:6akeeping them alive for thousands of generations. <As is written,> "He (God) keeps the covenant and favor with <those who love him> and who observe <his commandments> for a thousand generations" (Deut 7:9).

7:6bAnd if they reside (in) camps as was the rule of the land formerly (in the wilderness), they shall take 7:7wives in accordance with the custom of the Torah, and father children, and they shall walk in accordance with the Torah and the ordinance 7:8on chastisements according to the rule of the Torah, just as He said: "Between a man and his wife, and between a father 7:9and his son" (Num 30:17).

But pertaining to all those who despise the commandments and statutes, these wicked will be requited 7:10aduring God's remembrance of the land when the written word (19:7) of Zechariah the prophet will find fulfillment: "Oh sword, awake against (19:8)my shepherd and against my fellow man says the Lord. Strike the shepherd so that the sheep will scatter. (19:9)And I will turn my hand against the young shepherds" (Zech 13:7). Those who guard him (the shepherd) are the poor of the flock. (Zech 11:7) . . . 7:10b. . . (When that which was written) by Isaiah, son of Amoz, the prophet (will be fulfilled): 7:11who said, "Days will come upon you and upon your people and the house of your father, the likes of which have <not> 7:12transpired since the time that Ephraim split off from Judah" (Isa 7:17) when the two houses of Israel separated (and will do so again), 7:13the prince of Ephraim from Judah. And all the laggards were handed over (and will be so again) to the sword, but those who held fast (to the Torah)

---

[88] CD-B 19:7 reads .... אשר כתוב ביד זכריה הנביא.

[89] הַצֹּעֲרִים MT.

[90] MT reads יָבֵא. MTA's change to יבוא might have been intentional, since it stresses the futuristic element of the message: that there will be a new split in the future. It will occur again in the north. This future rift predicted by Isaiah, combined with Elijah's wandering to the wilderness of Damascus in 1 Kings 19:15 discussed above, may have served as an inspiration for MTA's central thesis of the exile to Damascus.

באו מיום סור אפרים מעל יהודה בהפרד שני בתי ישראל 7:12

שר אפרים מעל יהודה וכל הנסוגים הַסַגרו לחרב והמחזיקים 7:13

נמלטו לארץ צפון vacat כאשר אמר והגליתי את סכות מלככם⁹¹ 7:14

ואת כיון צלמיכם מאהלי דמשק vacat ספרי התורה הם סוכת 7:15

המלך כאשר אמר והקימותי את סוכת דוד⁹² הנופלת vacat המלך 7:16

הוא «נשיא» הקהל «וכינויי הצלמים» וכיון הצלמים הם ספרי הנביאים 7:17

אשר בזה ישראל את דבריהם vacat והכוכב הוא דורש התורה 7:18

הבא אל דמשק {כאשר} כאשר כתוב דרך כוכב מיעקב וקם שבט 7:19

מישראל השבט הוא נשיא⁹³ כל העדה ובעמדו וקרקר 7:20

את כול בני שת אלה יִמָלטו⁹⁴ בקץ הפקודה הָראישן⁹⁵ 7:21

והנשארים ימסרו לחרב⁹⁶ בבוא משיח 19:10b

אהרן וישראל: כאשר היה בקץ פקרת הראשון אשר אמר [יחזקאל] 19:11

ביד יחזאל וְהִתְוּ להתות התיו על מצחות נאנחים ונאנקים vac 19:12

והנשארים הסגרו לחרב נוקמת נקם ברית: 19:13

וכן משפט כול באי⁹⁷ בבריתו אשר 8:1b

לא⁹⁸ יחזיקו באלה החקים לפקידם⁹⁹ לכלה ביד בליעל הוא היום 8:2

אשר יפקדו אל כאשר דבר היו שרי יהודה כמשיגי גבול [ב]◌◌ אשר 8:3
עליהם אשפך כמים העברה¹⁰⁰

כי באו בסו בברית תשובה . . . «וי»יחלו למרפא¹⁰¹ «וידקמום» «וידרקמום» 8:4
כול מורדים¹⁰² מאשר¹⁰³ . . . לא סרו מדרך

---

⁹¹ The understanding of סְכּוּת מַלְכְּכֶם is problematic. The Septuagint renders the phrase as τὴν σκηνὴν τοῦ Μολοχ (the tent of Moloch). However, the author of CD reads it as positive, since he identifies the המלך (the סכות מלככם of Amos 5:26) as the ספרי התורה (the books of the Torah). As does the Septuagint, the author of MTA renders סכות as "tent." Unlike the Septuagint, however, which translates מלכככם as Μολοχ, the author of MTA understands it as המלך (the king), paralleling it with Amos 9:11 סֻכַּת דָּוִיד הַנֹּפֶלֶת, and identifying it as the "the books of the Torah." The phrase ספרי הנביאים (the books of the prophets) is a midrash on כיון הצלמכם.

⁹² Baumgarten restores שֻׁ[וכת דויד to the beginning of 4Q266 F3iii:17 (DJD XVIII, 44). Nothing remains of line 17. A צ survives at the beginning of line 18.

⁹³ נשי 4Q266 F3iii:21.

⁹⁴ מלסו CD-A 7:21.

⁹⁵ הראשון CD-A 7:21.

⁹⁶ CD-A 8:1 reads והנסוגים ה[סגיר]ו. 4Q266 F3iii:23 reads ו[ה]נסוגים הסגירו לחרב.

⁹⁷ כול באי הברית CD.

⁹⁸ לו 4Q266 F3iii:24.

⁹⁹ לפוקדם CD-B 19:14; לפקדם A-8:2.

¹⁰⁰ CD-A 8:3b reads CD-A 8:3b reads העברה עליהם תשפוך אשר שרי יהודה היו 4Q266 F3iii:25–3iv:1 may be reconstructed אשר ב[יום תשפוך] עליהם [שרי יהודה] היו העברה.

7:14escaped (and will do so again) to the land of the north, just as he said, "Then I will exile" the Sikkut of your king 7:15and the Kiyyun of your images "away from the tents of Damascus." (Amos 5:27). The books of the Torah are equivalent to the booth 7:16of the king as it says, And "I will raise up the fallen booth of David" (Amos 9:11). The king 7:17refers to the <prince> of the congregation and the Kiyyun of their images are the books of the prophets 7:18whose words Israel has despised. The star is the interpreter of the Torah 7:19who is to come to Damascus, as it is written, "A star has stepped forth from Jacob and a scepter has arisen 7:20from Israel" (Num 24:17). The scepter is the leader of the entire congregation, and when he will arise he will shake up 7:21all the sons of Seth . . . (19:10a)These will escape during the first period of redemption. And those who will remain will be given over to the sword when the Messiah (19:11)of Aaron and Israel will arise, as it was during the first period of remembrance (in Egypt) as He (God) said (19:12)through Ezekiel: "To make a mark upon the foreheads of the distressed and moaners" (Ezek 9:4). (19:13)But those who remain will be handed over to the avenging sword, a vengeance of the covenant.

CD 8:1bAnd thus will be the fate of all who will have entered His covenant who 8:2will not cling to these statutes resulting in them being handed over to Belial for destruction. That is the day 8:3when they will be summoned (by) God, as He spoke (through Hosea), "The princes of Judah (will) have become like the Shifters of the Boundary" [on] the day when "I will pour out anger[7] upon them like water" (Hos 5:10). 8:4For they will have entered into the covenant of repentance. . . and will begin to heal, and all fearers (of God) will weave them apart

---

[7] MT reads עֶבְרָתִי.

---

[101] Baumgarten reconstructs 4Q266 F3iv:1 [כי יחלו ללו מרפא] (for they shall be sick with no healing), stating, ". . .we assume the loss of the negative לו by haplography" (DJD XVIII, 46).

[102] כול מורדים 4Q266 F3iv:2; or כל מורדים "all the rebels" CD-A 8:4. Qimron reads "wounds excreting pus (ריר)" (Qimron, "The Text of CDC," 25).

[103] CD-B 19:16b–17a reads באו בסו בברית תשובה ולא סרו מדרך בוגדים, "(For) they will have entered a covenant of repentance but will not have turned aside from the way of the treacherous."

8:5 בוגדים ויתגוללו בדרכי ‹‹זונות›› ‹זָנוֹתָ› ובהון הָרִשְׁעָה ונקום ונִטור[104]

8:6 איש לאחיהֶו ושנוֹא איש את רֵעהוֹ ויתעלמו איש בשאר בשרוֹ

8:7 וַיִּגְּשׁ לזמה ויתגברו להון ולבצע ויעשו אִ⸻ איש הישר בעיניוֹ

8:8 וּבחרוֹ[105] איש בשרירות לבו ולא נזרו מעם וְמֵחַטָּאתָם‪:‬ ויפרעו ביד רמה

8:9 ללכת בדרכֵי רשעים‪:‬ אשר אמר אל עליהם חמת תנינים יינם

8:10 וראש פתנים אכזר‪:‬ vacat התנינים הֵם מלכי העמים וְיִינם הוא

8:11 דרכיהם וראש הַפְּתנים[106] הוא ראש מלכי יון הבא

8:12 עליהם לַעֲקָם נקמה[107] ובכל אלה לא הבינו בוני החיץ וטחי הַתָּפֵל כי

8:13 הוֹלֵךְ רוּחַ ושׁקֵל סַפָּת סוּפוֹת[108] ומטיף אָדָם לכזב הטיף להם

אשר חרה אף אל בכל עדתו‪:‬ vacat

8:14 ואשר אמר משה ליִשְׂרָאֵל לא בצדקתך ובַיוֹשֵׁר[109] לבבך אתה בא לרשת

8:15 את הגוים האלה כי מאהבתו את אבותֶיךָ[110] ומשמרו את השבועה‪:‬

8:16 וְכֵן הַמשפט לשבי ישראל סרו מדרך העם באהבת אל‪:‬ את

8:17 הראשנים אשר הֵעִידוּ[111] עַל הָעָם אחרי אֵל וְאָהַב[112]

את הבאים אחריהם כי לָהֶם

8:18 ברית הָאבות vacat וְשׁוֹנֵא[113] וְמִתְעַב אֶל את בוני החיץ וְחָרָה אַפּ

אפו בם וּבכל הַהֹלְכִים אַחֲרֵיהֶם וכמשפט

8:19 הזה לכל המוֹאֵס במצות אל ּּּּּ ויעזבם ויפנו בשרירות לבם

8:20 vacat הוא הדבר אשר אמר ירמיהו לברוך בֶּן נֵרייה ואלישע

8:21 לגֵחֲזִי נערוֹ vacat כֵּן כל האנשים אשר באו בברית החדשה בארץ דמשׂק

---

[104] ונסור CD-B 19:18.

[105] ויבחרו CD-A 8:8 and CD-B 19:20.

[106] פתנים CD-B 19:23.

[107] A-8:11b–12a הוא ראש מלכי יון הבא בהם נקמה לעשות.

[108] שׁקֵל רוח CD-A 8:13.

[109] ובישר CD-A 8:14.

[110] אבותך CD-A 8:15.

[111] Qimron, following CD-B 19:30 (העידו), reads הועידו (make the people assemble before God). See Qimron, "The Text of CDC," 25.

[112] היעידו אחריו אהב CD-A 8:17.

[113] CD-A 8:18 reads ובשונאי, which Qimron emends to ובשונאו (Qimron, "The Text of CDC," 25).

from those who have not turned away from the way [8:5]of traitors. But (changing directions) they will wallow in the paths of whoredom, and in the property of wickedness, and vengeance, and will bear a grudge [8:6]each against his brother, and hate his fellow man, being oblivious to their close kin. [8:7]And they will approach whoredom and make an effort to acquire ill-gotten wealth through exploitation, and each will do what is pleasing in his own eyes. [8:8]And each one will choose the corruption of his heart and will not keep apart from the people and their sins. And they will act haughtily in a vicious way [8:9]to follow the paths of the wicked, concerning whom God said, "Their wine is the poison of serpents, [8:10]and the cruel venom of asps" (Deut 32:33). The serpents are the kings of the nations and their wine is [8:11]their way of life. And the head of the serpents is the leader of the kings of Greece who is coming [8:12]to exact vengeance upon them. And in all these things the builders of the wall and those who plaster it with whitewash will not have understood, that [8:13]the one who walks by wind and weighs the whirlwind, and he who preaches lies to man will have preached to them what has provoked the anger of God against his whole congregation.

[8:14]Now as for what Moses said to Israel: "Not on account of your righteousness or the uprightness of your heart are you coming to inherit [8:15]these Gentile lands, but because of His love for your forefathers and His keeping the oath" (Deut 9:5; 7:8). [8:16]And thus will be the destiny for the penitent of Israel who will have turned from the way of the people. On account of God's love for [8:17]the ancestors who testified against the people since they followed God, He will love those who succeed them, because [8:18]the covenant of the forefathers belongs to them. But God will hate and abhor the builders of the wall, and His anger will be kindled against them and against all who follow them.

And this judgment [8:19]will apply also against all who will despise God's commandments and will leave them and turn in the stubbornness of their heart. [8:20]This is the matter that Jeremiah commanded to Baruch, son of Neriah, and Elisha [8:21]to Gehazi, his amanuensis. Thus are all the people who enter into the new covenant in the land

CD 19:34b–20:34
Parallels: 4Q267 F3:1–7 (underline)
           4Q266 F4:7–8 (overbar)
           paleo script is in DSS only
           extant and restored text unique to DSS (outline)

19:34b                         ושבו ויבגדו ויסורו מבאר מים החיים

19:35 לֹא יחשבו בסוד עם ובכתבם לא יכתבו מיֹום האסף יורֿ־מֿורֿה

20:1 {מֿיֿוֿֿם}⁹ מֿורֿה היחיד עד עמוֿד משיח מאהרֿן ומישראל vacat וכן המשפט

20:2 לכל באי עדת אנשי תמֹים הקדש ויקוץ מעשות פקודי ישֹרים

20:3 הוא האיש הנתך בתוך כור : ה בהופע מעשיו ישלח מעדה

20:4 כמֹוֿ¹¹⁴ שלא נפל גורלו בתוך למודי אל כפי מעלו יח יוכיחוהו אנשי

20:5 דעות עד יום ישוב לעמד במעמד אנשי תמים קדש «אשׁ»רֿ־אֿין

20:6 גֿורֿלֿו־בֿתֿוֿך־אֿ ובהופע מעשיו כפי מדרש התורה אשר יתהלכו

20:7 בו אנשי תמים הקדש אל יֿת יאות איש עמו בהון ובעבודה

20:8 כי אררוהו כל קדושי עליון וכמשפט הזה לכל המאס בראשונים

20:9 ובאחרונים אשר שמו גלולים על לבם וישֿימֿ וילכו בשרירות

20:10 לבם אין להם חלק בבית התורה : כמשפט רעיהם אשר שבו

20:11 עם אנשי הלצון ישפטו כי דברו תועה על חקי הצדק ומאסו

20:12 בברית ה^sch ואמנה אשר קימו בארץ דמשק והוא¹¹⁵ ברית החדשה :

20:13 ולא יהיה להם וֿ ולמשפחותיֿהֿם חלק בבית התור<ה>ה vacat ¹¹⁶ ומיום

20:14 האסף יורה היחיד עד תם כל אנשי המלחמה אשר שבו

20:15 עם איש הכזב כשנֹים ארבעים : ובקץ ההוא יחרה

20:16 אף אל בישראל כאשר אמר אין מֹלך ואין שר ואין שופט וֿ]אֿ]יֿן

20:17 מוכיֿח בצדק לֿ ושבי פשע יעֿקֿב שמרו ברית אל אז נֿדֿברֿו איש

---

¹¹⁴ Read כמי.
¹¹⁵ Read והיא.
¹¹⁶ Rabin restores ה. See Rabin, *The Zadokite Documents*, 38–39.

of Damascus <sup>CD 19:34b</sup>but will change (their minds) and act treacherously and turn away from the well of living waters; <sup>19:35</sup>these shall not be counted in the assembly of the people, and shall not be recorded in their records beginning from the day of the assembling <sup>CD 20:1</sup>by the Unique Teacher until the Messiah from Aaron and from Israel will arise.

Thus also will be the rule <sup>20:2</sup>for all who will be entering the perfect congregation which is holy, but will despise the observances of the commandments of the upright. <sup>20:3</sup>This is the person 'who shall be melted in the crucible' (Ezek 22:21). When his acts become evident, he is to be expelled from the congregation <sup>20:4</sup>as one who had not put his lot among God's learned. The people of knowledge shall chastise him in accordance with his acts of profanation <sup>20:5</sup>until he repents to stand in the position of the leaders of perfect holiness. <sup>20:6</sup>And during the time that his (evil) acts appear to be contrary to the Midrash on the (Eschatological) Torah by which <sup>20:7</sup>the people of perfect holiness shall live, let none of the members (of the community) join with him in wealth or labor, <sup>20:8</sup>since all the sacred of the Most High have cursed him.

And this rule applies also to anyone who will despise either the early <sup>20:9</sup>or the latter (words of the two Torahs), who will have placed abominations upon their heart and live by its stubbornness. <sup>20:10</sup>They shall not have a portion in the covenant of the Torah. They shall be judged by the rule of their (evil) associates who will have joined <sup>20:11</sup>with the scoffers, since they will have spoken deceptively concerning the righteous statutes. And they will despise <sup>20:12</sup>the covenant and faith which they will have established in the land of Damascus, this being the New covenant. <sup>20:13</sup>And they and their families shall not have a portion in the house of the Torah.

And from <sup>20:14</sup>the day of the assembling by the Unique Teacher until the destruction of all the warriors who will have joined <sup>20:15</sup>with the man of lies, will elapse about forty years. And at that time God's anger will be kindled <sup>20:16</sup>against Israel, as He says, "There will be neither king, nor prince" (Hos 3:4) nor chastiser nor <sup>20:17</sup>reprover in righteousness.

20:18 אל רעהו להצדיק איש את אחיו לתמך צעדם בדרך אל ויקשב

20:19 אל אל דבריהם וישמע ויכתב ספר זכרון לפניו ליראי אל ולחושבי

20:20 שמו ֯w עד יגלה צ ישע וצדקה ליראי אל ושבתם וראיתם בין צדיק

20:21 ורשע בין עבד אל לאשר לא עבדו : ועשה חסד לאלפים לאהביו

20:22 ולשמריו לאלף דור : [וכול אלה]w מביתֿ[117] פלג אשר יצאו מעיֿר הקדש

20:23 וישענו על אל בקץ מעל ישראל ויטמאו את המקדש ושבו עודq

20:24 אל דרדֿq העם בדברים מעטים כולם איש֯ לפי רוחו ישפטו בעצת

20:25 הקדש :    וכל אשר פרצו את גבול התורה מבאֿי הברית בהופע

20:26 כבודֿ אל לישראל יכרתו מקרב המחנה ועמהם כול מרשיעֿי

20:27 יהודה בימי מצרפותיו [ובוגדים בתֿ]קֿי הבריתֿ[ בעבור הןֿ ובצֿא][118]

vacat                    [                                            ]

וכל המחזיקים במשפטים האלה לצֿאת

20:28 ולֿבֿוֿא על פי התורה וישמעו לקול מורה ויתודו לפני  /ℓ  [ח]שֿאנוq

20:29 רשענו גם אנחנו גם אבותינו בלכתנו קרי בחקי הבֿרֿיֿתֿ[119 sch]

20:30 ואמת משפטיך בנו : ולא ירימו יד על חקי קדשו ומשפטיֿ

20:31 צדקו ועדות אמתו : והתיסרו במשפטים הראשונים אשֿֿ

20:32 נשפטו בם אנשי היחיד והאזינו לקול מורה צדק : ולא ישֿיֿבֿו

20:33 אֿת חֿקי הצדק בשֿמֿעֿםֿ אתם ישישו וישמחו ויעז לבם ויתגברו

20:34 עֿל כל בני תבל וכפר אל בעדם [כברית ֿרישֿוֿנֿם֯] וראו בֿיֿשועתו

כי חסו בשם קדשו

---

[117] Rabin transcribes בית [           ]; Qimron °בית [           ] (Rabin, *The Zadokite Documents*, 41; Qimron, "The Text of CDC," 47).

[118] Baumgarten restores [מחזי]קי הברית֯] (DJD XVIII, 99). I thank Tim Undheim for the alternate reconstruction which draws on 1QpHab 8:10–11.

[119] See also Schwartz in James H. Charlesworth, ed., *Damascus Document, War Scroll, and Related Documents* (vol. 2 of *The Dead Sea Scrolls: Hebrew, Aramaic, and Greek Texts with English Translations*; ed. James H. Charlesworth; Tübingen/Louisville: J. C. B. Mohr [Siebeck] and Westminster John Knox Press, 1995), 36. Rabin and Qimron read הברית צדק (Rabin, *The Zadokite Documents*, 43; Qimron, "The Text of CDC," 49).

But those who repent of the transgression of Jacob will have kept God's covenant. "Then each will speak 20:18to his associate" to declare righteous his brother to follow their step in the path of God. "Then God will hearken" 20:19to their words "and will pay attention, and a memorial book will be written before Him on behalf of those who fear God and honor 20:20His name" (Mal 3:16). Then He will reveal salvation and righteousness to the God fearing. "And you will repent and see to differentiate between the righteous 20:21and the wicked, between one who worships God and one who does not" (Mal 3:18). "And He will act lovingly for thousands, to those who love Him 20:22and to those who observe Him (His commandments) for a thousand generations" (Deut 7:9).

[And as for all those] from the house of Peleg (divisiveness) who will leave the holy city (Jerusalem), 20:23and lean upon God at the time of Israel's profanation as they will defile the sanctuary, but will turn once again 20:24to the way of the people in some (evil) matters: each and every one of them according to his inclination shall be judged within the holy council. 20:25And all of those who will be entering the covenant, who will have breached the boundary of the Torah when God's glory will appear 20:26to Israel shall be cut off from the camp, and with them all those of Judah who act wickedly 20:27during the time of their cleansing [and betray the sta]tutes of the covenant [for property and gain . . . ]

But all who will cling to these injunctions by living 20:28a life of Torah shall be obedient to the Teacher and shall confess to God, "'We have sinned 20:29and acted wickedly' (Dan 9:15) 'both we and our ancestors' (Gen 46:34; 47:3) by walking in a defiled way against the statutes of the covenant. 20:30And Your verdicts against us are correct." And they shall not raise their hand (rebel) to alter His holy statutes and His righteous injunctions 20:31and His true testimony. And they shall be chastised by the rules set down by the forefathers in which 20:32the men of the Unique One will have been adjudicated. And they shall obey the Just Teacher. And they shall not reject 20:33the true statutes. When they hearken to them they shall be happy, and rejoice and their heart shall be glad. Then they shall be supreme 20:34over all the people of the world. And God will forgive them [in

4Q266 F4:9–13

9 [כול אלה ישישו וישמחו במצותיו[ʷ ]וחזק°[ʷ ו]120 [

10 ] [°° ] והיקים[ʷ

11 אל את רו[עה אחד] ורעם ב[מרעה[ᵇ טוב את עבדי דויד הוא ירעם[ʷ

12 ו[הוא?]ʷ יהיה[ʷ 121 [לרועם[ʷ וברר לו [אנשי אמת ויראי אל משפט[ʷ

13 [אמת ישפטו חדס[ʷ ו]רחמים[ʷ יעשו איש את אחיו [

(possible ending to the column preceding 4Q267 F7)

] וכי יגור אתכה גר בארצכם לוא תונו אותו[

4Q267 F7:1–3

1 ואהב לו [כמוהו כי גרים הייתם בארץ מצרים vacat ואלה[ʷ

2 [החו]קים 122 [והמשפטים אשר תשמרון לעשות בארץ vacat ʷ [

3 וזה פרוש [המשפטים אשר יעשו בקץ הפקודה וזה משפט שנת[ʷ

4Q271 F3
Parallels: 4Q270 F5 (underline)
         4Q267 F7:4–14 (overbar)
         4Q269 F9 (lower underline)

1 [החמשים ישיב את אחזתו[ʷ ]בכסף] וזהב ואשר אמר[ʷ ו]קרא]תם דרור בארץ[ʷ

2 [ליושביה ואם[ʷ לוא ה]שיגה דיו לה]שיב לו] והגיע[ה 123 [שנת ה[יובל

3 [וישא את חובו[ʷ ואד[ם? ואל124 ]יעזוב ל[ו כול] עוונותיו vacat אל [י]הי[ה[ʷ כלי

4 [גבר על איש ואשה] כאחת כי תועבה היא vacat ואשר אמר כי [תמכור

---

120 Supplants וחזקו[ in Wacholder-Abegg, *Fascicle One*, 9.

121 Baumgarten transcribes והיה[    ]° (DJD XVIII, 46).

122 Baumgarten transcribes °ים[   ] (DJD XVIII, 103).

123 Baumgarten transcribes והגיש]ה (DJD XVIII, 175).

124 Hempel reads אל as a negative particle and, based upon her paleography and a presumed parallel in Jer 11:9–10, transcribes ישוב instead of יעזוב, rendering this clause as "And he shall not return to [ ] his sins," (Charlotte Hempel, *The Laws of the Damascus Document* [ed. F. García Martínez and P. W. Flint; Leiden: Brill, 1998], 65–66). However, these readings are less plausible since, although the negative אל does

accordance with the ancestral covenant]. And they will witness His salvation because they have relied upon His Holy Name. **4Q266 F4:9–13** [All of them will be happy and rejoice in His commandments] and statutes [ . . . ]

<sup>10</sup>[ . . . And] God [will set up] <sup>11</sup>[a unique] shep[herd] and will feed them in [a good pasture; My servant David, he will feed them] <sup>12</sup>and [he] will become [their shepherd (Ezek 34:23).] And he will select for himself [men of truth and God fearers.] <sup>13</sup>[They shall execute true justice. Kindness and] acts of mercy [they shall perform towards each other . . . ]

*The Elaboration of the Eschatological Torah*

[And if a proselyte dwells with you in your land, you shall not defraud him,] **4Q267 F7:1–3** <sup>1</sup>but each shall love him [as himself, since you were proselytes in the land of Egypt (cf. Lev 19:33–34) . . . Now these] <sup>2</sup>[are the sta]tutes [and the judgments which you shall observe to do in the land (Deut 12:1a).] <sup>3</sup>And this is the elaboration [of the judgments which they shall observe in the era of redemption.

*Jubilee; Intermingling Garments; Business and Marriage Disclosures*
Now this is the rule for the] **4Q271 F3** <sup>1</sup>[fiftieth year. He (the lender) shall restore his (the borrower's) possessions] with silver [or gold (for the loan). And where it says, "And you shall] proclaim [liberty in the land] <sup>2</sup>[for its inhabitants" (Lev 25:10): If he (the borrower) cannot] afford to [pay back his indebtedness] and the year of [jubilee] arrives, <sup>3</sup>[then he (the lender) shall forgive his loan; and both ma]n(?) (the lender) and God will forgive hi[m all] his transgressions.

[Let] not [a garment] <sup>4</sup>[of a man] b[e worn by man and woman] in common, for it is an abomination (cf. Deut 22:5). And what he (Moses)

---

occur at the end of this line, MTA as far as I can tell employs לוא rather than אל in apodoses (cf. לוא תונו on line 5). Moreover, the context as reconstructed here, requires a positive. Furthermore, her transcription ישוב is paleographically less likely than יעזוב of the Preliminary Concordance and Baumgarten. What she reads as ש diverges somewhat from the standard solidity of this letter in this manuscript. The letters עז are more likely since there appears to be a slight internal separation, thus suggesting two graphs. Finally, וֹאֲשֶׁר אמר בשנת הֵיוֹבֵל . . . לעזוב להמה 11QMelch 2:2–6 משא [כֹל עוונותיהמה ] lends additional support to the reading of יעזוב rather than ישוב.

5 [ממכר או קנה מיד [עֲמִיתך לוא תונו איש את עמיתו *vacat* וזֹה פרוֹ[ש הונאה[ʷ

6 [כול איש אשר יונהʷ] בכול אשר הוא יודע אשר ימצא אֹבֹדֹה?] והוא לואʷ [יתן

7 [לבעליו ואשר ישקʾ]ל̇ʷ והוא יודע אשר הוא מועל בו באדם ובֹהֹמה ואם

8 [את בתו יתן איש לאי[שֹ את כול מומיה יספר לו למה יביא עליו את משפט

9 [הארֹרֹה אֲשֶׁר אמֹ]ר̇ (ארור) משגֹה עור בדרך וגם אל יתנהֹ לאשר לוא הוכן לה כי

10 [הוא כלאים שֹ]ֹר וחמור ולבוש צמר ו<<ו>>פֹשתים יחדיו *vac* אל יבא איש

11 [אשה בברית הקו]דֹש אשר ידעה לעשות מעשה בֹדֹבר[125] ואשר ידעה

12 [מעשה בבית] אֹביה או אלמנה אשר נשכבה מאשר התארמלה וכול

13 [אשר עליה שֹ]ם רע בבתוליה בבית אביה אל יקחה איש כי אם

14 [בראות נשים] נאמנות וידעות ברורות ממאמר המבֹקֹר אשר על

15 [הרבים ואֹחֹ]ר̇ יקחנה ובלוקחו אותה יעשה כמ[ש]פֹ̇ט [ולוא] יֹגֹיֹד עלֹי[ה

16 [שם רעʷ      ] ° ° ° ° ° ° ° ° ° ° ° ° ° ° °לֹ° [

## 4Q266 F5i

Parallel: 4Q267 F5ii (underline)
        4Q273 F1 (overbar)

1 [     ] ואם אמרה אנוסה היתי אזʷ [תנק]ה[ °° א[     ]

2 [     ] וֹא[ם אנוס אל יֹ]ומתʷ

3 [°ר] את המשפטי[ם  על כול ישראלʷ לשמ]וֹ

4 [האלהʷ     [°°ם *vacat*]אל יבֹ [     ]

5 [     ] קץ הפקודהʾʷ [האחרון לֹ]בדורʷ ואלה המשפטים

6 [     ]° עֹם [°ֹם     ]

7 [     ]°  שֹ[     ]

8 [     ]ה[בנגגֹל ואמיצי כוחʷ מרוב אונים

9 [     ]ֹם בשם קוד[שו ה[°126]טימוא]ה וכול אלה ה   ʷ מֹן התורהʷ

10 [רֹ] שֹק [צא  נֹ]ה כי ביהודה[היʷ אנשי הלצון אשר בירושלים כאשרʷ

---

[125] What originally was a letter מ was corrected by a later hand to ב.
[126] Baumgarten restores המחזי[קים ] (DJD XVIII, 47).

said: "When [you make] [5][a sale or purchase from] your neighbor you shall not defraud each other" (Lev 25:14). And this is the definit[ion of "cheating":] [6][anyone who acts fraudulently] in any matter of which he is aware (that he is doing so); who finds a lost object [but does not] restore it [7][to its owner; and who lie]s and is aware that he is transgressing in the matter whether relating to man or beast. And if [8][one betroths his daughter to a ma]n, he must tell him all her defects. Why should he bring upon himself the fate [9][of the cursed one (*soṭah*)? Concerning which he (Moses) sai]d, "(Cursed) be one who misdirects a blind person in his path" (Deut 27:18). Moreover, he shall not marry her to one who is not appropriate for her, for [10][it is like a "prohibited mixture" (Lev 19:19; Deut 22:9), like plowing with an o]x and a donkey, and wearing wool and flax together.

A man may not bring [11][into the ho]ly [covenant a woman] who has willingly violated a sexual taboo, or who has willingly [12][(had sexual relations) in] her father's [house], or a widow who has had relations after having been widowed, or any [13][woman of] ill [re]pute concerning her virginity while in her father's house. One should not marry her unless [14]trustworthy and knowledgeable and expert [women examine her] under the order of the Supervisor who is over [15][the many. Thereaf]ter he may marry her. But when he marries her he must follow the ru[l]es (of any other marriage). He may [not] spread [16][bad words] concerning [her] . . .

*Duress; Eschatology of the Return; The Sage*

**4Q266 F5i** [1][and if she says, "I was forced," then] she is innoc[ent. . . ] [2][ . . . and i]f a man claimed that he was under duress he likewise shall not [be put to death . . . ] [3][ . . . upon all Israel to ke]ep [these] injunction[s . . . ] [4][ . . . ] let him not [ . . . ]

[5][ . . . And] these are the rules during] the eschatological [generation] for the [epoch of redemption . . . ] [6–7][ . . . ] with [ . . . ] [7][ . . . ] . . . [ . . . ] [8][ . . . mighty in power] and full of strength in what has been reve[al]ed [9][from the Torah . . . But as for all these who will despi]se [His] Hol[y] Name, [th]ey are [10][the followers of the Scoffer who will be in Jerusalem just as] it was formerly. For in

11 [לָשׁוּב על עונת אבותם[b בקץ רשע[w [לישראל בעומד[ו דו[א[w 127

12 [האחרון[w לעשות כרשעי ירושל[ם vacat וכול הנשא[רים]

13 [בה ימסרו[128 לחרב[w            [°° איש <<לי>> לפי רוח[ו יקר[בו

14 [אל תוך המחנה ורמי ר[w]זח ירחק{ן} או לפי המבקר ו[כו]ל

15 [שומרי מצוות אל[w יתהל[כו בם vacat כול שבי ישראל ה[יוצאים[w

16 [מארץ יהודה ועמהם[w ב[ני צדוק הכהנים הנה המ[ה על[w

17 [ספר[w מדרש ה[תורה הא̇ח̇ר̇ו̇ן vacat ואלה התו̇[ק[ים למש[כיל]

18 [להתהלך[w [בם לכול ישראל כֵ̇ לו יוש̇[יע אל[b את[w] כל ה̇[וט[א129

19 [והמחזיק[w [בד̇ר̇כ̇ו להתהלך תמ[ים[b בכול חוקי קודשו ומשפטי[w [

20 [צדקו ועדוות אמתו[w                                           [

## 4Q266 F5i(c-d)[130]

1 [ ]    ואז[w [w]ישפ[טו ב[ר[ו[ח[ ]°[ ]ם[
2 [ ]    [כי לכול ישרי לבב בי[ש[ראל
3 [ ]    [את חוקן הצדיקו ב[          [
4 [ ]    [°° יעו ל[                   [

## 4Q267 F5iii:1–2

1 [ ]    וכ[ו]ל ה[יותו אויל וכול משוגע[w[131
2 [ ]    [וכ[ו]ל שוגה[w[132 וכול כהה [עיני]ם או [חרש[w וכול אשר איננו[133]

## 4Q266 F5ii[134]

Parallels: 4Q267 F5iii (underline)
        4Q273 F2; 4i (overbar)

1 [ ]    [(אשר איננו) ממהר להב[י]ן וכול א[שר נקל בלשונו או בקול טרוד]

---

127 Baumgarten transcribes ל̇[ ] (DJD XVIII, 47).
128 Or יסגרו (CD 19:13)
129 Baumgarten transcribes א[ ]°° (DJD XVIII, 48).
130 These two mini-fragments potentially form the last four lines of 4Q266 F5i.
131 Baumgarten restores [      שר א[ו]ל וכ] (DJD XVIII, 102).
132 Baumgarten transcribes [            ]°[ ] (DJD XVIII, 102).
133 Baumgarten restores אינו (DJD XVIII, 102).
134 Because of the allusion to death in line 3 of this column, Baumgarten postulates that 4Q273 F3, ]ה לא ימות[, may parallel a portion of this pericope (DJD XVIII, 195).

Judah there will b[e a sche]me [11][to turn to the sins of their fathers (cf. Jer 11:9b–10a) during the epoch of wickedness] in Israel when [12]the [last genera]tion will arise [to act like the wicked of Jerusale]m. And all who rema[in] [13][in it shall be delivered over to the sword . . . ] . . . Each according to [his] spirit [will be broug]ht [14][into the camp, but the haughty in sp]irit will be expelled, (all) at the command of the Supervisor. And [al]l [15][who keep the commandments of God shall liv]e by them. As for all the penitent of Israel who [will exit] [16][from the land of Judah and with them the so]ns of Zadok, the priests: behold they are (described) [in] [17][the book of the Midrash on the] Eschatological Torah.

And these are the stat[ute]s for the Sa[ge] [18]by which [to guide] all of Israel, for [God] will not sa[ve] any s[i]nner. [19][But as for the one who clings] to his way by walking upright[ly in all His holy statutes, righteous injunctions] [20][and true testimony . . . ] **4Q266 F5i (c–d)** [1][ . . . and then] they [will be jud]g[ed] in the [s]pirit (?) of [ . . . ] . . . [2][ . . . ] for all the upright of heart in I[s]rael [3][ . . . ] they declared righteous His statutes [ . . . ] [4][ . . . ]

*Public Recitation of the Torah; Defrocking a Priest; Procedures in Both Cities and Camps*
**4Q267 F5iii:1–2** [1][ . . . and a]nyone w[ho is a fool, and any mentally deficient person,] [2][and a]n[y who is prone to err] and any dim-[eye]d or [deaf; or anyone who is not] **4Q266 F5ii** [1][quick to under]stand, and anyone o[f soft speech or who speaks with a stut-

2 [דבר לו ו]לֹא פֵצֵל דברו להשמיע [קולו איש מאלה לֹא יקרא בספר]

3 [התורה ]לֵמה ישוג בדבר מות] *vacat* ?וגם איש מכול עֲרֹתוֹ תֵמִֹים[135

  קודש לא יקרא עמוֹ[w 136

4 [אצֹ]ל[w אחו הכהנים בֹעֲבוֹדֹה [וא]ל[ֹ] ישרת עמו במקדש[w *vacat* ואיש[

5 מבני אהרון אֲשר ישבֹה לגואים] וישתחוה לפסילים ויקלל את התורה[w]

6 לחללה בטמאתם אל יגש לעבודת] הקודש[b *vacat* ואל יצא ואל יבוא[w]

7 מבית לפרוכת *vacat* ואל יֹזֵכל את קודש הֹ[קודשים[b ואל יגע בטהרה[w]

8 איש מבני אהרון אשר ינדד לעֹב[וֹד וישרת[w את הגואים[b אל יאות איש[w]

9 לֹהורות עמו בישוד עם וגם לבגו‹ד› עֲמוֹ |ׂ ‏    איש מבני]

10 אהרון אשר הֵוֵפֵ{י}ל שמו מן האמֱוֱֹת וֹ[עשה את הישר בעיניו ובחר[w 137

11 בשרירות לבו לאכול מן הקודש] לוא ישוב עוד וכול אשר ימרה[w]

12 מישראל את עצת בני אהרון תֵמֹש]רתים את בני ישראל לוֹא יגע[w]

13 את האוכל וֵהֵבֹו *vacat* וחב בדם [יכרת זרעו מן הארץ ולוא יכתב[w]

14 ביחֹש{י}ם *vacat* וזה סרך מוֹשֵב [הרבים לכול יושבי אנשי תמים[w 138

15 הקוֹד[ש מחני]הֹם 139 [וֹ]עֲרֹיהם בכ]ל[b וֹלֹי קץ חרון עד עמוד משיח[w]

16 וֹ[איש אשר[w יצחק[w 140 בֹמו[שֹב א]נֹשֹי הרבים בסכלות להרים שמיע[w]

17 [קולו והובדל שלושים[ יום ונענש חמשה עשר ימים[w ?‏   [

---

135 Baumgarten transcribes ]הֹ עֲלֹה[ in 4Q267 F5iii:6 (DJD XVIII, 102).

136 4Q267 F5iii:5b–6 apparently contained more text than did its parallel in 4Q266 F5ii:3. Postulating that 4Q266 is defective at this point, we provide a reconstruction corresponding to the larger spacing of 4Q267.

137 Baumgarten restores [(?)הלךֹ   ] (DJD XVIII, 50).

138 Baumgarten restores [אנשי   עֵרֵי ישראל מוֹשֵב] (DJD XVIII, 50).

139 Baumgarten restores הקוֹד[ש במחני]הֹם (DJD XVIII, 50).

140 The root צחק occurs in MTA only in 4Q273 F4i:9 with the adjoining words having perished, evidently connected to what we have in the variants סֹ[וח]ק[ in 4Q266 F10ii:12 and ק]חֹושֹ in 4Q269 F11ii+15:1. This verb occurs also in 1QS 7:14.

ter] [2][and] does not articulate his expressions so as to be audi[ble: none of these may recite from the book] [3][of the Torah] lest he err in a case involving the death penalty. [And likewise anyone from his entire congregation who is perfectly upright may not recite with him] [4][alongsi]de his brothers, the priests, in worship. [And] he may [no]t [minister with him in the sanctuary.

And anyone] [5]of the sons of Aaron who is taken captive by the pagans [and bows down to graven images and curses the Torah,] [6]profaning it with their impurities, may not lead the [holy] service. [And he may not exit or enter] [7]in front of the veil. He may not eat any food belonging to the holy of [holies. Nor may he touch anything belonging to the Purity.] [8]As for anyone from among the sons of Aaron who travels to wor[ship or serves the pagans, no one may participate] [9]in teaching with him (the one who practiced idolatry) in the foundation of the people, thereby joining in his betra<yal>... [ . . . Anyone from the sons] [10]of Aaron who removes his name from the membership roll, [doing whatever is pleasing in his eyes, and choosing] [11]the corruption of his heart by eating from the sacred food [cannot return (to the Purity). And anyone who violates] [12]from Israel the council of the sons of Aaron who se[rve the sons of Israel shall not touch] [13]the food. Guilty of consuming blood, [his seed will be cut off from the earth and he will not be recorded] [14]in their genealogy.

And this is the rule of the habitation [of the many for all the inhabitants of] [15]hol[y perfection, for] their [camps and] their cities during the en[tire epoch of anger until the Messiah arises.] [16]And [anyone who jests in the habit]ation of the m[any in a foolish manner, loudly raising] [17][his voice, shall be separated thirty days and punished fifteen days . . . ]

4Q272 F1i–ii

Parallels: 4Q266 F6i (underline)

         4Q269 F7 (overbar)

         4Q273 F4ii (lower underline)

          text unique to 4Q269 or 4Q273 (outline)

i:1   [אדם כי יהיה[w שאת א[ו ספחת או ב[הרת[b בעורו[w מה היא]

i:2   [והספחת מכת עץ וא[ו]בן וכול מכה בבוא הרו[ח ואחזה]

i:3   [בגיד ושב הדם למ]עלה ולמטה והגיד רו[חו עולה ויורדת[w]

i:4   [אחר הדם וראהו הכוהן והסגירו[w] ל[חוץ 141 המחנה שבעת ימים[w]

i:5   [וראה הכוהן את העור [החי ואת המת[w] אם נמעט[w] [המת מן

i:6a  [החי בשבעת ימים ואם י[שוב 142 הדם לגיד [ברוח[w] ואח[ר] ישוה

         [בו כאשר א[מר והסגיר[ו] הכוהן]

i:6   [שבעת ימים[w] h/ עד[143 אשר יצמח] הבשר וראה[ הכוהן ב[יום]

i:7   [השביעי אם[w רו[ח144 החיים עולה ו]ירדת [ו]הבשר צמח [נרפא144

i:8   [מן השאת ומן[w ה[ספחת לוא יראנה הכוהן לעור הבש[ר[b ואם[w]

i:9   [לוא יצמח הבשר[w] ואם ישפל השאת או הס[פחת[b בשפה[w]

i:10  [עורן[w 146 וראה הכוהן [אותו כמראי הבשר החי ו[כנגע[w]

i:11  [צרעת147 היא148 האוח[זה[ בעור החי וכמשפט [הזה לכול נגע[w]

i:12  [צרעת[w וראה הכוהן ביום השב[יעי [ו]הנה נוסף מ[ן החי]

i:13  [אל149 המת[b והסגירו[w צרעת מ[מארת היא vacat

i:14  [ומשפט נתק הראש והזקן vac(?) ו[ר]אה הכוהן וה[נה ]

i:15  [באה הרוח בראש או בזקן באוחזה בג[י]ד ופרח הנגע[ מתחת השער150

i:16  [והפך מראה[ו[w לדק צוהב כי כעשב] הוא אשר [ב[ו151 הרחש

i:17  [תחתו ויקיץ שורשו ויבש פרחו vacat ואש[ר א[מר וצוה הכוהן]

---

141 Baumgarten sees the remnant of a letter immediately preceding ל (DJD XVIII, 188).

142 Baumgarten restores [עד אשר י[שוב (DJD XVIII, 188).

143 Baumgarten restores [החי והסגירו עד] (DJD XVIII, 188).

144 Baumgarten restores ח[השביעי והנה רו[ (DJD XVIII, 188).

145 Baumgarten places נרפא on line 8 for the reading הנגע(?) טהורה(?) ה[ספחת, נרפא] (DJD XVIII, 188).

146 Baumgarten reconstructs ן[לכ]ה in 4Q266 F6i:2 (DJD XVIII, 52).

147 Baumgarten restores צרעת to 4Q266 F6i:3, but not here (DJD XVIII, 52).

148 היאה 4Q266 F6i:3.

149 The following vertical inter-columnar crossed-out text occurs between columns 1 and 2 of 4Q266 F6: שפח[ת] ג[ב]חת תח o o (scab of the forehead . . . ). Baumgarten transcribes שפח[ת] גבחת חת הבﬞ (DJD XVIII, 52).

150 I present here a conflation of this line and 4Q266 F6i:6a–7a. The lacuna of line 15 accommodates perhaps ten letters less than we have included from its parallel. Baumgarten concludes the lacuna with באוחזה.

*Leprosy; Bodily Emissions*

**4Q272 F1i–ii** <sup>i:1</sup>[As for a man who has a swelling o]r scab or
dis[coloration in his skin (Lev 13:2): what is it (i.e. "what are the
rules")?] <sup>i:2</sup>[If the scab is the result of a blow from wood or st]one or
of any other kind of blow, when the spiri[t] enters [and takes hold]
<sup>i:3</sup>[of the artery and the blood recedes u]pward and downward, and
the spir[it] of the artery [goes up and down] <sup>i:4</sup>[after the blood, the
priest shall examine him and quarantine him outside the camp for
seven days.] <sup>i:5</sup>[Then the priest shall examine] the living and the dead
[skin (to see) whether] the dead part [has receded] from <sup>i:6a</sup>[the living
during the seven days (of quarantine). And if] the blood return[s] to
the artery [through the spirit, the]n he shall compare [it (the two types
of skin), as he (Moses) s]ays, "'And [the priest] shall quarantine' [him]
<sup>i:6</sup>['for seven days'" (Lev 13:4, 31) until the flesh] grows. [Then] the
priest [shall examine (him] on the [seventh day] <sup>i:7</sup>[(to see) whether]
the living [spir]it goes up and down [and] the flesh has grown. [He
has been healed] <sup>i:8</sup>[of the swelling and the] scab. The priest shall
no longer examine the skin of the fle[sh. But if] <sup>i:9</sup>[the flesh does
not grow] and the swelling or the s[cab] becomes lower [than their
surrounding] <sup>i:10</sup>[skin, the priest shall examine] it as a likeness of
living flesh; [it is as an affliction] <sup>i:11</sup>[of leprosy which has taken hol]d
of the living skin. Now [this] is the rule [for any leprous affliction.]
<sup>i:12</sup>[The priest shall make an examination on the sev]enth [day; and]
if [the dead flesh] is enlarged fr[om the living,] <sup>i:13</sup>[he (the priest)
shall quarantine him.] It is [m]alignant [leprosy.]

<sup>i:14</sup>[And now the rule for the scall of the head or the beard:] The
priest [shall] examine (it), particularly i[f] <sup>i:15</sup>[the spirit has entered
the head or the beard as it takes hold of the artery and the affliction
spreads] under the hair, <sup>i:16</sup>[and &lt;its&gt; appearance turns to a light
yellow; since] it is [like grass] which [has] worms <sup>i:17</sup>[under it which
cuts its root, making its blossom dry up.] As for what he s[ays, "Then

---

<sup>151</sup> Baumgarten restores ט[·] in 4Q266 F6i:8 and transcribes ·[ ] in the parallel
4Q272 F1i:16 (DJD XVIII, 52, 188).

i:18 ‏[וגלחו את הרוש‏152 ואת‏] הנתק לוא יגלחו ‏[למען אשר יסף‏]וֹר ‏[הכוהן‏]

i:19 ‏[את השערות המתות והחיות וראה אם יוסף‏] מֹן החי אל הֹמֹ[ת‏]

i:20 ‏[בשבעת הימים טמא הוא‏153 ואם לוא ליוסף מֹ]ן החיות אל‏154 ‏[המתות‏]

ii:1 ‏[‏ו]הֹגיד נמלא ֹדֹם ורוח החיים עולה וי‏[‏ו]רֹדֹת בו נרפא מן‏]

ii:2 ‏[הנ‏]גֹע זה ‏[משפט תורת הצֹ]רֹעֹ[ת לב‏]נֹי אהרון ‏[להבדיל לנגע צרעת‏ᵂ]

ii:3 vacat ‏[זאת תורת הזב והזבה‏ᵂ] וֹמֹשֹ[פט הזב את זו‏]בֹ כֹ[ול איש‏]

ii:4 ‏[אשר ‏]זֹ[ו‏]בֹ יזוב מבשרו‏155 או אשר יעלה עליו מֹ[חשבת זמה או אשֹר‏

ii:5 יֹתור במחשבות יצר אשמה בעני זנות יטמא‏ᵂ ‏[מגע כמגע הֹזֹֹבֹ]ֹזֹ[ועֹ]ᵂ‏156

ii:6 ‏וֹכבס בֹגֹ[ד‏]יֹו ‏[ורחץ במים‏ᵇ vacat כול אשר ימשול רוח בליעל‏ᵂ]

ii:7 ‏בו הנוגע בו יֹ[חזק‏]157 וכבס בגדיו‏ᵂ ו‏[משפט ‏[הזבה כול אשה‏]

ii:8 ‏הזבה דם שבֹ[עת ימים תהיה בנד‏]תֹה בֹ[טמאתה‏ᵂ ת‏[שֹב אֹ[ת‏]

ii:9 ‏שבעת הימיֹםֹ האלה וכול כלי אשר‏ᵂ ‏יֹ[היה בו דם‏ᵂ ‏[הֹנדה וכ‏]וֹ[ל‏]

ii:10 ‏[הנו‏]גֹע בֹהֹ‏ יזו עליו מי חטאת ביום השלישי וביום השביעי‏ᵂ]

ii:11 ‏ובעֹ[ב‏158 יום השמיני יטהר‏ᵂ                ואם‏[ᵂ]

ii:12 ‏תקוֹן ‏[דם זובה‏ᵇ וטמאה שבעת ימים‏ᵂ              ‏[

ii:13 ‏המיֹם‏]                                          ‏[

ii:14 ‏]°°°°                                            ‏[

ii:15 ‏ובמי הנדהֹ‏]                                     המים‏[

ii:16 ‏החיֹיֹ[ם‏] שנֹיֹ[ת‏ᵂ                               ‏[

ii:17 ‏יֹדֹהֹ‏]                                          ‏[

ii:18 ‏]ֹ°                                             ‏[

4Q266 F6i(a–e)‏159

| | |
|---|---|
| (a):1 | ‏]ֹ[ ‏]ֹ[ |
| (a):2 | ‏[מ‏]שפחת ‏]° |
| (b):1 | ‏[הֹבשר ] |
| (b):2 | ‏[משפט ] |
| (c):1 | ‏[ש‏]רֹ ‏]יֹסֹוֹדֹוֹ |

---

152 What was originally a ‏ב in 4Q266 F6i:9 was transformed into a ‏ר plus a supralinear ‏ו. The word ends with an additional ‏ר, apparently a remainder of the original ‏בשר.

153 הואה 4Q266 F6i:11.

154 על 4Q266 F6i:12.

the priest shall ordain (Lev 13:54)] <sup>i:18</sup>[that they shave the head, but] the scall they shall not shave off" (Lev 13:33) [so that the priest will be able to cou]nt <sup>i:19</sup>[the number of the dead and the living hair. And he (the priest) shall see whether] any of the living hair [has been added] to the de[ad] <sup>i:20</sup>[during the seven days. (And if they have,) he shall declare him defiled. But if there has been no increase fr]om the living to [the dead hair] <sup>ii:1</sup>[and] the artery is filled with blood and the spirit of life goes up and d[own in him, he has been healed of] <sup>ii:2</sup>[the aff]liction. This is [the rule for the Torah of le]pro[sy for the so]ns of Aaron [with regard to quarantining the affliction of leprosy.]

<sup>ii:3</sup>[This is the law for the male or female who has a discharge.] Now the ru[le for the male who has a disch]arge: A[ny man] <sup>ii:4</sup>[whose body emits a ]hea[vy discharge, or into whom a th]ought of whoredom [enters], or whoever <sup>ii:5</sup>[turns towards thoughts inclining towards transgression with eyes of harlotry, is defiled.] His touch is like that of the lep[er,] <sup>ii:6</sup>and he shall launder his cloth[ing and wash in water. As for any who is taken over by the spirit of Belial:] <sup>ii:7</sup>he who touches him must w[ash and launder his clothing.

Now for the] rule of [the female who has a discharge: Any woman] <sup>ii:8</sup>who has a discharge of blood [shall be in] her [impur]ity sev[en days. She shall] remain in [her uncleanness] fo[r <sup>ii:9</sup>[those] seven days [along with any utensil upon which] there i[s a drop of blood of] defilement. And as for a[nyone] <sup>ii:10</sup>[who tou]ches her, [they shall sprinkle upon him water of purification on the third and the seventh day,] <sup>ii:11</sup>and in the even[ing of the eighth day he shall be declared clean . . . And if] <sup>ii:12</sup>she emits [the blood of her discharge she shall be unclean for seven days . . . ] <sup>ii:13</sup>water [ . . . ] <sup>ii:15</sup>and with the waters of purification [ . . . ] <sup>ii:16</sup>[living] wate[r agai[n . . . ] <sup>ii:17</sup>her hand[ . . . ] <sup>ii:18</sup>and [ . . . ] **4Q266 F6i(a–e)**<sup>8</sup> <sup>(a):1</sup>[ . . . ] <sup>(a):2</sup>[ . . . ] the family of [ . . . ] <sup>(b):1</sup>[ . . . ] the flesh [ . . . ] <sup>(b):2</sup>[ . . . ] rule [ . . . ] <sup>(c):1</sup>[ . . . ] . . .

---

<sup>8</sup> These pieces are not necessarily sequential.

---

<sup>155</sup> Baumgarten restores אשר יזוב מבשרו] (DJD XVIII, 190).
<sup>156</sup> Baumgarten restores הׄ°°° (DJD XVIII, 190).
<sup>157</sup> Baumgarten transcribes וׄהׄ]חׄץ (DJD XVIII, 190).
<sup>158</sup> Baumgarten transcribes [          ]°ובע (DJD XVIII, 190).
<sup>159</sup> Possibly positioned in F6ii:14 to the end of the column, these sub-fragments as arranged are not necessarily sequential.

[והבדל ואם °°°]    (c):2

[להֹטֹאֹ] [ ] וּיכבס בגד[וֹ]<sup>b</sup> ורחץ<sup>w</sup>    (c):3

[° [ [° ]    (c):4

[הֹ שב הֹרֹם]    (d):1

[ אֹוֹ °]     (d):2

[עֹל    (e):1

[כֹוֹל נגע    (e):2

[לֹעבור    (e):3

[לֹ    (e):4

**4Q266 F6ii**

[ ]   [° [ [ה אֹ°הֹאֹשֹׁ]ה °° [אשר יֹ]קֹרֹב [איש<sup>w</sup>]    ii:1

[אליה ע]וֹן נדה עלו ואם ראתה [עו]דֹ והיאה לו [בנדתה<sup>w</sup>]    ii:2

[וטמאה<sup>w</sup> ]שבעת ימים<sup>160</sup> והיאה אל תוכל קודש ואֹל תֹ[בוא]<sup>161</sup>    ii:3

אֹל המקדֹש עד בו השמש ביום הֹשמיני *vacat*    ii:4

ואשה אשֹר [תזרי]עֹ וילדה זכר [וטמאה אֹ]ֹת שבעת [הימים]    ii:5

[כֹ]יֹ[מי] נֹדֹת [דאותה ובוֹם השמיני ימול בשר] עֹרֹלֹתֹ[וֹ]    ii:6

[ושלשים יום ושלשת ימים תשב בדם<sup>162</sup> טוהרה ואם נקבה תלד]    ii:7

[וטמאה שבועים כנדת ד]אותה וֹ[ששים וששה יום תשב בדם<sup>163</sup>]    ii:8

[טוהרה והיאה ]לֹא תוֹ[כ]ֹלֹ קודש ולא תבו אל המקדש]    ii:9

[כי מ]שפט מות הוֹא ואם לא יכולה להיניק ונתנה<sup>w</sup> את]    ii:10

[הי]לֹד למנקת בטוה]רה תטמא עד הערב והביאה שה לעולה<sup>w</sup>]    ii:11

[ו]אם לוֹא הֹשֹיגה יֹד[ה די שה ולקחה בן יונה או תר לעולה]    ii:12

[ו]המירה [א]ֹת ה[שה]<sup>b</sup> לתר או לבן<sup>w</sup>] יונה<sup>164</sup> [     [    ii:13

[ ו]כֹן משפט [     [    ii(a):2

[° אֹוֹ ] [°     [    ii(a):3

---

<sup>160</sup> Baumgarten restores והיאה [בעת נדתה לו שבעת ימים, to read the following in the broader context: "If she ag[ain] sees (blood), and it is not [at the time of her menstruation] of seven days, she shall not eat anything hallowed, nor co[me] into the sanctuary until sunset on the eighth day" (DJD XVIII, 55–56). My restoration follows the syntax of Lev 15:19 wherein an accompanying verb specifies the period of seven days the menstruant is to remain impure, phraseology restored also to 4Q272 F1ii:7b–8.

<sup>161</sup> Baumgarten restores [תֹבו] (DJD XVIII, 55).

<sup>162</sup> For בדם סוהרה rather than בדמי סהרה of Lev 12:4 cf. 4Q265 F7:17.

<sup>163</sup> Baumgarten restores דם (DJD XVIII, 55).

<sup>164</sup> Transcribed from 4Q266 F6ii(a):1.

[ . . . ] (c):2[ . . . ] and to keep separate. And if . . . [ . . . ] (c):3[ . . . ]
. . . [ . . . ] and wash [his] clothing [and cleanse . . . ] (c):4[ . . . ]
(d):1[ . . . ] . . . the blood recedes [ . . . ] (d):2[ . . ] or [ . . . ] (e):1[ . . . ]
. . . (e):2[ . . . ] . . . (e):3[ . . . ] to transgress (e):4[ . . . ] . . .

*Menstruation; Childbearing*
**4Q266 F6ii** [1] . . . [one who] comes near [2][her] must bear upon
himself the [s]in of a menstruant. And if she sees (blood) [aga]in
and it is not [during her menstrual period,] [3][she shall be defiled]
for seven days and she may not eat sacred food nor [enter] [4]the
sanctuary until the sunset of the eighth day.

[5]And a woman who [concei]ves and gives birth to a male [shall be
defiled] for seven [days] [6][as] during the da[ys of] her menst[ruation.
And on the eighth day the flesh of his] foreskin [shall be circumcised.] [7][And thirty-three days she shall remain in her time of blood
purification (Lev 12:2b–4a). However, if she gives birth to a female,]
[8][she shall be unclean for two weeks, as during her period of] her
[mens]truation. And [sixty-six days she shall remain in the period of
her blood] [9][purification (Lev 12:5). She] shall not e[a]t [sacred food
nor enter the sanctuary (Lev 12:4b),] [10][as] i[t] is a capital [o]ffense.
[And if she cannot nurse she shall give] [11][the c]hild to a nurse during her period of purifica[tion. She shall be impure until the setting
of the sun and she shall bring a lamb for a burnt offering.] [12][But] if
she cannot afford [a lamb, she shall take a young dove or a pigeon
for a burnt offering (Lev 12:8a).] [13][And] she may replace the [lamb
with a pigeon or a young] dove [ . . . ] (a):2[ . . . and] thus the rule
[ . . . ] (a):3[ . . . ] . . .

4Q270 F3i:17–21[165]

| | | | |
|---|---|---|---|
| | ]∘ ה̇ ∘[ | חזה מן[ | ] 17 |

vacat　　18

] ואלה[ו]  חוק̇[י]ו̇  אד̇מ̇ת ה̇[קודש̇  תספור לכה שבעה[ו  19

[ו]שבועות חמש[י]ם יום ול[חר]מ̇ש קציר לרע̇ף̇ן תספור עד[ו  20

[אשר יצמח ג]ן ושדה ל[פרי ומים ו  א̇שר ישקו א̇[ת האדמה[ו  21

(4Q270 F3ii:1)

[　　　　　　　　　　　　　　　　　　　　　לדשנה[ו

4Q266 F6iii
Parallels: 4Q267 F6:1–6 (underline)
　　　　　4Q270 F3ii:12–16 (overbar)

| | | |
|---|---|---|
| [ | ]בד̇[∘ | ] iii(a):1 |

על פרי הגן[ו  ]והקציר[ שיש שנים יזרע איש[ו  ] iii(a):2

[שדהו ושיש שנים יזמור[ו  עץ פר]יו ובשנה השביעית לוא[ו  iii(a):3

[יזרע ועץ פריו לוא[ו  ]זמו[ר שבת שבתון יהיה לארץ[ו  iii(a):4

ה̇ אשר  ] iii(b):1

]לה מפר[י  iii(b):2

ובשנת היובל תשבות הארץ ]שנית̇  ו  [העצים[ו  iii(b):3

∘ ∘ ∘ [　ו̇ישב איש אל אחזתו[ו  iii(b):4

ו[ו̇]ו̇ם [הכפורים הואה סוף היובל ובקודש תקצרו[ם̇ו  iii:1

[כי]ו  את מי הנדה̇ [לא תגעו כאשר כתוב בתורת[ו  iii:2

על [ע̇ל̇  vacat[ א̇ל̇  iii:3

[הלקט ]ועללות הכ̇[רם עד עשרה גרגרי]ם̇  [העל]ל̇ת  iii:4

[הזית ]ו̇כול הלק̇ט̇ [עד סאה לבית ה[ס̇א̇[ה]  iii:5

[והיא ]אשר זרעה אין בה̇[  תרומה ו]פרט [אין[ו  iii:6

[בה]ו  ו̇בעוללתו עד עשרה ג[רגרים ]ובנק[וף  iii:7

[הזית ופר]י̇ תבואותו אם [שלמה הי]א̇ נ̇ק̇פ̇ה̇  iii:8

[אחת מ]של̇ל̇ו̇]שי̇ם̇ ש[אה]ו  ואם ימעט מ[מטע̇ו  iii:9

[　]∘ה̇ בשרף[וגנו ואם רפוס השדה או יקרה  iii:10

[165] With slight modifications I follow Baumgarten's more recent transcription of this column as presented in "Corrigenda to the 4Q MSS of the *Damascus Document*." *Revue de Qumran* 19 (1999): 217–18. He transcribes

*The Raising of the Omer*
**4Q270 F3i:17–21** [superscript 17][ . . . ] he saw by[ ] [superscript 18]. . . [superscript 19][ . . . These] are
His statute[s] (for) the [Holy] Land. [You shall count seven] [superscript 20][weeks,
fif]ty days. And for [the rea]ping of everyone's harvest [you shall reckon
(fifty days) until] [superscript 21][gar]den and field [produce fruit and (until) the
waters (accumulate)], irrigating [superscript (ii:1a)][the land to enrich it . . . ]

*The Sabbatical Year; Gleanings; Items Requiring Tithing*
**4Q266 F6iii** [superscript (a):1][ . . . ] [superscript 2][ . . . Concerning the fruits of the garden]
and the harvest: [Six years one shall plant] [superscript (a):3][his field and for six
years prune his] fruit trees. [But in the seventh year he may neither]
[superscript (a):4][plant nor] prun[e his fruit trees. The land shall have a solemn
Sabbath . . . ] [superscript (b):1][ . . . ] which [superscript (b):2][ . . . ] from the fruit[s] [superscript (b):3][of
the trees . . . And in the jubilee year the land shall rest] again.
[superscript (b):4][And each shall return to his inheritance . . . ] [superscript 1][Now the] Day
[of Atonement is the end of the jubilee. And in holiness you shall
harvest] them (the inadvertent growth during the sabbatical and
jubilee years), [superscript 2][for] the water of purification [you shall not touch,
just as is written in the Torah of] [superscript 3]God.  [ . . .

Concerning] [superscript 4][the field] and the vi[neyard] gleanings: [the glean]ing
[of olives may be up to ten berrie]s. [superscript 5]And all the field gleanings [may
be up to the seed volume needed to plant a] *sea*[*h.*] [superscript 6][However, where]
the planting of the seed has resulted in no growth, [there shall be
neither tithing of the field nor] gleaning of fallen berries. [superscript 7]But when
one does glean, (he may pick) up to ten be[rries.]

Now as for when [the olives] are squ[eez]ed [superscript 8][with the yield] of
its produce: if [i]t [is intact], its sacred yield shall be [superscript 9]one (*seah*) out
of] thirty *se*[*ahs.* And if] the planting [superscript 10][of its garden has decreased or
if the field is trampled or consumed by fir]e, **4Q270 F3ii:17–21** [superscript 17]its

| | | |
|---|---|---|
| [ | [ חֹזה מִ° ]°ח °[ | ] 17 |
| | *vacat* | |
| [ | חוקֹיֿ [ ] אדֹמַֿת הֹ[קודש | ] 19 |
| [ | [וֹם יום ולֹ[ה]מֹשֿ קצֿיר לֿרֹעֿ°] | ] 20 |
| [ | [ן ושֹרֹה לֹ[ [אֲשֶׁר יْשׁקן אֹ]ת | ] 21 |

4Q270 F3ii:17–21
Parallels: 4Q267 F6:7 (underline)
4Q266 F6iii:10 (overbar)

17 [(בשרפה) ונפרס] מ̇סאה לבית ס̇א̇ה מעשדה[^166] בה ואם תלקוט

18 [נפש אחת סאה] אחת ממנו ביום אחד תרומה בה בה עשרון

19 [ולוא תלקוט עוד^w] חלות התרומה לכל בתי ישראל אוכלי לחם

20 [הארץ^b עליהם^w ל]הרים אחת בשנה עשרון אחד תהיה האחת

21 [לחם בכורים לאל^w לפני] ה̇שלמו לישראל אל [י]רם איש

4Q270 F3ii(a)[^167]

1 [את ידו לאכול חטים חדשים^w וא]ת [לח]ם המצ̇[ו]ת עד יום^w]

2 [בוא לחם הבכורים^w   א]ת חלב הדגן ]   [

(last line of 4Q266 F6iii)

]   וכי יטע איש כרם כול פריו בשלוש^w]

4Q266 F6iv

iv:1 [^w השני[ם] הרישונ]ו̇ת לכהנים יהיו ערלה היא לאל וכול^w]

iv:2 נטעי הכר[ם ‹‹ו]כ̇ול›› עצי̇ הפר̇י̇ וכל עצ̇י̇ ה̇מ[אכל ל]ה̇ם [יהיו]

iv:3 כמשפטם [באדמ]ת הקודש ובארץ מגורים ואחר ימכ[רו]

iv:4 מהם לקנ̇[ו]ן פרי^w הע[צ]ים[^168] וא̇[ם w, m/t w, m/t]י̇ט̇ע[^169] איש בשנה הרביעית לו̇ יוכ[ל]^w

iv:5 [כי [ק]דשו בש[נ]ה הזאת^b הלולים המ[ז]ת[^w] ואם יקריב איש^w]

iv:6 מ̇מ̇נחה וג[ר]ש כרמל אביב קלוי באש יהיו בכוריו ולו^w]

iv:7 [יוכ]ל̇[ א[ת] ט̇[בל תבואתו ובשנה החמישית יוכל את פריו^w]

iv:8 [להו]ס̇י̇ף לו ת̇[בואתו ]   [

iv:9 [ ]שה ה̇א̇[·]ה̇[   [

iv(a):1 [^w וה]ל̇רים אשר] מן המנחה לאזכרה לאשה לאל ואל^w]

iv(a):2 [יסור אי]ש̇^w לימין ואשר ל[שמאול מכול אשר יורו הכהנים^w]

iv(a):3 [ באחרית הימים^w

---

[^166]: Read מעשרה.
[^167]: This small piece with reconstruction conceivably formed the first two lines of 4Q270 F3iii.
[^168]: Baumgarten transcribes ∘∘[ ]לקנ̇ (DJD XVIII, 59).
[^169]: Baumgarten transcribes טע[ ]י̇ (DJD XVIII, 59).

portion [should be reduced] to its tenth from the seed volume needed to plant a *seah*. And if [a person] gleans [18]one [*seah*] from it in one day, its tithing shall be a tenth [19][but he may glean no more.] As for the loaves of *terumah* required of all the houses of Israel who consume the food [20][of the land: it is incumbent upon them to] set aside (the loaves) once a year, one tenth per loaf [as first fruits to the Lord. Before] its completion by Israel, [let] no one raise **4Q270 F3ii(a)** [1][his hand to eat the new wheat and] unleaven[ed bre]ad [until the day] [2][of the coming of the firstfruits . . . ] the best of the grain [ . . . ]

*The Orlah*
**(last line of 4Q266 F6iii)–4Q266 F6iv** [ . . . And if one plants a vineyard, all its fruit that grows during the] [iv:1][fi]r[st three year]s [shall belong to the priests. It is *orlah* to the Lord. And all] [iv:2]the plantings of the vineya[rd] and all that is grown on the [fruit bearing] trees (during these years) [belongs to] them [iv:3]in accordance with their rights [in] the Holy [Land] and in (their) dwelling places. And thereafter [they] may sel[l] [iv:4]from them for the pur[chase of (other) fruit of the tr]ees. And i[f] one plants in the fourth year [he may] no[t ea]t (of them) [iv:5][for] they have been sanctified in [that] y[ear. They are (holy) hymns (Lev 19:24). And if one presents] [iv:6]a kind of meal offering, [his first fruits shall be] g[rits of fresh grain, young ears parched with fire. But] [iv:7][he may not ea]t[ the] g[ood of the untithed of his produce. However, in the fifth year he may eat its fruit] [iv:8][so that] he might have an increment from [its] p[roduce (Lev 19:25). . . ] [iv(a):1][ . . . Then he (the priest) shall r]aise a part [of the meal offering as a memorial as a burnt offering to the Lord. And on]e [shall not] [iv(a):2–(3)][turn] to the right nor to [the left from what the priests will instruct at the end of days . . . ]

4Q271 F2
Parallels: 4Q269 F8i–ii (underline)
          4Q270 F3iii:13–21 (overbar)

[וְעַל כּוֹל‏ᵂ תבוא‏תֿ‏ᵇ השרה‏ᵂ‏]¹⁷⁰

1 [וּמעשר כול אשר יביא‏ᵂ] מגורן יוֿרד את העשרון מן הֿחֿ[וֿמר ומן הא]‏יֿפֿה

2 [וֿהבת כאשר הקים אל ]הֿאיפה והבֿת‏{ב} תכון אחד שניהֿן ומֿןֿ[ החטים ש]‏שֿית

3 [האיפה לחמר ומעשר הבת לפֿרֿי ]הֿ[עֿ]‏יֿן אל יבדל איש להרים לשֿ[אֿ]‏דֿ מן הֿמֿאֿה

4 [וֿאל ]‏יֿאכל איֿשֿ מאומה‏ᵂ מן הגורן ומן הגנה טרם ישלחו [הכוה]‏נֿים את ידם

5 [לבר]‏ךֿ לריאשונֿהֿ[ל] ואחר יאכל ואם‏ᵂ בֿית לאיש ימכור ובחסֿנֿ[ו נס]‏חֿ‏ᵂ ואז ינקה

6 [    ]‏קֿ[    ]          [וֿאת הֿ‏]‏◦          [שרה המעורב

7 חֿ[טים ושורים הוא כלאים ואלה החוקים יכתבו‏ᵂ מֿמֿשֿפֿטי הי]‏חֿד שֿלֿוֿשֿ פעמים בֿ[סֿפֿרֿ

8 אֿל יבֿא‏] אֿיֿש את בהמות פן עבדו הגוים בֿמֿᵂ בֿדֿם זבֿחֿם וֿכֿסֿ[תֿו‏]¹⁷¹ בֿטֿהֿרֿתו ומכוֿ[לֿ‏]‏לֿ

9 הֿזֿהֿב וֿהֿכֿסֿףֿ[ והנחשת ומןᵂ ה]‏בֿ[ֿב]‏דֿיֿל‏¹⁷² וֿהֿעֿ[ֿפֿרת אשר עשו הגוים פֿ]‏סֿל אל יביאהו

10 איש אל טהרֿ[תו כי אם מֿןֿ החֿדֿ‏שֿ הבא מן הכֿבֿכֿ[שֿ‏]‏◦ ]‏◦‏ᵐ/ᵗ[¹⁷³ אֿלֿ יֿבֿ]‏יֿא איש
    כֿוֿל עור ובגד ומן

11 כֿל הֿכֿלֿ[ֿים אשר תעשה‏ᵂ מ‏]‏לֿאֿכה בהם‏¹⁷⁴ אשר יטמאו לנפֿשֿ[ אדם כי ]‏אֿם הוֿזֿו כמשפט

12 [טהרת‏ᵇ אנשי הקודש במיᵂ ]‏הֿנדה בקֿןֿ הרֿשֿע ‹מֿ?›‏איש טֿהֿ[וֿר מכול טמֿאֿ‏]‏חֿ‏וֿ אשר

13 [יעריב את השמש וכול נער אשר לוֿ[א מֿלֿאו ימֿיו לעבור על הֿפֿ[קודים אֿלֿ יֿזֿ[¹⁷⁵

14 [את מי הנדה על טמאי נפש‏ᵂ        ]‏הֿ לֿ[          [

---

¹⁷⁰ Conjecturally such a rendition drawn from a reconstruction around אֿתֿ[ of
4Q270 F3iii:13 would have ended the column preceding 4Q271 F2.

¹⁷¹ Baumgarten restores סֿ[תֿו    בֿדֿם זבֿחֿם    [אֿיֿש אֿת (DJD XVIII, 173).

¹⁷² Baumgarten restores וֿהֿנֿחֿשֿת וֿהֿ[בֿדֿיֿל (DJD XVIII, 173).

¹⁷³ Baumgarten transcribes הֿבֿוֿרֿ◦◦◦ (DJD XVIII, 173).

¹⁷⁴ Baumgarten restores הֿכֿלֿ[ֿי אשר יעשה מ]‏לֿאֿכה בהם (DJD XVIII, 173).

¹⁷⁵ Baumgarten restores יזה (DJD XVIII, 173).

*Dimensions for Tithing; Priestly Blessing; Illicit Mixtures; Idolatrous Objects; Defilement From a Corpse*
**(4Q270 F3iii:12b–13a)** [Now concerning any prod]uce of [the field] **4Q271 F2** [^1][and the tithe of anything which one brings] from the threshing floor: one shall deduct a tenth of the *ḥ*[*omer*—which is an *e*]*phah*, [^2][or a *bat* as God has established], "the *ephah* and the *bat* being "the same measure" (Ezek 45:11a)—and from [the wheat a si]xth [^3][of an *ephah* per *ḥomer* (Ezek 45:13b) and a tenth of a *bat* from the fruit] of the [tr]ees. Let no one separate himself from offering (as a tithe) [on]e lamb per hundred.

[^4][And let no] one eat [anything from the threshing floor] or from the garden before [the prie]sts stretch out their hand [^5][to make the ble]ssing first. [Then he may eat.

Now if] one sells (his) house and, while in [its] solidity [it collap]ses, he is not liable.

[^6][ . . . ] A field consisting of mixed produce [^7]of w[heat and barley is under the prohibition of *kil'ayim*. And these are the statutes that shall be recorded among the injunctions of the com]munity three times in the book.

[^8][No one] shall bring [domesticated animals lest the pagans worship them in their sacrificial blood. Neither (may he bring)] his [garme]nt into his Purity, nor of any [^9]gold, silver [and bronze or t]in or le[ad of which the pagans have made an i]dol. One shall not bring them [^10]into [his] Puri[ty except] those made [ane]w from the fur[na]ce . . . No [man] shall br[ing] any material made from skin or a garment or [^11]any [manu]factured utensil[s] which have become defiled by a [human] corpse [un]less they have been sprinkled in accordance with the injunctions [^12][of the purification of the men of holiness with waters] of purification during the period of wickedness <by> a man puri[fied from all] his [defilement], who [^13][has waited for sundown. And any youth who has no]t reached the time of mem[bership shall not sprinkle] [^14][the waters of purification upon the unclean . . . ]

4Q266 F7i–iii
Parallel: 4Q267 F8 (underline)

[ ] ל̊ל̊ °[ ] i:1
ואל יקו[ם̊ ʷ[176]    [מנ]ו[ס]ʷ אבד אליה[ם ואין דורש לנפשםʷ i:2
«ו»עלו אל יסור איש את[ ʷרעהו וידבר באהבה לבנ[177]ע̊מ̊ו כי א̊[ם i:3
[ו]נו̇שה עו[ן]    נוצר חסד לאלפיםʷ בהוכח ענות צדק אליה[ם i:4
[ופשע] ו[ל]ו אבה ל[כו]ל יו[רדי דומהʷ i:5

ממנו °[ ] ii:1
ם̊[ ] ii:2
[ ] ii:3
ל[ ] ii:4
[ ] ii:5
[כול המחנה ] ii:6
ונענש בלחמוʷ [רובעוʷ vacat ] ii:7
[°°ר את [ ] ii:8
ואשר יטור את רעהוʷ א[שר לו במש̊[פט ] ii:9
ה̊איש אשר[ ] ii:10

(final two lines of 4Q266 F7ii)

ואל יקר[ב ]
[לברית אנשי הקודש ואל יודיעוהו את המשפטים האלהʷ לפני]

בוא[ם[178] אל המבקר ואחר ילמדוהו לשוב אל תורת מושה להתהל[ךʷ] iii:1
לפני ה[מבק]ר ה[מחנהʷ [ iii:2
למבק[ר א]שר על המחנה vac וכי ידור איש נדר ולוא ישלמו או[ʷ] iii:3
ל[נדבה דרושʷ ידרוש מידו [מ]י[ן נכסיוʷ [ iii:4
[את ושונאʷ את המוא[ס בת]ורה [ואשר לוא ישוב אל תורתʷ] iii:5
[ʷ מושה ולאל ישרא[ל ל]עשותʷ מ[ן]עשים [ישרים[179] iii:6
] ̊הואה מ̊ °[ iii:7

---

176 Baumgarten transcribes °[ . See DJD XVIII, 61.
177 Baumgarten restores בנ[ אל̊[ (DJD XVIII, 61).
178 Baumgarten transcribes ]°בוא[ (DJD XVIII, 62).
179 Baumgarten transcribes ] ל̊ל[ מ]ע̊שים [ (DJD XVIII, 63).

*The Supervisor of the Camp*

**4Q266 F7** <sup>i:1</sup>[ . . . ] <sup>i:2</sup>[esca]p[e] has failed the[m and no one looks for them . . . And let him not aven]ge <sup>i:3</sup>him. No one shall keep a grudge against [his neighbor, but must speak lovingly to] his people, excep[t] <sup>i:4</sup>when reproving, responding righteously to th[em . . . who keeps devotion for thousands] and bears iniqui[ty] <sup>i:5</sup>[and transgression] and does no[t] wish that [an]y de[scend to hell . . . ] <sup>ii:1</sup>[ . . . ] from it <sup>ii:2–5</sup>[ . . . ] <sup>ii:6</sup>[ . . . ] the entire camp <sup>ii:7</sup>[ . . . and he shall be punished in his rations] by a fourth. <sup>ii:8</sup>[ . . . ] <sup>ii:9</sup>[ . . . and whoever keeps a grudge against his neighbor] unjus[t]ly <sup>ii:10</sup>[ . . . ] the man who . . . **(final two lines of column ii)** [ . . . And let him not approach the covenant of the men of holiness. And let them not inform him of these injunctions before] <sup>iii:1</sup>they come [to the Supervisor. And afterwards they shall instruct him to return to the Torah of Moses to live (by them)] <sup>iii:2</sup>in the presence of the [Supervis]or of the [camp . . . ] <sup>iii:3</sup>to the Supervis[or] of the camp. [And if one makes a vow and does not fulfill it or <sup>iii:4</sup>(promises) a [gift offering (to God), He will surely] requite it from him [fr]om [his possessions . . . ] <sup>iii:5</sup>[the . . . and hates] anyone who despi[ses the T]orah [and who does not turn to the Torah of] <sup>iii:6</sup>[Moses nor to the God of Israe]l to [do upright d]eeds [ . . . ] <sup>iii:7</sup>[ . . . ] he [ . . . ]

4Q267 F4

]תֿתֿ°°[     1

4Q270 F2i–ii
Parallel: 4Q267 F4:2–15 (underline)
          6Q15 F5 (overbar)

i:1   [    בעבור אשר דרשו בחלקות ויבחרו במהתלות ויתעוˮ] בם¹⁸⁰

i:2   [    ה וינבאו שקר על אל ועודˮ יצעדו נגד כולˮ דב]לֿיֿ

i:3   [    אלˮ   וכול טמאˮ מחול¹⁸¹ לוא יביאנו אל הטהרהˮ   ]לֿ[

i:4   [    את      ולוא          ויחסו בשם קודשוˮ]

i:5   [

i:6   [    ש   ה   כמותו   כל הבאˮ בברית יאהב את רעהוˮ]

i:7   [ואל יתיצב לפניוˮ   ˮכול אל יתן הוא את כפוˮ בערובות ואת כספו]

i:8   [    בנשך ואת אוכלוֿ בתרבית אל יתן הואˮ מכה בהבלֿ כי]

i:9   [    וכול איש אשרˮ] ישלˮ[¹⁸² זבחו או ישתחוהˮ לש]מֿש

i:10   [או לירח או יזבח ˮ לשע]ורים או ידרוש באוב ובידעונים¹⁸³

i:11   [או אשר ישאל אל המתיםˮ ]וֿהˮ[וחו]ת או אֿ אשר יחלל את השם

i:12   [או אשר ידבר עצהˮ סרה כאשר יעשו הגויםˮ כו]לֿ [אשר יעשהˮ] ? ¹⁸⁴

i:13   [אלה ביד רמה ישפט ואישˮ אשר

i:14   [    ים

i:15   [°°°°נֿיֿן

i:16   [    או אשרᵇ עלהˮ עליה שם רע ב]בֿתולֿיֿה בבית

i:17   [אביהᵇ אם שכב עמה אישˮ או אלמנה אשר ]ישכב אחר עמה

i:18   [כול אלה לא יומתו vac וכל איש אשרˮ יק]רֿב אל אשתו ביום

i:19   [השבתˮ ᵇ או יעשה מלאכה או יעבוד את האדמ]הֿ¹⁸⁵ או אשר י[חלל] ?

i:20   [את יום השבת ואת המועדות לא יומת כי על בני האדםˮ]

i:21   [משמרוˮ            כ]ל

ii:1   [°°     עלֿ קֿדֿ[שהˮ]

---

¹⁸⁰ Based upon Milik's identification of the ends of lines 1–3 with text from CD
20:32–33, Baumgarten conjecturally restores

       שפטו] בם                               [ 1
       לקול מן]דֿי                              [ 2
       יעז] לֿ[בם]                             [ 3

See DJD XVIII, 142.

¹⁸¹ Abegg, following Baumgarten, parses מחול as an imperative of מחל (to forgive).
Martin G. Abegg, Jr., *Qumran Sectarian Manuscripts: Qumran text and grammatical
tags* (1999–2005), 4Q267 F4:4.

*Capital and Non-Capital Offenses; A List of Transgressions and the Eschatological Punishment of Transgressors*

**4Q270 F2i–ii / 4Q267 F4** i:1[since they will interpret (Him) with flattering words, choosing farce, and going astray] by them i:2[ . . . and will prophesy falsely against God and furthermore, behave contrarily to all the comman]ds of i:3[God . . . And as for anything that has been defiled of ordinary matter, let him not bring it into the Purity . . . ] i:4[ . . . And not . . . And they shall rely upon His Holy Name . . . ] i:5[ . . . ] i:6[ . . . anyone who enters into the covenant shall love his neighbor as himself . . . ]

i:7[and no one shall rebel against him in any manner. One may not put out his hand as security, nor his money] i:8[as interest, nor his food for an increase. One shall not strike another for no reason, because . . . ]

i:9[ . . . And as for anyone who] worships, or sends [his sacrifice (to worship), or prostrates himself to the s]un i:10[or the moon, or sacrifices to the go]at demons, or inquires by means of a medium or wizards, i:11[or who consults the dead] and the sp[irit]s, or who profanes God's name, i:12[or who gives deviant counsel, as do the pagans: any]one [who does] i:13[these things in a haughty manner shall be condemned (to death). And he who . . . ] i:14–15[ . . . ] i:16[ . . . or who has acquired an evil name while in] her virginity in the house of i:17[her father if a man has lain with her, or a widow] with whom another man lies: i:18[none of these shall be put to death. And any man who ha]s sexual relations with (literally, comes near) his wife during the [Sabbath] day, i:19[or does labor or plows the fiel]d, or who p[rofanes] i:20[the Sabbath day and the festivals shall not be put to death. Rather, it is the duty of man to place him] i:21[in detention . . . ] . . . ii:1concerning sanc[tity . . . ]

---

182 Baumgarten transcribes י־שׁל[ ((DJD XVIII, 142).

183 4Q267 F4:11–12 reads ידרו[שׁ את א[ו]בות וא]ת ידעוני[ם.

184 The tops of several letters appear shortly after the ל.

185 Baumgarten transcribes ח, providing no reconstruction in the lacuna preceding it (DJD XVIII, 143).

ii:2 ‫°את הק]‬ ‫ואיש אשר ישכב את אשה דוה וגלה את ערותה[‬

ii:3 ‫אל מקור[ה‬ ‫ יערה‬ ‫[°°]‬ [

ii:4 ‫[ו]א[ל]‬ ‫[°°ק]‬ [

ii:5 ‫ או אשר י[מחא להרים [את הקודשים כפרוש‬ ]

ii:6 ‫[תורת מושה לתת ]ל[בני אהרון ה[מטעת [הכרם וכל עצי‬

ii:7 ‫[המאכל] וראש[י]ת כל אשר להם ומעשר ב[ה]מתם מן הבקר‬

ii:8 ‫והצון ופדו[י] בכור הבה[מ]ה הטמאה ופדוי בכ[ור אדם וראשית גז‬

ii:9 ‫הצון וכסף הערכים לפדוי נפשם vacat [וכל אשם מושב אשר‬

ii:10 ‫אין להשיב[ה וחומשה עליה או ]מ[שולו בם רוחות בליעל ויכתבו‬

ii:11 ‫בשמותם לטמא את רוח קודשו [או אשר יגע בכל טמא נפש‬

ii:12 ‫או ינוגע בנגע צרעת או זוב טמ]א או כל אשר יגע בו הזב או‬

ii:13 ‫אשר יגלה את רז עמו לגואים או יקלל א[ת עמו או ידבר‬

ii:14 ‫סרה על משיחי רוח הקדש ותועה ב[חוזי אמתו בהמרותו‬

ii:15 ‫את פי אל או ישחט בהמה וחיה עבר[ה או אשר ישכב עם‬

ii:16 ‫אשה הרה מקיץ דם [או יקרב א]ל בת[ו] אחיהו או ישכב איש עם זכר‬

ii:17 ‫משכבי אשה vac עוברי א[ת ]ת מצות התור[ה] וא[ת] חוקיה[186‬

ii:18 ‫בם חקק אל להעביד[187 בת[ה]רון אפו בק[ץ [הפקורה עד עמוד משיח‬

ii:19 ‫ועתה שמעו לי כל יודעי צדק ו[בינו] תור[ת אל188 בלבבם ואגלה‬

ii:20 ‫לכם דרכי חיים ונתיבות שחת אפתחה ל[עיניכם ובמוקשי שחת‬

ii:21 ‫אל תתפשו ובהבינכם במעשי דור ודור] תבינו במעשי אל‬ [

---

[186] Baumgarten restores ‫ב[ וא]ת‬ ‫א]ה‬ (DJD XVIII, 145).

[187] 6Q15 F5:4 contains the infinitive ‫להבעיר‬.

[188] Baumgarten restores [‫שימו]ו‬ ‫תור[ה אל בלבבם‬) (DJD XVIII, 145). The presumed
parallel in 6Q15 F5:5 reads ‫בל[בית אל בלבבם‬.

ii:2the . . . [ . . . and whoever lies with a menstruating woman and exposes her nakedness,] ii:3[pouring] into [her] vagina (Lev 20:18) [ . . . ] ii:4. . . [ . . . ] ii:5[ . . . or whoever] declines (?) to raise up [the holy tithings in accordance with the interpretation of the] ii:6[Torah of Moses to apportion] to the sons of Aaron the planting [of the vineyard and all that is grown on the] ii:7[fruit bearing trees, the fir]st fruits of all tithings belonging to them, the tithing of [their] ca[ttle from the herd] ii:8and sheep and [those] redeemed [of the firstborn of] the unclean [catt]le as well as the redeemed of the fir[stborn of man, the first of the wool of] ii:9the sheep, and the silver that is equivalent for their redemption, [and any guilt restitution that] ii:10cannot be restored (to the owner, which must be given to the priest—Num 5:7–8; CD 9:13–14) with an additional fifth (of its value if he knew the owner and did not return it); or [any whom the spirits of Belial take sway of, and hence are recorded] ii:11by name for defiling His Holy Spirit; [or whoever touches any defiled person (Lev 22:4)]; ii:12or anyone stricken with the affliction of leprosy or uncle[an] flux, [or anyone who touches the person who has a flux (Lev 15:11)]; ii:13or anyone who reveals the secrets of his people to the gentiles, or curses [his people or speaks] ii:14deviantly against those anointed with the Holy Spirit; and who goes astray against [the seers of His truth by rebelling] ii:15against the command of God; or who slaughters an animal or beast that is pregnan[t]; [or who lies with] ii:16a pregnant woman, emitting blood; [or he who approaches] the daughter [of his brother or lies with a male] ii:17as if lying with a woman: it is (these) transgressors [of the commandments of the Tora]h and [its statutes] ii:18against whom God has legislated to render destruction by [His] w[rath during the epo]ch [of redemption until the Messiah arises.] ii:19And now, hear me all who know righteousness (truth) and [discern] the Tora[h of God in your heart. And I will reveal] ii:20–21to you the ways of life and the paths of hell I will open for [your eyes so that] you not be caught [by those ensnared by the pit.] And when you discern the events of each generation [you will understand the acts of God . . . ]

4Q273 F5[189]

| | | | |
|---|---|---|---|
| [ 1 | [ | ] ∘ ∘ [ | ] |
| [ 2 | ∘∘[הֿאֿתֿרֿוֿגֿהֿ | ] [כֿל שבה וכסתה אֿ]ת פניה[ʷ | ] |
| [ 3 | [לֿא יֿשֿא פֿנֿיֿ? רֿעֿ וֿהֿנהʷ הֿיֿא אשר הוא יֿ]ספר להם[ʷ | |
| [ 4 | [ʷ כול חוק]וֿת עולם המה אל יקח איש את האֿשֿ]ֿה לצרר בחייה[ʷ 190 |
| [ 5 | [אל יקחʷ מֿיֿמֿיֿ ספרה191 את דֿם בֿשֿרֿהֿ? עד אשר תֿ]טהר מזובה[ʷ |

4Q270 F4
Parallel: 4Q266 F12 (underline)

| | |
|---|---|
| [ 1 | וכיʷ [יֿבא איש אשה להאלותה |
| [ 2 | [והיה לו עד אחד במעשה והעידʷ ]הרואה אם יראה אשת |
| [ 3 | [רעהוᵇ שוכבת עם איש וטמאהʷ ואם] אֿמֿרֿה אֿנֿוֿסֿהֿ הֿיֿתֿי |
| [ 4 | [אז תנקה ושבה אל בעלה אלʷ יב]יֿאֿהֿ כי אם דמֿ יצֿוֿא |
| [ 5 | [לא יצאᵃ והמבקרʳ יביאה לפני אי]שֿ [מן] הֿכֿהנים ופרע |
| [ 6 | [הכהן את ראשה והשביע את ]הֿאֿשה והשקה את |
| [ 7 | [האשה את מי המרים המאררים] לֿא תקח מידֿ]וֿ כֿ[ל |
| [ 8 | [מאכל קודש ולא תגע במים∘ המרים] הקדושים |
| [ 9 | [ואמר הכהן יתן אל אותך לאלהʷ וא]לֿ יתן איש אֿ[ת |
| [ 10 | [המים המרים לאישה אשר שכבה עם אישʷ לֿ]פֿני∘ |
| [ 11 | [עדים שנים כי אם אין עד וצבתה בטנה א]םֿʷ יֿשֿ |
| [ 12 | [האלה לה כאֿשר אמר השכילו הוסרוʷ ]הֿמֿלֿכֿיֿםֿ192 |
| [ 13 | [ושופטי ארץʷ אל יקרב ואל ישכב איש]193 עם אשה |
| [ 14 | [שכבת זרע והיא שופחה וגם לאישʷ שֿופחה החֿרופֿה הֿיֿא |
| [ 15 | [והביאה לביתו חדש ימיםʷ כאשר] אמר לא תֿ[געʷ |
| [ 16 | [לכה בטהרה עד שבע שנים אםʷ י]קֿחֿנה אֿו לב]נֿו] |
| [ 17 | [ייעדנה כמשפט הבנות הוא יעשהʷ לֿ]הֿ אֿתֿ אֿשֿרֿ לֿ]הֿ∘ʷ] |
| [ 18 | [יתן לה שארה כסותה ועונתה לא יגרעʷ]∘∘∘∘∘[ |
| [ 19 | שבע שנים לא תאכלʷ [מן הקֿדֿ]שֿ] לֿחמו |

---

189 The placement of this fragment is uncertain and does not necessarily sequentially precede 4Q270 F4. It does, however, contain material related to that of this larger fragment; hence its location in the general context of 4Q270 F4.

190 For the reconstruction of this line, see above CD 4:20–5:2.

191 See 4Q274 F1i:7.

192 4Q266 F12:4 appears to read לֿ מֿלֿכֿיֿםֿ.

193 Spanning lines 5–6 of 4Q266 F12, the clauses ואל[ ישכב א]יֿש ]∘ [אל י]קֿרב ]∘ and [אשה] עֿ]ם form part of a text which appears to be more expansive than my reconstruction of 4Q270 F4:13.

*The Straying Wife; Bigamy; Marriage during Menstruation*

**4Q273 F5** ¹[ . . . ] ²[ . . . ] last[ . . . ] for she shall turn and cover [her face . . . ] ³[ . . . ] He (God) does not favor the wicked. And behold that is what He w[ill relate to them.] ⁴They are [all the] eternal [statute]s. No man may marry a wom[an (in addition to his wife) to be (her) rival during her lifetime (Lev 18:18).] ⁵[He may not marry (a woman)] during the time that she counts her menses until she is c[leansed from her flow.]

*The Straying Wife; A Slave Marrying a Priest*

**4Q270 F4** ¹[ . . . When] a man comes to impose a curse on (his) wife (under suspicion of adultery) ²[having a single witness to the act, and] the one who saw [testifies] if he (really) saw the wife ³[of his neighbor lying with (another) man, then she should be declared defiled. But if] she says, "I did the act under compulsion," ⁴⁻⁵[then she shall be declared innocent and shall return to her husband. He may not br]ing her (to the court) unless her (virginal) blood [does not flow] at all. [(As for the oath), let the Supervisor bring her before on]e [of] the priests. And [the priest] shall expose ⁶[her head (Num 5:18a), make] the woman [swear] (Num 5:19a, 21a) and make [the woman] drink ⁷[the waters of bitterness that induce the curse (Num 5:24a).] (Until then), she may not take from [him a]ny ⁸[holy food, nor may she come in contact with the] sacred [waters of bitterness.] ⁹[Then the priest shall pronounce, "May God place you under a curse" (Num 5:21b). But no] one shall give ¹⁰[the waters of bitterness to a woman who has slept with a man] in the p[resence] ¹¹[of two witnesses; rather only if there is no testimony at all. And if her womb swells (Num 5:27b) as a] consequence ¹²[of her curse, it is as the Scripture says, "Be skillfull, act prudently] O kings ¹³[and judges of the land" (Ps 2:10).

One (who is a priest) should not touch, nor have sexual intercourse] with a woman ¹⁴[who is a slave,] she being a slave betrothed [to (another) man.] ¹⁵Rather, he shall bring her to his house for one month as] it says, "She may not tou[ch ¹⁶[your (priestly) Purity for seven years." If h]e marries her, or to [his] so[n] ¹⁷[he betroths her, he shall treat he]r [according to the prerogatives of (Israelite) daughters (Exod 21:9);] (every right) belonging to [her] ¹⁸[he shall grant her; he may not diminish her food, her clothing nor her conjugal rights (Exod 21:10)] . . . [ . . . ] ¹⁹[ . . . For seven years she may not eat] from his

20 [ו) בשנה[ᵂ] הש[מיני]ת[ᵂ] תאכל מלחמו ואל[ᵂ [וישכב עם

21 [ᵂ] שופחה הב[עו]לה לא[או]יש? ]¹⁹⁴

(presumed ending of the final line of
the Genizah column preceding CD 15)

[ᵂ]ביזד והי לא               ]

## CD 15

Parallels: 4Q266 F8i  (underline)
          4Q270 F6i:20–ii:10 (overbar)
          4Q271 F4i:4–ii:3a (lower underline)
          text unique to DSS (outlined)

15:1 ⁹ישבע וגם באלף ולמד וגם באלף ודלת כי אם שבועת הבנים⁹

15:2 באלות הברית vacat ואת תורת משה אל יזכור כי בה כל פרוש השם⁹ ¹⁹⁵

15:3 vacat ואם ישבע ועבר וחלל את השם vacat ואם באלות הברית ישבעᵂⁱ ¹⁹⁶

15:4 השפטים vacat אם עבר אשם הוא והתודה והשיב ולא ישא חטא⁹ה⁹

15:5 [ויו]מות vacat והבא בברית לכל ישראל לחוק עולם את בניהם אשר יגיעו

15:6 לעבור על הפקודים בשבועת הברית יקימו עליהם vacat וכן

15:7 המשפט בכל קץ הרשע לכל השב מדרכו הנשחתה ביום דברו

15:8 עם המבקר אשר לרבים יפקדוהו בשבועת הברית אשר כרת

15:9 משה עם ישראל את דב⁹רי⁹ ¹⁹⁷ לש[וב ]אל תורת משה בכל לב ו[ב]כ[ל]

15:10 נפש אל הנמצא לעשות בכ[ל] קץ ל[מ]רᵂⁱ ¹⁹⁸ ואל יודיעהו איש את

15:11 המשפטים עד עמדו לפני המבקר ל⁹מה¹⁹⁹ יתפתה בו בדרשו²⁰⁰ או⁹תו

15:12 וכאשר יקים אותו עליו²⁰¹ לשוב אל תורת משה בכל לב ובכל נפש

---

¹⁹⁴ Baumgarten transcribes [          ]ᵒᵒ עו]לה[          ] (DJD XVIII, 153).

¹⁹⁵ Baumgarten transcribes what might be the upper left corner of a ם at the end of 4Q271 F4i:4 (DJD XVIII, 177).

¹⁹⁶ Baumgarten transcribes ישבעׄוׄתׄ . See Charlesworth, ed., *Damascus Document*, 36.

¹⁹⁷ Rabin read הברית. See Rabin, *The Zadokite Documents*, 73.

¹⁹⁸ The paleography of this word is not clear. Rabin bracketed it as a reconstructed הרשע, Qimron presents it as ק[ר]בׄו, Baumgarten has ל[הרש]. See Rabin, *The Zadokite Documents*, 73; Qimron, "The Text of CDC," 39; and Charlesworth, ed., *Damascus Document*, 38.  I thank Tim Undheim for suggesting the possibility ל[מ]רׄו.

¹⁹⁹ למה CD.

²⁰⁰ בה בדרשה 4Q266 F8i:2.

²⁰¹ עלו 4Q266 F8i:3.

sacr[ed] food. [20][But in the e]ight[h year she may partake of his food.] He may [not] have sexual relations with [21][a slave-maiden who has been ma]rried to a m[an . . . ]

*The Covenant and Other Oaths Or Vows*

[ . . . By the *yod* and *hē* (YHWH) one should not][9] CD 15:1swear, nor by the *aleph* and *lamed* (Elohim), nor with the *aleph* and *dalet* (Adonai), except for (in) "the oath of the youths" 15:2during the covenantal curses (at the time of the admission ceremony). Neither shall he make mention of the Torah of Moses, since in it The Name (YHWH) is enunciated. 15:3And if he does take an oath (using God's name explicitly), he is in violation and profanes the name (of God). But if the judges make (him) swear with the curses of the covenant, 15:4if he transgresses, he is guilty and must confess and make amends so as not to bear sin 15:5–6[and] die.

And each and every one who is entering the covenant of all of Israel by the eternal statute shall impose the oath of the covenant upon their sons who reach (the appropriate age) to be counted in the muster.

The same 15:7rule applies during the whole era of wickedness for anyone who repents from his corrupt way. On the day that he speaks 15:8with the Supervisor in charge of the Multitude, they shall enroll him (as a member of the Community) with the oath of the covenant which Moses established 15:9with Israel, his (the candidate's) promise to tu[rn] to the Torah of Moses with all (his) heart and al[l] 15:10(his) soul to what is found (therein) to observe during the enti[re] period of his in[struc]tion. And no one shall make known to him (the enrollee) the 15:11rules (of the community) until he appears before the Supervisor lest he be misled by him when he examines him. 15:12But when he (the candidate) imposes upon himself to turn to the Torah of Moses with

---

[9] This phrase presumably was on the final line of the previous page preceding CD 15 in the Genizah text.

15:13 [נק]ֹֿאׄים הֵֿם מֵמנו אם ימֹעֵֿל *vacat* וֿכֹוׄל אשר נגלה מן התורה לרֹוב

15:14 הֿמֿחֿנֿה וֿהֿוֿא שֹנֿה בה[202] יֹוׄר[י]ֿעׄה[9 המבקר אותו ויֿצותו עׄליו ויֹל[מד]ֹֿהֿ

15:15 עַד שנֿה תמֿימה ולֿפֿי דֿעׄתֹו יֹקֹרׄבׄ וֹכֹֿל היותו אויל ומשֹוגע אֹל יֿבֹֿ
וֿכֹוׄל פֿתֹ[י] וֿשֹֿו[גֿ]ֿנֿה[203]

15:16 וֿכֿה עׄינֿוׄם[204] לֿבֿל[תֿ]ֿי ראות וחגר או פסח או חרש[ אֿ נֹעׄר[205] ז]ֹֿעׄטוֿֿט אל

15:17 יבוא אֿיֹ[ש מֿאׄ[ש אל תֹוֹך העדה כי מלאכי ה]ֿקֹֿ[וֿ]ֿרֿׄש ? ל ת בֿ[206]

15:18 [כי אחר ימי המבול[w] מֿעׄטו שני האדם בחרון אף אל שב]ֿעׄ[י]ֿ[ם[w] [אֿֿשׄר[w] לׄהֿם[207]

15:19 [ובהופע כבוד אל בעֿמֿוד משיח אהרן וישראל הם יחֿיו אלֿף[w] דֹֿוֹׄד[208]

15:20 [לא ירפם ולא ישחיתם ולא ישכח את ברית אבותם בשממם בֿֿקֹֿוֹׄל[ו][w]

15:21 וֿיׄאמֿר אל להם כֿי[w] יכרות את בית ישראל ואת בית יהודה ברֿית (חדשה)[[w]

15:22 [וֿעׄל הברית הֿזׄות כאשר אמר אלֿי[w] לֿאמֿור על פי הדברים הֿאׄלֿה כרתי]

## CD 16
Parallels: 4Q266 F8ii:1b–8a (underline)
　　　　　4Q270 F6ii:17–21; iii:13–15 (overbar)
　　　　　4Q271 F4ii:3b–17 (lower underline)
　　　　　extant and restored text unique to DSS (outlined)

16:1 עמכה[209] ברית ועם כל ישראל על כן יקום[210] האיש עַל נפשו[211] לשוב אל

16:2 תורת מֿוׄשה {פֿ|} כי בה הכֹֿוׄל מדוקדק ופרוש קציהם לעורון

16:3 ישראל מכֹֿוׄל אלה הנה הוא מדוקדק על ספר מחלקות העתים

16:4 ליובליהם ובשבועותיהם *vacat* וביום אשר יקים[212] האיש על נפשו לשוב

16:5 אל תורת מֿוׄשה יסור מלאך המשטמה מאחריו אם יקים את דבריו

16:6 על כן נמֹוׄל[213] בֿ אברהם ביום דֿעׄתו *vacat* ואשר אמר מוצא שפתיך

16:7 תשמור להקים[214] כֹֿוׄל שבועת אסר אשר יקום[215] אַיש עַל נפשו

---

[202] בֿ CD.

[203] פֿֿוׄתה ושוגה 4Q270 F6ii:8. Qimron (CD) restores שֿֿ[וֿ]ֿנׄה פֿֿתֿ[י]. Abegg provides a more paleographically defensible פֿֿתֿ[י] וֿ[מֹֿֿשֿֿ]ֿוֹׄנׄה for CD. See Qimron, "The Text of CDC," 39; and Martin G. Abegg, Jr., *Qumran Sectarian Manuscripts*, CD 15:15.

[204] וכֿֿ הׄ עׄינֿוׄם CD.

[205] וֿׄנׄער CD.

[206] Compare also כֿיא מלאכי קודש [בעד]ֿֿהֿֿם (For the sacred angels are [in] their [congrega]tion) in 1QSa 2:8–9. It seems that my reconstruction based upon 4Q266 F8i:9 may contain more text than there was in the medieval parallel.

[207] This reconstruction takes account of the proportional space in 4Q270 F6ii: 9–10, a restoration that may exceed that of CD. Rabin and Baumgarten read אמֿ[ֿוֿׄ|ֿ ל]ֿֿהֿם　　　　　] (Rabin, *The Zadokite Documents*, 75; Charlesworth, ed., *Damascus Document*, 38).

all (his) heart and with all (his) soul, <sup>15:13–14</sup>they (those who examine him) will be [ab]solved if he transgresses. Should he err in any matter which has been revealed from the Torah for the Many of the camp, let the Supervisor in[form] him concerning it, command him about it, and te[ach] him <sup>15:15</sup>for a complete year. And let him come in (to the community) in accordance with his mental abilities.

But no one who is a fool or mentally deficient may enter (the community). And as for any simple[ton] or one [prone] to err, <sup>15:16</sup>one who is dim-eyed, no[t being able to see, or a limper, or lame, or deaf] or a youngster: none <sup>15:17</sup>of [them] may be admitted [to the community, since the] sa[c]red [angels] . . . with them, <sup>15:18</sup>[for following the flood the years of humanity were reduced on account of God's anger to the se]v[e]nty allotted to them. <sup>15:19</sup>[But when the glory of God appears as the Messiah of Aaron and Israel arises, they will live for a thousand] generations. <sup>15:20</sup>[He (God) will not leave them alone nor destroy them nor forget the covenant of their fathers as long as they hearken] to [His] voice. <sup>15:21</sup>[But God will announce to them that He will make a (new) covenant with the house of Israel and the house of Judah (Jer 31:31).] <sup>15:22</sup>[And concerning this covenant as God has said, "In accordance with these commandments I hereby make] CD <sup>16:1</sup>a covenant with you and with all Israel" (Exod 34:27b).

Therefore, the candidate shall obligate himself to turn to <sup>16:2</sup>the Torah of Moses, for everything in it is perfect. And as for the elaboration of their epochs pertaining to Israel's blindness <sup>16:3</sup>in all these matters, behold it is perfect in the Book of the Divisions of the Times <sup>16:4</sup>by their jubilees and their septal cycles. And on the day that a candidate obligates himself to accept <sup>16:5</sup>the Torah of Moses the Angel Mastema will release him from his grasp if he keeps his words. <sup>16:6</sup>Therefore, Abraham was circumcised on the day when he came to know (God).

And when it says, "Keep what comes forth from your lips (fulfilling what you have vowed)" (Deut 23:24), <sup>16:7</sup>this means to uphold any

---

[208] This line is reconstructed on the basis of 4Q267 F3:2.

[209] עמכם CD.

[210] Read יקים here and in line 7 (cf. יקים in 4Q271 F4ii:6, paralleling יקום of CD 16:4).

[211] נפשך CD; נפשׁו 4Q271 F4ii:4.

[212] יקום CD.

[213] נימול CD.

[214] A vacat follows להקים in CD but not in 4Q271 F4ii:8.

[215] Read יקים.

16:8 ‫לעשות דבר מן התורה עד מחיר מות אל יפדהו‬ *vacat* ‫כל אשר‬

16:9 ‫[יק]ים איש על נפשו לסור מן התו]רה[216 עד מחיר מות אל יקימהו‬

16:10 ‫[ע]ל שבועת האשה אשר אמ]ר ל[אישה להניא את שבועתה אל‬

16:11 ‫יניא איש שבועה אשר לא [י]דענה הם להקים היא‬ *vacat* ‫ואם להניא‬

16:12 ‫אם לעבור ברית הוא217 יניאה ואל יקימנה‬ *vacat* ‫וכן המשפט לאביה‬

16:13 *vacat* ‫על משפט הנדבות‬ *vacat* ‫אל ידור איש למזבח מאום אנוס וגם‬

16:14 ‫ה[כ]הנים אל יקחו מיד218 ישראל219*vacat* אל] יקדש איש את מאכל‬

16:15 ‫פיהו [לא]ל כי הוא אשר אמר איש את רעיהו יצ]ו[דו חרם‬ *vacat* ‫אל220‬

16:16 ‫יקד[ש] איש מכל א[חזה אשר קנה מיד אונס‬w 221 *vacat* ‫ואם מ]שדה אחזתו‬

16:17 ‫יקדש ל[אלw9 ג]ם ה[משפט הזה וכי יפלא איש נדר בערכך‬w ‫ו]נענש‬

16:18 ‫הנודר [את חמישית כסף ערכו ואם משנת היובל יקדש שדהו‬w]

16:19 ‫לשופט]ים לשפט צדק ולהעריכו9 222 עד אחר השנים (?) הנותרות ביובל‬w]

16:20 ‫אם] אנוס הוא עד אשר יוסר ושלם האונס אם לא דבר אמת]‬

16:21 ‫[עם רעהו ועד אשר ישלם(?) והביא איל אשמו‬w ‫מב]חתו‬w(?) ‫כמוה כי‬]

16:22 ‫[לו הקים את דברו לדברb אמת‬ *vacat*               ‫ואשר אמר]‬


CD 9:1–11:2

Parallels: 4Q266 F8ii:8b–iii:10 (underline)

          4Q267 F9i (lower underline)

          4Q270 F6iii:16–21, iv, v:1–4 (overbar)

          5Q12 F1 (dotted underline)

          extant and restored text unique to DSS (outline)

          paleo script is in DSS only


9:1 ‫כל אדם223 אשר יחרים אדם מאדם בחוקי הגויאים להמית הוא‬

9:2 226 ‫איש מבא‬ ‫ואשר אמר224 לא תקום ולא תטור את בני עמך כל225‬ *vacat*

---

216 ‫לסור את התורה‬ 4Q271 F4ii:9–10.

217 ‫היא‬ 4Q271 F4ii:12.

218 4Q271 F4ii:12.

219 A word appears to follow ‫ישראל‬ in the lacuna of CD.

220 ‫ואל‬ CD.

221 There are remnants of the top portions of the unidentifiable words here.

222 Qimron restores ‫ולהעריך‬ (Qimron, "The Text of CDC," 41).

223 With Rabin and Qimron, read ‫חרם‬ (Rabin, *The Zadokite Documents*, 44; "Qimron, The Text of CDC," 27).

224 ‫מ‬ is corrected from ‫ש‬ in antiquity.

225 ‫וכל‬ CD.

226 ‫מביאו‬ CD.

prohibitive oath one takes upon himself 16:8to observe anything commanded in the Torah. Even at the price of death he shall not annul it. (However), anyone who 16:9[obli]gates himself to turn away fr[om the To]rah shall not fulfill it even at the price of death.

16:10[Con]cerning a woman's oath about which it sa[ys that] her husband may annul her oath (Num 30:9). A man may not 16:11interdict an oath of which he is not certain whether to uphold or to annul it. 16:12If it would violate the covenant he should annul and not approve it. The same rule applies to (the annulment) by her father.

16:13The rule concerning gifts: no one may devote to the altar anything acquired by force. Neither 16:14may the priests take anything from an Israelite (unless it is voluntary). [No] one may consecrate the food 16:15of his mouth [to G]od (food which is *herem*, totally dedicated to God), for this is what it (Scripture) says (Mic 7:2), "Each together with his neighbor h[u]nt *herem*."10 Let no one 16:16–18consec[rate] any po[ssession which he has purchased from an extorter. And further]more, the [same rule applies if one] consecrates to [God from] a field of his own inheritance. [And if one explicitly vows one's own estimated value, an additional fifth of his worth] shall be exacted from the one who made the vow. [And if he consecrates his field from the year of jubilee] 16:19it is the responsibility of the judge[s to judge rightly and to assess its value until after the remaining years in the jubilee.] 16:20If [it was extorted, until he is disciplined the extorter shall (first) compensate (for what was illegally acquired) if he did not speak truthfully] 16:21[with his neighbor. And when he (finishes) paying he shall bring the ram of his guilt offering (Lev 5:25) from his property comparable to it (the ram), for] 16:22[he has not fulfilled his promise to speak truthfully. And as it says:] CD 9:1Any devotion in which a person proscribes11 another person by the statutes of the pagans, shall be put to death.

*Justice*
9:2And when it says: "Neither avenge nor keep a grudge against

---

10 Food that is totally dedicated to the Lord (Lev 27:28).

11 The reading of כל חרם instead of the manuscript's כל אדם draws on Lev 27:29.

9:3 הברית אשר יביא על רעהו דבר אשר לא בהוכח [ע]ל פי[227] עדים

9:4 והביאו בחרון אפו או ספר לזקניו להבזתו[228] נוקם הוא ונוטר

9:5 *vacat* ואין כתוב כי אם נוקם הוא לצריו ונוטר הוא לאויביו[229]

9:6 אם החריש לו מיום ליום ו[ב]מחרש לחדש ובחרות[230] אפו בו דבר בו

9:6a בדבר מות [יומת הנקם שקר ענה בו אם]ׁ דבר כן ו[ד]בר בלא[ᵂ

9:6a שׁפ[ט מׁשׁפט

9:6b היו [ᵂהשׁפפׁפים אם]ת ל[ה]מׁחיᵂ

9:6c השׁ[פ]פ[י]ᵂ[ם] יהי [וׁקׁא[י]ם כי שקר]

9:7 ענה בו יען אשר לא הקים את מצות   ∠✲   אשר אמר לוׁ[א231] הוכח

9:8 תוכיח את רעיך ולא תשא עליו חטא *vacat* עׁל השבועה אשר

9:9 אמר לא תושיעך ידך לך איש אשר ישביׁעׁ עׁל פׁנׁי השׁדׁה

9:10 אׁשׁר לא לפני<<מ>>ᵂ השפטים או מאמרם הושיע ידו לׁוׁ וכׁלׁ הׁאׁוׁבׁד

9:11 ולא נׁודע מי גנבו ממאד המחנה אשר גנב בו ישביׁע בׁעׁלׁיׁו

9:12 בשבועת האלה והשומע אם יודע הוא ולא יגיד ואשם

9:13 *vacat* כל אשם מושב אשר אין בעלים והתורה[232] המישׁב[233] לכהן

9:14 והיה לו לבׁד מאיׁל האשם *vacat* {הׁכל}ᵠ וכן כל אבדה נמצאת ואין

9:15 לה בעלים והיתה לכהנים כי לא ידע מוצאיה את משפטה

9:16 אם לא נמצא לה בעלים הם ישמרו *vacat* כל דבר אשר ימעל

9:17 איש בתורה וראה רעיהו והוא אחד אם דבר מות הוא וידיעהו

9:18 לעיניו בהוכיח למבקר והמבקר יכתבהו בידו עד עשותו

9:19 עוד לפני אחד ושב והודיע למבקר אם ישוב וניתפש לפני

9:20 אחד שלם משפטו *vacat* ואם שנים הם והם מעידים על

[227] לפני CD.
[228] להבזותו CD.
[229] לאויביו CD.
[230] ובחרון CD.
[231] לוא = לו.
[232] Read והתודה.
[233] Read המשיב.

your people," (Lev 19:18) anyone of [9:3]the covenanters who brings
a charge against his neighbor that is without any attestation [b]y
witnesses [9:4]and does so in anger or gossips it to his elders for the
purpose of embarrassing him falls under the biblical description of
being an avenger and one who holds a grudge. [9:5]And Scripture does
not sanction vengeance except that He (the Lord) "may avenge those
who trouble Him and He may carry a grudge against His enemies"
(Nah 1:2). [9:6]And, if he was silent from day to day [or] month to
month, but when he ignited his anger against him (the accused) he
charged him with a capital offense, [the avenger shall be put to
death. He has testified falsely against him. If] he has asserted thusly,
sa[ying so without the testimony of two witnesses, the judges] shall
be [faith]ful [by condemning him to death . . . and the judges shall
be] absolved [since falsely] [9:7]he has testified against him, for he has
not upheld the commandments of God. (This is the meaning when)
it says concerning him, [9:8]"You shall surely reprove your neighbor so
that you shall not bear sin on account of him" (Lev 19:17). Concerning the oath, when [9:9]it says, "You may not help yourself on your
own (??)," anyone who makes someone swear in the field concerning
a contention [9:10]not in the presence of judges or by their command
has acted on his own.

And as for any lost object [9:11]of which it was not known who stole it
from the property of the camp wherein it was robbed, its owner should
proclaim [9:12]a maledictory oath, and anyone who hears (the oath),
while knowing (a suspect) and does not report (it) shall be culpable.
[9:13]And as for any object about which an offense was committed but
whose ownership is not known, the (offender) who restores it shall
confess to the priest [9:14]and it will belong to him (the priest), except
for the ram of guilt offering. And the same rule applies to any lost
object [9:15]which has no claim of ownership. It shall belong to the
priest, since its founder does not know its correct place. [9:16]If the
owner cannot be located, they (the priests) shall have custody of it.

Any matter wherein a person is in violation [9:17]of the Torah, and
his neighbor witnesses it, being only a single witness, and it concerns a
capital offense, let him make it known [9:18]in his (the offender's) presence together with the evidence to the Supervisor. And the Supervisor
shall record it in writing until he commits [9:19]the same offense again
in the presence of another single witness. Then he shall return and
inform the Supervisor if he repeats it and is caught in the presence
of another [9:20]single witness. His case is complete. But if there are

9:21 דבר אחר והובדל האִיש מן הטהרה לבד vacat אם נאמנים

9:22 הם וביום ראות האיש יודיעה למבקר ועל ההון יקבלו שני

9:23 עידים נאמנים vacat ועל אחד להבדיל (מן)ʷ הטהרה ואל יקובל

10:1 עיד לשופטים להמית על פיהו אשר לא מלאו ימו[234] לעבור

10:2 על הפקודים ירא את אל vacat אל יאמן איש על רעהו

10:3 לעד עובר דבר מן המצוה ביד רמה עד זכו לשוב

10:4 vacat וזה סרך לשופטי העדה עד עשרה אנשים ברורים

10:5 מן העדה לפי העת ארבעה למטה לוי ואהרון ומישראל

10:6 ששה מבוננים בספר ההגי[235] וביסודי הברית מבני חמש[236]

10:7 ועשרים שנה ועד בן[237] ששים שנה ואל[238] יתיצב עוד מבן

10:8 ששים שנה ומעלה לשפוט את העדה כי במעל[239] האדם

10:9 מעטו ימו ובחרון אף אל ביושבי הארץ אמר להס[ו]ר[240] את

10:10 דעתם עד אשר לא ישלימו את ימיהם vacat על הטהר במים אל

10:11 ירחץ איש במים צואים ומעוטים מדי מרעיל איש

10:12 אל יטהר במה כל vacat כלי וכל גבא בסלע אשר אין בו די

10:13 מרעיל אשר נגע בו הטמא וטמא מימיו במימי הכלי

10:14 על הש[ב]ת לשמרה כמשפטה vacat אל יעש איש ביום

10:15 מ̇ה̇ השישי מלאכה מן העת אשר יהיה גלגל השמש

10:16 רחוק מן השער מלואו כי הוא אשר אמר שמור את

10:17 יום השבת לקדשו וביום השבת אל ידבר איש דבר

---

[234] ימיו CD.

[235] ההגו CD; ההגוֹי 4Q418 F43–45i:13 and ההגוֹי 4Q267 F9v:12.

[236] 4Q270 F6iv:17 can be restored to ח[מ]ש. CD reads חמשה.

[237] בני CD.

[238] ולא 4Q270 F6iv:18.

[239] במועל 4Q270 F6iv:18.

[240] לסור CD.

two witnesses testifying, each attesting to a ⁹:²¹different incident, the offender shall be separated from the Purity only, providing the witnesses are trustworthy. ⁹:²²And on the day that one sees the offense, he shall inform the Supervisor. Likewise, in offenses relating to property they shall accept the testimony of two ⁹:²³trustworthy witnesses. However, if there is only one, it suffices to separate (the offender from) the Purity. And no witness shall be accepted CD ¹⁰:¹before the judges to condemn one to death by his testimony prior to his passing CD ¹⁰:²⁻³the muster (at the age of twenty), as well as fearing God. One who violates the commandment (of God) publicly shall not be accepted as a trustworthy witness against his neighbor, unless he has merited restoration.

¹⁰:⁴And this is the rule for the judges of the congregation: a minimum of ten expert men ¹⁰:⁵from the congregation for the occasion—four from the tribes of Levi and Aaron and six from Israel—¹⁰:⁶who are experts in the book of Haguy and in the foundations of the covenant, from ¹⁰:⁷twenty-five to sixty years of age. No one who is over ¹⁰:⁸sixty years of age shall hold the office of judging the congregation, for when man ¹⁰:⁹became corrupted his longevity was reduced. And when God's wrath burned against the earth's inhabitants He determined to weaken ¹⁰:¹⁰their mental abilities so that they would not be able to reach the fullness of their lifetime.

*Bathing*

On the purification by water: ¹⁰:¹¹A man shall not bathe in waters which are soiled or insufficient to cover a man. ¹⁰:¹²He shall not purify any vessel in them. And as for any cistern in a rock in which there is insufficient water ¹⁰:¹³to cover a person, which an unclean person has touched, he defiles its waters as if by the (defiled) waters of a vessel.

*Sabbath*

¹⁰:¹⁴Concerning the Sa[bb]ath, to keep it in accordance with its precepts: One may not do ¹⁰:¹⁵any labor on Friday from the moment the sun's disk ¹⁰:¹⁶faces the gate in its fullness. For this is what He said, "Keep the ¹⁰:¹⁷Sabbath day by sanctifying it" (Deut 5:12).

10:18 נבל ורק אל ישה ברעהו כל אל ישפוכו[241] על הון ובצע

10:19 אל ידבר בדברי המלאכה והעבודה לעשות למשכים

10:20 vacat אל יתהלך איש בשדה לעשות את עבודת חפצו

10:21 השבת אל יתהלך חוץ לעירו א על אלף באמה[242]

10:22 vacat אל יאכל איש ביום השבת כי אם המוכן ומן האובד

10:23 בשדה vacat ואל יאכל ואל ישתה כי אם היה במחנה

11:1 בדרך וירד לרחוץ ישתה על עומדו vacat ואל ישאב אל

11:2 כל כל<י>[w] אל ישלח את בן הנכר לעשות את חפצו ביום השבת

CD 11:3–11

Parallels: 4Q267 F9ii:2–3 (lower underline)
　　　　　4Q270 F6v:12–16a (overbar)
　　　　　4Q271 F5i:1–7a (underline)
　　　　　extant text unique to DSS (outlined)

11:3 vacat אל יקח איש עליו בגדים צואים או מובאים בגז כי אם

11:4 כובסו במים או שופים בלבונה vacat אל יתערב איש מרצונו

11:5 בשבת vacat אל ילך איש אחר בהמה[243] לרעותה חוץ מעירו כי

11:6 אם אלפים באמה vacat אל ירם את ידו להכותה באגרוף vacat אם

11:7 סוררת היא אל יוציאה מביתו vacat אל יוציא איש מן הבית

11:8 לחוץ ומן החוץ לבית[244] ואם בסוכה יהיה אל יוצא ממנה

11:9 ואל יבא אליה אל יפתח כלי טוח בשבת vacat אל ישא איש

11:10 עליו סמנים לצאת <<ולביא>>[w] <ולבוא> בשבת vacat אל יטול בבית מושבת

11:11 סלע ועפר vacat אל ישא האומן את היונק לצאת ולבוא בשבת

---

[241] Read ישפוט. See Qimron's transcription ישפוט in "The Text of CDC," 29.

[242] על אלף באמה א is in bold letters, possibly to stress that it is one thousand rather than the customary two thousand cubits.

[243] הבהמה CD.

[244] אל בית CD.

And no one should utter 10:18a lewd or empty word[12] during the day of the Sabbath.

He may not lend anything to his neighbor.[13]

One may not adjudicate in matters of property and wealth. 10:19He shall not discuss matters related to work or labor that will be done on the morrow. 10:20A person may not walk around the field during the Sabbath to plan the necessary weekly tasks. 10:21Neither may he walk about outside his city more than a thousand cubits on the Sabbath.

10:22One may not eat on the day of the Sabbath except what has been prepared beforehand or from something found 10:23in the field. Furthermore, he may neither eat nor drink except for what has been (brought) into the camp. CD 11:1(But, if he is) on a journey, and he goes down to wash (bathe?), he may drink while standing, but he may not draw the water into 11:2any utensil.

He may not dispatch the son of a foreigner (proselyte) to accomplish his wishes during the day of the Sabbath.

11:3One may not wear garments which have been soiled or brought into contact with wool shearings unless 11:4they have been laundered in water or rubbed with incense.

One may not famish himself voluntarily 11:5on the Sabbath.

A man may not follow a pasturing animal on the Sabbath 11:6beyond two thousand cubits. He shall not raise his hand to strike it with his fist; if 11:7it is rebellious he may not let it out of his estate. One may not take anything from (his) 11:8house to the outside, nor anything from the outside into his house. And if he is in a tent he shall neither take out 11:9nor bring anything in to it.

He may not open plastered-over vessels on the Sabbath.

One may not carry 11:10drugs upon himself going out or coming in on the Sabbath.

He should not carry 11:11rock or soil inside housing quarters.

A nurse may not lift an infant to go out or come in on the Sabbath.

---

[12] Compare ריקה in rabbinic literature and ῥακά in Matt 5:22.

[13] Or, as suggested alternatively by Rabin, "press his neighbor for repayment of anything" (Rabin, 52).

CD 11:12–18
Parallel: 4Q266 F9i:1–4 (lower underline)
　　　　　4Q267 F9ii:8 (italics)
　　　　　4Q270 F6v:16b–21 (overbar)
　　　　　4Q271 F5i:7b–12 (underline)
　　　　　　text unique to CD (outline)
　　　　　　extant text unique to DSS (outline + lower underline, overbar or underline)

11:12 *vacat* אל ימרא[245] את עבדו ואת אמתו ואת שוכרו ביום השבת
11:13 אל אל ייׄלד איש בהמה ביום השבת *vacat* ואם תפול[246] אל בור
11:14 ואל פתח אל יקימה בשבת *vacat* אל ישבות[247] איש במקום קרוב
11:15 לגוים בשבת *vacat* אל יחל איש את השבת על הון ובצע בשבת
11:16 *vacat* וכול נפש אדם אשר תפול אל מים מקום מים ואל [בו]ר[248]
11:17 אל יעלה איש בסולם וחבל[249] וכלי אל יעל איש למזבח בשבת
11:18 כי אם עולת השבת כי כן כתוב מלבד שבתותיכם *vacat* אל ישלח

CD 11:19–14:2
Parallel: 4Q266 F9i:16–17, ii, iii; F10i (underline)
　　　　　4Q267 F9iii, iv, v:1–6a (lower underline)
　　　　　4Q269 F10i–ii:8 (italicized)
　　　　　4Q271 F5i:13–21, ii (overbar)
　　　　　　extant and restored text unique to DSS (outline)
　　　　　　paleo script is in DSS only

11:19 איש למזבח עולה ומנחה ולבונה ועץ ביד איש טמא באחת
11:20 מן הטמאות להרשותו לטמא את המזבח כי כתוב זבח
11:21 רשעים תועבה ותפלת צדיקים[250] כמנחת רצון *vacat* וכל הבא אל
11:22 בית ההשתחוות[251] אל יבוא טמא כבוס ובהרע חצוצרות הקהל <לא>[w]
11:23 יתקדם או יתאחר ולוא ישביתו את העבודה כולה (כי)[w] בי[ת][252]
12:1 קודש הוא *vacat* אל ישכב איש עם אשה בעיר המקדש לטמא

---

[245] CD ימרא איש את; 4Q271 F5i:7 ימר את.
[246] CD תפיל; 4Q270 F6v:18 יפול.
[247] CD ישביה. This clause is omitted entirely in 4Q270 F6v:18.
[248] CD אל מים מקום מים ואל מקום.
[249] 4Q270 F6v:20 ובחבל.
[250] CD צדקם.
[251] CD השתחות.
[252] Qimron reads בׄיׄתׄ and Baumgarten בׄיׄת[ ]. See Qimron, "The Text of CDC," 31; and Charlesworth, ed. *Damascus Document*, 50.

11:12One shall not command his man servant, his maid servant or his hireling (to perform tasks) on the Sabbath day.

11:13One may not assist an animal in giving birth on the Sabbath. And if it falls into a pit 11:14or a trap, he shall not lift it out on the Sabbath.

One may not celebrate the Sabbath in a place near 11:15pagans. One may not profane the Sabbath for wealth or business.

11:16And as to a person who falls into a ditch of water or into a [pi]t: 11:17one may not raise him up with a ladder, a rope or a tool.

One may not offer any sacrifice on the altar on the Sabbath 11:18except for the Sabbath sacrifice, for so it is written "on your Sabbaths" (Lev 23:38).[14]

*Sanctification of the Temple and the House of Worship*

No one may dispatch 11:19to the altar a burnt, a grain, a frankincense or a wood offering through a person who has been contaminated 11:20by any of the defilements, allowing him to defile the altar, since it is recorded, "the sacrifice 11:21of the wicked is an abomination, but the prayer of the righteous is like a freewill offering" (Prov 15:8).[15] And anyone who comes to 11:22the house of worship may not come defiled, (but) washed. But when the trumpets of the congregation blast 11:23he shall <not> come early or late so that they will not disturb the whole service, (for) it CD 12:1is a sacred house. A man may not

---

[14] MT reads מִלְּבַד שַׁבְּתֹת.

[15] MT reads זֶבַח רְשָׁעִים תּוֹעֲבַת יְהוָה וּתְפִלַּת יְשָׁרִים רְצוֹנוֹ (The sacrifice of the wicked is an abomination to the Lord, but the prayer of the upright is His delight).

12:2 את עיר המקדש בנדתם *vacat* כל אֵישׁ אשר ימשׁ̇לו בו רוחות בליעל

12:3 ודבר סרה כמשפט האוב והידעוני ישפט וכו̇ל אשר יתעה

12:4 לחלל את השבת ואת המועדות לא יומת כי על בני הָאֽדם

12:5 משׁמרו ואם ירפא ממנה ושמרוהו עד שבע שנים ואחר

12:6 יבֽוֹא לַקָהָל[253] *vacat* אל ישלח ﬞﬞﬞ את ידו לשפוך̇ דם לאיש מן הגוֺים

12:7 בעבור הון ובצע *vacat* וגם אל ישׁא ﬞﬞ[ﬞ] מהונם כל בעבור אֲשׁר לא

12:8 יגֽדפו כי אם בעצת חבור̇ ישראל *vacat* אל ימכר איש בהמה

12:9 ועוף טהורים לגוים בעבור אשר לא יזבחום *vacat* ומגורנו

12:10 ומגתו אל ימכר להם בכל מאדו ואת עבדו ואת אמתו אל ימכור

12:11 להם אשר באו עמו בברית אברהם *vacat* אל ישקץ איש את נפשו

12:12 בכל החיה והרמש לאכל מהם מעגלי הדבורים עד כל נפש

12:13 החיה אשר תרמוש במים ודהגים אל יאכלו כי אם נקרעו

12:14 חיים ונשפֿך דׇמ̇ם וכל החגבים במיניהם יבאו באש או במים

12:15 עד הם חייֺם כי הוא משפט בריאתם *vacat* וכל העצים והאבנים

12:16 והעפר אשר יגואלו בטמאת האדם לגֻאולי שמן[q] בהם כפי

12:17 טמאתֽם יטמא הנ[ו]נֽגע בם *vacat* וכל כלי מסּמֻר מסמר או יתד בכותל

12:18 אשר יהיו עם המת בבית וטמאו בטמאת אחד כלי מעשה

12:19 *vacat* (וזה)[w] [254] סרך מושב ערי ישראל על המשפטים הֳאלה להבדיל בין

12:20 הטמא לטהור ולֽהודיֽע בין הקודש לחול *vacat* ואלה החקים

12:21 למשכיל לֽהֽתֽהֽלֽך בם עם כל חי למשפט עֵׄת ועת וכמשפט

12:22 הזֶה יתהלכו זרע ישראל ולא יוארו *vacat* וֽזֽה סרך מושב

[253] אל הקהל CD.
[254] Cf. line 22.

sleep with a woman in the city of the Temple, thereby defiling 12:2the city of the Temple by their uncleanness. Any man whom the spirits of Belial take sway of 12:3and who speaks waywardly as the mediums and wizards do shall be condemned (to death). However, anyone who strays 12:4by profaning the Sabbath and the festivals shall not be put to death; rather let the people 12:5keep him in custody. And if he desists from it (from going astray) they shall watch him for seven years, and afterwards 12:6he is to be readmitted to the congregation.

*Relations with Pagans; Prohibited Foods*
No one shall stretch out his hand to spill the blood of any of the pagans 12:7because of property or gain. Likewise on[e] shall not take anything from their possessions so that 12:8they not blaspheme (Israel), unless (authorized) by the association of Israel. One may not sell edible cattle 12:9or fowls to pagans so as not to enable them to use them for sacrificial purposes. And furthermore he shall not sell to them from his threshing floor 12:10and vat (or) from anything he possesses. Nor shall he sell to them his male and female slave 12:11who have entered with him into the covenant of Abraham.

One should not abominate himself 12:12with any (prohibited) creature or creeping thing by eating of them, including the larvae of bees or any 12:13living thing which creeps in the water. And they shall not eat fish unless they have been cut open 12:14while alive and their blood has been emptied out. All kinds of locusts shall be passed through fire or (dipped in) water 12:15while still alive, for this is the nature of their creation. And as for any wood, stone 12:16or soil which are defiled by a human corpus, such as those defiled by oil, 12:17the one who touche[s] them is defiled by their type of contamination. And any vessel, nail or peg within the wall 12:18which are together with the corpse in the house will defile any manufactured utensil in the same degree of defilement.

*Organizational Structure of the Cities*
12:19(And this) is the procedure for the habitation of the cities of Israel. By these rules they shall differentiate between 12:20the unclean and the clean and tell between the sacred and the ordinary. And these are the statutes 12:21by which the Sage is to conduct himself together with all living persons, each injunction for its own occasion. And according to this formula 12:22the seed of Israel shall conduct themselves so that they will not be cursed.

12:23 הֻמִתֻ[נו]ֻת הֻמִתֻהֻלֻכֻיֻם בֻּאֻלֻה בקץ הרשעה עד עמוד משוח אהרן

13:1 וישראל עד עשרה אנשים למועט לאלפים ומיאיות וחמשים

13:2 ועשרות ובמקום עשרה אל ימש איש כהן מבונן בספר ההגי על

13:3 פיהו ישקו כולם *vacat* ואם אין דיא בחון בכל אלה ואיש מהלוים בחון

13:4 באלה ויצא הגורל לצאת ולבוא על פיהו אֻ[לֻ]255 כל באי המחנה *vacat* ואם

13:5 משפט לתורת נגע יהיה באיש ובא הכהן ועמד במחנה והבינו

13:6 המבקר בפרוש התורה *vacat* ואם פתי הוא הוא יסגירנו כי להם

13:7 המשפט *vacat* וזה סרך המבקר למחנה ישכיל את הרבים במעשֻי

13:8 אל ויבינם בגבורות פלאו ויספר לפניהם נחיות עולם בפתריהם256

13:9 ועליהם ירחם257 כאב לבניו וישֻקֻוֻדֻb לכל מדהובם כרועה עדרו

13:10 יתר כל חרצובות קשריהם לבלתי הֻיֻות עשוק ורצוץ בעדתו

13:11 *vacat* וכל הנוסף לעדתו יפקדהו למֻעֻשיו ושכלֻו258 וכוחו וגבורתו והונו

13:12 וכתבוהו במקומו כפי נחֻלֻתו בגורל האֻוֻר *vacat* אֻל ימשול איש

13:13 מבני המחנה להביא איש אל העדה זולֻתֻ9 פי המבקר אשר למחנֻת

13:14 *vacat* ואיש מכֻל באי ברֻיֻת אֻל אֻל ישא ואֻל יתן לבני השחֻ9259 כֻי

13:15 אם כף לכף *vacat* ואל יעש איש למקֻח ולמֻמֻכֻר [ד]ֻבֻֻ260 כֻי אם הודֻיֻע

13:16 למבֻקֻר אשר במֻחֻנֻה ועשה בעצה ֻֻולֻֻא יֻשֻ[וגו וכן] לֻ[כו]ֻלֻ לֻ[וק]ֻח אֻֻש[ה]

13:17 והֻ[וֻ]אֻ[ה] wֻיֻעֻ[שה]w 261 בֻ[עֻ]צֻה וכן יֻבֻ262 למגרש ֻוֻהֻיֻא יֻֻסֻ[וֻ]ֻֻר את בניהם וֻבֻנֻותֻיֻהֻֻם[w263]

13:18 [וֻטֻפֻם bברוח ]עֻנֻוֻה264 ובאהבת חסד אֻל יֻטוֻר לֻהֻ[ם ] בֻא[ף]

255 Baumgarten restores [ה]א in 4Q266 F9ii:14 (DJD XVIII, 69).

256 בפרתיה CD.

257 וירחם עליהם CD.

258 ושוכלו CD.

259 CD reads שחר. Rabin noted that the context requires שחת (perdition) on the basis of CD 6:15 (Rabin, *The Zadokite Documents*, 66–67). שחר is preferable, however, in that it is stronger than שחת. The prohibition of dealing with the sons of darkness would be expected. However, our text seems to be saying the authority of the Supervisor extends to prohibiting transactions with the children of light as well. For the use of בני שחר compare 4Q298 F1–2i:1. See also Baumgarten in Charlesworth, ed., *Damascus Document*, 55, n. 203.

260 CD places דבר before למקח.

261 CD plausibly reads יֻעֻ[שה], paralleling ועשה בעֻצֻה in line 16. However, it is absent in 4Q266 F9iii:5.

262 והוֻאה בעצה וֻכֻן יֻבֻן 4Q266 F9iii:5.

263 The extant parchment at the end of line 17 does not allow for extra letters after the restoration את בניהם. However, there is sufficient space in 4Q266 F9iii:6 for either ובנותיהם (or ובנותם as suggested by Baumgarten). See DJD XVIII, 70.

264 יענוהו CD.

*Organizational Structure of the Camps*

Now this is the procedure for the habitation 12:23of the cam[p]s who conduct themselves by these commandments during the epoch of wickedness until the rise of the Messiah of Aaron CD 13:1and Israel. (There shall be) a minimum of ten men for the thousands, hundreds, fifties 13:2and tens. (And where there are ten) there shall not be absent a priest who is expert in the book of Haguy. By 13:3his authority all of them shall be guided (Gen 41:40). But if he is not competent in all these matters, but one of the Levites 13:4is, the lot of when to go out and to come in shall shall follow his command fo[r] all members of the camp.

But if 13:5there is a case regarding the law of leprosy, the priest shall come and stand up in the camp (to take charge), and (if the priest lacks competence) the Supervisor shall explain to him 13:6the details of the Torah. And even if he (the priest) is a fool, nevertheless he (the priest) must be in charge of quarantining him (the leper), for they alone have the 13:7authority to do so.

This procedure pertains to the Supervisor of the camp. He shall enlighten the many in the acts of 13:8God, and explain to them His mighty wonders and tell them of the events of eternity with their explanations. 13:9He will have compassion upon them as a father has for his children, and will attend to all their mishaps as does a shepherd for his flock. 13:10Let him loosen all the knots of their cords so that no one in his congregation be oppressed or crushed. 13:11And he (the Supervisor) shall rank anyone who joins the congregation as to his actions, his intellect, vigor, power and possessions. 13:12And they shall record him by his position in accordance with his succession in the lot of Light. No other member of the camp has the authority 13:13to bring anyone into the congregation without the sanction of the Supervisor of the camp. 13:14And one who has entered the covenant of God may neither buy (from) nor sell to the Sons of Dawn 13:15except from hand to hand (by bartering). However, no one may initiate any [ma]tter relating to buying and selling unless he has informed 13:16the Supervisor of the camp, doing so by (his) counsel so that [they] will not e[rr. The same procedure] governs [any]one who t[ak]es a wif[e]. 13:17He shall d[o so with] counsel. And in the same manner he shall enlighten one who initiates a divorce. And he (the Supervisor) shall discip[line their sons, daughters] 13:18[and infants with] a humble [spirit] and gracious love. He shall not keep a grudge

13:19 [וֹעברה על פ]שֹׁעֹיהם[b] ואת אשר איננוֹ נקשר בשֹֹׁב[ועת הברית[w]265

13:20 [עלˉw משפטיהם] vacat וֹזֹה, מושב המחנות לֹכֹל זֹ[רע?[b]ישראל266

13:21 [ואם267 לא יחזיקו בא]לֹה לא יצליחו לֹשבת בארץ ו[לֹא יצילוˉs[i]268

13:22 [ממצוקותם] vacat ואˉ/לֹה המשפטים לֹמשֹכֹיֹל [להתהלך בםˉb בקץ[w]

13:23 [פקוד269 אל את הארץ בֹבוֹא הדבר אשר דֹבר יבואו על עמכה ימים[w]

14:1 אשֹר לֹא[270 בֹאו מֹיֹוֹם סֹר אפרים מעל יהודה וכֹוֹל המתהלכים באלה

14:2 ברית /✡ נאמנת271 לֹהם להנצילם מכל מוקשי שחת כֹיֹ אֹ פתֹאוֹם272

עֹבֹרֹ[ו]273 וֹיֹעֹנֹשֹוֹ

CD 14:3–21

Parallels: 4Q266 F10i (underline)

4Q267 F9v:6b–14 (lower underline)

4Q268 F2 (dotted underline)

4Q269 F10ii:9–12; F11i:1–7 (overbar)

1QS 6:24b–25a (superscript numerals)

extant and restored text unique to DSS (outline)

14:3 vacat וסרֹך מושב כֹוֹל המחנות יפקדו כלם בֹשֹמֹוֹתיהם הכֹוֹהֹנֹים לֹלֹאˉsˉiֹשֹׁוֹנֹה

14:4 וֹהֹלֹוים שנֹיֹם ובני ישראל שלֹשים274 והגר רביע וֹיֹכֹתבו בֹשֹֹׁמֹוֹתיהם

14:5 אֹישֹ אחר אחיהו הכֹוֹהֹנים לֹראֹישֹונה והלֹוֹיֹˉiֹם שֹנֹים ובני ישראֹל

14:6 שֹלֹישֹׁיˉ[i]ם275 והגר רביעֹיֹ וכֹן ישבו וכֹן ישֹׁאלו לכֹוֹל276 והכֹוֹהֹן אֹשֹר יֹפֹקֹד

14:7 בֹֹרֹˉ[i]אֹש הֹרֹבים מבן שלושים שנה וֹעֹד בֹן ששים [שֹׁ]הֹ מבונן בֹסֹפֹר

14:8 הֹֹֹהֹגֹˉiֹ276 וֹבֹכֹוֹל משֹׁפֹטֹיֹ התורֹה לֹדברם277 vacat כֹמֹשֹׁפֹטֹם וֹהֹמבקֹר אֹשֹׁר

---

265 Rabin transcribes [    ]ב; Qimron and Baumgarten [    ]שׁב (Rabin, *The Zadokite Documents*, 67; Qimron, "The Text of CDC," 35; Charlesworth, ed., *Damascus Document*, 54).

266 What survives of the first letter following לֹכֹל does not appear to be a portion of a usual ז in CD mss A. However, our reconstruction follows 4Q266 F9iii:11.

267 Baumgarten restores ואם to 4Q266 F9iii:12 (DJD XVIII, 70).

268 Rabin transcribes nothing after בארץ. Qimron sees בֹ before the lacuna. See Rabin, *The Zadokite Documents*, 67; Qimron, "The Text of CDC," 35. Our restoration follows that of Stegemann in 4Q269 F10ii:4. See Hartmut Stegemann, "4QDamascus Document[d] frgs. 10, 11 (Re-edition), 15, 16," *Qumran Cave 4.XXVI: Cryptic Texts and Miscellanea, Part 1* (DJD XXXVI. Oxford: Clarendon, 2000), 204.

269 Rabin restores lines 22b–23a [להתהלך בם עם כל חי עד אשר יפקד אל את הארץ] (Rabin, *The Zadokite Documents*, 67).

270 לו 4Q266 F9iii:18.

271 CD has נאמנת. נאמנת is attested in 4Q267 F9v:4.

272 On the basis of the alleged reading in 4Q267 F9v:5, Qimron reads פתאום, as do Martínez-Tigchelaar. However, the reading פ[ת]אֹ[ם] is equally plausible.

against them [with anger] 13:19[or rage for] their [trans]gressions even (against) that which is not bound by [the covenantal] oa[th] 13:20[pertaining to their disciplinary rules.]

And this is (the procedure for) the habitation of the camps for all the off[spring of Israel.] 13:21[And if they do not adhere to th]ese (commandments) they will not succeed in dwelling in the land, and [will not be delivered] 13:22[from their oppressions.

And th]ese are the rules [by which] the Sage [is to conduct himself during the epoch] 13:23[when God will remember the land (and) when the matter which He spoke of will transpire, "There shall come upon your people days] CD 14:1which have not transpired since Ephraim split off from Judah" (Isa 7:17). But as for those who conduct themselves in these ways, 14:2the divine covenant will remain faithful to them, saving them from those ensnared by the pit, since suddenly [they] (those who are ensnared) will have transgressed and been punished.

14:3Now for the procedure of the camp sessions. All of them shall be organized by their names: first the priests, 14:4the Levites second, the Israelites third and proselytes fourth. And they shall be recorded by their names 14:5one after another: the priests first, the Levites second, the Israelites 14:6third and the proselytes fourth. And thus they should be seated, and thus should they inquire about any matter. And the priest who will be appointed 14:7as leader of the Many, shall be between thirty and sixty years of age, an expert in the book 14:8of Haguy and in all the injunctions of the Torah to interpret them cor-

273 ונענשו CD.

274 שלשתם CD.

275 שלושתם CD.

276 ישאלו על 4Q268 F2:2.

276 Baumgarten transcribes ההוגי (Charlesworth, ed., *Damascus Document*, 56).

277 לרבים 4Q267 F9v:12.

14:9 לְכֹל הַמַחֲנות מִבֶּן שְׁלֹושִׁים שנָה עַד בֶּן חֲמִשִׁים שנה בעול בְכֹל

14:10 סוד אנשים וְלכֹל לְשׁון רמ[ ] פרִיה‎[278] על פיהו יבאו‎[279] באי העדה

14:11 אִישׁ בתרו וְלכֹל‎[280] הַדָבַר אֲשֶׁר יִהֵיה לְכֹל האדם לְדַבֵר לַ[עֵדַה‎] למבקר ידבר

14:12 לְכֹל רִיב ומשפט vacat וְזֶה סֵרֶך הַרֵבֵים לְהָכִין כֹל חפציהם שכר

14:13 שְׁנֵי ימִים לכל חדש לִמֵֿעֵֿט וְיֵנתֵן‎[281] על יד הַמְבֵקֵר‎[282] והשופטים

14:14 מִמֵֿנוֿ יתנו בעד [פ]צֵֿעֵֿם‎[9] ומֵמֵנו יחזקו בעד‎[283] עני וֵהֵאביון ולזקן אֲשֶׁר

14:15 יִכר[עֵ] ולְאִישׁ אשר ינו[ג]ע ולאשר ישבה לגוי נכר ולבתולה אשר

14:16 [אֵי]ן לֵה גֵֿ[וֵא]ל וֵלֵנֵעֵר[] א[שֵ]ר אֵין לו דֵורֵֿש וֵלכֹל עבודת הֵחֵֿבֵֿר ולא

14:17 [יִכרת בית החבר מִיד[ֵם‎] vacat וְזֶה פֵרֵֿוֵֿשׁ מֵוֵֿשֵׁב הֵמֵֿ[חנות‎][9] ואֵלֵה יֵסֵֿודֵֿות‎[284]

14:18 [אֵנֵשֵׁי‎[285] הֵקֵ[הֵֿל‎] vacat וֵֿזֵה פֵרֵֿוֵֿש המשפטִים אֲשֵׁ[ר ישפטו בם‎][286]

14:19 [עֵד עמֵוֵֿד‎[287] מֵשֵׁ[יֵח אֵהֵֿרֵֿן‎] וֵישֵׁראֵל וִיכֵפר עֵונם מֵֿ[נֵחה וחֵטֵאת ונדבה‎w]

14:20 vacat‎][6:24b וֵהֵאֵי[סֵֿ‎m/w] אֵֿ[שֵֿ]רֵֿ[9] יֵֿישֵׁ>קֵֿרֵֿ[9] 6:25a] בֵממון וֵהֵוֵא יֵודֵע וֵ[ֿ]ת[בֵֿדִילֵֿוֵחֵוֵֿ מֵן הֵֿטֵֿהֵֿרֵֿה‎]

14:21 [שֵׁנה אֵחֵֿת‎w וֵנֵ[עֵֿנֵֿש שֵׁשֵׁ]ים יֵוֵם‎[288] וֵאֵֿשֵֿׁר יֵֿדֵבֵֿ]ר אֵת רֵעֵֿהֵֿו במֵֿרֵֿוֵֿם‎b אֵו[רֵֿ‎w]

14:22 [יֵֿטֵוֵֿר לֵֿרֵֿעֵֿהֵֿו אֲֿשֵֿׁר] לֵֿא בֵֿמֵֿשֵֿׁפֵֿטֵֿ וֵֿֿנֵעֵֿ[נֵֿ]שֵֿׁ‎w וֵֿהֵֿ[וֵֿ]יֵה מֵֿשֵֿׁפֵֿטֵֿו כֵֿמֵֿוֵֿהֵֿוֵֿ‎w [

14:23 [ ]·[ ] לֵֿ[ ] ]··[ [

---

[278] The transcription of the letters following לשון is problematic. Ginzberg read רמיה פרך; Rabin למשפחותם; and Baumgarten רמשפחותם. Qimron transcribes [ ] רמ‎| פרִיה, speculating that it might be a corrupt version of למשפחותם. Louis Ginzberg, *An Unknown Jewish Sect* (New York: The Jewish Theological Seminary of America, 1976), 90; Rabin, *The Zadokite Documents*, 69; Charlesworth, ed., *Damascus Document*, 56; Qimron, "The Text of CDC," 37. In light of Gen 10:5, אִישׁ לִלְשֹׁנוֹ לְמִשְׁפְּחֹתָם, we adopt the emendation of Rabin and Qimron.

[279] יבאו 4Q266 F10i:3.

[280] וֵלכֹל 4Q266 F9iii:4.

[281] ונתנו CD 16:13.

[282] המבקר 4Q266 F9iii:6.

[283] יחזקו ביד CD.

[284] Qimron reads הֵמֵֿ[חנה (Qimron, "The Text of CDC," 37).

[285] אֵנֵשֵׁ[י‎·] 4Q266 F9iii:11.

[286] Qimron restores ישפטו] בהם בקץ הרשעה עד עמוד מֵשֵׁי[ח to CD 14:18b–19a (Qimron, "The Text of CDC," 37).

[287] מֵמוֵֿד 4Q266 F10i:12.

[288] וֵנֵ[עֵֿנֵֿש ימֵֿים שֵׁשֵׁה can be restored in CD.

rectly. And the Supervisor 14:9of all the camps shall be between thirty and fifty years of age, accomplished in every 14:10mystery (revealed to) men and in every tongue as (spoken) by their families. By his authority the members of the congregation shall enter, 14:11each in his turn. And in any concern that a person may encounter, in which he wishes to address the congregation, let him speak (first) to the Supervisor 14:12pertaining to any legal conflict.

And this is the procedure of the 'Many' to fill all their needs. (Let there be) a wage withholding of 14:13at least two days per month; and let it be administered by the Supervisor and the judges. 14:14From it they shall provide for (the healing of) their [wo]unded. And from it they shall assist the poor and the destitute, the elderly man who is 14:15[bent do]wn, him who suffers from lep[ro]sy, him who is taken captive by a foreign nation, a maiden who 14:16[does no]t have a re[dee]mer, a lad [w]ho has no guardian, and all the services provided by the association, so that 14:17[the association] not [perish for lack of] their [support.]

And this is the elaboration concerning the habitation of the c[amps. And these are the founding rules] 14:18[of the people of the com]munity.

*Camp Discipline*
And these are the verdicts [by which they shall be judged] 14:19[until the Anoint]ed of Aaron and Israel [arises] and atones for their transgressions by an of[fering, a sin offering or a gift.]

14:20[And any]one w[h]o knowingly <speaks fa>lsely in matters of business, [they shall separate from the Purity 14:21for one year, and] he shall [be] fine[d] for sixty days.

And he who addre[sses his neighbor haughtily or] 14:22[holds a grudge against his neighbor] unjustly should be fi[n]ed and [his sentence] shall b[e like that of the preceding case . . . ] 14:23[ . . . ]16

---

16 What follows is text of approximately eight lines that has not survived, material that would have spanned from lines 18–25 of 4Q266 F10i.

(4Q266 F10i:25)

 והובדל[ᵂ

] 10i:25

4Q266 F10ii
Parallels: 4Q270 F7i:1–6a (underline)
    4Q269 F11i:8–ii:2 (overbar)
    1QS 7:8–16a (superscript numerals)

[מאת]ᵒֶ̇ם ימים ונענש מאה יום ואם בֿדבר מות ⁷:⁸ינטור ולוֿ] יֿ[שוב    10ii:1

[עוד ואשֿ]לֿ [יצֿ]חֿתֿ את רעהו שלֿ²⁸⁹ בעצה [והוֿ]בֿדל שנה אחת ונע]שֿ    10ii:2

שֿ]שה חודשים ⁷:⁹[ואשר ידבֿר בפיֿהֿ]וֿ ]דבר נבל ונענש עֶ̇]שֿ̇רֿ]י̇ם    10ii:3

[יוֿם והובדל] שלושה חודשיֿ[ם ואשר יֿ]דבר בתוך דֿבֿ]רי רעהו ו]פרע    10ii:4

[ונענש ⁷:¹⁰עשרת ]ימים[ ואשר ישכֿ]בֿ [וֿ]ישן ב[מוֿ]שֿ[ב הרבים ᵂ שלושֿ]הֿ    10ii:5

[והובדל] שלושים יום [וֿ]נֿענש עשרת ימים[ וכן לאיש הנפֿ]טֿר    10ii:6

[אשר ]לֿוֿ בעצת הרֿ[בֿ]יֿ[ם וֿ]חֿ[נֿם] עֶ̇רֿ שלוש פעֿ[מים על מושב ]אחד    10ii:7

וֿ]נענש עשרה ימים אֶ̇ם [יזקפֿו] ⁷:¹²[ונפטֿרֿ] במושב ונענש שלושים[    10ii:8

יוֿ[ם] ואשֿ̇ר יהלך לפני רעֿ]הו ערום בבית או בשדה הלך עֶ̇רום לפני]ֿ    10ii:9

הֿ[בֿ]רֿיאות והובדל ששה [חודשיםᵇ ואשר ירוק אל תוך המושב ⁷:¹³וֿאוֿ²⁹⁰[ᵂ    10ii:10

[יוֿ]צֿא אֶ̇ת ידו מתחת בגדֿוֿ[ן והואה ⁷:¹⁴פוֿחֿוֿ?²⁹¹ [ונראתה ערותו והובדל    10ii:11
שלוֿ[שים

[יוֿ]ם ונענש עשרֿה והֿסֿ[וֿ]חֿ[קֿ²⁹² בסכלוֿ[ת להשמיע²⁹³ קולו והובדל]    10ii:12

[שֿ]לֿושים <יום>ᵂ ונעֶ̇נֿשֿ חֿמשתֿ] עשֿ̇רֿ ימיֶ̇ם ⁷:¹⁵[הֿמוציא את יֿ]דֿו השֿ̇מֿ]אלֿית[    10ii:13

[לֿשֿ̇חֿֿת בה ונענֿש] עשרֿה ימים[ והובדל שלושיםᵂ והאיש [אֿ]שֿ̇ר ילך [רכיל]    10ii:14

---

²⁸⁹ 4Q269 F11i:7 has בֿלוא. It evidently places this injunction subsequent to . . . ואשר יֿ]דבר בתוך of 4Q266 F10ii:4.

²⁹⁰ Baumgarten restores ואשר from 1QS 7:13 (DJD XVIII, 74).

²⁹¹ Remnants of several letters have survived above [בסכלו אֶ̇[ of PAM 43.398 (supplying the center of 4Q266 F10ii:12). We tentatively transcribe the letters פוֿחֿ, a word that Baumgarten reconstructs from 1QS 7:14.

²⁹² Baumgarten transcribes [והֿ]סֿ[וֿ]חֿקֿ (DJD XVIII, 74). 4Q269 F11ii+15:1 reads והשֿוֿחֿ]קֿ.

²⁹³ 4Q270 F7i:4 reads בסכלות להרים ]קולו with a supralinear correction of שמיע above רים of the infinitive להרים. 1QS 7:14 seems to reflect the corrected reading בסכלות להשמיע קולו.

**(4Q266 F10i:25b)** (and shall be separated) **4Q266 F10ii** [1]for two [hundred] days and fined for one hundred days. And if he holds a grudge involving a capital offense he [shall] not be permitted to return [2][(to the Purity).

Any]one who [mo]cks his neighbor without authorization of the counsel [shall be] separate[d] (from the Purity) for one year and be fi[n]ed [3]for s[ix months.]

One who uses lewd speech shall be fined for t[wen]ty [4][days and separated] (from the Purity) for three month[s.

One who] talk[s] on top of [his neighbor] disruptively [5][shall be fined ten] days.

[One who lies dow]n [and] sleeps during the [ses]si[ons of the Many thre]e (times) [6][shall be separated] (from the Purity) for thirty days [and] fined for ten days.

[And the same applies to one who lea]ves [7]without the permission of the M[a]n[y.

And] he who [dozes off] up to three ti[mes during] one [session] [8]shall [be fined] for ten days. And if [when they arise], he leaves [the session (without permission), he shall be fined for (an additional) thirty] [9]da[ys.]

One who walks around naked [in the house] in front of [his] neigh[bor or parades naked in the field before] [10]p[e]ople shall be separated (from the Purity) for six [months.

One who spits into the session, or] [11][draws o]ut his hand from under [his] garment [which has] holes so that [his penis becomes visible, shall be separated (from the Purity) for thir]ty [12][da]ys and fined for ten.

And anyone who stupid[ly] j[es]ts, [loudly raising his voice, shall be separated (from the Purity) for] [13][t]hirty <days> and fined for fif[tee]n days.

[One who takes out] his le[ft ha]nd [14][to uri]nate with it shall be fined [for ten days and separated for thirty.

10ii:15  [בר]‏[עֹהֹ]ו‏<sup>7:16a</sup>‏והבדילהו <u>מן הטהרה שנה אחת ונענש ששה</u>‏<sup>294</sup> חורשים[

4Q270 F7i:6b–16a
Parallels: 4Q267 F9vi (underline)
　　　　　　1QS 7:16b–21 (superscript numerals)

6  [  ‏<sup>7:16b</sup>ואיש ברבים <sup>b</sup>אשר <sup>w</sup>ילך[‏<sup>b</sup>]

7  אשר לא במשפט‏<sup>7:18</sup>‏[ישוב עֹ]וד ואם על רעהו ילון‏<sup>7:17</sup>‏ולא [‏<sup>w</sup>‏295 רכיל לשלחו]
ונענש ששה[

8  וללכת‏<sup>7:19</sup>‏לבגוד באמת‏<sup>w</sup> הרבים מלפני‏<sup>b</sup>[רוחו אשר תזוע ‏שֹ[חורשים והאי]
בשרירות לבו[

9  לו‏<sup>7:21</sup>‏ובמלאות‏<sup>7:20</sup>‏[ונ]עֹנֹש ששים [יום ‏<sup>w</sup>‏רשֹ‏[רֹ]‏297 ואם ישוב ‏‏[פֹו]‏ ולא‏[בדל]‏<sup>bb</sup>[וֹ]‏[ר]
ששים יום‏<sup>w</sup> ישאלו הרבים[

10  [　　　　　　אל המשפט ישאל ואחר בתכונו ‏[בוהו]‏וֹ‏[כתוֹ]‏ ואם יקרב ‏‏[רוֹ]‏‏[דֹבֹ]‏ על

11  *va*]cat ואיש <u>אשר</u> ימאס [א]ת משפט הרבים ויצא ו[לא <u>ישוב עוד</u> ואיש אשר יקח[

---

<sup>294</sup> A one year separation is associated with a six month fine in 4Q266 F10ii:2–3 (4Q269 F11i:8).

<sup>295</sup> Following 1QS 7:16, Baumgarten restores לשלח הוא (DJD XVIII, 162).

<sup>296</sup> Baumgarten restores מיסוד היחד (DJD XVIII, 162). The completion of the wording והאי[שֹ אשר תזוע draws on the parallel, 1QS 7:18. However, we depart from the Community Rule in our reconstruction of MTA in an important point. מיסוד היחד (from the foundation of the community), is a reading unlikely here, since, although יחד is a standard term in the Community Rule, it evidently occurs only once in all of MTA (cf. 4Q270 F3iii:19 as supplemented by its parallel 4Q271 F2:7). In other words, the author of MTA does not know of the technical sense of יחד as an appellation for the community. Moreover, in one instance where the disciplinary injunctions of MTA parallel those of 1QS, the latter (1QS 6:24) has יחד, but not the former (CD 14:18b–19). Furthermore, in several clauses of this pericope there exists a clear divergence between the two texts. 1QS 7:1–2 contains עצת היחד (the counsel of the community) in a clause which is absent in MTA. 1QS 7:5b–6 has בהון היחד (in the property of the community) in an injunction likewise not found in MTA. Neither does MTA have the formula כול אנשי היחד (all the men of the community) (1QS 7:19b–20). Finally, the presence of four occurrences of יחד in 1QS 7:22–25 find no place in the last clauses of the משפטים of MTA (4Q270 F7i:11–15a). Hence, the two texts clearly diverge in their use of this technical term. The wording על (against the foundation of the community) in 1QS 7:17–18a might perhaps be interpolated into 4Q270 F7i:7. However, it is implausible since its apodosis would then be ישלחהו ולא ישוב, a clause that would not correspond to the general wording of this section of MTA. It is more likely that the verdict followed that of the second clause of its parallel, pertaining to the issue of complaining. All in all, there is no compelling reason to suppose that 4Q270 F7i:8 contained the reading מיסוד היחד as Baumgarten supposes.

<sup>297</sup> Our reconstruction reflects two reading options explained in greater length in the commentary. The original scribe may have written והובדל ואם ישוב ונענש ששים יום

And as for anyone] who goes around [gossiping] [15][about] his
[neigh]bor, [they shall separate him from the Purity for one year and
he shall be fined for six months.]

**4Q270 F7i:6b–16a** [6b][One who goes around] [7][gossiping about
the Many shall be expelled and] shall [not] be r[e]admitted. [And if
he complains unjustly against his neighbor, he shall be fined for six]
[8][months.

And any]one whose [spirit] is vain [before the many by repudiating the Truth and walking in the stubbornness of his heart] [9][shall]
be se[parated (from the Purity). And if he should be readmitted] he
shall be fined for sixty [days. When the sixty days have passed, the
Many shall deliberate][17] [10]concerning [his] statu[s. And if he is to
be readmitted, they] should list [him in his rank. Thereafter, he shall
inquire into the verdict.]

[11][The man] who despises the (final) verdict of the many shall exit
and [never again return.

---

[17] or the supralinear alternative: "shall] be se[parated (from the Purity) and not
readmitted, but shall be ex]pelled . . . (*omit*) . . . [When the sixty days have passed,
the Many shall deliberate . . ."

---

(. . . he shall be separated. And if he returns he shall be fined for two years), a reading
reflected in part in the *Rule of the Community* parallel, 1QS 7:19. A later emender,
sensing excessive leniency in the punishment, leaving the original reading intact, may
have augmented the text to increase the punishment, reading והובדל ולא ישוב ופורש
(. . . he shall be separated and may not return, but shall be expelled).

12 אוכלו חוצה מן המשפט והשיבו לאיש אשר לקחו מ[מנו va[cat וֹאֲשֶׁר יקרֹ[ב]

13 לֹזֹנות לאשתו אשר לא כמשפט ויצא ולֹא ישוב עֹוד va[ca]t ואשר ילו[ן] על האבות

14 [ישלח] מן העדה ולא ישוֹב [ואם] על האמות ונֹעֹנֹש עֹשֹרֹ[ת] ימים כי אין

לֹאֹמֹ[ו]ת רֹוקמֹהֹ[298] בתוך

15 [העדה] vacat [ואלה המ[שפטים א]שר ישפטו ]בֹם כל המחזסרים כל אֹין[ש] אשר

16 [לֹאֵ]ʷ התיס[ר299] יבוא וידיעהו לכוהֹן [הֹמ]וֹפֹקֹר

**4Q266 F11**

Parallels: 4Q270 F7i:16b–21; F7ii (underline)

4Q269 F16 (overbar)

text unique to 4Q266 (plain outline)

text unique to 4Q270 (underlined outline)

text unique to 4Q269 (overbarred outline)

1 עֹל הרביֹם וקבל את משפטו מרצונו כאשר אמר ביד

2 מֹוֹשׁה עֹל הנפש אשר תחטֹא בשיגגה אשר יביאו אֹת

3a חטֹאֹתֹוֹ [ו]אֹת אשמו

## 2.3. Finale

3b ועֹל ישראל כתוֹב אלכה לי

4 אֹל קציֹ[300] [ה]שמים ולו אריח בריח ניחוחכם ובֹמקום אחר

5 כתוֹב לשוב אל אל בבכי ובצום וֹבֹמקוֹ‹ם› [אח]רֹ[ʷ] ? כתוֹב[301] קרעו לבבכם

וֹאֹל בגדיכם[302] וכוֹל המואס במשפטים

6 האלה על פֹי כוֹל החוקים הנמצאים בתורת מושה לו יחשב

7 בכוֹל בני אמתו כי גֹעֹלה נפשו בֹיסוֹרי הצדק וֹבמרד מלפני vacat

8 הרבים ישתלח וידבר בו הכוהן המופקֹדֹ[] עֹ[ל] הרבים וענֹה

9 [וא]מֹר בֹרוֹך אתֹ אֹוֹן הו הכול וֹבֹידיךֹהֹ הכול ועושה הכוֹל אשר יסדתה

---

298 For the word רוקמה as "gloriously woven art" see 1QM 5:5–14; 4Q161 F8–10:19; 4Q287 F2:5; 4Q403 F1ii:1; 4Q405 F14–15i:3–6; 4Q405 F19:5; 4Q405 F20ii–22:11 and 4Q405 F23ii:7. For an alternative view that this term is a phonetic variant of Akkadian *rugummû* (legal claim), see Victor Avigdor Hurowitz, "רוקמה in Damascus Document 4QDᵉ (4Q270 7 i 14)," *DSD* 9-1 (2002): 35.

299 Baumgarten reads כל אין[ש] אשר יתיס[רʷ] (DJD XVIII, 163).

300 קצה 4Q270 F7i:18.

301 Baumgarten reads וֹבֹמקוֹם כתוֹב (DJD XVIII, 76).

302 Instead of לשוב . . . בגדיכם of 4Q266, 4Q270 F7i:19 alternatively reads קרעו לבבכם ואל בגדיכם וכתֹוֹב לשוב אל אל בבכי ובצום]

One who appropriates] ¹²food illicitly shall return it to the man from [whom] he took it.

And one who approa[ch]es ¹³his wife to have sexual relations contrary to the law shall exit and not return.

[Any one who rebe]ls against the fathers ¹⁴[should be expelled] from the community and not return. [But if] he rebels against the mothers, he shall be fined for ten days, for mothers do not have the ornate glory¹⁸ (as do the fathers) [in] ¹⁵[the community.

These are the in]junctions by wh[ich] all who are disciplined [shall be judged].

Anyon[e] who ¹⁶[has violated a disciplinary ru]le shall come and relate it to the priest [who is in c]harge **4Q266 F11** ¹of the Many and shall accept his verdict willingly as it was said through ²Moses concerning "the person who sins unwittingly" (Lev 4:2): they shall bring ³their sin [and] guilt offering.

## 2.3. Finale

*Convocation of the Camps*
And concerning Israel it is also written, "I will go ⁴to the 'ends of [the] heavens' (Deut 30:4) 'and I will not savor your sweet smelling odors'" (Lev 26:31). And in a different passage ⁵it is written "to return to God with weeping and fasting" (cf. Joel 2:12). In yet [a differen]t pass<age> it is written "rend your hearts and not your garments" (Joel 2:13). But anyone who despises these precepts ⁶which are in accordance with all the statutes that are found in the Torah of Moses will not be reckoned ⁷among all the sons of his Truth, for he has repudiated the righteous chastisements. Because of his rebellion against ⁸the Many he should be expelled. And the priest who is in charge [o]f the Many shall speak concerning him, responding ⁹[and s]aying, "Blessed are

---

¹⁸ i.e. status.

10 [ע]מים למשפחותיהם ולשונות לאומותם ותתעם בתהו ולו

11 ‹‹ולו›› דרך ובאבותינו בחרתה לזרעם נתתה חוקי אמתכה

12 ומשפטי קודשכה אשר יעשה האדם וחיה וגבולות הגבלתה

13 לנו אשר את עובריהם ארותה ואנו עם פדותכה וצון מרעיתךה

14 אתה ארותה את עובריהם ואנו הקימונו ויצא המשתלח והאיש

15 אשר יוכל מהונם ואשר ידרוש שלומו ~~המשתלח~~ ואשר יאות עמו

16 ונכתב דברו על פני המבקר בחרת ושלים משפטו *vacat* וכול ה

17 [יושבי ]המחנות יקהלו בחודש השלישי וארדו את הנוטה ימין

18 [ושמאול מן ה]תורה *vac* והזה פרוש המשפטים אשר יעשו בכול קץ

19 [הפקודה את אשר יפק]דו [בכו]ל קצי החרון ומסעיהם לכול

20 [יושב מחניהם וכול יושב עריהם הנה הכו]ל נ[כתב ע]ל[303] [מ]דר[ש] התורה

21 [האחרון *vacat* ]

[303] Baumgarten transcribes כ[תוב] על in 4Q270 F7ii:14b–15a (DJD XVIII, 166).

You, Almighty Lord of all, in whose hands is everything, and who creates all. You are the one who founded [10][na]tions by their families and national tongues, and led them astray in a [11]trackless wilderness. But You have chosen our ancestors, bestowing upon their seed statutes of Your truth and [12]sacred commandments, which a person must observe and live by. You made limits [13]for us, whose transgressors You cursed. But we are the people of Your redemption, the sheep of Your pasture. [14]You cursed their sinners, but we have upheld (Your commandments)." And let the one who is expelled depart. And as for anyone [15]who partakes of their property and greets or welcomes any one of them, [16]his action shall be recorded in the presence of the Supervisor, etched in ink. Thus his condemnation is complete. And all [17][the inhabitants] of the camps shall assemble on the third month and curse anyone who deviates either to the right [18][or to the left from the] Torah.

*Epilogue*
And this is the elaboration of the injunctions which they shall observe during the entire epoch [19][of redemption which they shall remem]ber [during al]l the epochs of anger and their journeys, for every [20][inhabitant of their camps and everyone who dwells in their cities. Behold, every]thing has been [written up]on "the Mi[d]ra[sh] on the [21][Eschatological] Torah."

# CHAPTER THREE

# COMMENTARY

### 3.1. *Preamble (4Q266 F1; F2i:1–6a / 4Q268 F1:1–8)*

4Q266 is unique among the Dead Sea Scrolls in that it preserves the leading edges of both the beginning and ending of the manuscript. As will be shown, these archaeological vestiges assure the modern reader that these remains emanate from an ancient copy more complete than the medieval Cairo Genizah text. Thus, for the first time the document gives us a more comprehensive picture of what was available in antiquity but is absent in CD.

The first portion of our composite text consists exclusively of Cave textual witnesses, preserved mainly in 4Q266 and 4Q268, with limited attestation by 4Q267. I call this introductory pericope the preamble to the document. Herein the author provided what was likely the title of the book in parchment which has not survived. He then presents the goal of his composition, followed immediately by the anticipation of the downfall of the opposition of the sect. From there the author promises his readers that the mysteries of history will be revealed therein. Following a lengthy prayer our writer introduces the document's base text, the book of *The Divisions of the Times*, a work conventionally known as *Jubilees*.

### 3.1.1. *Prologue: The Title and Aim (4Q266 F1:1–3a)*

Only the center of the document's first line survives. Baumgarten has restored its beginning as [פרוש המשפטים למשכיל לב]נֵ֯י אור which he renders "[The elaboration of the laws by the Sage for the s]ons of light."[1] His restored title, as argued below, is not persuasive. The proposed clause פרוש המשפטים does appear in CD 14:18–19 and 4Q266 F11:18–19 (repeated in 4Q270 F7ii:12–13), but not as a title; nor is it followed by למשכיל.

As proposed independently by Stegemann and by me, it is more likely

---

[1] Joseph M. Baumgarten, *Qumran Cave 4.XIII: The Damascus Document (4Q266–273)* (DJD XVIII; Oxford: Clarendon, 1996), 31–32.

that the beginning of the work contained the phrase מדרש התורה האחרון, a formula that occurs at the end of the composition—present in 4Q270 F7ii:15 and partially extant in 4Q266 F11:20–21. Stegemann expands this formula to begin the work with [מדרש התורה האחרון על ב[נ' אור, translating it, "This is the final midrash of the law for all the children of light."[2] It is more likely, however, that the book began with the interjectory particle הנה, a word which harmonizes with both extant occurrences of the formula מדרש התורה האחרון (hereafter usually referred to as "MTA").[3] The statement הנה מדרש התורה האחרון (Here is the 'Midrash on the Eschatological Torah') displays a syntax similar to that of הנה פרוש שמותיהם לתולדותם (Here is a listing of their names by their ancestry) in CD 4:4b–5a. As will be argued below, MTA presents itself as an amplification of the book of *Jubilees*, whose author gives the title of his work מחלקות העתים (*The Divisions of the Times*) in both the very beginning and ending of his book.[4] As stated, MTA repeats the formula מדרש התורה האחרון in 4Q266 F5i:17.[5] 1QS 6:24 may add support to the reading of מדרש התורה האחרון in the opening

---

[2] As quoted by Joseph M. Baumgarten, "Corrigenda to the *Damascus Document*," *RevQ* 19 (1999): 222; Hartmut Stegemann, "Towards Physical Reconstructions of the Qumran Damascus Document Scrolls," in *The Damascus Document A Centennial of Discovery: Proceedings of the Third International Symposium of the Orion Center for the Study of the Dead Sea Scrolls and Associated Literature, 4–8 February, 1998* (ed. Joseph M. Baumgarten, Esther G. Chazon, and Avital Pinnick; Leiden: Brill, 2000); Vol. XXXIV in *Studies on the Texts of the Desert of Judah* (ed. F. García Martínez and A. S. van der Woude; Leiden: Brill), 193–94.

[3] See my reconstruction הנה המֹ]ה על ספר מדרש ה[תורה האֹחֹרֹוֹן in 4Q266 F5i:16–17 and my proposed composite reading הנה הכול נ[כתב] על מדרש התורה האחרון based on 4Q270 F7ii:15 and 4Q266 F11:20–21 at the end of the document. Cf. also 4Q269 F16:16–19, a reconstruction published by Hartmut Stegemann in "4QDamascus Document[d] frgs. 10, 11 (Re-edition), 15, 16" in *Qumran Cave 4.XXVI: Cryptic Texts and Miscellanea, Part 1* (DJD XXXVI; Oxford: Clarendon, 2000), 201–11. For the restoration נכתב instead of Baumgarten's כתוב or Stegemann's נמצא (is found), see my comments in "The Preamble to the Damascus Document: A Composite Edition of 4Q266–4Q268," *HUCA* 69 (1998): 47. The proposed beginning הנה מדרש התורה האחרון and the succeeding reconstruction departs somewhat from that of page 35 in my article.

[4] *Jub.* 1:4 and 50:13 as translated from the Ethiopic. Additionally, it seems likely that MTA drew heavily from *Temple Scroll*.

[5] Although the formula does not occur in its entirety in CD, it seems to me that two of the three words survive in CD 20:6. The context of this line asserts that the מדרש התורה should serve as the code (יתהלכו בו) for the אנשי תמים הקדש (the people of perfect holiness). It appears likely that the phrase מדרש התורה is a shortened form of מדרש התורה האחרון, since the formula in MTA survives in part in 4Q266 F5i:14–17 in a similar context. In this text the partially extant verbal phrase יתהלכו בם was

line of our document. It introduces the list of disciplinary injunctions taken mostly from MTA with an allusion to this formula.

*vacat* ואלֶה המשפטים אשר ישפטו בם במדרש יחד על פי הדברים

> And these are the verdicts by which they shall be judged through the *Midrash-Yachad* according to (their) commands. (1QS 6:24)

This line suggests that מדרש here is the source from which these injunctions were taken, and יחד is the title given to what we call *Rule of the Community*, thus linking the works MTA and *Rule of the Community* as a hybrid.

What makes מדרש התורה האחרון a literary title is that these extant occurrences are preceded by the emphatic particle הנה. That the word הנה in MTA is used to mark a literary work is attested in line 3 of CD 16 which introduces the Hebrew title of *Jubilees*.[6] This mode of citation suggests a heading for the composition rather than its reduction, *a la* Baumgarten, to merely a "source from which the laws derived."[7]

The significance of the above point is twofold. First, ever since the original publication of CD by Schechter, scrollists have alluded to it with many appellations. To cite a few, Schechter named it "Fragments of a Zadokite Work," Rabin, "The Zadokite Documents," and more recently, Baumgarten, "The Damascus Document."[8] Presumably, we now have the author's title for the work, מדרש התורה האחרון. Secondly, this is the beginning of a revolutionary understanding of

---

probably preceded by the reconstructed clause [ו,[כו]ל [שומרי מצוות אל], a synonymous phrase to אנשי תמים הקדש, to read "And [al]l [who keep the commandments of God shall liv]e by them."

[6] See Hartmut Stegemann, *The Library of Qumran* (Grand Rapids: Eerdmans, 1998), 117. Our author emphasizes the authoritativeness of the book of *Jubilees* and his dependence upon it by way of his extraordinary praise, wherein he calls it the Torah of Moses which is מדוקדק (perfect), repeating the word מדוקדק twice (CD 16:1–3). The emphatic phrase הנה הכול כתוב בלוחות אשר... (... behold everything is written in the tablets which . . .) appears in 4Q177 F1-4:12, likewise suggesting a literary composition such as לוחות האבן (the tablets of stone).

[7] Baumgarten, DJD XVIII, 78.

[8] Joseph A. Fitzmyer, ed. *Documents of Jewish Sectaries* (New York: Ktav, 1970; Rep., with "Prolegomenon," of Solomon Schechter, *Fragments of a Zadokite Work*. Cambridge: Cambridge University Press, 1910); Chaim Rabin, *The Zadokite Documents* (2d rev. ed.; Oxford: Clarendon, 1958); Baumgarten, DJD XVIII; Baumgarten in James H. Charlesworth, ed., *Damascus Document, War Scroll, and Related Documents* (vol. 2 of *The Dead Sea Scrolls: Hebrew, Aramaic, and Greek Texts with English Translations*; ed. James H. Charlesworth; Tübingen/Louisville: J. C. B. Mohr [Siebeck] and Westminster John Knox Press, 1995).

MTA. Standard scholarship posits a collection of extracts without a single topic or unitary theme. However, al-Qirqisani, the tenth century Karaite writer, who gives an account of a work such as MTA, regarded it as a document authored by either a single writer, Zadok, or by two men, Zadok and Boethus.[9] The attribution of MTA to Zadok used to be discussed by early scrollists such as Schechter, but recent scholarship generally ignores him altogether.

In a duel of different eras, Qirqisani bests modern scholarship. The close similarity of the extant twelve manuscripts of MTA provides probative evidence for the essential unity of the composition. Had it been a collection of extracts without a single topic or unitary theme, as many scholars spanning from Schechter to Hempel assume,[10] it is likely that the DSS, with their rich collection of sectarian versions, would have presented a more divergent documentary tradition. With some exceptions, the evidence for general uniformity in the extant remains is overwhelming. That MTA was a unitary composition can also be seen in CD 20:6, where it was designated to serve as the code of the community. As will be shown over and over, it is safer to presume that MTA originated from a single author, or as Qirqisani asserts, from two authors, than to describe it as a collection of various extracts.

MTA could be translated as is generally done, "the final midrash of the Torah." This implies a midrash prior to this document. More likely, however, the term אחרון here modifies תורה or rather התורה (ספר) as the syntagm in CD 5:2, בספר התורה החתום (in the sealed book of the Torah). As to the translation of אחרון, rather than "final," I render it as "eschatological," conveying what I perceive was the broad expectation of an era of messianic dimension.[11] Hence, the formula as a whole reads "The Midrash on the Eschatological Torah."

In the previous section, I presented the respective arguments pertaining to the book's title. Yet, whether one accepts Baumgarten's appellation, פרוש המשפטים למשכיל, or mine, מדרש התורה האחרון, what follows remains ambiguous. The preserved wording begins with [ב]נֹי אור ([the s]ons of light). Nevertheless, how does any proposed title link

---

[9] Leon Nemoy, "Al-Qirqisani's Account of the Jewish Sects and Christianity," *HUCA* 7 (1930): 326.

[10] Fitzmyer, ed., *Documents of Jewish Sectaries*, X; Charlotte Hempel, *The Laws of the Damascus Document* (ed. F. García Martínez and P. W. Flint; Leiden: Brill, 1998), 18.

[11] Cf. the clauses עד (ע)(מוד מש(י)ח (until the rise of the Messiah) in CD 12:23; CD 20:1; 4Q266 F10i:12.

with the preserved words? Baumgarten's title, ‏[פרוש המשפטים למשכיל‏
‏לב[נ]י אור‏ ([The elaboration of the laws by the Sage for the s]ons of
light), and Stegemann's naming,[12] ‏[זה מדרש התורה האחרון לכול לב[ני‏
‏אור‏ ([This is the final midrash of the law for all the chil]dren of light),
closely knit the introductory formula with the material that follows.
Alternatively, however, what comes after the title ‏מדרש התורה האחרון‏
may be taken as the beginning of a new sentence, ‏על ב[נ]י אור ל. . .‏
(It is incumbent upon the sons of light to . . . ). In this rendition,
after giving his title the author begins again with the message of his
work, ‏[להנזר מדר[כי‏ (to keep separate from the wa[ys of...]), literally,
"to become a Nazirite." Support for the alternate reading comes from
a parallel construction in a version of *Rule of the Community*:

‏(1) מדרש למשכיל על אנשי התורה המתנד(ב)ים להשיב מכל‏
‏רע ולהחזיק בכל אשר צוה (2) ול(ה)בדל מעדת אנשי העול‏

The Midrash by the Sage. It is incumbent upon the people of the Torah
who enter freely (into the community) to turn away from all evil and
to cling to everything that (God) has commanded and to separate from
the congregation of injustice. . . .[13] (4Q258 1:1–2a)

The last words of line 1 of 4Q266 fragment 1 have perished.
Baumgarten restores ‏[מדר[כי רשעה‏ (. . . from the way[s of wicked-
ness]). However, although ‏רשעה‏ is a frequent word in the DSS, the
reconstruction lacks contextual support. More plausibly, the final
portion of the line and the beginning of line 2 was ‏בני חושך‏ (the
sons of darkness), a clause which provides a deliberate contrast to
the children of light.[14] Furthermore, this restoration finds support
in 1QS 1:9b–10 where ‏בני אור‏ contrasts with ‏בני חושך‏.

1 ‏ולאהוב כול בני אור איש‏
2 ‏כגורלו בעצת אל ולשנוא כול בני חושך איש כאשמתו‏

---

[12] As quoted more recently by Baumgarten, in "Corrigenda," 222.

[13] Cf. also 1QpHab 7:10–11. In my translation a colon follows the formula,
to suggest that the next word ‏על‏ is really the first word of the composition itself,
giving the theme of this manuscript of *Rule of the Community*. This translation presents an alternate rendition to that of Charlesworth in *The Rule of the Community and
Related Documents* (vol. 1 of *The Dead Sea Scrolls: Hebrew, Aramaic, and Greek Texts with
English Translations*; ed. James H. Charlesworth; Tübingen/Louisville: J. C. B. Mohr
[Siebeck] and Westminster John Knox Press, 1994), 73.

[14] This resembles Stegemann's ‏[מדר[כי חושך‏ (Stegemann, "Physical Reconstructions," 193).

. . . and to love all the sons of light each according to his station in the
council of God, and to hate all the sons of darkness each according to
his transgression. (1QS 1:9b–10)

Thus, lines 1–2a of MTA may be restored as follows:

[הנה מדרש התורה האחרון על ב]נֵ֯י אור להנֹזֹר מדֹרֹ[כי בני חושך]

[Here is "The Midrash on the Eschatological Torah." It is incumbent
upon the so]ns of light to keep separate from the wa[ys of the sons
of darkness . . . ]

The term להנזר occurs again in CD 6:14b–15 להבדל מבני [העו]ל
ולהנזר מהון הרשעה הטמא בנדר ובחרם (It is imperative to separate from
the sons of [injus]tice and to "nazirite" by means of a vow and ban
from the defiling wealth of wickedness). Combined with the clause
containing להנזר of the preamble, this text may give us a clue to
the origin of the group that is known from the classical sources as
the Essenes. As far as we know, this movement did not exist before
the composition of MTA. According to al-Qirqisani, it was Zadok
and Boethus who founded the sectarian movement. As was noted,
al-Qirqisani attributes the authorship of a work very much like MTA
to Zadok. If we read להנזר as urging a withdrawal from the sons of
darkness as separation from the majority of the people, these words
may have constituted a call to organize an association that would be
the sons of light. We find an echo of this call in CD 13:12, which
specifies that the inclusion of new members be recorded in writing:
"And they shall record him by his position in accordance with his
succession in the lot of Light (בגורל האוֹר)." *Rule of the Community*
often alludes to the יחד as the בני אור. Line 1 of MTA may then
preserve the call for the foundation of the Essene movement.

Let us now study the meaning of these reconstructed clauses. The
introduction to the book divides itself into two parts: 1) the title מדרש
התורה האחרון, and 2) its purpose, על בני אור להנזר מדרכי בני חושך. Rabin
renders the words מדרש התורה as "the investigation of the Law"[15]
and Schwartz "the interpretation of the Torah."[16] Translators have
rendered the whole formula מדרש התורה האחרון, first made available
in Baumgarten's recent edition, as follows. Baumgarten translates it

[15] Rabin, *The Zadokite Documents*, 38.
[16] Charlesworth, ed., *Damascus Document*, 35. Cf. also "the interpretation of the
Law" in G. Vermes, *The Complete Dead Sea Scrolls in English* (New York: Penguin Press,
1997), 140.

as "the final interpretation of the law,"[17] Martínez-Tigchelaar and Vermes, "the last interpretation of the law,"[18] Cook, "the most recent interpretation of the Law,"[19] and Stegemann, "the last midrash of the Torah."[20] However, as I go on to explain, it should be rendered "The Midrash on the Eschatological Torah," where Torah includes both the Mosaic Pentateuch and *Jubilees*.

We will now analyze the meaning of this formula in two ways: each of the three components of MTA independently as well as in tandem. The word מדרש, ubiquitous in rabbinic literature, occurs about thirteen times in the DSS, three of which are in MTA. However, it appears in Scripture only twice, first in relation to the historical traditions about king Abijah attributed to the prophet Iddo in 2 Chr 13:22—"The rest of the acts of (king) Abijah, his ways and his sayings, are written in the *midrash* of the prophet Iddo." The second occurrence, in 2 Chr 24:27, pertains to King Ahaz: "Accounts of his sons, and of the many oracles against him, and of the rebuilding of the house of God are written in the *midrash* on the Book of the Kings."[21] Besides its use as a source for the chronicler, what the biblical texts meant by מדרש remains unclear. The term as used by the rabbinic sages goes far beyond what appears in DSS. The word תלמוד, frequently synonymous to מדרש in rabbinic literature, does not occur in DSS except once where it is a pejorative term.

(8) פשר[ו ע]ל מתעי אפרים אשר בתלמוד שקרם ולשון כזביהם ושפת
(9) מרמה יתעו רבים מלכים שרים כוהנים ועם עם גר נלוה ערים
(10) ומשפחות יובדו בעצתם נ[כ]בדים ומוש[לים] יפולו [מז]עם לשונם

[Its] eschatological interpretation pertains to those who lead Ephraim astray, who through their lying Talmud, specious tongue, and deceitful lip mislead many: kings, princes, priests, and the populace together with the proselyte. Cities and clans will perish by their counsel, nobility and rulers will fall on account of their ferocious tongue.[22] (4Q169 F3–4ii:8–10a)

---

[17] Baumgarten, DJD XVIII, 167.

[18] Florentina García Martínez and Eibert. J. C. Tigchelaar, eds. and translators, *The Dead Sea Scrolls Study Edition, Volume One: 1Q1–4Q273* (Leiden, Brill: 1997), 587, 617; Vermes, *The Complete Dead Sea Scrolls*, 153.

[19] Michael O. Wise, Martin G. Abegg, Jr., and Edward M. Cook, *The Dead Sea Scrolls: A New Translation* (San Francisco: Harper Collins, 1996), 74.

[20] Stegemann, *Library*, 117.

[21] *RSV* modified. See G. Porton, "Midrash," *ABD* 4:818.

[22] Pesher on Nah 3:4. See Ben Zion Wacholder, "A Qumran Attack on the Oral Exegesis? The Phrase *'šr btlmwd šqrm* in 4Q Pesher Nahum," *RevQ* 5 (1966): 575–78.

Not so the term דרש. Both the verb דרש and its nominal form as well as midrashic method, appear throughout MTA. The verbal form occurs one hundred and thirty-eight times in the DSS, about twenty of which are in MTA. The importance of דרש in CD is reflected in its use as another term for מורה צדק (or) יורה צדק. Opinion differs over whether the דורש התורה in CD 6:7 is identical to the מורה צדק.[23] An analysis of the passages makes it clear, however, that the מורה צדק and the דורש התורה are the same person. A correlation of CD 6:4–8; 7:18–20 and 19:33–20:1 serves to equate these two sobriquets.

> The well is the Torah and its excavators are the penitent of Israel who will exit from the land of Judah and dwell in the land of Damascus, all of whom God called "princes," for [they] all will have interpreted it (the words of Moses) and their glorious (interpretation) cannot be challenged by anyone. And the lawgiver is the *interpreter of the Torah* (דורש התורה) about whom Isaiah said, "One who brings forth an instrument for his works." (CD 6:4b–8a)

> The star is the *interpreter of the Torah* (דורש התורה) who is to come to Damascus, as it is written, "A star has stepped forth from Jacob and a scepter has arisen from Israel." (CD 7:18b–20a)

> Thus are all the people who enter into the new covenant in the land of Damascus but will change (their minds) and act treacherously and turn away from the well of living waters; these shall not be counted in the assembly of the people, and shall not be recorded in their records beginning from the day of the assembling by the *Unique Teacher* (מורה היחיד, i.e. the *Just Teacher*) until the Messiah from Aaron and from Israel will arise. (CD 19:33b–20:1a)

The דורש התורה and the מורה צדק must refer to the same individual since both will serve the community in the *land of Damascus*. What has prompted the speculation that the interpreter of the Torah was distinct from the Just Teacher has been the entrenched opinion that the מורה צדק was a figure of the past while the דורש התורה is futuristic. However, if both represent *eschatological* figures, as I believe they do, there exists no basis for positing two distinct personages.

Nevertheless, the exact denotation of מדרש in the DSS is not clear. As the title of a book it appears on the back of papyrus manuscript 4Q249 as מדרש ספר מושה (Midrash of the book of Moses). Unfortu-

---

23 See Davies who argues that the דורש התורה is not the Teacher of Righteousness. P. Davies, *The Damascus Covenant: An Interpretation of the "Damascus Document"* (JSOTSup 25; Sheffield: JSOT Press, 1983), 18.

nately, very little survives of this large text. Nevertheless, the two-fold occurrence of the word משפט suggests it dealt with legal subject matter. *Rule of the Community* likewise begins with an exhortation, לדרוש אל (to seek God). The use of the infinitive construct here corresponds to Ezra 7:10 which urges the study of the Torah of the Lord.

It is conventional to designate the biblical commentaries known as *pesher* as midrash-like writings. In fact, not only did they use the midrashic hermeneutics, but they also named their works *Midrash*. In our reconstructed text the term מדרש is the first word of the title of the work, with cross references to it throughout the composition. Presumably, the title may also have been used in the lost portions of MTA. The name מדרש התורה האחרון certainly forms an important concept that extends beyond the references. For more discussion see the comments on CD 4:12b–5:19 in section 3.2.1.4.2 below.

Thus, the first portion of the introductory line as reconstructed from [   ]אור נ', although only partially preserved, gives us an inkling of the author's concept of the work as a whole more than two millennia ago. As noted, it divides itself into two parts. It is a midrash on a Torah that has two scriptural canons: 1) the standard canon of the *Tanakh* and 2) a second that is sectarian. The first, which keeps this group apart from the sinners, consists of other writings delivered to Moses, the prophets, and to David. As to Moses, the Pentateuch in both its senses, historical and legal, forms an integral part of Judaism. Yet, it is not the most authoritative text. The other book by Moses, the book of *Jubilees* (although not available for centuries and hidden in the ark) is just as authoritative as the first, if not more so. In fact, often the injunctions found in the sectarian Torah, such as bigamy, incest, marriage of nieces, purity, tithing and leprosy, radically modify the traditions found in the first Torah, the Pentateuch. The name of *Jubilees*, מחלקות העתים (*The Divisions of the Times*) and our author's own work known conventionally as the *Damascus Document*, but whose Hebrew name מדרש התורה האחרון, thus gives a midrash on the Second Torah. In other words, one can understand MTA only if he has before him both Torahs—the traditional first law telling the story of creation up to and including the life of Moses, and the second revealing many of the mysteries not exposed in the first. The introductory lines of MTA disclosing the name of the work can be understood in still another way. Scholars have divided CD into two themes: the admonition (chapters 1–8 and 19–20) and the laws (chapters 9–16). This view seemed plausible prior to the discovery of the fragmentary remains of 4Q266–273. These texts have enriched us by providing the original beginning and ending plus large sections of legal material absent in CD. They also afford us a new view of the book as a whole. Reading MTA as a sequel to *Jubilees* makes us see that a division between admonitory and legal materials is artificial. One needs only to peruse *Jubilees* to note that Torah and admonition are constantly interfused into a single unit, a feature seen also in MTA. Similarly the five passages that begin with the formula "Now hear me," tell us the purpose of these two works is to reveal the wonders of the acts of creation from the *Urzeit* to its *Endzeit*. They provide a key for unlocking not only *Jubilees* and MTA, but to a large extent the Dead Sea Scrolls as a whole, by opening for us the mysteries of the sect's first and second Torah.

Only four words and a single letter survive from line 2: וֹם המו פ ו ה ב . Baumgarten completes the line with רו ולה, to read "until the completion of the fixed time for visitation upon [the spirit of iniquity"]. Although plausible, his proposed reading does not convey the element of time in the extant portion of the line. The words וֹם מו may have been preceded by a temporal clause with lines 1–4a reading as follows.

1:1 [הנה מ רש ה ורה הא רו    ל ב]נֹי אור להנ̇ר מ ר[כי בני]

1:2 [ וש ומ    רו ב רב האר   [    ום מו    /ה\פ ו ה ב]   ה ול]

1:3 [ מ ו ם י י  בול vac ובפ ]ו  אל א  כול מ ש י ה להבי כל]ה]

1:4 ב [בל לוא ישאיר שאירי | למ י י  בול

[Here is "The Midrash on the Eschatological Torah." It is incumbent upon the so]ns of light to keep separate from the wa[ys of the sons of darkness. Now from the Age of (God's) Anger during the desolation of the land] until the completion of the period of remembrance at [the end of the epoch of evil there have arisen the Shifters of the Boundary. But] God, [rememb]ering each and every deed, (and) wreaking hav[oc] against the e[arth, will not leave a remnant] to the Shifters of the Boundary . . .

This rendition would serve to introduce the opposition, the time of their inception and rise to prominence. However, more defensible paleographically, less redundant, and utilizing a greater amount of terminology found in MTA is the reconstruction in our text and translation, a variation of Stegemann's wherein וֹם מו is preceded by a verbal clause specifying further activity incumbent upon the sons of light. Hence, the proposed restoration, ולה הל   ל פי ה ורה (and to walk in accordance with the Torah . . .," a reading resembling

CD 7:7 (19:4), and whose word התורה resumes the force of the primary word of the title in line 1.[24] My reconstruction קץ הרשעה at the end of line 2 and beginning of line 3, based on CD 12:23 and 15:7, preserves the temporal framework of this section. Thus, lines 2 through the beginning of 3 may have read originally ולהתהלך על פי התורה עד תום מועד הפקודה בקץ הרשעה (and to walk in accordance with the Torah until the completion of the period of remembrance at the end of the epoch of wickedness), whose terminology also resembles that of CD 12:23. Read in this manner, the phrase בקץ הרשעה would parallel the words תום מועד הפקודה, the conclusion of the four hundred and ten years following the destruction of Jerusalem (CD 1:5–6), just preceding the anticipated messianic era known elsewhere as the אחרית הימים. Foreshadowed by the very title of the book, מדרש התורה האחרון, lines 2–3a as reconstructed evince the necessity of separation from wickedness and conformity to Torah life, all within the author's chronological framework.

### 3.1.2. *The Downfall of the Opposition (4Q266 F1:3b–5a)*

Baumgarten reconstructs lines 3b–5a as

$$\text{3 [} \qquad \text{ישמי]ד אל את כול מעשיה להבי כל]ה]}$$
$$\text{4 בת]ועי רוח} \qquad \text{[למסיגי גבול וכלה יעשה] לפועלי]}$$
$$\text{5 [ רשעה ]}$$

He translates them "God [will destroy] all her works, bringing rui[n] upon [the errant in spirit ] those who move boundaries, and he will wreak ruin [upon those who work] wickedness . . . " His transcription מעשיה (her works) provides a framework for his restoration רוח עולה (the spirit of iniquity) at the end of line 2 as well as the

---

[24] This is an abbreviation of Stegemann's proposal, ולהתהלך תמים על פי התורה (and to walk uprightly in accordance with the Torah). My rendition may find support in its relation to the following contrastive clause in lines 5b–6a of 4Q266 F11 in the book's finale: וכול המואס במשפטים האלה על פי כול החוקים הנמצאים בתורת מושה . . . (But anyone who despises these precepts which are *in accordance with* all the statutes that are found in *the Torah* of Moses . . . ). This similarity seemingly resembles other features of the book's introduction and conclusion that mirror each other either comparatively or contrastively. Cf. especially the inclusio מדרש התורה האחרון restored in the first and extant in the last lines of the work. See also the supplication of 4Q266 F1 (especially lines 19–25) and 4Q266 F11:9–14a. Within the prayers we may compare the glory of the divine acts of creation (fragment 1:5–6) and the Creator of all (fragment 11:9). In addition, we may parallel the community's commitment to follow the Torah in small and large matters (fragment 1:16b–18a) with the specification that the annual assembly curse those who turn to the right or left from the Torah (fragment 11:16b–18a).

proposed reading ישמיד of line 3. However, the erasure dot above the *yod* of מעשיה excludes a feminine antecedent. In fact, מעשה does not refer primarily to the previous line, but more fully to what follows. Moreover, that the finite verb was likely some form of פקד, whose root appears on the previous line in the word פקודה, finds support from CD 5:15b–16a which reads כי אם למילפנים פקד אל את מעשיהם ויחר אפו בעלילותיהם (For formerly God recalled their deeds and God was angry with their misdeeds). Stegemann's reconstruction כי בחרון אפו in the first lacuna of line 3 resembles ויחר אפו in this same Cairo text, further buttressing my notion that the verb at the end of the lacuna is some form of פקד.[25] The reconstruction in the first lacuna of line 4, לאין שירית ופליטה] למסיגי גבול [ , a variation of לאין שאירית ופליטה למו ואין שרית ופליטה, compares with of CD 2:6b–7a, incorporating orthographic peculiarities of 4Q266. Baumgarten's proposed reading [לפועלי] רשעה from the end of the line to the beginning of line 5 is too redundant. As for the phrase לעוזרי which I insert here, see עוזרי רשעה in 4Q299 F59:4. The short vacat following רשעה, including the noun בנים[26] after the conjunctive adverb ועתה, is paleographically more tenable than עד בוא משיח הצדק (until the coming of the Righteous Messiah) proposed in my article in *HUCA* 69, 33.

The introductory lines 3–5a serve to introduce the polemical aspect of MTA against the Shifters of the Boundary and their associates for misleading Israel. Although scholars plausibly identify the מסיגי (ה)גבול as Pharisees, if accurate, the dating of this group by the author of MTA conflicts with that of modern scholarship. Conventional opinion supposes the Pharisaic movement began during the Antiochan persecution in the second century B.C.E.[27] However, CD 5:20–6:2a (partially preserved in 4Q266 F3ii:7–9 and 4Q267 F2:4–7) definitively places the origin of the מסיגי (ה)גבול following the destruction of the first temple.

5:20 *vacat* ובקץ חרבן הארץ עמדו מסיגי הגבול ויתעו את ישראל
5:21 ותישם הארץ כי דברו פ̇צ̇ו̇[28] סרה על מצות אל ביד משה וגם
6:1 במשיחי הקודש וינבאו שקר להשיב את ישראל מאחרי
6:2 אל

---

25  Cf. also ובחרון אף אל ביושבי הארץ in CD 1:8b–9a.

26  See Stegemann, "Physical Reconstructions," 193.

27  See Albert I. Baumgarten, "Pharisees," *EDSS* 2:657–63.

28  4Q267 F2:5.

Now during the epoch of the desolation of the land (587 B.C.E.) the Shifters of the Boundary arose and misled Israel. And the earth has turned into wilderness because they spoke deviant counsel against the ordinances of God through Moses, and even through the anointed holy ones. And they have prophesied falsehood to make Israel turn away from God. (CD 5:20–6:2a)

The fact that the author's introductory lines begin with the attack on the Boundary-Shifters reveals that polemics constituted an important element of MTA. See my comments on CD 5:20–6:2a for a further explication of the nature of this opposition.

This Mosaic legacy in MTA, so contrary to modern scholarship, corresponds fully with that described in *Mishnah Avot* 1:1 which states,

משה קבל תורה מסיני. ומסרה ליהושע. ויהושע לזקנים. וזקנים לנביאים. ונביאים מסרוה לאנשי כנסת הגדולה. הם אמרו שלשה דברים. הוו מתונים בדין. והעמידו תלמידים הרבה. ועשו סיג לתורה:

Moses received the Torah from Sinai; and he handed it over to Joshua, and Joshua to the elders, and the elders to the prophets; and the prophets handed it over to the leaders of the Great Assembly. They (the leaders of the Great Assembly) uttered three principles: Be lenient in matters of law, produce many disciples, and make a hedge around the Torah. (*Mishnah Avot* 1:1)

While MTA and the Mishnah agree over the time frame, a wide gulf separates the two. According to the sages, the Assembly carried on the legacy of Moses on Sinai. However, in view of MTA, the great leaders left an infamous legacy when they led Israel astray, brought devastation, spoke rebellion and prophesied falsely. Nevertheless, contrary as these two views are with regard to the authority of this assembly, they agree that the assembly or the Pharisees came into being at the time of the destruction of the first temple.

It is important to remember that, although פקד and פקודה are sometimes used negatively as here at the beginning of MTA, they never fully lose their fundamental sense which is positive. After all, the fact that Israel's behavior, whether good or bad, has consequences, shows that her conduct is always under divine scrutiny. God punishes those who mislead the people and their adherents, but will remember the faithful remnant, preserving them. This positive sense of פקד is brought out in Exod 3:16.

לֵךְ וְאָסַפְתָּ אֶת־זִקְנֵי יִשְׂרָאֵל וְאָמַרְתָּ אֲלֵהֶם אֱלֹהֶם יְהוָה אֱלֹהֵי אֲבֹתֵיכֶם
נִרְאָה אֵלַי אֱלֹהֵי אַבְרָהָם יִצְחָק וְיַעֲקֹב לֵאמֹר פָּקֹד פָּקַדְתִּי
אֶתְכֶם וְאֶת־הֶעָשׂוּי לָכֶם בְּמִצְרָיִם

> Go gather the elders of Israel and say to them, "The Lord God of
> Abraham has appeared to me, the God of Abraham, Isaac and Jacob,
> saying, '*Surely I have remembered you* and what has been done to you in
> Egypt.'"

Thus, the oppression in Egypt had positive consequences. Although
the sons of Jacob had suffered oppression and, according to the
tradition of MTA had erred (compare CD 3:4b–12a), walking in
the stubbornness of their heart against God's commandments, God
would deal kindly with them. Here too at the beginning of MTA,
the anticipated destruction of the Pharisees and those siding with
them would bring redemption to the remainder of Israel as stated
immediately below.

### 3.1.3. *The Promise to Reveal the Mysteries of History (4Q266 F1:5b–9)*[29]

Whereas lines 1–5a present the author's introductory remarks in the
third person, beginning with line 5b the document changes into an
oral address given by a master to his disciples or a wider fellowship. The formula לִ֯י שמעו בנים ועתה ["But now O children, hear]
me . . ." and four other similar clauses repeated throughout this work
draw on Isa 51, a passage wherein God summons the returned exiles
of Israel who know and pursue righteousness to heed His Torah.[30]
For a work that apparently imitates this style in MTA, see 4Q298.
Compare fragment 1-2i:1–3.

1   [דבר]י֯ משכיל אשר דבר לכול בני שחר האזי֯[נו לי כ]ול אנשי לבב
2   [ורוד]פֿי צדק הבי֯[נ]ו֯ במלי ומבֿקשי אמונה שֿ[מע]ו֯ למלי בכול
3   [מ]ו֯צֿא שפֿתֿ[י ]י֯ וי֯[ל]רעים דר[ש]ו֯[י א]ל֯ה וֿהֿשֿיבֿו֯ לאורח [חיים

---

²⁹ This section could have extended beyond line 9. Little of lines 10–15 has
survived.

³⁰ שְׁמְעוּ אֵלַי רֹדְפֵי צֶדֶק מְבַקְשֵׁי יְהוָה (Hear Me you who pursue righteousness, who
seek the Lord)—v. 1a; הַקְשִׁיבוּ אֵלַי עַמִּי וּלְאוּמִּי אֵלַי הַאֲזִינוּ כִּי תוֹרָה מֵאִתִּי תֵצֵא (Hearken
to Me My people and give ear to Me, My nation, for the Torah issues forth from
Me)—v. 4a; שְׁמְעוּ אֵלַי יֹדְעֵי צֶדֶק עַם תּוֹרָתִי בְלִבָּם (Hear Me you who know righteousness,
O people in those heart is My Torah)—v. 7a.

[The word]s of the Sage which he spoke to all the Sons of Dawn: Hear[ken to me a]ll men of heart. [And you who purs]ue righteousness, understand my words. And you seekers of truth, h[ear] my words, everything [ut]tered from [my] lip[s. And] you who understand, inter[pret] [t]hem and turn [to the path] of life.

Repeated four more times in our work, the verb שמעו in this clause is always connected with the conjunctive adverb ועתה. The five formulas vary slightly but as a whole make up a structural unity.

1. The first, partially reconstructed, reads:

5 רשע=ה [ ] ועתה בנים שמעו[ ] לי ואודיעה לכם מֹעֹ[שי אל]

6 הנורא[ים בגבורות] פלאו וֹאֲספר{ר}ֹה לכֹ[ם נהיות עולם הנסתרות]

7 מאנוש

[ But now O children, hear] me and I will make known to you the awesome ac[ts of God] along with His [miraculous] powers. And I will relate to yo[u the events of eternity hidden] from man.[31] (4Q266 F1:5b–7)

2. The second reads:

vacat 1 ועתה שמעו ⳑ[32] כֹּל יודעי צדק ובינו במעשי

2 אל

And now, heed me all you who know righteousness and discern the acts of God. (CD 1:1–2a)

3. The third reads:

2 ועתה שמעו אלי כל באי ברית ואגלה אזנכם בדרכי

3 רשעים

And now, heed me all who are entering the covenant and I will reveal to you the ways of the wicked. (CD 2:2–3a)

---

[31] Baumgarten proposes reading [ועתה שמע]ו לי ואודיעה לכם מֹהֹ[שבות אל] הנורא[ות which he translates "[ And now hearken unto] me, and I will make known to you the awful [devices (?) of God. . .]" However, what remains of the second letter following the medial מ resembles more the top portion of an ע than it does that of a ה. Hence, our reading מֹעֹ[שי אל] הנורא[ים. Moreover, the similarly constructed passages CD 1:1 and 2:14 have מעשי אל in their formulation.

[32] 4Q268 F1:9.

4. The fourth reads:

14 vacat ועתה בנים שמעו [א]ל־<sup>33</sup> ואגלה עיניכם לראות ולהבין במעשי

15 אל

And now, hear me O children that I may open your eyes to see and
to understand the acts of God. (CD 2:14–15a)

5. The final formula, slightly more expansive, may be reconstructed
as follows:

19 ועתה שמעו לי כל יודעי צדק ו[בינו] תור[ת] אל בלבבכם ואגלה]

20 לכם דרכי חיים ונתיבות שחת אפתחה ל[עיניכם

And now, hear me all who know righteousness (truth) and [discern] the
Tora[h of God in you heart. And I will reveal] to you the ways of life
and the paths of hell I will open for [your eyes]. (4Q270 F2ii:19–20)

These five formulas have common features. 1) As stated above, they
begin with the conjunctive adverb ועתה. 2) Speaking authoritatively
in the first person through the words שמעו לי, the author addresses
an audience of either disciples or a wider fellowship. In the first
formula the author promises to reveal to them the acts of God and
the hidden events of eternity, bridging both the past and the future.
Three of these fives passages seem to contain the phrase מעשי אל
(the acts of God). By the acts of God, the author means creation,
perhaps alluding to the twenty-two acts of creation in *Jub.* 2. In the
second he addresses them as those who know righteousness or truth
and tells them of these acts. In the third he salutes them as those
who are ready to enter the covenant and is about to tell them of
the ways of the wicked. In the fourth he speaks to them as a father
or master who once again will reveal to them the acts of history. In
the beginning of the fifth formula the author reiterates what he said
in the second and additionally promises to reveal to them the ways
of life for the righteous and the paths of hell for the wicked.

   Taken together, the author's five addresses reveal an I-thou relationship between the addressor and the addressees. The addressor is a
knower of mysteries. He is cognizant of how God created the world,
the epochs of history, and the ways of the righteous and the wicked,
which he promises to reveal to his disciples and sympathizers. What he
does not tell is whence he got this knowledge. It could be that the title

---

<sup>33</sup> [א]ל֯֯ 4Q268 F1:9.

מדרש התורה האחרון resolves this problem. By the phrase "Eschatological Torah" our writer means the mysteries revealed in *Jubilees*, the second Torah, which along with the traditional Pentateuch forms the תורת מושה (the Torah of Moses), as will be shown more fully below in comments on CD 16:1b–6a (see entry *c* under section 3.2.2.9.9.1.4).[34]

Baumgarten reads [וֶאֲסּפּר‹ר›ה לכ]ם אשר נסתרו} in lines 6b–7a. My reconstruction [וֶאֲסּפּר‹ר›ה לכ]ם נהיות עולם הנסתרות] (And I will relate to [you the events of eternity hidden]), based on similar language in CD 13:8, provides an object for the verb and embraces the range of God's wonders from creation to the time of judgment. As stated above, a reading of *Jub.* 1–6 lies behind this introductory section of MTA and permeates the work from beginning to end. Lines 6b–7a demonstrate that the author's own generation stands on the threshold of a new era where man finally perceives perennial mysteries concerning the nature of God and man. They describe the reduction of human longevity, a theme developed at length in *Jub.* 23, but implicit in the age span of the early biblical figures. Although the extant portions of these lines do not explicate the cause of man's increased mortality, CD 10:7b–10a offers a rationale for the shortening of human life:

ואל יתיצב עוד מבן | 7
ששים שנה ומעלה לשפוט את העדה כי במעל האדם | 8
מעטו ימו ובחרון אף אל ביושבי הארץ אמר לה[ס]‹ר›[י] את | 9
דעתם עד אשר‹‹ לא ישלימו את ימיהם | 10

No one who is over sixty years of age shall hold the office of judging the congregation, for when man[37] became corrupted his longevity was reduced. And when God's wrath burned against the earth's inhabitants He determined to weaken their mental abilities so that they would not be able to reach the fullness of their lifetime. (CD 10:7b–10a)

The onus for man's diminishment falls on man himself and represents God's wrath against the inhabitants of the land. CD does

---

[34] For an explication of this view see also my article entitled "The 'Torah of Moses' in the Dead Sea Scrolls: An Allusion to the Book of Jubilees" in *Proceedings of the Thirteenth World Congress of Jewish Studies* (Jerusalem, 2001).

[35] לה[ס]יר 4Q266 F8iii:8.

[36] 4Q270 F6iv:19.

[37] Cook (*The Dead Sea Scrolls*, 68) translates "Adam" rather than "man," thereby giving the text a different thrust wherein diminishment of years relates to the consequences of *Adam's* original sin where God limited the duration of man's life. Yet, this rendition does not explain man's further reduction to seventy years (Ps 90:10) from the hundreds of years present in the early biblical figures.

not specify the occasion for the burning wrath of God. A more developed explanation, however, appears in *Jub.* 23:8–9 and 26, passages which the author of MTA never directly cites:

> (8) And he (Abraham) lived three jubilees and four weeks of years, one hundred and seventy-five years, and completed the days of his life, being old and full of days. (9) For the days of the forefathers, of their life, were nineteen jubilees; and after the Flood they began to grow less than nineteen jubilees, and to decrease in jubilees, and to grow old quickly, and to be full of their days by reason of manifold tribulation and the wickedness of their ways, with the exception of Abraham . . . (26) And in those days the children shall begin to study the laws, and to seek the commandments, and to return to the path of righteousness. And the days shall begin to grow many and increase amongst those children of men till their days draw nigh to one thousand years.[38]

The story of the flood marks the watershed point of God's wrath where man's wickedness diminishes his longevity. However, a spiritual renewal in the eschatological era will return the period of man's life-span back to one thousand years, even extending it beyond its former limit (*Jub.* 23:26–27).

As reconstructed, lines 6b–7a of our text invoke *Jub.* 23 in two ways. 1) They allude to lines 8–9 cited above which state that human longevity was reduced because of mankind's wickedness before the flood. 2) Just as *Jub.* 23:26 promises that the study of the Torah will increase human longevity, so the pledge to relate to the community the events of eternity hidden from mankind further suggests that when the righteous observe the Eschatological Torah, ancestral longevity will be renewed once again. This is the first example in MTA where the author uses *Jubilees* to bolster his argument, which as we shall see, he does repeatedly. *Jubilees* then is not just a convenient source for this writer, but a pivotal instrument in the composition of the book. It suggests further, that much of MTA rests on it. Stegemann provides the following alternative restoration beginning with the first lacuna of line 6, suggesting that the "wisdom of heaven" is descriptive of the book of *Jubilees* or, perhaps, *Enoch*.[39]

---

[38] R. H. Charles, trans., *The Book of Jubilees or the Little Genesis* (London: Adam and Charles Black, 1902), 145, 149.

[39] Stegemann, "Physical Reconstructions," 193, 195.

6    וגבורות] פלאו אֲסֻפְרֲדה לכ]ם ולוא נסתרה עוד[

7    מאנוש] חכמת ש[מים אשר חי בֹ[ו]לֹ[ל] אוהבה . . .

I will relate to yo[u] his [mighty] wonders. [Now the wisdom of he]aven
through which eve[ry]one [who loves] lives [had not yet been hidden]
from mankind.[40]

The reconstructed amplification in lines 7b–8a, [ואין אחר זולתו להביט]
בעמקתֿ] רזיו ([There is no one but He who can fathom] the profundities of [His mysteries]), is taken from 1QS 11:18–19, which forms
part of a supplicatory praise. This presumes that our text served as
the source for this passage in *Rule of the Community*. Beginning with
[    ]חֿק[            ] in line 8 through [        ] חתם of line 9, we
continue with wording based upon two anterior texts from *Hodayot*[a]
(1QH[a] 21:12–13 and 4Q427 F7i:18–19), both containing laudatory
praise of God. The supposition that *Hodayot* preceded MTA rests on
the fact that nothing in it reflects a borrowing from either MTA or
works such as *Rule of the Community* and the pesher commentaries. The
word חתם (He has sealed), telling us that God has withheld from
man mysteries that will be revealed, may echo the incident told below
in CD 5:2–5 (see commentary section 3.2.1.4.2.2.2). Cognates of
חתם and גלה reappear in this passage as החתום and נגלה, describing
the book of the Torah of Moses concealed by Eleazar, Joshua and
the elders, but revealed in the time of Zadok. Thus, the words [חֿק]ק
(He has etc[hed]) and חתם allude once again to the formation of
Moses' Torah, the Pentateuch, on the one hand and to *Jubilees* on
the other.[41] What MTA supposes here in our text is that all mysteries
belong to God. Yet the speaker feels confident that the unfolding
of God's acts (line 5) will be realized by humanity in the messianic
epoch, a fitting opening for the material contained in MTA. God
reduced human longevity but length of life will be restored once
again. Those who have stumbled will be raised up. He sealed up His
mysteries, (withholding them) from the patriarchs and the prophets,
hidden things that He will reveal to humanity. The first words of CD,
וֹעֹתֹה שמעו לי in 4Q268 F1:9, have therefore an antecedent context
in MTA's introduction, projecting the work as eschatological from

---

[40]  The translation is mine.
[41]  See comments on CD 5:2–5 in section 3.2.1.4.2.2.2 below.

the beginning of the composition to its end. Stegemann, however, furnishes the following reading for lines 7b–8a.[42]

7                       [ואבינה אתכם]

8    בעמקת] כול רז[י הקוד]ֿש אשר היו נסתרים מקדם . . .

[And I will give you understanding] into the profundities [of all the] hol[y myster]ies [which have been hidden since antiquity . . . ][43]

Whatever followed our reconstruction of line 9, a complex problem confronts us now. Lines 9–14, represented by sub-fragments *a-b*, could be left blank as an irretrievable loss as in the preliminary edition, editio princeps and subsequent publishings (except for that of Stegemann, discussed below in a note). Or, as Baumgarten conjectures, Milik's combination of sub-fragments *c-f*, possibly five partial lines, may belong here.[44] As Baumgarten and a few subsequent publishers have done, I have chosen to leave lines 10–14 unrestored. Positioning sub-fragments *c-f* here would greatly distance the prayer surrounding their first line from the extant supplication further down the page preserved in fragments *a-b*.[45] Instead, I locate these pieces between lines 20 and 25 of fragments *a-b*.

---

   [42] Stegemann, "Physical Reconstructions," 193, 195–96. He modifies Milik's earlier reading, הקוד[ש   ° [ , in line 8.

   [43] The translation is mine.

   [44] Baumgarten, DJD XVIII, 34.

   [45] Restoring the first line of this small composite as ל[וֿחות ה]ברית (the t]ablets of the [covenant), Stegemann positions portions of it as follows from lines 9–13.

8                              [כי אל]

9               חתם [את ל]וֿחות ה]ברית

10             [אשר [צֿוֿה ביד מוש]ה

11   [על התב]ֿל הֿוֿ היֿום [אשר יפקד אל את הארץ והצדיקים]

12    [יספרו בש[מ]חה את מע]שֿי אל הגדולים

13            [     ] דֿ̇רֿ̇ך אל נב]

[ . . . for God] has sealed [the t]ablets of the [covenant . . . which] he commanded through Mose[s . . . upon the eart]h. That is the day [that God will punish the earth; but the righteous will relate with j[oy] the [great] ac[ts of God . . . ] (The translation is mine.)

In contrast to Stegemann, I restore סל]וֿחות of the editio princeps to the first line, a word attested in CD 2:4.

### 3.1.4. *Supplication (4Q266 F1:14–25)*[46]

The suggested reading of lines 14b–15 is a paraphrase of what
survives in *Rule of the Community* (1QS 9:26–10:6; 4Q256 19:4 and
4Q258 9:3). What is significant about these passages is that the
phrase זכרון במועד, generally translated as "memorial (or reminder)
during (a) season," is instead construed in the DSS as a celebratory
prayer through the offering of lips. 1QS 9:26b–10:6a reads:

(9:26). . . [בתרומת] שפתים יברכנו  (10:1) עם קצים אשר חקקא ברשית
ממשלת אור עם תקופתו ובהאספו על מעון חוק ברשית  (10:2) אשמורי
חושך כיא יפתח אוצרו וישתהו עלת ובתקופתו עם האספו מפני אור
באופיע  (10:3) מאורות מזבול קודש עם האספם למעון כבוד במבוא
מועדים לימי חודש יחד תקופתם עם  (10:4) מסרותם זה לזה בהתחדשם
יום גדול לקודש קודשים ואות נ למפתח חסדיו עולם לראשי
(10:5) מועדים בכול קץ נהיה ברשית ירחים למועדיהם וימי קודש
בתכונם לזכרון במועדיהם  (10:6) {°°} תרומת שפתים הברכנו
כחוק חרות לעד . . .

> [With the offerings of] lips He will bless us during the times which He
> had legislated at the beginning of the dominion of light with its (annual)
> cycle, and at its gathering into its assigned abode at the beginning of
> the vigils of darkness when He opens His storehouse and designates it
> as burnt offerings, and in its cycle at its ingathering from the light at the
> appearance of the luminaries from the sacred dwelling at their gathering
> into the glorious dwelling place at the entrance of the seasons on the
> days of the month together with their circuits with their turnings one
> to another when they are renewed (during) the great day for the holy
> of holies, and as a sign to the opening of His eternal favors, for the
> beginnings of the festivals during all the future epochs at the beginning
> of the new moons, for their festivals and sacred days in their setting.
> With prayers during their festivals with an offering of lips (I) will bless
> Him according to a statute engraved forever. (1QS 9:26b–10:6a)

These passages presumably reference the so-called sectarian calendar
detailed in *Jub.* 6. MTA and *Rule of the Community* suggest an additional
aspect, alluding to the cosmic order since creation: how the monthly
and festive seasons invariably recur not only on the same day of the
month, but also on the same day of the week. Moreover, set as part
of the creation, the festivals fall on the fourth day of the week, which
always begins the new year.

---

[46] This section could have started before line 14, as virtually nothing of lines
10–14 has survived.

Aside from their calendric importance, the festive days had liturgical significance. The authors of MTA and *Rule of the Community* promise a special liturgy for each of these festive days (תרומת שפתים). Column 27:2–10 of 11QPs^a (11Q5) ascribes to David 4,050 compositions, each of which functioned as a daily and festive psalm. The fragmentary remains of the *Songs of the Sabbath Sacrifice* (4Q400–407) remind us that, in addition to psalmic works, there also existed a kind of Ezekielian composition that could be called mystical, assigned for specific Sabbaths during the year. Note that the term עלת in 1QS 10:2 cited above, which is generally rendered as an extension of the preposition על, may instead be celestial songs connected with the burnt offerings.

The surviving words of lines 15b–18a plausibly continue the affirmative spirit of the prayer in the preceding lines wherein the text, molded into the first person plural seen in הודיענו נא in line 19, may have read "[And we will hearken] to the voice of Moses, [ . . . and we will not go around] slandering [those] who seek refuge [in Him (God)], God's commandments [and in His covenant . . . ]"[47] Our reading [בחוס[י בו (compare Ps 2:12) diverges from the editor's transcription בחוק[י] (against the statute[s]).[48] The phrase קטנה וגדולה (in small or large matters) is not recorded elsewhere in the DSS.[49] However, it echoes the concluding lines of MTA. There, the annual assembly on Pentecost is enjoined to curse those who turn to the right or left from the Torah (4Q266 F11:16b–18a). When paired with "God's commandments," our text expresses the need to embrace the totality of the Torah.

As presented, lines 18b–25 continue this lengthy supplication. The surviving words הודיענו נא (please let us know) on line 19 suggest that lines 18b–19a paraphrase the prayer of Moses in Exod 33:13. Our author and his audience, like Moses, wish to know the way God is acting, divine acts being quoted three or four times in MTA.[50] The words שיחתך אם (meditating about You when) at the beginning of line 20 may echo Ps 119:97. Note also that the underlined אם calls attention to the first extant word of 4Q267 fragment 1 and subse-

---

[47] Note also the first person plural occurring throughout the concluding prayer of the document (4Q266 F11:9–14a).

[48] I thank David Maas for suggesting the reading בחוס[י.

[49] Genesis 48:19 contains these two terms in the clause אָחִיו הַקָּטֹן יִגְדַּל מִמֶּנּוּ (his younger brother shall be greater than he), however not as a merism as apparently here.

[50] Cf. CD 1:1b–2a; 2:14b–15a; 13:17b–18a. In addition the phrase מעשי אל likely formed the end of 4Q266 F1:5.

quently 4Q268 fragment 1. The parallelism continues in the letters
דתה of עמדתה on line 21 of 4Q266 F1. As suggested above, but with
one alteration, Milik's combination of sub-fragments *c-f* plausibly
restores the ends of lines 20–25. Our restoration utilizing line 1
of these pieces parallels CD 2:4, only with a pronominal change.
The phrase עמדתה ותתבונן (You have attended to and analyzed) in
line 21 echoes the sapiential wording found in Job 30:20 and 37:14
(אֲשַׁוַּע אֵלֶיךָ וְלֹא תַעֲנֵנִי עָמַדְתִּי וַתִּתְבֹּנֶן בִּי "I cry out to you but you
do not answer me; I stand up but you did not consider me" and
עֲמֹד וְהִתְבּוֹנֵן נִפְלְאוֹת אֵל "Stand still and consider God's wonders"). The
verbal root בין (to perceive) recurs twice again three lines later. All in
all MTA employs this verb some eighteen times, making this work in
part at least a sapiential composition. Related wisdom terminology
occurs throughout it; the verb גלה (to reveal) appears fourteen times,
the noun דעת (knowledge) four times and דעה once, the participle
נהיה (event) three times, the nouns רז (secret) and בינה (insight) twice
each, שיחה (meditation) once (in the preceding line), חכמה (wisdom)
once and the phrase ידע דרך (to know the way of) once (compare
הודיענו נא א]ת דרככה in line 19 of our text). This similar vocabulary tends
to support the supposition that MTA has a sapiential flavor. Moreover,
as will be explained below, it cites three times the book of Haguy, a
major sapiential composition, associating it with the foundations of
the Torah. Thus, our text, whose author in alluding to Exod 33:13
pleads to know the ways of God, gives us a glimpse into his mental
makeup through his fusion of Torah and wisdom. Extending back to
אין אחר זולתו להביט] בעמקת[ רזיו] of lines 7–8, the material here too
bears sapiential characteristics. Line 21 continues the sapiential element
of this work by linking the laws of Moses with wisdom.

Important as wisdom is in MTA, it does not match the work's
more general theme of the observance of the law. The first line of
the book contains the phrase להנזֹר מֹ(ן) "to keep separate from . . . "
The sense of the separation here is that of keeping a distance from
those of Israel who do not follow the Torah as commanded. Attacks
on the opposition in the DSS are generally legal. Thus the famous
*Miqṣat Maʿaśê ha-Torah* which deals with infringements on Jewish laws
and customs. Likewise, in MTA's introduction the argument against
the opposition rests upon their departing from the rules of the Torah
in minor or major matters (lines 17–18a).

It is fashionable among scrollists to separate the Damascus Document from other scrolls, in that it is allegedly divided into admonitions

and legal material. However, this acute separation is a modernistic tendency. In fact, in my opinion, the admonitory material is full of law. The observances of the commandments of Moses appear twice on this introductory page. Terms such as מושה, which occurs about fifteen times (two of which are on the first page), תורה, appearing forty some times and the numerous occurrences of אמר citing legal texts make up a vocabulary which fills the so-called admonitory passages. For example, CD 4:15–5:10 intermingles biblical citations, partisan polemics and legal subject matter. The main focus of these texts is זנות (whoredom), particularized by bigamy and the marriage of one's niece. In fact, niece marriage is repeated in line 16 of the list of offenses of 4Q270 F2ii. The division between admonition and legal material is also objectionable on other grounds. As is generally recognized, the admonition is full of polemics against the sect's opposition. The primary cause for these arguments is that the adversary does not follow the law as it is prescribed in the Torah. Thus, if we look deeper into the problem, the division between admonition and laws as two distinct parts of MTA is superficial.

The word ישיבו in line 22 was likely preceded by the infinitive absolute שוב, since it is attested in 4Q267 F1:4. Baumgarten, following Milik, transcribes lines 3–4 of sub-fragments *c-f* as follows:

3 ‏[°‏שה [הא̇ד̇ם]°°ל[

4 ‏[ מחה את מע]ה [ להבי ]

3) ] man [    ] 4) blot out her [    ] to bring [

For spatial reasons I have moved the independent sub-fragment *f* (‏שה°) directly over (‏ה להבי) to the right of the interconnected pieces *c-e* to connect with lines 22 and 23 of the larger fragment *a*, for the reading ‏ומי קד̇ו̇[ש כמוכ]ה להבי [כלה] and ישיבו את א̇[שר צוה מ̇[ו̇]שה. Lines 21b–22 of our text then continue in the wisdom style, imploring the sincerity of those who express repentance.

The reconstruction ‏[ונחנו מ]ה in 4Q267 F1:5, inserted into line 22b of our text, draws on Exod 16:7–8. The phrase עפר ואפר (dust and ashes) immediately following the above reconstruction occurs in Gen 18:27, וְאָנֹכִי עָפָר וָאֵפֶר (but I am but dust and ashes), Job 30:19, וָאֶתְמַשֵּׁל כֶּעָפָר וָאֵפֶר (and I am like dust and ashes) and 42:6, עַל־עָפָר וָאֵפֶר וְנִחַמְתִּי (and I repent in dust and ashes). Our suggested composite is incorporated into the author's supplications. As a metaphor, "dust and ashes" expresses man's mortality and insignficance when compared to God (compare 1QH^a 18:5; 4Q301 F4:3; 4Q511 F126:2). The reading in line 23, כמוכ[ה‏ קד[ו]ש‏ ומי (and who is as holy [as Yo]u?) rests on Exod 15:11 and Ps 111:9. As to the wording לחבי [כלה, see line 3 above. Moreover it coheres with the continuing word, מחה (to wipe out), in sub-fragment *b*. This line is one more element of the nomistically based polemical stance seen in the prefatory material and exposed throughout MTA as a whole. MTA here uses vocabulary of the account of the giants and the flood in Gen 6–8 (*Jub.* 5–7), also described below in CD 2:14–21. In line 25 of our text, as reconstructed, the author praises God for leaving a remnant of humanity when destroying mankind.

The reconstruction in line 24, התבונ[נתה ‹ה‹לוא הבינותה אל משכל]ים (You have anal[yzed, and surely You have imparted understanding to the sage]s), gains support from 4Q418 F81+81a:17.

התבונן מודה ומיד כול משכילכה הוסף לקח]

Investigate well and by every one of your sages add instruction.

Baumgarten, followed by Martínez-Tigchelaar, understand the לוא preceding הבינותה restored from 4Q267 F1:6 as a negative, with the resultant translation, "you did not understand."[51] Such a resolution of this material is unlikely. Nowhere in the Jewish tradition do we find an assertion denying God's insight into human affairs. Hence, our addition of ה to form an emphatic positive, a feature appearing several lines later in 4Q268 F1:1.

Buttressing the positioning of the sub-fragments *c–f* near the end of fragment 1 is the coherence of לדבר ר‹א›ב‹ר in line 5 of these mini-pieces and ובפ‹י[ותכה in line 25 of sub-fragment *a*. Juxtaposed, they provide a logical sequence to the prayer as will be shown below. Line 24 depicts how God imparts learning to humanity. The acquisitions of prophets and sages are ultimately subjected to that which God imparts to mankind. The central idea in the so-called מוסר texts (4Q415–418) of understanding and thought evidently occurs here. As will be discussed, MTA three times credits the book of Haguy mentioned in 4Q417 F1i:16–17.[52] The tandem use of the root בין dramatizes God's dissection of human behavior and thought.

Apparently metathesized as ובפויתכה in 4Q267 F1:7, the restoration ובפ‹י[ותכה in line 25 of 4Q266 F1 literally means "in your mouths."[53]

---

[51] Martínez and Tigchelaar, *Scrolls Study Edition*, vol. 1, 599.

[52] J. Strugnell, D. J. Harrington, and T. Elgvin, in consultation with J. A. Fitzmyer, *Sapiential Texts, Part 2: Cave 4.XXIV* (DJD XXXIV; Oxford: Clarendon, 1999), 3ff. Strugnell refers to these documents as a work with sapiential themes.

Note that the biblical plural of פֶּה (פִּיוֹת or פִּיפִיוֹת), meaning a dou-
ble-mouthed (bladed) sword, here refers to a double (or sincere)
prayer. Thus the restoration וּבִפִּי]וֹתחכה נודך, when taken together with
line 25, portrays that prayer is an expression of God's own words
and attributes. Praise and prayer are not an artificial creation of
humans. The basis for the supplication is evidently God's history of
forgiving sin, both unintentional and intentional.[54] Our reconstruction
אשמתם (?)[ח]טֿאת[ה] ([the s]in of their guilt) draws on the atonement for
inadvertent sin (שְׁגָגָה) explicated in Lev 4:2–3 and 5:15–18. Note also
the parallel phrase עֲוֺן אַשְׁמָה (the iniquity of guilt) in Lev 22:14–16 which
also deals with sin committed unwittingly. Restored from 4Q267 F1:8,
[ולא תשמיד כול בשר ובריאה] (and You do not destroy all flesh and
creation) evidently refers to the intentional sins of humanity preceding the flood wherein God did not destroy mankind completely. The
word פיות may allude to the psalms. The author and his associates
are praising God for leaving a remnant. Tacitly, this foreshadows
Israel's eschatological role in the next pericope. After all, had the
flood left no remnant there would have been no Israel and time itself
would have ceased.

Much of the vocabulary in this section, such as ידע דרך (occurring
once),[55] בין (three times)[56] and שיחה (once) acknowledges God's wisdom in His acts and that He imparted to humanity elements of His
wisdom.[57] This links our text to the above cited 4Q415–418, what I
understand to be the book of Haguy, three times cited in MTA.

### 3.1.5. *A Tribute to the "Divisions of the Times": The Calendation of the Book of Jubilees (4Q268 F1:1–8 / 4Q266 F2i:1–6a)*

At this point, 4Q266 F1, the main manuscript and 4Q267 F2, its
more fragmented but very helpful supplement, ends. 4Q268 F1 now
becomes the main source, supplemented by 4Q266 F2. Let me remind
the reader that 4Q268 diverges in its orthography from that of CD
and the other Cave 4 texts. It tends to lengthen third person mas-

---

53  Abegg transcribes ובפויתכה in 4Q267 F1:7; Ben Zion Wacholder and Martin
G. Abegg, Jr., reconstructors and eds., *A Preliminary Edition of the Unpublished Dead Sea
Scrolls. The Hebrew and Aramaic Texts from Cave Four. Fascicle One* (Washington, D.C.: Biblical Archaeology Society, 1991), 28. Baumgarten transcribes וּבִ‹‹[ in 4Q266 F1:25.
54  The restoration תסלח follows from ורוב סל‹חות] restored to line 20.
55  הודיענו נא א[ת דרככה.
56  הבינותה, התבונ]נתה, and ותתבונן.
57  The word מעשה occurs repeatedly throughout this work.

culine plural pronominal suffixes. For instance, בם is spelled במה.
What remains in these two documents generally overlaps, corresponding to each other. There are exceptions, however. As far as
we can tell, 4Q268 appears to contain approximately two lines of
text absent in 4Q266.[58]

That line 1 of 4Q268 F1 likely begins with the title of *Jubilees*,
מחלקות העתים (*The Divisions of Times*) (compare CD 16:3), is supported
by content and grammar. That this phrase was apparently present in
our text becomes evident from the close relationship between *Jubilees* and our remnants. 4Q268 F1 lines 3 and 8 contain two phrases
referring to the future: [את עד] אשר יבוא במה and עד מה יבוא במה.
Baumgarten notes that these lines correspond to what Josephus reports
about the Essenes as foretellers of what is to come.[59]

That מחלקות העתים begins the page is buttressed also by the feminine gender of the extant word אחרונות immediately following the
lacuna. In my opinion, the author of *Jubilees* presents his work as a
Super Canon, vis-à-vis the traditional five books of Moses.[60] That
MTA accepts this view is attested in CD 16:2–3 wherein *Jubilees*
is considered מדוקדק (literally "most precise" or "perfect"), that is
to say, more precise and perfect than the traditional canon. Since
Louis Ginzberg, some scholars such as Rabin have speculated that
these lines are a late intrusion. Ginzberg and Baumgarten have also
tended to minimize the importance of these lines by rendering the
twice-repeated מדוקדק respectively as "exactly given" and "specified"
instead of what is contextually required—"perfect."[61]

Much of MTA is not only dependent on *Jubilees*, but can best be
understood as its amplification. Note, for example, the importance

---

[58] Line 1 of 4Q266 F2i ends with the words עד אשר. Based on the location
of this same אשר on line 3 of 4Q268 Fi, we might plausibly reconstruct line 1 of
4Q266 F2i as [עד אשר ואת [ס]האחרונות ואת הראישונים את אל והגיד ובריאה [בשר, to
continue on line 2 with . . . [כי אין [לעולם בם יבוא], a combination of the middle of
lines 3 and 4 of 4Q268 F1.

[59] Baumgarten, DJD XVIII, 120. Cf. Josephus, *J.W.* 2.159 (Thackeray, LCL).

[60] For a defense of this view see my above cited paper, "The 'Torah of Moses'
in the Dead Sea Scrolls" as well as my article "*Jubilees* as the Super Canon: Torah-
Admonition versus Torah-Commandment," in *Legal Texts and Legal Issues: Proceedings
of the Second Meeting of the International Organization for Qumran Studies: Cambridge 1995* (ed.
M. Bernstein, F. García Martínez and J. Kampen; Leiden: Brill, 1997), 195–211.
See also my comments on CD 16:2–4.

[61] Louis Ginzberg, *An Unknown Jewish Sect* (New York: The Jewish Theological
Seminary of America, 1976), 95; Baumgarten in Charlesworth, ed., *Damascus Document*, 39.

of ראשונים, אחרונים and עד אשר יבוא in both *Jubilees* (compare 1:4 and 26) and our document. Moreover, the book's presumed title מדרש התורה האחרון emphasizes the end of time and the beginning of the future, elements also echoed in our passage.

What is more certain, however, is the end of line 1 and the beginning of line 2 of our text. "Surely they (the Divisions of the Eschatological Epochs) will occur" points to the fact that the calendric system should be celebrated according to what is prescribed in *Jubilees*.[62] Any change in the calendar constitutes a violation of divine law. The reckoning of time is unalterable. Our restoration [ככול ימיו וכ]ול [תקופות מועדי]ו ([according to all its days and a]ll [the cycles of] i[ts festivals]) is based in part upon terminology from lines 4b–5a which explicitly affirms the author's agreement with the polemics of *Jub.* 6:32.[63]

> And command thou the children of Israel that they observe the years according to this reckoning—three hundred and sixty-four days, and (these) will constitute a complete year, and they will not disturb its time from its days and from its feasts; for everything will fall out in them according to their testimony, and they will not leave out any day nor disturb any feasts.[64] (*Jub.* 6:32)

Our reading in lines 4b–5, כי אי[ן] לקדם [ו]ל[א]חר ממועדיה]מה ומחודשיהמה ומ[שב]תות[ם] ([since one may neith]er advance [nor post]pone th[eir] festivals, [their months or] their Sabb[aths]), if correct, contains the jubilean fixation of the days of the month and implicitly disputes the Pharisaic calendation of adding a month to certain years.[65] Thus, the first day of the year always falls on a Wednesday and the Day of Atonement on a Friday, etc. It is an ideal calendar and diverges radically from standard Jewish and general reckoning of time. The Gregorian year, on the other hand, consists of 365.24 days. The date of January 1st shifts by one day every year, for instance from Sunday to Monday in a year, and every four years by two days. In the nineteen-year cycle of Jewish calendation the days of the week change

---

[62] Although Baumgarten does not reconstruct the first word of line 2, he does presume it in his notes. Baumgarten, DJD XVIII, 120.

[63] For תקופת מועדים (or תקופות מועדים) cf. 1QS 10:6; 1QH[a] 20:8 and 4Q427 F8ii:14.

[64] Charles, 56–57.

[65] An example of intercalation is 2 Chr 30, which documents Hezekiah's postponing the Passover to the second month.

radically. Thus, during the intercalary years an additional month of thirty days is added.

This Pharisaic calendation was objectionable to the sectarians. By contrast, in that advocated by *Jubilees* and here in MTA, the years resembled each other without alteration. Since God, at the time of creation established the reckoning of time which He imparted to Noah, it may be neither advanced nor postponed (4Q268 F1:3b–5a). This view, however, departs from prevailing opinion which maintains the sectarian calendar likewise added extra days in order to correspond to the three hundred and sixty-five day astronomical number.[66]

Thus, both MTA and *Jubilees* mandate a three hundred and sixty-four day calendar. However, MTA continues to add mysticism to its reckoning.

[וה]וא[ חקק קצי ח[רון לעם לא ידעהו] 5
6 והוא הכ[ין [מועדי] רצון לדורשי מצוותיו ול[הולכים בתמים]
7 דרך ויגל ע[יניה]מה בנסתרות ואוזנמה פתחו [וישמעו עמוקות]
8 ויבינו בכול נהיות עד מה יבוא במה

And H[e] decreed the epochs of a[nger for a people who knew Him not,] but proclaimed agreeable [festivals] for those who observe His commandments faithfully and for [those who keep to the straight] path. And He will (yet) open their e[ye]s to the hidden mysteries, and they will open their ears [so that they will hear profound matters.] And they will perceive all events to eternity (before) they occur to them . . . (4Q268 F1:5b–8a)

Although the writer of MTA follows *Jubilees* in chronology, history and calendation, he supplements it with additional matters—the eschatological revelations for each epoch. Time and its mysteries, therefore, becomes an elevated topic in MTA. See, for example, the focus on the shortening of human longevity at the time of the flood in lines 6–7 of the first page of MTA.

4Q268 F1:8 (preserved in part by 4Q266 F2i:5) is the second time our text speaks of revealing profound things. In the first, 4Q266 F1:8, just subsequent to the allusion of the shortening of human life following the flood, it alluded to the mysteries of creation. Here in the second occurrence it deals with futuristic events, those of the eschaton

---

[66] Interestingly, in the 1920s the League of Nations proposed an alteration to the Gregorian calendar by declaring one day of the year and two days every four years as universal days not to be counted among the weekly days of the year, exactly as articulated in the DSS more than two millennia ago.

and messianic epochs. Thus, the continuity of calendation and the events of history are interwoven into a single theme and made part of creation. They are unalterable.

### 3.1.6. *Summary of What the Cave Manuscripts Add to CD*

Let us now summarize what the introduction to MTA reveals in the face of commonly held opinions. According to the editor, the new texts (4Q266, 267 and 268) underscore the legal component as the title of the book "The Elaboration of the Laws by the Sage." He contends the Damascus Document emerges as an essentially legalistic opus with "a hortatory preface and conclusion."[67] In my opinion, this nomistic view falters on a number of fronts.

As we argued, Baumgarten's title should be exchanged for מדרש התורה האחרון, a formula that appears within the work, as well as at its ending. As I understand MTA, the author proposes his work as a midrash on the eschatological Torah—i.e. on the book of *Jubilees*, one of two interwoven portions of the broader תורת מושה (a combination of this perfect work designed for the eschaton, and the traditional Pentateuch). For him, *Jubilees* forms a Super Canon. If Genesis–Deuteronomy were addressed to the Israelites in the wilderness and at Moab, *Jubilees* and, perhaps, *Temple Scroll* would become law at the end of time. MTA, therefore, in its title, מדרש התורה האחרון, promises to deal with eschatology.

The word תורה in MTA and throughout the work has a dual sense. Not only does it claim superiority to Genesis–Deuteronomy, but it also adds another branch of law frequently known as משפטים. Whereas MTA contains some rules that diverge from the Pentateuch, such as prohibition of bigamy, additional rules of cleansing and observance of purity, and leprosy, the משפטים concern the rules of a sectarian community that lives beyond biblical law.

This view becomes apparent in the second part of line 1 (4Q266 F1): "It is incumbent upon the so]ns of light to keep separate from the wa[ys of the sons of darkness." These words may be read in two manners: 1) as a call for piety, as part of the hortatory preface (Baumgarten), or, 2) as I understand them, as a call for absolute separation, the creation of a new sect. In other words, [על ב]נֹי אור להנזֹר מד[רֹ]כֹי בני חושך] is not only a call for piety but is a proclamation for the creation of a new Israel. True, prior to MTA

---

[67] Baumgarten, DJD XVIII, 7.

there existed many writings that supplemented and modified the biblical canon, such as the book of *Enoch*, the *Testaments of the Twelve Patriarchs* in their original version, *Jubilees* and *Temple Scroll*. However, MTA is the first to proclaim a new organization that keeps itself apart from Israel socially, religiously, and economically.

MTA is an organization for the eschaton. It does not as yet prohibit marital relations. In fact, it prescribes stringent rules for them. Nevertheless, the book's call for separation may have led to asceticism, including abstention from sexual relations altogether.

While scholars rightly regard what they call the Damascus Document as an important work, it is also, in my opinion, nascent Essenism. What is new is a midrash or reinterpretation of both the old and new Torahs as well as time itself. The old Torah belonged to the ראשונים. *Jubilees* and, perhaps, *Temple Scroll* are for the אחרונים as well as for the עד אשר יבוא, the messianic age. These three epochs project a division of history that rewrites the past, the present and the future. Time is now divided by a calendar of three hundred and sixty-four days ascribed to Enoch and Abraham during the ראשונים, but stretching all the way through the אחרונים and into the עד אשר יבוא.

In addition to its eschatological connotations, this introductory portion contains headings of the work as a whole. Scrollists take it for granted that the Damascus Document consists of a collection of extracts from a variety of sources. I believe this view is mistaken. An analysis of this book's contents will reflect its general uniformity. That MTA's title presumably occurs at its beginning and certainly at its end hints that this is a composition produced by a single author. 4Q266 F1:1–2a speaks of a separation from evil, an important theme throughout. Much of the book describes the cities and the camps as set apart from sinful Israel. As explained for example in CD 6:14–15, it is incumbent upon the righteous to keep apart from injustice by means of a vow and ban. Other passages describe the procedure for admitting members by special examinations and tests. Membership is restricted to those who pass an examination overseen by the supervisor of the community. As reconstructed, lines 2b–3a of the book's preamble continue the obligations of the community begun in line 1, this time with a positive tenor and qualifying the duration of these requirements—until the completion of the period of remembrance at the end of the epoch of wickedness (the conclusion of the era of the אחרונים). Lines 3b–5a announce the impending future, revealing that God will destroy the inhabited earth, including those who have gone astray in Israel. A large portion of this book deals with the eschaton, the age of the Messiah, as well as the destruction of the opposition against whom much of MTA's polemics are directed. In lines 5b–7a the author tells his listeners that this work will reveal to them the mysteries of the universe as well as the laws of the Torah. He repeats the formula ועתה שמעו four more times. Our writer continues in line 7 by telling us that human life was shortened. Elsewhere in the book we hear that ancient longevity will be restored to humanity so that man might live for a thousand generations. Having mentioned the shortening of human life, lines 7b–9, according to our reconstruction, go on to describe the mysteries that God will reveal to humanity. Much of this work, beginning with CD 1 amplifies this wisdom motif. Following a lacuna of some five lines, the text records a prayer whose ideas likewise mirror the contents of the book. A sizable portion of this supplication is a commitment to listen to the voice of Moses and not to depart from the Torah in any matter, both of which refer to the punctilious observance of the laws contained in the large volume of legal material in MTA. The Divisions of the Epochs introduced in 4Q268 F1:1–8 come back again and again throughout the work under the formulas ראשונים and אחרונים.

Furthermore, the preamble and the concluding sections of the work contain similar ideology and vocabulary, forming a literary inclusio. Each contains a prayer, a feature not found elsewhere in the work. As has been noted, both have the same title. Line 2 of the beginning has the term פקודה, God's remembrance of Israel. The third to the last line contains יפקידו and probably also פקודה. Some form of the verb פקד evidently appears also on line 3 of the introduction. The importance of observing the minutiae of the law is stressed in lines 17–18 of both the introduction and conclusion. Thus, the preponderance of the material points not to a collection of disparate passages as is generally contended, but to an ideological and literary unity. A work such as this shows all signs of a single authorship.

*3.2. BODY (CD 1:1–7:5a; CD 7:5b–8:21 / 19:1–34a;*
*CD 20:1–32a; 20:33b–34 / 4Q266 F4 . . . 4Q270 F4 / 4Q266*
*F12; CD 15–16; 9:1–14:17; CD 14:18–23 / 4Q266 F10ii:1–8;*
*4Q266 F10ii:8–15 / 4Q270 F7i:1–6a; 4Q270 F7i:6b–17 /*
*4Q266 F11:1–3a)*[68]

3.2.1. *An Introduction to the Eschatological Torah (CD 1:1–7:5a; CD 7:*
*5b–8:21 / 19:1–34a; CD 20:1–32a; 20:33b–34 / 4Q266 F4)*

The two texts, 4Q266 F2 line 6, and line 9 of 268 F1 coincide with
the very beginning of what has survived in the Genizah text: ועתה
שמעו (לי) (And now, heed me). Formerly it had been presumed that
this formula begins the Damascus Document. Now that we see it is
a continuum of the preamble which we just read, the clause ועתה
שמעו לי assumes a new sense. Although no longer the beginning of
MTA, it is still of great significance, since it commences a large
section that may be defined as the general introduction to the legal
section, which, as we suggest and will elaborate on below in section 3.2.2, begins shortly after CD 20 in 4Q267 F7:3 with the text
וזה פרוש [המשפטים אשר יעשו בקץ הפקודה] (And this is the elaboration
[of the judgments which they shall observe in the era of redemption]).
In this elaborate introduction spanning from CD 1–8:21 (manuscript
A) to 19:1–20:34 (manuscript B) and 4Q266 F4 to 4Q267 F7:1–2,
we can follow the theoretical raison d'etre for the new features in the
eschatological Torah, absent in the traditional Pentateuch.

3.2.1.1. *Announcing the Coming Eschatology (CD 1:1–2:1)*
The author of MTA commences this lengthy introduction to the
eschatological Torah with a concise reference to Israel's history. In
the second half of line 4 and continuing to the beginning of CD 2,
however, he launches into a rendition of God's plans for His people—a
promise to leave a remnant who will inherit a fructified land and be
guided by a Just Teacher. On the other hand, those who side with
the opposition will suffer divine wrath.

---

[68] See the text layout for a representation of all texts that form this corpus,
including the Cave material bridging from CD 20 to 15.

### 3.2.1.1.1. *God's Quarrel with Israel (1:1–4a)*

As was noted above, the remains of MTA contain five formulas commencing with ועתה שמעו. One appears in the preamble (4Q266 F1:5–7), one begins the body of the work (CD 1:1–2) and two follow shortly thereafter (2:2, 14). A fifth (4Q270 F2ii:19–20) occurs near the middle of the composition where the author stresses the "Torah of Moses" with its ideological bent.

The phrase יודעי צדק (those who know righteousness), here and in 4Q270 F2ii:19, is one of the names of the group known by various appellations. It is parallel to באי ברית (CD 2:2) and בנים (CD 2:14). This illustrates that the name יחד still was not known to the author. In fact, it suggests the titles באי ברית, יודעי צדק and בנים antedate that of יחד, so ubiquitous in *Rule of the Community* and elsewhere in the DSS.

Thus, the יודעי צדק whom he addresses here are the members of the same audience addressed above in 4Q266 F1:5–6a ([But now hear] me and I will make known to you the awesome ac[ts of God] along with His [miraculous] powers). Thus, the יודעי צדק, those who know righteousness, are no longer only people who are knowledgeable, known to us in other related texts, but enlightened members who expect mysteries and revelations. What is new in the phrase ועתה שמעו לי is the next clause ובינו במעשי אל (and discern the acts of God). These words seem to go back to Exod 34:10.

וַיֹּאמֶר הִנֵּה אָנֹכִי כֹּרֵת בְּרִית נֶגֶד כָּל־עַמְּךָ אֶעֱשֶׂה נִפְלָאֹת אֲשֶׁר לֹא־נִבְרְאוּ
בְכָל־הָאָרֶץ וּבְכָל־הַגּוֹיִם וְרָאָה כָל־הָעָם אֲשֶׁר־אַתָּה בְקִרְבּוֹ אֶת־מַעֲשֵׂה יְהוָה
כִּי־נוֹרָא הוּא אֲשֶׁר אֲנִי עֹשֶׂה עִמָּךְ

> Then he said I am making a covenant. In front of your entire people I will perform wonders that have not occurred in the entire earth and all the nations. And all the people in whose midst you are will see the wonders of the Lord, for what I am doing with you is awesome. (Exod 34:10)

The entire text which we have read so far in MTA builds on the idea that, according to the emerging Essene sect, Exod 34:10, 27 and 28 refer not only to the covenant of the wilderness, but to the future covenant in *Jubilees* as well. Column 2 of *Temple Scroll* likewise has the same biblical text with some variance.[69] It follows that the introductions to MTA and *Temple Scroll* connect with Exod

---

[69] See Ben Zion Wacholder, *The Dawn of Qumran* (Cincinnati: Hebrew Union College Press, 1983), 20–21.

34:10–28. These three texts—MTA, *Temple Scroll* and the biblical source—therefore, suppose that, in addition to the covenant with the patriarchs, there was a special covenant with Moses, and that this covenant embraced not only the Sinaitic covenant of Exodus, but also a Mosaic covenant which is attested in *Jubilees* and elsewhere, referring to the futuristic epoch. However, this institution is most prominent in MTA wherein it is known as the ברית החדשה, the new covenant (in the land of Damascus).

CD commences with "For He is in contention with all flesh and will execute justice upon all who vex Him." The time element for כי ריב לו is the present, for it continues the author's imperative ועתה שמעו לי (And now, heed me). The text continues with "for in their treachery, having deserted Him, God hid His face from Israel and His temple and put them (Israel) to the sword." Although our text deals with both the past and the future—Israel's treachery and God's punishment and awaiting redemption—the context here begins with the present time. The exiles are awaiting redemption. The word translated here "treachery" is from the root מעל, occurring six times in MTA. In Leviticus the noun מַעַל refers to a profanation that requires a sin offering. מעל generally refers to what the rabbis call מעילה, the profanation of the temple. However, the passage alluded to by our writer must be Ezek 39:23–24.

23 וְיָדְעוּ הַגּוֹיִם כִּי בַעֲוֹנָם גָּלוּ בֵית־יִשְׂרָאֵל עַל אֲשֶׁר מָעֲלוּ־בִי
וָאַסְתִּר פָּנַי מֵהֶם וָאֶתְּנֵם בְּיַד צָרֵיהֶם וַיִּפְּלוּ בַחֶרֶב כֻּלָּם
24 כְּטֻמְאָתָם וּכְפִשְׁעֵיהֶם עָשִׂיתִי אֹתָם וָאַסְתִּר פָּנַי מֵהֶם

And the nations will know that the house of Israel had gone into exile because of their treachery against me. So I hid my face from them, handing them over to their oppressors, and all of them fell by the sword. According to their uncleanness and transgressions I dealt with them, hiding my face from them. (Ezek 39:23–24)

CD's paraphrase preserves Ezekiel's three motifs—the treachery of the house of Israel, God's hiding his face, and handing them over to the sword—features which are in the past tense.

### 3.2.1.1.2. God's Promise to Israel's Righteous Remnant and the Date of the Eschaton (1:4b–7a)

Although what follows in CD 1:4b–7a diverges from Ezek 39:25–29, the prophet's main idea is still echoed in our text—God's pity on the remnant of Israel. The idea of a remnant for Israel may have its origin in 1 Kgs 19 where the prophet Elijah is commanded to anoint Elisha who would slay any of Israel's wicked who might survive the sword of King Jehu. However, seven thousand who had not worshipped Baal would survive as a remnant of true Israel. Here too in MTA God intends to establish a remnant led by the מורה צדק for the people who kept faith (CD 1:10b–12). The Just Teacher, as will be argued below, is an Elijah and Elisha type figure, whose coming, according to the writer, will announce the advent of the Messiah.[70]

With the infinitive construct ובזכרו in line 4, the situation shifts from the past to the future. The author is looking ahead to the conclusion of the three hundred and ninety years after Nebuchadnezzar's conquest of Jerusalem in 597 B.C.E. At this point God *will* remember the covenant of the ancestral generation.[71] This futuristic understanding diverges from conventional opinion which renders this three hundred and ninety year period as having already elapsed: e.g. "And towards the end of the epoch of anger—three hundred and ninety years following God's handing them over to Nebuchadnezzar, king of Babylon—He remembered them." Schechter, Rabin, Schwartz and Baumgarten take it for granted that the verb and object פקדם (He remembered them) in conjunction with בקץ (at the end) refers to the past. In other words God's minding of Israel has already occurred and has transpired some time ago. Therefore, the next clauses dealing with the sprouting of the plant refer also to the past. Hence, the twenty years of blindness and the germination of the plant both necessarily reference bygone times. All these lines as rendered by the scrollists are regarded as having already occurred at the time of the composition of MTA.

Grammatically, the word השאיר is in the suffixed conjugation and is generally understood to refer to the remainder of Israelites following the Babylonian invasion in 597 B.C.E. and the destruction of the temple in 586 B.C.E. However, the action described suggests a futuristic tone, since in the past God did not destroy the wicked nor save the righteous. According to our writer this verb means that God will draw a sharp distinction between good and evil at the time

---

[70] Cf. Mal 3:23.

[71] Let us remember that the basic ideas of dividing time into the ראישונים, the אחרונים and the עד אשר יבוא of 4Q268 F1:2–3 go back to *Jub.* 1:26. However, the referent of the term ראישונים in our passage differs from that of 4Q268. In the former text it denotes the broad spectrum of historical events. Here it shifts specifically to the personalities of history, namely the patriarchs, the generations in the wilderness and Israel's leaders during the settlement of Canaan and the monarchy.

of the advent of the Messiah. As the text proceeds, at that time all the righteous will have confessed with a perfect heart that they are guilty. God will discern their complete sincerity. At this point the Messiah will arise.

The above scrollists and others never pose the possibility that the words קץ and פקד refer not to the past, but to the present and future—that God is beginning to remember Israel, and that the author of MTA composed his work prior to the end of the three hundred and ninety year epoch, looking forward to the future redemption of his people. What was the actual time interval from this writing until the completion of this period of time? Our text does not give a precise length of time, but does devote an extended account of what would occur during this interval. From this point onward the author is not telling his readers the chronological sequence of the *past*, as is generally supposed, but is announcing a radical break in the history of Israel, the advent of a new epoch. At the end of the epoch of anger God will begin to change the land of Israel from a wilderness into miraculous prosperity, a righteous teacher will arise to guide the nation, and God will forgive its transgressions. It is at that time that there will be an opportunity for members to enroll in this community. CD 4:7b–13a marks the completion of this era:

וכל הבאים אחריהם 4:7

4:8 לעשות כפרוש התורה אשר התוסרו בו הרי°שנים עד שלים

4:9 הקץ [כמספ] ⁷² לשנים האלה כברית אשר הקים אל לראשנים לכפר

4:10 על עונותיהם כן יכפר אל בעדם ובשלום הקץ למספר השנים

4:11 האלה אין עוד להשתפח לבית יהודה כי אם לעמוד איש על

4:12 מצודו נבנתה הגדר רחק החוק ובכל השנים האלה יהיה

4:13 בליעל משולח בישראל

Now as for all who succeed them, continuing to act in accordance with the elaboration of the Torah by which the forefathers were disciplined until the completion of the epoch [according to the number] of these years, in accordance with the covenant which God had established for the ancestors to atone for their sins, so God will atone for them. And at the end of the epoch by the reckoning of these years one may no longer join the (new) house of Judah, but instead every person shall remain at his stand (literally "stand upon his fortress"). The fence has been completed; the statute is distant. And during all these years Belial will be let loose against Israel. (CD 4:7b–13a)

---

⁷² Restored to 4Q266 F3i:3.

Note that the phrase שלים הקץ, occurring twice in CD 4:8–10, concludes the author's chrono-messianic scheme which began in CD 1:5, and should be read as MTA's chronological schema.

### 3.2.1.1.3. *The Fructification of the Holy Land (1:7b–10a)*

The futuristic understanding of CD 1:4b–7a is inescapable for another reason. There had as yet been no redemption, since the next clauses, ויצמח מישראל ומאהרן שורש מטעת לירוש את ארצו ולדשן בטוב אדמתו, make little sense as referring to the past. Surely at the writer's time Israel's desert had not yet disappeared. Let us remember that the clauses "to inherit His land" and "to grow fat in the fertility of his soil" allude to a promise presaged in Ezekiel 47. In the second part of this chapter (verses 13–23) the prophet predicts a new re-division of the tribal lands. These reapportionments would ultimately include not only the twelve tribes, but also the proselytes who would share in the tribal divisions of their habitations. In the first part of the chapter Ezekiel speaks of a lake that would emerge from the threshold of the sanctuary, filling the dry lands of Israel from the north in Damascus to all corners of the land, including the oasis of En-gedi. The lifeless Dead Sea would henceforth contain abundant fish as does the great sea, the Mediterranean. Israel's trees would produce crops monthly. The clause . . . ויצמח מישראל must be read as the Ezekielian promise of a transformed land. In all, the prophet presages that much of Israel that was desolate would turn into marvelous fertility. In standard translations of CD these events refer to the past. But surely at the time of the composition of MTA the מדבר and the ערבה prevailed in the Holy Land. Clearly Ezekiel's promises paraphrased in CD 1:7–8 had not as yet been realized in the days of the authorship of MTA and must be understood as futuristic. It follows that the rendition of ויצמח as a consecutive past syntagm (וַיִּצְמַח) is not exact. It should be read as וְיִצְמַח.

CD 1:8b–10a describes Israel's emerging awareness of their sinfulness and their groping in the darkness for twenty years. In this passage too, all the verbs—ויבינו, וידעו, ויהיו, and ויבן—have been universally rendered as events of the past, their *waws* being read as so-called conversives.[73] In fact, however, all these verbs can, and I believe must be taken as imperfects with their *waws* as simple conjunctions,

---

[73] For the commonly presumed vocalization see Eduard Lohse, *Die Texte aus Qumran* (München: Kösel-Verlag, 1971), 66.

referring to the future. Surely the author of this composition does not presume to say that all of Israel had already repented. We are still in the period of the קץ חרון (the period of wrath). The three hundred and ninety years had not as yet elapsed; neither had the twenty years of groping in the darkness. God, at the end of this four hundred and ten year period is minding them with a call to return to Him, still in the future. After all, CD does not presume to say that Israel's repentance had occurred in the past. Rather, the author is calling his audience to turn to God. In other words, in this chronological scheme, the point in time is 597 B.C.E. plus three hundred and ninety years, which equals 207 B.C.E., with an additional twenty years of blindness to arrive at 187 B.C.E. as the anticipated year of Israel's full repentance.[74]

*3.2.1.1.4. The Rise of the Just Teacher (CD 1:10b–12)*
Consistent with the previous lines, conventional scholarship without dissent renders the verb ויקם as וַיָּקֶם (then He raised up). As to the tense of ויקם, two possibilities exist depending on the vocalization. If one points the verb as וַיָּקֶם, it does mean that the raising had occurred in the past. But, if we vocalize it with a *schewa* under the *waw* as וְיָקֶם or וְיָקֶם,[75] the "raising up" or "rising up" of the מורה צדק would occur in the future. Which is the correct vocalization of the connective in this context? The מורה צדק introduced here in MTA, a term drawn from יֹרֶה צֶדֶק in Hos 10:12, is the most important personality mentioned in the Dead Sea Scrolls. The text continuing with להדריכם בדרך לבו (to guide them in the way that will please Him) favors the futuristic rendition as does the next clause, ויודע לדורות אחרונים את אשר עשה בדור אחרון (. . . and He will make known to the eschatological generations what He will have done to the final generation).[76] Here the word אחרונים, contrary to that of the restoration in 4Q268 F1:3 where this term described the *historical events* from the חרבן (the destruction of the temple whose process

---

[74] See James VanderKam, *The Dead Sea Scrolls Today* (Grand Rapids: Wm. B. Eerdmans Publishing Co., 1994), 100 for a discussion of the sequencing of this material. He sets the 587 B.C.E. conquest as the beginning of the four hundred and ten year period, arriving at 177 B.C.E. as the conclusion of the twenty years of groping.

[75] The medieval scribe who sometimes adds vowels or ambiguous words has placed a *segol* under the *quf*, reading the verb as a *hif'il* stem.

[76] The perfect עשה is to be rendered as prophetic (i.e. what He will have done in the last generation). See Schwartz in Charlesworth, ed., *Damascus Document*, 13, note 8.

began with Nebuchadnezzar's second invasion of Jerusalem in 597
B.C.E., Ezekiel's deportation) until the time of the writer, assumes
an *eschatological* denotation, as does אחרון in the title of the book,
מדרש התורה האחרון. Likewise, דור אחרון (the final generation) which
follows it alludes to the last survivors of the traitors, a group whose
fate will be sealed with the coming of the Messiah.

The terms ויודע and עשה should be understood in tandem וְיוֹדַע
לדורות אחרונים את אשר עשה בדור אחרון, translated "and he (the Teacher)
*will make known* to the eschatological generations what He *will have
done* to the last generation." The adjective אחרונים here in CD 1:12
functions in the same manner as does ראישונים eight lines earlier
in 1:4 (4Q268 F1:12), both referring to groups of people within
Israel—the first to the *ancestors* whose covenant God will remember
and the second to the *coming* generation of penitent Israel to whom
God will reveal His dealings with mankind. The terms ראישונים and
אחרונים (although functioning differently from those reconstructed in
4Q268 F1:2b–3a mentioned above) draw on *Jub.* 1:4 and 26. The
author of *Jubilees* exegetes Exod 24:12, calling on Moses,

עֲלֵה אֵלַי הָהָרָה וֶהְיֵה־שָׁם וְאֶתְּנָה לְךָ אֶת־לֻחֹת הָאֶבֶן
וְהַתּוֹרָה וְהַמִּצְוָה אֲשֶׁר כָּתַבְתִּי לְהוֹרֹתָם

> Come up to me on the mountain and tarry there, and I will give you the
> stone tablets and the Torah and commandments which I have inscribed
> to teach them. (Exod 24:12)

As expounded in *Jubilees*, "come up to me and tarry there" refers
not only to the mountain, but also above the summit to the cloud
where God's glory had descended. The phrase "and tarry there"
suggests the forty days, the period that Moses would remain above
the mountain. The futuristic sense of the infinitival phrase להדריכם
בדרך לבו in CD 1:11 cited above, draws on that of לְהוֹרֹתָם of Exod
24:12 quoted in *Jub.* 1:1. The clauses ". . . the stone tablets, the
Torah and the commandments which I have inscribed to teach them"
refers to three texts that God gave Moses: a) the stone tablets,
b) the Torah (apparently the Pentateuch) and c) the "commandments,"
which *Jubilees* sometimes renders as "testimony" (1:4, 8, 26, 29; 2:33
and 3:14), cited as תעודה in 4Q416 2:4–5 (apparently another name
for the מחלקות העתים, the work commonly known as the book of
*Jubilees*). MTA has already made several allusions to this work. As
was noted above, while paraphrasing Ezek 39:23 that God will hide
His face, the author of MTA also alludes to *Jub.* 1:12–13.

I will send witnesses to them so that I may testify to them, but they
will not listen and will kill the witnesses. They will persecute those too
who study the law diligently. They will abrogate everything and will
begin to do evil in my presence. Then I will hide my face from them.
(*Jub.* 1:12–13)[77]

Note also that the division of time into the three epochs: a) "early,"
b) the "last" and c) the "future" formulated in *Jub.* 1 reappears
throughout MTA. As stated above, the first allusions are plausibly
in the preamble to the work (4Q268 F1:2b–3a). A similar mention
of the future occurs a few lines later in line 8 (בכול נהיות עד מה יבוא
במה), translated "all events to eternity (before) they occur to them."
The allusion to the early and latter periods as two epochs of the
two covenants and their Torahs occurs in CD 20:8–10.

וכמשפט הזה לכל המאס בראשונים                          20:8

20:9 ובאחרונים אשר שמו גלולים על לבם וישׂימֿוּ וילכו בשרירות

20:10 לבם אין להם חלק בבית התורה: כמשפט רעיהם אשר שבו

And this rule applies also to anyone who will despise either the early
or the latter (words of the two Torahs), who will have placed abominations upon their heart and live by its stubbornness. They shall not have
a portion in the covenant of the Torah. (CD 20:8b–10)

Finally, as I argue elsewhere, MTA both begins and ends with the
three words מדרש התורה האחרון, where the word אחרון modifies
not מדרש, as translated by Baumgarten and Stegemann, "the last
midrash," but תורה, rendered "the last (eschatological) Torah." This
falls under the historical rubric of the ראישונים (the first events) and
the אחרונים (the latter events), reflecting the outlook of *Jubilees*. MTA
entitles itself as the amplification or midrash of this work, which
CD 16:2–3 describes as מדוקדק (perfect) i.e, more so than the first
Torah. Hence, these clauses that deal with both the plant and the
מורה צדק are predictive and were so understood by the author's audience, telling them what God will do on the one hand to the penitent
generations as well as to the congregation of traitors, not what had
already occurred to these entities as is generally assumed.

   As to the origin of the sobriquet מורה צדק, as stated above, it goes
back to Hos 10:12.

זִרְעוּ לָכֶם לִצְדָקָה קִצְרוּ לְפִי־חֶסֶד נִירוּ לָכֶם נִיר

וְעֵת לִדְרוֹשׁ אֶת־יְהוָה עַד־יָבוֹא וְיֹרֶה צֶדֶק לָכֶם

---

[77] VanderKam, *The Book of Jubilees*, Vol. 1, (Louvain: Peeters, 1989), 3–4.

> Spread seed for righteousness; harvest for love; draw a planting line. It is the time to search for the Lord until He comes and teaches righteousness to you. (Hos 10:12)

Likewise the clause preceding that which introduces the Just Teacher, ויבן אל אל מעשיהם כי בלב שלם דרשוהו (CD 1:10b), rendered "And God, noting their (righteous, loving) deeds that *they will have searched for Him* with a perfect heart," resembles the first part of Hos 10:12, "Spread seed for righteousness; harvest for love; draw a planting line. It is the time *to search for the Lord* . . .'' דרש can also in its technical meaning be rendered "to midrashize, interpret (the Lord's name)."

### 3.2.1.1.5. *The Rise and Fall of the Scoffer and His Associates (CD 1:13–2:1)*

The author then relates the destruction of the wicked generation and their leader, a description that stretches from CD 1:13–2:1. This sinful generation will turn away from the right path. It will occur during the time about which had been prophesied by Hosea: כפרה סוררה כן סרר ישראל (Like a belligerent heifer, so Israel will have rebelled).[78] That is to say, so Israel will behave. The author transforms the prophetic past of סָרַר to the future, reading Hosea's words as a prediction of things to come. The nemesis of the מורה צדק is introduced as the איש הלצון (the Scoffer . . . who will have dripped lying waters on Israel). The author of MTA has given two lines to describe the Just Teacher but devotes nine to depict his opponent. This passage pictures the scoffer as a futuristic figure, as is the מורה צדק. Thus the word ויתעם, which Lohse vocalizes with a *patah* under the *waw*, making it a consecutive past, should be read with a *schewa* under the *waw*, as futuristic. This would generate an eschatological framework for the remaining lines 15–19.

1:15  ויתעם בתוהו ולֹוֹא[79] דרך להשח גבהות עולם ולסור
1:16  מנתיבות צדק ולהֹסיע גבול אשר גבלו ריֹשֹוֹנֹים בנחלתם למען
1:17  הדבק בהם את אלות בריתו להסגירם לחרב נקמת נקם
1:18  ברית בעבור אשר דרשו בחלקות ויבחרו במהתלות ויצפו
1:19  לפרצות ויבחרו בטוב הצואר ויצדיקו רשע וירשיעו צדיק

---

[78] Cf. Hos 4:16. The Masoretic text does not contain כן. This alteration may have been prompted by MTA's author to stress its futuristic sense.

[79] ולוא 4Q266 F2i:19. Lines 15 and 16 are supplemented by 4Q266 F2i:18–20.

Thus, He will lead them astray into a landless wilderness without an escape route, both lowering the heights of the world by turning away from the paths of justice and by removing the boundary that the ancestral generations had set in their inheritance, so that the curses of His covenant cling to them, resulting in them being handed over to a sword which will fiercely avenge (the violation of) the covenant. For they will have interpreted Him with flattering words, choosing farce and looking for loopholes favoring the fine neck, that will result in declaring the wicked as righteous and the righteous as wicked. (CD 1:15b–19)

Both figures, the מורה צדק and the איש הלצון are, therefore, Elijah type personalities of the eschaton, presaged in Mal 3:23, "Behold I will send you Elijah the prophet before the advent of the great and awesome day of the Lord."

The figure here named איש הלצון is described again in CD 20:13–15 as איש הכזב (the Man of Lies) and in CD 8:13 as מטיף כזב (the Spewer of Lies). These sobriquets refer to the same individual, since our text indicates that he will have preached false waters (מימי כזב). CD 20:13–15 correlates the destruction of the warriors who will have joined the "Man of Lies" as transpiring forty years after the formation of the Teacher's *assembly* (האסף).[80] In other words, according to that text, the Teacher's convocation and his opposition will have come to prominence at the same time, a period that corresponds to the rise of Moses and the destruction of the wilderness generation that wandered for forty years. The Just Teacher's opponent could conceivably be understood as a reference to the leader of the Pharisees, a group whom the author labels as the (ה)גבול מסיגי.

### 3.2.1.1.6. *Pesherite References to the Just Teacher and His Nemesis*

The figure, איש הכזב, appears again in the pesherite commentaries on Habakkuk and Psalms. The above-cited phrase, מטיף כזב, occurs in the commentaries on Habakkuk and Micah. *Pesher Habakkuk*, which has survived only in one manuscript, consists of a commentary on the first two chapters of the biblical book. Each comment begins with a quotation from the biblical source and is elaborated on with the words פשרו or פשר הדבר (its eschatological interpretation). The word פשרו, so ubiquitous in the pesharim, appears for the first time in CD 4:14, these commentaries being posterior to and drawing on the vocabulary of MTA. The author of *Pesher Habakkuk* tells us the

---

[80] For this translation of האסף see my discussion on the deserters of the sect (CD-A 8:1b–21 [paralleling CD-B 19:13b–33a]; CD-B 19:33b–20:17a).

words of the prophets of Israel were intended not so much for their own times, but for the הדור האחרון,"the last generation" (1QpHab 2:7; 7:2), apparently meaning the final generation of the era of the אחרונים to be followed by the אחרית הימים (the end of days), that is to say the messianic age.

### 3.2.1.1.6.1. Pesher Habakkuk

These comments have two main themes: 1) the מורה צדק and his nemesis, the איש הכזב, and 2) a subordinate theme, the conquest and destruction of the Kittim. Scholars have understood the Kittim as referring to the Romans. However, while the Romans might be included, the word Kittim as it is defined by the author really has a wider scope, referring to the conquering nations among the gentiles, Ezekiel's Gog and Magog. The definition of Kittim is given in 1QpHab 9:4b–7.

9:4      פשרו על כוהני ירושלם

9:5      האחרונים אשר יקבוצו הון ובצע משלל העמים

9:6      ולאחרית הימים ינתן הונם עם שללם ביד

9:7      חיל הכתיאים vacat כיא המה יתר העמים

> Its eschatological interpretation concerns the last priests of Jerusalem who will amass wealth and gain from the plunder of the peoples. However, at the end of days their wealth with their plunder will be given to the armies of the Kittim, for *they are the most powerful* (literally "remainder") of the nations. (1QpHab 9:4b–7)

The pesher's author understood Habakkuk's purpose as to elucidate the eschatological age by showing that the two figures were not merely his inventions, but were presaged by the prophets. He chose to give his visionary comments on the biblical book because its theme depicts the prophet's complaint of why God allows the wicked to oppress the righteous. Moreover, Habakkuk introduces the theme of the coming of the Chaldeans as an instrument to punish the wicked, but the prophet also predicts their ultimate demise. Our commentator believed Habakkuk referred to the two figures of MTA, namely that the righteous are the coming מורה הצדק and the wicked his nemesis, the איש הלצון, referred to variously throughout his pesher as the איש הכזב (1QpHab 2:1–2; 5:11) and the מטיף הכזב (1QpHab 10:9). Ultimately the Chaldeans are the Kittim who will perish at the end of time. This theme appears at the very beginning of our pesher.

     The first comment is highly fragmentary, but its meaning is nevertheless discernible. Quoting Hab 1:1–2, the commentator says,

פשרו על ת[]חלת דור       1:2

[אחרון]     1:3     כול הבא[]ות עליהם

"[ . . . Its eschatological interpretation refers to the beg]inning of the [final] generation [ . . . all events that will co]me upon them."[81] (1QHab 1:2b–3)

Much of the text is missing on page 1 of *Pesher Habakkuk*, but enough survives to give an inkling of the major theme, the conflict between the righteous and the wicked. The pesherite author shows how the biblical book depicts the oppression and perhaps the attempt of the wicked figure to murder the Just Teacher. 1QpHab 5:8–12a serves to describe the theme lost in the missing text, but elaborated on further throughout the book.

למה תביטו בוגדים ותחריש בבלע      5:8

רשע צדיק ממנו *vacat* פשרו על בית אבשלום    5:9

ואנשי עצתם אשר נדמו בתוכחת מורה הצדק   5:10

ולוא עזרוהו על איש הכזב *vacat* אשר מאס את   5:11

התורה בתוך כול עדתם       5:12

"Why do you traitors look and are silent as the wicked swallows up one who is more righteous than he?" (Hab 1:13b) Its eschatological interpretation refers to the house of Absalom and their council who will have fallen silent at the (time of) the reproof by the Just Teacher, not assisting him against the Man of Lies who will have despised the Torah within their entire congregation. (1QpHab 5:8–12a)

The author claims that the conflict between the righteous and the wicked goes back to David and his nemesis, the house of Absalom. It will reach a climax in the eschatological epoch.

The pesherite writer transforms the phrase בבלע רשע צדיק ממנו in his commentary on Hab 1:13, to refer to the house of Absalom who

---

[81] Horgan and Brownlee restore [תו]חלת דור ] ([the expec]tation of the generation of . . . ) and Nitzan, [אחרון] [תו]חלת דור [ ([the expec]tation of the [last] generation). James H. Charlesworth, ed., *Pesharim, Other Commentaries, and Related Documents* (vol. 6b in *The Dead Sea Scrolls: Hebrew, Aramaic, and Greek Texts with English Translations*; ed. James H. Charlesworth; Tübingen/Louisville: J. C. B. Mohr [Siebeck] and Westminster John Knox Press, 1995), 160; W. H. Brownlee, *The Midrash Pesher of Habakkuk* (Missoula: Scholars Press, 1979), 37; Bilhah Nitzan, *Pesher Habakkuk* (Jerusalem: Bialik Institute, 1986), 150. The phrase דור אחרון suggests a time element, and hence my reconstruction תחלת. We supply the word כול before Horgan's reading הבא[]ות עליהם.

would become quiet at the reproof delivered by the Just Teacher
for not providing him assistance against the attack of his opponent.
The pesher continues to use the verb בלע three more times. Brownlee interprets לבלעו בכאס חמתו in 1QpHab 11:5 "in order to make
him (the Just Teacher) reel through the vexation of his wrath."[82] In
fact בלע, as in Hab 1:13, means "to swallow" and is another term
to denote "slaying." This verb is used again several lines later in
1QpHab 11:6b–8.

ובקץ מועד מנוחת                              11:6

11:7 יום הכפורים הופע אליהם לבלעם

11:8 ולכשילם ביום צום שבת מנוחתם . . .

> And during the time of resting on the Day of Atonement he will appear
> to them to swallow them up and to make them sinful (literally "stumble")
> on the day of fasting, during their Sabbath rest.[83] (1QpHab 11:6b–8)

Just as in Hab 1:13, all uses of בלע in the pesher expand upon the
sense of slaying found in the biblical *Vorlage*, that the wicked besieges
the more righteous than he. All in all, *Pesher Habakkuk* shows that,
just as Absalom plotted to kill David, so the Wicked Priest's intent
is to slay the righteous. As God saved David, so will He deliver the
Just Teacher. Whether the author meant that the Wicked Priest will
actually slay the Just Teacher or merely have the intention to do
so is not absolutely clear. Nevertheless, since the writer repeats בלע
three times, all in relation to the Scoffer, it suggests that he actually
will attempt to or even succeed in carrying it out. This understanding of Habakkuk differs from standard exegesis. Scrollists see in
this text contemporary figures, where the Kittim are the Romans
and the Just Teacher is one of the Hasmonean rulers. Common is
the view that the Man of Lies is Jonathan or the anonymous high
priest that ruled Judea prior to Jonathan's ascent in 152 B.C.E.
As I understand it, however, the author is not referring to specific
individuals of his age, rather to the apocalyptic figures as I argue
are present in MTA.[84]

---

[82] Brownlee, *Midrash Pesher*, 179. This meaning misconstrues the context. As
to the function of לכשילם, it has been rendered as "to cause one to trip." In this
context, however, it refers not to literal stumbling, but to causing a failure in the
observance of a most sacred occasion.

[83] הופע, when used for a person, can refer to the appearance of God (cf. CD
20:25–26). Here it pertains to the Wicked Priest.

[84] See Ben Zion Wacholder, "The Righteous Teacher in the Pesherite Commentaries," *HUCA* 73 (2002): 1–27.

The sobriquets, the איש הכזב and מטיף הכזב, appear to draw directly on MTA. Other passages in *Pesher Habakkuk* refer to him as הכוהן הרשע (the Wicked Priest). This designation does not diverge from MTA, since MTA also refers to the Just Teacher as a priest. Our text then is saying the Just Teacher and the Scoffer will be priests, in consonance with the general name given to this sect, בני צדוק הכוהנים (4Q266 F5i:16; 1QS 5:2, 9; 1QSa 1:2, 24; 2:3; 3:22). Following are more texts that continue to describe the Wicked Priest's persecution of the Teacher. Although הכוהן הרשע does not occur in the extant portions of the first, 1QpHab 1:10b–13, most scrollists restore it to line 13.

10 [ עַל כן תפוג תורה
11 [פשרו על מטיף הכזב[85] ואנשי עדתו [אשר מאשו בתורת אל
12 [ולוא יצא לנצח משפט כיא רשע מכתי]ר את הצדיק *vacat*
13 [פשרו הרשע הוא הכוהן הרשע והצדיק] הוא מורה הצדק

"So, the Torah becomes numb" (Hab 1:4a). [It refers to the Spewer of Lies and his congregants] who will have despised the Torah of God. ["And judgment will not come forth truthfully, for the wicked will be besie]ging the righteous" (Hab 1:4b). [Its eschatological interpretation: the wicked refers to the Wicked Priest, and the righteous] to the Just Teacher.[86] (1QpHab 1:10b–13)

---

[85] An alternative reading is איש הכזב (the Man of Lies). Cf. 1QpHab 5:11–12a.

11 ולוא עזרוהו על איש הכזב *vacat* אשר מאס את
12 התורה בתוך כול עצֹתֹם
And will not have assisted him against the *Man of Lies who will have despised the Torah* within their entire congregation.

[86] Brownlee, 43–45; Horgan (p. 150) proposes an alternate reconstruction.

10 [ עַל כן תפוג תורה [
11 [ולוא יצא לנצח משפט     פשרו [אשר מאשו בתורת אל
12 [ כיא רשע מכתי]ר את הצדיק
13 [פשרו הרשע הוא הכוהן הרשע והצדיק] הוא מורה הצדק

Timothy Lim provides another rendition of line 13.

13 [פשרו הרשע הוא איש הכזב והצדיק] הוא מורה הצדק

[Its interpretation: *the wicked* is the man of the lie and *the righteous*] is the Teacher of Righteousness.

He argues that in 4QpHab 5:8–12 the Teacher of Righteousness is equated with the צדיק of the biblical text whereas the רשע of the biblical lemma is interpreted as the איש הכזב. He concludes that, whereas הכוהן הרשע does appear later in *Pesher Habakkuk*,

The first extant reference to the Wicked Priest in this pesher is found in 1QpHab 8:8.

8    פשרו על הכוהן הרשע אשר *vacat*
9    נקרא על שם האמת בתחלת עומדו וכאשר משל
10   בישראל רם לבו ויעזוב את אל ויבגוד בחוקים בעבור
11   הון

It (Hab 2:5–8) refers to the Wicked Priest who will have been called by the True (God's) Name[87] at the beginning of his accession; but after becoming a ruler in Israel his heart will become vain and he will forsake God and will act treacherously against the statutes for the gain of wealth. (1QpHab 8:8b–11a)

Note that ויעזוב is an imperfect verb. It should be remembered that a large number of the verbs in this work employ the prefixed conjugation to convey the future tense. As we have seen, in accordance with their understanding of MTA, most commentators have interpreted Habakkuk as referring to the past or contemporary times, taking the figure of the Just Teacher as the founder of the Essene movement. However, as argued above, the author of MTA likewise placed the Just Teacher באחרית הימים (at the end of days). *Pesher Habakkuk*, which was composed at least a generation or more after MTA, still envisages the contending figures as operating at the end of days.[88]

2:5    וכן פשר הדבר] על הבו]גדים לאחרית א
2:6    הימים המה עריצ̇י̇ הבר]ית אשר לוא יאמינוא
2:7    בשומעם את כול הבא]ות ע]ל הדור האחרון מפי

---

"the adjective 'wicked' when it occurs in the biblical lemma is never equated with the title 'the wicked priest' anywhere else in the pesher." See Timothy Lim, "The Wicked Priest or the Liar?" in *The Dead Sea Scrolls in their Historical Context* (ed. Timothy Lim, et al.; Edinburgh: T&T Clark, 2000), 49–50.

[87] For the ambiguity of this clause see Brownlee, *Midrash Pesher*, 134–37, who cites nine possible renditions. It is likely, however, that the sobriquet שם האמת "the Name of Truth" alludes to the deity. For שם, cf. CD 15:1–2, especially the concluding clause:

(לא) י̇שבע וגם באל̇ף ולמד וגם באל̇ף ודלת כי אם שבועת הבנים
באלות הברית *vacat* ואת תורת משה אל יזכור כי ב̇ה כל פרו̇ש השם

... one should (not) swear, nor by the *aleph* and *lamed* (Elohim), nor with the *aleph* and *dalet* (Adonai), except for (in) "the oath of the youths" during the covenantal curses (at the time of the admission ceremony). Neither shall he make mention of the Torah of Moses, since in it The Name (YHWH) is enunciated.

[88] This may account for the fact that the appellation, Essenes, found in the classical writers, occurs neither in MTA nor in the pesherite writings. In the time of these commentators the Essene movement had not as yet appeared.

2:8 הכוהן אשר נתן אל ב[לבו בינ]ה לפשור אׄת כול

2:9 דברי עבדיו הנׄביאיׄם[ אשר ]בׄידם ספר אל את

2:10 כול הבאות על עמו וׄעׄ]דתו . . .

And thus is the eschatological meaning [concerning the tr]aitors toward the end of days. They are the breacher[s of the cove]nant who will not trust when they will hear all the (miraculous) event[s] that will come to pass [up]on the ultimate generation by the words of the priest [whom] God had endowed with [understand]ing to presage all the words of his prophetic servants through [whom] God had foretold all the (miraculous) events that will occur concerning His people and [His] con[gregation . . . ]. (1QpHab 2:5–10a)

Commentators who take it for granted that the priest, identical with the Just Teacher, is a historical figure and therefore, that his prophecies speak of the current scene, have difficulty with this passage which is blatantly eschatological in nature. Note the words לאחרית א הימים (toward the end of days), אשר לׄוא יאמינוא (who will not trust), כׄול הבאות על הדור האחרון (all the events that will come to pass upon the ultimate generation) and לפשור (to exegete concerning the eschatological epoch). This phraseology is the most eloquent proof that the Just Teacher and the Wicked Priest are depicted not as historical, but as futuristic figures in MTA and the pesherite commentaries.

The next passage deals with retribution that awaits the Wicked Priest.

9:8 מדמי אדם וחמס אׄרׄץ קריה וכוׄל יׄושבׄיׄ בה

9:9 פשרו על הכוהן ה[ר]שׄע אשר בעוון מורה

9:10 הצדק ואנשׄי עצתו נתנו אל בׄיׄד אׄויביו לענוׄתׄו

9:11 בנגע לכלה במרורי נפש בעבור [א]שׄר הרשיע

9:12 על בחירו . . .

". . . on account of the blood shed by man and the crime of the land, the city and all its inhabitants" (Hab 2:8b). Its eschatological interpretation refers to the [Wi]cked Priest who on account of his sinning against the Just Teacher and the men of his council, God will have handed him over to his enemies to torture him with strikes to wear him out with afflictions because he will have acted wickedly against His (God's) elect. (1QpHab 9:8–12a)

In the previous verses we already saw that the Wicked Priest would plot to destroy the Just Teacher. Here the pesherite commentator predicts the destruction of the Wicked Priest as a punishment for his persecution of the Teacher.

The next passage draws up the most dramatic scene of our work

and perhaps of the DSS as a whole: the Wicked Priest's confronta-
tion of the מורה הצדק on the Day of Atonement.

11:2          הוי משקה רעיהו מספח
11:3 חמתו אף שכר למען הבט אל מועדיהם
11:4 vacat פשרו על הכוהן הרשע אשר
11:5 רדף אחר מורה הצדק לבלעו בכעס
11:6 חמתו אבית גלותו ובקץ מועד מנוחת
11:7 יום הכפורים הופע אליהם לבלעם
11:8 ולכשילם ביום צום שבת מנוחתם . . .

> "Woe to him who serves his friend drink, erupting in his anger, even
> intoxicated so as to check their holy days" (Hab 2:15). Its eschatological
> interpretation concerns the Wicked Priest who will have pursued the
> Just Teacher to swallow him in his fierce anger in the house of his exile.
> And during the time of resting on the Day of Atonement he will make
> an appearance to swallow them and to make them stumble on the day
> of fasting, their Sabbath rest. (1QpHab 11:2b–8)

This passage has provoked a vast literature dealing with its exegetical
and theological problems. For our purpose it suffices to note that our
text stresses the calendar wars between the three hundred sixty-four
day and the three hundred sixty-five day year.[89] As understood by
scrollists, these lines suggest that the Wicked Priest is here the High
Priest who appeared in an intoxicated state on the Day of Atonement
to swallow the Just Teacher in his house of exile (אבית גלותו). If the
passage refers to the High Priest, he came from Jerusalem to the
land of Damascus, which current opinion identifies as Qumran. In
fact, however, as was noted, in my interpretation our passage must be
construed as prophetic. That is to say the calendar wars depicted here
refer not to events which had occurred already for which no plausible
dating can be found, but to the struggle that will take place during the
eschaton.[90] As argued in the introductory material, Damascus refers
not to Qumran, but to Syria's capital to where the Israelites would
migrate and where God would rescue them from sin and oppression,
just as He did their forefathers who had descended to Egypt. Contrary
to what has generally been maintained, the exile to Damascus is not

---

[89] See Ben Zion Wacholder, "Calendar Wars Between the 364 and the 365-Day
Year," *RevQ* 20 (2001): 207–22.
[90] For recent probative debates concerning this text see Brownlee, *Midrash Pesher*,
179–89.

an occurrence of the past, but a futuristic expectation.

The pesherite text that follows likewise exposes the eventual fate of the Wicked Priest.

כיא חמס לבנון יכסכה ושוד בהמות[    ]    11:17

יחתה מדמי אדם וחמס ארץ קריה וכול יושבי בה    12:1

פשר הדבר על הכוהן הרשע לשלם לו את    12:2

גמולו אשר גמל על אביונים כיא הלבנון הוא    12:3

עצת היחד והבהמות המה פתאי יהודה עושה    12:4

התורה אשר ישופטנו אל לכלה    *vacat*    12:5

כאשר זמם לכלות אביונים . . .    12:6

"[For the violence of Lebanon will cover you, and the spoil of the beasts] will frighten (them) on account of the blood shed by man and the crime of the land, of the city and all of its inhabitants" (Hab 2:17). The eschatological interpretation of this matter refers to the Wicked Priest (whose acts) will be requited for the fate that he will have bestowed on the destitute, since Lebanon refers to the council of the community, and the beasts to the simple of Judah, the observer(s) of the Torah. (It is the Wicked Priest) whom God will condemn to destruction[91] just as he will have plotted to destroy the destitute. (1QpHab 11:17–12:6a)

Our text finds in Hab 2:17 a reference to the council of the community here identified as Lebanon, whose members are the simple of Judah, the observers of the Torah. The identification of Lebanon here as the עצת היחד is an indication that the pesher is dependent in part on *Rule of the Community*, since this phrase occurs about a dozen times in it, but never in MTA. As stated above, *Rule of the Community* came into being subsequent to MTA. In other words, the composition of this pesher appears to have followed not only MTA, but 1QS as well, in which the men of the עצת היחד are a standard allusion the sect. Quoting I. Rabinowitz, Brownlee argues that the phrase פשר הדבר...לשלם לו foretells the doom of the Wicked Priest.[92] This insight is right, except that the prediction is not a reference to what had happened in history as he presumes but refers to an event that is yet to take place.

The penultimate comment of *Pesher Habakkuk* continues to deal with the Wicked Priest.

---

[91] For כלה in MTA see 4Q266 F1:3, 4, [23]; CD 1:5; 8:2 (19:4).
[92] Brownlee, *Midrash Pesher*, 198.

12:6    ואשר אמר מדמי

12:7    קריה וחמס ארץ פשרו הקריה היא ירושלם

12:8    אשר פעל בה הכוהן הרשע מעשי תועבות ויטמא את

12:9    מקדש אל וחמס ארץ המה ערי יהודה אשר

12:10   גזל הון אביונים . . .

> And which (Habakkuk) said, "On account of the shedding of blood of
> the city and the crime of the land." Its eschatological meaning: The city
> is Jerusalem in which the Wicked Priest will have executed his abomi-
> nable acts and defiled God's sanctuary. The crime of the land refers
> to the cities of Judah wherein (the Wicked Priest) will have robbed the
> destitute. (1QpHab 12:6b–10a)

Interesting in these passages is the author's dual interpretation of the
blood of man and the city and its inhabitants, where he fuses Hab
2:8 with 2:17. The interpretation of 2:8 links the biblical passage to
the Wicked Priest who will have sinned against the Just Teacher and
will have been requited for acting wickedly against God's chosen.
Commenting on Hab 2:17, the pesherite writer resumes his midrash
on the same wording, on the shedding of the blood of man and
the crime against the sanctuary committed by the Wicked Priest.
Here the Wicked Priest is requited for his acts against the destitute.
It is worth noting that the word אביון (poor) although frequent in
Scripture, is relatively rare in the DSS. Nevertheless, the pesher on
Psalms twice employs the sobriquet עדת האביונים (the council of the
poor) as another name for the community of the יחד. The Habakkuk
commentator, however, applies the term אביונים three times, not as a
name for the community, but as an amplification of the oppression
committed by the Wicked Priest. In other words the latter apparently does not know of the designation עדת האביונים, a nickname that
evidently came into being only in the pesher on Psalms. It may be
supposed then that comments on Psalms were composed subsequently to those on Habakkuk.

Two geographic terms in these pesher texts need explanation: 1) the
fact that the commentator understands the קריה as Jerusalem where
the Wicked Priest resides and commits abominable acts and 2) the
phrase אבית גלותו, where אבית is an Aramaicism for בבית denoting "in
his house of exile," that is to say the Teacher's exile. As is frequently
alluded to in MTA, the Teacher will be exiled to the land of Damascus
where he will assemble his adherents. If we read this text correctly,
the Wicked Priest will have to travel a distance from Jerusalem to
Damascus. Such an itinerary may involve several days, perhaps a

week to reach the Just Teacher during the Day of Atonement, especially considering that an individual must refrain from travel on the Sabbath and the holidays. In other words, even a most speedy journey from Jerusalem to Damascus would involve almost the entire interval from the first to the tenth day of the seventh month. Of course, the two calendars observed by these opponents would conflict. Let us not forget 1QpHab 11:6–8 which stresses their divergent calendations: "And during the time of resting on the Day of Atonement he will make an appearance to swallow them and to make them stumble on the day of fasting, during their Sabbath rest." Such an itinerary presumes an ambitious task for a high priest and his entourage.

The phrase מטיף הכזב, is another sobriquet for the nemesis of the מורה צדק. It occurs in *Pesher Habakkuk* once.[93]

| | |
|---|---|
| הוי | 10:5 |
| בונה עיר בדמים ויכונן קריה בעולה הלוא | 10:6 |
| הנה מעם יהוה צבאות יגעו עמים בדי אש | 10:7 |
| ולאומים בדי ריק ייעפו  *vacat* | 10:8 |
| פשר הדבר על מטיף הכזב אשר התעה רבים | 10:9 |
| לבנות עיר שוו בדמים ולקים עדה בשקר | 10:10 |
| בעבור כבודה לוגיע רבים בעבודת שוו ולהרותם | 10:11 |
| במ[ע]שי שקר להיות עמלם לריק בעבור יבואו | 10:12 |
| למשפטי אש אשר גדפו ויחרפו את בחירי אל | 10:13 |

"Woe unto him who builds a city by bloodletting and constructs a metropolis with injustice. Behold this is from the Lord of hosts. They make weary nations by poles of fire and they tire the people with vanity." (Hab 2:12–13) The eschatological meaning of the passage concerns the Spewer of Lies who will have misled the community (literally "the many") to construct an otiose city by bloodletting and to establish a congregation with lies on account of its glory to weary the community with empty services and to teach them with false observances that their toil might be in vain so that they come to fiery rules by which they will have blasphemed and shamed the chosen of God. (1QpHab 10:5b–13)

Otherwise the verb נטף is found almost exclusively in MTA, appearing only once elsewhere in the DSS in the phrase מטיף הכזב in *Pesher Micah*. By contrast, MTA has the verb נטף six times and once as the phrase מטיף כזב (Spewer of Lies). There is also a resemblance between this Habakkuk pesher and CD 1:14b–15a where both employ the roots נטף, כזב and תעה.

---

[93] It can perhaps be restored in 1QpHab 1:11.

בעמוד איש הלצון אשר הטיף לישראל 14

15 מימי כזב ויתעם בתוהו ו‍לוא דרך

. . . when the Scoffer arises, who will have dripped lying waters on Israel. Thus, he will lead them astray into a landless wilderness without an escape route. (CD 1:14b–15a)

### 3.2.1.1.6.2. Pesher Micah

As stated above, the phrase מטיף הכזב also appears in *Pesher Micah*, in an extended passage that provides commentary on the Just Teacher.

[בפשע                                                                    ] F8-10:1

[יעקב כול זאת ובחטאות בית ישראל מה פשע יע]קב הלא F8-10:2

[שומרון ומה במות יהודה הלא יר]ו‍[ש]לם ושמתי שומרון] F8-10:3

[לעי השדה למטעי כרם              פשרו על מטיף הכזב F8-10:4

[אשר הואה התעה[94] את ה]פתאים ומה במות יהודה F8-10:5

[הלא ירושלם פשרו ע]ל מו[רי הצדק אשר הואה F8-10:6

[יורה התורה לעצת]ו ולכ[ו]ל המתנדבים לוסף על בחירי F8-10:7

[אל עושי התורה] בעצת היחד אשר ינצל[ו] מיום F8-10:8

[משפט . . . F8-10:9

["All this is] for the transgression [of Jacob and for the sins of the House of Israel. What is Jac]ob['s transgression?] Is it not [Samaria? And what are the high places of Judah? Are they not Jer]usa[lem?" (Mic 1:5). "I will make Samaria as a ruin of the field, and as places for planting vineyards . . . " (Mic 1:6).] Its eschatological interpretation pertains to the Spewer of Lies, [who will have led astray] simple. "And what are Judah's altars? [Are they not Jerusalem?" (Mic 1:5). Its eschatological interpretation refers to] the Just Teacher who himself [will teach the Torah to] his [Council] and to all those who will volunteer to be added to the chosen of [God, those ones who will observe the law] in the council of the Yahad who will be saved on the Day of [Judgment . . . ] (1Q14 F8–10:1–9)

---

94  Milik restores יתעה, apparently on the basis of *Pesher Nahum* (4Q169) F3–4ii:8.

פשר[ו ע]ל מתעי אפרים אשר בתלמוד שקרם ולשון כזביהם ושפת מרמה יתעו רבים

[Its] eschatological interpretation pertains to those who lead Ephraim astray, who in their lying Talmud, specious tongue, and deceitful lip *mislead* many.

The reading התעה is more likely here. Cf. 1QpHab 10:9 cited immediately above pertaining to the מטיף הכזב.

This passage, too, lends further support to our thesis that the Just Teacher is a figure of the future. The verb [ו]נצּל in line 8 describes a futuristic salvation of those who choose to join the new community.

Returning to *Pesher Habakkuk*, on the whole, its author expands greatly the theme begun by the writer of MTA. In MTA, the offense of the Spewer of Lies is leading a community against the Just Teacher. Nothing in this work suggests that he personally attacks the מורה and his community. He is corrupt and wicked, but he does not threaten personally the Just Teacher. In Hab 1:13b the prophet asks, "Why are you silent when the wicked swallows the more righteous than he?" Taking the prophet as a theme, this pesherite writer construes this question as his chief concern.

The pesher has a beginning and an ending, both of which unify the author's vision for the end of time. He apparently started with תחלת דור אחרון (the beginning of the apocalypse) and concludes with the final destruction of paganism from the earth. *Pesher Habakkuk*'s wording and format help to unify it, just as those of MTA demonstrate the unity of this prior work.

### 3.2.1.1.6.3. Pesher Psalms

Two pesherite commentaries on the psalter are attested: 4Q171 with 101 lines on Ps 37, 45 and 60, and 4Q173 with 21 lines on Ps 127, 129 and 118. Let us not forget that the ancient authors and scribes regarded David as a prophet whose words presaged the future. A single topic dominates these pesherite texts: the מורה הצדק, here frequently called the priest, and, as in *Pesher Habakkuk*, the איש הכזב and the כוהן הרשע. The author of *Pesher Psalms* amplifies MTA which introduces these figures in CD 1:10b–2:1. On several points, however, the pesherite commentator somewhat extends MTA with other minor themes. The sobriquet עדת האביונים, reconstructed at the beginning and recurring twice, is unique to the commentary on Psalms. Note, however, the phrase עצת אביונים in the *War Scroll* text 4Q491 F11i:11. The next passage ascribes to the עדת האביונים the reward for accepting the sectarian date of the Day of Atonement.

וענוים ירשו ארץ והתענגו על רוב שלום פשרו על F1-2ii:8

עדת האביונים אשר יקבלו את מועד התעות ונצלו מכול פחי F1-2ii:9

בליעל ואחר יתענגו כול ב[נ]י הארץ והתדשנו בכול תענׄוׄגׄ F1-2ii:10

*vacat* בשר F1-2ii:11

"And the meek will inherit the land and enjoy the abundance of peace"
(Ps 37:11). Its eschatological interpretation concerns the congregation
of the destitute who will accept the Day of Atonement (literally "fasting") and will be rescued from the snares of Belial. And thereafter (as
a reward) all the s[on]s of the earth will be joyful and fattened with all
the pleasure of flesh.[95] (4Q171 F1-2ii:8–11a)

The Psalms commentator singles out the rewards given to the righteous who will celebrate the Day of Atonement in accordance with
the sectarian calendation. This whole passage castigates those who
celebrate the festivals by the reckoning of the opposition.

    Just prior to this passage is a text that deals with the chronology of
the sect, also taken from MTA.

F1-2ii:5                             ועוד מעט ואין רשע

F1-2ii:6     ואתבוננה על מקומו ואיננו פשרו על כול הרשעה לסוף

F1-2ii:7     ארבעים השנה אשר יתמו ולוא ימצא בארץ כול איש

F1-2ii:8                                         ש[ר]ע

"But in a short while the wicked will be no longer. I will search for his
place but he will not be there" (Ps 37:10). Its eschatological interpretation concerns all the wickedness at the end of the forty years when
they will be exterminated and no [wi]cked man will be found in the
land. (4Q171 F1–2ii:5b–8a)

Whence comes the idea of a period of forty years? The source seems
to be CD 20:13b–15a.

20:13                                                  ומיום

20:14     האסף יורה היחיד עד תם כל אנשי המלחמה אשר שבו

20:15                               עם איש הכזב כשנים ארבעים:

And from the day of the assembling by the Unique Teacher until the
destruction of all the warriors who will have joined with the Man of
Lies will elapse about forty years. (CD 20:13b–15a)

Scrollists translate האסף to mean the *ingathering* (i.e. the death) of
the Unique Teacher. I have argued, however, that this term in CD

---

[95] Some scrollists translate תענית as "error" or "distress." See respectively Cook,
in *The Dead Sea Scrolls*, 221 and Martínez and Tigchelaar, *Scrolls Study Edition*, vol.
1, 343. However, it is clear that the phrase מועד התענית here has the same meaning
as it does in CD 6:18–19.

    and to observe the day of the Sabbath including its elaborations and the festive
    seasons and the day of fasting (Atonement) in accordance with the practice of
    those who will enter the new covenant in the land of Damascus . . .

20:14 as well as in 19:35 does not refer to the Teacher's death, but to the *assembling* of the people under his leadership, and that at its completion (תם) all the warriors who had rebelled will meet their demise.[96] CD 20:14 employs the wording of Deut 2:14.

וְהַיָּמִים אֲשֶׁר־הָלַכְנוּ מִקָּדֵשׁ בַּרְנֵעַ עַד אֲשֶׁר־עָבַרְנוּ אֶת־נַחַל זֶרֶד
שְׁלֹשִׁים וּשְׁמֹנֶה שָׁנָה עַד־תֹּם כָּל־הַדּוֹר אַנְשֵׁי הַמִּלְחָמָה מִקֶּרֶב הַמַּחֲנֶה
כַּאֲשֶׁר נִשְׁבַּע יְהוָה לָהֶם

> The time that we spent in travel from Kadesh-barnea until we crossed the wadi Zered was thirty-eight years, until the complete (תם) demise of the whole generation of warriors from the camp, as the LORD had sworn to them. (Deut 2:14)

It stresses that just as those who rebelled in the wilderness against Moses died out after thirty-eight years, so those who will not join the Teacher when he assembles the people in Damascus (resembling Moses' gathering the Israelites in Egypt for liberation) will perish after about forty years.

Drawing on MTA, our pesherite writer makes the same point. Indeed, all three texts (Deut 2:14; CD 20:14 and 4Q171 F1–2ii:6–8) employ the same verbal root תמם. Each designates a similar chronology of approximately forty years. Thus we may be assured that the pesher's period of forty years draws on MTA. Moreover, the pesherite writer attests to the fact that האסף in MTA does not, as many have argued, allude to the *death* of the Just Teacher, but refers to his act of *assembling* the exiles in Damascus, resembling Moses' gathering the elders of Israel (Exod 3:16; 4:29) and eventually the entire nation for their liberation from oppression. As to the number forty, it is traditional to divide the life of Moses into three periods of forty years. Scripture tells us that Moses was eighty years of age at the time of the exodus and lived to one hundred and twenty. Rabbinic and New Testament literature, likewise, divide his life into three periods of forty years each. Hence, here too our text is modeled after the life of Moses.

Returning to the pesher's main theme, the struggle between the Man of Lies and the Just Teacher, the commentator, like that of *Pesher Habakkuk*, expands upon Ps 37:7.

---

[96] Ben Zion Wacholder, "The Teacher of Righteousness is Alive, Awaiting the Messiah: האסף in CD as Allusion to the Siniatic and Damascene Covenants," *HUCA* 70–71 (1999–2000): 75–93.

F1-2i:17 [דו]ם ל[י]הוה ו[ה]תחולל לו ואל תחר במצליח דרכו באיש
F1-2i:18 [עוש]ה מזמות [פשר]ו על איש הכזב אשר התעה רבים באמרי
F1-2i:19 שקר כיא בחרו בקלות ולוא שמ[עו] למליץ דעת למען
F1-2ii:1 יובדו בחרב וברעב ובדבר

["Be sil]ent before [the Lord and] wait for Him; and be not jealous of the (wicked) who is successful in his way, with the man [who plo]ts schemes" (Ps 37:7). Its [eschatological interpretation] concerns the Man of Lies who will mislead the masses with deceitful words, since they will choose trivial matters and will not hear[ken] to the interpreter of understanding. Hence, they will perish by the sword, famine and pestilence. (4Q171 F1–2i:17–ii:1a)

Note the phrase מליץ דעת, a sobriquet for the Just Teacher. That the מורה הצדק represents the core of this psalmic commentary becomes evident in its amplification of verses 23–26 of the biblical text in Fragment 1+3-4iii:14–19a.

14 כיא מיהו]ה מצעדי גבר כונ[נו בכ]ול דרכו יחפץ כיא יפ[ו]ל[ל] לוא]
15 יוטל כיא י[הוה סומך ידו] פשרו על הכוהן מורה ה[צדק אשר]
16 [ב]חר בו אל לעמוד ו[אשר] הכינו לבנות לו עדת[ האביונים 97[
17 [ודר]כו ישר לאמת [ נער היי]תי וגם זקנתי ולוא] ראיתי צדיק]
18 נעזב וזרעו מבקש לח[ם] כול היום] חונן ומלוה וזר[עו לברכה פשר]
19 הדבר על מו]ר[ה הצדק אשר ]אל מ[לוה בכול דרכיו98[

"For [the steps of a man are estab]lished from the Lo[rd]. He delights in all his way. If he stu[mb]les he does [not] go down, for the L[ord] supports his hand"] (Ps 37:23–24). Its eschatological interpretation concerns the Priest, the [Just] Teacher [whom] God [will have ch]osen to rise to office and [whom] He will have prepared to establish for Himself a congregation [of the destitute . . . ] and He straightens his [pa]th for truth. "I [was a youngster] and I also have aged, but I have not [seen the righteous] forsaken, and his seed begging for bread. [All day] he is gracious and lends, and [his] see[d becomes a blessing" (Ps 37:25–26) Its eschatological [interpretation] concerns the [Just] Teach[er whom ]God will ac[company in all his ways . . . ] (4Q171 F1+3–4iii:14–19a)

The pesherite writer continues his diatribe against the Wicked Priest through his prophetic interpretation of verses 32–33 in Fragment 3–10iv:7–10a.

---

97 Martínez and Tigchelaar reconstruct instead בחירו באמת (*Scrolls Study Edition*, vol. 1, 344). There is no such extant phrasing in the DSS, but עדת האביונים appears in 4Q171 F1–2ii:9 and 4Q171 F1+3–4iii:10.

98 My reconstruction of this lacuna draws on an alternative rendering of the participle מלוה in the preceding line for the pesher of the biblical text.

7 צופה רשע לצדיק ומבקש] להמיתו יה[וה [לוא יעזבנו בידו ולוא י]רשיענו

בהשפטו   8 פשרו על [הכו]הן הרשע אשר צ[ופ]ה הצד[י]ק ומבקש] להמיתו

[ בגלל התוכח]ת והתורה אשר שלח אליו ואל לוא יע]זבנו בידו] ולוא

9 [ירשיענו ב]ה[שפטו ולו י]שלם] אל ג[מולו לתתו   10 ביד עריצ]י] גואׄ֯ים

לעשות בו] משפט . . .

"The wicked man spies on the righteous man and attempts [to slay him.
The Lo]rd [will not entrust him into his hand, n]o[r will] he declare him
guilty at his judgment." (Ps 37:32–33). Its eschatological interpretation
concerns [the] Wicked [Pri]est who will be sp[y]ing on the righte[ous,
attempting to] slay him [on account of the rebuk]e and the Torah which
he will have sent him. But God will not le[ave him in his hand] and
[will] not [declare him guilty during] his judgment. Rather, [God will]
pay [him] (the Wicked Priest) his [re]compense by giving him into the
hand of the ruthless of the nations to execute [judgment] (death) upon
him. (4Q171 F3–10iv:7–10a)

These lines are interesting and perhaps explain why its author chose
to compose his commentary on this psalm describing the mortal
struggle between the צדיק and the רשע. The Wicked Priest will attempt
to kill the Just Teacher, thus bringing about his own destruction. My
reconstruction להמיתו [בגלל התוכח]ת והתורה אשר שלח אליו in line 8
compares to similar terminology in 1QpHab 5:8–12a cited above
pertaining to the conflict between the מורה הצדק and the איש הכזב.

8        למה תביטו בוגדים ותחריש בבלע

9 רשע צדיק ממנו vacat פשרו על בית אבשלום

10 ואנשי עצתם אשר נדמו בתוכחת מורה הצדק

11 ולוא עזרוהו על איש הכזב vacat אשר מאס את

12 התורה בתוך כול עצׄתׄם

"Why do you traitors look and are silent as the wicked swallows up
one who is more righteous than he?" (Hab 1:13b) Its eschatological
interpretation refers to the house of Absalom and their council who
will have fallen silent *at the (time of) the reproof by the Just Teacher*,[99]
not assisting him against the Man of Lies who will have despised the *Torah*
within their entire congregation. (1QpHab 5:8–12a)

---

[99]  See Brownlee's extended discussion as to whether the מורה הצדק is here a
subjective or an objective genitive (Brownlee, 93–94). My rendering this phrase as
a subjective genitive accords with the use of תוכחת in biblical wisdom literature and
the DSS, where God, wisdom and true justice function as the reprovers of those in
need of reproof. Cf. especially Prov 3:11: מוּסַר יְהוָה בְּנִי אַל־תִּמְאָס וְאַל־תָּקֹץ בְּתוֹכַחְתּוֹ
(My son, do not despise the correction of the Lord; nor loathe His reproof), a text
containing terminology similar to that of our Habakkuk pesher.

As reconstructed and interpreted in light of *Pesher Habakkuk*, the above
cited clause להמיתו [בגלל התוכח]ה והתורה אשר שלח אליו in *Pesher Psalms*
is interesting. The reason for the animosity of the Wicked Priest is that
the Just Teacher will have reproved him through a Torah which he
detested. What specifically that Torah was is of course not given. Yet,
the fact that this pesherite work follows MTA, which as I have argued
elsewhere is an amplification of the book of *Jubilees* described in
CD 16:1–3 as מדוקדק "perfect," suggests, perhaps, that the Torah
employed for the rebuke and dispatched by the Teacher to his opponent would be the book of *Jubilees*.[100] A related text in the so-called
*Catena*[a], which is really a pesher composition, contains the same idea.

תקעו שופר בגבעה השופר הואה ספר [התורה ראישונה הח]צ[ו]צרה הי[אה
ספר התורה שנית אשר מאסו כ]ול א[נ]שי עצתו וידברו עליו סרה

"Blow the *shofar* in Gibeah." (Hos 5:8). The *shofar* refers to the book [of
the first] Torah. "The tr]u[mpet" (Hos 5:8) i]s the book of the second
Torah which a[ll the me]mbers of the council will have despised and
spoken of in a deviant manner. (4Q177 F1–4:13b–14a)

This "pesherite" work as reconstructed here[101] reiterates the idea of
two Torahs, apparently the Pentateuch and *Jubilees*. The rejection of
the second Torah recalls the animosity of the Wicked Priest toward
the צדיק (the Just Teacher) in the above cited pesher on Ps 37:32–33
for having reproved him, dispatching to him a copy of the Torah.

4Q171 F3–10iv:13–14, a pesher on Ps 37:35–36 likewise continues to deal with the איש הכזב, but because of its fragmentary nature
we omit it here. On the other hand, two of the final three texts in
*Pesher Psalms* which refer to the מורה הצדק, although only partially
extant and whose state does not allow for a confident reconstruction,
nevertheless deserve attention. The comments on Ps 45:2 in lines
26–27 of the above listed 4Q171 F3–10iv composite and in line 1
of fragment 11 of the same manuscript, are interesting. The latter
section relates to CD 15, which repeatedly uses the clause "to return

---

[100]  See my above cited article "*Jubilees* as the Super Canon: Torah-Admonition
versus Torah-Commandment."

[101]  Allegro transcribes this text as follows:

[תקעו שופר בגבעה השופר הואה ספר]          [    ]ו[ הו]אה

ספר התורה שנית אש]ל[          א]נ[שי עצתו וידברו עליו סרה

John M. Allegro, *Qumran Cave 4.1 (4Q158–4Q186)* (DJD V; Oxford: Clarendon,
1968), 68.

to the Torah of Moses with a whole heart and soul . . ."

[ ולשוני עט                                                    F3-10iv:26

[102סופר מהיר פשרו ]על מורה[ הצדק אשר ידבר ל]פני(?) אל במעני לשון[102    F3-10iv:27

F11:1    . . . לשוב יחד לתורה ב]כול לב ובכול נפש [103

"And my tongue is the stylus [of an expert scribe" (Ps 45:2). Its eschatological interpretation] concerns [the Just] Teacher [who will speak
be]fore God with a confessional tongue . . . to return together to the
Torah with[ a whole heart and soul.] (4Q171 F3–10iv:26b–27; 4Q171
F11:1)

My reconstruction for the pesher portion of the second of these fragmentary texts containing the phrase מורה הצדק draws on Ps 56:6.[104]

[                                ] שו[א לכם] משכימי קום מאחרי שבת אוכלי לחם העצבים כן יתן לידידו שנא

[                         (?)פשרו א[שר יבקשו] לעצב את דברי הצדיק כול היום

[                    ב[הן לאחרית הק]ץ     ] נס[תרות מורה הצדק

["It is vai]n for you [who rise up early, to stay up late, to eat the bread
of painful sorrow; for so he gives sleep to His beloved." (Ps 127:2). Its
eschatological interpretation concerns those w]ho will seek [to distort the
words of the righteous all day long . . . hid[den] by the Just Teacher[ .
. . in] them toward the end of the er[a . . . (4Q173 F1:2–5)

The third of these fragmentary references to the Just Teacher in *Pesher
Psalms*, 4Q173 F2:2, contains little that is helpful for constructing its
context, save that the subject matter continued to be concerned with
this leading eschatological personality.[105]

---

[102]  Allegro (DJD V, 45) transcribes

[ ולשוני עט                        ]ס[פרי[           ] 26

[ו[ אל במעני לשון                ]סופר מהיר פשרו[ על מורה[ הצדק      27

[103]  For my restoration cf. CD 15:9; 16:4–5.

[104]  Allegro (DJD V, 51–52) provides no reconstruction for what he presumes to
be the pesher. He transcribes lines 4–5 as follows.

[                ]ע[תרות מורה הצדק[           ] 4

[                כו[הן לאחרית הק]ץ           ] 5

*sup]plications* of the Teacher of Righteousness [ . . . [5] . . . pri]est at the end of
ti[me . . .

[105]  See the different reconstructions in Allegro, 52 and in Martínez and Tigchelaar, *Scrolls Study Edition*, vol. 1, 350.

### 3.2.1.1.6.4. Pesher Nahum

*Pesher Nahum*, of which portions of 61 lines have survived, has aroused much interest on account of some of its unique content. It diverges from the other pesherite writings in that it alludes to contemporary figures such as the Seleucid rulers, Antiochus and Demetrius. In some respects it resembles them, but in several features it is unique. It repeatedly interprets the destruction of Nineveh as presaging the downfall of the Kittim, a common topic in these biblical commentaries. Unique to *Pesher Nahum* is the repetition of דורשי החלקות (interpreters of smooth things), a polemical phrase which occurs five or six times. These preachers are associated with Menasseh and the house of Peleg on the one hand and Ephraim on the other. The sobriquet דורשי החלקות probably draws on אשר דרשו בחלקות in MTA (CD 1:18). Other works such as *Hodayot*[a], *Pesher Isaiah* and 4Q177 (4QCatena[a]) likewise have this phrase, but in none of them does it receive the emphasis given to it in *Pesher Nahum* where it occurs six times. Unique to this commentary as well as to the DSS on the whole is a polemic against a "Talmud" ascribed to the Ephraimites.

> פשר]ו ע]ל מתעי אפרים אשר בתלמוד שקרם ולשון כזביהם ושפת מרמה
> יתעו רבים

> Its eschatological interpretation pertains to those who lead Ephraim astray, who through their specious Talmud, their *lying* tongue, and deceitful lip will mislead many. (4Q169 F3-4ii:8)

כזבים calls attention to the איש הכזב of *Pesher Habakkuk* and *Pesher Psalms* on the one hand, and on the other to the מימי כזב of CD 1:15. Compare also יתעו רבים with ויתעם of CD 1:15. Scrollists have rendered the term תלמוד here as "teaching." In my opinion, however, the fact that the word תלמוד is preceded by the preposition ב suggests that the meaning here is a literary composition; and since it is followed by the parallel phrase ולשון כזביהם, it alludes to an oral composition that was important to the sect's opponents, probably an early form of our Mishnah. The Mishnah was edited by Rabbi Judah Ha-Nasi (c. 200 C.E.), but the term תלמוד in our text apparently goes back to the second or early first century B.C.E. Certainly this is the oldest reference to this literature by name. The entire comment on Nah 3:4, "Its eschatological interpretation pertains to those who lead Ephraim astray, who through their specious Talmud, their lying tongue, and deceitful lip will mislead many," consists of a polemic against the

Pharisees. As to the temporal relation of *Pesher Nahum* to the other pesherite writings, it probably is one of the last of these commentaries in the DSS. Like the others, it speaks of אחרית הימים (the end of days) or אחרית הקץ (the end of the epoch), making its eschatological stance manifest. The extant part of *Pesher Nahum* does not contain the sobriquet מורה הצדק, but its entire language makes it a part of the pesherite literature related to the Just Teacher in MTA.

### 3.2.1.1.6.5. Pesher Isaiah

The remains of five commentaries from the peshers of the book of Isaiah survive (4Q161–165). In essence, they resemble the pesher on Habakkuk which is virtually complete and, like *Pesher Habakkuk*, are dependent on MTA. These works deal with two themes which are amplifications of MTA: 1) the Just Teacher and 2) the Scoffer and his followers. An additional theme common to the pesherite works, preserved also in *Pesher Nahum*, deals with the Kittim, the pesher's sobriquet for the mighty pagan nations, and their eschatological defeat by the Just Teacher. However, one text, 4Q165 F1–2:3, although fragmentary, presents a novel idea that someone, probably the Just Teacher, will disclose a תורת הצדק (a just Torah), giving a legal stance to the instructions of the Teacher, as well as, perhaps, revealing the etiology behind the sobriquet מורה (ה)צדק. In other words, the name "Just Teacher" originated with his presentation of a just Torah to Israel.

These texts emphasize the defeat of the Kittim and the downfall of those who will follow the Scoffer. In the midst of this, the author gives great attention to Isa 10–11 and other Isaianic passages that form an eschatological theme. However, what has survived is so fragmentary that no detailed account can be derived. In one such passage, the author appears to allude to David's conquest when he was ascending from the valley of Akko to make war against the Philistines (4Q161 F5–6:11). Although David is not found in what survives of this passage, he is recorded in 4Q161 F8–10:17–18a, another fragment commenting on Isa 11:1–5.

17 [פשרו על צמח] דויד העומד באח[רית הימים [
18 [לכלות את או]יבו[106]

---

[106] The reconstruction לכלות את is mine.

> [The eschatological interpretation of the passage concerns the sprout]
> of David which will arise in the la[st days . . . to defeat] his [en]emy.
> (4Q161 F8–10:17–18a)

The common denominator of all these pesherite passages is their eschatological stance. Prophecies are not contemporary statements, but futuristic expectations. As we have seen, the authors of both MTA and *Pesher Habakkuk* describe at length the two figures, the מורה הצדק and the איש הכזב. One would be remiss not to repeat that these figures appear also in three other pesherite works (Psalms, Isaiah and Micah) but nowhere else in the DSS.

This analysis of virtually all phrases that allude to the מורה הצדק and the איש הכזב and its related sobriquets shows the importance of these two personalities in MTA and the pesherite writings wherein they play a vital role. Indeed, scroll scholarship makes the Teacher the founder of the Essene movement and the Man of Lies a Pharisaic leader. Much literature has been devoted to their identification. Louis Ginzberg, writing before the discovery of the DSS, viewed the role of the מורה צדק of CD as a model for the Elijah found in later rabbinic and Talmudic literature, especially his role as the true arbiter in legal subject matter relating to *halakah*. It is the Elijah modeled after the מורה צדק that will answer all unresolved questions raised by the Talmudic sages. Note, however, that Ginzberg, in his lengthy discussion, ignores altogether CD's mention of the conflict between the Just Teacher and his nemesis, the איש הלצון. By contrast, for the pesherite writers it is the struggle between these two personalities and the attempt of the Wicked Priest to destroy, if not murder, the Just Teacher that characterizes their extraordinary role. As we noted above, modern scholarship views the significance of the Just Teacher in MTA as that he was the founder and ideologue of the Essene movement. Nothing in MTA or the pesherite accounts of the מורה הצדק suggests that they saw him as the founder of a movement. On the contrary, what we find in these writings is his millennial role. In the words of CD 7:4b–6a, the life and practices of the Just Teacher will serve as a model for the eschaton: "As for all who walk in these rules in perfect holiness, in accordance with all His chastisements, the divine covenant will remain faithful to them, keeping them alive for thousands of generations." What the pesherite writers understand in these two personalities is the dualism, the conflict between good and evil. It is this dissonance that reflects the author's interest in MTA.

### 3.2.1.2. *A Review of History (CD 2:2–3:12a)*

The perspective of CD 1:1–2:1 has been God's discord with mankind, those who know righteousness and those who do not. The prototypes for these groups are the two personalities, the מורה צדק and the איש הלצון. The text also displays a twofold definition of epochs: first the ריאשונים (the ancestors) who are a mixture of the righteous and the wicked, whose presence in Israel ends with the חרבן (the entire era of the destruction of the first temple), presumably beginning in 597 and continuing until 586 B.C.E.[107] The second period is that of the אחרונים, the succeeding generations commencing with this devastation and continuing to the קץ (ה)רשעה (restored into line 2 of the preamble)—the "end of the epoch of wickedness" also rendered as אחרית הקץ (the end of time) in 4QpNah (169) F3–4iii:3 and the קץ חרון (the 'end' of the epoch of anger) in CD 1:5—which marks the beginning of the messianic age exposed in part in CD 1:7–12.

### 3.2.1.2.1. *God's Providence from Creation until the End of Time (2:2–13)*

CD 2:2–13 begins with a new address to the audience, commencing with the formula ועתה שמעו אלי (and now, heed me), a variant of ועתה שמעו לי, addressed once again to all the covenanters. Note that the epithet יודעי צדק in CD 1:1 is now altered to באי ברית (those who are entering the covenant). The phrases יודעי צדק and באי ברית are essentially synonymous, except that the covenanters are part of a new organization. ברית in MTA has two senses: a) emphasizing those who enter the traditional covenant of Moses (באי ברית), and b) accentuating its newness (ברית (ה)חדשה). Each of these phrases appears seven times in what remains of MTA. The latter receives its proper explication in CD 19:33b–34.

כֿן כל האנשים אשר באֿוֿ בבריֿת    33

34 החדשה בארץ דמשק ושבו ויבגדו ויסורו מבאר מים החיים

This will also apply to all those who will have entered into the *new covenant* in the land of Damascus but will have changed (their minds)

---

[107] The inception of this period is the date of Nebuchadnezzar's second deportation of residents of Judah (Ezek 1:2), the first having been in 605 B.C.E. (Dan 1:1–2) and the third one being in 586, the razing of the temple and turning of the city. This date appears preferable for the starting point, since the author seems to build his chronography on the book of Ezekiel, dating the exile to that of Jehoiachin.

and acted treacherously and turned away from the well of living waters.
(CD 19:33b–34)

In this sense, the old covenant is reinterpreted in the light of apocryphal, pseudepigraphic and other writings, the remains of many
of which have survived in the DSS. It is this fusion of the old
and the new ברית which became the kernel out of which arose the
אנשי היחד (the men of togetherness) of *Rule of the Community* and
the Essene movement of the classical sources Philo of Alexandria,
Flavius Josephus and Pliny the Elder.[108]

Prior to MTA, dissenting views representing a variety of opinions
and a multiplicity of biblical amplifications reflected the suppositions
of isolated writers and their readers. Such is the case in the book
of the Giants, *Enoch*, *Jubilees*, and even *Temple Scroll.* Now we hear
the author of MTA urging the formation of a distinct grouping, a
sect only beginning to take shape. A name for the members of this
emerging group, באי (ה)ברית, a term frequent in MTA, occurs only
once in *Rule of the Community*, a work that more often uses the above
mentioned sobriquet, אנשי היחד. Except for perhaps one reference,
MTA does not employ the name יחד. Hence, in my opinion, *Rule of
the Community*, so much influenced by MTA, is posterior to it. The
composition of our document occurred subsequent to that of *Jubilees*
but prior to *Rule of the Community* and before the pesherite commentaries on Scripture, as we noted in our discussion on CD 1:13–2:1.

The essence of CD 2:2–13 may be described as a historiographic
panorama of God's purpose in creating the universe. The author
claims to reveal the origins of wickedness. This philosophy is not mere
theory, but has as its purpose keeping the people away from evil. God
has destroyed wickedness throughout history, but in every generation
has preserved a righteous remnant to populate the earth. Our author
goes on to stress divine foreknowledge, declaring that God knew the
acts of humanity prior to their birth, hating especially those genera-

---

[108] This designation gives us the birth of the sect that is partly comparable to
the Pharisees and Sadducees. It is not what Schiffman proposes to argue, linking
the Essenes with an offbreak of the Sadducees, although the term צדק is indeed
rooted to both the Sadducees and the Sons of Zadok. The origins of Sadduceeism
extend back to the Zadokite priests of the First Temple. The sons of Zadok emanate from Ezek 40–48 where they are depicted as those who observed the commandments of the Lord while all of Israel had gone astray.

tions that shed blood (CD 2:7b–8a).[109] God's providence extends to all of history, *Urzeit* and *Endzeit*; He reveals to us His concept of the historical process, the sequence of the events yet to come (CD 2:9–10). On this point, our writer had earlier noted, ". . . for [(God)] has fore[told the firs]t [as well as the latter things and] what will transpire thereafter in them (the Divisions of the Eschatological Epochs) . . ." (4Q268 F1:2b–3a).

### 3.2.1.2.2. *Those Who Lived Righteously and Those Who Did Not (2:14–3:12a)*

The phrases יודעי צדק in CD 1:1, באי ברית in 2:2 and בנים here in 2:14 are employed for a group in the process of formation (as mentioned earlier), rather than as names for an existing organization such as אנשי היחד of *Rule of the Community*. The formula here, ועתה בנים שמעו לי, draws on the same wording in Prov 5:7 and 7:24, in whose contexts personified wisdom exhorts the young naive males of the community of Israel to heed her wise counsel so as not to be trapped in sin. The same formula occurs in Prov 8:32 wherein wisdom emphasizes the reward for observing her ways.

Prov 5:7  וְעַתָּה בָנִים שִׁמְעוּ־לִי וְאַל־תָּסוּרוּ מֵאִמְרֵי־פִי
Prov 7:24  וְעַתָּה בָנִים שִׁמְעוּ־לִי וְהַקְשִׁיבוּ לְאִמְרֵי־פִי
Prov 8:32  וְעַתָּה בָנִים שִׁמְעוּ־לִי וְאַשְׁרֵי דְּרָכַי יִשְׁמֹרוּ

And now O sons, hear me and do not depart from the words of my mouth.
And now O sons, hear me and give heed to the words of my mouth.
And now O sons, hear me, for happy are they who observe my ways.

The sapiential terminology of each of these passages compares to that of our text. Note especially the exhortation in CD 2:16 not to turn away toward thoughts inclining toward transgression with eyes of whoredom (זנות). This compares with wisdom's warning about the זונה (whore) of Prov 6:26 and 7:10. כי רבים תעו בם (since many have gone astray through them), the immediately succeeding clause in CD 2:16b–17a, echoes Prov 7:26—כִּי־רַבִּים חֲלָלִים הִפִּילָה וַעֲצֻמִים כָּל־הֲרֻגֶיהָ (for she has toppled many wounded; and mighty are all

---

[109]  For the inclusion of a phrase dealing with the shedding of blood, see *Jub.* 6:38, where the author concludes his injunctions concerning calendation with a single clause on the eating of blood. It might be that our writer refers here also not to the shedding of blood, but to its consumption (cf. CD 3:6 below).

her slain). Personified wisdom's compassion toward the young men
of the sapiential texts is transformed in MTA into that of a caring
father for his children in need of enlightenment. בנים is here a term of
endearment as it is CD 13:9 in the phrase וירחם עליהם כאב לבניו (And
he will have compassion upon them as a father has for his children).

The author goes on in CD 2:14–15 to show that God wants not
only the observance of the commandment, but the sapiential element
as well. In the first ועתה formula as reconstructed in 4Q266 F1:5–6
in the preamble, the author tells of the mighty acts of God and the
details of how the world came into being. The story of how eternity
came into existence in the context of this formula reappears in CD
1:1–2 and here in the phrase ולהבין במעשי אל (and to understand
the acts of God).

The giants and the flood, the destruction of the rebellious wilderness generation and the desolation of the land in the text that
follows serve as examples of divine retribution in history. On the
other hand Noah and the patriarchs Abraham, Isaac and Jacob,
God's favorites, are recorded as lovers of God. A close reading of
these lines shows not only the author's historiography, but also some
of the contemporary lore that he may have used in constructing this
survey. Certainly, the mention of the עירי השמים (the Watchers of
Heaven) echoes material in the *Book of the Giants* and *Enoch*. The writer
shows an awareness of *Genesis Apocryphon* as well as the last section
of the book of *Enoch* where the figure of Noah as an extraordinary
giant is described in great detail. However, whereas *Genesis Apocryphon* makes Noah phenomenal in this respect, our writer depicts the
entire pre-flood generation as people whose height was like that of
cedars and mountains. More significantly, the author reflects in his
use of extra-biblical texts what we find elsewhere in MTA: a close
awareness of the chronological scheme preserved in *Jubilees* as it is
evidenced in MTA's classification of history into epochs along with
a detailed chronology of the antediluvian generations.

### 3.2.1.3. *The Sons of Zadok and Their Adherents (CD 3:12b–4:10a)*
With CD 3:12b the author begins to present a more vivid picture of
the righteous and the wicked. Whereas the previous segments dealt
with these contrasting groups of the past, beginning here the author
returns to his favorite theme, the organization that he proposes to
form. He links these addressees to the righteous of the past as well
as to the forerunners of the new epoch.

### 3.2.1.3.1. *Ezekiel 44:15 and Its Eschatological Exegesis: the Sons of Zadok (3:12b–4:7a)*

He refers to his listeners as מחזיקים במצות אל אשר נותרו מהם (those who are clinging to God's commandments, the remnant).[110] For them God will establish the covenant, presumably the ברית החדשה. This group will be the privileged ones. מחזיקים refers to those who would be joining the new group. That the author repeatedly identifies his audience with this epithet suggests that at the time of this composition this group had as yet not acquired a name. As mentioned above, the tag יחד, so prevalent in *Rule of the Community* and elsewhere, occurs perhaps only once or twice in this large text. It must have come into vogue posterior to the composition of MTA.

Thus, MTA has five leading themes: 1) God and His covenant, 2) the historical ראשונים, ancestors who are divided into the righteous and the wicked, 3) the audience to whom the work is addressed (known also as the אחרונים), 4) the opponents, the מסיגי הגבול (the Shifters of the Boundary) against whom the author thunders over and over, and 5) the eschatological generations when the Messiah of Aaron and Israel will arise to form the eternal era.

As to the נסתרות (the hidden matters), also restored into the preamble in 4Q266 F1:6 and parallel to רזים in 1QHᵃ 26:1, lines 13–15 identify what they refer to in this context, namely the Sabbath and the festive seasons in which Israel had gone astray. These clues suggest that the hidden matters pertain to the disputations concerning the calendar. In contrast to the lunisolar reckoning of a three hundred and sixty-five day year, the author refers here to a three hundred and sixty-four day calendation by which the appointed seasons (מועדים) should be reckoned as examples of the נסתרות.[111] Interestingly enough, the rabbis also refer to the setting of the festive calendars as סוד העיבור (the mystery of calendation). By this they mean that the setting of the length of the month and the year is the prerogative of the court and those appointed by them. However, the author of MTA may mean that the matters of calendation under the sectarian reckoning had resulted from direct revelation and must not be interfered with by courts or any other human institution.

---

[110] See CD 1:20; 3:20; 7:13 and 20:27 for the use of מחזיקים. The wording מחזיקי בברית from 1QSb 1:2 seems to belong to 4Q266 F2i:24 which is restored from CD 1:20–21, resulting in a somewhat longer line matching the surrounding text.

[111] For the calendric meaning of מועד, cf. 4Q268 F1:4.

MTA's stress here on the reckoning of time may help resolve a
problem in the sect's history of calendation. Whereas the books of
*Enoch* and *Jubilees* devote considerable space to the three hundred and
sixty four day year, they make no mention of the משמרות (courses).
Despite the lengthy treatment of the sectarian calendation in these
writings, nothing in these traditions links this reckoning to the priestly
courses that took turns in the service of the sanctuary. CD 3:21–4:2a
goes on to cite Ezek 44:15 concerning the priests of the sons of Zadok
who observe the משמרת of the temple. Although the clause שמרו את
משמרת מקדשי may convey in Ezekiel the maintenance of the service
of God's sanctuary (see NJPS), the sense given to this clause in CD
4:1, by reason of what follows in lines 2b–7a describing the listing
of the sons of Zadok, is identical to that found in the Mishnah and
Talmud—the weekly courses from one Sabbath to another kept by
the descendants of Zadok. We now have a number of scrolls that
list the calendars with their משמרות, the twenty-four priestly courses
bearing the names of the sons of Zadok and Abiathar found in the
מחלקות (divisions) of 1 Chr 24.[112] The catalogue of names in the
weekly courses of the DSS differs in one minor point from that of
the chronicler. Whereas the latter begins with Jehoiarib, its order in
the scrolls starts with Gamul as the first course, perhaps because,
whereas the name Jehoiarib echoes contention and conflict, Gamul
denotes recompense or retribution, an idea favored in MTA. The
question arises, at what point did the sectarian calendation adopt
these priestly courses, completely absent in *Enoch* and *Jubilees*? It is
likely that our passage in MTA interprets the מִשְׁמֶרֶת of Ezekiel's Sons
of Zadok as the calendation of the Sabbath and the festive seasons,
and created the impetus to link the element of the weekly courses
into sectarian calendation. Hence, the number of sobriquets found
here which tell about the Sons of Zadok in a list of names alludes
to the introduction of the weekly courses into the sect's calendric
system. If this was indeed the case, it was of great importance, for
by setting the weekly courses to the three hundred and sixty-four day
year, each week assumed an additional element of priestly interest
and made it possible to have a system of reckoning which made the
holidays always fall on the same day of the year.[113] Thus the sobri-

---

[112] Cf. 1QM 2:2–6; 4Q320–330.

[113] As mentioned on p. 137, the League of Nations deliberated on creating such
a reckoning for modernity so that the New Year and all other festive occasions would

quet "called by name, who will arise at the end of days. Here is a listing of their names by their ancestry and the time of their offici- ating" (CD 4:4–5a) found in this text may have given rise to linking the three hundred and sixty-four day year with the chronicler's list of divisions. Note that whereas the chronicler calls these divisions מַחְלְקוֹת, the (priestly) divisions, our writer and the sectarian calendar makers refer to them as משמרת or משמרות.[114]

The issue of calendation in our text becomes especially important in the preceding clauses of CD 3:14–16 with the injunction that life is dependent upon the following: 1) observance of the festive seasons, 2) His righteous testimony and 3) the desires of His will by which man shall observe and live and dig a well of many waters. The sec- tion goes on to say the negative: ומואסיהם לא יחיה (. . . but He will not let those who despise them live). The text continues והם התגוללו בפשע אנוש ובדרכי נדה ויאמרו כי לנו היא (since they wallowed in man's transgression and in the ways of impurity, saying, 'It belongs to us'). This passage too refers to the sinfulness of the past. The meaning of ויאמרו כי לנו היא in CD 3:18 could mean that Israel claimed that *God* had commanded their evil acts, a rendition that is implausible. There- fore, it is more likely that כי לנו היא denotes their claim to be righteous.

CD 3:18–20a continues by teaching that, despite Israel's continued record of wickedness, God in His mysterious ways is acting magnani- mously with her (albeit the remnant) by forgiving her sins and will erect for her a new sanctuary, a faithful house (בית נאמן), the likeness of which has never been—a claim that the futuristic temple will be more glorious than that of the highly endowed Solomonic sanctuary. Standard translations take these clauses as referring to the temple of the past, that God had forgiven Israel's sins and built a faithful sanc- tuary, the likes of which had never existed. Rabin adduces support for this interpretation by referring to the phraseology in 1 Sam 2:35, paraphrases of which he finds in *Rule of the Community* 8:9, *1 En.* 91:13 and *Jub.* 22:24. It follows that the reading וַיִּבֶן in the consecutive past, "then he built" for them a faithful house, refers to that established by David and Solomon. This interpretation is implausible. True enough, Rabin's citations are unchallengeable. However, it does not follow that ויבן or, for that matter the other intertestamental references, necessarily

---

fall on the same day from year to year. It abandoned its endeavors on the so-called 13-month calendar plan in 1937.

[114] See "Calendrical Documents and Mishmarot" in DJD XXI (2001).

refer to it. The concluding clause in CD 3:19, "the likeness of which had never existed from earliest time until now," where "now" refers to the time of the author's book, could not have meant the first temple. Secondly, CD 3:21–4:2a, citing Ezek 44:15, does not refer to the first temple, but to a futuristic sanctuary. Incidentally an awareness of this tendency in MTA is very important for the understanding of the DSS. Scholars tend to mistranslate meaning when they become slavish to the biblical original. We must necessarily read, not וַיִּבֶן as a past consecutive, but וְיִבֶן (and he will build), a future tense verb which the author takes to refer to Ezekiel's sanctuary.[115] Again, the phrase "the likeness of which had never existed from earliest time until now" also excludes the possibility that the faithful house refers to the post-exilic temple, a sanctuary inferior in quality to that which Solomon had erected.[116] Furthermore, the citation from Ezek 44:15 in CD 3:21–4:2 which follows makes this view a certainty. The last nine chapters of Ezekiel depict a new sanctuary, built not by Zadok of David and Solomon, but by his descendants during the post-exilic period. This section proposes a new division of the tribes of Israel, a new epoch of prosperity, and the creation of a new nation that will prosper in its fertility. The future intent of the author's use of Ezek 44:15 will be discussed in greater length below.

Our text which continues in line 20, המחזיקים בו לחיי נצח וכל כבוד אדם להם (The people who cling to Him are destined to eternal life and all human glory will be accorded to them), summarizes the preceding section. Scholars have taken the word בו as referring to the temple. It is more likely, however, that it here refers to the deity, since the sanctuary is God's house and it is God who will give eternal life to those who cling to Him. With המחזיקים, the author continues the theme which extends throughout the work, describing the righteous which is the organization ultimately named Essenes, but here stressing the contrast with the wicked, the מסיגי (ה)גבול, "the Shifters of the Boundary."

As stated above, CD 3:20b–4:2a goes on to cite Ezek 44:15.

כאשר                                                              3:20
3:21 הקים אל להם ביד יחזקאל הנביא לאמר הכהנים והלוים ובני

---

[115] Cf. also Dan 11 wherein conventional biblical verbal patterns of regular imperfects and perfects consecutive are frequently ignored in favor of shortened imperfects preceded by ן to indicate future time.

[116] Cf. Ezra 3:12 and Hag 2:3.

4:1 צדוק אשר שמרו את משמרת מקדשי בתעות בני ישראל

4:2 מעלי הם יגישו לי חלב ודם *vacat* הכהנים הם שבי ישראל

> ...just as the Lord has established them by Ezekiel the prophet saying,
> "As for the priests and the Levites and the sons of Zadok who have kept
> the courses of My sanctuary when the children of Israel strayed from
> Me, they shall offer me fat and blood." (CD 3:20b–4:2a)

The mode of citation used in CD 3:20a–21 deserves a comment.
On the surface כאשר is another term used for quoting the prophets
Hosea, Amos and Isaiah, et al. In fact, however, as a citation formula
in MTA, כאשר הקים אל is used only for referencing Ezekiel.[117] The
other prophets are introduced with the phrases כאשר אמר or אשר
כתוב. The citation כאשר הקים אל fronts an extended clause in which
both the deity and the prophet are joined in a lengthy elaboration
that goes on to be interpreted word by word in 4:2–7. It seems that,
although MTA quotes Isaiah frequently, it is Ezekiel that receives the
greatest emphasis in MTA as we shall see. It is the role of the priests
of the house of Zadok in the land of Damascus that is elaborated
on over and over from this point to the end of the work.

Ezekiel 44:15 is well known in historical scholarship. Abraham Gei-
ger and Julius Wellhausen cited it to show that the book of Ezekiel,
which mentions priests and Levites, had not known the Pentateuch as
we have it, referring to the sons of Zadok as both priests and Levites.
In other words, the composition of the five books of Moses, especially
the priestly code, is presumed to be posterior to that of Ezekiel. Furthermore, as Wellhausen sees it, Ezekiel's sons of Zadok refer to the
high priests of the Solomonic temple.

Although, for the author of MTA, the sons of Zadok likewise have
an extraordinary role, they do not refer (as contended by Wellhausen
et al.) to the priesthood of the past, but to that of the future. For
MTA, the sobriquet "sons of Zadok," defined by Ezekiel four times
as being especially near to God (קרוב) while Israel as a whole went
astray (תעה), is a new priesthood for a new Israel.[118]

Let us now see how MTA exegetes Ezek 44:15.

הכהנים הם שבי ישראל CD 4:2

היוצאים מארץ יהודה והנלוים עמהם *vacat* ובני צדוק הם בחירי CD 4:3

---

[117] Cf. also 4Q271 F2:2a, restored from 4Q270 F3iii:14. The phrase הקים אל
occurs in CD 3:13 and 4:9, but not to quote a biblical text.

[118] Cf. 40:46; 43:19; 44:15 and 48:11.

CD 4:4 ישראל קריאי השם העמדים באחרית הימים הנה פרוש

CD 4:5 שמותיהם לתולדותם וקץ מעמדם ומספר צרותיהם ושני

CD 4:6 התגוררם ופירוש מעשיהם ‹אנשי› קודש ‹הרי›שונים אשר כפר

CD 4:7 אל בעדם ויצדיקו צדיק וירשיעו רשע

> The "priests" are the "penitent of Israel" who will depart from the land of Judah, and those who will accompany them. And the "sons of Zadok"[119] are the chosen of Israel, called by name, who will arise in the end of days. Here is a listing of their names by their ancestry and the time of their officiating and the number of their troubles and the years of their sojourn and the elaboration of the deeds of their holy <anc>estors whose (sins) God has atoned for. And they will declare the just righteous and the sinful wicked. (CD 4:2b–7a)

The priests refer to the contrite of Israel who will leave Judah and who, according to CD 6:5, will dwell in the land of Damascus. It is generally taken for granted that this passage refers to the priests of the past. However, it is clear that our text places them in the future. The basis for our futuristic understanding, however, rests in the succeeding clause. The prepositional phrase באחרית הימים in line 4 marks events yet to come, as necessarily does the participle העמדים associated with it. The parallel participial phrase, היוצאים מארץ יהודה, on line 3 must therefore also mark a future event. This means not that the exodus to Damascus had already occurred, but that it would take place in a time to come. This entire passage from lines 2–7 connotes an eschatological era. As was stated above, conventional reading takes this clause and those that follow to refer to the past.[120]

Many scrollists argue that the two words, והלוים הם (and the Levites are) preceded the phrase והנלוים עמהם in CD 4:3 to read "(the Levites are) those who accompanied them." I believe this misinterprets the text. On the contrary, the phrase והנלוים עמהם is a pun on Levites and places them as subordinate to the priests. In other words, it is the priests and not the Levites that will serve as the chieftains in the futuristic sanctuary. בני צדוק (sons of Zadok) is a sobriquet which

---

[119] 4Q266 F5i:15–17 quotes this text in part. It may be reconstructed as follows: כול שבי ישראל ה[יוצים מארץ יהודה ועמדם ב]ני צדוק הכהנים הנה המ]ה על ספר מדרש ה[תורה האחרון (As for all the penitent of Israel who [will exit from the land of Judah and with them the so]ns of Zadok, the priests: behold they are (described) [in the book of the Midrash on the] Eschatological Torah).

[120] Martínez-Tigchelaar, for example, translate lines 2–4 "The priests are the converts of Israel who left the land of Judah; and <the levites are> those who joined them; *Blank* and the sons of Zadok are the chosen of Israel, the men of renown, who stand (to serve) at the end of days" (Martínez and Tigchelaar, *Scrolls Study Edition*, vol. 1, 556–57).

receives much attention in MTA. It depicts the "sons of Zadok" as the "chosen of Israel." The term בחיר is usually an epithet given to Saul, David and the children of Jacob. קריאי השם (listed by name) may also be rendered "called by God," a phrase resembling פרוש השם in CD 15:2 and וחלל את השם in 15:3, both of which denote the divine name. However, the epithet בני צדוק normally refers to the tribal leaders named in Scripture. It also makes it apparent that the original text gave the actual names of the sons of Zadok.

The clause הנה פרוש שמותיהם (Here is a listing of their names) in lines 4–5 suggests that originally this passage was followed by the actual names of the "sons of Zadok," material that is absent in the extant text. As has been explained, it is an allusion to the list of Zadok's progeny given in 1 Chr 24 which names sixteen of his descendants plus eight of the sons of Abiathar for a total of twenty-four "sons of Zadok." If so, the "sons of Zadok" here in MTA function in the system of time reckoning, a feature that is fundamental in the DSS documents and also attested in the Aramaic and Ethiopic books of *Enoch* and *Jubilees*. Note that *Enoch* and *Jubilees* show no awareness of linking the sons of Zadok with the calendar. MTA, however, does. Furthermore, our author's lengthy elaboration on the sons of Zadok seems to make an additional point. His ignoring the descendants of Abiathar given in 1 Chr 24 gives exclusive credit to the "sons of Zadok," pointing to a pun on צדוק with צדק. The reiteration of the root צדק some two dozen times in the extant remains of MTA indicates the extreme importance of this concept for the author, and seems to link up with the epithet "sons of Zadok." In addition, it may buttress the rejection of the commonly held view that supposes MTA to be a sheer collection of disparate extracts. On the contrary, much of MTA's vocabulary points to a singular *tendance* and authorship. And, what is true of צדק could be true of other terms so frequently used in this treatise. Another word, for example, that deserves attention for its frequent usage is פרוש, a term that occurs in our passage twice—in lines 4–5 as פרוש שמותיהם (a listing of their names) and in line 6 as פירוש מעשיהם (an elaboration of their deeds). The word פרוש is a term not recorded in Scripture, but is ubiquitous in rabbinic literature. Significantly it appears to occur some twenty-one times in the extant remains of MTA with several senses, resembling the usage it frequently has in rabbinic literature.

As to לתולדותם וקץ מעמדם...ופירוש מעשיהם in lines 5–6, the itemization of the "sons of Zadok" must have consisted of naming their high priestly pedigree to David and Solomon. These phrases commenting

on the "sons of Zadok" suggest that our text is abbreviating what had
originally been an extensive narration of the history of the Zadokite
tribe. The Qumran texts, longer in some parts than the later medieval
parallels, may have contained the משמרות of the Sons of Zadok, perhaps beginning near the end of 4Q266 F2iii and continuing in a
fragment that has not survived. As has been noted, at this point the
text of 4:6 has fallen into disarray, as the next two words הקודש שונים
lack coherence. Perhaps שונים should read הרישונים. Lines 6–7 explain
that the priests of Zadok will be accorded distinction not only on
account of their prominence, but also because God has forgiven
whatever sins they have committed. He will recognize that their acts
follow the rules of the Torah.

### 3.2.1.3.2. *The Successors to the Sons of Zadok during the Eschaton (4:7b–10a)*

Lines 7b–10a assert that the prominence of these descendants of
Zadok will continue not only among those who are part of the
audience, but also to the succeeding generations. Prior to this point,
our author refers to the מחזיקים, the present audience whom he was
addressing. Now he speaks to those who will follow them (כל הבאים
אחריהם), the next generation. As long as they will continue to be
under the discipline of the Torah which the patriarchal generations
endured, God will extend His atonement until the completion of
these years. Note that the writer presumes the present generation
will experience the discipline of those of the past (the ראשונים). This
is an important line in our text since it reveals much of the outline
of MTA. Repeatedly we hear what will happen to the future generation. They will go to the north (Damascus). Many will continue
being penitent, will establish a new covenant and will receive another
Torah of Moses, apparently a reference to *Jubilees* and *Temple Scroll*.
Finally, the future generations will await the apocalypse wherein all
the wicked will be destroyed (resembling those who left Egypt and
were destroyed at Kadesh-barnea), but the righteous will live for
a thousand generations. It will be the end of the epoch and the
beginning of a new.

### 3.2.1.4. *Israel's Decline: The Past and Impending Crisis (4:10b–6:2a)*

The term שלום occurs twice in CD 4: first as שלים in lines 8–9 marking the completion of the epoch when God will forgive the sins
of Israel and second in line 10 as the new period when it will no
longer be possible to join the new association, a view also expressed

in portions of CD 20:1b–17a. However, what is the significance of these two epochs? The first completes the period of divine anger. The second marks the beginning of the eschatological age. The question arises, at what point do these eras divide? What is the nexus of "these years"? MTA articulates this same division again in CD 19:28b–20:1a (paralleled in part in CD 8:16–21). The phrase עד שלים הקץ [כמספר] השנים האלה (until the completion of the epoch [according to the number] of these years) probably refers to the קץ defined by our author in CD 1:5 as the epoch of three hundred and ninety plus twenty (=410 years) which was to transpire from Nebuchadnezzar's second entrance into Jerusalem in 597 B.C.E. until its conclusion in 187 B.C.E.[121] 187 then, is the anticipated date of Israel's future repentance, after which the Messiah of Aaron and of Israel was expected to appear to inaugurate the eschatological era and the Just Teacher was to emerge to lead the community. This outlines the chrono-Messianic epochs presented in MTA. As stated above, the first is the ראשנים, the beginning period of Israel's history starting with Adam and the rebellion of the fallen angels, that continues through the age of the patriarchs until the Ezekielian חרבן of 597 B.C.E. The second, that of the אחרונים, began with this conquest and would end four hundred and ten years later. The third period was expected to commence with the debut of the divine appearance in the futuristic temple. The community expected that God would at that point reveal Himself to the righteous, whose longevity would extend for a thousand generations. The author of MTA is living in the last period of the second epoch.

### 3.2.1.4.1. *Demarcating the New Age (4:10b–12a)*

Lines 10b–12a stress that there will be a solid curtain between the epoch of the אחרונים, the age of the writer's audience, and that which follows it, the eschatological era. The fence has been built around the אחרונים. The present age will be separated from the future by a fortress with a fence that will demarcate current life from that of the miraculous eschaton. One will no longer be able to construct new laws. נבנתה הגדר רחק החוק (The fence has been built, the statute is distant) paraphrases Mic 7:11: יוֹם לִבְנוֹת גְּדֵרָיִךְ יוֹם הַהוּא יִרְחַק־חֹק

---

[121] The reconstruction of the temporal [… קץ]ב הרשעה in lines 2–3 of the document preserves the temporal framework of the preceding clause, עד תֹּם מוֹעֵד הַפְּקוּדָה, the conclusion of the four hundred and ten years marking the inception of the eschaton.

(The day to build your fences. On that day the statute will be far away). It is likely, however, that our author adds a new sense to this biblical reference. נבנתה הגדר suggests there no longer will be an exit. רחק החוק implies that it may no longer be modified, since each person will become part of a fortress. What was once near and expansive will now remain afar and unalterable. This idea follows the previous sentence, wherein it is warned that the opportunity to join the community is now in the present only, not in the future. Let us remember that the author dates this separation in the near future, which for him in this chronology corresponded to four hundred and ten years after Nebuchadnezzar's first conquest of Jerusalem.

### 3.2.1.4.2. *A Midrash on Isaiah 24:17 Announcing the Role of Belial (4:12b–5:19)*

Having told of the divisions of the epochs, the writer resumes his description of the critical situation at hand, the last days of the אחרונים just prior to the eschaton when Belial will still hold sway over Israel. 4:12b introduces this crisis with the familiar formula ובכל השנים האלה (and during all these years), emphasizing the critical situation facing the nation. The author communicates that during this epoch they will be reaching a turning point. Israel's sinfulness will witness a point of no return. MTA quotes Isa 24:17, introducing it with special emphasis. This formula כאשר דבר אל ביד ישעיה הנביא בן אמוץ לאמר (as God has spoken through Isaiah the prophet, son of Amoz saying) recalls the introduction to Ezek 44:15 stated above: כאשר הקים אל להם ביד יחזקאל הנביא לאמר (just as the Lord has established them by Ezekiel the prophet saying). Both citations, כאשר דבר אל and כאשר הקים אל, enable the writer to present an expansive midrash on the impending crisis.

### 3.2.1.4.2.1. Isaiah and the Testament of Levi: Three Categories of (Un)righteous Deeds (4:12b–19a)

The discovery of the presumed title מדרש התורה האחרון in the DSS adds additional weight to the midrashic technique used in this work. Now that we know the importance of the term in the Damascus Document we gain new insight into the author's midrashic methodology. As stated above, numerous passages in this volume begin with אשר and כאשר אמר or כתוב, serving as markers for interpreting ancient passages and corresponding to the ubiquitous term שנאמר in rabbinics. The term פשרו (its interpretation), so characteristic in the biblical commentaries of the DSS, occurs first in MTA, likely the *Vorlage* from which these later commentaries drew this term. The passage that contains the word פשרו helps illustrate what our author meant by מדרש.

וּבכל השנים האלה יהיה CD 4:12

בליעל משולח בישראל כאשר דבר אל ביד ישעיה הנביא בן CD 4:13

אמוץ לאמר פחד ופחת ופח עליך יושב הארץ *vacat* פשרו CD 4:14

שלושת מצודות בליעל אשר אמר עליהם לוי בן יעקב CD 4:15

אשר הוא תפש בהם בישראל ויתנם פניהם לשלושת מיני CD 4:16

הצדק הראשונה היא הזנות השנית ההין השלישית CD 4:17

טמא המקדש העולה העולה מזה יתפש מזה והניצל מזה יתפש CD 4:18

בזה CD 4:19

And during all these years Belial will be let loose against Israel as God has spoken through Isaiah the prophet, son of Amoz, saying, "Fear and the pit and the snare are upon you, inhabitant of the land" (Isa 24:17). Its eschatological meaning (פשרו) is the three nets of Belial concerning which Levi son of Jacob said "with which he (Belial) trapped Israel and paraded them as if they were fronts for three classes of (un)righteous deeds": the first is whoredom, the second wealth (and) the third the defiling of the sanctuary. He who escapes from one will be trapped in the next; and whoever is saved from that will be trapped in the other. (CD 4:12b–19a)

In this text the author of MTA quotes Isa 24:17, then paraphrases the first part of verse 18.

פַּחַד וָפַחַת וָפָח עָלֶיךָ יוֹשֵׁב הָאָרֶץ וְהָיָה הַנָּס מִקּוֹל הַפַּחַד

יִפֹּל אֶל־הַפַּחַת וְהָעוֹלֶה מִתּוֹךְ הַפַּחַת יִלָּכֵד בַּפָּח

Terror and pit and trap are upon you who inhabitant the earth. It will happen that he who flees from the sound of the terror will fall into the pit; and he who escapes the pit will be caught in the trap. (Isa 24:17a)

MTA understands the prophet as if he were addressing the writer's contemporaries. However, it quotes Levi, son of Jacob, to explicate Isaiah's three traps as referring to the three abominations with which Belial had ensnared Israel. The citation of Levi presumably refers to the *Testament of Levi*, which, however, is not present in our Greek version of the *Testaments of the Twelve Patriarchs*. We do not know, therefore, whether Levi cited Isaiah, or as is more likely, that the author of MTA uses Levi's three traps of Belial as metaphor for the prophet's terror, pit and snare. In our text Isaiah's three traps are referred to as three classes of (un)righteous deeds which are euphemistically referred to as צדק (righteousness): whoredom, wealth (or exploitation) and the defiling of the sanctuary. Note that Levi is used as if he were the father who had been designated for the priesthood. This citation of Levi within the exegesis of Isa 24:17 illustrates the presence of a midrashic couplet in our author's composition. The composite makeup of this passage shows that the midrashic pesher, as used by our writer, diverges from the standard pesher, which is a simple substitution of terminology.

### 3.2.1.4.2.2. The Ensnarement of the Builders of the Wall (4:19b–5:19)

בוני החיץ (builders of the wall), a phrase found several times in MTA but only once in the Bible, serves as one of several appellations for the malevolent spiritual leaders of the era of Belial's sway over Israel. Their poor model of service is exposed through a description of their transgressions and a vilifying discourse on their character.

### 3.2.1.4.2.2.1. An Exegesis of צו: (4:19b–20a)

Describing the overall character of the בוני החיץ, MTA here expands upon an intertextual midrash on צו stretching from Hos 5:10–11 to Isa 28:9–14 and ending with the בוני החיץ of Ezek 13:1–16. צו is punned from קו, "a (construction) line," but used here as the spewing gibberish of a foreign tongue. The author of MTA employs both monosyllabic terms to illustrate the nonsense of the people of Judah. Hos 5:10–11 relates that the leaders of the nation follow after צָו, a (useless) commandment, and therefore become the מַסִּיגֵי גְּבוּל (the Shifters of the Boundary), a sobriquet appearing in line 4 of the preamble and also described below in CD 5:20 (see section 3.2.1.4.3).

10  הָיוּ שָׂרֵי יְהוּדָה כְּמַסִּיגֵי גְּבוּל עֲלֵיהֶם אֶשְׁפּוֹךְ כַּמַּיִם עֶבְרָתִי
11  עָשׁוּק אֶפְרַיִם רְצוּץ מִשְׁפָּט כִּי הוֹאִיל הָלַךְ אַחֲרֵי־צָו

The princes of Judah have become like the Shifters of the Boundary. I will pour out my wrath like water upon them. Ephraim is oppressed. Justice is trampled, for he has chosen to follow after a *useless commandment* (צָו). (Hos 5:10–11)

Expanding upon צו and קו, Isaiah relates of mocking the drunkards of Ephraim with gibberish.

(28:9) אֶת־מִי יוֹרֶה דֵעָה וְאֶת־מִי יָבִין שְׁמוּעָה גְּמוּלֵי מֵחָלָב עַתִּיקֵי מִשָּׁדָיִם
(28:10) כִּי צַו לָצָו צַו לָצָו קַו לָקָו קַו לָקָו זְעֵיר שָׁם זְעֵיר שָׁם (28:11) כִּי
בְּלַעֲגֵי שָׂפָה וּבְלָשׁוֹן אַחֶרֶת יְדַבֵּר אֶל־הָעָם הַזֶּה (28:12) אֲשֶׁר אָמַר אֲלֵיהֶם
זֹאת הַמְּנוּחָה הָנִיחוּ לֶעָיֵף וְזֹאת הַמַּרְגֵּעָה וְלֹא אָבוּא שְׁמוֹעַ (28:13) וְהָיָה

לָהֶם דְּבַר־יְהוָה צַו לָצָו צַו לָצָו קַו לָקָו קַו לָקָו זְעֵיר שָׁם זְעֵיר שָׁם
לְמַעַן יֵלְכוּ וְכָשְׁלוּ אָחוֹר וְנִשְׁבָּרוּ וְנוֹקְשׁוּ וְנִלְכָּדוּ פ (28:14) לָכֵן שִׁמְעוּ
דְבַר־יְהוָה אַנְשֵׁי לָצוֹן מֹשְׁלֵי הָעָם הַזֶּה אֲשֶׁר בִּירוּשָׁלָ‍ם

Whom will He teach knowledge? And, to whom will He expound what
He heard? Those weaned from milk, just separated from the breast. For
*commandment* upon *commandment*, line upon line, a bit here a bit there (gibberish). For with stammering lips and divergent words He speaks to this
people. To whom he said, "This is the resting place, let the weary rest.
And this is the place of repose." However, they refused to hear. The
word of the Lord will come to them, "*Commandment* upon *commandment*,
line upon line, a bit here a bit there." And so they will go on, but will
stumble backward and be broken and hurt and captured. Therefore,
hear the word of the Lord O men of mockery who rule this people of
Jerusalem. (Isa 28:9–14)

Ezekiel 13:1–16, a vision against the false prophets of Judah who
misled the people, claiming peace when there was no peace, labels
them as the בונה חיץ, "the builder(s) of the wall," who plastered
it with vanity. There will be a terrible storm that will remove the
plaster from the wall, destroying it and ultimately the false prophets
themselves in the pile.

Drawing on these biblical prophecies, MTA builds a case against
the current so-called "builders of the wall" who, pursuing their
own measuring standard in their edifications, spew false legislation.
These are the Pharisees who, according to MTA, arose after the חרבן,
corresponding to the tradition in *Avot* which depicts the rise of the
leaders of the Great Assembly. As explained above, this assessment
diverges from modern scholarship which tends to set the rise of the
Pharisees during the period of the Hasmoneans. The builders of
the wall are charged with having been ensnared by two offenses:
1) whoredom (4:20b–5:6a) and 2) defilement (5:6b–19). These *two*
offenses are an abridgement of the above cited *three* traps of Belial,
the classes of (un)righteous deeds with which he ensnared Israel
(CD 4:14b–19a).

## 3.2.1.4.2.2.2. Whoredom (4:20b–5:6a)

Nineteenth and twentieth century rabbinic scholars have divided
midrash into two categories: the more ancient *midrash-halakah* and
the subsequent *midrash-agadah*. The *halakah* dealt with matters of law,
whereas *agadah* had a much wider scope. The following question arises.
Does the Qumran author use *halakah* for legal exegesis of Scripture?
Our passage of Belial's three nets—terror, pit and snare—followed

by his exegesis of צו, after which he defines whoredom (using both
*halakah* and *agadah*), suggests that for him there was no stringent
division between the two types of midrash.

The first midrashic truth arguing against whoredom (which here
pertains to bigamy) draws on זָכָר וּנְקֵבָה (male and female) in Gen 1:27.
God created Adam and Eve and they were created male and female.
These are two singularities that may not be violated by expansion
into bigamy of more than one pair.

The second proof comes from באי התבה. Our text is not a direct
quote of Gen 7:9, but a slight amplification of it. Compare the two
clauses: שְׁנַיִם שְׁנַיִם בָּאוּ אֶל־נֹחַ אֶל־הַתֵּבָה (By pairs they came to Noah
into the ark) and its expansive formulation in CD: באי התבה שנים שנים
באו אל התבה (Those who entered the ark came in pairs to the ark).
The idea that the entrance into the ark was by pairs ironically serves
as more authoritative than the practices of the patriarchs who were
polygamous, reflecting a subjective use of Genesis.[122] The account of
the flood supersedes that of the actual practice of Abraham. Note
also that the author changes the biblical formulas to his own style.
A phrase such as באי התבה, a construct participle with its object, is
rare in Scripture. In contrast, this syntagm is characteristic of MTA.
Compare phrases such as באי ברית, באי המחנה, באי העדה, and יודעי
צדק to name a few.

The argument against acquiring more than one wife continues
with a third proof.

*vacat*          ועל הנשיא כתוב לא ירבה לו נשים

And concerning the leader (of the tribes and the head of the priests) it
is written, "He shall not multiply wives for himself." (CD 5:1b–2a)

Many scholars including Baumgarten note that CD quotes here Deut
17:17.[123]

וְלֹא יַרְבֶּה־לּוֹ נָשִׁים וְלֹא יָסוּר לְבָבוֹ

Neither shall he multiply wives for himself, so that his heart will not
turn away (from Me). (Deut 17:17)

Baumgarten, moreover, is amazed that the author of CD ignores the

---

[122] Our author's text of Genesis may not have contained Gen 7:2, which says
that the animals came to the ark by pairs of seven. Or, just as the writer ignored the
patriarchs, he may have disregarded Gen 7:2.
[123] Baumgarten, DJD XVIII, 12.

protasis of Deut 21:15, "If a man has two wives" (כִּי-תִהְיֶין֩ לְאִישׁ֙
שְׁתֵּי נָשִׁים). However, the assertion that MTA is quoting Deut 17:17,
a text which finds no objection to polygamy, lacks precision. It is
noteworthy that while Deut 17:15 uses מלך, MTA has נשיא, a term
favored by *Temple Scroll*.[124] I believe that our author is quoting not
Deuteronomy, but *Temple Scroll*, which, while citing Deut 17:17,
emends it radically as follows:

לוא ירבה לו נשים ולוא יסירו לבבו מאחרי

> He shall not multiply wives for himself lest they turn his heart away
> from Me. (11QT 56:18b–19a)

The royal charter goes on a page later to explicate Deut 17:17 as
modified in the above text:

ולוא יקח עליה אשה אחרת כי היאה לבדה תהיה עמו כול ימי חייה

> He may not take another wife in addition to her, for she alone shall live
> with him during all of her lifetime. (11QT 57:17b–18a)

The words "all of her lifetime" here embrace the prohibitions of both
bigamy and divorce. Marriage is regarded as an indissoluble contract.
The importance of this citation from *Temple Scroll* becomes clear from
11QT 56:18b–19a cited above, where it explains the words of Deut
17:17. Hence, CD 5:1b–2a is a quote from *Temple Scroll* which cites
Deut 17:17. However, *Temple Scroll* adds a rationalization for it, namely
that the many wives might turn his heart away from God. The author
of CD, however, goes much further, ascribing to Belial the temptation
of polygamy, since he holds sway over Israel.

Although the author cited three passages against bigamy, he is
not yet finished with this subject. While ignoring the polygamous
relations of Abraham and Jacob, he is not silent about the marital
practice of David whose many wives are recorded in the book of
Samuel, but nevertheless is exalted throughout Scripture.

CD 5:2      ודויד לא קרא בספר התורה החתום אשר

CD 5:3      היה בארון כי לא {נפתח} נפתח בישראל מיום מות אלעזר

CD 5:4      ויהושע ‹‹ויושֻׁעַ›› והזקנים אשר עבדו את העשתרת

---

[124] Cf. ושנים עשר נשיי עמו עמו (and twelve leaders of the people with him, i.e.
the king) in 11QT 57:11–12.

> As to David, he could not read in the book of the Torah which had
> been sealed since it was in the ark, for it (the ark) had not been opened
> in Israel since the day of the death of Eleazar, Joshua and the elders
> who worshipped the Ashtoroth. (CD 5:2b–4a)

In other words, David was not obliged to observe the rule of monogamy
which was not in his possession, since the book of the Law had been
sealed in the ark. However, why was the Law not available to him?
VanderKam argues that the reason David could not know Deut 17:17,
the text prohibiting bigamy, is because 1 Sam 5–6 records that the
ark which contains the Torah had been seized during the Philistine
invasion of Israel. Hence, the king could not read the text prohibiting bigamy.[125]

VanderKam's explanation is not persuasive. The wording אשר היה
בארון (which was in the ark) does not allude to the absence of the
ark. If it were to have meant so, the author would have qualified it
with אשר היה ביד פלשתים (which was in the hand of the Philistines).
Moreover, David's practice of polygamy extended throughout virtually all his adult life and was not restricted to the seven months of
the Philistine seizure of the ark. Furthermore, the text goes on to
say כי לא נפתח בישראל מיום מות אלעזר (For it had not been opened in
Israel since the day of the death of Eleazar). It should have said,
according to VanderKam, כי לא נפתח בישראל כי היה ביד פלשתים (For
it had not been opened in Israel since it had been in the hand of
the Philistines). What do Eleazar and Joshua have to do with the
affair of the Philistines? This phrase אשר היה בארון actually draws
on Deut 31:26 which states:

לָקֹחַ אֵת סֵפֶר הַתּוֹרָה הַזֶּה וְשַׂמְתֶּם אֹתוֹ מִצַּד
אֲרוֹן בְּרִית־יְהוָה אֱלֹהֵיכֶם וְהָיָה־שָׁם בְּךָ לְעֵד

> Surely take this book of the Torah and place it on the side of the ark
> of the covenant of the Lord your God and it shall remain there as a
> witness against you. (Deut 31:26)

The reason for placing the book of the Torah on the side of the ark
becomes apparent in the seeming repetition of Deut 31:19 and 22.
In verse 9 of this chapter Moses inscribed the scroll of the Torah
and delivered it to the priests and the twelve tribes of Israel. In
verses 22–26 he wrote another Torah which he entrusted to the

---

[125] James VanderKam, "Zadok and the SPR HTWRH ḤḤTWM in Dam. Doc.
V, 2–5," *RevQ* 44 (1984): 567–70.

Levites who carried the ark. Various traditions have found it difficult to reconcile verse 9 where Moses autographs the Torah and
distributes it among the Levites and the elders of Israel with verses
22–26 which tell about placing the Torah in the ark. According to
Maimonides, verse 9 refers to the twelve copies which Moses prepared for each of the tribes of Israel, whereas verses 22–26 pertain
to an extra copy which Moses prepared to be placed in the ark in
case any of the common copies became questionable. The author of
CD, however, has an original response to this apparent redundancy.
He makes no comment here on verse 9, but apparently troubled by
the sense of this phrase, he explains Deut 31:25–26 where Moses
tells the Levites to place the scroll on the side of the ark (מצד ארון).
Why does the text say מצד ארון (on the side of the ark) rather than
בארון (in the ark)? He evidently resolves the problem by presuming
that, while the traditional Mosaic Pentateuch was deposited in the
ark itself, that of another Torah also inscribed by Moses himself,
but intended for the latter generations and the eschatological epoch,
was placed on the side of the ark. And, since in verses 25–26 it is
Moses who commands the Levites to place this Torah in the ark, it
must have been at first available to Eleazar, Joshua and the elders.
This explains why CD claims that the eschatological Torah was
still available to Eleazar, Joshua and the elders, since Eleazar and
Joshua were among those whom Moses, prior to his death, charged
to place it in the ark.

There is another problem. Why is this Torah which had been
hidden since the days of Eleazar and Joshua revealed now in the
author's time? The sentence ויטמון נגלה עד עמוד צדוק in lines 4b–5a
responds to this question. As will be explained below, an allusion to
a hidden Torah may already have appeared in the introduction to
this work.[126]

CD 5:4b–5a is problematic. Virtually every word has been con-
tested. According to Rabin, the verb ויטמון, although an active form,
is translated as if it were a passive, "and it was hidden." He adds a
negative after ויטמון to read ויטמון (ולא) נגלה עד עמוד (בן) צדוק with the
rendition, "and it was hidden (and was not) revealed until (the son
of) Zadok arose."[127] The idea of reading ולא was first suggested

---

[126] The reconstruction of 4Q266 F1:8–9 speaks of the concealment and revelation of God's divine mysteries.
[127] See also Davies who supplies "and not" (Davies, *The Damascus Covenant*,
245).

by Schechter. As to בן צדוק, this notion goes back to Ginzberg.[128] Schwartz translates "and that which had been revealed was hidden until Zadok arose," rendering ויטמון as a relative clause.[129] Schiffman discusses נגלה at some length, analyzing it from its appearance in the DSS. He regards נגלה as synonymous to תורה (i.e. the Pentateuch) and as a contrast to נסתר (the hidden). He translates lines 4b–5a as "Since they (Israel) worshipped Ashtoret, the נגלה (i.e. the Torah) was hidden until the arising of Zadok."[130] The first problem with all these renditions is that ויטמון is not a passive verb. It is a Qal third person form. None of these translations, moreover, provides the identity of the alleged concealer. Additionally, none explains the purpose of citing Eleazar and Joshua. In my translation, he (Eleazar) hid the Torah as he was commanded by his master, Moses (the Levites in Deut 31:25). It was Moses who goes on to explain in verses 26–30 that Israel would become corrupt after his death. Our text, then, presumes that Eleazar and Joshua carried out this order. Therefore, it is Eleazar who was the Levite who executed Moses' will.

As to the נגלה, Schiffman correctly translates it as referring to Torah. For him, however, the word Torah refers to the Pentateuch. Although נגלה in the DSS can mean the standard Law, in my opinion this term denotes the sectarian Torah. This sectarian Law known as *Torah* and *Teʿudah* according to *Jubilees*, was delivered to Moses during his forty days in the cloud of Mt. Sinai.[131] A text from *Rule of the Community* serves to elucidate the term נגלה.

5:8 . . . ויקם על נפשו בשבועת אסר לשוב אל תורת מושה
5:9 ככול אשר צוה בכול לב ובכול נפש לכול הנגלה ממנה
לבני צדוק הכוהנים שומרי הברית ודורשי רצונו ולרוב אנשי
5:10 בריתם המתנדבים יחד לאמתו ולהתלך ברצונו . . .

He should take it upon himself by an obligatory oath to turn to the Torah of Moses according to all that he commanded with all (his) heart and with all (his) soul, to everything that has been revealed to the Sons of Zadok, the Priests, those who have observed the covenant and who do

---

[128] See Ginzberg, *Unknown Jewish Sect*, 21.

[129] Charlesworth, ed., *Damascus Document*, 21.

[130] Lawrence H. Schiffman, *The Halakhah at Qumran* (Leiden: E. J. Brill, 1975), 30.

[131] For this rendition of ויטמון נגלה, see my article "The 'Sealed' Torah versus the 'Revealed' Torah: an exegesis of Damascus Covenant V 1–6 and Jeremiah 32:10–14," *RevQ* 12 (Dec. 1986): 351–68.

His will and the multitude of the people of their covenant who volunteer together for His truth and live by His will (1QS 5:8b–10a).

The נגלה in line 9 of this text applies to the sons of Zadok, priests who according to CD 4:3–4 as stated above, *will arise* at the *end of days* as the chosen of Israel, called by God. Three pages later *Rule of the Community* continues with another amplification of this term.

8:14 כאשר כתוב במדבר פנו דרך יייי ישרו בערבה מסלה לאלוהינו

8:15 היאה מדרש התורה א[ש]ֿר צוה ביד מושה לעשות ככול הנגלה עת בעת

8:16 וכאשר גלו הנביאים ברוח קודשו

As it is written, "Prepare the way of the Lord in the wilderness; make straight the highway of our God in the desert" (Isa 40:3). It (the way) is the Midrash of the (Eschatological) Torah which He commanded by Moses to do according to all that has been revealed from time to time, just as the prophets have presaged through His Holy Spirit. (1QS 8:14–16a)

This passage, too, definitely has a sectarian echo, in that the Torah will be revealed "from time to time," a clear allusion to the emergence of the subsequent Law.

Two other passages in MTA containing נגלה may likewise pertain to the sectarian Scripture. CD 15:13–14 reads "and everything *revealed* from the Torah to the multitude of the camp." The phrase, "the multitude of the camp" evidently alludes to that of the sectarians. Likewise 4Q266 F5i:8–9 may be read " . . . [mighty in power] and full of strength in what has been *reve[a]led* [from the Torah . . . "

Scholars have differed as to the identity of Zadok in the clause of CD 5:5, עד עמוד צדוק (until Zadok arises). Schechter supposed that it must refer to an unidentified biblical personage.[132] Ginzberg, followed by Rabin and Schiffman emend the text to עד עמוד בן צדוק, identifying this Zadok as the (grand)father of Hilkiah who found the book of the Torah (2 Kgs 22 and 2 Chr 34).[133] Hilkiah, along with the scribe Shaphan discovered the book of the Torah in the days of Josiah, a corpus which modern scholarship identifies as Deuteronomy. This Hilkiah who is said to have discovered the lost scroll is, according to 1 Chr 9 and Neh 11, the grandson of Zadok.

The identification of this Zadok as the grandfather of Hilkiah, the alleged discoverer of this biblical text, lacks persuasion. First,

---

[132] Schechter in Fitzmyer, ed., *Documents*, 68.

[133] Rabin, *The Zadokite Documents*, 18–19; Schiffman, *The Halakhah*, 30–31.

the passage says עד עמוד צדוק (until Zadok arises). It does not say עד
עמוד בן צדוק (until the *son* of Zadok arises). Furthermore, I doubt that
the author of CD would have ascribed the book of Deuteronomy to
anyone but Moses. And, if he did regard another as the author, he
would have disclosed his identity. Hence, the Zadok of this text could
be one of two possibilities: 1) the high priest of David or 2) a figure
contemporary with the author of the document. The supposition
of identifying the Zadok of our text as David's high priest is also
problematic, however. How could David have practiced polygamy
while Zadok served as his priest for virtually a lifetime, having access
to the Torah prohibiting it? It is necessary, therefore, to presume
that Zadok here is a figure from the period of the Second Temple.
Alluding to the tradition found in *Avot d'Rabbi Natan* 5, al-Qirqisani
designates Zadok as the author of a work such as MTA. However,
the formula "until the rise of Zadok" can only mean a figure other
than the author himself. It follows that, according to him, he attributed not MTA, but other more ancient works such as *Jubilees* and
*Temple Scroll* to this personage.

On the other hand, it is possible to conjecture the identity of this
Zadok textually. The central question in this passage is this. At what
point in time did the prohibition of multiplying wives (Deut 17:17)
become an absolute command for the observance of monogamy?
Our text makes it clear that monogamy became part of the Torah
only after the death of David and presumably Solomon. Our writer
says that the prohibition is old, going back to Moses, but was not
made public until the rise of Zadok. The answer to this question may
lie in *Temple Scroll* 56–57. As was stated above, 11QT 56:18–19 cites
Deuteronomy's prohibition against multiplying wives. And, in 11QT
57:17, the author of *Temple Scroll* amplifies this line, stating, "he shall
not take another wife." It is necessary to assume, therefore, that the first
text which prohibits bigamy and commands the marrying of a single
wife is attributed to Zadok, the presumed author of *Temple Scroll*.[134]

---

[134] See Wacholder, *Dawn of Qumran*, 99–140. However, I no longer hold that
Zadok is the author of the Damascus Document, what we now call MTA. Qirqisani's
attribution of MTA to Zadok should be modified to *Temple Scroll*, for the attack
on polygamy in CD can only refer to it. No other work interprets Deut 17:17 "to
marry two wives" as does 11QT 57. Furthermore, in this connection, I want to
make it clear that I no longer think as I claimed in *The Dawn of Qumran*, that Zadok
may have been the Teacher of Righteousness. I believe now that the מורה צדק was
for the author of MTA a future messianic figure.

The problem with this identification, as noted by Baumgarten, is the prevalent presumption that the DSS authors, unlike the Talmudic sages, never cite post-biblical figures.

The above supposition, however, is no longer true. 4Q513 F3–4:5 cites a certain sectarian sage named Anani in an argument against the opponent whose views do not accord with the Torah of Moses: ‏[וֹלא מתורת משה . . .‏     ‏[כ]אשר הר[א]ה עננין‏], ‏"‏. . . [as] Anani has sho[w]n [(that the opinions of the opposition in regard to the raising of the omer)] do not accord with the Torah of Moses."[135] Hence, the attribution of the citation of *Temple Scroll* in CD to a sage named Zadok is no longer unique. Moreover, al-Qirqisani identifies the founder of the sect as Zadok, whom as stated above, *Avot d'Rabbi Natan* regards as one of two disciples of Antigonus. Al-Qirqisani makes Zadok the author of a work such as MTA and Boethus, the other disciple, the founder of the sectarian calendar. The common assumption that al-Qirqisani's attribution of the foundation of the Zadokite movement to Zadok and Boethus was based exclusively upon rabbinic sources is a mistake. He seems to have had access the works of Zadok and Boethus which are now lost. He says that a work such as MTA was composed by Zadok, and that Boethus, his colleague, formulated the thirty day month of the sectarian calendar. However, nothing in the DSS knows of such an attribution. And, the DSS do not identify Zadok as the author of MTA. Nevertheless, as argued by Abraham Harkavy, al-Qirqisani had access to the original composition of what we now know as the *Damascus Document*. In ignoring al-Qirqisani as an important source for the history of the Essene movement, modern scholarship is missing rich lore, much of which may be historical. After all, al-Qirqisani quotes many passages that are now verified in MTA and attested among the remains of the DSS.

Our author continues with his defense of David in CD 5:5b–6a.

‏ויעלו מעשי דויד מלבד דם אוריה ויעזבם לו אל‏

And the acts of David became acceptable (before God) aside from (the king's guilt pertaining to) the blood of Uriah, as God made him responsible for them. (CD 5:5b–6a)

---

[135] That this line reflects a polemical statement can be deduced also from the previous line ‏תעות עורון‏ (misleading blindness). See Baillet in *Qumrân Grotte 4.III (4Q482–4Q520)* (DJD VII; Oxford: Clarendon, 1982), 290; Wacholder, "The Omer Polemics in 4Q513 Fragments 3–4: Is Ananni Their Author?" *RevQ* 77 (June, 2001): 93–108.

These two clauses have caused much difficulty to commentators, whose renditions tend to ignore the context. See for example translations cited by Jacqueline C. R. de Roo.[136] She interprets both verbs עלה and עזב as pertaining to מעשי דויד (the deeds of David)—in the first clause מעשי דויד functions as a subject; in the second as the direct object.[137] Actually, however, the two verbal clauses diverge in these matters. ויעלו מעשי דויד pertains to David's style of life, including his polygamous practices which God overlooked, since the rules against it had not yet been disclosed to him. On the other hand, the object in ויעזבם relates to the דם אוריה—the blood (killing) of Uriah—a heinous act contrived by David and the nearest potential antecedent in the sentence. Its plural number alludes not to the acts of polygamy as many have construed, but to the several violations against Uriah—covetuousness, adultery and murder. As to the exact meaning of ויעזבם לו אל, there could be two possible senses: 1) that God *forgave* David for his heinous deeds because of his other virtues,[138] or 2) a more literal meaning—that God did *not* absolve him for his despicable acts, but *left them to him*, i.e., made him responsible for them, punishing him for them through the death of his son through Bathsheba. Rabin cites Rab (*Bavli Shabbat* 56a) who exonerates David for the Bathsheba affair. In fact, however, the cited Talmudic text attributes to Rab two opinions that are contradictory—one exonerating him and the other charging him with accepting לשון הרע (evil information). MTA here is likewise balanced, however, in regard to both categories of offense cited in our text. It grants the king absolution for all other misdeeds he may have committed, but makes him responsible for the blood of Uriah. As severe as this text seems to be toward David, it need not be considered contradictory to other passages in the DSS that tend to glorify him, as claimed by de Roo. The rabbis likewise present a balanced view and would not otherwise hesitate to exult the king. After all, David was a mortal.

The lengthy treatment of David's polygamy in lines 2–6 is revealing

---

[136] Jacqueline C. R. de Roo, "David's Deeds in the Dead Sea Scrolls," *DSD* 6–1 (1999): 44–65.

[137] In addition to de Roo, see Rabin, *The Zadokite Documents*, 18; Schwartz in Charlesworth, ed., *Damascus Document*, 21; Davies, *The Damascus Covenant*, 245; Martínez-Tigchalaar, *Scrolls Study Edition*, 557; Vermes, *The Complete Dead Sea Scrolls*, 130.

[138] See Cook on CD 5:5b–6a who translates the clause positively: "Nevertheless the deeds of David were all excellent, except the murder of Uriah and God forgave him for that" (Wise, Abegg and Cook, *Scrolls*, 55).

in several respects. First, it tells us that the writer did not hesitate to interrupt his narrative with a lengthy defense of the king's practices, citing first the creation of Adam and Eve, second Deut 17:17, and third, David's affair with Bathsheba. Our author had a special regard for David, as he finds it necessary to deal at length with his marital transgressions. However, it also gives us a glimpse into the writer's midrashic methodology. In a few words the author draws a comprehensive account of David's role as the king. The king committed several terrible acts and these cannot be fully excused by the mere absence of an injunction against polygamy. After all, David did have access to the accounts of creation, Noah and the flood. Yet even his affair with Bathsheba did not suffice to erase his wonderful accomplishments. Furthermore this text sets forth for us the claim that *Temple Scroll's* prohibition of polygamy overrides any Pentateuchal suggestion such as Deut 21:15 which sanctions bigamy, or for that matter, the practice of David and, shall we say, other patriarchs. It also intimates that some texts that became available only as late as Zadok, whoever that Zadok might be, go back to Moses at Sinai. This helps us understand more clearly CD 16:2–3 which labels *Jubilees* as מדוקדק, more perfect and precise than the traditional Pentateuch.

In addition, this lengthy defense of the king may also suggest that the writer regarded David's psalter and even other compositions attributed to him as authoritative biblical text.[139] It is worth noting that the theology of much of Qumran, and especially that of MTA, can be understood as an amplification of the psalter, presenting it as the psalmist's way of life. A striking example of the psalm-like perspective is lines 1–2a of the preamble of our work. It contains the term דרך used throughout the psalter's introductory chapter: להנזר מדר[כי בני חושך] (to separate from the wa[ys of the sons of darkness]).[140] Indeed, much of MTA and the DSS as a whole reflect the way of life of the צדיקים and the wickedness of the רשעים, contrasted in Ps 1. The basic difference between the theologies of the Psalter and those of the DSS is that in the former the two camps, the righteous and the wicked, are portrayed as intermingled within a single community. On the other hand, in the DSS and especially

---

[139] Cf. 11QPs^a 27:10, which ascribes to David 4,050 compositions. J. A. Sanders, *The Psalms Scroll of Qumran Cave 11 (11QPs^a)* (DJD IV; Oxford: Clarendon, 1965), 92.

[140] Or as Baumgarten (DJD XVIII, 31) suggests: להנזר מדרכי רשעה (to separate from the ways of wickedness).

in MTA, the two groups are viewed as distinct entities—the children of light and the children of darkness, or as in other terms, the
children of God and those of Belial. These are separate in place
and theology, and in some sense even in time, in that the wicked
are seen as excluded from the messianic era.[141] Furthermore, they
are also divergent in their literature. The crucial word then in line
1 of MTA (4Q266 F1:1) is להנזר, an infinitive construct suggesting a
sharp line of demarcation wherein all links between two groups are
severed absolutely. In the Bible the verb נזר sometimes functions in a
more restricted sense to connote an individual's abstaining from wine,
letting one's hair grow and refraining from touching a corpse. Here,
however, להנזר seems to connote the sense of living by special rules
as a whole congregation apart from Israel and remaining separate
from the community of sinners who do not accept the commandments of Moses destined for the last days.[142] As reconstructed, lines

---

[141]   The last word of the formula מדרש התורה האחרון serves to call attention to
the future separation of the two contrasting camps. The adjective אחרון depicts the
social and literary aspects of the community of the new era coming to the fore, the
final epoch to which the righteous will enter and from which the wicked will be
excluded. Hence, the righteous and wicked living at the end of the era of the אחרונים
are not only distinguished in behavior. They will also be separated following the end
of days. Whereas Jacob and Esau, the two brothers, serve as a contrast between the
two types inhabiting the same womb, whose progeny coexisted during the eras of
the ראשונים and the אחרונים, the true community envisaged for the eschaton is one
wherein only the righteous will live. One is reminded of the anticipated futuristic
demarcation of the wicked and the righteous in Ps 1:4–5.

לֹא־כֵן הָרְשָׁעִים כִּי אִם־כַּמֹּץ אֲשֶׁר־תִּדְּפֶנּוּ רוּחַ
עַל־כֵּן לֹא־יָקֻמוּ רְשָׁעִים בַּמִּשְׁפָּט וְחַטָּאִים בַּעֲדַת צַדִּיקִים

Not so the wicked; rather they are like chaff which the wind drives away.
Therefore the wicked will not stand up in (survive) the judgment, nor sinners
in the congregation of the righteous.

[142]   Cf. CD 6:14–16 where נזר follows בדל.

אם לא ישמרו לעשות כפרוש התורה לקץ הרשע ולהבדל
מבני השחת ולהנזר מהון הרשעה הטמא בנדר ובחרם ובהון המקדש

. . .if they will not take heed to do according to the explanation of the Torah
during the epoch of wickedness. *It is imperative to separate* from the sons of [injus]tice
*and to "nazirite"* by means of a vow and ban from the wealth of wickedness that
is defiling  as well as from the property of the sanctuary.

Cf. also 4Q418 F81:2

ואתה הבדל מכול אשר שנא והנזר מכול תעבות נפ֯ש֯] כי[א הוא עשה כול

1–2a of the book's preamble combine into a single idea to create a generation of light by making the Torah a psalmic Torah, a psalmic way of life, a Torah for the end of time. MTA is not, as is generally taken for granted, only a work that consists of admonitions and law. Rather it is a unified idea where Torah becomes transformed into righteous living.

### 3.2.1.4.2.2.3. Defilement (5:6b–19)

The author continues his attack on the religious leadership of Israel with a pericope on defilement. Not only were the builders of the wall ensnared in whoredom as explicated above, but they were also entrapped in contaminating practices that defiled both the sanctuary and the spirit.

### a. Defilement of the Temple (5:6b–11a)

CD 5:6b–11a deals with three prohibitions: 1) having sexual intercourse in the temple (presumably in Jerusalem); 2) lying with a woman during her flux; and 3) marrying the daughter of one's brother or sister.

The first of these defilements (CD 5:6b–7a) is amplified later in CD 12:1b–2a.

12:1        אל ישכב איש עם אשה בעיר המקדש לטמא

12:2 את עיר המקדש בנדתם

A man may not sleep with a woman in the city of the Temple, thereby defiling the city of the Temple by their uncleanness. (CD 12:1b–2a)

Prior to the discovery of the Dead Sea Scrolls, scholars were divided as to the meaning or basis for the first prohibition.[143] However, the sense of this clause has become very clear with the publication of *Temple Scroll*. The reference to the עיר המקדש (city of the Temple) in CD 12:1 draws on 11QT 45:11–12a, including its common redundancies.

45:11    ואיש כיא ישכב עם אשתו שכבת זרע לוא יבוא אל כול עיר

45:12 המקדש אשר אשכין שמי בה שלושת ימים . . .

A man who lies with his wife, having sexual relations, shall not enter any place in the city of the Temple wherein I dwell for three days. (11QT 45:11–12a)

---

And as for you, *separate* from everything which He hates and *nazirite* yourself from every abomination of the sou[l, for] He has created everything.

[143] See Ginzberg, *Unknown Jewish Sect*, 349.

The city of the Temple in *Temple Scroll* undoubtedly refers to Jerusalem, from which not only sexual activity was excluded, but also from which the blind, one having had a recent seminal emission or contact with a corpse, or who was a leper were restricted (compare 11QT 45:12b–18). However, the extra wording several pages later in 11QT 47:3–6a and 48:14b–17a implies that sexual relations may also have been forbidden in cities other than Jerusalem.

47:3 [והיו ]ע֯ריהמה טהורות וש֯[כנתי אני בתוכמ]ה לעולם והעיר
47:4 אשר אקדיש לשכין שמי ומקד֯[שי בתוכה] תהיה קודש וטהורה
47:5 מכול דבר לכול טמאה אשר יטמאו בה כול אשר בתוכה יהיה
47:6 טהור וכול אשר יבוא לה יהיה טהור . . .
48:14 ובכול עיר ועיר תעשו מקומות למנוגעים
48:15 בצרעת ובנגע ובנתק אשר לוא יבואו לעריכמה וטמאום וגם לזבים
48:16 ולנשים בהיותמה בנדת טמאתמה ובלדתמה אשר לוא יטמאו בתוכם
48:17 בנדת טמאתם

. . . [And] their cities [shall be] pure. And [I will dw]ell [in their midst] for ever. And the city that I will sanctify to dwell therein; and [my] temple [that is therein] shall be sacred and pure from anything in it that is defiling. Anyone (and anything) in it must be pure. And anyone who enters it must be pure . . . And in each and every city you shall construct places for those suffering with leprosy, an affliction or scall that they might not enter your cities, contaminating them; also for men having a discharge, for women during menstruation as well as for those having given birth, that they not contaminate with their menstrual uncleanness in their midst. (11QT 47:3–6a; 48:14b–17a)

Indeed, the descriptions of the categories of cities in these lines from *Temple Scroll* are similar. Both Jerusalem and the other cities are to be טהור (pure). God would dwell in each grouping. Entry restrictions into the temple city are similar to those of the others.

If sexual activity was barred from the cities of Israel, the following question arises. What were the proper locations for procreative activity in the view of the sectarians? It is noteworthy that the author of MTA elsewhere stresses the differentiation between living by the rules of the *cities* and those of the *camps* (e.g. CD 12:19–13:4). As stated above pertaining to CD 7:6b–9a (19:2b–5a of Ms B), procreation and the raising of families was the way of life prescribed for the residents of the camps. Indeed the מבקר על המחנה (the Supervisor over the camp) was to regulate marriage and divorce in the camps (CD 13:16–17), status changes never attributed to residents of the cities, whose responsibilities were limited to differentiating between the unclean

and the clean and telling between the sacred and the ordinary (CD
12:19b–20a). In contrast to the cities, life in the camps was modeled
after that of the מחנות of old in the wilderness, a community in which
all categories of society lived.[144] Whereas sectarian literature may
have forbidden procreative activity in all cities of Israel, the ascription of קודש in addition to טהור to the city of the Temple (11QT
47:7) suggests that there were two levels of purity in Israel's ערים,
Jerusalem having the highest level of sanctity.

The second prohibition in our text pertaining to defiling the temple,
that of lying with a woman during her flux (CD 5:7b), had likewise
been obscure prior to the discovery of the fragments from Cave 4 as
well as *Temple Scroll*.[145] This proscription is problematic on account
of its paucity, but its sense, by reason of its similar vocabulary and
corresponding defilement, is related to 4Q266 F6i:14–15a, the rule
concerning the male with a seminal discharge. The two texts are as
follows.

ושוכבים עם הרואה את דם זובה CD 5:7b

And they lie with a menstruating woman . . .

[ומ]שׁפּט הזב את זובו כול איש א[שר זו]ב[ יז]וב]  vacat ○ 4Q266 F6i:15
מבשׁר]ו 4Q266 F6i:15

[Now the r]ule for a male who has a discharge: Any man w[hose] body
em[its a [hea]vy dis[charge] . . .

In these passages, MTA is altogether dependent on *Temple Scroll*.

---

[144] Qimron regards the singular and plural number of מחנה in the DSS as
connoting communities of different design. He cites 4Q394 F8iv:9b–10a (כי ירושלים
היאה מחנה הקדש "For Jerusalem is the camp of holiness"), arguing that מחנה in the
DSS refers to Jerusalem, the city in which celebacy was to be the rule. On the other
hand, the מחנות signify those cities wherein marriage was sanctioned. See Elisha
Qimron, "Celibacy in the Dead Sea Scrolls and the Two Kinds of Sectarians,"
in vol. 1 of *Proceedings of the International Congress on the Dead Sea Scrolls Madrid 18–21
March, 1991* (ed. Julio Trebolle Barrera and Luis Vegas Montaner); Vol. XI,1 of
*Studies on the Texts of the Desert of Judah* (ed. F. García Martínez and A. S. van der
Woude; Leiden: E. J. Brill, 1992), 289. This distinction between the singular and
the plural is not compelling, at least as far as MTA is concerned. Our author uses
both pertaining to sectarians who were to practice family life. The supervisor of
the מחנה regulated marriage and divorce (CD 13:16–17). By the same token, the
מחנות were communities where the sectarians were commissioned to take wives and
procreate children (CD 7:6b–9a; 19:2b–5a).

[145] See Ginzberg, *Unknown Jewish Sect*, 349–50 for the problems in understanding the CD passage.

This Cave 11 text also contains several references to the second prohibition of the זב cited above, a male with a discharge.

45:15 וכול איש אשר יטהר מזובו וספר לו שבעת ימים לטהרתו ויכבס ביום
45:16 השביעי בגדיו ורחץ את כול בשרו במים חיים אחר יבוא אל עיר
45:17 המקדש

And any man who cleanses himself from his discharge shall count seven days for his purification, and shall launder his garments on the seventh day and shall wash all of his flesh with running water; subsequently he may enter the city of the Temple. (11QT 45:15–17a)

46:16 ועשיתה
46:17 שלושה מקומות למזרח העיר מובדלים זה מזה אשר יהיו
46:18 באים המצורעים והזבים והאנשים אשר יהיה להמה מקרה
47:1 [לילה . . .

And you shall make three locations to the east of the city, each apart from the other into which lepers and those who have a discharge and men with a [nocturnal] emission shall reside . . . (11QT 46:16b–47:1a)

48:14 ובכול עיר ועיר תעשו מקומות למנוגעים
48:15 בצרעת ובנגע ובנתק אשר לוא יבואו לעריכמה וטמאום וגם לזבים
48:16 ולנשים בהיותמה בנדת טמאתמה ובלדתמה אשר לוא יטמאו בתוכם
48:17 בנדת טמאתם

And in every city you shall make places for those who are afflicted, whether with leprosy, or with wound, or with scab who may not enter into your cities lest they contaminate them. And likewise, for men who have a discharge, as well as for women being in their menstrual defilement, and those having given birth, who should not defile in their midst with their menstrual defilement. (11QT 48:14b–17a)

Interestingly, CD differs from *Temple Scroll* in not listing leprosy (צרעת) together with the defilement of the זוב, replacing it instead with polygamy. The latter issue, according to CD, then, constitutes a major offense, being addressed especially to the princes with their customary harems. However, according to our text this prohibition applies to ordinary people as well. One senses the polemical stance against polygamy by the author's citation of creation and the flood which, by depicting in CD 4:21b–5:1a their idealized monogamous state, must have implied that bigamy might have been the cause of the deluge.

The text prohibiting one from lying with a woman during her flux is relatively brief. In 4Q270 F2ii:15c–16a it occurs in a long list of transgressions for which God will destroy those who commit any of them.[146] What is so interesting is that the catalogue of transgressions, as does CD, includes both lying with a menstruating woman and marrying one's niece—the second and third temple defilement. It seems that all of these trespasses, including having sexual intercourse in the temple, are considered by the author of MTA as offenses subject to capital punishment.[147]

It is the third prohibition, marrying the daughter of one's brother or sister (CD 5:7b–11a), upon which MTA expounds at length.

| | |
|---|---|
| ולוקחים | 5:7 |
| איש את בת אחיהֶם ואת בת אחותו vacat ומשה אמר אל | 5:8 |
| אחות אמך לא תקרב שאר אמך היא ומשפט העריות לזכרים | 5:9 |
| הוא כתוב וכהם הנשים ואם תגלה בת האח את ערות אחי | 5:10 |
| אביה והיא שאר | 5:11 |

And they marry the daughter of one's brother or sister. However, Moses said, "You shall not come near the sister of your mother; she is a relation of your mother." And the rules of incest are in male language, but they apply to women as well. Hence, if the brother's daughter uncovers the nakedness of her father's brother, she is a (forbidden) relation. (CD 5:7b–11a)

Scholars have noted that some rabbinic texts not only diverge from the prohibition of marrying the daughter of one's sister, but commend it as halakically desirable, perhaps to stress their disagreement with views such as are found in MTA. The disputative stance of MTA becomes evident in the reappearance of the prohibition in at least one more passage—that which forms part of the so-called catalogue of transgressions mentioned above.

---

[146] 4Q270 F2ii:17–18 seems to preserve the punishment in the apodosis: בם חקק אל להעביר בח]רון אפו בק]י[ן . . . (. . .against whom God has legislated to render destruction by [his] w[rath during the epo]ch . . . ).

[147] Whereas levitical law contains numerous references to capital crimes, the terminology of the transgression in Lev 18:21 of offering one's children to Molech is interesting. The infinitive construct להעביר appears here as the offense; in 4Q270 F2ii:18, the conclusion to the so-called catalogue of transgressions, it denotes capital punishment. As the Israelites of antiquity made their children pass through the fire to Molech, so God will make Israel's transgressors during the period of the אחרונים pass through, as it were, His divine anger. Some rabbinic sources interpret the reference to Molech in Leviticus metaphorically as referring to intermarriage of Jews and pagans. For more discussion on the issue of capital crimes in MTA, see the comments on 4Q270 F2i:7–20 (and the parallel 4Q267 F4:11–15) in section 3.2.2.9.6.1 entitled "Capital and Non-Capital Offenses."

[או יקרב א]ל בת[ אחיהו או ישכב איש עם זכר]  4Q270 F2ii:16

4Q270 F2ii:17 משכבי אשה vac עוברי א]ת מצות התור[ה וא]ת חוקיה]

148[  בם חקק אל להעביר בח]רון אפו בק[ץ [הפקודה  4Q270 F2ii:18

> [or he who approaches] the daughter [of his brother or lies with a male]
> as if lying with a woman. It is (these) transgressors [of the command-
> ments of the Tora]h and [its statutes] against whom God has legislated
> to render destruction by [His] w[rath during the epo]ch [of redemption
> . . . ]149 (4Q270 F2ii:16b–18)

As has been noted, al-Qirqisani, quoting from a work attributed
to Zadok, states that the analogy in CD 5:7b–11a is a unicum in
Zadok's writings.

> Zadok was the first who exposed the Rabbanites and disagreed with
> them; he discovered part of the truth and wrote books in which he
> strongly rebuked and attacked them. He did not adduce any proofs for
> anything he said, but limited himself to mere statements; excepting one
> thing, namely the prohibition of (marrying) the daughter of the brother
> and the daughter of the sister, which he inferred by the analogy of the
> paternal and maternal aunts.150

As to the statement given by the author of MTA in CD 5:9b–10a
which proclaims that biblical texts, although using masculine language, are intended to incorporate also women, it opens new vistas
into the history of biblical hermeneutics. Prior to the discovery
of CD in 1887, the earliest biblical hermeneutic principles were
attributed to Hillel, who flourished in the first century B.C.E., and
Rabbi Ishmael, a century or two later. The former is said to have
enunciated seven principles, which the latter increased to thirteen.
Of course, it is not necessary to presume that these sages were the
earliest to apply such maxims. It might be that they are credited
with assembling and organizing them. At any rate, it can no longer
be assumed that the establishment of such principles was a new
phenomenon in Judaism. The date of composition of MTA probably
goes back to the third century B.C.E.151 The question that arises is,

---

148 See the text and translation for the rendition of the editio princeps.

149 For the other prohibition see the reconstruction אל יקח איש את בת [א]חותו
in 4Q266 F14d:1 (Baumgarten, DJD XVIII, 146). In addition to MTA see 11QT
66:17 and 4Q251 F17:2–3.

150 Nemoy, "Jewish Sects and Christianity," 326.

151 See my comments in section 1.2.1 of the introduction pertaining to the date
of composition.

was the author of MTA, presumably Zadok, the first to announce this principle? Note that, unlike Hillel and Rabbi Ishmael who give names like קל וחומר and גזירה שוה, our text offers no specific appellation for the principles. As is implied in the lengthy description, the Talmudic term היקש (analogy) and the like had not as yet been coined at the time of the composition of MTA. Nevertheless, the principle was known to its author. Yet, I do not know whether he was its first expounder. What was used was a technical explanation of how this principle should be applied not only here to matters of the prohibition of the niece, but to other Scriptural passages as well which are formulated in the masculine and, according to MTA, are equally applicable to females.

What is technical in our text is the phrase משפט העריות (the rule of incest). עריות is ubiquitous in rabbinic literature, but its earliest attestation is in MTA. In Lev 18 and 20 ערוה, from which the plural עריות is drawn, precedes each prohibition. However, the term משפט in the construct state with a noun pertaining to a legal issue, as in משפט העריות, is somewhat foreign to rabbinic terminology, the more common expression being דין or דיני.[152] Our author's statement on the rules of incest in CD 5:9b–11a is the oldest illustration of scholarly exposition of Scripture on this issue. The same may be said of his citation of Adam, Eve and the flood, as well as Deut 17:17, from which he deduces the prohibition of bigamy. Strictly speaking, therefore, al-Qirqisani's statement that marriage of a niece was the only point for which Zadok, the presumed author of MTA, brought proof, is not accurate, for our author does cite at least three passages for the prohibition of polygamy. It might be, however, that what al-Qirqisani meant by the uniqueness of Zadok's treatment of the marriage of a niece, is that the author of our text extends the argument beyond biblical citations. After all, he frequently buttresses his arguments with the formulas אשר כתוב and אשר אמר fronting biblical citations. For example, compare CD 10:14–17 from which the writer derives that rest from labor must cease at the moment the circuit of the sun passes through the (heavenly) gate in its (the sun's) fullness.[153] He

---

[152] משפט עריות does appear later in *Rashi Ketubbot* 46:1.

[153] See *1 En.* 72:4 for "its fullness" as referring to the sun. The standard interpretation that שער here refers to an earthly gate is unacceptable. See Ginzberg (*Unknown Jewish Sect*, 55) who rightly alludes to *1 Enoch*, who speaks of twelve heavenly gates through which the sun enters and exits the heavens. It follows that Ginzberg's argument that this text may correspond to the rabbinic extension of sabbath rest by an

seems to draw proof from the word יום, meaning apparently that the cessation of labor begins at the instant the day changes from Friday to Saturday.[154] That is why he uses the word שמור (Deut 5:12) rather than זכור (Exod 20). One must be on guard to observe the very moment of the sun's transition through the heavenly gate and its disappearance from the sky.

### b. Defilement of the Spirit (5:11b–19)

What follows is a lengthy diatribe against the religious leadership extending from lines 11b–19. MTA contains many passages in which the opponents are castigated. This, however, is the most powerful. It divides itself into two parts—one of them specific and the other general. Let us begin with reading the first.

|  | |
|---|---|
| וגם את רוח קדשיהם טמאו ובלשון | CD 5:11 |
| גדופים פתחו פה על חוקי ברית אל לאמר לא נכונו ותועבה | CD 5:12 |
| הם מדברים | CD 5:13 |

And they (the opponents) also have defiled their holy spirit, and have opened (their) mouth with blasphemous language against the statutes of God's covenant, saying, "They are not right," and speak of them as an "abomination." (CD 5:11b–13a)

So far, the author has listed specific misinterpretations such as polygamy and marriage to a niece. These lines move from the specific to the general. There are many disputations with the opposition. However, this passage is unique, in that the author cites the actual wording of the enemy with the terminological quote לאמר.

---

hour and a quarter before sunset on Friday is not plausible. The point at which the sun goes into its prescribed gate really matches what we call sunset.

|  | |
|---|---|
| אל יעש איש ביום | CD 10:14 |
| מן השישי מלאכה מן העת אשר יהיה גלגל השמש | CD 10:15 |
| רחוק מן השער מלואו כי הוא אשר אמר שמור את | CD 10:16 |
| יום השבת לקדשו | CD 10:17 |

One may not do any labor on Friday from the moment the sun's disk faces the gate in its fullness. For this is what He said, "Keep the Sabbath day by sanctifying it."

[154] As explicated in comments on CD 10:14–17a (section 3.2.2.9.12.1) which mandates the cessation of labor at sunset, the majority of DSS scholars have stressed that lines 15b–16a ordain the prohibition of labor on Friday sometime prior to sunset, the length of time which elapses during the sun's descent to the horizon from a distance of its diameter above it. Comments on this text display my rationale for understanding מן העת אשר יהיה גלגל השמש רחוק מן השער מלואו as the very moment in which the sun in its fullness passes through the *heavenly* gate, a concept drawn from *1 En.* 72.

*Rule of the Community*, 1QS 4:9–11a, apparently exegetes lines 11b–17a of CD 5 with some expansion.

9 *vac* ולרוח עולה רחוב נפש ושפול ידים בעבודת צדק רשע ושקר
10 גוה ורום לבב כחש ורמיה אכזרי  ורוב חנף קצור אפים ורוב
אולת וקנאת זדון מעשי תועבה ברוח זנות ודרכי נדה בעבודת טמאה
11 ולשון גדופים עורון עינים וכבוד אוזן קושי עורף וכיבוד לב . . .

> However, to the spirit of injustice belong excess, slackness in the service of justice, wickedness, lying, pride, haughtiness of heart, falsehood, cruel deceit, immense hypocrisy, impatience, abundant folly, willful jealousy, abominable acts in the spirit of whoredom, defiling manners in the service of impurity, a blasphemous tongue, blindness, refusal to hear, stiffness of neck and hard heartedness . . . (1QS 4:9–11a)

Another text which seems to echo our MTA passage is *Pesher Nahum*.

פשר[ו ע]ל מתעי אפרים אשר בתלמוד שקרם ולשון
כזביהם ושפת מרמה יתעו רבים

> [Its] (Nah 3:4) eschatological interpretation refers to those who lead Ephraim astray, who through their lying Talmud, their specious tongue, and deceitful lip will mislead many. (4Q169 F3-4ii:8)

The Pesherite text cited above ascribes to Nah 3:4 a polemic against the Pharisees. It is conceivable that the blasphemous tongue refers to a proto-Talmud, whose later form the rabbis called the תורה שבעל פה (the oral Torah).[155]

The quote לא נכונו (They are not right) in line 12 seems to charge that, according to the Pharisees, the covenantal ordinances, if taken literally without an oral exegesis, would be false.[156] According to the author of MTA, however, this is equivalent to blasphemy. Our text might echo Pharisaic attacks on the book of *Jubilees*, to which it ascribes a covenantal character as the Torah of Moses. The whole Pharisaic methodology of interpreting the biblical text is regarded by the sect as blasphemous against the Bible. The diatribes against Pharisaism, therefore, did not begin with the New Testament (compare Matt 23). They go back at least to the Zadokite invectives.

---

[155] As stated earlier, *Pesher Nahum* is apparently a late commentary, closer to the rabbinic era than other DSS sectarian texts.

[156] The unlikely alternative is that the Pharisees rejected not an exegesis of them, but the very ordinances themselves.

The vilification continues in lines 12b–13a with the clause ותועבה הם
מדברים בם (and they speak of them as an 'abomination'). This may be
interpreted in one of two ways. It could be a claim by the sect that the
Pharisaic interpretations of Scripture are abominable. On the other
hand, and more likely, it is the opposition who charges that the sect's
legislation is an abomination. This would make sense as stated above,
that the opposition was using blasphemous language against the sect's
legal system, regarding it as abhorrent. As we have stated elsewhere,
much of MTA is devoted to a defense of the sectarian law, the book of
*Jubilees* which is called "perfect" and other schismatic legal texts.

The preceding denunciation was not sufficient for our writer. In
his aroused state he expands upon it in lines 13b–15a with a number
of pronouncements.

כלם קדחי אש ומבערי זיקות קורי                          CD 5:13
עכביש קוריהם וביצי צפעונים ביציהם הקרוב אליהם          CD 5:14
לא ינקה כהר ביתו יאשם כי אם נלחץ                       CD 5:15

All of them (the opponents) kindle fire and burn firebrands. Webs of
a spider are their webs and eggs of vipers are their eggs. Anyone who
comes near to them will not be innocent. As he increases (his transgressions) he will be declared guilty, unless under duress. (CD 13b–15a)

The wording of these lines draws on Isa 50:11 and 59:5 respectively.
Here they are paraphrased to denounce the sect's opponents and their
nonsensical teachings. The construction of the last phrase, הקרוב אליהם
לא ינקה (Anyone who comes near to them will not be innocent) draws
on the image of adultery used in Prov 6, which concludes with its
consequences in verses 26–29, "Can a man take fire in his bosom,
and his clothes not be burned? Can one go upon hot coals, and
his feet not be consumed? So he that goes in to his neighbor's wife;
whoever touches her shall not escape punishment."[157] The words
כהר ביתו יאשם have been supposed to denote "As (at) the mountain,
his house will be held guilty."[158] However, it is more reasonable to
read the two words כהר ביתו as a singular כהרבותו[159] "as he increases
(his transgressions)," which is to say the violator will incur more
guilt. The text concludes with כי אם נלחץ, saying that no one will

_____

[157] לֹא יִנָּקֶה, literally "shall not be clean."
[158] See Schwartz in Charlesworth, ed., *Damascus Document*, 21.
[159] Rabin, *Zadokite Documents*, 21.

escape punishment unless acting under duress. Only those who were forced to follow the opposition will be absolved. These are called דיני אונסין in rabbinic literature, sins committed under duress (compare *Mekilta Vayasa'* 1). The phrase in our text, יאשם כי אם נלחץ (he will be declared guilty, unless under duress), concludes the pericope that began with 4:12, the period when Belial will have dominance in Israel, that is to say the epoch in which the author lived. It ends with the punishment awaiting the enemies of the sect.

Whereas קץ (CD 5:20) points to a specific date, למילפנים (line 15) is more general, lacking the definite time alluded to in קץ.[160] מלפנים, then, here refers to the beginnings of Israel's history commencing with Abraham and continuing to the exodus and the giving of the first Torah. Lines 15b–19 are a general statement that embrace the whole period of Israel's history from the formation of the nation to the author's own time. It asserts that the opposition to the Torah did not begin in the exilic period. Rather, elements of it go back to the very formation of the law at Sinai. More specifically it shows that Moses and Aaron confronted the opposition, just as the author and his entourage to whom this work is addressed must likewise do. Facing more opposition than did his ancestor Abraham who had contented with Mastema, Moses dealt not only with Pharaoh, but also Belial (introduced in 4:12–13) and those whom he raised up, יחנה and his brother. Moses was, of course, the victor since he was

---

[160] An important term in this section as elsewhere in CD is מלפנים. We find it first in CD 2:17. Wickedness, according to the writer, started at the very beginning of creation when the watchers came down from heaven and corrupted the human daughters.

> And now hear me O children that I may open your eyes to see and to understand the acts of God, to choose what He desires, and to despise what He hates, [to observe the statutes of God with the loving covenant], to walk perfectly in all His ways and not to wander into thoughts inclining towards transgression with eyes of whoredom, since many have gone astray in these matters. Mighty warriors have stumbled into them *since the time of old* until now. (CD 2:14–17)

These lines open the pericope that deal with the fall of the giants, the corruption of the flood and how the men of the wilderness lost their way to enter the holy land. CD 3:19–20a contains the next occurrence of מלפנים, speaking of the sanctuary that God will build in the future when He will atone for all sin.

> And he will erect for them a faithful temple in Israel, the like of which has never existed *from earliest time* until now.

The temporal term מקדם (CD 2:7 and 19:3) is a synonym of מלפנים.

guided by the Prince of the Urim (and Thummim).[161]

Note the three-fold emphasis on Israel's lack of wisdom in lines 16–17. The theme of understanding is a characteristic of MTA. Although much of this document deals with theological and legal subject matter, wisdom and sapiential issues remain an essential part of the composition, alluded to already in the preamble of the work.

Lines 18–19 draw on *Rule of the Community* (1QS) 3:20 and 4Q164 F1:5, both of which ultimately paraphrase the levitical blessing in Deut 33:8 concerning the function of the divinatory Urim and Thummim. The idea here in the DSS is pointing to Exod 7:11–12 where the Egyptian magicians duplicated the miraculous acts performed by Moses. Belial in our text retorts to Moses by raising up the magicians יחנה and his companion. According to Targum Yerushalmi, the names of the Egyptian magicians were יַנֵּיס and יִמְבְרֵיס. Talmud *Bavli Menahot* 85a spells these names יוחנא and ממרא. 2 Tim 3:8 refers to Ἰάννης and Ἰαμβρῆς challenging Moses. The Targum and 2 Tim 3:8 are similar. The spelling of יחנה in CD most closely resembles יוחנא of *Bavli Menahot*. At any rate, CD, *Bavli Menahot* and Paul's letter to Timothy make the same point—the attempt of the Egyptian magicians to outwit Moses and Aaron with their magical skills. In CD it is Belial, a synonym to Mastema (Satan), who is the master of יחנה and his brother, whereas in rabbinic texts יחנה and his brother may be assistants to Balaam. Our text in CD, however, gives only one name, יחנה, identifying the second magician as his brother, apparently paralleling the kinship of Moses and Aaron.[162]

### 3.2.1.4.3. *The Shifters of the Boundary (5:20–6:2a)*
Whereas hitherto we have dealt with Egypt and the Exodus, these lines move from the ancient epoch when Israel had become wicked

---

[161] Cf. Deut 33:8 and Isaiah Pesher[b] (4Q164) F1:4–5. Schechter identified the שר אורים of CD 5:18 as the שר הפנים. Ginzberg argues for שר העירים (Prince of the Watchers), the term עירים occurring in CD 2:18 as angels (Ginzberg, *Unknown Jewish Sect*, 26). However, it could not refer to the "watchers," since they ultimately became the fallen angels, negative figures. The אורים should be identified with the oracular instruments, first utilized by Moses in his disputations with Belial. The central idea of the אורים in CD 5:18 is that Moses and Aaron themselves used the Urim and Thummim to combat Belial.

[162] The fact that three traditions (MTA, the rabbinic and Paul) know of these brothers' rivalry with Moses and Aaron suggest the existence of a pseudepigraphon now lost which elaborated on this subject.

the first time (הראשונה) to the more recent era that approximates the contemporary scene after the destruction of Jerusalem and the Temple in 586 B.C.E. This period, as will be explicated in the next section, led ultimately to the beginning of the apocalyptic epoch when the Messiah of Aaron and Israel was to arise, in which the righteous were expected to have a longevity of a thousand generations (CD 7:6). Here in 5:20 the text deals with the rise of the opposition, the מסיגי הגבול (the Shifters of the Boundary), a sobriquet for the Pharisees or Rabbanites,[163] introduced earlier in this section as בוני החיץ (the builders of the wall). The juxtaposition of the era of the ראשונים seen again in 6:2 (the beginning of the next section describing Israel's rise)[164] with the time when the מסיגי הגבול came to prominence draws on Deut 19:14 which prohibited one from moving a boundary established in antiquity.

לֹא תַסִּיג גְּבוּל רֵעֲךָ אֲשֶׁר גָּבְלוּ רִאשֹׁנִים בְּנַחֲלָתְךָ
אֲשֶׁר תִּנְחַל בָּאָרֶץ אֲשֶׁר יְהוָה אֱלֹהֶיךָ נֹתֵן לְךָ לְרִשְׁתָּהּ

Do not *shift the boundary* of your neighbor which the *ancestors* have set, in the property which you shall inherit in the land which the Lord your God is giving you to possess. (Deut 19:14)

In interpreting the Shifters of the Boundary as the Pharisees, our author regards this group as having fashioned their own system of interpreting Scripture, a technique which had departed from the plain meaning of holy writ. The opposition had altered, as it were, the hermeneutical boundaries fixed by the writers in antiquity.

CD 5:21–6:1a ties the current events to what had taken place in the wilderness following the reports of the spies in Kadesh-barnea, preparing the reader for the description of the Shifters of the Boundary. Just as the rebellious Israelites perished in the wilderness prior to the nation's entry into Canaan, so also the Shifters of the Boundary and their followers, having spoken evil against the commandments of God through Moses, will perish.

The assumption behind the clause "And the earth has become desolate" is that Israel's wilderness occurred as a result of her rebelliousness following the report in Num 13 of the spies who, despite their

---

[163] See al-Qirqisani's description of the Rabbanites in *HUCA* 7, 325–26.
[164] ריאשונים in this case is a composite spelling of components preserved in CD 6:2; 4Q267 F2:7; 6Q15 F3:5.

negative report on the size and strength of the people of Canaan, claimed that the land was זָבַת חָלָב וּדְבָשׁ (flowing with milk and honey). However, it was Israel's lack of faith in God's enabling them to conquer the land that was the cause of the loss of its fructification. Nevertheless, with Israel's redemption at the end of time, the milk and honey of previous epochs would be restored. This point is radical, since it claims that even the settlement in Canaan under Joshua was not the utopia that it might have been. Israel of the ריאשונים did not as yet possess a perfect Torah. The work of Belial and his entourage had succeeded even in corrupting parts of the Law, rendering the first as imperfect and relegating the ideal Torah of Moses to a future age.

Conventional scholarship emends CD's reading משיחו (6:1) to a plural, משיחי, and understands it as alluding to two messiahs.[165] Indeed, both 4Q267 F2:6 and an unclear script in 6Q15 F3:4 seem to have a second *yod* at the end, not a *waw*. If we read CD's במשיחו, the text refers to Moses ("as God has commanded through Moses, even by his holy anointed"). On the other hand, as was noted by Rabin, the introductory section to *Rule of the Community* has כאשר צוה ביד מושה וביד כול עבדיו הנביאים (as He commanded through Moses and all His servants, the prophets), a passage that tends to support the reading במשיחי הקודש. As the author of CD understood our text, the phrase "anointed holy ones" includes Moses, the first prophet, against whose transcribed divine laws the Israelites had rebelled in the wilderness. Reading the word משיחי gains confirmation in its conceptual parallel in 4Q270 F2ii:14, suggesting another correction in CD 2:12 to read ויודיעם ביד משיחי רוח קדשו (And He has informed them through those who were anointed by His Holy Spirit). The plural in the clause following in CD 2:13, וחוזי אמת, "and (by) the seers of truth," a phrase parallel to משיחי רוח קדשו, lends additional support for the plural of "anointed" both here and in 6:1.

A distinction should be drawn between these clauses containing the word משיח in the plural and that of משיח (מ)אהרן ו(מ)ישראל (the Messiah from Aaron and Israel) which occurs four times in MTA (CD 12:23–24; 14:19; 19:10–11; 20:1), wherein the term "messiah" is in the singular. The plural refers to those that have been sanctified with oil, set apart for a particular task within historical Israel, whereas the singular pertains to the anticipated Messiah of the future.

---

[165]  See Qimron, "The Text of CDC," in *The Damascus Document Reconsidered* (Ed. Magen Broshi; Jerusalem: The Israel Exploration Society, 1992), 21.

Incidentally the clause "Messiah from Aaron and Israel" is unique to MTA and contains, so to speak, the author's "signature," supporting the view that this composition constitutes a unity, not a mere collection of extracts.

Coming back to CD 5:20, our text says, "Now during the epoch of the desolation of the land the Shifters of the Boundary arose and misled Israel." This passage is interesting since, as was stated, it dates the rise of the Boundary-Shifters during the period of the חרבן, the destruction of the temple and the land. Who were these offenders? The epithet מסיגי (ה)גבול appears three times in MTA, first in the preamble in 4Q266 F1:4, second in CD 5:20 and finally in CD 19:15–16. As mentioned above, scrollists have presumed that the sobriquet מסיגי (ה)גבול attacks the Pharisees. If so, our author sets the rise of this group during the exilic period, an opinion contrary to the standard view which dates their formation during the Macabbean age. Let us not forget that the Talmudic tradition likewise sets the rise of the Pharisees in the exilic and post-exilic age, as does al-Qirqisani, the 10th century Karaite writer. In this connection it is clear that in their view, the sectaries regarded themselves as Israel *veritas*, and that they were those whom God had left as a remnant in the past when the others perished (CD 1:4–5).

The era described thus far depicts the post-exilic epoch when the writer anticipates another rebellion by the Pharisees, this time against the יורה הצדק mentioned just below in 6:11. Hence, our whole passage binds together two periods of history: 1) the epochs of the wilderness when Israel, prompted by the reports of the spies, gave deviant counsel (דברו עצה סרה) against Moses, and 2) the author's period of history when the sect's opponents, the Pharisees, will repudiate the leader of the covenanteers (see the text to follow in CD 6:2–11).

This leads us to a more general point in MTA and other Dead Sea Scrolls. There is a constant intermingling of past, present and future—everything that happened in bygone days (ריאשונים) is only a model for what is transpiring currently and for what will occur in the coming era. In other words, all history serves as a blueprint for the אחרית הימים (the end of days). Thus, when MTA speaks of the fall of the giants during the antediluvian age and the events leading to the flood, it is not a mere retelling of the past but a stern warning for comparable retribution in the present and future resulting from the non-observance of the Torah. Heeding the commandments serves as a control for desolation and fertility of the land. MTA's futuristic tendency and its focus on the אחרית הימים prompts us to recognize that verbal conjugations alone are not the sole determinants as to whether a narrative refers merely to the past or to both past and future. As was noted above, the allusion to Moses as one of the holy anointed, refers, of course, to the events in the wilderness. However, the entire passage "they spoke deviant counsel" may also point to the future. Therefore the words כי דברו סרה עֹצ̇ה לׁבׁרוֹ in 4Q267 F2:5 (כי דברו סרה in CD 5:21) could equally be rendered "because they will have spoken deviant counsel."

The clause וינבאו שקר להשיב את ישראל מאחרי אל (And they have prophesied falsehood to make Israel turn away from God) may also be rendered, "and they are, and will be prophesying falsehood to turn Israel away from God." The Israelites in the wilderness claimed that they would not be able to conquer the land, since its masters were too mighty. The contemporary Pharisees likewise have spoken deviously against the covenanters, disregarding their interpretations of the Torah and prophesying falsehood resulting in a national departure from God. Our text disputes the Pharisaic concepts of messianism and perhaps attacks the opinion that the people should collaborate with the occupying Ptolemaic authorities.

### 3.2.1.5. *Israel's Rise: The Life of the New Covenant in Damascus (CD 6:2b–7:5a; 7:5b–8:21 / CD 19:1–34a; 19:34b–20:32a; 4Q266 F4)*

At this point the text shifts from the negative to the positive, to a verbiage describing the *rise* of a new movement inspired to observe the Torah as guided by the new leadership. The heads of this new community, like the patriarchs of old, will be princes and men of understanding who will know how to interpret the ancient past for the immediate and future epochs. The present is an age when the sinners will be more sinful, but, at the same time, there will arise princes inspired enough to draw living waters from the well of the Torah, both the traditional and the eschatological laws. Incidentally, it would appear that the author of MTA regarded himself as one of these emerging inspired sages. The author then presents a digest of the new sectarian Torah, to be elaborated on by him in the second part of the body of the composition. A future migration from Judah to Damascus and the camp life in this new locale pictures the life of this new community that will await the Just Teacher who will lead them into the messianic epoch.

### 3.2.1.5.1. *Those Committed to Live a Righteous Life in Damascus (CD-A 6:2a–7:5a, 5b–6a / CD-B 19:1–2a)*

Damascus becomes a prominent theme at this point in the book's development, a city to which the searchers pursuing the truth of the Torah will migrate. As stated above, this municipality will become the habitation of the new community awaiting the Messiah and the salvation he will bring.

### 3.2.1.5.1.1. The Rise of the New Interpreters of the Torah (CD-A 6:2–11a)

This text interprets in a new way Num 21:18. As was introduced above, the text beginning with ויזכר אל ברית ראשונים (But God will remember the covenant of the patriarchs) shifts to the future and introduces the new era that will bring about the foundation of a new Israel. The nation had reached an impasse, sinking deeply into an abyss. It was only by divine grace that she would receive salvation through the rise of new leaders. These anticipated guides would not be the masters of the past who had misled Israel, but would be a new group with a new understanding of the sense of divinity, whose advent would lead the people to the end of time.

וישמיעם (and He will inform them) pertains in line 3 to the explication of the pesherite meaning of Num 21:18 which follows. Having refuted the argument of the opposition, presumably the Pharisees, the author of MTA now addresses the adherents. He does so with a pesherite midrash on this biblical passage which, as he understands it, foretells the coming rise of the community to whom this work is addressed. The text preceding this verse tells of the Israelites' wandering in the wilderness thirsting for water. God told Moses, "Assemble the people that I might give them water." Our author apparently takes the following phrase in verse 17, אָז יָשִׁיר יִשְׂרָאֵל (Then Israel sang), not only as the past tense of this clause in Exod 15:1, but as futuristic, "Then Israel *will* sing," addressing his assembly and that of the end of days. The two imperative phrases, עֲלִי בְאֵר (Rise, O well) and עֲנוּ־לָהּ (Sing to it), are also taken to anticipate the coming era. עֲנוּ־לָהּ could also mean "Repeat it," a phrase, which in our writer's opinion, would be directed to the Israel of his time, carrying the repetitive aspect in which the rabbis read the verbs of the שְׁמַע (Deut 6:6–9), thus giving an inspiration to the pesherite exegesis that follows. The water of the well stands for the words of the Torah, and its diggers are its transcribers and instructors. They are identified

here as the penitent members of the new group who will migrate to
Damascus. נדיב links up with מתנדב, especially in *Rule of the Community*,
where it forms the core of the membership of the community. For
example 1QS 5:1–3a reads

1 וזה הסרך לאנשי היחד המתנדבים לשוב מכול רע ולהחזיק בכול
אשר צוה לרצונו להבדל מעדת 2 אנשי העול להיות ליחד בתורה
ובהון ומשיבים על פי בני צדוק הכוהנים שומרי הברית וַעל פי רוב אנשי
3 היחד המחזקים בברית

> And this is the rule for the members of the community who freely take
> upon themselves to repent from all evil and to accept all that He has
> commanded by His will. It is incumbent that they keep apart from the
> council of the men of evil, becoming a community in (the study of)
> Torah and in possessions. And they shall respond in accordance with
> (the principles) of the Sons of Zadok, the priests, the guardians of the
> covenant and in accordance with the majority of the members of the
> community who hold fast to the covenant. (1QS 5:1–3a)

This introductory passage to *Rule of the Community* presents itself as an
umbilical cord of MTA, using נדב as it is interpreted in נדיבי העם.

The word במחקק (by the Lawmaker) in CD 6:4 may have seemed
out of place in a line that deals with well diggers. For the pesherite
interpreter, however, במחקק refers not only to Moses the lawgiver,
but to the more abstract מחוקקות of CD 6:9, legislation in general.
The tendency to change nouns into their abstract sense occurs elsewhere in MTA, such as גבהות (CD 1:15) and השתחוות (CD 11:22).[166]
Apparently the author of MTA believed himself to be a linguist
who could not only interpret Scripture, but also transform ordinary
words of Torah into their more abiding sense.

The מחוקק (the Lawgiver) is here not a mere transmitter of divine
legislation, but also a searcher of the law who expands upon what
God had commanded, that is to say making new law. As was stated
above, the law refers not only to the Pentateuch, but to other works
as well such as *Jubilees*. The pesherizing of the biblical text continues
by identifying the well of Num 21:18 as the Torah. Note, however,
that it does not specify which Torah it is, apparently referring here
to both that given by Moses at Sinai and *Jubilees* said to have been
composed by him during his forty day stay on top of the cloud resting

---

[166] In addition the following occur elsewhere in the DSS: אלוהות ("divinity"—
4Q287 F2:8; 4Q400 F1i:2 and 4Q403 F1i:33), ארמלות ("widowhood"—4Q176
F8-11:6), חזות ("vision"—PAM 43.692 F80:1), צבות ("will"—1QH^a 18:18) and תעות
("error"—1QS 3:21; 1QH^a 10:14; 12:12, 16, 20; 4Q381 F79:5).

on the mountain. חופריה (its excavators) are "its interpreters."

Moses, together with the people of Israel, searched for the meaning of Torah through their digging. The excavators are not only Moses and Aaron and their associates who interpreted the divine legislation; as was stated before, the present diggers of the Torah are also the future penitent of Israel "who will exit from the land of Judah and dwell in the land of Damascus" (CD 6:5). They are the princes whose glorious hermeneutics no one can challenge.

The clause ולא הושבה פארתם בפי אחד has troubled translators. Schechter already noted the problematics of these words. Assuming that our text is related to Ezek 31:12, he understands פארתם as a bough of a tree.[167] Hence, the translation "and their bough was not turned back in the mouth of one." Ginzberg, quoting Isa 20:5, emends our text from הושבה to הובשה (a verb from the root בוש "shame, embarrassment"), understanding the clause as "because the objects of their pride did not become a cause of shame."[168] Rabin, followed with the same sense by Cook, Davies, Vermes, Martínez-Tigchelaar and Schwartz, renders it "and their fame was not rejected by the mouth of anyone."[169] The meaning still is obscure, however. To whom exactly does "their fame" refer and what does it mean? It might be that this difficult clause is parenthetical, commenting on the complex exegesis of the pesherite interpretation of Num 21:18. After all, we see here a chain of aggressive hermeneutics played out with this interpretation. The well means the Torah and its diggers are its interpreters. And perhaps, most significantly, the מחוקק refers now both to the lawgiver Moses and to the דורש התורה, the futuristic sectarian interpreter of the law known also elsewhere as the מורה צדק. Our phrase in 6:6, כי כולם דרשוהו, meaning "for they all *midrashized* it" might have aroused scorn among the sect's opponents. Possibly responding to such a critique, the author becomes defensive, saying that no one can reasonably repudiate this pesherite exegesis. Their glorious interpretation may not be challenged. If this is its real meaning, MTA displays a method of argumentation that is somewhat rare in that, anticipating the criticism, it attempts to refute it in advance.[170] Our text now continues with the exegesis to account for its purpose.

---

[167] Schechter in Fitzmyer, ed., *Documents*, 70, note 11.
[168] Ginzberg, *Unknown Jewish Sect*, 28.
[169] Rabin, *Zadokite Documents*, 22.
[170] Cf. also Jer 13:21 and Rom 9:19.

The association of the infinitive להדריכם (to lead them) with the phrase מורה צדק (the Just Teacher) found in CD 1:11, when compared with that of the similar infinitival phrase להתהלך בם (to walk by them), and the phrases דורש התורה (the interpreter of the Torah) and יורה צדק (the True Lawgiver) in CD 6:6–11, suggests that these sobriquets refer to the same personality. Another passage in the Florilegium (4Q174) confirms this impression.

F1-2i:11    אני אֱהֹיֶה לוא לאב והוא יהיה לי לבן הואה צמח

דויד העומד עם דורש התורה אשר F1-2i:12 [יקום [בצי]ון בא]חרית
הימים כאשר כתוב והקימותי את סוכת דויד הנופלת היאה סוכת
F1-2i:13 דויד הנופלֹ[ת א]שר יעמוד להושיע את ישראל

> I will be a father to him, and he will be a son to me. He is the sprout of David who will come to prominence together with the Interpreter of the Torah who will arise in Zion at the end of days, as it is written, "and I will raise up the fallen tent of David." The fall[en] tent of David is (a way of referring to David) [w]ho will arise to deliver Israel. (4Q174 F1-2i:11–13)

Modern researchers, however, diverge widely as to the identity of these figures. Some, as Frank Cross, fuse all the passages dealing with these personalities into a single construct, historicizing them into what we know of the Hasmonean high priests such as Simon, John Hyrcanus and Alexander Janaeus.[171] Others, like Philip Davies, posit two different personas.[172] The first is the מורה צדק who is regarded as the founder of the movement, the second the יורה הצדק who will arise at the end of time.

Either opinion, relegating both figures into a single historical setting, or making the מורה צדק historical and the יורה הצדק eschatological, makes little sense. As these and other writers say, these texts (and there are many of them) mention no names, leaving the task of identifying them to modern scholarship. Some have taken their identity as far back as Ezra and Nehemiah. No personal name, however, is given to any of these figures in the DSS.[173] In fact, neither is there an allusion to the Seleucid persecution and Hasmonean liberation.

---

[171] Frank Moore Cross, *The Ancient Library of Qumran* (3d ed. Minneapolis: Fortress Press, 1995), 88–120, 156–65.

[172] Davies, *The Damascus Covenant*, 173–79.

[173] Solome Alexandra, the Hasmonean queen (76–67 B.C.E.), is mentioned, but only in the *mishmarot* texts that deal with Pompei's conquest of Jerusalem.

Lines 7–11 amplify the function of the יורה הצדק, known also as the דורש התורה. Our text appears to draw on elements of Gen 49:10 and Hos 10:12. The following elucidates the integration of these components.

לֹא־יָסוּר שֵׁבֶט מִיהוּדָה וּמְחֹקֵק מִבֵּין רַגְלָיו עַד כִּי־יָבֹא
שִׁילֹה וְלוֹ יִקְּהַת עַמִּים

The scepter will not depart from Judah, nor the *lawgiver* from between his feet *until he comes to Shiloh* and the people render him homage. (Gen 49:10)

זִרְעוּ לָכֶם לִצְדָקָה קִצְרוּ לְפִי־חֶסֶד נִירוּ לָכֶם נִיר וְעֵת
לִדְרוֹשׁ אֶת־יְהֹוָה עַד־יָבוֹא וְיֹרֶה צֶדֶק לָכֶם

Spread seed for righteousness; harvest for love; draw a planting line. It is the time to search for the Lord *until He comes* and *teaches righteousness* to you. (Hos 10:12)

עד עמד יורה הצדק באחרית הימים (until the True Lawgiver arises at the end of time) paraphrases עַד כִּי־יָבֹא שִׁילֹה (until he comes to Shiloh) in Gen 49:10 and עַד־יָבוֹא (until He comes) in Hos 10:12. Our author takes the מְחֹקֵק from the first and יֹרֶה צֶדֶק from the latter, fusing them into one text. The purpose of this legislator in our passage is broad and precise—to follow the laws during the epoch of wickedness that will continue until the end of days when the righteous will live for a thousand generations. Whereas the sectarian text apparently identifies the well as both the Torah given to Moses on Sinai and that which he inscribed during his forty days while on top of the cloud resting on the mountain, the biblical word מחוקק might have been understood as referring to Moses alone.

The author links these exegetes to creators of art by citing Isa 54:16 which depicts the craftsman as the מוציא כלי למעשיהו (One who brings forth an instrument for his works). As interpreted by our writer, both Moses and the דורש התורה made the Torah as an instrument for reinterpretation to create new meanings. Our text then refers to the members of the community (נדיבי העם) as those who will come to dig the well (the Torah) in the land of Damascus. They perform their excavations through legislative mastery (מחוקקות) throughout the entire epoch of wickedness and thus help bring about the coming of the True Lawgiver. On the other hand, those who stand apart from this select community will not perceive its meaning. However, its truth will become apparent to all when the True Lawgiver will arise at the end of time.

### 3.2.1.5.1.2. Those Who Shun the Temple on Account of Its Defilement (6:11b–14a)

Lines 11b–14a are difficult both textually and conceptually. It is likely that the idea of closing the sanctuary in this passage interconnects with the more central idea on this page beginning with line 5 and ending in 19, namely that those who leave Judah will be the wise men who will have the new covenant in the land of Damascus, a contract superior to the traditional Sinaitic covenant. In other words, the pesherite interpretation of Num 21:18 which makes the wise men of Jerusalem leave the holy land to sojourn in Damascus (and I mean Damascus, not Babylon or Qumran) created a problem—that these שבי ישראל would lose all access to the holy temple. The citation of Mal 1:10 in CD 6:13–14 responds to this problem, since according to the prophet, God and not only the prophet (כאשר אמר אל "as God has said") had commanded them to abandon the sanctuary. This would require the penitent of Israel to abandon the holy place if only temporarily prior to the coming of the Messiah of Aaron and Israel.

The clause at the beginning of this section, וכול אשר הובא בברית (and anyone who has been brought into the covenant), addresses once again the uniqueness of each member of this group who commits himself to the observance of the new Torah. The prerequisite demands that he not enter the temple to kindle the altar which had been defiled during the period of wickedness. This is a radical requirement for which apparently the writer felt compelled to look for Scriptural support. He found substantiation for it in Malachi. As taken by our author, Mal 1:10 not only sanctions not entering the temple, but requires it, given the deviant leadership of its contemporary leaders. After all, those who have been in charge of the sanctuary have not observed the laws of the entire Torah. However, not all of the members of the community will leave Judah for Damascus, thereby abandoning the defiled sanctuary. Those who elect to remain in the land of Judah will still be dependent upon the temple and its errant personnel and will not take on the obligation to reject it.[174] Yet many

---

[174] *Pesher Habakkuk* describes the activities of the latter priests in Jerusalem who in the final days will amass wealth (1QpHab 9:4b–7a), and those of the Wicked Priest

others, those who will have joined the exodus, will be subject to the
ברית החדשה בארץ דמשק (the new covenant in the land of Damascus)
explicated in the next section which describes the digest of the sectarian Torah and in what follows pertaining more specifically to the
migration from Judah and the forewarned apostasy. The idea that
the obligation to abandon the sanctuary is part of the exodus further
illustrates the importance of the temple in our document.

The question anticipated pertains to the duration of the forsak-
ing of the Jerusalem temple. As disclosed in the above paragraph,
the subject of the clause אם לא ישמרו לעשות כפרוש התורה לקץ הרשע in
CD 6:14 (if they will not take heed to do according to the explanation of the Torah during the epoch of wickedness) refers not to
the members of the community,[175] but to the authorities in charge
of the sanctuary.[176] In other words the author is not suggesting
that they ought to reject the sanctuary in total, but must distance
themselves from it as long as the sons of perdition are in charge of
its worship during the epoch of wickedness. For despite its defilement, the standing temple retains its sanctity. In line with what we
said above, the idea of abandoning applies fundamentally to those
who will have participated in the exodus from Judah to Damascus;
but certainly, those who remain in the holy city and live under its
apostate priests are not excluded. All are invited to partake in the
new covenant life in Damascus.

---

who will have committed despicable deeds, defiling the temple in Jerusalem (1QpHab
12:7b–9a). *Pesher Nahum* likewise depicts the wealth that the Jerusalem priests will
have gathered (4Q169 F3-4i:11b–12a). The presence of these religious leaders presumes an active community in Jerusalem. 4Q162 2:6b–10 (*Pesher Isaiah*) describes
the activities of the scoffers of Jerusalem, part of this community, evidently those
who side with the איש הלצון (the Scoffer), the nemesis of the מורה צדק who was
expected to lead the community of the exodus in Damascus.

[175] See Rabin, *Zadokite Documents*, 22–24. As Rabin reads it, the community has
breached the covenant by profaning the temple and not keeping the laws of the
Torah.

[176] See Davies, Schwartz and Martínez-Tigchelaar who interpret these lines as
an admonition. The covenanters are prohibited from participating in the worship
of the temple because of the illicit offerings of the sanctuary personnel (Davies, 249;
Charlesworth, ed., *Damascus Document*, 23; Martínez-Tigchalaar, *Scrolls Study Edition*,
559).

3.2.1.5.1.3.  A Digest of the Sectarian Torah (CD-A 6:14b–7:5a,
        5b–6a / CD-B 19:1–2a[177])

The following digest serves as a summary of and a link to the detailed
elaborations on the Eschatological Torah exposed after its lengthy
introduction extending from CD 1:1–8:21; 19:1–20:34 to 4Q266 F4
and 4Q267 F7:1–2. It constitutes the epitomic requirements of those
commissioned to forsake the Jerusalem temple explicated above and
live under the directives of the Damascene covenant (CD 6:19).

    The subject of להבדל in CD 6:14b are those who have been brought
into and will continue entering the covenant introduced in 6:11b.
This infinitive bears a close resemblance to להנזר in lines 1–2 of the
prologue to our document, [כי בני חושך]‎ [על ב]נ֗י אור להנז֗ר מדר֗ (‎[It is
incumbent upon the so]ns of light to keep separate from the wa[ys of
the sons of darkness]), serving to succinctly present the general contents of this work. It is not merely to emphasize differences of opinion
within the collective, but to separate themselves from Israel as a whole,
those who remain in Judah under the jurisdiction of the temple. It is
necessary that these covenanters who refrain from presenting offerings
in the sanctuary defiled by the priests keep away from these transgressors who have profaned the holy place. The two infinitive clauses
להבדל מבני [הַשֻּׁ]‎[178] followed by להנזר מהון הרשעה have a legal dimension, each stressing the demand to separate. These phrases apparently mark the beginning of the movement known from the classical
sources as the Essenes.

    These verbs also introduce the idea of a separation from Israel, the
formation of a new community or sect. In other words as stated before,
we are no longer dealing with mere differences of opinion among
the collective of the nation, but what we have is a redefinition of the
sense of the term Israel. It includes only those who have joined the
new movement and yet others who *will* embrace the developing community in the future, a constituency which makes a radical separation
from non-adherents in Judah. This suggests that MTA introduces the
pivotal idea of creating a new sect, the Essenes, a group which will
have separated itself from the body of Israel.

---

[177]  As will be shown, at CD 7:5b (Mss A) there begins a correspondence with
CD 19:1 (Mss B) which continues through CD 8:21 (19:34a). However, the B-text is
expansive at this juncture, containing a peroration from Deut 7:9, "And know that the
Lord God your God is the only God, the faithful who keeps the covenant and love
to those who love him and keep his commandments for a thousand generations."
[178]  4Q266 F3ii:21; השחת CD.

The rendition in line 15, "and to 'nazirite' by means of a vow and ban from the defiling wealth of wickedness," diverges from the standard translations which understand the vow and ban as describing the illicit mode of acquisition. As I understand them, however, they affirm the means through which the covenantal community must separate itself from those who have violated the Torah. In my rendition the vow and ban refer to the obligation taken by the members of the covenant to keep apart from the community of the pit. Our text, therefore, describes how Israel must separate from the children of perdition. As to the type of vow involved in the separation, see the broader explication on the covenant and other oaths or vows in CD 15:1–16:22 and continuing into 9:1.

Nevertheless, even in describing themselves as the children of light and defining the others who are not part of the movement as children of darkness, those Israelites who are not part of the new covenant are not to be equated with the pagans. Those who remain in Judah are still part of the "greater" covenant in that they keep the rules of the first Torah, in contrast to the Gentiles who do not follow them at all.

The phrase הון המקדש in line 16 could be perceived in one of three ways: a) as a rejection of the contemporary sanctuary, b) that the non-priests may not touch the holy or defiled objects, or c) wealth of outsiders which is deposited in the sanctuary. CD 4:17 lists הון along with זנות (whoredom) and טמא המקדש (the defilement of the temple) as the three cardinal transgressions which Israel is guilty of. Our text gives הון הרשעה and הון המקדש as the פרוש (the detailed sense) of הון.

ולגזול את עניי עמו (to rob the poor of his people) is presumably another item of the list in CD 4:17. The verb גזל occurs nowhere else in MTA, but is frequent in the DSS. Admonishing judges not to accept bribes to pervert justice, *Temple Scroll* states,

57:20 ולוא יקח שוחד להטות משפט צדק ולוא יחמוד

57:21 שדה וכרם וכול הון ובית וכול חמוד בישראל וגזל. . .

One shall not take a bribe to pervert righteous justice and shall not covet field or garden, and any property or house or anything covetable in Israel, and robbery . . . (11QT 57:20–21)

11QT 58 goes on to speak of a gentile nation. The king should make war against any pagan people that robs the Israelites.

58:3 כי ישמע המלך על כול גוי ועם מבקש לגזול מכול אשר יש

58:4 לישראל ושלח על שרי האלפים ועל שרי המיאות הנתונים בערי

58:5 ישראל

When a king hears about any nation or people trying to rob any possessions of Israel, he should send for the princes of the thousand and
for the princes of the hundred stationed in Israel's cities . . . (11QT
58:3–5a)

Attacking robbery, 1Q27 (Mysteries) becomes rhetorical:

מי גוי חפץ אשר יעושקנו חזק ממנו מי                    F1i:10

יחפץ כי יגזל ברשע הונו מי גוי אשר לוא עשק רעה]ו[ איפה עם אשר לוא    F1i:11

גזל הו]ן[ ל]אחר                    F1i:12

What nation wants to be plundered by one that is stronger than it.
Who desires that someone should rob his property wickedly? Is there a
nation who that has not plundered [its] neighbor? Where can one find
a people that has not ravaged proper[ty] belonging to [someone else?]
(1Q27 F1i:10b–12a)

The sequence of עני (poor), אלמנות (widows) and יתומים (fatherless)
from lines 16–17 of our text resembles that of Isa 10:2.[179]

לְהַטּוֹת מִדִּין דַּלִּים וְלִגְזֹל מִשְׁפַּט עֲנִיֵּי עַמִּי
לִהְיוֹת אַלְמָנוֹת שְׁלָלָם וְאֶת־יְתוֹמִים יָבֹזּוּ

To turn the judgment of the destitute, and to rob my people's poor of
justice, that widows may be their prey, and that they may plunder the
fatherless! (Isa 10:2)

However, the author of CD combines this Isaiah passage with Ps 94:6,
changing the verb from בז (to plunder) to רצח (to murder).

אַלְמָנָה וְגֵר יַהֲרֹגוּ וִיתוֹמִים יְרַצֵּחוּ

They kill the widow and the proselyte and murder the fatherless. (Ps
94:6)

By fusing biblical lines, our text shows how the author of MTA drew
his charges against the Pharisees. For other sectarian rules applying
to widows, see 4Q269 F9:5, 4Q270 F5:19 and 4Q271 F3:12.

    The prohibitions in lines 17–18, "and to distinguish between what
is defiling and pure and to tell between what is sacred and ordinary,"
fall under the third category of (un)righteousness in CD 4:16–18,
טמא המקדש (the defiling of the sanctuary). They interpret the sense
of what the Shulchan Aruch calls הלכות גזילה (the rules of theft),

---

[179] Cf. Zech 7:10 for a different sequence and number of groups.

detailing what one may not appropriate, issues discussed in 4Q270 F2ii:9b–10a, CD 15:3b–5a and 9:10b–16a.

As stated earlier, the noun פרוש never occurs in Hebrew Scripture, but is ubiquitous in the Talmud and rabbinics, and especially so in MTA wherein it occurs sixteen times. The participle מְפֹרָשׁ, however, does occur in Neh 8:8:

וַיִּקְרְאוּ בַסֵּפֶר בְּתוֹרַת הָאֱלֹהִים מְפֹרָשׁ וְשׂוֹם שֵׂכֶל וַיָּבִינוּ בַּמִּקְרָא

> Then they read in the book of the Torah of God, elaborating upon it and giving attention to its sense, and they perceived (the deeper meaning) of Scripture. (Neh 8:8)

Rabin renders פרוש "exact rules," Davies "details," Schwartz, "exact details," and Martínez-Tigchelaar "exact interpretation." However, פרוש really serves as a term which amplifies the word מדרש, elaborating on biblical rules such as here, the Sabbath, the festivals and the Day of Atonement, including the calendar. It differs from its synonym פשר, in that the latter alludes to the prophetic meaning of Scripture. At any rate the general sense of פרוש is the elaboration given to it by those belonging to the author's circle.

What the author of MTA means here in 6:18 pertaining to the elaboration of the Sabbath rules, however, becomes clear in CD 10–11 where many details concerning the observance of the Sabbath are listed. For a more general statement concerning it see 4QApocryphon of Jeremiah C$^e$ (4Q390) F1:7b–8.

7        ומתום הדור ההוא ביובל השביעי

8 לחרבן הארץ ישכחו חוק ומועד ושבת וברית ויפרו הכול . . .

> And at the end of that generation during the seventh jubilee after the destruction of the land they (Israel) will forget the laws and festivals and Sabbath and covenant. And they will abrogate all.

Our text and 4Q390 appear to allude to *Jub.* 1:10; 2:31–33 and the entire chapter 50 (verses 1–13) dealing with the observance of the Sabbath. Interestingly, some of the rules of the Sabbath found in *Jubilees* are mentioned in MTA. For example, *Jub.* 50:5 records the prohibition against sexual relations on the Sabbath, as does CD 12:1. *Jubilees* 50:5 mentions contamination as does MTA טמאות (impurities).

In one point, however, MTA diverges sharply from *Jubilees*. *Jubilees* 50:8 reiterates the biblical injunction that labor on the Sabbath constitutes a capital offense. CD 12:3b–5a on the other hand says,

וכל אשר יתעה                                        12:3

12:4    לחלל את השבת ואת המועדות לא יומת כי על בני האדם

12:5    משמרו

Anyone who goes astray to profane the Sabbath and the festivals shall
*not be put to death*; rather it is the duty of man to place him in detention.
(CD 12:3b–5a)

MTA's dissent from a direct statement in *Jubilees* is interesting in view
of CD 16:2–3, which characterizes the book called *The Divisions of
the Times* as מדוקדק (perfect). This softening of the biblical stringency
with regard to the Sabbath and the festivals appears to be unique in
the sectarian writings, which in general hold to a more severe mode of
punishment.

What is also apparent pertaining to our passage dealing with the
Sabbath, festivals and the Day of Atonement, is its polemical nature,
evidenced in part in the word כפרושה (according to its elaborations).
The festivals and the Sabbaths are mentioned in the preamble (4Q268
F1:4–5) and again in CD 3:13–15a. Like our text these passages contain an argumentative flavor. The apologetic stance of our passage
further emerges in the next clause ואת יום התענית כמצאת באי הברית
החדשה בארץ דמשק, "and the day of fasting (i.e. Day of Atonement)
in accordance with the practice[180] of those who will enter the new
covenant in the land of Damascus." The word תענית occurs elsewhere
in the DSS in the pesher on Ps 37.

F1-2ii:8          ועניים ירשו ארץ והתענגנו על רוב שלום. פשרו על

F1-2ii:9    עדת האביונים אשר יקבלו את מועד התענות ונצלו מכול פחי

F1-2ii:10    בליעל

And the meek will inherit the land and will rejoice in the abundance
of peace. It refers to the congregation of the meek who will accept
the season of the fast,[181] and thus be saved from any of the snares of
Belial. (4Q171 F1-2ii:8–10a)

This disputatious language in regard to the Sabbath, the festivals and
the Day of Atonement indicates that our text refers to the disputation

---

[180] Ginzberg reads כמצות (Ginzberg, *An Unknown Jewish Sect*, 31), Qimron כמצוות,
"in accordance with the commandments" (Qimron, "The Text of CDC," 21). The
manuscript reading, כמצאת (as is the practice) is more likely. כמצאת corresponds
to פרוש.

[181] תענית occurs also in 4Q508 F2:3; 4Q509 F16:3; 4Q510 F1:7–8; 4Q511
F8:5; 4Q511 F10:4, 6; 4Q511 F121:2.

concerning the calendar. The sectarian calendar placed the Day of Atonement always on Friday and the festivals during the days of the week, thus never coinciding with the Sabbath day. Likewise, the Sabbath in the sectarian reckoning played an important role in the setting of the fifty-two week year. Each week had a name taken from the Sons of Zadok in 1 Chr 24. It should perhaps be emphasized that, although *Enoch* and *Jubilees* deal at length with calendric subject matter, they make no mention of the role of the Zadokite names in the reckoning of time. One may suppose then, that the introduction of Zadokite week names may have begun with the author of MTA or perhaps as stated by al-Qirqisani, with Zadok's companion, Boethus.[182]

The clause in CD 6:19b, "the practice of those who will enter the new covenant in the land of Damascus," is of special interest for the understanding of MTA. It anchors the three-fold legal traditions found in this work (the biblical and the sectarian bible such as *Enoch, Jubilees* and *Temple Scroll*) with the author's innovation of the new rules that will be observed under the new covenant in the land of Damascus. Thus, Damascus is recorded seven times in MTA, five of which are ארץ דמשק (the land of Damascus) and is contrasted with ארץ יהודה (the land of Judah). The באי הברית will have left the land of Judah to go to the land of Damascus. As was noted in the introductory material, some scrollists identify the land of Damascus as Qumran. The context of these passages, however, obviates such an interpretation. Why would ארץ יהודה be literal and ארץ דמשק figurative? Moreover, it is unreasonable to suppose that the author would choose ארץ דמשק, a region geographically far to the north, as a symbol for Qumran, contrasting it with ארץ יהודה, which might include the very area of the Dead Sea where Khirbet Qumran is located. Likewise, as amplified above, the sobriquet ברית החדשה which occurs in MTA three times and once in Pesher Habakkuk where it is a derivative of this work, points to the foundation of the sect. Additionally CD 7:13–15 identifies Damascus as located in the land of the north in connection with Amos 5:27 which mentions the exile to Damascus. Furthermore, CD 7 continues to pesherize both Amos 5:27 and 9:11, but makes no attempt to alter the sense of דמשק as meaning something other than its northern locus. Let us remember that these words are said to have been uttered while the prophet was in the north.

---

[182] Nemoy, "Jewish Sects," 326.

As in 2 Chr 30 and 35, the verb הרים in line 20 refers to the תרומה, the produce set aside for the priests and poor. The rules of tithing are prominent in MTA as is evident in the surviving Cave 4 manuscripts of MTA (266–273), but were omitted in the Cairo texts. Note that the term פרוש here as in line 14 makes up a thematic linkage of the legal texts, showing that their mention here is an attempt to present the important legal concepts regarding the Sabbath, the festivals, and now, the priestly portions (תרומה). What is striking is that some of the headings in MTA bear a close resemblance to those found in the Mishnah and some of its tractates.[183]

The section spanning from CD 6:20b to 7:6 consists of a list of personal obligations, either between one and his neighbor or pertaining to himself alone. For anyone who lives by the aforementioned precepts, it concludes with the promise that God will make a life of a thousand generations (i.e. the messianic epoch will have arrived). MTA sounds ambiguous concerning the concept of immortality. Does a thousand generations denote life for eternity, or is it merely longevity? I discuss this issue below.

The clause "to love each his companion like himself" (6:20) para-phrases Lev 19:18, וְאָהַבְתָּ לְרֵעֲךָ כָּמוֹךָ (And you shall love your neighbor as yourself). The formulas following it amplify how one should love one's neighbor: by supporting the needy and being concerned with his physical and mental wellbeing. להחזיק ביד עני ואביון וגר (and to support the poor, destitute and proselyte) in CD 6:21 is an important heading for many passages in MTA. It relates to the preceding lines where the sect is commanded to refrain from robbing the poor of God's people. CD 14:12–17a lists the poor and destitute as among the deprived group for whom the wages of two days per month are withheld. This passage contains the social structure of the com-munity.

וזה סרך הרבים להכין כול חפציהם שכר[184]                    14:12

---

[183] Note for example 4Q266 F6iii:7b–10 and 4Q270 F3ii:17–F3ii(a) (items which require tithing, a section which provides a definition of תרומה), subject matter reflected in Mishnah *Terumot*. See also the legislation on the ערלה in 4Q266 F6iv and iv(a) (Mishnah *Orlah*), the Sabbath regulations in CD 10:14–11:18a (Mishnah *Shabbat*), the issue of the straying wife in 4Q270 F4:1b–13a (Mishnah *Sotah*), rulings on leprosy in 4Q272 F1i:1–ii:2 and 4Q266 F6i:1–13 (Mishnah *Nega'im*) and bodily emissions explicated in 4Q272 F1ii:3–18, 4Q266 F6i:14–16 and ii:1–4 (Mishnah *Niddah* and *Zavim*).

[184] Outlined text is from 4Q266 F10i.

14:13 שְׁנֵי יָמִים לְכֹל חֹדֶשׁ לְמַמְעֹט וּ֯נָתַן עַל יַד הַמְבַקֵר וְהַשׁוֹפְטִים

14:14 מִמֶנוֹ יִתְנוּ בְעַד [פ]צֻעָם וּמִמֶנוּ יַחְזִקוּ בְעַד עָנִי וְהָ֯אֶבְיוֹן וְלִזָקֵן אֲשֶׁ֯ר

14:15 [יִכר]עַ֯ וְלָאִישׁ אֲשֶׁר יִנֻ֯[גַ]עַ וְלָאֲשֶ֯ר יִשָׁבֶה לְגוֹי נֵכָר וְלַבְתוּלָה אֲשֶׁר

14:16 [אֵי]ן לָהּ גֹ[וא]ֵ֯ל וְלְנֻעַ֯ר֯ אֲ[שֶׁר] אֵין לוֹ דוֹרֵשׁ וְ֯לְכֹ֯ל֯ עֲבוֹדַת הַחֶבֶר וְלֹא

14:17 [יִכָרֵת בֵית הַחֶבֶר מִיָד]֯ם

And this is the procedure of the 'Many' to fill all their needs. (Let there be) a levy from the wages of at least two days per month apportioned by the Supervisor and the judges. From it they shall provide for (the healing of) their [wo]unded. And from it they shall assist the poor and the destitute, the elderly man who is [bent do]wn, him who suffers from lep[ro]sy, him who is taken captive by a foreign nation, a maiden who [does no]t have a re[dee]mer, a lad [w]ho has no guardian, and all the services provided by the association, so that the association not [perish without] their [support] (CD 14:12b–17a).

The above itemization expands on the short list of the membership of the community given in our passage. However, this long enumeration does not contain the גר of CD 6:21. That the proselytes were considered an integral part of the sectarian structure is attested in CD 14:3–7, wherein they are listed twice—fourth in the social sequence following the priests, Levites and the Israelites making up the camp of Israel. Evidently the term גר, meaning "proselyte" (not "stranger" or "sojourner"),[185] so common in rabbinics and attested in MTA, may go back to Ezek 48. The following question arises. How large a segment of the sectarian community were proselytes or manumitted slaves, some of which joined the status of foreigners who became members of the community?[186] Since these groups are not listed within the stipulations on social welfare toward the end of MTA, one wonders if their numbers were not significant enough to warrant their placement in the legislation (actual legislation indicating historical prominence). Nevertheless, the emphasis given to the גרים in this composition might suggest that their air of devotion hinted at in the DSS was in part due to an influx of converts, perhaps

---

[185] "Stranger" more correctly translates זָר or נֵכָר. Whereas "sojourner" and perhaps "resident alien" are adequate renditions of גר, "proselyte" is a transliteration of the LXX προσήλυτος and denotes the foreigner who resides within Israel, adopting the way of life of her people.

[186] The injunction against selling slaves who have entered into the covenant of Abraham (CD 12:10–11), undoubtedly the (ה)ברית (ה)ראשנים "the ancestral covenant" of CD 1:3, 4:10 and 6:2, suggests that a portion of the proselyte sector was released slaves.

some of them being released slaves who wished to display zeal for their newly acquired faith. The list of benefits of CD 14:12b–17a which included a minimum of two days of monthly wages for the sick and deprived opens a new dimension of social aid. It seems to resemble the biblical מעשר עני, the tithe of the poor to be collected every third and sixth year of the sabbatical cycle. These and the other social benefits of which the judges and the Supervisor were in charge should be noted as unprecedented until modern times.

The requirement ולדרוש איש בשלום אחיהו in lines 21b–22a, "that each be concerned with the welfare of his neighbor," continues to amplify the theme that began with how to love one's neighbor. What follows the clause ולא ימעל איש בשאר בשרו in 7:1, "and that no one should adulterate his near kin," widens further the concept of brotherly love. Up to now, our text has amplified the *positive* aspects of loving one's neighbor. Beginning with this phrase the author lists *negative* facets in expressing love, by setting down general injunctions against sexual transgressions. The statement להזיר מן הזונות כמשפט (to keep apart from prostitutes in accordance with the rules) alludes to other passages in MTA which prohibit sexual transgressions.

As to the chastisement in 7:2b–3a להוכיח איש את אחיהו כמצוה ולא לנטור מיום ליום (to reprove each his neighbor in accordance with the commandment and not to bear a grudge from day to day), note CD 9:7b–8a.

הוכח תוכיח את רעיך ולא תשא עליו חטא

> You shall surely reprove your neighbor and not bear sin because of him (compare Lev 19:17).

A more ample paraphrase on the two clauses "to chastise" and not to avenge one's neighbor appears in CD 9:2–8, which fuses Lev 19:17–18 with Nah 1:2. The difference between our passage and that of CD 9 consists in the brevity of our text and its amplification in the latter. Both texts, however, contain the concept that vengeance applies to keeping a grudge the following day.

להבדל in the clause "and to keep away from all kinds of defilement in accordance with their rule . . . " (CD 7:3) forms part of the vocabulary designating the community as separate from Israel.[187]

---

[187] Cf. the composite test of CD 6:14–15 להבדל מבני [העו]ל ולהנזר מהון הרשעה הטמא. See also lines 1b–2a of MTA as reconstructed, [להנזר מדרֹ[כי כול בני חושך].

The plural טמאות embraces a wide number of acts that degrade the person—not only defilements of which there are many in this text, but other violations of the law which likewise reduce one's path to holiness. The verb שקץ occurs once again in CD 12:11 in reference to partaking of prohibited foods such as beasts, creeping things, bee honey and fish not properly slaughtered. Our text and CD 12 suggest a polemical stance against the views attributed to the Pharisees and those expressed by their successors, the rabbis and the sages of the Mishnah, who sanction the eating of bee honey.

As to the phrase רוח קדש in 7:4, we gain a sense of its meaning in CD 2:11–13a.

2:11  ובכולם הקים לו קריאי[188ם שם למען התיר פליטה לארץ ולמלא

2:12  פני תבל מזרעם *vacat* ויודיעם ביד משיחו רוח קדשו וחוזי

2:13  אמת ובפרוש «שמו» שמותיהם

> And during all (these epochs) He has raised up for Himself well known people in order to preserve a remnant in the earth and to fill the world with their descendants. And He has informed them through those who were inspired by His *Holy Spirit* and (through) the seers of truth by elaborating on their names. (CD 2:11–13a)

Our text emphasizes that the people who violate these prohibitions shrink the presence of the Holy Spirit on this earth. The formulation הבדיל אל attributes to God the separation of the community from all of Israel, going on to explain that those who separate faithfully by observing the covenant will flourish for a long time. The verb התהלך appears about fifteen times in various forms in MTA, virtually always as a description of the righteous way of life as described by God. All these repetitions seem to echo the introductory clause of the book of Psalms where the Qal form of the root הלך is used.

אַשְׁרֵי־הָאִישׁ אֲשֶׁר לֹא הָלַךְ בַּעֲצַת רְשָׁעִים

> How happy is the man who has not walked in the council of the wicked. (Ps 1:1a)

This passage stresses the necessity of their remaining apart from the community of the wicked, an entity that, according to the last verses of Ps 1 will suffer separation from the righteous.

The word נאמנות (CD 7:5), an abstract noun, appears in both the

---

188 Outlined text is from 4Q266 F2ii:11.

A and B texts of CD, as in CD 14:2 where it occurs in the same
construction. However, as explained in the textual notes, I follow the
reading of 4Q267 F9v:4 which parallels CD 14:2, a passage whose
content and syntax matches that of our text. Hence, the participle
נאמנת, a reading which is buttressed by the use of the participle נֶאֱמָן
in Deut 7:9, the biblical text from which CD 19:1–2 (Manuscript B)
is drawn and which supplements our A text.

וְיָדַעְתָּ כִּי־יְהוָה אֱלֹהֶיךָ הוּא הָאֱלֹהִים הָאֵל הַנֶּאֱמָן שֹׁמֵר הַבְּרִית
וְהַחֶסֶד לְאֹהֲבָיו וּלְשֹׁמְרֵי מִצְוֹתוֹ לְאֶלֶף דּוֹר

Know, therefore, that the Lord your God is God, *the faithful* God who
keeps the covenant and love for those who love Him and keep his commandments for a thousand generations. (Deut 7:9)

The statement ברית אל נאמנת להם לחיותם (the divine covenant will
remain faithful to them, keeping them alive . . . ), draws on the
account of Joshua's covenant with the Gibeonites.

וַיַּעַשׂ לָהֶם יְהוֹשֻׁעַ שָׁלוֹם וַיִּכְרֹת לָהֶם בְּרִית לְחַיּוֹתָם וַיִּשָּׁבְעוּ לָהֶם נְשִׂיאֵי הָעֵדָה

So Joshua established peace with them and made *a covenant allowing them
to live.* And the leaders of the congregation made an oath with them.
(Josh 9:15)

Note also that CD 19:1–2 presents two versions of our text: 1) אלף
דור in the singular as in CD 7:6 as well as in Deut 9:7, Ps 105:8
and 1 Chr 16:15, and 2) the plural אלפי דורות here in CD 19:1. The
divergence may be explained in two ways: that the plural דורות אלפי
is a paraphrase, whereas אלף דור in CD 19:2 is a literal quote of
Deuteronomy. The two alternate readings, then, may serve to reflect
two meanings. The singular אלף דור might be understood literally,
that as Adam's descendents lived virtually a *thousand* years, so will
the covenanters live a *thousand* generations. The plural אלפי דורות, on
the other hand, may be a metaphorical plural denoting a very long
life. At any rate, both the singular and the plural may call attention
to the fact that extreme longevity rather than immortality will be
part of the messianic age, a concept not apparent in MTA.

3.2.1.5.2. *The Migration From Judah (CD-A 7:6b–8:1a / CD-B 19:
2b–13a)*

What follows in CD 7:6–8:21 (Mss. A) parallels parts of CD 19:1–
19:34 (Mss. B). As scholars have noted, manuscript A emanates from
the 10th century and B from the 12th. The many differences in read-

ing have given rise to two questions. First, how did these divergences arise? Second, when differing, which of them appears to have greater authenticity? As to the differences, the most significant are the citations of biblical texts. For example, whereas manuscript A quotes Isa 7:17, B has Zech 13:7 at this point. Quotations from Amos 5:27 and 9:11 are present in manuscript A but absent in its parallel, B. On the other hand, A quotes Jeremiah and Elisha, references not found in B. In addition, B quotes Hos 5:10 and Ezek 9:4, quotations absent in A. As to the presence or absence of biblical citations, it is likely that MTA quoted both Isaiah and Zechariah. But, copyists intentionally omitted some.

Furthermore, as to the variant readings, by and large B contains more words than does A. For example, compare manuscript A 7:6b–8a with manuscript B 19:2b–4. The first reads:

ואם מחנות ישבו כסרך הארץ ולקחו נשים והולידו בנים
והתהלכו על פי התורה וכמשפט היסורים כסרך התורה

And if they reside (in) camps according to the rule of the land, they shall take wives and father children and walk in accordance with the Torah and the ordinance on chastisements according to the rule of the Torah. (17 words in the Hebrew text)

The second on the other hand is more expansive.

ואם מחנות ישבו כסרך הארץ אשר היה מקדם ולקחו נשים כמנהג התורה
והו[ל]ידו בנים ויתהלכו על פי התורה *vacat* וכמשפט היסורים כסרֿך התוֿרֿה

And if they reside (in) camps as was the rule of the land formerly (in the wilderness), they shall take wives in accordance with the custom of the Torah, and father children, and they shall walk in accordance with the Torah and the ordinance on chastisements according to the rule of the Torah. (22 words in the Hebrew text)

Some of the variants in the two manuscripts reflect a divergence in verbal conjugation patterns. Whereas A often employs the perfect, B sometimes uses the imperfect, conventionally conveying the future tense. For example, A uses התהלכו (7:7) and מלטו (7:21) whereas B has יתהלכו (19:4) and ימלטו (19:10). In addition, A employs הסגירו (8:1) whereas B has ימסרו (19:10).

As to which text is more authoritative with regard to differences in expression, the following questions arise. Can it be said that there existed a tendency to enlarge upon the original? Or, *aux contraire*, does A reflect a tendency to abbreviate? In keeping with our general method of preferring the more expansive text witnessed in the Cave

manuscripts as well as reading some suffixed conjugation verbs as
conveying the future tense, yielding readings which better accord
with the historical allusions of the work, we will follow the B-text
as a more reliable attestation to the MTA tradition. However, when
the B-text is incoherent and the A is more readable, the latter is
preferred. Although our rendition of the text favors B readings, the
line numbering of this section generally follows that of the more
highly represented A-manuscript (except for when a portion of B is
not present in A). Indeed, this format fits with greater ease into the
sequencing pattern of the Cairo text as a whole.

### 3.2.1.5.2.1.  Living in Camps as in Mosaic Times (CD-A 7:6b–9a / CD-B 19:2b–5a)

Scrollists have understood the word מחנות in CD-A 7:6 (CD-B 19:2)
as the members of the group who lived in Judea, including those who
preserved the Dead Sea Scrolls in Khirbet Qumran. Actually, this
term has a technical meaning in MTA, differentiating its inhabitants
from those who lived in the cities including Jerusalem. The campers
in MTA correspond to those of the exodus in the wilderness. Some
Qumran scholars think that CD-A 7:6a–9a (CD-B 19:2b–5a) is an
intrusion into our text due to its different style and lack of context.
Davies defends that these few lines of legislation possibly formed part
of the original composition, maintaining that they serve to mandate
that even those who are born in the camps must follow all the other
rules prescribed in the community, just as must those who enter the
community by conversion.[189] However, the fact that the broader section on the migration from Judah (CD-A 7:6b–8:1a) is found in both
the A and B Cairo manuscripts as well as in portions of 4Q266 suggests that this short camp legislation was in the earlier manuscripts
from the Judean desert and is a relevant part of MTA as a whole. The
point of this passage was not so much to include children in the halakah of the community as it was to require that every member of the
camp structure be part of a procreative family. Taken this way, family
life was not an option for the campers as Davies implies. Moreover,
the idea of the distinctions that existed between camps and cities articulated here is crucial for understanding several other passages, as
was explained above, in MTA, as in other DSS works. As I see it,

---

[189]  Davies, *The Damascus Covenant*, 142.

MTA divides the community into city dwellers and campers. Note the clauses found in the B-text omitted in the A-text: "as it was in former times" and "in accordance with the Torah" (CD-B 19:3), both of which defend the practice of regular family life in the camps. What the A-text omits is the emphasis given to the fact that family life in the camps was modeled after Israel of old (specifically the mode of living during the wilderness wanderings) and was presumably the official life of the sect of the early Essenes. However, in some passages preserved *only* in A, the sectarian campers are subdivided into the thousands, hundreds, fifties and tens just as their ancestors were depicted in the wilderness (CD 12:22a–13:2a). The minimal counting of ten is synonymous to the word *minyan* in modern Judaism, but its etiology is accounted for in MTA as a memorial of the past. What distinguishes the campers from the city dwellers is the matter of celibacy. This status was required only of those who lived in the cities among the general population. As was explained, this was to keep the city dwelling Essenes separate and pure. By contrast, as our composite text goes on to say, the campers were commanded to marry and procreate as was the custom when Israel camped in the wilderness.

3.2.1.5.2.2. The Community's Escape to Damascus (CD-A 7:9b–
8:1a / CD-B 19:5b–13a)

In this section the author returns to his main theme—the community of Damascus and its legal structure that would inaugurate the messianic age. It consists of three elements: 1) Israel's divisions of the past; 2) the fulfillment of the promise of the prophets; and 3) the ultimate destruction of evil. As was discussed above, it is my opinion that Damascus in CD is the city in Syria, not Qumran or Babylon, as many scrollists believe. Our passage here, which culminates with Damascus, makes this yet more evident. The author emphasizes in CD-A 7:13–14 (text not available in CD-B) that those who cling (to the commandments) escaped (and will escape) to the land of the north (not to Qumran which is to the southeast). The author dealt with this theme in CD 6:2–11. In that passage God recalled the ancestral covenant and established the wise men who dug the Torah—the princes who interpret the law, those forming the community which would migrate from Judah to the land of Damascus. Here in CD-A 7:14b–21a, the author presents more fully the pesher on Num 21:18 developed earlier in CD 6:2–11. What is so interesting is that both pages which together comment on Num 21:18 and 24:17 plus Amos

5:27 and 9:11 are among few DSS texts which pesherize biblical verses term by term.[190] In CD 6:4–11, the words pesherized are "the well," "the diggers," "the princes," and "the Lawgiver." That pesher serves to introduce the דורש התורה, rendered "the interpreter (or searcher) of the Torah" and the more general theme, those who will depart from Judah to Damascus. Our text in CD-A 7:18–21 makes a subsequent verse from Numbers (24:17) into an eschatological midrash. Here the pesherized word "star," anticipating the biblical quote, is the "interpreter of the Torah" who will come to Damascus to organize the community. Note, however, that in CD 6:7–11, the word מחוקק (Lawgiver) is taken to be the דורש התורה. Another term interpreted in our text is the word שבט (scepter), which is taken here to be the prince or king of Israel. As to the question why the writer employs duplicate words from two different texts to refer to the same figure, the "interpreter of the Torah," perhaps it was inadvertent. Another possibility is that there is an attempt to link the מחוקק and שבט to two parallel words in Gen 49:10, where the terms together within the blessing of Jacob, a crucial text in biblical tradition, depict the regal status of Judah among the tribes of antiquity, thereby authenticating the leadership roles of the נשיא כל העדה (CD-A 7:20) and the מחוקק of the sectarian community.

לֹא־יָסוּר שֵׁבֶט מִיהוּדָה וּמְחֹקֵק מִבֵּין רַגְלָיו

The scepter shall not depart from Judah, nor the ruler's staff from between his feet. (Gen 49:10a)

Other terms interpreted in this fashion are the סכות (Amos 5:26), read in CD-A 7:15–16 as סוכת (tent), and pesherized together into סוכת דוד (tent of David) in Amos 9:11 and ספרי התורה (the books of the Torah).[191] The word מלך in Amos 5:26 is pesherized as the

---

[190] But, compare CD 4:14–18 which presumably pesherizes a passage in the Testament of Levi: "'Fear and the pit and the snare are upon you, inhabitant of the land.' Its eschatological meaning is the three nets of Belial concerning which Levi son of Jacob said 'with which he (Belial) trapped Israel and paraded them as if they were fronts for three classes of (un)righteous deeds': the first is whoredom, the second wealth (and) the third the defiling of the sanctuary."

[191] The understanding of סִכּוּת מַלְכְּכֶם (the *Sikkut* of your king) is problematic. The Septuagint renders the phrase as τὴν σκηνὴν τοῦ Μολοχ (the tent of Moloch). But, the author of CD reads it as positive, since he identifies the סוכת המלך (the סִכּוּת מַלְכְּכֶם of Amos 5:26) as the ספרי התורה (the books of the Torah). As does the Septuagint, the author of MTA renders סִכּוּת as "tent." Unlike the Septuagint, however, which translates מַלְכְּכֶם as Μολοχ, the author of MTA understands it as המלך (the king),

"(prince) of the congregation." The words כיון הצלמים are said to correspond to the ספרי הנביאים (the books of the prophets). This passage is remarkable, not only in its midrashic pesher, but also in its extraordinary content. Let us remember that, although the plural ספרי התורה occurs neither in the Hebrew Scriptures nor elsewhere in the DSS, ספרי הנביאים has a duplicate in *Miqṣat Maʿaśê ha-Torah*[d] which may, perhaps, shed light on our text.

[כתב]נו אליכה שתבין בספר מושה [ו]בספר[י הנ[ב]יאים ובדוי]ד        [

We have written to you that you might understand the book of Moses [and] the book[s of the pr]ophets and Davi[d . . . ][192] (4Q397 F14-21: 10)

As pointed out by Qimron and Strugnell, 4QMMT[d] attests to ספר מושה in the singular, an old reference to the Pentateuch, the ספרי הנביאים (the prophets), and to [. . . ]דוי[ד, the latter of which they take to be a reference not only to the psalter, but to the Hagiographa as well.[193] If so, our text, which employs ספרי התורה in CD-A 7:15 and ספרי הנביאים in 7:17, may have referred to the prophets without an allusion to the Hagiographa. On the other hand, it could be that our text included the psalter as part of the the books of the prophets, or that MMT's mention of David resembles our text by stressing that the Psalms should also be considered part of the prophets.[194] The difference between our text, which uses ספרי התורה in the plural, and ספר מושה of MMT may be important. The author of MTA emphasizes in several passages his dependence on *Jubilees*. The plural ספרי התורה in our text, therefore, might refer to both the Pentateuch and the book of Division of Times (*Jubilees*), the latter of which is described in CD 16:2–3 as "perfect." This dual Torah was known by the sectarian community as the תורת משה.[195]

The pesherite passages of CD 6 and 7 cited above culminate with the central idea of this text: the new exodus from Judah to Damascus. It is interesting that these two passages stand out in MTA by reason of their lengthy midrashic exegeses, both leading to the

---

paralleling it with Amos 9:11 סֻכַּת דָּוִיד הַנֹּפֶלֶת, and identifying it as the "the books of the Torah."

[192]  This is seemingly an early attestation of the tripartite division of the canon.
[193]  Qimron and Strugnell, DJD X, 59.
[194]  For David as a prophet, see 11Q5 27:11.
[195]  Wacholder, "The 'Torah of Moses' in the Dead Sea Scrolls."

advent of the Messiah. The author once again takes up the theme of the escape to Damascus in the concluding section of MTA preserved in 4Q266 F11.

16 וכול יִד

17 [יושבי ]הֹמֹחֹנות יקהלו בחודש השלישי ואררו את הנוטה ימין

18 [ושמאול מן ה]תֹּוֹרֹה ¹⁹⁶<sub>vac</sub> והזֹה פרוש המשפטים אשר יעשו בכול קץ

19 [הפקודה את אשר יפק]ֹדו [בכו]ֹל קצי החרון ומסעיהם לכול

20 [יושב מחניהם וכול יושב עריהם הנה הכו]ֹל ﬠﬡ[ﬨ]ﬨ ﬠ]ֹל [מ]ֹ[ד]ֹ[ש] התורה

21 [האחרון]   *vacat*   [

And all [the inhabitants] of the camps shall assemble on the third month and curse anyone who deviates [from the] Torah, either to the right [or to the left]. And this is the elaboration of the injunctions which they shall observe during the entire epoch [of redemption which they shall remem]ber [during al]l the epochs of anger and their journeys, for every [inhabitant of their camps and everyone who dwells in their cities. Behold every]thing has been [written up]on "the Mi[d]ra[sh] on the [Eschatological] Torah." (4Q266 F11:16b–21a)

Note that the gathering on the third month addresses those who live in the camps, apparently not the city dwellers. However, the concluding lines of the book stress that the injunctions of the work as a whole apply to both groups. This once again distinguishes that, while the book contains injunctions for both, the sect recognizes as official members of the group only those who live in the camps, that is to say those who practice a normal family life after the pattern of ancient Israel in the wilderness.[197] It could be that Josephus had in mind a group like this, a community which outrightly condemned celibacy.

> They think that those who decline to marry cut off the chief function of life, the propagation of the race, and, what is more, that, were all to adopt the same view, the whole race would very quickly die out. (Josephus, *J.W.* 2:160 [Thackeray, LCL])

### 3.2.1.5.3. *The Deserters (CD-A 8:1b–21 / CD-B 19:13b–33a; 19:33b–20:17a)*

This large pericope concerns itself with what was an important theme for the writer: the anticipation of being abandoned by some of its adherents. It is also important in modern scholarship, because

---

[196] Outlined vacat and text is unique to 4Q270 F7ii.

[197] See Cross, 71, who denies the distinction between the camps and the cities. However, he does mention so-called "secular" camps that had a family life.

it contains two occurrences of the infinitive האסף, once in CD-B 19:35 and again in 20:14, both of which supposedly refer to the death of the מורה, the founder of the Essene movement. However, in my understanding of האסף in these passages the text relates to the "assembling" of the sectaries by the Just Teacher in Damascus. This futuristic assembly corresponds to Moses' gathering of the Israelites in Egypt, which culminated with the death of the disobedient generation and the entry of their descendants into Canaan after forty years.[198] Two occurrences of האסף in *Rule of the Community* lend additional support to my rendition of this term as a description of the new organization: 1QSa begins with

וזה הסרך לכול עדת ישראל באחרית הימים בהספם [ליחד

> And this is the rule for the entire congregation of Israel at the end of days when they will assemble [for the *Yachad* . . . (1QSa 1:1)

Note that this introduction to this version of *Rule of the Community* speaks to the assembly that will take place during the eschaton. The next passage likewise employs האסף for the organizing of the legal structure of the יחד.

ואלה תכון דרכיהם על כול החוקים האלה בהאספם ליחד

> And this is the structure of their paths pertaining to all these statutes when they will assemble for the *Yachad*. (1QS 5:7)

In other words, the term האסף never refers to the demise of the Teacher, but rather to his planned assembly inaugurating the messianic age.

This large segment dealing with the forewarned desertion begins with those who will enter the covenant community, but will become disappointed. The text chronicles this period as forty years from the time of the assembling by the Unique Teacher until the appearing of the Messiah of Aaron and Israel (CD-B 19:35–20:1, 12–15). As stated above, the author parallels the forty years of this account with the time of the Israelite sojourn in the wilderness.

My rendition of CD-A 8:3b is a combination of the A and B Cairo manuscripts and scattered cave portions preserved in 4Q266 F3iii:25b–iv:1a. It represents the differences between the medieval versions, each of which diverge from the biblical text, Hos 5:10, from

---

[198] For support for this view see Wacholder, "The Teacher of Righteousness," 75–93.

which they derive. Displayed below are the four versions beginning with the biblical base. The fifth is the conflated reading of the MTA witnesses.

1    הָיוּ שָׂרֵי יְהוּדָה כְּמַסִּיגֵי גְּבוּל עֲלֵיהֶם אֶשְׁפּוֹךְ כַּמַּיִם עֶבְרָתִי

The princes of Judah were like the Shifters of the Boundary upon whom I will pour out my anger like water. (Hos 5:10)

2             היו שרי יהודה אשר תשפוך עליהם העברה

The princes of Judah were those upon whom wrath shall (be) pour(ed). (CD-A 8:3b)

3    כאשר דבר היו שרי יהודה כמשיגי גבול עליהם אשפך כמ̇י̇ם̇ עברה

. . . as he spoke (through Hosea), "The princes of Judah were like the Shifters of the Boundary against whom I will pour out wrath like water. (CD-B 19:15b–16a)

4    כאשר [דבר] היו [שרי יהודה ב]י̇ום אשר [אשפוך עליהם העברה

. . . as [He spoke] (through Hosea), "[The princes of Judah] were in the day that [I will pour out wrath upon them.] (4Q266 F3iii:25b–iv:1a)

5    כאשר דבר היו שרי יהודה כמשיגי גבול [ב]י̇ום אשר עליהם
אשפך כמ̇י̇ם̇ העברה

. . . as He spoke (through Hosea), "The princes of Judah (will) have become like the Shifters of the Boundary" [on] the day when "I will pour out anger upon them like water." (CD-A 8:3b with CD-B 19:15b–16a and 4Q266 F3iii:25b–iv:1a)

Note that the citation in the composite rendition employs the word אשפך, implying that the time of the pouring out of God's anger upon the aberrant leaders is seen as futuristic. CD-A 8:4–5 which follows (corresponding to CD-B 19:16b–17), a grammatically difficult and somewhat enigmatic text which I likewise have conflated from three sources, appears to say that the princes of Judah upon whom God will execute His anger will have entered the covenant of repentance and will begin the restoration process, even being assisted by the godly, but will return once again to the vices of their ancestors.

CD-A 8:9, a passage which is pesherized, might refer to the change of control from the Persians to the Macedonians, whose head is Alexander, the ראש מלכי יון (the leader of the kings of Greece). According to common opinion, Alexander never entered Jerusalem. Josephus' *Antiquities* 11:329–39, which depicts Alexander's prostration before Judas, the high priest, is commonly branded as part of Pseudo-

Alexander. Our text, however, apparently supposes that Alexander treated Jerusalem as his enemy.

The בוני החיץ (the builders of the wall), mentioned twice in our pericope, draws on Ezek 13:10. The first mention of this entity in MTA (CD 4:19) attacks them for their practice of bigamy and for marrying their brothers' and sisters' daughters. In our passage they are a segment upon whom God will pour His wrath, an element of the earlier mentioned מסיגי (ה)גבול (the Shifters of the Boundary), apparently the Pharisees, who will suffer the same fate (CD-B 19:15–16; CD-A 8:3). In our passage these builders are linked with the Spewer of Lies, whose teachings will provoke God's anger. They form part of the author's polemic against the followers of the איש הכזב, the nemesis of the Just Teacher.

In CD-A 8:14–18a (CD-B 19:26a–31a), a parenthetical section presenting the destiny of the followers of the Just Teacher, the author makes Deut 9:5 and 7:8 refer to the righteous of Israel as part of the ancestral promise to the patriarchs. The righteous here are the author's audience who, according to our writer, are beloved of God as were Abraham, Isaac and Jacob (lines 16b–18a). This thesis is a pivotal point in this work that constantly intertwines the *Urzeit* with the *Endzeit*, the eschaton. The followers of the Just Teacher are regarded as part of the ancestral promise to the patriarchs, the inheritors of the pagan lands.

CD-A 8:18b–19 (CD-B 19:31b–33a) shows that, in contrast to patriarchs and their successors who were objects of divine love, God despises the deserters, known here once again by the epithet "the builders of the wall" and those who follow them. Among them are those who despise the commandments of God. Our text stresses that one cannot love God without observing His commandments. The two actions are necessarily intertwined.

CD 8 concludes with a succinct but enigmatic statement: "This is the matter that Jeremiah said to Baruch, son of Neriah and Elisha to Gehazi, his amanuensis." This presents an enigma. To what is our author referring in his allusions to Jeremiah and Elisha? Scholars have not resolved this issue. Writing in 1910, Schechter suggested that the quotes cited here must have been a reference to passages in lost apocrypha. Indeed, Ginzberg found a reference to Jeremiah's statement in the Syriac Apocalypse of Baruch (*2 Bar.*) 84:5. However, Rabin found this implausible, suggesting instead, that it possibly refers to Jer 45:4–5. Neither of these solutions are satisfactory. In my opinion, what scholars have not stressed is the nature of this citation. They presume that אשר אמר here quotes a passage as the formula כאשר אמר in the frequent citations in MTA usually does. Our text, however, says "*asher amar* personal name #1 *l*-personal name #2 *w*-personal name #3 *l*-personal name #4." It appears to me that the formula ... אשר אמר ל does not refer to textual citations, but to general statements emerging from the biblical accounts of the disciples of Jeremiah and Elisha—namely, that the author has just told us that the group which will go to Damascus will consist of two sorts: 1) those who will remain faithful and thus live to witness the coming of the Messiah of Aaron and Israel and 2) others who will join those believers but later will decide to turn back and desert the faithful. Baruch, ben Neriah, despite all the threats against his life as detailed in the book of Jeremiah, remained faithful. On the other hand, Gehazi who accepted gifts from Naaman against the prophet Elisha's wishes, characterizes the deserters, those who, although becoming part of the covenant, will abandon it on account of their avarice.

CD-A 8:21b, the last clauses of the A-text, links up with CD-B 19:33b and following to amplify what occurred to Gehazi and his master. Our passage condemns all those who, like Gehazi, accepted God's covenant and subsequently turned away from the well of the living waters in the land of Damascus. These people and the like of them will neither be regarded as part of the sect nor recorded in the list of faithful Israelites. As was explained above, the author weaves this condemnation into his chronological scheme of the forty years of CD 20:14–15, and stated in 19:35–20:1 as "from the day of the assembling by the Unique Teacher until the Messiah from Aaron and from Israel will arise." The author apparently has in mind the larger chronology of Israel in their 430 years of sojourn in Egypt mentioned in Exod 12:40. Here too, three hundred and ninety years after Nebuchadnezzar's conquest of the land (CD 1:5–6) plus the forty years of the period of the assembly until the rise of the Messiah will total four hundred and thirty years. As stated earlier, the chronology of the forty years reappears in *Pesher Habakkuk*, commenting on Ps 37:10.

ועוד מעט ואין רשע                    F1-2ii:5
ואתבוננה על מקומו ואיננו פשרו על כול הרשעה לסוף F1-2ii:6
ארבעים השנה אשר יתמו ולוא ימצא בארץ כול איש F1-2ii:7
[ר]שע F1-2ii:8

"But in a short while the wicked will be no longer. I will search for his place but he will not be there" (Ps 37:10). Its eschatological interpretation concerns all the wickedness at the end of the forty years when they will be exterminated and no [wi]cked man will be found in the land. (4Q171 F1–2ii:5b–8a)

Conceivably the author of the psalmic pesher understood the word האסף here in CD 19:35 and in 20:14, the latter of which is followed by כשנים ארבעים (about forty years), as referring not to the death of the Teacher, but to the end of the wicked in the wilderness who deserted after the evil reports of the spies on the one hand after the assembling of the people by Moses at Sinai (the *Urzeit*), and on the other to the inception of the period of forty years for those who will have joined the Teacher at the time of his assembly, but who subsequently will desert (the *Endzeit*). Both groups, that of the Bible and the rebels of the eschaton, will have been destroyed.

The last two words of CD 19 require comment. The reason for the strike through of יור מורה can perhaps be explained by the following scenario. The scribe began to write יורה היחיד as he did later in 20:14, but changed his mind to write the more usual מורה (20:28, 31 as well as CD-A 1:11). Not wishing to split the phrase מורה היחיד across pages, he crossed out both words, wishing to place them both on the next page. Forgetting he had already written מיום האסף on the previous page, he accidentally began page 20 with מיום. Erasing this third error he continued with מורה היחיד.

In CD 20:1b–17a the author applies what he said above to the membership of the community. Anyone who has been accepted as a member, but goes on to reject the Torah shall be expelled as if he were one who had never joined. Being a member does not bestow upon anyone irrevocable privileges. Unless he repents and acts accordingly, such a person shall be excluded as if he were one who had never placed his fate with those who were instructed by God (20:3–6). This entire pericope deals extensively with the deserters who must have been a constant sore for the faithful leadership. People would join the community and, not being able to stand its rigor, would leave. Even the property of such people must be rejected. One's great wealth was not to be a mitigating factor in keeping him within the group.

Lines 8–9 stress that the member in the group must accept unconditionally both the first and latter things (Torahs). In other words, acceptance of the traditional text alone does not suffice. Only those who keep what modern scholarship calls the apocryphal Torah as faithfully as the old sacred text shall be part of this society. The so-called *Catena*ᵃ (4Q177)[199] cited above likewise refers to two Torah's, probably the Pentateuch and *Jubilees-Temple Scroll*.

תקעֹו שופר בגבעה השופר הואה ספר [התורה ראישונה הח[שֹ]ֻֿ[וצרה הי]אה
ספר התורה שנית אשר מאסו ב[ול א]ֻֿנשי עצתו וידברו עליו סרה

"Blow the *shofar* in Gibeah." (Hos 5:8). The *shofar* refers to the book [of the first Torah. "The tru]m[pet" (Hos 5:8) i]s the book of the second Torah which a[ll the me]mbers of the council will have despised and spoken of deviantly.[200] (4Q177 F1-4:13–14)

The author of our MTA text makes no distinction between what is conventionally known as canonical and apocryphal or pseudipigraphic texts. Both have the same sanctity and are binding upon each of the members. Those who reject any of these principles shall be condemned as if they had joined the opposition to the Teacher, since they will have abrogated the divinely ordained injunctions of the new covenant established in the land of Damascus.

As noted, the author reiterates his chronology once again in CD 20:13b–15a. The period of destruction would be during the forty years of faithless Israel, a group that, like the Israelites of old who had been part of the Sinaitic covenant but transgressed, would receive the Damascene (the new) Covenant but would desert to be ultimately destroyed. Our writer confirms this linkage between the desertion at Sinai and that of the Damascus community by citing Hos 3:4, "There will be neither king, nor prince nor chastiser nor reprover" in *righteousness*. Righteousness constitutes the centrality of both the Sinai and Damascus covenants. MTA asserts that many in Israel rejected the leadership of Sinai and will do so once again by abrogating that of the Damascene assembly.

### 3.2.1.5.4. *Salvation in the Messianic Epoch (CD-B 20:17b–34; 4Q266 F4)*

With CD 20:17b, MTA returns to one its major topics, the righteous of Israel who will repent of their transgressions, that is to say, the community whom the author addresses. It is these who, having confessed their sins, will rejoice in the salvation God has prepared for them at

---

[199] Also known as *Midrash on Eschatology*ᵇ.
[200] See the comments pertaining to this text in my amplification of CD 1:13–2:1. See also my remarks on CD 7:15 pertaining to ספרי התורה as referring to both the Pentateuch and *Jubilees-Temple Scroll*.

the advent of the Messiah during the eschaton. However, those who desert the community, departing from the Torah, will be cut off. This text understands the Midrash on the Eschatological Torah as a song of Israel's triumph of the righteous over sinners.

### 3.2.1.5.4.1. The Book of Remembrance (CD-B 20:17b–20a)

The author paraphrases and expands Mal 3:16, amplifying it with extra clauses. The additions make the point that brethren must assist each other in their righteous paths, supporting one another. Only then will God record their names in His book of memory. 4Q417 F1i:13b–18a likewise exegetes our citation of Mal 3:16, but somewhat differently.

ואתה
13
14 מבין רוש פעלתכה בזכרון הע[ים ]בא חרות חַחוק{כה} וחקוק כול הפקודה
15 כי חרות מחוקק לאל על כול עֲוֺנֺֺֹת בני שֿוֿת וספר זכרון כתוב לפניו
16 לשֿמרי דברו והואה חזון ההֺגוֿי לֹספר זכרון וינחילונֿו לאנוש עם עֹם רוח כֹֿי̇ ]א
17 כתבנית קדושים יצרו ועוד לוא נתן הגוֿי לרוח בשר כי לא ידע בין
18 [טוֺ]בֿ לרע כמשפט [ר]וֿחו

And you understand the beginning of your (God's) creation in the remembrance of the e[pochs.] In it[201] (the remembrance) the statute is etched, and the entire command is decreed (in it), because it was etched to God's lawgiver (Moses ?) pertaining to all the epochs for the sons of Seth. A memorial volume is written before Him for those who keep His word; and it is the *vision of Haguy* for the memorial volume; and they (the sons of Seth) bequeathed it forthwith to Enosh together with the people of the spirit, be[ca]use he fashioned it as a sacred blueprint. But Haguy had not as yet been given to the spirit of flesh, for it (the spirit of flesh) had as yet not known the difference between [goo]d and evil in accordance with his [spi]ritual nature . . . (4Q417 F1i:13b–18a)

Whereas this Haguy text pesherizes Mal 3:16 as part of a dialogue concerning the origin of good and evil, lines 17–18 of CD 20 interpret the clause, "each spoke to his associate," as referring to mutual instruction of righteousness in the future. Thus, God will observe man's obedience which will bring about the messianic age exposed toward the end of this section.

---

[201] Strugnell and Harrington render בא as "comes." DJD XXXIV, 155.

### 3.2.1.5.4.2. Salvation for the God Fearers (CD-B 20:20b–22a)

Teaching each other righteousness will enable one to adjudicate between the just and the wicked and between the one who worships God and him who does not. Our text weaves Mal 3:18 with Deut 7:9 into God's love toward the righteous thousands that they might flourish for a thousand generations. As was stated, the phrase אלף דור has some ambiguity. It may be understood either literally or figuratively, "a thousand generations" or "forever."

### 3.2.1.5.4.3. Punishment of the House of Peleg (CD-B 20:22b–27a)

The problematic readings and syntax following the word דור in line 22 have divided translators. Schechter linked מבית פלג (from the house of Peleg) as part of the thousand generations and read נסיך העם (the prince of the people)[202] at the beginning of line 24 as the beginning of a sentence extending to הׄקׄדׄש of line 25.[203] Rabin, after some missing words, has בית פלג, and read עד instead of the conventional עוד at the end of line 23. He translated the next word אל not as a preposition, but as the deity. Instead of the standard דרך of line 24, he proposed to read ו[יׄשׄ]ך (and let him appease).[204] Both these and other translators understand the verbs ויטמאו, וישענו, יצאו and ושבו as historical, but diverge widely as to the role of "the house of Peleg." Some assume that this was a group that split off from the Just Teacher, which gives it a negative stance. Others take it as a positive move on account of the defilement of the Jerusalem sanctuary. In my view, however, these complex debates have no historical basis whatsoever. These lines do not describe history, but concern the prophecy of those who will leave the land of Judah for the land of Damascus mentioned in CD 4:2–3 and 6:5.[205] As to the connotation of the sobriquet "the house of Peleg," it has the same sense as the phrase in *Pesher Nahum.* Interpreting Nah 3:9, which deals with the many nations where Israel will migrate, and anticipating Nah 3:10 which speaks of exile, the pesherite writer says,

פשרו הם רשׁׄעׄ]י מנשׁ]ה בית פלג הנלוים על מנשה

---

[202] Qimron reads דרך העם (Qimron, "The Text of CDC," 47).
[203] Fitzmyer, ed., *Documents of Jewish Sectaries,* 77, note 48.
[204] Rabin, *Zadokite Documents,* 40–41.
[205] Cf. also 4Q266 F5i:15–16 discussed below in section 3.2.2.5.

> Its eschatological interpretation concerns the wicked of Manasseh as well as the house of Peleg that will join with Manasseh. (4Q169 F3-4iv:1)

It would seem that the author of this pesher draws on our text wherein he understood this reference to "the house of Peleg" as a negative statement. In other words, as taken by him, those who will leave Judah to go to Damascus will eventually split off from the righteous group and join the wicked. The words בית פלג then resemble in meaning בית אבשלום (the house of Absalom) occurring in 1QpHab 5:9, a phrase which refers to the treacherous act committed by a son against his father, not to a historical group as generally supposed. בית פלג in our text does not allude to a group in history, but to anticipated fractures during this whole period of exile. It refers to contemporary Judah who, after leaving Jerusalem with the other exiles, will splinter again. The author of MTA alludes to a similar group in CD 20:26–27 by the words מרשיעי יהודה ביומי מצרפותיו (those of Judah who act wickedly during the days of their cleansing). In other words, as understood by the author of MTA, the process of catharsis will be traumatic and enduring, in that this will be a group not united. During their sojourn they will retain their zeal for God, but will retract in some matters to the way of the populace. God will treat each of them according to their individual inclination.

Scrollists also diverge as to the import and sense of the defilement of the sanctuary in line 23. The clause ויטמאו את המקדש explicates the preceding phrase בקץ מעל ישראל. Those who will defile the Jerusalem house of worship are those who have been unfaithful during the era of Israel's lengthy period of profanation extending throughout the epoch of the אחרונים. On the other hand, those exiles who will have intended to conduct themselves in accordance with the rules of God under the Damascene covenant, but who will have violated the laws of the Torah, will be cut off from the faithful camp at the coming of the Messiah. Included in this group are the wicked of Judah who, during the epoch of cleansing, deserted the statutes of the covenant for avarice. Note that our reading rests on combining CD 20:27 with the fragmentary remains of line four of 4Q267 F3. CD 20:27b–28 fuses with 4Q267 F3, and lines 33–34 with fragment 4 of 4Q266.

## 3.2.1.5.4.4. Confession of Sins (CD-B 20:27b–32a)
Following the above parenthetical section describing the future fracture of Israel, our text continues to depict the spiritual awakening that will occur at the advent of the messianic age. The term מחזיקים

beginning this segment is common in MTA. However, here it has a special connotation, referring to people who will have withstood all temptations and distractions and will have emerged steadfast in their trust in the new organization. This proposed entity are those who will accept the new covenant in the land of Damascus under the guidance of the Just Teacher. They will cling not only to the commandments of the Torah, but also to the injunctions recorded only in MTA. The word אלה qualifying משפטים emphasizes the rules that were special to this community (important elements such as study and decorum listed in our text). Translators render the phrase לצאת ולבוא על פי התורה literally as going out and coming in according to the Torah. What it does denote is that one must live entirely by the stipulations of the Law. This affirmation bears a close resemblance to what the leaders of Talmudic Judaism advocated. In this respect, although they may have diverged in many details, the goal of this organization agreed fully with the sages of the Mishnah and Talmud.

Our text then goes on to describe their way of life. A primary point is the obedience to the Just Teacher and asking forgiveness for any transgression. The wording that describes it bears also a close resemblance to the more expanded confession prevailing in Judaism. Both our text and rabbinic Judaism echo the confession in Dan 9:15, "we have sinned, we have been wicked . . . may your wrath and anger turn away from your city Jerusalem, your holy mountain." As emphasized by Baumgarten, our text has a legal dimension throughout. Here in the confession too, Israel stresses that they have lived contrary to the statutes of the covenant. The text goes on to affirm that Israel's punishments will have been fully warranted. The author divides their Torah into three categories: a) His holy statutes (apparently a reference to the commandments found in the Pentateuch), b) His righteous injunctions (special rules innovated by the community) and c) His true testimony (the admonitory material that forms the glue of our text). In these three phrases, the author voices the motto of the Damascene Covenant. As stated in the preamble and throughout the work, in spite of the many innovations introduced by these injunctions, our author insists ironically that their legal system, in contrast to that of their opponents, had not departed in any way from the nomistic tradition of the Hebrew Scriptures. The clause "and they shall be chastised by the rules set down by the forefathers" emphasizes that remembering the past is not merely a cognitive operation. Rather, many of the trials and punishments endured by the patriarchs will reoccur over and over.

### 3.2.1.5.4.5. Hearkening to the Just Teacher and Rejoicing in the Law (CD-B 20:32b–33a)

The clause והאזינו לקול מורה צדק (And they shall obey the Just Teacher) confirms once again what is emphasized throughout this work—that the Teacher is not in MTA a historical personality and certainly that he had not died as is supposed according to CD 19:35–20:1 and 20:13–14. Instead, he is the futuristic figure who will become the interpreter of the Torah and his decisions must be followed to the letter. The clause "And they shall not reject the true statutes" apparently emphasizes the importance of the social rules innovated to create a more righteous society by maintaining the poor and destitute. These rules should not be abrogated.

Some scholars read the words בשמעם אתם in line 33 as part of the previous sentence, meaning that the covenanters shall not reject the words of the Torah when they hear them.[206] However, this understanding would add nothing to what has already been said. On the other hand, if we link this phrase with what follows, it adds *gusto* to the admonition, emphasizing the joyful consequences of obeying the law. Heeding the statutes of the Torah will bring satisfaction and happiness. In addition, the adherents to the covenantal life style will attain a life that is superior to that of any other group.

### 3.2.1.5.4.6. Salvation for the Righteous (CD 20:33b–34; 4Q266 F4:9)

For lines 33b–34a see 1QSb 5:27b–29a, which likewise affirms Israel's rule over the nations.

27. . . . כיא אל הקימכה לשבט 28 למושלים לפ[ניכה יקדמו וישתחוו
וכול לא[ומים יעובדוכה ובשם קודשו יגברכה 29 והייתה כא]ריה

For God has raised you up as a scepter over the rulers; [they shall come] befo[re you and prostrate themselves and all peo]ples will serve you. And through His holy name He shall make you supreme; and you shall be like a li[on . . . (1QSb 5:27b–29a)

The next two sentences of CD reiterate a central theme of this work: God and His forgiveness of those who live by the Torah. CD 4:9b–10a asserts that on account of the ancestral covenant, God will forgive

---

[206] Rabin, *Zadokite Documents*, 42; Martínez and Tigchelaar, *Scrolls Study Edition*, vol. 1, 581; Schwartz in Charlesworth, ed., *Damascus Document*, 37.

Israel's sins. Based upon 4Q266 F4:7 and its corresponding wording in CD 20:33, line 8 of 4Q266 F4 contained ten to fifteen spaces more than its CD parallel וכפר אל בעדם וראו בישועתו. Thus it is plausible that, based upon CD 4:9b–10a, the extra spacing in the Cave 4 text likewise contained the phrase כברית רישונים, to read "And God will forgive them in accordance with the ancestral covenant."[207]

The construction from now until we return to 15:1 of CD draws almost exclusively on what survives in 4Q266–273. What exactly follows the end of the B manuscript and how it links up with the parts of MTA preserved in the fragments is uncertain. As cited by Baumgarten, Milik maintained that textual and paleographic evidence support the conjoining of the words found in the sub-fragments a–d of 4Q266 F4 with CD 20:33–34. Milik also supported the supposition that 4Q270 F2i:1–3 joins with the end of CD 20.[208] Baumgarten wants to place the catalogue of transgressions (4Q270 F2i–ii) immediately after CD 20, since the clause ועתה שמעו לי found in column 2 line 19 immediately following the catalogue introduces the subsequent laws. However, this formula, which occurs four times elsewhere in MTA, does not introduce legal texts. As I see it, the marking for nomistic sections does have a standard formula in our work: זה פרוש המשפטים, a clause which appears in CD 14:18 and 4Q266 F11:18 (paralleled in 4Q270 F7ii:12). This phrase was probably present in 4Q267 F7:3, a fragment which conjoins with text introducing the subject of integrity in commerce and marriage, legal material. A sub-specification of this broader nomistic subject appears in 4Q271 F3:5 shortly after the conjoin as וזֿה פרו[ש הונאה] (And this is the definit[ion of cheating]). This fragment appears then to link up thematically with 4Q266 F5i, a passage which may begin with marital offenses. Whereas Milik's joining of 4Q270 F2i:1–3 with CD 20:32–33 is not in itself implausible, it is problematic to parallel 4Q266 F4:9–13 with any of what spans from 4Q270 F2i:(6) to the beginning of column 2 (the maximum textual parameter of the four sub-fragments in 4Q266 F4, assuming the entire fragment was as many as twenty-five lines in length).[209] For, whereas the former contains positive content, corre-

---

[207] For ברית ראשונים cf. also CD 1:4 and 6:2.

[208] Stegemann does not dissent from this positioning of this fragment. See Hartmut Stegemann, "Physical Reconstructions," 180, 190–91. However, as explained below, it seems to me that placing this fragment here is tenuous if not unacceptable.

[209] If 4Q266 F4 was a page of twenty-five lines, as many as eighteen may have separated sub-fragments a–b from c–d. 7–13, the numbers assigned within the editio

sponding to the tenor of the end of CD 20, the latter is negative. The four lines of 4Q266 F4:10–13 (two sub-fragments evidently drawing on the terminology of portions of Ezek 34:23–24, Exod 18:21–22 and 11QT 57:8–9) does not satisfactorily parallel any four lines of extant text from column 1 line 9 of 4Q270 F2 to the beginning of column 2. One must then choose the beginning of either 4Q266 F4 or 4Q270 F2i as conjoining with the end of CD 20, but not both. A more plausible locus for the list of offenses, the so-called catalogue of transgressions (all of 4Q270 F2), is toward the end of the interior section bridging pages 20 and 15 of CD. The placement of the list there has reasoning behind it. The material that would then precede it (4Q266 F7) concerns itself largely with the Supervisor's modes of admission of candidates to the Purity. The purpose of the list at this point would be to present to the new members an outline of the traditional law as perceived by its author. Hence, the function of the catalogue would be pedagogic.

Let us consider now 4Q266 F4, the text which, as was stated above, most likely bridges the ending of CD 20 with what follows. The word חוק read by Baumgarten in line 9 of this text is ubiquitous in MTA. כול אלה ישישו וישמחו במצוותיו (All of them will be happy and rejoice in His commandments), our reconstruction prior to it, is based upon what precedes it in our context. The salvation that God has made available to the righteous of Israel will generate joy in the Torah.

### 3.2.1.5.4.7. The Advent of the Shepherd Messiah (4Q266 F4:10b–13)

Missing material, a line or perhaps as many as eighteen (the potential range of the lacuna of this fragment), separates וחוק[י]ו from the succeeding sub-fragments. These two crumbs of parchment contain paraphrases from Ezek 34. The lacuna preceding the extant text may have contained elements of the theme of this chapter. Chapter 34 begins with the prophet's vision of the coming eschaton. Much of

---

princeps to the seven lines represented by these four miniscule pieces, are in my opinion arbitrary ascriptions. Not only do we not know how long the lacuna was between a-b and c-d, but we are not certain of how many lines preceded a-b in this fragment. Stegemann notes that the shape of 4Q266 F4 "resembles rather closely the shape of the left edge of (4Q266) frg. 3 iv(a) with lines 1–4 of its column." Hence, he reasons that 4Q266 F4:7–9 of Baumgarten's numbering should be labeled as lines 1–3 of 4Q266 F4 (see Stegemann, "Physical Reconstructions," 180).

this text revolves around the term רועה, the shepherd being God or king David.

The theme of Ezekiel's shepherd frequently appears throughout MTA. For example, in CD 19:7–9, the citations taken from Zech 13:7 and 11:7 link with Ezekiel's metaphor here in 4Q266 F4:10–13 of God and Israel as a shepherd and his sheep. The prophet's use of דרש four times in Ezek 34 may have inspired the sobriquet דורש התורה in MTA. More significantly, MTA appears to draw a notion from Ezek 47:7–12 (a text which extends conceptually back to Deut 11:7–17 and 28:1–18) that the fertility or desolation of the Holy Land will depend upon Israel's obedience to the Torah. In this prophetic book God promises to gather the dispersed of Israel to their own land where the mountains will contain fertile pastures and fat grasslands prior to David's reascent as the prince of Israel (Ezek 34:13–24). Building on this idea, MTA prefaces the rise of the Just Teacher with the future fertility of Israel.

CD 1:7      ויצמח מישראל ומאהרן שורש מטעת לירוש

CD 1:8      את ארצו ולדשן בטוב אדמתו . . .

CD 1:11      ויקם להם מורה צדק להדריכם בדרך לבו

And He will cause to sprout forth from Israel and from Aaron roots of a plant to inherit His land and to grow fat in the fertility of His soil . . . and will raise up for them a Just Teacher so as to lead them in the way that will please Him. (CD 1:7–8a, 11a)

Conversely, when Israel would disobey God, the land would become desolate.

CD 5:20      ובקץ חרבן הארץ עמדו מסיגי הגבול ויתעו את ישראל

CD 5:21      ותישם הארץ

Now during the epoch of the desolation of the land (587 B.C.E.) the Shifters of the Boundary arose and misled Israel. And the land has turned into wilderness. (CD 5:20–21a)

Returning to our text, what survives plausibly continues with "[And] God [will set up a unique] shep[herd] and will feed them in [a good pasture; My servant David, he will feed them] and [he] will become [their shepherd.] And he will select for himself [men of truth and God fearers. They shall execute true justice. Kindness and] acts of mercy [they shall perform towards each other...]" The reconstruction following ובדר לו draws on 11QT 57:8–9 combined with Exod 18:21–22 and Zech 7:9. The author of MTA not only required that judges be truthful men who feared God, but that they be compassionate as well. CD 10:6 lists an additional qualification; a judge must be an expert in the book of Haguy and in the foundations of the covenant.

This passage adds a new dimension to the messianic theme of MTA. Without it, the idea of messiah in this work is obscured by the question of whether the Qumran community anticipated a single messiah or two, an issue that has divided scrollists. Some have taken CD 12:23–13:1, 14:19, 19:10–11 (משיח אהרן וישראל) and 20:1 (משיח מאהרן ומישראל) to allude to a single Messiah. However, with the publication of *Rule of the Community* the majority of scrollists shifted to a dual messiah theory, largely because of 1QS 9:11 which mentions עד בוא נביא ומשיחי אהרון וישראל (until the prophet and Messiahs of Aaron and Israel come). Proponents argue that the alleged references to the singular messiah in CD resemble in syntax the phrase מֶלֶךְ־סְדֹם וַעֲמֹרָה in Gen 14:10, whose corresponding verbs are plural, and hence that משיח אהרן וישראל refers to two personages—a priestly and a lay messiah.[210] However, quoting from Ezek 34, our text makes it apparent that David and David alone is the Messiah anticipated by the author of MTA, רֹעֶה אֶחָד (one shepherd) being a messianic phrase. If so, the word משיחי appearing above in CD 6:1 (paralleled in 4Q267 F2:6 and 6Q15 F3:4), should not be understood as "messiahs," but as the "anointed," in the sense of the anointing of kings and prophets.[211] The plural משיחי אהרן וישראל in *Rule of the Community* may be construed as a plural form with a singular intent.[212]

3.2.2.  *The Elaboration of the Eschatological Torah (4Q267 F7 / 4Q271 F3 . . . 4Q270 F4 / 4Q266 F12; CD 15–16; 9:1–14:17; CD 14:18–23 / 4Q266 F10ii:1–8; 4Q266 F10ii:8–15 / 4Q270 F7i:1–6a; 4Q270 F7i:6b–17 / 4Q266 F11:1–3a)*[213]

What follows the text of messianic dimension exposed above is uncertain. As was stated, 4Q267 F7 and the conjoining 4Q271 F3 con-

---

[210] James VanderKam, "Jubilees and the Priestly Messiah of Qumran." *Revue de Qumran* 13 (1988): 353–65. See Schiffman, *The Halakhah*, 51 for a brief bibliography on the two-Messiah concept.

[211] Cf. also elsewhere in the DSS 1QS 9:11; 1QM 11:7 and 4Q287 F10:13 for other uses of משיחי conveying this sense.

[212] Some would see it as reflecting a later development in the Essene community, the expectation of two messiahs.

[213] These references reflect only select primary textual witnesses for what continues to the end of the Cave material that bridges from CD 20 to 15. In similar fashion,

tain the phrase זה פרוש, a formula which apparently marks nomistic material and which here likely fronts the legal text that bridges CD 20 and CD 15. If we are right, this commences the second major section of the body of our work. As was noted above, the book evidently begins with the title מדרש התורה האחרון, which inaugurates the preamble continuing up to 4Q268 F1:8 of the composite text. The first part of the body, beginning with CD 1:1, concludes with the immediately preceding lines dealing with the advent of the Messiah (4Q266 F4:10–13). Now begins an extensive list of laws which are to govern Israel during the eschatological epoch. The first section deals with the inability of a debtor to repay the loan prior to the jubilee year so that he could repossess his inherited land. It evidently continues with the parental responsibility to present a daughter to a prospective groom honestly.

Preceding these laws is a short pericope in 4Q267 F7 containing the phrase ואהב לו (and he shall love him). These words in line 1 presume a subject matter which corresponds to the גר (proselyte) in Lev 19:33–34, the basis for our reconstruction. CD 6:20–21 contains similar wording: "that each love his companion as himself," and continues with the clause, "and support the poor, destitute and proselyte (גר)." This buttresses the presumed injunction here concerning loving the proselyte. The גר is a favorite topic in this work. In several passages proselytes are cited following the priests, Levites and Israelites as part of the four-fold division of the community. The first proselyte, Abraham (CD 16:6), is labeled אוהב (lover), as are Isaac and Jacob (CD 3:2–3). Love likewise forms an important theme in MTA. Compare CD 13:9, "He will have compassion upon them as a father has for his children." This serves to bridge from the introduction to the eschatological Torah (the first part of the body of our text) to the elaboration of the injunctions that follows. The inclusion of the proselytes at this point tells us the converts are as much an integral part of Israel as are the Israelites themselves. This corresponds to Ezek 47:22 which prescribes that in the messianic age the legal rights of the proselytes will be equal to those of the tribes of Israel in regard to land allotment.

My continued reconstruction, ואלה החו[קי]ם [והמשפטים אשר תשמרון] [לעשות בארץ] (Now these are the sta]tutes [and the judgments which

---

I cite only the main witnesses of that which continues in CD 15 to the end of this section, text which extends beyond the conclusion of the medieval version.

you shall observe to do in the land]), whose wording is taken from Deut 12:1, resembles אֶת־חֻקֹּתַי תִּשְׁמֹרוּ (You shall keep my statutes) immediately following the injunction to love one's neighbor as oneself (compare Lev 19:18b–19a); hence, our choice for filling the lacuna of line 2.

### 3.2.2.1. *Restoration of Land in the Jubilee Year (4Q267 F7:3b; 4Q271 F3:1–3a)*

The lost text in 4Q271 F3:1 makes it impossible to give the context of the isolated word בכסף (with silver). It probably dealt with the injunction to lend money to one's neighbor, which leads to the rules that govern sabbatical and jubilee years found in the next line. My reconstruction וזה משפט החמשים (Now this is the rule for the fiftieth year) at the end of 4Q267 F7:3 and continuing to the first line of 4Q271 F3 serves as a prelude to the jubilee legislation evident in line 2. Lev 25:10, the basis for our reconstruction for much of line 1 and the beginning of line 2 of 4Q271 F3, prescribed that Hebrew slaves were to be released in the sabbatical years, and debts cancelled prior to the jubilee year when any land sold during that period would be restored to the original owner. However, line 2 of this text is concerned with a problem not recorded in the Hebrew Scriptures. The legislator here presumes that the purchase money paid for the land precedes its restoration to the original owner. If so, what happens if the original owner lacks the means to restore the money? What is the status of this property? Unfortunately a portion of our text is lost. It is noteworthy, however, that the problem legislated here does not cohere with the rabbinic understanding of jubilee law. According to the Talmud, there exists no indebtedness during the restoration of the land, because a buyer pays only the prorated cost in proportion to the number of years that he will have actual possession of it. However, it could be that the author of MTA deals here not with a buyer of land, but with a borrower who placed his property as a surety. Now, when the jubilee year arrives and the loan has not been repaid, is that guarantee cancelled or not? A related passage in 11Q13 (Melchizedek) 2:6, like our text, speaks of forgiveness of indebtedness. וקרא להמה דרור, conventionally translated "And he shall proclaim liberty to them," is to be understood here as the announcement of release of the obligation of repayment of debts as is amplified in the succeeding clause, לעזוב להמה] משא [כול עוונותיהמה (to forgive them [of the debt] of all their transgressions), a wording corresponding to the extant portion of line 3 of our text.[214] The word עוונות, generally rendered as "transgressions," is problematic given the fact that the context refers to forgiveness of *debts*. How does the incurring of a *debt* amount to a *sin*? Whereas these passages do authorize the cancellation of indebtedness when the jubilee year arrives, they apparently do not sanction free and unlimited resort to the absolving of debts in the fiftieth year. The arrears incurred are still considered by these authors as transgressions if not paid off, especially for people of means for whom repayment would not be a burden. MTA and 11Q13 agree that the advent of the jubilee year involves the cancellation of debts.

Line 3 of our text is a mess. The identity of the letter emerging from the first lacuna is uncertain. It could be a remnant of a *waw*, to read from the end of the previous line והגיעׂ[ה] [שׁנת הׂ]יובל וישא את חובו מעלי[ו] (and the year of [jubilee] arrives, [then he shall forgive him] his [loan]). But, if so, we would have to suppose that the letters which Baumgarten transcribes וׂאלׂםׂ preceding [יעזוב] אל[ו] in the parallel 4Q267 F7:6 were a scribal error for the word אל[ו] which follows it. Alternatively, instead of reading [מעלי]ו, we insert וׂאד[ם], restored from its parallel in 4Q267. In our restoration the lender will forgo his loss and both he and God will forgive the borrower's indebtedness. What this means is that not only does the lender not collect his rightful money, but he must hold no grudge against the non paying debtor. Nevertheless, I present this interpretation with some hesitancy, inasmuch as I am uncomfortable with the notion of aligning God with man in the matter of forgiveness. Baumgarten takes a different stance concerning what is being forgiven. On the basis of the above cited passage from Melchizedek, he presumes that "the release from sins refers to the divine reward for those who redeem their brother from bondage."[215] The problem with this understanding, however, is that the wording in line 3 of our text speaks of release from *iniquities* rather than a *reward* for good deeds. Furthermore the text of 11QMelch 2:5–6 is unclear. See the discussion in DJD XXIII, 230–31, where the editors assemble a variety of textual and interpretative possibilities. As to the clause in our text, "[and both man] and God will forgive hi[m all] his transgressions," it is conceivable that MTA would not

---

214   קרא דרור is rendered in the LXX translation of Lev. 25:10 as διαβοᾶν ἄφεσιν; in Isa 61:1 as κηρύξαι ἄφεσιν and in Jer 34:8, 15, 17 as καλέσαι (or) καλεῖν ἄφεσιν (to proclaim forgiveness).

215   DJD XVIII, 176.

object to the voluntary repayment of such debt *following* the jubilee year, especially by those debtors who are not truly indigent.

### 3.2.2.2. *Intermingling Male and Female Garments (4Q271 F3:3b–4a)*

The reading in lines 3b–4a, "[Let] not [a garment of a man be worn by man and woman] in common, for it is an abomination," paraphrases Deut 22:5. Another rendition of this passage occurs in 4Q159 (Ordinances[a]) F2-4:7, where it links up with related subject matter. The reading יהיה here follows that of MT, whereas Baumgarten's יהיו accords with 4Q159. On the other hand, both our text and 4Q159 omit the mention of the deity found in the expansive formulation of the MT: כִּי תוֹעֲבַת יְהוָה אֱלֹהֶיךָ כָּל־עֹשֵׂה אֵלֶּה (For anyone who does such things is an abomination to the Lord your God). The word כאחת (in common), unique to our text, is puzzling. Does it prohibit only the interchanging of clothing between men and women, or does it forbid also any unisex garment worn by either man or woman? On the intermingling of garments see more comments below on lines 9–10 of 4Q271 F3.

### 3.2.2.3. *Honesty in Business (4Q271 F3:4b–10a)*[216]

MTA changes the reading את of Lev 25:14 to עמית in line 5, perhaps to clarify that honest business dealings are required of anyone rather than merely one's kin. Baumgarten wonders whether the word פרוש in line 5, referring to the explication of Lev 25:14, is restricted to the issue of excessive profits or to not disclosing defects in goods for sale.[217] He then cites *Bava Metzi'a* 4:3–12 which defines the term אונאה (defrauding). However, it is likely that the word פרוש here is intended to explicate the immediately preceding citation of Lev 25:14, and that our text embraces both: profiteering and hiding defects. In fact, this passage itemizes still another kind of אונאה not mentioned in *Bava Metzi'a*: not restoring lost objects to their owner.

Let us take a closer look at MTA's list of fraudulent activity. Examples are a) not returning a lost object to its owner (lines 6–7a), b) conscious lying in business transactions whether concerning people or animals (line 7b), c) not disclosing the defects of a bride to her groom or vice versa (line 8), d) misdirecting people in any matter (line 9a), e) mar-

---

[216] Parallels 4Q270 F5:14–17a and 4Q269 F9:1–2.
[217] DJD XVIII, 176.

rying off one's son or daughter to someone who is unfit (line 9b) and
f) incorrectly pairing objects in any other matter (line 10).

As to a), in rabbinics the tractate *Bava Metzi'a* 1–2 deals with the
issue of not returning a lost object to its owner apart from אונאה
treated in pericope 4. The author of MTA on the other hand makes
it part of his list of fraudulent activity. The role here of the word
בָּאדם in example b) may refer to slavery or perhaps to dealings in
matters of commerce, whereas וּבְהֵמה clearly refers to defects in trading. With reference to example c), MTA goes beyond the Talmudic
tradition in its definition of אונאה. Marriage laws are very extensive
in rabbinics, but I am not aware of requiring the parent to disclose
his daughter's defects. The listing of example d) is indirect, because
what the text actually does is to link the defrauding in business matters to the *soṭah*, the adulterous woman, here called the אר(ו)רה (the
cursed one) who is punished for her deceit. This prompts the author
to cite a related verse in Deut 27:18, אָרוּר מַשְׁגֶּה עִוֵּר בַּדָּרֶךְ (Cursed be
one who misleads the blind in his way). Note however, that although
the word אָרוּר that begins the biblical citation seems to be missing
in our MTA text, it was clearly intended. Perhaps the omission was
due to haplography. By linking the two Deuteronomy passages with
the *soṭah*, the author of MTA suggests the severity of fraudulent
dealings. Especially interesting in this list is the joining of examples
e) and f), namely the marrying of one's daughter to an unfit groom
with plowing with an ox and a donkey and mixing together wool
and linen together.[218] See also the intriguing references to rabbinic
literature cited by Baumgarten in DJD XVIII, 177. Compare also
Paul's apparent drawing on this text in 2 Cor 6:14: Μὴ γίνεσθε
ἑτεροζυγοῦντες ἀπίστοις τίς γὰρ μετοχὴ δικαιοσύνῃ καὶ ἀνομίᾳ
. . . (Do not be unequally yoked with unbelievers; for what partnership has righteousness with lawlessness? . . . ).[219]

### 3.2.2.4. *Marriage and Adultery (4Q271 F3:10b–16a; 4Q266 F5i:1–2)*

For the phrase [בברית הקו]דש ([into the ho]ly [covenant]) restored in
line 11 as defining marriage, compare CD 12:11 which uses "the
covenant of Abraham" as the act of manumission of a slave. Both

---

[218] Cf. 4Q271 F2:6–7; [כלאים הוא ושורים ח]טים שדה המעורב (A field that is mixed
with w[heat and barley is under the prohibition of illicit mixtures']). See section
3.2.2.9.3.4 below.

[219] I thank Clark Brooking for this suggestion.

marriage and manumission change the status of a person in that each becomes sanctified by being obliged to observe additional commandments. Hence, the use of the phrase ברית קודש or ברית אברהם. As Baumgarten notes, the rabbis likewise designate marriage as an act of sanctification (קדושין). The text goes on to deal with a maiden or widow who has sexual relations with a man outside of marriage. No one may marry her. She is like an adulteress. This opinion differs from the rabbinic tradition that restricts adultery to a married woman (not a maiden or widow) who has sexual relations with another man. Furthermore, in rabbinic exegesis the violation of virginity is restricted to cases of women suspected of adultery at the beginning of their marriage. It would not be applicable to a widow or an unmarried maiden. Unique to our text is the detailed description of examining the presence of virginity by expert women, a process which is, as far as I know, absent in Talmudic literature. 4Q159 (Ordinances[a]) F2-4:8–10 explains that if the women find her guilty of illicit sexual relations, she has committed a capital offense. On the other hand, if her husband lies about her, he shall be fined two *minas*. Interestingly, the amount of two *minas*, equaling two hundred *zuz*, corresponds to what the Mishnah defines as the amount which a groom marrying a maiden is contractually obliged to pay. The phrase יעשה כמ[ש]פֿטֿ (he should follow the ru[l]e) in line 15 lacks specification. However, it most likely refers to Exod 21:9–10, "And if he betroths her to his son he (the son) shall treat her in accordance with the prerogatives of maidens (כְּמִשְׁפַּט הַבָּנוֹת יַעֲשֶׂה־לָּהּ). . . . He may not diminish her food, her clothing and her conjugal rights." MTA might have in mind here additional wifely rights beyond those listed in Exodus. See 4Q270 F4:16–18 (see commentary section 3.2.2.9.8.2.3) where these prerogatives are reconstructed into a passage dealing with a priest marrying a maiden.

Whereas the material just discussed is fragmentarily attested in four manuscripts, most of what follows is irretrievably lost. Our setting of the word תנק[ה] (she is innoc[ent]) in 4Q266 F5i:1 as sequential to 4Q271 F3 rests on the presumption that the two texts dealt with the case of an adulterous woman. The words [ואם אנוס אל יֿ[ומת] ([and i]f a man claimed that he was under duress he likewise shall not [be put to death]) following it a line later may have dealt with a married man who faced capital punishment on account of his relations with another woman. If he claims that he acted under threat, he is absolved as well. Interestingly, according to the Talmud, while duress would exonerate a woman in a case of illicit sexual relations, it would not do so to a man, perhaps since a woman is more likely to be coerced than a man.

### 3.2.2.5. *Eschatology of the Return (4Q266 F5i:5–17a)*

As to what preceded האחרון in line 5, based on line 17, Baumgarten speculates that it might have been מדרש התורה, to read [מדרש התורה] האחרון. However, it is more likely that this introduces the short eschatological theme in these lines that would occur with the apocalyptic era. Hence, our reading [בדור] האחרון, conceivably a parallel to 4Q273 F1:1[220] and arguably reconstructed as well in lines 11–12 of our text as [דו]ל[ ] האחרון]. This section then presumably concludes with הנה המ]ה על ספר מדרש ה[תורה האחרו]ן in lines 16–17. As has been noted elsewhere, מדרש התורה האחרון both begins and concludes the title of the book. Its place here in the middle of the work, however, is puzzling, but may be accounted for perhaps as a tentative conclusion. In other words, the author had thoughts of ending the book at this point, but subsequently changed his mind to enlarge it further. This supposition, then, would explain why the next pericope begins with an introductory formula, ואלה החוקים (line 17). This indication of a serial composition of the work is then another hint that this large opus is a unitary endeavor by a single author, rather than a composite text as is generally taken for granted.

As to line 8, the reading מרוב אונים draws on Isa 40:26. However, what is interesting in these lines is the phrase [בנגלה] מן התורה. The term נגלה has a technical sense in MTA (compare CD 5:4–5, "And he (Eleazar) hid the *Niglah* until Zadok arose"). The context here in CD accounts for David's failure to heed the commandment against bigamy in Deut 17:17: "The king shall not have many wives." Indeed, *Temple Scroll* which forms part of the dual Torah and which prohibits polygamy had not as yet been penned. In our line too, בנגלה מן התורה refers to the legal text in *Jubilees* and *Temple Scroll*.

In line 9 Baumgarten reconstructs [המחזי]ק[ים בשם קוד]שו] ([who hold f]ast to [his] holy name). However, the context makes this reconstruction implausible, since it goes on negatively to depict a conspiracy against turning to the Torah. Hence, our reconstruction based upon

---

[220] 4Q273 F1 consists of small portions of three lines. I have not attempted to utilize the scattered letters remaining in this piece to reconstruct any portions of lines 6 or 7 of 4Q266 F5i.

[וכול אלה המואָ[סים בשם קוד]שו ה[ם [אנשי הלצון ]
[היה [אשר בירושלים כאשר (But as for all these who will despi]se [His] Hol[y] Name, [th]ey are [the followers of the Scoffer who will be in Jerusalem just as] it was formerly).

Several words after our reconstruction based upon CD 19:10 at the beginning of line 13, the text refers to those who should be treated each according his demeanor. Depending on his attitude toward the Torah, he should be either accepted or rejected from the camp.

4Q266 F5i:15–17 deals with the sons of Zadok depicted at length in CD 4:1–10 which pesherizes Ezek 44:15, thereby extending this reference to the entire contents of the last nine chapters of Ezekiel. This prophetic material describes the eschatological sanctuary, the restructuring of the tribal boundaries and Judea's extraordinary fertility in the eschatological age. If we are right as was mentioned above, that these lines had momentarily been the author's intended valedictory for the work, they might have served as a fitting conclusion, with the exodus from Judah to Damascus as its central theme. Note that the idea of assembling in Damascus is alluded to once again just prior to the book's conclusion in 4Q266 F11:17–18 which leads to its formulaic ending, "The Midrash on the Eschatological Torah."

3.2.2.6. *The Leadership of the Sage (4Q266 F5i:17b–19; 4Q266 F5i c-d)*
After this provisional conclusion, line 17b begins the additional peri-cope which ascribes the injunctions by the משכיל (the Sage). A similar introductory clause appears in CD 12:20b–21, "And these are the statutes for the Sage to be guided by with all living persons, each injunction for its own occasion," and subsequently in CD 13:22b–23a, "[And th]ese are the rules [by which] the Sage [is to conduct himself during the epoch when God will remember the land (and) when the matter which He spoke of will transpire]." Each of these three pas-sages stresses the Sage's role as a model which all of Israel should emulate. His exact function and identity are somewhat obscure. Is he a distinct personality, or does this epithet refer to a specialized function of the Supervisor? That the Sage is probably another appel-lation for the מבקר is seen in CD 13:7, which assigns the function of enlightening (ישכיל) to the Supervisor. If the two terms refer to the same personality, why the change in names? Perhaps when he con-trols the camps he is called the מבקר, whose primary role is pastoral (compare Ezek 34:12); when he functions as the spiritual ideal of

all righteous Israel, for those in both cities and camps, he is called the משכיל.[221] That the responsibilities of the Sage are sandwiched between the procedures of the cities and those of the camps in this passage may lend some support to this notion.

This section pertaining to the Sage also introduces the rules applicable to the recitation of the Torah that follows, a duty which Baumgarten understands as restricted to priests. This ascription, however, is not entirely evident in the text. The matter of the priesthood appears in a later section. MTA does not necessarily restrict the public recitation of the Torah to a priest. This section, absent in CD, tells us that the author attached great importance to public rhetoric. No one defective in speech or recitation was allowed to read the Scripture in public. It might result in an erroneous interpretation of the Torah that would bring about capital punishment. In other words, part of the recitation of the law was to interpret its legal ramifications.

At the suggestion of Milik, Baumgarten places two small pieces of leather under the label 4Q266 F5i(c-d) immediately prior to the text on public recitation. However, Baumgarten goes on to question this positioning on paleographic grounds. I too follow Milik, not knowing where else to place them. The readable words in this passage, כי לכול ישרי לבב בי[ש]ראל (for all the upright of heart in I[s]rael) and את חוקו הצדיקו (they declared righteous His statutes), suggest that these lines were part of a prayer, not legal subject matter.

### 3.2.2.7. *Qualifications for Public Recitation of the Torah (4Q267 F5iii:1–2; 4Q266 F5ii:1–4)*

What follows this text in 4Q267 F5iii:2 and continues in 4Q266 F5ii:1–4 lists the qualifications for public reading from the Torah.[222] The phrase ספר התורה (book of the Torah), restored in 4Q266 F5ii:2–3 from 4Q273 F2:1, certainly refers to the five books of Moses. However, as has been frequently stated, it has a larger sense that would include also the books which the sect regarded as Scripture, such as *Jubilees* and *Temple Scroll*. The extant lines here make no mention

---

[221] Cf. כול ישראל (4Q266 F5i:18) and זרע ישראל (CD 12:22), both of which have the משכיל as their heading.

[222] Hempel links this section and what follows from 4Q266 F5ii:5–16 under priestly rules (Hempel, *The Laws of the Damascus Document*, 38–41). However, the qualification [ואיש] מבני אהרון (lines 4–5) suggests that the preceding rules were not restricted to priests, but included any Israelite.

of the Sabbath. It is likely, therefore, that our author refers to the daily use of Scripture for prayer and study. The fact that the text is concerned about erroneous readings which might inappropriately result in condemning someone to death would indicate that the recitation of Scripture was part of daily routine for liturgy and study and that, moreover, they studied the legal imputations of the text. A closer look at these lines gives the headings in which the sect expressed special interest. It begins with the blind and the deaf and probably includes other handicapped and unqualified people cited in CD 15:15b–17.

15 וכ̇ל̇ היותו אויל ומשוגע אל̇ י̇ב̇ וכו̇ל פת̇[י] ד̇ש̇[ו]גה̇[223]

16 וכה ע̇ו̇ו̇ת̇ לב̇ל̇[תי ראות וחגר או פסח או חרש] א̇ש נ̇ער ז̇[עטו]ט אל

17 יבוא אי̇[ש מאלה אל תוך העדה כי מלאכי ה̇[ק̇]ו̇דש̇ ? ל ת בם

And no one who is a fool or mentally deficient may enter (the community). And as for any simple[ton] or one [prone] to err, one who is dim-eyed, no[t being able to see, or a limper, or lame, or deaf] or a youngster: none of [them] may be admitted [to the community, since the] sa[c]red [angels] . . . with them. (CD 15:15b–17)

If our reconstruction of 4Q266 F5ii:3a–4 is correct, the requirement of literacy is applicable not only to reading Scripture, but to other holy services as well. People whose literacy was not perfect were unfit to lead in the sacred service. Perhaps it is worth comparing this brief passage dealing with the reading of Torah with the more extensive text composed by Maimonides in paragraphs 8–9 of his first chapter on the rules pertaining to the study of Torah. Whereas our text disqualifies the handicapped from public recitation, regardless of their mastery of the text, Maimonides says that blind and deaf scholars may serve as leaders in interpreting the tradition.

8. כל איש מישראל חייב בתלמוד תורה בין עני בין עשיר בין שלם בגופו בין בעל יסורין בין בחור בין שהיה זקן גדול שתשש כחו אפילו היה עני המתפרנס מן הצדקה ומחזר על הפתחים ואפילו בעל אשה ובנים חייב לקבוע לו זמן לתלמוד תורה ביום ובלילה שנאמר והגית בו יומם ולילה. 9. גדולי חכמי ישראל היו מהן חוטבי עצים ומהן שואבי מים ומהן סומים ואף על פי כן היו עוסקין בתלמוד תורה ביום ובלילה והם מכלל מעתיקי השמועה איש מפי איש מפי משה רבינו

Every Israelite is obliged to study (Talmud) Torah, whether he is destitute or wealthy, whether he is perfect in body, whether he is a man of sufferings, whether a youngster or a very old man whose strength

---

223 Outlined text is supplemented from 4Q266 F8i.

has declined, even if he is so poor that he is supported by charity and begs from door to door. And even if he is married and has children, nevertheless he is obligated to set apart times for the study of Torah day and night. For it is written, "And you shall meditate in it (the study of Torah) day and night" (Josh 1:8). Some of the greatest sages of Israel were choppers of wood and drawers of water; some of them were blind, but nevertheless, they were engaged in the study of Torah day and night. And these people were among those who transmitted the tradition sage after sage going back to the mouth of Moses our Master (Rabbi). (*Talmud Torah* 1:8–9)

Our MTA text emphasizes the importance of understanding Scripture for its correct interpretation. It diverges from the Talmudic tradition whose emphasis is the proper transmission of Scripture, its precise readings. For example, the Masorah stresses the importance of distinguishing between כת (*ketib*) and קר (*qere*), the spelling of words and their oral equivalence, or between the מלא and the חסר. One may argue that these features are part of a later development and had not as yet existed. This may be true. However, even at this earlier stage during the pre-Christian centuries, it would seem that the cultural levels of approaching Scripture diverged between the two traditions. Whereas the concern of MTA centers on the proper understanding of words of Scripture, the Pharisaic tradition had gone beyond understanding to its accurate transmission. In the tradition of the Pharisees, proper understanding is taken for granted. For example, neither the Talmudic tradition nor Maimonides mention the requirement of mastering the proper understanding of textual passages, as our lines do. In other words, the author of MTA presumes a lower level of literacy than does the Pharisaic tradition.

### 3.2.2.8. *Causes for Defrocking a Priest (4Q266 F5ii:5–14a)*

The theme of captive priests follows. Lines 5–7 are one of two passages in MTA which deal with captivity. CD 14:15 obliges the community to redeem any Israelite seized against his will by pagans. In other words, it seems that no matter how he behaved, his redemption was unconditional. Our passage here, however, qualifies this, stating that if the redeemed captive was a priest, his sacerdotal conduct in captivity was to be scrutinized. If he worshipped idols, he would forfeit his priestly privileges. The text itemizes these forfeitures: a) leading in the temple's worship, b) touching the curtain of the holy of holies, c) partaking of the sacred food and d) handling the purities of the community.

Whereas the previous lines deal with someone who has been taken by force, the text continues by devoting a special injunction against priests who migrate to serve in pagan worship voluntarily (lines 8–9a). This second category of priests differs from those listed first. The former includes any son of Aaron. The latter addresses rituals pertaining to select individuals such as those who minister the Urim and Thummim or serve in the courts that interpret the laws of the Torah, rituals specified in Deut 33:8–10. The term להורות (to teach) in our text capsulizes Moses' blessing on Levi, but here specifically prohibits anyone who served gentiles from being part of Israel's legal system. As reconstructed, lines 9b–11a ban from membership and appear to bar from reinstatement anyone who has withdrawn his name from the priestly roster and lived against the rules of the priesthood.

The preceding material dealt with priests who acted wrongly. The concluding portion of this section (lines 11b–14a) lacks a clear subject, but seems to address the Israelite who disobeys the rules of the priestly council. Note that the council is restricted to priests. Our reading [לוא יגע] את האוכל ([ . . .shall not touch] the food) prohibits the violator from partaking of the food of the community. The phrase וחב בדם (and guilty of blood) is obscure. Baumgarten points to the clause דָּם יֵחָשֵׁב לָאִישׁ הַהוּא in Lev 17:4, "it will be accounted to that man as the shedding of blood." Compare, however, the words of CD 3:5–7, "and their sons in Egypt followed the willfulness of their heart to plot against the commandments of God, each doing as his eyes pleased. And they consumed blood and He cut off their males in the wilderness in Kadesh." By sequencing the eating of blood and the cutting off of the violators' offspring, our text seems to paraphrase what was said in CD 3:5–7 and Lev 17:4.[224]

The last extant word of this section, ביחש{י}ם (their genealogy), stands in isolation. Based upon CD 19:33b–35a, our reconstruction [ולוא יכתב] ביחש{י}ם ([and he will not be recorded] in their genealogy) is an attempt to make sense of what is present in the text.

כֹּן כל האנשים אשר בֹאֹוֹ בברֹית 33

החדשה בֹארֹין דמשק ושבו ויבגדו וֹיסֹורו מבאר מים הֹחיים 34

לֹא יחשבו בסוד עם ובכֹתֹבֹם לא יכתבו 35

"Thus are all the people who enter into the new covenant in the land of Damascus but will change (their minds) and act treacherously and turn

---

away from the well of living waters; these shall not be counted in the
assembly of the people, and *shall not be recorded in their records . . .* "

Alternatively, our text could have read ולוא יחשב ביחשם (and he will not
be counted in their genealogy).

### 3.2.2.9. *Procedures in Both Cities and Camps (4Q266 F5ii:14b–17 . . .*
###              *4Q270 F4:21; CD 15–16; 9–12:18)*[225]

The words זה סרך in MTA introduce new sections (compare also
4Q266 F5ii:14; CD 10:4; 12:22; 13:7 and 14:12), here drawing attention once again to the legal structure that will be in force in the
community. The phrase וזה סרך מושב . . . appears to precede injunctions
that are neither based upon scriptural texts nor derived from them,
but draw upon organizational decorum. Compare the phrase (וזה) סרך
מושב in CD 12:19 and 22 which serves to set off another subsection on
the organizational structure of the community. In our text, this phrase
continues a list of injunctions that will be in force during the eschatological epoch (lines 14–15). Our reconstruction in line 14, differing
from [ערי ישראל . . . אנשי] of Baumgarten, draws on וזה סרך הרבים
(And this is the procedure of the 'Many') in CD 14:12 and אנשי תמים
הקדש (leaders of perfect holiness) in CD 20:2, 5 and 7.

### 3.2.2.9.1. *Interrupting the Assembly (4Q266 F5ii:16–17)*

The reconstruction [וֹ]אֹיש אשר יצחק במוֹ[שֹב אֹ[נשי הרבים . . .] (And
[anyone who jests in the habit]ation of the m[any . . .]) in lines 16–17
draws on what is extant in our text and 4Q273 F4i:9 combined
with wording from 1QS 7:14–15 and elsewhere in MTA, primarily
4Q266 F10ii:12–13. What is problematic about this reconstruction is
that the supplementary text from MTA occurs near the end of the
composition. I suppose that the author placed this material here and
then later repeated it. Repetitions of legal material occur throughout
MTA.[226] As to the substance of these lines, they resemble material
found in rabbinic works such as *Derekh Eretz Zuta.* However, unlike
the rabbinic material, our text presumes the formation of a new
community whose members must follow the prescribed discipline.

---

[225] See the text layout for the full list of texts including parallels in this heading.
[226] CD 5:7–8 mentions the marriage to one's niece and 4Q270 F2ii:16 seems to
include illicit relations with one's niece in a list of transgressions. Sabbath legislation
appears in CD 6:18 and 10:14–12:5. CD 5:7; 12:2; 4Q272 F1ii:3–18 and 4Q266
F6ii:1–4 contain regulations pertaining to bodily discharges.

3.2.2.9.2. *Classes of Defilements (4Q272 F1i–ii; 4Q266 F6i:1–ii:13)*
This section deals with the broad subject of contamination spanning
skin diseases, sexual emissions and childbearing. Our text consists of
a fusion of Leviticus and *Temple Scroll*, but follows the organizational
structure of the latter. It begins with the most complex, the issues of
skin diseases, and concludes with what is most regular in society, the
bearing of children.

3.2.2.9.2.1. Leprosy (4Q272 F1i:1–ii:2 / 4Q266 F6i:1–13)
Two manuscripts, 4Q272 and 4Q266, have preserved extensive
pericopes dealing with leprosy (Lev 13–14). Two others have only
fragmentary remains. Interestingly, nothing of these larger sections
has survived in the Genizah A-B manuscripts, showing that the Cairo
texts omit extensive themes of MTA, since most of these rules were
no longer applicable in the Middle Ages. These leprosy passages are
interesting from another point of view. They show how the author of
MTA paraphrased Lev 13–14 into an essay. The essay is introduced
by a question, "As for a man who has a swelling or scab or discoloration in his skin: what is it?" This inquiry draws on the wording of
Lev 13:2, " . . . a swelling, a scab or a discoloration." However, the
answer extends also to the נתק (Lev 13:29–37), which the author of
MTA exposes in 4Q272 F1i:14–ii:2 (4Q266 F6i:5–13) with a gener-
alization, "This is [the rule for the Torah of le]pro[sy for the so]ns
of Aaron [with regard to quarantining the affliction of leprosy.]"
The organization in MTA apparently follows that of *Temple Scroll*.

48:14         ובכול עיר ועיר תעשו מקומות למנוגעים
48:15    בצרעת ובנגע ובנתק אשר לוא יבואו לעריכמה וטמאום וגם לזבים
48:16   ולנשים בהיותמה בנדת טמאתמה ובלדתמה אשר לוא יטמאו בתוכם
48:17      בנדת טמאתם והצרוע אשר בו צרעת נושנת או נתק ויטמאנו הכוהן

And in every city you shall make places for those stricken with leprosy,
affliction and scall who may not enter your cities thereby defiling them;
and also for those who emit a discharge and for women during their
menstrual impurity and when they give birth as well, so that they may
not defile in their midst with their menstrual impurity. And the leper
who has malignant leprosy or scab the priest shall declare as unclean
(11QT 48:14b–17).

The following chart illustrates the sequence of the categories of
uncleanness in the Temple Scroll 48:15 and those of the two main
MTA witnesses on this subject, 4Q272 F1i–ii and 4Q266 F6i:1–ii:13.

| Temple Scroll<br>1QT 48:15 | MTA<br>4Q272 F1i-ii; 4Q266 F6i:1-ii:13 |
|---|---|
| affliction of leprosy | 4Q272 F1i:1–13; 4Q266 F6i:1–5 |
| scall | 4Q272 F1i:14–ii:2; 4Q266 F6i:5–13 |
| bodily emissions | |
|    seminal emissions | 4Q272 F1ii:3–7a; 4Q266 F6i:14–16 |
|    menstruation | 4Q272 F1ii:7b–18; 4Q266 F6ii:1–4 |
| child bearing | 4Q266 F6ii:5–13 |

The text's response to the difficult terms שאת, ספחת and בהרת, that they are the result of "wood, stone or any other kind of blow," is surprising. Both ancient and modern commentators take it for granted that these terms pertain to some kind of skin disease resulting from an infectious malady. However, there is a problem with this explanation, since the text goes on to amplify the definition as "when the spirit enters and takes hold of the artery," suggesting that leprosy results from the spirit, an internal factor. As to the exact meaning of רוח throughout this section, Baumgarten argues that it is not a moralistic term as it is in biblical and rabbinic exegesis. In his words, "it is the infiltration of the רוח which disturbs the normal flow of the blood in the arteries, causing it to recede."[227] The circulatory aspect of the blood causes disorders in the skin. Conversely he supposes that it is the return of the blood to the arteries by the רוח החיים which fosters healing. In other words, according to Baumgarten, the author of MTA, like Hippocrates and the Jewish writer, Asaph, presents the רוח as if it were the physiological factor in the health or sickness of the body.[228]

As I see it, however, our text appears to follow closely Ezek 37 which, like MTA, presents the גידים (the arteries), the רוח and the verb בוא in tandem. In Ezek 37:10 the רוח functions as the *spirit* that *comes in*, generating life (וַתָּבוֹא בָּהֶם הָרוּחַ וַיִּחְיוּ, "Then the spirit entered them and they came alive"). However, רוח can also be negative, bringing sickness and death. An example of רוח bringing leprosy is Job 2:7, articulated in Job 4:15 as the result of a spirit. Depending on what it is commanded to do, the spirit may bring health or

---

[227] Charlesworth, ed., *Damascus Document*, 62.

[228] Baumgarten's point that passages in Asaph may draw on MTA is perceptive. In fact, Asaph uses the chronology of *Jubilees*, reflecting an awareness of the Essene literature.

sickness. The dual aspect of רוח is described at length in *1 En.* 76. 4Q270 F2ii:12 catalogues נגע צרעת and the זוב in a list of transgressions. Finally, it is interesting that our text castigates the one whose thoughts turn to whoredom as being defiled like the זב and adds that his touch is as defiling as that of the leper (4Q272 F1ii:4–5). This indicates that our author, like Scripture and the Talmud, regarded leprosy as a consequence of moral lapse. Miriam's defamation of Moses brought about her leprous fate, a condition which was healed by prayer (Num 12:1–15). King Uzziah contracted leprosy either because of his condoning of idolatry according to 2 Kgs 15:3–5, or, as the chronicler presents it, because as a king he assumed the role of a priest by burning incense on the altar (2 Chr 26:16–21). Likewise, Gehazi's craving for worldly goods from Naaman prompted Elisha to castigate his avarice by afflicting him with the same leprosy which had afflicted the Syrian military commander, now healed (2 Kgs 5:20–27). Two passages in MTA may suggest the connection of Gehazi and leprosy. One is CD 8:20–21, which seems to allude to his transgression resulting in his affliction. Interestingly, what precedes the second passage, 4Q270 F2ii:12 mentioned above, is misappropriation of stolen or lost property (4Q270 F2ii:9b–10a), the combination bearing a resemblance to the vice of Gehazi. This is followed in lines 10b–11a by anyone who defiles one's holy spirit. There also the spirit is the one that could be either holy or defiling, and, in this manner, resembles our text wherein the רוח either contaminates or heals.

The author repeatedly emphasizes the role of the priest in the treatment of the leper. This recalls CD 12:23–13:7 which says that wherever there is a community of ten men, one of them must be a priest who is expert in the book of Haguy. The text elaborates on this matter by pointing out that "By his authority all of them shall be guided," and goes on to note,

> But if he is not competent in all these matters, but one of the Levites is, the lot of when to go out and to come in shall shall follow his command for all members of the camp. But if there is a case regarding the law of leprosy, the priest shall come and stand up in the camp (to take charge), and (if the priest lacks competence) the Supervisor shall explain to him the details of the Torah. And even if he (the priest) is a fool, nevertheless he (the priest) must be in charge of quarantining him (the leper), for they alone have the authority to do so. (CD 13:3b–7a)

### 3.2.2.9.2.2. Bodily Emissions (4Q272 F1ii:3–18 / 4Q266
### F6i:14–16; 4Q266 F6ii:1–4)

This subsection dealing with sexual discharges resulting in contamination both modifies and amplifies the biblical references to bodily emissions. Its sequencing after the section on skin diseases follows that of both the Hebrew Scriptures and *Temple Scroll*.

### 3.2.2.9.2.2.1. Seminal Emissions (4Q272 F1ii:3–7a / 4Q266
### F6i:14–16)

As to the זוב (seminal emission), it appears that our text modifies יָזוּב זוֹב of Lev 15:25 which states, . . . וְאִשָּׁה כִּי־יָזוּב זוֹב דָּמָהּ יָמִים רַבִּים. (A woman who experiences a discharge of her blood for many days . . .") to זוֹב יָזוּב, apparently making the point that the flow of blood must be intensive. It is fascinating how our text conjoins the זוב of Lev 15:2–18 with the clause "or into whom a thought of whoredom enters," thus coupling the mental and physical aspects of seminal emissions. Does this conjunction imply that the discharge results from unclean thinking? In any case, MTA's idea that whorish thoughts result in a seven-day period of defilement is radical.[229] This indicates that the author of MTA regarded mental deviation as corresponding to physical defilement legislated in Leviticus.

### 3.2.2.9.2.2.2. Menstruation (4Q272 F1ii:7b–18; 4Q266 F6i a–e;
### 4Q266 F6ii:1–4)

The pericope pertaining to menstruation extends from 4Q272 F1ii:7b until the end of the column, little of which has survived. It resumes with what is preserved in the first four lines of 4Q266 F6ii. It is not implausible that 4Q266 F6i-c, a sub-fragment containing the clauses והבדל ואם, followed a line later by [וי]וכבס בגד (and be separated, and if . . . and he shall wash [his] clothing . . . ), parallels this lost text. Perhaps it came shortly before the clause [אשר י]קרב [איש אליה ע]ון נדה עלו ([one who] comes near [her] must bear upon himself the [s]in of a menstruant) in 4Q266 F6ii:1–2. The phrasing on the זבה and נדה in MTA departs from the corresponding injunctions in Leviticus. In its description of the purification following childbirth, Lev 12:4 states, "she may not touch the holy and may not enter the sanctuary." MTA replaces the biblical verb נגע with אכל (to eat) and transplants these

---

prohibitions to the *nidah* section in 4Q266 F6ii:3–4, absent in our biblical source. It is not that MTA softens the interdiction that only eating is prohibited but touching is allowed. Other phrasings make it clear that both touching and consumption are prohibited by MTA. See for example the phrase [וע]מגעו כמגע הצר (his touch is like that of the lep[er]) in 4Q272 F1ii:5. The only way to account for this paraphrasing of the biblical text is the author's use of rhetoric.

3.2.2.9.2.3. Childbearing (4Q266 F6ii:5–13; ii[a])
4Q266 F6ii:5–9 paraphrases Lev 12:2–4. Note that the author places this section following the זוב and the נדה rather than preceding them as in Lev 12 and 15. What is worth noting is that this long pericope on giving birth strengthens my opinion that MTA does not approve of celibacy as many scholars have presumed. On the contrary, marriage and procreation form part of the community's lifestyle, specifically that of the camps. The statement in lines 9–10 that entering the temple during her period of defilement is a capital offense is extreme. Baumgarten cites Num 19:20 which states, "But a man that is unclean, and has not been cleansed, that person shall be cut off from among the congregation because he has defiled the sanctuary of the LORD: the water of purification has not been sprinkled upon him; he is unclean." If so, the author of MTA read the term כרת (to cut off) as denoting a capital offense. All the biblical passages which prescribe being "cut off" are similarly capital in nature. This runs contrary in spirit at least to another statement in MTA which absolves capital punishment from all who have done prohibited labor on the Sabbath, an offense which according to rabbinic law is capital. CD 12:3–5 states, "Anyone who goes astray to profane the Sabbath and the festivals shall *not be put to death*; rather it is the duty of man to place him in detention." Here our author replaces capital punishment with incarceration. However, the issue of death penalty constitutes an important theme in MTA, since it is frequently alluded to, and is dealt with elsewhere in this work.[230] The mention in line 11 of a מנקת to nurse the infant adds a point not in Leviticus. Baumgarten explains that the handing over of the child to a nurse was a necessity, since the mother "was held to be ineligible for nursing her offspring during

---

[230] CD 15:4–5; 16:8–9; 9:1, 6; 12:4; 4Q266 F5ii:3; 6ii:10; 10ii:1–2 and 4Q273 F3:1. Cf. also 4Q270 F2i:13.

the days of purification."[231] This view suggesting that all infants be under the care of a wet nurse is unreasonable. In my opinion, the requirement of a wet nurse refers only to situations where a mother is unable to suckle her child; hence my reconstruction in line 10.

### 3.2.2.9.3. *Harvest Laws (4Q270 F3i:19–21; 4Q266 F6iii a-b; 4Q266 F6iii / 4Q270 F3ii:17–21; 4Q270 F3ii a; 4Q266 F6iv; 4Q271 F2:1–7)*

What immediately follows the section on childbirth is difficult to determine. The presence of the term קציר (harvest) in the pieces of parchment forming 4Q270 F3i:17–21, assembled by Milik and now followed by Baumgarten, suggests that this material relating to harvest follows the passage that dealt with nursing in 4Q266 F6ii and connects to 4Q266 F6iii(a) and (b), two small sub-fragments that also contain the term קציר.[232] These two pieces and the first three lines of 4Q266 F6iii proper provide the ten or eleven lines of intervening text between 4Q270 F3i:21 and 4Q270 F3ii:12 (the latter of which parallels 4Q266 F6iii:4). This arrangement makes the rules of harvest, some forty-nine or fifty lines if not more, a lengthy theme in MTA. It suggests that for the people our author was addressing, agriculture was of paramount interest. This, however, does not cohere with the generally accepted thesis that the CD Cave manuscripts were composed in the wilderness of Qumran, serving its inhabitants. This document speaks of camps and cities, entities that seemingly spanned the entire country. Qumran, on the other hand, was merely one area, a community in the wilderness that later transcribed MTA and other documents. In my opinion Qumran was primarily a scriptorium, an enterprise that copied and disseminated sectarian texts.

### 3.2.2.9.3.1. The Raising of the *Omer* (4Q270 F3i:19–21)

This heading follows a vacat of one line whose red ink, according to Stegemann, serves as a marker within 4Q270 for new headings on agriculture.[233] The author of MTA seems to introduce this new section on the harvest and priestly prerogatives with the rules for the

---

[231] DJD XVIII, 57.

[232] In his DJD edition Baumgarten departed from Milik's placement of the two fragments in PAM 42.398 and 43.295. However, in his article "Corrigenda to the 4Q MSS of the *Damascus Document*" in *RevQ* 74, 217–225 he reverted to their original positioning by Milik. In general my reconstruction follows their sequence.

[233] Stegemann, "Physical Reconstructions," 189–90.

Holy Land. The phrase [קודש]ה אדמת (the [Holy] Land) in 4Q270
F3i:19[234] and repeated below in 4Q266 F6iv:3 occurs in Zech 2:16
where the text introduces it and its high priest, Joshua. Our author
seems to transform this short section to present the Holy Land and
its produce, which serve to list the priestly prerogatives. The text as
reconstructed begins with a paraphrase of Deut 16:9 which appears to
treat the counting of the seven weeks of the עֹמֶר, at the conclusion of
which the festival of the first fruits is celebrated. Leviticus and Deuteronomy require the raising of the *omer* which begins the reckoning
of the seven weeks, concluding with the celebration of the Pentecost.
Although described at length in Scripture, the biblical text does not
explain the function of the *omer* and its counting. On the other hand,
our text, although not containing the word עומר, seems to describe it.
It evidently promises that the bringing of the *omer* will result in the
land receiving an abundance of water, suggesting that the raising of
the bundle of the blossoming grass which begins the counting of the
seven weeks will result in a blessing for the Holy Land, thereby making
it fertile. Other passages in MTA speak of the eschatological fertility
of the land (compare CD 1:7–8), as does Ezek 47 and 48.

### 3.2.2.9.3.2. The Sabbatical Year (4Q266 F6iii a–b – iii:3a)

What follows is troublesome since much of the text has perished.
Moreover we are not certain as to the placement and sequence of the
small fragments *a* and *b*. They cannot be established paleographically.
I have chosen to place *a* before *b* because it relates linguistically to the
immediately preceding 4Q270 F3i.[235] Having dealt with the *omer* and
the first fruits, judging from the scattered surviving words of 4Q266
F6iii(a-b)–iii:3a, it is likely that our text presented here rules of the
sabbatical and jubilee years, some of which are explicated elsewhere.
We assume that much of these scantily preserved lines follows Lev 25
with additions taken from 11Q Melchizedek; hence, the reconstruction. Note that sabbatical and jubilee terminology is rather frequent
in DSS. As cited in CD 16:3–4, the Hebrew title of the so-called
book of *Jubilees* is מחלקות העתים ליובליהם ובשבועותיהם. In the *Apo-*

---

[234] My reconstruction for this line follows in part that of Baumgarten in
"Corrigenda," 217–18. Baumgarten reverses the sequence of the two pieces of
this fragment from that of the editio princeps wherein he originally transcribed
[ ] אֹת [ ]אֹרָצֹֽ[ ]ֹֹ[ ] (DJD XVIII, 147).

[235] Cf. the word קציר in 4Q270 F3i:20 and 4Q266 F6iii a:2.

*cryphon of Genesis* Noah relates that ". . . in my days, when there had been completed for me - according to the calculation that I calculated . . . ten jubilees, then my sons finished taking wives for themselves for . . ."[236] A prayer in *Rule of the Community* likewise deals with the author's celebration of דרור (freedom) which is the jubilee year. 1QS 10:8b–9 states, ". . . the season of the harvest up to summer, the season of seed-time up to the season of the grass, the seasons of the years up to their seven-year periods. At the commencement of the seven-year periods up to the season for freedom (מועד דרור). And in all my existence the precept will be engraved on my tongue . . ."[237] Coming back to the MTA readings, our author appears to modify Lev 25:5 and 11 which prohibit the harvesting of inadvertent growth (ספיח) during the sabbatical and jubilee years. Our text seems to prohibit even the touch of this inadvertent growth, likening it to the waters of purification, a subject frequently discussed in MTA.

3.2.2.9.3.3.   Prerogatives of the Poor and the Priests (4Q266
              F6iii:3b–10; 4Q270 F3ii:17–21; 4Q270 F3ii a; [last
              line of 4Q266 F6iii]; 4Q F6iv; iv a; 4Q271 F2:1–5a)
In several passages MTA deals with the problem of assisting the destitute and the orphans. CD 14:12–14 prescribes two days of wages per month to be set aside for the destitute and the elderly, an idea not recorded in Scripture. This may be historically important since it is probably the first instance of what is called in the United States "Social Security." The text here dealing with harvest and tithing is more traditional, and in general corresponds to what is included in the first division of the Mishnah, זרעים. The dominant theme of this lengthy rubric under the harvest laws deals with the portions of the harvest and flock given to the priests. In rabbinics the most common term is מעשר, technically a *tenth*, and is used for all kinds of tithing, not necessarily one part out of ten. However, this word is rather infrequent in MTA. The technical meaning for a tenth used in our text is עשרון. Otherwise the tithing here generally follows that of Ezekiel and, as in Ezek 45:13, is specified as one sixth.

---

[236] Martínez and Tigchelaar, vol. 1, 33.
[237] Martínez and Tigchelaar, vol. 1, 95. מועד דרור is my addition.

### 3.2.2.9.3.3.1. Gleanings for the Poor (4Q266 F6iii:3b–7a)

Leviticus 19:9–10 and 23:22 require that the corners of the field and isolated fallen berries of the vineyard be left for the poor and proselytes. Our text amplifies this commandment by giving the dimensions and limitations of the amounts to be yielded. It specifies the maximum that the poor may collect in the field and the vineyard. Ten berries are considered the most that could be gleaned. The reconstruction [הזית] [העל[לת] ([the glean]ing [of olives]) in 4Q266 F6iii:4–5 draws on [ובנק]וף הזית] (Now as for when [the olives] are squ[eez]ed) in lines 7–8 (restored by the parallel extant text נקוף הזית in 4Q270 F3ii:15). For the field, the maximal gleaning is restricted to the amount necessary for the planting of a *seah* of corn. MTA makes no apparent mention of what the rabbis called שכחה, inadvertently ungathered produce (Deut 24:19). Perhaps it is included in the לקט of our text. Lines 6–7a apparently convey the idea that the owner is not required to compensate the poor for the failure of growth. Taken as a whole, these passages dealing with ownership are puzzling in a work about a group whose land was kept in common and who saw צדקה as a serious responsibility. The clause [ובעוללתו עד עשרה ג[רגרים] can be paraphrased in two ways: 1) as I do wherein it serves as an inclusio to ועללות הכ[רם עד עשרה גרגרי[ם of line 4 (restored from 4Q270 F3ii:1 and 4Q267 F6:2), or 2) by attaching the clause to the end of the preceding sentence as Baumgarten renders it, "a (field) which does not yield its s[eed] is not subject to *teru*[*mah* and fallen berries,] nor its single grapes up to ten b[erries.]" In his translation this clause relates to defining the field as empty if it has only ten berries.

### 3.2.2.9.3.3.2. Items Requiring Tithing (4Q266 F6iii:7b–10; 4Q270 F3ii:17–21; 4Q270 F3ii a)

The text goes on to provide a definition of תרומה. The rabbis recommend that the תרומה be in the range of one part out of forty to sixty. However, if one had given only one seed of corn, it fulfilled the biblical requirement. This view is attributed to the latter prophets Haggai, Zechariah and Malachi (*Bavli Hullin* 137 b). In MTA the תרומה is one *seah* out of thirty. However, if parts of the field have been trampled or scorched, the volume of tithing is reduced from the standard תרומה which is a *seah* of produce per *seah* of planting to a normal tithe (i.e. one tenth). The subject matter here is whether a field requires tithing, if damaged. Tithing, itself, and its dimensions are treated below in 4Q271 F2:1–3a (see commentary section 3.2.2.9.3.3.4).

Baumgarten translates נפרס as "was left," referring to what remained of the field. However, פרס, as in Dan 5:28, denotes "reduced," and refers not to what was left of the field, but to the proportion of the tithing. This word is hinted at three lines earlier in 4Q266 F6iii:8 where the words אם שלמה היא, translated "if (the field) is intact (i.e. not damaged)," suggest that the volume of tithing is larger when the harvesting covers the entire field than when parts of it have been damaged. 4Q270 F3ii:17b–19a makes a new point, requiring the poor to tithe what they have gleaned from the fields.[238]

4Q270 F3ii:19–21 and what immediately follows, dislocated wordage which I classify as the beginning of fragment 3, could be reconstructed in two ways. As Baumgarten regards it, based on 1QSa 2:18–19, it refers to the blessing at the beginning of the meal. However, this understanding ignores altogether the wording חלות התרומה in 4Q270 F3ii:19, which requires that the subject matter here deal with the separation of the loaves. חלה occurs in Lev 2:4; 7:12–13; 8:26 and 24:5, but never in connection with the בכורים. However, 4Q256 F9:5–6 does cite the בכורים in connection with the חלות; hence our reconstruction. In rabbinics a piece of each loaf of dough was required to be given to the priest.[239] Our text appears to mandate that a loaf be presented to the priest every year as part of the first fruit offering.

### 3.2.2.9.3.3.3. The Orlah ([last line of 4Q266 F6iii]; 4Q266 F6iv; iv a)

How to reconstruct these scattered lines is problematic. The complexity of this text goes back to Lev 19:23–25 and *Jub.* 7:35–37. Leviticus designates the fruit of a tree's first three years as ערלה, translated variously as "defiled" (ἀκαθαρσία, LXX); "forbidden" (NJPS) and "(un)pluck(ed)" (Milgrom).[240] The rabbis understand ערלה as completely inedible, *Jubilees* as unpicked produce.[241]

Leviticus classifies the fruit of the fourth year as קֹדֶשׁ הִלּוּלִים,[242] a phrase whose exact meaning is difficult, as the Samaritan text reads חלולים (profanation, redemption). The sages refer to it as כרם רבעי (a

---

[238] See Maimonides in *Gifts for the Poor* 7:5.

[239] *Halah* 1:1.

[240] Jacob Milgrom, *Leviticus 17–22* (New York: Doubleday, 2000), 1678–79.

[241] Vanderkam, *Jubilees*, vol. 1, 49. Charles translates "will not be gathered"; *Jubilees*, 64.

[242] Milgrom maintains the *'atnaḥ* belongs under קֹדֶשׁ rather than כָּל־פִּרְיוֹ as in the MT. Milgrom, 1683.

garden in the fourth year), and understand that it is to be brought to Jerusalem, as are other first fruits. *Jubilees* 7:36 states that the fruits of the fourth year will be sanctified, [offered as firstfruits].[243] What exactly does "as first fruits" mean? Charles suggests two possibilities: "(*a*) If we omit the words in brackets, our text directs that all the fruit of the fourth year is to be accounted holy and offered to God. (*b*) If the bracketed words are genuine, the text directs that, while all the fruit is to be accounted holy, only the first-fruits are to be offered to God."[244]

As to the sense of עורלה in MTA, unfortunately the line dealing with the first three years is lost. It appears to me that Baumgarten maintains that our text contains no allusion to the first three years, but does designate the first fruit of the fourth as sanctified, not to be eaten by the owner, but given to the priests as first fruits. Let us observe what the actual text does say and what it implies. What we have in Baumgarten's transcription and reconstruction for 4Q266 F6iv:4b–5a is:

‏4‏.] [טע איש בשנה הרֿבֿיעית לֿו יוכ]לֿ [כי [קֿדשו בשֿ]נה הזאת

a man may [p]lant, in the fourth year he [may not eat of it for] they are sanctified in [that y]ear.

He takes the first three words of the above text as referring to the planting of fruit trees outside of עורלה.[245] However, a closer examination of the sequence of the extant wording in lines 3–8 suggests otherwise. The clause in line 3, [ואחר ימכו[רו] (and thereafter they may sell . . .), the phrase in line 4, בשנה הרֿבֿיעית (in the fourth year), and the restored text of line 7, ובשנה החמישית ([however, in the fifth year]), wording which is secure because of the allusion in line 8 to Lev 19:25, strongly indicates that lines 1–3a, as do Lev 19:23 and *Jub.* 7:36, dealt with the produce known as עורלה grown during the first three years of planting. Moreover, the phrasing of lines 1–3a which contains the word לֿהֿ[ל] (line 2) must have as its subject the priests. It follows that what Leviticus and, perhaps, our text called עורלה was designated to belong to the priests for exchanging other

---

[243] The Ethiopic text is bracketed.

[244] Charles, *Jubilees*, 64.

[245] Martínez and Tigchelaar read the beginning of the sentence as I do, but understand the word קדשו as a D-stem verb with a suffix pronoun and translate the last clause as "but he shall consecrate it in (that) year" (Martínez and Tigchelaar, *Scrolls Study Edition*, vol. 1, 591).

produce or for commerce within the confines of Jerusalem. Support for this reconstruction emerges from the reading in 4QMMT wherein it seems to catalogue the difference between the opposition and the sect on the issue of עורלה.

ואף על מטעת עצי המאכל הנטע בארץ ישראל כראשית הוא לכוהנים

And also concerning (the fruits of) trees for food planted in the land of Israel: they are to be dealt with like first fruits belonging to the priests. (a composite of 4Q394 F8iv:12–13; 4Q396 F1-2iii:2–3 and 4Q397 F6-13:4–5)[246]

Qimron understands this passage as referring to the fruit of the fourth year. However, the wording in MMT suggests that this is a definition of עורלה during the first three years as well as the fourth, as MTA seems to indicate. In our reconstruction, then, the injunction "And i[f] one plants in the fourth year [he may] no[t ea]t (of them) [for] they have been sanctified in [that] y[ear]" applies to one who plants in the fourth year the produce which belongs to the priests. The crop is not edible inasmuch as its planted seed is sacred. The question arises as to how the holiness of the fourth year diverges from the עורלה. The difference seems to be that, whereas the produce of the first three years may be exchanged in the fourth by the priests for other fruit or for commerce, the crops of the fourth year may not. It is apparent, as noted by M. Kister, that these sources reflect a divergence of traditions on the status of עורלה during both the first three years and the fourth.[247]

Lines 5b–6 which contain the word מְמִנחה (from a meal offering) are reconstructed on the basis of Lev 2:14 as dealing with a meal offering as first fruit and which our text specifies must be offered as בכורים (first fruits) of the fourth year. Thus our text follows *Jub.* 7:36 which asserts that the fruit of a tree's fourth year be offered on *Shabuot*. These lines make another point—that the rules of עורלה during the first three years and the fourth are applicable only within the realm of Israel ("in accordance with their rights [in] the Holy [Land]").[248] The extant wording pertaining to the fifth year (lines 7b–8a) echoes Lev 19:25. Finally, 4Q266 F6iv(a):1–2, a small fragment whose place-

---

[246]  Qimron in DJD X, 52–55.

[247]  Menahem Kister, "Some Aspects of Qumranic Halakhah," in *The Madrid Qumran Congress*, vol. 2 (ed. F. García Martínez and A. S. van der Woude); vol. XI, 2 in *Studies on the Texts of the Desert of Judah* (ed. Julio Trebolle Barrera and Luis Vegas Montaner; Leiden: Brill, 1992), 576–86.

[248]  See line 3.

ment is uncertain, seems to belong in this general area, serving as an epilogue to the peroration on the *orlah*. Our reconstruction in line 1 of this piece draws upon Lev 2:9a, וְהֵרִים הַכֹּהֵן מִן־הַמִּנְחָה אֶת־אַזְכָּרָתָהּ (Then the priest shall raise up from the meal offering its memorial). Line 2 assumes a polemical tone. The rules of the fruits of newly planted trees must be followed punctiliously, not to be departed from in any manner. Interestingly, these lines dealing with עורלה suggest a tendency to interpret biblical passages for the benefit of the priestly class. That these texts have an argumentative tendency is evident in line 2 of this small fragment: "[And on]e[ shall not turn] to the right nor to [the left from what the priests will instruct . . . "].

### 3.2.2.9.3.3.4. Dimensions for Tithing (4Q270 F3iii:13a; 4Q271 F2:1–3)

The next theme deals with priestly tithing and its dimensions. But, how precisely this section begins is somewhat complicated, since the material fuses 4Q271 F2 with a small piece of parchment of 4Q270 F3iii, the miniscule beginning of which precedes what is extant in 4Q271 F2:1. Line 13 of 4Q271 F2 contains the letters את, plausibly reconstructed as תבואת based upon 4Q266 F6iv:8 immediately above. The entire clause would then possibly rest on 2 Chr 31:5. What follows it are the dimensions used to measure the priestly tithings, a subject partly anticipated above. Its emphasis, as in the preceding section, serves to highlight the generous portions made available for the priests. The program of measuring the tithing draws largely on Ezek 45–46. See for example הָאיפה והבת תכון אחד שניהן (line 2) which compares to הָאֵיפָה וְהַבַּת תֹּכֶן אֶחָד יִהְיֶה (the *ephah* and the *bat* have the same measurement) in Ezek 45:11. Verse 13b of the biblical text says, שִׁשִּׁית הָאֵיפָה מֵחֹמֶר הַחִטִּים (a sixth of an *ephah* from a *homer* of wheat) which corresponds to [וּמִן] החטים ש[שׁ]ית [האיפה לחמר] (and from [the wheat a si]xth [of an *ephah* per *homer*) in lines 2–3 of our text. Line 3b is ambiguous since it might be read in one or two ways: "Let no one separate himself from offering (a tithe) of one lamb per hundred (not one per two hundred as specified in Ezek 45:15)," or alternatively, "Let no one separate himself (from what Ezekiel says) by offering (as a tithe) one lamb per hundred (but follow the words of Ezekiel which is one lamb per two hundred)." Baumgarten suggests the latter alternative. This raises a question. If his understanding is right, why did the author not assert simply that the tithe of sheep is two hundred as required by Ezekiel? However, as was noted above, my understanding that the author tends to deviate from the biblical requirement by specifying larger shares for the priest would accord with the first rendition, namely requiring a double portion of the flock.

### 3.2.2.9.3.3.5. Priestly Blessing of the Bread (4Q271 F2:4–5a)

The hierarchical order at the table recorded in our text is more elaborate in 1QS 6:4b–6a. 1QSa 2:17–22 presents a yet more lengthy sequence: 1) the priest's blessing, 2) the blessing by the Anointed (Messiah) of Israel, then 3) the blessing of each member of the יחד according to his rank. It is apparent that the author of MTA does not know of this hierarchical seating at the meal. This accords with my general supposition that *Rule of the Community* was composed subsequently to MTA, and that 1QSa is a yet further literary development.

What survives of line 5b is incoherent.[249] My reconstruction posits that this line deals with a person selling a house after which it collapses. Could the buyer ask for compensation? The answer seems to be negative. If my rendition is correct, the subject matter here is parenthetical to the general theme dealing with the harvest and the priestly prerogatives.

### 3.2.2.9.3.4. Illicit Mixtures (4Q271 F2:6b–7)

Baumgarten translates the words שדה המעורב "mixed(?) field," Cook as "field mixed" and Martínez-Tigchelaar as "the mortgaged field."[250] In my opinion these words refer to כלאים. MTA dealt with this subject in 4Q271 F3:9–10 in connection with illicit sexual affairs or mismatched marriages, which are compared to illicit mixtures of produce and garments. A similar discussion is found in 4Q418 F103ii:6b–9.

```
[          ב]מסחורכה אל תערוב אשר] לרעכה          6
7 למה יהיה כלאים כֶּבְּפרד והייתה כלוב]ש שעטנז [בצמר ובפשתים ועבודתכה
כחור]ש[  8 בשור ובח]מו[ר] ו[י]חד[ו] ו[גם תבואתכה תה]יה לכה כ]זורע כלאים
```

---

[249] Baumgarten translates "house (belongs(?)) to the man, he may sell and with [ ] and then will he be guiltless," Martínez-Tigchelaar, "a house to someone sells and with . . . [ . . . ] and then he is innocent," and Cook, "to a man, he may sell it and when he [ . . . ] and then he shall be free of obligation." Baumgarten, DJD XVIII, 174; Martínez and Tigchelaar, *Scrolls Study Edition*, vol. 1, 619; Wise, Abegg and Cook, *Scrolls*, 64.

[250] Baumgarten, DJD XVIII, 174; Wise, Abegg and Cook, *Scrolls*, 64; Martínez and Tigchelaar, *Scrolls Study Edition*, vol. 1, 619.

אשר הזרע והמלאה̊ ותבוא̊[ת] 9 ה[כרם] יקד̊[ש יחדו ? וג[ם הונכה עם בשרכה
[יטמא̊<sup>251</sup> חייכה יתמו יחד ובחייכה לוא תמצא

... In] your business transactions do not intermingle (תערוב) what [belongs to your neighbor (with what belongs to you) . . . ] Why should it be *kil'ayim* as in the case of a mule or like one who wea[rs a mixed material] of wool and flax; and your field work (be) like plo[wing] with an or and a do[nke]y [to]geth[er]? And likewise your produce will b[ecome for you like] planting a mixture of *kil'ayim* in which the seed and the full vat and the produce [of] the [vineyard together] will become hol[y (forbidden). And like]wise your property with your sexual relations [will defile] your life. They will come to an end together. And you will no longer be living. (4Q418 F103ii:6b–9)

Like MTA and the above cited Musar text, MMT fuses the theme of illicit sexual affairs with the intermingling of illicit mixtures.

| | |
|---|---|
| ועל בה̊[מתו הטהורה] | F1-2iv:5 |
| כתוב שלוא לרבעה כלאים ועל לבושו[ כתוב שלוא] | F1-2iv:6 |
| יהיה שעטנז ושלוא לזרוע שדו וכ̊[רמו כלאים] | F1-2iv:7 |
| [ב]:גלל שהם קדושים ובני אהרון ק[דושי קדושים] | F1-2iv:8 |
| וא̊[ת̊ם יודעים שמקצת הכהנים וה̊[עם מתערבים] | F1-2iv:9 |
| [והם ]מתוככים ומטמא̊י̊[ם ]את זרע̊ [ם הקודש ואף] | F1-2iv:10 |
| את ]זרע[ם ע̊ם הזונ̊ות כ] | F1-2iv:11 |

And it is written with regard to [his clean an]imal not to intermingle illicit mixtures (*kil'ayim*). And concerning [one's] garments [it is written not] to wear *shatnez* and neither may one plant his field or [his] vi[neyard with *kil'ayim* be]cause they (Israel) are holy and the sons of Aaron are h[oly of holies. And y]ou are aware that some of the priests and the [people intermingle (מתערבים) and they] interbreed and defile the [holy] progeny [and moreover] (they defile) their [seed] with whores, f[or . . . ] (4Q396 F1-2iv:5b–11).

Unfortunately, virtually nothing survives from our text concerning the mixed field. Nevertheless, the DSS regard כלאים as a major rubric.

One of the most enigmatic passages in MTA is what survives in 4Q271 F2:7b and its parallels, 4Q269 F8:3 and 4Q270 F3iii:19. Baumgarten regards the juxtaposition of these fragments as tentative. The resulting composite, ממשפטי היחד, is interesting since the term יחד, so ubiquitous in *Rule of the Community* and elsewhere, would

---

<sup>251</sup> The restoration is mine.

only occur here in MTA.[252] שלוש פעמים that follows it is problematic. Our reconstruction of this sentence reflects an attempt to resolve the puzzle. It might to be a concluding remark to the harvest laws. The statement, "[ . . . And these are the statutes that shall be recorded among the injunctions of the com]munity three times in the book," proposed here might be a concluding remark to the harvest laws. Alternatively, it could qualify the next subject, the acquisition of animals and metals from pagans. In any case, this comment has a special interest of its own, as it is an internal remark of the author on the composition of MTA as a whole.

### 3.2.2.9.4. *Prohibition of Idolatrous Objects and Defilement from a Corpse (4Q271 F2:8–14)*

This section presents two issues: the prohibition of objects used by pagans and the cleansing of defiled matter. The first of these subjects introduces a topic dealt with later in CD 12:8b–11a. There the prohibition of trading with pagans is absolute, extending to any possessions including slaves. The question arises. What does our passage add to that text? It is likely that this injunction here attempts to stress the prohibition against acquiring not only animals, but also metals (objects favored in pagan worship). Is it possible that this ban exemplifies the previous injunction that certain laws must be recorded several times? Many rabbinic texts are devoted to the prohibitions against the use of idolatrous objects, especially in the Mishnah and Talmud of tractate עבודה זרה. The second subject pertaining to materials defiled by a corpse is likewise treated later in CD 12:15b–18.

These two sets of injunctions draw on a combination of Num 31:18–24 and 19:11–22. The first of these cited texts contains a list of Midianite metals taken by the Israelites. Verse 23 prescribes that any metal that can withstand fire must pass through it. Other objects must be cleansed with water. Line 10 of our text specifies that only metals which have emerged anew from the furnace can be brought into the holy community. Evidently MTA is more stringent than is the biblical text. The list of items in our pericope which have been defiled by a corpse (lines 10b–11), seem also to echo Num 31:20. However, the apodosis draws on Num 19. The requirement in our passage that

---

252 Note that the term היחד might occur in 4Q270 F7i:8 as restored from 1QS 7:18. However, given the general absence of this word in MTA in contrast to its frequency in *Rule of the Community*, the restoration of היחד here is questionable.

only a perfectly clean person can do the sprinkling (lines 11b–13a) is found in Num 19:18–19. MTA equates the state of purity of the cleanser to that of the person being cleansed in this biblical text. The cleanser in our passage must have been purified from any taint of defilement in the same manner that Scripture prescribed for the one being purified. Moreover, these lines have the addition that a minor— that is to say one who has not attained the age of twenty—may not perform the required sprinkling. Another supplement here, the clause ומן כל הכלֹי̇ם אשר תעשה מ[לֹ]אֹכה בהם (or any [manu]factured utensil[s]) consists of an amplification of the subject matter treated in the above cited text from CD dealing with materials defiled by a corpse. The basic idea of both passages is that objects made by people become defiled by their very presence in a house containing a corpse.

The rule of purification in MTA applies to both priests and laymen. On the other hand, the rabbinic sages were more lenient, restricting defilement from a corpse to priests only. These rules point to how grave MTA considered idolatry and corpse defilement.

### 3.2.2.9.5. *The Supervisor of the Camp (4Q266 F7)*

Much of column 1 of 4Q266 F7 has perished, with some letters and words surviving here and there. Problematic also is the placement of this fragment, as there are no parallel texts to sufficiently position it within a certain sequence. Baumgarten positions it at the end of the passages presumably bridging pages 20 and 15 of CD.[253] It is more likely, however, that in the material immediately preceding CD 15 the author dealt with the matter of oaths as does the top of that page. If so, 4Q270 F4 (paralleled in 4Q266 F12), the oath of the *soṭah*, is more appropriate for that linkage. The passage in our text seems to have as its main subject, admonition pertaining to the way of life in the camp dominated by its supervisor, a paramount personality initially mentioned in 4Q266 F5i:13b–14. This preceding text defines his position in the camp. According to this passage it is the מבקר who had the power to either admit or exclude members. He controlled the purse and was the lay expert who guided the priests who officially at least were in charge of the camp. Thus, for example, in matters of leprosy and other technical problems, the Supervisor would advise the priest on when to isolate or release a leper (CD 13:3b–6a).

---

[253] Baumgarten, DJD XVIII, 4.

Several passages in MTA deal with the issue of rebuke and some link it with the prohibition against keeping a grudge.[254] CD 9:2–5 relates to the moral order of the community led by the מבקר, similar to what is presumably behind our defective fragment. These passages draw on Lev 19:17–18.

17 לֹא־תִשְׂנָא אֶת־אָחִיךָ בִּלְבָבֶךָ הוֹכֵחַ תּוֹכִיחַ אֶת־עֲמִיתֶךָ וְלֹא־תִשָּׂא עָלָיו חֵטְא
18 לֹא־תִקֹּם וְלֹא־תִטֹּר אֶת־בְּנֵי עַמֶּךָ וְאָהַבְתָּ לְרֵעֲךָ כָּמוֹךָ אֲנִי יְהוָה

> You shall not hate your brother in your heart. You shall always reprove your friend so that you might not be sinning because of him. You shall not avenge nor bear a grudge against your people, but you shall love your neighbor as yourself. I am the Lord. (Lev 19:17–18)

Lines 4b–5a of our text appear to draw on a combination of Exod 34:7 and Ps 115:17. My reconstructions on column 1, although conjectural, do seem plausible in light of their biblical background.

The extant word רובעו (its fourth) at the end of line 7 of column 2 does not occur elsewhere in what survives of MTA. However, its cognate רביעית does appear in 1QS 6:25 where it relates to violations of camp discipline, a subject taught to candidates requesting admission, and presumably dealt with in the lost lines near our reconstruction. The two extant phrases in lines 9 and 10, reconstructed on the basis of 1QS 7:4, 8, 15, 17 and 18 may indicate that my reconstruction on line 7 has plausibility. Yet, its placement here is puzzling, for the subject matter of discipline spans from CD 14:18 (4Q266 F10i:11) to 4Q266 F11:3. Why these injunctions relating to discipline are positioned here in a pericope that does not seem to deal with this subject matter is not clear.

What precedes column 3 of our text fragmentarily survives in 4Q267 F8:1–2. What seems to remain by juxtaposing the extant portions of both 4Q266 F7iii:1 and 4Q267 F8:2 are the phrases לפני] בואם ([before] they come) and לפני ה[מבק]ר ה[מחנה] (in the presence of the [supervis]or of the [camp]), both of which relate to עד עמוד לפני המבקר (until he appears before the Supervisor) in CD 15:11. My reading of 4Q266 F7iii:1 and what immediately precedes it draws on that text.

The extant part then of 4Q266 F7ii and what follows until column 3 appears to be part of what MTA calls משפטים, injunctions governing the behavior of the candidates, such as speaking out of turn and frivolous conduct, actions which led the author to deal with the mat-

---

254  Cf. CD 7:2; 8:5–6 (19:18) and 9:2–5.

ters of disrespect of superiors and fellow members. What follows this gap is a matter pertaining to discipline—that candidates for admission as well as their associates learn how to exercise self-control prior to being taken into the association. It is the מבקר who is in charge of training novitiae to master the discipline of the camp.

MTA evidently responds to an implicit problem. Its basic premise stated repeatedly is to observe the commandments and precepts of the Torah. However, there are no biblical texts that directly deal with injunctions such as spitting or other capricious prohibitions prescribed in MTA and, by extension, *Rule of the Community*. Our text already alluded to this in the introductory section to this material on the מבקר (4Q266 F7i:3b–4a), suggesting that they come under the commandments in Lev 19:17, "You shall always reprove your friend . . . ," i.e. reprimanding them for breaches of good behavior. The allusion here to the admonition of righteous reproof reiterates this point.

Column iii:3b–4 seems to include the biblical injunctions to keep one's vows as part of this discipline and is a fitting conclusion to this subject matter. The use of the word [ס]המוא on line 5 gives us a clue as to the thought behind this line and what may have preceded it. It is characteristic of MTA to finalize various pericopes with a sentence that contains the verb מאס; hence the reconstruction that follows. The phrase [ישרים] מ[עשים מ[עשות ל (to [do upright] d]eeds),[255] if a valid reading, may be part of an introduction to MTA's list of offenses which might follow.

### 3.2.2.9.6. *List of Offenses (4Q267 F4 / 4Q270 F2i:1–14; i:15–21; ii:1–21 / 6Q15 F5)*

As was indicated above, Milik-Baumgarten proposed placing 4Q270 F2 just preceding the general laws bridging pages 20 and 15 of CD. Baumgarten makes the point that the formula ועתה שמעו לי found in 4Q270 F2ii:19 follows the catalogue of transgressors (F2i:9–ii:18) and necessarily introduces the legal material of this work. However, as I have argued, it is more plausible to front the nomistic subject matter and this list with the injunctions concerning integrity in business and marriage beginning with וזה פרוש זה (4Q267 F7:3), a phrase which probably was followed by המשפטים, forming a clause that the author of MTA characteristically uses to mark legal material.[256] Furthermore,

---

[255] Or, perhaps [נדולים] מ[עשים מ[עשות ל (to [do mighty d]eeds).

[256] זה פרוש המשפטים appears in CD 14:18 and 4Q266 F11:18 (paralleled in 4Q270 F7ii:12). Note however that in one instance זה פרוש is followed by מושב (CD 14:17).

it is not correct to presume as Baumgarten does that the formula
ועתה שמעו לי generally precedes law, since it occurs four other times
within so-called "admonition." Hence, we place the lists of capital
and non-capital offenses followed by a catalogue of other transgressions near the *conclusion* of the material spanning CD 20 and 15,
just before the oath of the *soṭah*. It seems that its positioning here
served an educational purpose. The preceding material concerned
itself primarily with the Supervisor's mode of admitting new members
to the Purity. The list of offenses that would follow itemizes to the
adherents the most important commandments of the Torah.

At this point, a general word should be should be said about the
list which both Baumgarten and Hempel discuss at some length.[257]
Baumgarten speculates that it resembles to some extent the list of
curses in Deut 27, a view accepted by Hempel. However in a later
article Baumgarten somewhat retracts this connection by stating
that "the curse formula, reflected in 1QS 2:11, is not found in
the D catalogue, and the nature of the transgressions is entirely
different."[258] Indeed, the curses of Deut 27 diverge also in syntax.
Hempel further speculates as to whether the list in our text constituted
an independent composition appended to MTA. She also wonders
whether the catalogue is sectarian. In my opinion, its *raison d'etre*
is to dispute conventional rules. For, as I show below, the sectarian
and Talmudic schools' understanding of many of the items in the list
diverge radically. The catalogue seems to be part of polemics against
the מסיגי (ה)גבול announced in line 4 of the book's introduction and
the דורשי החלקות cited in 4Qpap pIsaᶜ and 4QpNah,[259] mentioned
also in MTA in the phrase בעבור אשר דרשו בחלקות, "since they will
have interpreted (Him) with flattering words" (CD 1:18). As was
shown above, a number of the list's items are rules that contradict
the Pharisaic-Talmudic interpretation of the Torah. CD 5 with its
lengthy technical argumentation typifies the disputatious nature of
MTA's list.

Another matter concerns the placement of 4Q267 F4, an issue not
treated by Baumgarten. The reason for positioning its remains here
as a parallel to a portion of 4Q270 F2i rests on similar wording in

---

[257]  Baumgarten, DJD XVIII, 143–46; Hempel, *The Laws of the Damascus Document*, 161–70.

[258]  Joseph M Baumgarten, "The Laws of the Damascus Document—Between
Bible and Mishnah," in *The Damascus Document A Centennial of Discovery*, 18.

[259]  4Q163 F23ii:10; 4Q169 F3-4i:2, 7, ii:2, 4, iii:3.

4Q270 F2i:10 and 4Q267 F4:11–12.[260] Although there are differences, their general content is remarkably identical. There remain, however, problems of spacing in the alignment of parts of the surviving letters. 4Q270 F2i appears to be more expansive than is 4Q267 F4. Hence, our reconstruction of this primary text based upon 4Q267 F4 remains somewhat uncertain. Another problem relates to the fragmentary remnants of 6Q15 F5, whose wording may parallel 4Q270 F2ii:15–19. It is clear that fragments 1–4 of this document parallel portions of CD 4–7. Fragment 1 corresponds to CD 4:20–22, fragment 2 to CD 5:13–15, fragment 3 to CD 5:17–6:2 and fragment 4 to CD 6:21–7:2. It might be presumed then that fragment 5 matches a portion of text following CD 7:2, of which 4Q270 F2 is a part, albeit distant. This solution encounters some problems, however. חקק אל להעביר of 4Q270 F2ii:18 contains some variance from [עקב להבעיר of 6Q15 F5:4 as does [תור]ת אל בלבכם of 4Q270 F2ii:19 from ברי֯ת אל בלבב of 6Q15 F5:5.

## 3.2.2.9.6.1. Capital and Non-Capital Offenses (4Q267 F4:11–15 / 4Q270 F2i:7–20)

The first major subject treated in the combination posited above seems to have two basic categories: capital, followed by non-capital offenses. Lines 9–11 of 4Q270 F2i clearly describe cases that would warrant the death penalty. However, the two lines preceding them, drawn from 4Q267 F4:9–11, do not seem at first sight to cohere with the overriding subject. Nevertheless, what is interesting is that the phraseology of these two lines (displayed in the chart below) appear also in Ezek 18 and 22:1–17, passages whose offenses are designated as capital, the major theme of the former being individual responsibility. Line 7a of 4Q270 is difficult because of the sparsity of the extant words drawn from the presumed parallel. Yet, on the basis of *Rule of the Community* 1QSa 1:19–20, MTA here seems to have dealt with people who are excluded from holding public office on account of low intelligence, or perhaps, with unfit judges. The second matter relates to granting security for a debtor and the prohibition of usury. How these two subjects relate to what follows in a schema of capital offenses is unclear. It is possible that the matters of rebellion against leadership and taking usury were included among offenses warranting the death penalty.

---

[260] For wording in 4Q267 F4:11–12 that seems to be related to 4Q270 F2i:10: ידרו[ש את א]ו[ן]בות וא[א]ת ידעוני[ם את]ה.

How the last six words restored to 4Q270 F2i:8 (reconstructed from 4Q267 F4:10b–11a) would pertain to capital crime is also problematic. Baumgarten translates בהבל, a term not found in Ezekiel, as "for vanity." But, in our restoration אל יתן הוא מכ]ה בהבל may mean "[one] shall not [stri]ke (another) *for no reason*."[261] If this is a capital offense, it bears some resemblance to Lev 24:17: וְאִישׁ כִּי יַכֶּה כָּל־נֶפֶשׁ אָדָם מוֹת יוּמָת (And one who strikes any human being shall certainly be put to death). Yet, the *verb* in MTA would compare to that of the protasis of verse 19 in the biblical text, וְאִישׁ כִּי־יִתֵּן מוּם בַּעֲמִיתוֹ כַּאֲשֶׁר עָשָׂה כֵּן יֵעָשֶׂה לּוֹ (As for one who maims his neighbor: just as he has done, so it shall be done to him), a case which does not include the death penalty. If my rendition is correct, the noun מכה is used here in MTA rather than the verbal phrase אל יך (or אל יכה) to convey a strike *not* unto death, rather a more casual one that has been rendered frivolously, without thought, and which only wounds an individual. It is conceivable that a serious injury which becomes infected, ultimately resulting in death, would warrant the death penalty. It is interesting that, whereas Scripture calls for the so-called *lex talionis* (the law of retribution) for maiming an individual, the sages interpret it as monetary compensation, like that for killing another's animal (v. 21).

Although the above reconstruction is not alluded to in Ezekiel, much of the introductory portion of this list—which MTA appears to declare as warranting the death penalty—remarkably echoes the prophet.[262] Here follows a table which illustrates the words and concepts (either literal or conceptual) of this MTA text and related biblical passages, the majority of which are from Ezekiel.

| MTA Reference | Words | Bible Reference | Words |
|---|---|---|---|
| 4Q267 F4:10 | ע]רובות | Prov 17:18 | עֹרֵב עֲרֻבָּה |
| 4Q267 F4:10 | נש]ך | Ezek 18:8, 13, 17; 22:12 | נֶשֶׁךְ |
| 4Q267 F4:10 | תרבית | Ezek 18:8, 13, 17; 22:12; Prov 28:8 | תַּרְבִּית |
| 4Q267 F4:11 | מכ]ה בהבל | Lev 24:19 | מוּם |
| 4Q270 F2i:12 | [גוים] | Ezek 22:15 | גּוֹיִם |
| 4Q270 F2i:17 | [אלמנה] | Ezek 22:7 | אַלְמָנָה |
| 4Q270 F2i:9–ii:18 | (תועבה) | Ezek 22:2, 11 | תּוֹעֵבָה |
| 4Q267 F4:11–12/ 4Q270 F2r:10 | ידעונים, אוב/אובות | Ezek 18:12, 15; 22:3, 4 | גִּלּוּלִים |

---

[261] I thank Tim Undheim for suggesting the possibility of reading מכ]ה בהבל in 4Q267 F4:11.

[262] See the introductory section 1.4 dealing with capital offenses and my comments on CD 12:2a–3.

These parallel items are additional examples of the linkage between the composition of MTA and Ezekiel found in other parts of this work.[263] These lines may give us a clue that the injunctions listed in the so-called catalog frequently draw on the legal material in prophetic or haggiographic writings.

ידרוש באוב ובידעֹונים in 4Q270 F2i:10 (inquires by means of a medium or wizards) draws on Lev 20:6 where the punishment is being cut off from one's people, and Lev 20:27 where it is death through stoning. Maimonides reconciles the two texts by interpreting the former as referring to the sculpturing of these idols, whereas the death penalty is for actually worshipping them in the presence of witnesses (Rambam, *Laws of Idolatry* 6, 1). Unlike the sages of the Mishnah and Talmud, the author of MTA makes no distinction between what the rabbis called כרת (excision) and the death penalty. Apparently all commandments in Scripture whose punishment is not specified, result in death. Our text also resembles CD 12:2b–3a in condemning necromancy as a capital offense.

שם, referring to the name of God (4Q270 F2i:11), is frequent in MTA, sometimes occurring as שֹם קֹדֹ(וֹ)שו, "His Holy Name" (CD 20:34; 4Q266 F5i:9), but more often without any modifier.[264] The concept of profaning God's name occurs also below in CD 15:3. Note that both here and in that passage the text draws on biblical parallels. Our wording corresponds to Lev 20:3 where giving one's children to Molech profanes the holy name of God. CD 15:3 on the other hand follows Lev 19:12 in connection with false oaths. Note also that Lev 20:3 suggests that profaning God's name invokes the death penalty. CD 15:3–5 also indicates that taking a false oath entails punishment by death: "And if he does take an oath (using God's name explicitly) he is in violation and profanes the name (of God). But if the judges make (him) swear with the curses of the covenant, if he transgresses, he is guilty and must confess and make amends so as not to bear sin [and] die." In other words, if the violator fails to confess, he will lose his life.

The lost material of 4Q270 F2i:13b–16a and what continues in lines 16b through the end of the column presumably contrasted with the preceding material which we have placed under the rubric of offenses warranting death. Differing from crimes of idolatry, whose penalty

---

[263] See CD 3:21–4:2a.
[264] See also שם הנכבד (the Honorific Name) in 1QS 6:27.

according to Scripture is capital in nature, the offenses itemized
in this section—one of which seems to be profaning the Sabbath
(CD 12:3b–5a), immediately following the death penalty for necromancy (CD 12:2b–3a)—are exempted from the death penalty. As discussed below pertaining to legislation concerning the Sabbath in CD
10:14–11:18a (commentary section 3.2.2.9.12), the reasoning behind
the leniency concerning the Sabbath are its numerous legal categories,
the violation of any of which would result in death.

The clause spanning from lines 16b–17a, [בְּתֹולִיֹה בבית [אביה]]
([while] in her virginity in the house [of her father]), apparently dealt
with a woman who was suspected of having relations with a man previous to her marriage, amplified earlier in 4Q271 F3:11–13. Whereas
rabbinic law would not regard this as a criminal act, our text appears
to do so. Nevertheless, it would not be regarded as a capital offense
under sectarian law, since she had not been married to anyone. The
same applies to a widow who has relations with a man, whose wording
I also fill in from 4Q271.

Lines 18b–20, as reconstructed on the basis of CD 12:3b–5a; *Jub.*
50:8; Exod 34:21 and 35:2–3, stress that offenses done on the Sabbath
are not to be considered capital. Although MTA generally follows *Jubilees*, a work it describes as perfect (CD 16:2–4), its leniency concerning
sabbath labor is an outright dissent from this venerable source.

> And the man that does any work on it shall die: whoever desecrates that
> day, whoever lies with (his) wife, or whoever says he will do something
> on it, that he will set out on a journey thereon in regard to any buying
> or selling: and whoever draws water thereon which he had not prepared
> for himself on the sixth day, and whoever takes up any burden to carry
> it out of his tent or out of his house shall die. (*Jub.* 50:8)[265]

MTA diverges also from Talmudic legislation which, in accordance
with Exod 35:2–3, prescribes the death penalty for any of thirty-
nine kinds of sabbath labor if done in the presence of two witnesses
and "forewarning" (התראה). MTA's specific departure from Scripture is noteworthy. In general, its stringency contrasts sharply with
the rabbinic tradition. According to the rabbis, prohibitions whose
punishment is not specified in Scripture are subject to thirty-nine
lashes, not to death.

---

[265] Charles, 259–60.

## 3.2.2.9.6.2. A List of Transgressions and the Eschatological Punishment of the Transgressors (4Q270 F2ii:1–14, 15–21 / 6Q15 F5)

As we have seen, MTA divides the offenses into capital and non-capital violations. There is yet another category—transgressions whose doers will be punished in the eschatological age before the advent of the Messiah. The extant letters עֲל קְדוֹ (probably [עֲל קְדוֹ]שה) in line 1 of 4Q270 F2ii seem to suggest a heading for the material that follows up to line 18. This pericope, the first portion of which has perished, dealt with a variety of themes pertaining to sanctity, many of which are polemical: a) the sanctity of marriage and its violations (lines 2–3); b) the sanctity of priestly perquisites (lines 5–10a); c) the nature of idolatrous desecration (lines 10b–11a); d) general defilements (lines 11b–12; e) revealing Israel's secrets to pagans (line 13a); f) rebellion against Israel's leadership and commandments (lines 13b–15a); g) the holiness of food (line 15b) and h) illicit sexual relations (lines 15c–17a).

### 3.2.2.9.6.2.1. The Sanctity of Marriage and Its Violations (4Q270 F2ii:2–3)

The words [אֶל מְקוֹר[ה (into [her] source) at the beginning of line 3 suggest a reconstruction for lines 2–3 drawing upon Lev 20:18. The text likely continued with the subject of having relations with a menstruous woman.

### 3.2.2.9.6.2.2. The Sanctity of Priestly Perquisites (4Q270 F2ii:5–10a)

For our restoration in lines 5b–6a, compare CD 6:20. Baumgarten's reading הֻמַּטַּעַת [הרביעית] (the planting [in the fourth year . . . ]) in line 6b presupposes his opinion that MTA understood *orlah*, the status of the first three years of planting, to be completely prohibited as it is in rabbinics, whereas the produce of the fourth year was for the priests.[266] As I understand MTA, however, its author perceived *orlah* as belonging to the priests, a view also maintained in 4QMMT as was cited above in commenting on this subject in 4Q266 F6iv—"And also concerning (the fruits of) trees for food planted in the land of

---

[266] See Baumgarten, DJD XVIII, 59–61.

Israel: they are to be dealt with like first fruits belonging to the priests"
(a composite of 4Q394 F8iv:12–13; 4Q396 F1-2iii:2–3 and 4Q397
F6-13:4–5). Hence, our reconstruction [הכרם וכל עצי המאכל] הֵמְּטָעֵת
which borrows from [וְכֹל עֵצֵי הַפְּרִי וכל עֵצִי הֵמֹּאכל] in נטעי הכר[ם
4Q266 F6iv:2 (compare also עצי המאכל in the above cited 4QMMT
composite). It is interesting that the *orlah* is separated from the other
priestly perquisites given in lines 5–10a of our text. Perhaps it was
meant to be included under the rubric of the first fruits designated
for the priests (line 7). Returning to the beginning of this section,
as restored, it starts with a general statement [או אשר יְמַחֵא להרים
[     ], "[or whoever] declines (?) to raise up [ . . . ]"

The word פרוש restored into the lacuna following it hints at the
diversity of opinion that existed between this priestly sect and what
we know the Pharisaic-Talmudic sages ordained. As alluded in the
above paragraph, the priestly perquisite of the *orlah* was controversial.
Thus, Lev 19:23–25 defines fruit grown during the first three years of
a tree's life as *orlah*, which the sages interpret as not being able to be
consumed at all. The fruit of its fourth is regarded as קֹדֶשׁ הִלּוּלִים לַיהוָה
(holy, praises to the Lord)—what the sages understand as כרם רבעי (a
garden in the fourth year), produce to be carried to Jerusalem. On the
other hand, the sect regarded the fruit of the first three as belonging
to the priests, able to be exchanged in the fourth for other crops,
whereas the produce of the fourth year was sanctified and unable to
be eaten. Indeed, there arose divergences of interpretation pertaining
to most of the items detailed in this list of transgressions. A glaring
example of the differences between the schools is having relations
with one's wife during the Sabbath cited above. In the view of the
sages, this is a commendable act (a מצוה), while our text condemns it.
Another such divergence concerns the issue of pregnancy. Our text
below in line 15b prohibits slaughtering and consuming a pregnant
animal. It also bans having sexual relations with a pregnant woman
(lines 15c–16a). The sages of the Mishnah and Talmud sanction
both. CD 5:7b–10a refutes the Pharisaic position which permits
marrying one's niece. As was noted above, al-Qirqisani, writing in
the tenth century, called attention to this passage, pointing out its
exceptionality. According to him, Zadok did not adduce proofs to
any of his statements save this alone.[267]

---

[267] Nemoy, "Jewish Sects," 326.

Another perquisite mentioned here in lines 9b–10a for the first time relates to a found object whose owner cannot be identified. Whereas in the biblical and rabbinic tradition it would belong to the finder (Deut 22:1–3), MTA assigns it to the priest (CD 9:10b–16a). Both Lev 5:21–26 and MTA (4Q270 F2ii:10) prescribe that, if the finder fails to return the object he must pay an additional fifth of its value. However, whereas according to the Bible the fifth is to be given to the owner, based on CD 9:13–16 MTA evidently apportions it to the priest. Neither CD 9 nor our text specifies the identity of the sacerdote to whom it is to be given. Presumably the finder may designate it for any of the "sons of Aaron."

### 3.2.2.9.6.2.3. The Nature of Idolatrous Desecration (4Q270 F2ii:10b–11a)

Pertaining to the word בשמותם (by their names), Baumgarten cites *J.W.* 3:142 which asserts that the Essenes guarded the names of the angels, to which our text might refer. However, this linkage is unlikely since the extant wording following it deals with the defiling of God's Holy Spirit, and would not refer to angels. Our reconstruction או ⁱ[משולו בם רוחות בליעל ויכתבו] (or [any whom the spirits of Belial take sway of and hence, are recorded]. . . ) in line 10, taken in part from CD 12:2 and 14:4, provides a contrast to the clause רוח קודשו (His Holy Spirit) and a parallel to the infinitive לטמא (for defiling) in line 11.

### 3.2.2.9.6.2.4. General Defilements (4Q270 F2ii:11b–12)

The basis for our reconstruction at the end of line 11 is twofold. The roots טמא and נגע occur in the adjoining clauses. Furthermore Lev 22:4, from which we restore the lacuna, contains צָרוּעַ (leprous), טְמֵא־נֶפֶשׁ (a defiled person) and זָב (one who has a discharge), paralleling בנגע צרעת (with the affliction of leprosy) and זוב טמא[א] (uncle[an] flux) in line 12 of our text. The reading for the lacuna at the end of line 12 draws on Lev 15:11. As seen above, MTA devotes a large pericope to the issue of leprosy (compare 4Q272 F1, paralleled in 4Q266 F6i, 4Q269 F7 and 4Q273 F4ii).

### 3.2.2.9.6.2.5. Revealing Israel's Secrets to Pagans (4Q270 F2ii:13a)

The wording here resembles that of the Ein Gedi inscription: מן הי

דגלי רזה דקרתה לעממיה (or whoever reveals the secrets of the city to the pagans).[268] Compare also 11QT 64:6b–8a:

כי     6

7 יהיה איש רכיל בעמו ומשלים את עמו לגוי נכר ועושה רעה בעמו

8 ותליתמה אותו על העץ וימת

If one gossips against his people, handing over his people to a foreign nation, doing evil to his people, you shall hang him on a tree. Let him die. (11QT 64:6b–8a)

### 3.2.2.9.6.2.6. Rebellion against Israel's Leadership and Commandments (4Q270 F2ii:13b–15a)

In accordance with 11QT 64:10; CD 2:12–13 and 1QS 6:26 see Baumgarten for the restoration of these lines. For speaking evil against authority which would result in the fertile land turning into desert, see CD 5:21.

### 3.2.2.9.6.2.7. The Status of a Fetus (4Q270 F2ii:15b)

As we have stated above, the prohibition against slaughtering a pregnant animal differs from rabbinic tradition which sanctions it. On this ban, see also 11QT 52:5–7a:

5     ולוא תזבח לי שור ושה ועז והמה מלאות כי תועבה המה לי

6 ושור ושה אותו ואת בנו לוא תזבח ביום אחד ולוא תכה אם

7 על בנים

You shall not sacrifice to me an ox a lamb or a goat when they are full (pregnant), for (slaughtering) them is an abomination to me. And an ox or a lamb with its offspring you may not slaughter at the same time. And you shall not strike the mother with her offspring. (11QT 52:5–7a)

This text diverges from Talmudic tradition. According to the sages, the prohibition against slaughtering a young calf extends from birth to the seventh day of its life (*Hullin* 78:2). However, *Temple Scroll*, by linking Lev 22:28 and a paraphrase of Gen 32:12 which contains the phrase אֵם עַל־בָּנִים in the context of Jacob fearing that Esau might strike him together with all of his clan, suggests that ביום אחד means "at the same time." In other words, it is prohibited to slaughter a fetus when in its mother's womb.

---

[268] Benjamin Mazar, "כתובת רצפת בית־כנסת בעין־גדי," *Tarbiz* 40 (1971): 20. The translation is mine.

Interestingly, the item that follows this prohibition in MTA bans intercourse with a pregnant woman. Baumgarten speculates that the reason for both of these interdictions was concern for the fetus, an independent creation.[269] The ban in MMT pertaining to the fetus of an animal, a clause possibly elucidating this text, is puzzling.

ועל] האוכל [אנח]נו חושבים שאיאכל את הולד

[שבמעי אמו לאחר שחיטתו ואתם יודעים שהו]א כן והדבר כתוב עברה[270]

Qimron translates it, "[ . . . And concerning] eating (a fetus): we are of the opinion that the fetus [found in the (dead) mother's womb may be eaten (only) after it has been ritually slaughtered. And you know that it is] so, namely that the ruling refers (to) a pregnant animal."[271] His reconstruction of this text rests on the word שאיאכל, which he assumes is positive, i.e. that one may eat an embryo found in the womb of its mother if it has been slaughtered properly. He bases his reading on MMT's spelling שא for the relative -ש.[272] If so, this text would diverge from our line in MTA which clearly forbids the slaughtering (and presumably the consumption) of a pregnant animal. Moreover, given the broader biblical injunction in Lev 22:28 cited above, it is unlikely that this MMT text would devote a special clause authorizing its consumption. שאיאכל may, instead, be a combination of שאי and יאכל, i.e. that one may *not* eat the embryo. The next item in the list, that of prohibiting sexual relations with a pregnant woman, would seem to support our contention—that lying with a pregnant woman as well as eating the embryo of a pregnant animal are both banned according to MTA.

### 3.2.2.9.6.2.8. Illicit Sexual Relations (4Q270 F2ii:15c–17a)

As stated above, the clause prohibiting the marriage of a niece mirrors CD 5:7b–10a. The reappearance of this prohibition supports my contention that MTA is a unitary work, not a composite as is generally contended. Whereas the mention of the flow of blood in the prohibition of intercourse with a pregnant woman might allude to injury of the fetus as speculated above, the reference to the emission of blood more likely highlights the illicit nature of sexual activity

---

[269] Baumgarten, "The Laws," 20.
[270] A composite of 4Q394 F8iii:7–9; 4Q396 F1-2i:3–4 and 4Q397 F4:2.
[271] Qimron, DJD X, 50.
[272] Qimron, DJD X, 68–69.

during pregnancy.[273] The ban on homosexuality completes the list of
sexual prohibitions.

### 3.2.2.9.6.2.9. The Punishment of the Transgressors During the Eschaton (4Q270 F2ii:17b–18)

What follows in lines 17b–18 concludes the broader list of biblical
offenses that began in column 1 of 4Q270 F2. As reconstructed, it
serves to underscore the divinely decreed commandments in contrast
to the disciplinary injunctions found near the conclusion of MTA
(14:18b–22; 4Q266 F10ii:1–15; 4Q270 F7i:6b–16a; 4Q266 F11:1–3a).
Our text is a cautionary statement admonishing those who diverge
from the group's practice. The punishment of these transgressors will
be fatal during the eschatological epoch just prior to the advent of
the Messiah. For the reconstruction עוברי א[ת מצות] (transgressors [of
the commandments]) see the clause לָמָה אַתֶּם עֹבְרִים אֶת־מִצְוֹת יְהוָה (Why
do you transgress the commandments of the Lord?) in 2 Chr 24:20.
For the restoration חקק אל להעביר בח[רון אפו] (God has legislated to
render destruction by [His] w[rath]) compare [והו]א• חקוק קץ חרון
לעם לא ידעהו ([And H]e decreed epoch(s) of anger for a people who
knew Him not) above in 4Q266 F2i:3 (4Q268 F1:5). Baumgarten
notes the word play of עוברי and להעביר.[274] In displaying a purpose
of the divine law as to destroy evil at the end of time, these clauses
serve as a hortatory warning that, much like stated in Num 32:23b,
hidden transgressions will not go unpunished.

### 3.2.2.9.7. *The Acts of God in History (4Q270 F2ii:19–21)*

The author resumes here the phrase ועתה שמעו (לי), a topical clause
which has appeared once in the introduction to this work (4Q266
F1:5) and three times at the beginning of the body of MTA (CD
1:1; 2:2 and 14). Scrollists used to take the phrase ועתה שמעו to
characterize the work as a whole. Now, we can see that the writer
employs it to begin new themes wherein he addresses his audience.
Three of the four introductory passages containing this formula,
and possibly our text as well, have a single theme: revealing מעשי
אל (the acts of God), meaning what is now known as "theology."
Under this phrase, our author incorporates a number of concepts.

---

[273]  See also Joseph M. Baumgarten, "A Fragment on Fetal Life and Pregnancy
in 4Q270," in *Pomegranates and Golden Bells* (ed. D. P. Wright, D. N. Freedman and
A. Hurvitz; Winona Lake, Indiana: Eisenbrauns, 1995), 448.
[274]  Baumgarten, "The Laws," 21.

He refers first primarily to the acts of creation listed in *Jub.* 2 as the twenty-two acts of creation. To know what is good and evil or righteous and wicked is a second element of this general concept. It recalls what is stated in 4Q417 F1i:17–18, a text depicting the book of Haguy, a work mentioned three times in MTA. These two lines in 4Q417 expose the book of Haguy as the first to record the distinction between good and evil: "But Haguy had not as yet been given to the spirit of flesh, for it (the spirit of flesh) had as yet not known the difference between good and evil as part of his spiritual nature." A third feature of מעשי אל is the history of generations, or *Urzeit* and *Endzeit*. A fourth pertains to the legal material, the תורה as it is to be observed during the eschaton. Finally, מעשי אל applies to features of the messianic epoch itself.

What is new in the formula of our text is the clause ו[בינו] תור[ת] אל בלבבכ[ם] (and [discern] the Tora[h of God in you heart]).[275] As was stated, it underscores the legal aspect of this document, the תורה as it is to be observed during the eschaton, an idea also present in the title of this work, מדרש התורה האחרון, and whose era is restored plausibly in line 18b of our text. The author continues with wording familiar from MTA but in a new context. The extant portion concludes with understanding the acts of every generation, an important theme in MTA.[276] This new fragmentary reappearance in 4Q270 F2 is important in that it tells us the author used the formula ועתה שמעו לי elsewhere in his work, a clause that is unique to this composition. In other words, it shows that, contrary to the general assumption that the Damascus Document combines sections from a variety of sources, we have to suppose that the MTA composite is a unitary composition.

The five appearances of formulas beginning with ועתה שמעו ל(א)י strengthen the impression that the author regarded his audience

---

[275] Baumgarten interposes ו[שימו]. However, ו[בינו] is more likely. Cf. CD 1:1 and 2:14.

[276] It is conceivable that this text, which is partly cited in MMT (4Q397 F14-21:11), may have continued with בספר כתוב (in the book it is written), where the book refers to the מדרש התורה האחרון. If so, MMT alludes to our passage and is posterior to MTA. Alternatively, we might reconstruct the lacuna and what continues into the next page of 4Q270 with חסדי נביאים תזכרו ובמעשי חסידיכם תתפארו, sapiential terminology drawn from 11Q5 (11QPs^a) 22:3–6, to read, "And when you discern the events of each generation, [you will recall the pious acts of your prophets and you will be beautified by the deeds of your pious ones . . . ]." Our reconstruction תבינו במעשי אל (you will understand the acts of God) reflects ideology elsewhere in MTA.

as having a share in this work. The sobriquets באי ברית, יודעי צדק, and בנים indicate this was a new organization whose terminology was still fluent. The term יחד, so common in *Rule of the Community* but occurring only once in MTA, had as yet not been formulated. This further suggests the author was addressing a new structure just emerging, whose nomenclature had as yet not been set.

### 3.2.2.9.8. *Domestic Issues (4Q273 F5; 4Q270 F4 / 4Q266 F12)*

The placement of 4Q273 F5 and the parallel texts 4Q270 F4 and 4Q266 F12 is uncertain. The rationale for positioning the latter two parallel passages just before CD 15 rests on some similar wording between them and the medieval version. The Cave texts and CD 15–16 and 9:1 contain the subject of curses and oaths. However, the location of 4Q273 F5 within MTA is less certain. 4Q273 is unique among the MTA manuscripts, in that while the others are inscribed on parchment, it is a papyrus. Moreover, its remaining wordage is crumby. The words of fragment 5 of this manuscript are more faded than usual in this document. What remains is difficult to read and its subject matter is somewhat impenetrable. Part of the problem in identifying the location and content of this piece results from the fact that considerable sections of MTA have perished. See also the number of unincorporated fragments listed in chapter four. Its placement in the general context of 4Q270 F4 is provisional. However, as reconstructed, it does appear to contain material that relates to the domestic issues of 4Q270 F4 and 4Q266 F12, cited above. Yet, it does not necessarily sequentially precede these two parallel fragments. Lines 2–4a seem to conclude the unit of subject matter dealing with the *soṭah* (the straying wife), perhaps reflecting another variant version to this pericope. The phrase שבה וכסתה א]ת פניה] (she shall turn and cover [her face]) in line 2 appears to deal with the suspect who must conceal her face during the ordeal. Although the extant wording of these lines does not correspond to that of 4Q270 F4 and 4Q266 F12, its content is certainly parallel. This will be discussed below following my comments on 4Q270 F4:1b–13a (section 3.2.2.9.8.1) pertaining to the issue of the *soṭah*. 4Q273 F5:4b–5 continues with marital themes, matters also addressed in 4Q270 F4:13b–21.

### 3.2.2.9.8.1. The Straying Wife (4Q270 F4:1b–13a; 4Q266 F12:1–4; 4Q273 F5:2–4a)

4Q270 F4:1b–13a is a lengthy section relating to the *soṭah* (Num 5:12–31). As was mentioned and will be commented upon below, our rationale for positioning it and its parallels here rather than elsewhere in the MTA material not conjoining with CD rests in part on lexical similarities between it and CD 15. Both deal with the term אלה (curse) and the subject of oath taking. Hence, we sequence it following the formula ועתה שמעו לי of 4Q270 F2ii:19–21. By reason of the oath and covenantal terminology throughout and following into CD 15:1–16:22 and 9:1, it stands as *new* material in the legal portion of MTA. The matter of the straying wife is apparently introduced by the topical protasis " . . . כי" characteristic of legal material. The wording mainly deals with rules that are implied in the biblical text with important elucidations. Numbers 5:13 states that the ordeal proceeds when there is no single witness attesting adultery (וְעֵד אֵין בָּהּ). Our passage expands upon this by supposing a case where there is a *single* witness. Does it suffice to obviate the ordeal? The answer seems to be that two witnesses are not needed, provided that the single observer attests to the actual act of adultery rather than merely being suspicious of it. *Mishnah Sotah* 6:1–4 affirms the same interpretation of the biblical wording. Lines 3b–4a of our text state that if the suspected woman responds to the charge by claiming that she was under duress, she is absolved and may return to her husband. My reconstruction rests in part on 4Q266 F5i:1 which contains the word תנק[ה] (she is innoc[ent]), evidently connected with the term אנוס (under compulsion) in line 2.

4Q270 F4:4b–5a deals with a case involving the flow of blood. Citing Milik, Baumgarten inserts the negative לא to read כי אם דמה יצוא [לא יצא], translating it "unless her blood does [not] come forth," arguing that the absence of menstrual bleeding is evidence of pregnancy.[277] It is more likely, however, that the issue under consideration is the absence of the flow of virginal blood, a matter described at length in Deut 22:13–21 and in *Mishnah Ketubbot* 1:1. Deuteronomy asserts that in the case wherein a man who suspects that his bride has committed adultery, since he could not find her virginal blood, the parents of the bride may refute the claim by spreading out the (bloody) sheet

---

[277] Baumgarten, DJD XVIII, 153.

as evidence of her virginity. Our text makes a similar point that her husband may (not) bring charges of infidelity unless no (virginal) blood whatsoever was found. The wording אל יב[יאה] ([He may not br]ing her . . . ) in line 4 of our text returns to that of line 1 of our passage, "[ . . . When] a man comes to impose a curse on (his) wife (under suspicion of adultery) . . . "

It is my presumption that line 5 refers to the role of the Supervisor of the camp in the *soṭah* ordeal. He may not himself execute the oath upon the woman, but he should defer to a priest whether expert or not. This parallels the case of leprosy in CD 13:4b–7a which states that the מבקר may not deal with the matter at all, even in the absence of a competent priest.

CD 13:4                                          ואם
CD 13:5 משפט לתורת נגע יהיה באיש ובא הכהן ועמד במחנה והבינו
CD 13:6 המבקר בפרוש התורה *vac* ואם פתי הוא הוא יסגירנו כי להם
CD 13:7 המשפט

> But if there is a case regarding the law of leprosy, the priest shall come and stand up in the camp (to take charge), and (if the priest lacks competence) the Supervisor shall explain to him the details of the Torah. And even if he (the priest) is a fool, nevertheless he (the priest) must be in charge of quarantining him (the leper), for they alone have the authority to do so. (CD 13:4b–7a)

Here, in the matter of our *soṭah* case, it is the priest who is in charge of making the woman take the oath (line 6).

The wording ופרע [הכהן את ראשה] (And [the priest] shall expose [her head]) quotes a portion of Num 5:18, presuming that the reader can complete the biblical words "and place upon her hands the memorial offering . . . " Our text seems to continue with [והשביע את האשה] ([and he shall make] the woman [swear]), paraphrasing a clause picked up in verse 21. The succeeding words, והשקה את [האשה את מי המרים המאררים] (and make [the woman] drink [the waters of bitterness that induce the curse]), quote from verse 24.

Baumgarten understands the restored masculine suffix of מיד in line 7b as referring to the priest. The woman may not take anything from the priest's hand lest he or a vessel he is holding become contaminated.[278] If so, this text appears to contravene the wording of verse 25 of the biblical passage, which commands the priest to take

---

278 Baumgarten, DJD XVIII, 154.

the jealousy offering from the woman's hand וְלָקַח הַכֹּהֵן מִיַּד הָאִשָּׁה אֵת)
(מִנְחַת הַקְּנָאֹת, a clause which necessarily implies that the priest is not
defiled. It seems that our text is saying that, although she is to give
the offering to the priest, she may not touch any other food or the
bitter waters. This may mean that, whereas she hands over to the
priest the jealousy offering, it is the priest alone who may execute
the consumption of the bitter water.

Lines 9b–11a, partly supported by its parallel, 4Q266 F12:1–2,
articulates a point implied in lines 1–2, that if the adultery had been
committed in the presence of witnesses, there would be no need for
the ordeal, since this would warrant a capital offense.

The word המלכים at the end of line 12, as Baumgarten notes,
is puzzling. Our conjectural reading, drawing on Psalm 2:10, may
resolve the puzzle. If so, it accounts for magic ascribed in Num
5:27–28, a rite that enables the bitter waters to give a verdict of
absolute guilt or innocence. The psalmic citation וְעַתָּה מְלָכִים הַשְׂכִּילוּ
הִוָּסְרוּ שֹׁפְטֵי אָרֶץ (And now, O kings, be skillful; act prudently O judges
of the land) affirms the superiority of the Israelite court, which as
paraphrased here, buttresses the claim that the Israelite system of
justice is able to determine the woman's guilt or innocence.

4Q273 F5, the papyrus, has text which seems to pertain to the *sotah*
pericope, perhaps to its ending. Lines 2b–4a insinuate that she must
cover her face during the process. Lines 3b–4a, "And behold that is
what he will relate to them. They are [all the] eternal [statute]s," seem
to have two purposes: 1) to conclude this long section, and 2) to sustain
the validity of these rules, some of which perhaps were objectionable.
For example, the biblical rule that the drinking of the bitter waters
would, if guilty, result in death and, if innocent, in pregnancy, may
have been deemed unacceptable to some. However, our author stresses
that these rules are eternal and immutable.

### 3.2.2.9.8.2. Prohibited Marriages (4Q273 F5:2b–5; 4Q270 F4:13b–21)

As stated above, what follows in lines 13b–21 of 4Q270 pertains to
marital issues. Although impossible to place in the context of the
entire document, I include lines 2b–5 of the papyrus fragment with
the larger text from 4Q270, since they likewise appear to contain
directives pertaining to matrimony.

### 3.2.2.9.8.2.1. Bigamy (4Q273 F5:4b)

4Q273 F5 has another line and a half of text beyond that pertaining to the straying wife. Line 4b evidently deals with bigamy. CD 4:20–5:2 contains an attack against marrying two wives. As reconstructed, the text draws on Lev 18:18, וְאִשָּׁה אֶל־אֲחֹתָהּ לֹא תִקָּח לִצְרֹר לְגַלּוֹת עֶרְוָתָהּ עָלֶיהָ בְּחַיֶּיהָ (You shall not marry a woman as a rival to her sister, to uncover her nakedness in her lifetime). According to the sages of the Talmud, this verse prohibits a man from marrying two sisters during their lifetime. However, in sectarian texts the word אחות is taken to designate a "rival wife," and, in this sense, is a prohibition against bigamy. The possible reiteration banning polygamy reflects the author's tendency to repeat significant points.

### 3.2.2.9.8.2.2. Marriage during Menstruation (4Q273 F5:5)

The next point in this fragment is obscure, but appears to prohibit marrying a woman during her menses.

### 3.2.2.9.8.2.3. A Slave Marrying a Priest (4Q270 F4:13b–21)

At this point we return to 4Q270 F4:13b–21 which is partially paralleled in what remains of 4Q266 F12:5–9. Our text devotes eight fragmentary lines to the topic of a priest marrying an unredeemed slave. It fuses four biblical passages: Lev 19:20–22, Exod 21:7–11, Deut 21:10–14 and Lev 22:10–11. The first pertains to a man having relations with an unredeemed woman. He shall present a guilt offering for atonement. The text from Exodus deals with a man who has sold his daughter as a slave. He cannot treat her like any other slaves. He may not sell her as he would male servants. If he takes another woman, he may not reduce her rights, but must treat her like any other Israelite daughter. The third biblical text pertains to the marrying of a captive woman, a passage amplified in 11QT 63:10–15. She must stay in his home for one month, weeping for her family. Then he may marry her. The fourth relates to a priest acquiring a slave.

In Talmudic literature the injunction in Exod 21 refers to a Hebrew slave, whereas Lev 19 and Deut 21 pertain to a case where the servant or maiden is a pagan. As far as we can tell from the difficult text, MTA combines the four biblical themes into a single case, modifying it radically. Whereas Lev 19:20 has the verb יִשְׁכַּב, our text adds the phrase אל יקרב before ישכב [ואל], meaning that a priest may not come near her. What the Bible calls נֶחֱרֶפֶת, our text identifies as the passive participle חרופה, a term also used in Talmudic tradition. What is strange is the juxtaposition of the slave with the captive beauty. Deut 21:13 specifies that the man must bring her to his house for a month before marrying her. The *Temple Scroll*, evidently followed almost literally in our text, prescribes that for seven years she may not touch anything holy of the טהרה, the priestly Purity. As to the phrase [כאשר] אמר in line 15b, this clause in the DSS normally flags a biblical citation. However, as far as we can tell, here it appears to introduce a direct citation from *Temple Scroll* 63:14b–15a. In other words, MTA regards the *Temple Scroll* as authoritative Scripture.

ולוא תגע לכה בטהרה עד שבע שנים

Yet, she may not touch your Purity for seven years. (11QT 63:14b–15a)

Note that, whereas Deut 21 refers to warriors in general taking captives as wives, MTA here specifies that the woman cannot touch the priestly Purity (line 16a), suggesting that the subject here refers to a priest acquiring a slave as a wife. Lines 16b–18 then move to a paraphrase of Exod 21:9–10.[279] The clause [לא תאכל [מן הקד]ש] לחמו in line 19 draws on Lev 22:10–11, which allows the servant purchased by a priest to partake of the priestly emoluments.[280] However, our text, in accordance with *Temple Scroll*, modifies this in that the former slave receives the priestly perquisites only after seven years in her newly acquired home. Whereas *Temple Scroll* employs the words אחר תואכל following the seven years, line 20 of our text articulates it more precisely as the eighth year in which she may partake of his emoluments. As to the last four letters in line 21, transcribed by the editor as עׁוׁלׁה (burnt offering), the context here appears to require the construction of [ב]עׁוׁלׁה (*bĕʿûlāh*; married). Hence, the final clause in 20b–21a, "He may [not] have sexual relations with [a slave-maiden who has been ma]rried to a m[an]," is an inclusio that generalizes the contents of the preceding pericope dealing with priestly marriage to a slave. This section as well as 4Q251 (Halakha A) F16 are of interest, since both cases pertain to acquiring slaves. Other passages in MTA likewise deal with slaves. CD 12:10b–11a asserts "Nor shall he sell to them (pagans) his male and female slave who have entered with him into the covenant of Abraham." Another passage prohibits the owner from making his slaves do labor on the Sabbath (CD 11:12).

---

[279] See also 4Q271 F3:15 which deals with the marital rights of a woman.
[280] 4Q251 F16 uses some of the vocabulary of this text.

Our text suggests that the community was of some means, certainly not destitute.

### 3.2.2.9.9. *The Covenant and Other Oaths or Vows (CD 15:1–16:22; 9:1)*[sic!]

What follows 4Q270 F4 is problematic. However, several points seem to indicate that our text, perhaps with a few missing lines, connects back with CD 15. To begin with, as stated above, both 4Q270 F4 and the beginning of CD 15 deal with the term אלה (curse). In 4Q270 F4:1 it is the issue of bringing on the curse of the *soṭah*, whereas CD 15:2–3 contains the noun construct אלות הברית (the covenantal curses). Furthermore, both texts concern the issue of taking oaths. 4Q270 F4:6 refers to the oath taking of the straying woman. CD 15:1–8 prescribes several types of oaths that are discussed below.

As we have seen, the series of oaths begins with that of the *soṭah* (4Q270 F4:1b–13a and 4Q273 F5:2–4a). However, in CD 15:1–16:22 and immediately following in 9:1, the author particularizes a variety of oaths and vows. The first of these concerns oaths of admission to the covenant (15:1–16:6a). Then comes an oath concerning biblical commandments (16:6b–9). Rules pertaining to the annulment of a woman's oath by her husband or father follow (16:10–12). The text then treats gifts and other vows (16:13–22; 9:1).

### 3.2.2.9.9.1. Admission to the Covenant (CD 15:1–16:6a)

The main subject embracing CD 15:1–16:6a pertains to the covenant. The word ברית assumes a special meaning in MTA. People are admitted to or rejected from the covenant. Beginning with CD 15:5b and continuing to 16:6a, MTA delineates the obligations incumbent upon the candidates who take the covenantal oath.

### 3.2.2.9.9.1.1. Restrictions of the Tetragrammaton (CD 15:1–5a)

We come now to textual elucidations of CD 15. The first word on line 1 reads יֹשָבַע (he should swear . . . ). Schechter read it as a positive statement. However, most modern editors presume that the negative לא preceded it. Compare line 2 ואת תורת משה אל יזכור (but he shall not make mention of the Torah of Moses . . . ). The last word of line 1 is also problematic. Schechter read שבועת הברית, "the oath of the covenant," Ginzberg שבועה הכתובה, "the oath that is written (in the curses of the covenant)," Rabin שבועה ה[סכ]ם, "oath of agreement," Baumgarten שבועת הבאֹיֹם, "the oath of those who enter (by the curses of the covenant)"—i.e. those of Deut 28, and Qimron and

Martínez-Tigchelaar שְׁבוּעַת הַבָּנִים, "the oath of the youths."[281] An analysis of the paleography seems to confirm the last reading, and is adopted in our comments below. The first injunction appears to assert that one may not swear by using the names אלוהים and אדוני. Note that these appellations are here abbreviated respectively אלף ולמד and אלף ודלת. The context seems to require that the last line of the previous page ended with ביוד והי לא, to read ביוד והי לא ישבע וגם באלף ולמד וגם באלף ודלת, "By the *yod* and *hē* (YHWH) one should not swear, nor by the *aleph* and *lamed* (Elohim), nor by the *aleph* and *dalet* (Adonai) . . ."[282]

Scholars have been of the opinion that circumlocution of God's name originated in rabbinic literature. We now see that this concept is dealt with at some length in MTA. The author of this work makes a theme out of it. The text prohibits the use of YHWH and the like in certain oaths. Line 2 further prohibits the mention of the use of this name and the like when citing the Torah of Moses.[283] That the word שם is an attempt to avoid the overuse of God's name can be seen in CD 20:20, 34; 4Q266 F5i:9; 4Q270 F2i:11; 1QS 6:27; Ps 72:19 and 96:2, etc. Interesting is the word פרוש in the phrase פרוש השם, denoting the enunciation of the letters of God's name.

What exactly the clause "'the oath of the youths' during the covenantal curses" in lines 1–2 means is not clear, due to the lacuna of the preceding page. It may refer to the oath taken by children during the division of inheritance. Or it could allude to the father's role in annulling the vows of his children in accordance with Num 30:4–5. The phrase שבועת הבנים would amplify the biblical injunction whose wording limits it to the vows of a daughter (see below in CD 16:10–12; commentary section 3.2.2.9.9.2.2). Most likely, however, these words here refer to the oaths of the young men who enter the muster of the community as is stated in lines 5–6: "And each and every one who is entering the covenant of all of Israel by the eternal statute shall impose the oath of the covenant upon their sons who reach (the appropriate age) to be counted in the muster." It is likely

---

[281] Ginzberg, *Unknown Jewish Sect*, 91; Rabin, *Zadokite Documents*, 70–71; Fitzmyer, ed., *Documents*, 86; Martínez and Tigchelaar, *Scrolls Study Edition*, vol. 1, 563; Qimron, "The Text of CDC," 39.

[282] Qimron reconstructs וכל שבועה אל יש[בע וגם באלף ולמד וגם באלף ודלת; E. Qimron, "שבועת הבנים in the Damascus Covenant 15:1–2," *JQR* 81, no 1-2 (July–October 1990): 116.

[283] Ginzberg understands this phrase as one may not use the Torah as an oath (Ginzberg, *Unknown Jewish Sect*, 93).

that אלות הברית has the same meaning as does אלות בריתו (the curses of His covenant) in CD 1:17 and אלות הברית (the curses of the covenant) in 15:3, both of which denote the covenantal curses mentioned in Deut 29:20 and listed in Deut 27:13–26. As we understand these lines, the name of God, the tetragrammaton, should be used in the covenantal curses exclusively at the time of admission. One should not employ it in business and other kinds of adjurations.

The concept in CD 15:3 of profaning the divine name occurs likewise above in 4Q270 F2i:11 in the context of idolatrous practice, as it does in Lev 18:21 and 20:3 in relation to sacrificing children to Molech. The taking of false oaths here in CD 15 profanes God's name, as it does in Lev 19:12.

והשיב in line 4 of our text draws on Lev 5:23, requiring that the one who appropriated an object not belonging to him must restore it to its owner. However, lines 3b–5a are silent about the additional fifth as well as the guilt offering prescribed in verses 24–25 of the biblical text, if he does not restore the value of the stolen object immediately. MTA, however, does not ignore this requirement; the author does mention the fifth below on CD 16:18 and appears to have recorded the guilt offering in the reconstructed line 21. Furthermore, as was noted, 4Q270 F2ii:9b–10a, reconstructed on the basis of CD 9:13, asserts that anyone who has appropriated something not belonging to him must add a fifth as a fine, which is given to the priest. In addition, CD 9:14 prescribes that the offender must bring a ram as a guilt offering (איל האשם). The thought concludes with the assertion that if he restores the lost object he will not incur sin and die. The negative לא qualifies both verbs. The word וי[מות] is ambiguous. It may mean that if the judges find out that he is guilty they will condemn him; or perhaps more likely, the punishment is not capital, but refers to divine punishment. However, see above in comments on 4Q270 F2i:11 where profanation of the divine name might involve a capital crime.

### 3.2.2.9.9.1.2. The Initiation of Juniors (CD 15:5b–6)
Lines 5b–6 obligate those who enter the covenant community to bring their children with them into the congregation. It is interesting that our text, although discussing at length the joining of the covenant, does not employ the term יחד, so ubiquitous in *Rule of the Community* where 1QS uses the term sixty times. In other words, although the author of MTA may have used יחד once or twice, he did not

regard it as the appellation of the sect as do the authors of *Rule of the Community* and other Dead Sea Scrolls. The important term in MTA is ברית, illustrating that at the time of this composition there was not yet an organized community. Interestingly also, the sense of this expression undergoes a change. In the Hebrew Scriptures, it suggests an obligation to be faithful to God and His Torah. In MTA, ברית denotes a separation from Israel into the precepts of additional laws, a new Torah. Subsequently, in *Rule of the Community* it is defined as joining a separate organization.

The formula חוק עולם, as used in the Pentateuch, occurs in specific obligations such as the priestly perquisites. The phrase is relatively less frequent in the DSS, and appears only here in MTA. Its use in our text refers to the covenant in general, not to specific regulations as in the Torah.

### 3.2.2.9.9.1.3. Returning Apostates (CD 15:7–13a)

Lines 7–10a include those who turn back from their corrupt way, who are to retake their covenantal oaths as they return to the community. Our text now assigns a more significant role to the Supervisor, who must not only approve their return, but guide the procedure. Nevertheless, it is the many on the examining board who join in the teaching of the repentant member.

Translators have handled lines 10b–11 variously. Rabin, renders them, "And let no man let him know the rulings until he has stood before the overseer, lest he turn out to be a fool when he examines him."[284] Martínez and Tigchelaar translate, "But no-one should make him know the precepts before he stands in front of the Inspector: when he stands he should be persuaded by him when he tests him."[285] Cook provides the rendition, "No one is allowed to tell him the rules until he appears before the Overseer, so that he, the Overseer, is not fooled by him when he examines him."[286] Our translation tends to agree with that of Cook, that the subject of יתפתה is not the enrollee, but the Supervisor. Teaching the novice the rules prematurely may prevent the Supervisor from evaluating him objectively.

---

[284] Rabin, *Zadokite Documents*, 72. See also Baumgarten who translates "Let no one make the precepts known to him until he stands before the Examiner [ . . . ] °*m*°, (lest) he prove to be a fool when he questions him." Charlesworth, ed., *Damascus Document*, 39.

[285] Martínez and Tigchelaar, *Scrolls Study Edition*, vol. 1, 563.

[286] Wise, Abegg and Cook, *Scrolls*, 65.

The author of MTA here implicitly responds to a question of whether the Supervisor and those who examine with him could be blamed for misjudgment in the event that the candidate they approved returns to his evil ways. Lines 12–13a imply that they need not be concerned about misjudgment, for as long as they have performed their task faithfully they are not responsible for the subsequent apostasy of a candidate. What they must attest is that the returnee had committed himself to the absolute observance of the Torah of Moses. Note that the Mosaic Law here, as explained above and below, is not limited to the Pentateuch, but embraces the futuristic Torah.

### 3.2.2.9.9.1.4. The Rules for the Many (CD 15:13b–16:6a)

Up to this point the role of the מבקר has been noted somewhat incidentally. He provides guidance to the admission process, examining with his associates the returnees. The following lines portray his function in the life of the community as more prominent—personally teaching the sectarian law on a regular basis to adherents and excluding the unfit.

### a. The Eschatological Torah (15:13b–15a)

נגלה is here a finite verb, paralleling other passages where it is used as a substantive (CD 5:5 and 4Q266 F5i:8). In any case, the term is associated with the Torah, but is not limited to it as contended by Schiffman.[287] Rather, by reason of its context and its proximity to the description of the book of *Jubilees* mentioned in CD 16:2–3, it encompasses the eschatological Scriptures accepted by the sect. נגלה (revealed) serves as a contrast to נסתר (hidden), but not to the mystic concepts as stressed by Schiffman. Rather it alludes to the early stage of Jewish sectarianism when the second Torah had still been hidden prior to its publication by Zadok.[288]

MTA here appears to continue with a repenting candidate reentering the community. Such a person requires extra instruction from the Supervisor. Hence, the repetition of the verbs יוד[יעה]ו (he shall in[form] him), יצוהו (he shall command him) and ילמ[ד]הו (he shall te[ach] him). Each of these verbs refers to the different tasks of the community's leader—the first to pointing out the candidate's erroneous way, the second to showing him what is the proper path, and the

---

[287] Schiffman, *The Halakhah*, 22–32.
[288] Cf. CD 5:4–5.

third to ensuring that he has mastered the instruction. The clause עד שנה תמימה (for a complete year) has a technical sense in the DSS. Thus 1QS 6:16–17; 4Q256 11:12–13 and 4Q265 F4ii:6–7 reiterate the statement found in our text, namely that an erring candidate should be investigated a full year. שנה תמימה implies that the year should not be 365 days, but 364.[289]

### b. Excluding the Unfit on Account of Physical or Mental Defects (CD 15:15b–16:1a)

This list presents those who are to be excluded from the community due to physical or mental deficiencies. A variant parallel text in 1QSa 2:3–9 contains a somewhat longer list.

2:3 וכול איש מנוגע באחת מכול טמאות
2:4 האדם אל יבוא בקהל אל<‹ה›› וכול איש מנוגע באלה לבלתי
2:5 החזיק מעמד בתוך העדה וכול מנוגע בבשרו נכאה רג‹ל›ים או
2:6 ידים פסח או עור או חרש או אלם או מום מנוגע בבשרו
2:7 לראות עינים או איש זקן כושל לבלתי התחזק בתוך העדה
2:8 אל יב[ו]או [אלה להתיצב [ב]תוך עדת א[נ]ושי השם כיא מלאכי
2:9 קודש [בעד]תם

And no man who is afflicted in a single one of all human defilements may enter the congregation of God. And as for any man so afflicted that he lacks stability within the congregation; and anyone afflicted in his flesh such as one who is crippled in feet or hands, lame, blind, deaf, mute or one who has a defect in his flesh that is visible, or a stumbling old man who cannot take care of himself within the congregation: these may not en[ter] to take office [with]in the congregation of the m[e]n of God, because the holy angels are in their [congregati]on.

A striking difference between these two passages is in the main verbs employed. Whereas MTA begins with אל יבו(א) (may not enter)[290] and concludes with אל יבוא אי[ש] מאלה אל תוך העדה (none of them may be admitted to the community),[291] the corresponding prohibitions in *Rule of the Community* commence with אל יבוא בקהל אל (shall not enter the congregation of God)

---

[289] Cf. יצא נח מן התבה לקץ שנה תמימה לימים שלוש מאות ששים וארבעה, "Noah went out from the ark at the end of a complete year, three hundred and sixty-four days" (4Q252 2:2–30). See also my article, "Calendar Wars Between the 364 and the 365-Day Year" cited above.

[290] See the parallel 4Q266 F8i:7 which supplements CD 15:15.

[291] A composite of CD 15:16b–17a; 4Q266 F8i:8b–9a; 4Q270 F6ii:9.

and finish with אל יב[ואו ]אלה להתיצב [ב]תוך עדת א[נ]ושי השם (these may not en[ter] to take office [with]in the congregation of the m[e]n of God). Both clauses in the MTA text, therefore, may be understood as a prohibition against such people joining the new covenantal community. Whereas the two verbs in MTA might be construed as prohibiting such members from joining the new group, the corresponding wording in *Rule of the Community* echoes more closely Deut 23:2–9 where the main prohibition is against marrying foreigners. Interestingly enough, the author of MTA feels compelled to justify these prohibitions by referring to the period of the flood when, according to our text, human life was shortened apparently to seventy years. The basic idea goes back to Gen 6:1–7 where, on account of the cohabitation of the sons of God with the daughters of men, God in His anger circumscribed human longevity to one hundred and twenty years. Ps 90:9–11 asserts that because of His wrath, God reduced human life to seventy and only exceptionally to eighty years. The author of *Jubilees* (23:12) apparently had the psalmist in mind when he asserts that human life would be decreased to a jubilee and a half (approximately seventy-five years), a unit of time which is between the seventy and eighty years of Ps 90:10. If our restoration is correct, CD 15:18 gives the psalter's lesser period of seventy years.

The question arises as to how this shortening of longevity shed light on the roster of unqualified members. In CD 10:7–10 the writer restricts the period of functioning judges to sixty years on account of the shortened life of man in the antediluvian epoch. But, what is the relationship here? Perhaps the answer is that, just as according to *Jubilees* and the author of MTA God shortened human life, He also brought about human frailties such as blindness and deafness.[292] This would imply then, as our writer seems to go on, that during the messianic age human frailty and shortness of life will disappear (CD 15:19). The pericope adds to this discussion by invoking the holy angels. The implication appears to be that the physically unfit are restricted from the community because they cannot associate with immortal beings, that is to say that humanity prior to the flood as well as that of the messianic age had and will have an angelic lifestyle.

---

[292] Cf. the tradition that Abraham was the first person to contract old age and Jacob the first to become ill (*Bava Metzi'a 87a*).

Most of the last four lines of CD 15 have perished. Our reconstruction of this material, commented on in part above, draws on what survives at the end of lines 19–20, their scanty parallel letters in 4Q271 F4ii:1 and what continues in this scroll for the next two lines. We presume that the original page consisted of twenty-two lines. The suggested readings draw on CD 20:1, 25–26 and Deut 4:30–31. Note that, having introduced the idea of the reduction of human life in antediluvian times in line 18, the expectation of a renewal of longevity during the messianic age presumably follows in line 19. The remains of 4Q271 F4ii:1–3a provide us with the bricks to restore the last two lines of the page, connecting them with page 16.

Hence, although not articulated, the basic supposition in this pericope seems to be that prior to the flood humans were physically perfect with no senility and lived for nearly a thousand years, witness Methuselah. This leads the author to a pivotal point of the book—linking *Urzeit* and *Endzeit* and making human health dependent on the obedience to the Torah. Here the contrast of human frailties in the past and present with longevity in the idealized future suggests that not only will there be no more senility, but handicaps like blindness and deafness will disappear. See the composite reading of CD 8:4 and 19:16, where MTA stresses the linkage between the covenant of repentance and the process of healing. Lines 21–22 of our text and continuing on page 16 connect the covenant of Moses (Exod 34:27) with a (new) covenant. This is suggested by the clause reconstructed from 4Q271 F4ii:2, יכרות [את בית ישראל ואת בית יהודה] ברית, which echoes the prophet Jeremiah's announcement of a new covenant in Jer 31:31–34 (וְכָרַתִּי אֶת־בֵּית יִשְׂרָאֵל וְאֶת־בֵּית יְהוּדָה בְּרִית חֲדָשָׁה "And I will make a new covenant with the house of Israel and the house of Judah").[293]

### c. In Praise of the Book of Jubilees (CD 16:1b–6a)

The previous lines merge passages from Exodus and Jeremiah with the renewal of longevity and the healing of mankind. In CD 16:1b–6a the author articulates what is implicit elsewhere, but here stated directly. Throughout MTA we find frequent allusions to ideas appearing only in *Jubilees*. We have just read one of them in CD 15:18 (compare *Jub.* 23:8–9). Here in CD 16:1b–6a, the author goes out

---

[293] Cf. CD 6:19; 8:21 (19:33–34) and 20:12 for the phrase ברית החדשה (the new covenant).

of his way to emphasize the authoritative nature of this work. The linkage is assured by the introductory words על כן יקום האיש על נפשו לשוב אל תורת מושה (Therefore, the candidate shall obligate himself to turn to the Torah of Moses). Translators and commentators take the Torah of Moses axiomatically as referring to the Pentateuch, since it says that the Law of Moses is מדוקדק. Ginzberg noted a problem in these lines. Whereas the clause כי בה הכל מדקדק (for everything in it is perfect) refers allegedly to the five books of Moses, the lines that follow, . . . ופרוש קציהם (the elaboration of their epochs . . . ), pertain to *Jubilees*. He resolved the problem by hypothesizing that "כי בה הכל מדקדק is not to be taken literally, for in respect of the 'calendar,' פרוש קציהם, one must be guided by what is written on this subject in *Jubilees*. To the מדוקדק connected with the Torah is opposed the מדוקדק connected with the pseudepigraphon here mentioned."[294] Baumgarten agrees with Ginzberg.[295] At any rate, the problem alluded to in this passage by Ginzberg remains. Not embracing his solution, how can we reconcile the two consecutive clauses, the first concluding with כי בה הכל מדקדק, and the second with הנה הוא מדוקדק (behold it is perfect)? What is the connection between the statement "Therefore the candidate shall obligate himself to turn to the Torah of Moses, for everything in it is perfect" and what follows it that declares the book of *Jubilees* as perfect? The answer is that the תורת מושה here along with its five other occurrences in MTA encompasses both the Pentateuch and *Jubilees*, and perhaps *Temple Scroll* as well.[296] Indeed, as mentioned elsewhere, the author of MTA regarded his work as an amplification of *Jubilees*. For example, as reconstructed, 4Q268 F1:1–3a asserts,

1  [מחלקות העתים ה]אֹחֹרונות הלוא כן תבואינה] ככול ימיו וכ]וֹל
2  [תקופות מועדי]וֹ איזה תחלתו ואיזה סופו וֹהֹ[גיד את הראישו]נֹיֹ‹ם›
3  [ואת האחרונים ואת עד] אשר יבוא במה

"[As for the Divisions of the] Eschatological [Epochs]: Surely they will occur (as was presaged) [according to all (the number of) its days and a]ll [(the number of) the cycles of] i[ts festivals,] when its beginning (was)

---

²⁹⁴  Ginzberg, *Unknown Jewish Sect*, 95.
²⁹⁵  Baumgarten in Charlesworth, ed., *Damascus Document*, 39, note 132. However, he may have changed his mind on this point (see his article on the Damascus Document in the *Encyclopedia of the Dead Sea Scrolls*).
²⁹⁶  In my opinion, the same is probably true of the two mentions of תורת מושה in *Rule of the Community*, a satellite work of MTA.

and ending (will occur); for [(God)] has fore[told the firs]t [as well as the latter things and] what will transpire thereafter in them (the Divisions of the Eschatological Epochs) . . . "

Both here and in CD 16:1b–6a our author declares the jubilean calendar of the Sabbath and the festivals as authoritative.

Lines 4b–6a fuse several theological concepts. First, they continue the praise of the Torah of Moses which embraces *Jubilees*. Secondly, they present this sectarian Scripture as indispensable for the salvation of the candidate. Finally, the author gives the historical precedent that Abraham, when he fulfilled God's covenant of circumcision, was given the Torah of Moses as guidance. When a candidate becomes a member of this community and explicitly obligates himself to live by its precepts, the angel Mastema (elsewhere known as Belial) will lose his grip on the new covenanter.

The circumcision commandment appears above in 4Q266 F6ii:6 pertaining to childbearing. Yet, it is only here in CD 16:4b–6a (which has its basis in *Jub.* 15) that the author comments on its significance, noting that every entrant into the covenant must obligate himself to observe the law in accordance with the sectarian Scriptures. Our writer states that the principle linking the covenant with *Jubilees* dates back to Abraham who committed himself to its observance at the time of his circumcision. We must remember here that the patriarch was an adult when he was circumcised. The candidates for membership in the sectarian community must have entered the age of consciousness. More importantly, however, they must follow Abraham's mode of accepting the covenant, a point seemingly drawn from and based upon the chronology and text of *Jub.* 15. This chapter not only commands Abraham to circumcise himself and his household, but proceeds with a dissertation on its import, that it is the observance of the covenant of circumcision which will keep Belial (known as Mastema elsewhere in *Jubilees*) from the community.

The two occurrences of ביום in CD 16:4–6 could be translated "at the time," without referring to a precise day, but more probably mean "on the very day," pointing to *Jub.* 15:1 which dates Abraham's conversion to "the fifth year of the fourth week of this jubilee [1986]—in the third month, in the *middle of the month* . . . "[297] Perhaps this elucidates 4Q266 F11:17–18 where the renewal of the covenant should take place every year in the third month. This fragment, like Exod 19:1,

---

[297] VanderKam, *Jubilees*, vol. 1, 87.

does not mention on which day of the month it occurs, but CD
16:4b–6a, when aligned with *Jub.* 15, suggests that the annual renewal
of the covenant should take place during the sect's observance of
*Shebu'ot* on the fifteenth of the third month.[298] The text is not explicit
as to the kind of knowledge which the patriarch acquired on that day.
However, it would appear that יום דעתו is an additional reference to
*Jub.* 15 where God revealed to Abraham a series of covenantal bless-
ings: a) the celebration of *Shebuot* and its offerings, b) the covenant
with God wherein the patriarch's children would inherit the Holy
Land, c) the commandment of circumcision and d) the birth of a
son, Isaac. Thus, the commendation of *Jubilees* as perfect forms part
of this section which likewise deals with covenantal commitment (CD
15:5b–16:6a). The main point in this unit is that the covenant must
be accepted with the entire heart and soul, echoing Deut 6:5, which
according to MTA, was modeled after Abraham's covenant.

### 3.2.2.9.9.2. Other Oaths and Promises (CD 16:6b–22; 9:1)

This section deals with the broader subject of oaths and promises.
Lines 6b–9 deal with prohibitive oaths; 10–12 pertain to the annulment of that made by a woman; 13–22 and what follows sequentially
in CD 9:1 concern voluntary contributions and idolatrous vows.

### 3.2.2.9.9.2.1. Prohibitive Oaths (6b–9)

This segment consists of two statements: a person vowing to fulfill a
commandment already in the biblical text and a vow to depart from
it. Our text emphasizes the importance of these rules by repeating
the threat of a capital offense, עד מחיר מות. This view accords with
the opinion of Rabbi Judah ben Betherah, who in *Bavli Shebu'ot* 27a
maintained that if one swears to fulfill a commandment required
already in Scripture and does not do so, he has breached two commandments—one prescribed in the Torah and the other his own
oath. However, the majority of the Talmudic sages diverge in this
matter, arguing that one cannot improve upon an issue dealt with in
Scripture, even by an oath. What the Torah said stands and a personal vow in such a matter is irrelevant. Conversely, when one makes

---

[298]  See Baumgarten's remarks on 4Q266 F11:17. He disputes Milik's suggestion
that MTA required the renewal of the covenant on Pentecost, the fifteenth day of the
month. However, CD 16 does appear to substantiate Milik's hypothesis.

a vow to violate the Torah, his vow is not valid. On this matter the sages would be in accord.

### 3.2.2.9.9.2.2. Annulling a Woman's Oath (16:10–12)

These three lines summarize the subject dealt with at length in Num 30:4–17 and virtually reproduced in *Temple Scroll* 53:16–54:5. The formula [ר]אמו אשר, which in MTA generally constitutes a quote from Scripture, here is followed by [ל]אישה להניא את שבועתה [[for] her husband to annul her oath), a clause with no exact equivalence in Numbers. [ל]אישה להניא could be rendered in one of two ways: that a husband *may* annul the oath of his wife or, alternatively, that he *should* annul her oath. If the latter, our text would express the idea that it is not desirable for women to make a practice of vowing, and therefore her husband is encouraged to void them. What is interesting is that, whereas Scripture deals primarily with the vow of the father, appending to it the vow of the husband, MTA reverses the sequence, making the vow of the husband primary and adds to it that of the father. It is conceivable that the author of MTA had here before him another source which he followed. It might have been material taken from the sapiential work, the book of Haguy cited in CD 10:6, 13:2 and 14:7–8.[299]

בֹּ[רוחה]                                                          F2iv:6

המשׁילך להתהלך ברצׁוֹנֹכה ולא להוסיף נדר ונדב[ה]    F2iv:7

[       השׁב רוחכה לרצונכה וכל שבועת אסרה לנֹדֹר נֹדֹ[ר    F2iv:8

הֹפר על מוצא פיכה וברצונכה הניא[ה]    F2iv:9

He has given you control over [her] that she accord with your wishes and not make (frivolous) vows and gif[ts.] Follow your own desire and annul any prohibitive oath that she vows. By your own utterance and your desire disavow [her]. (4Q416 F2iv:6b–9a)

MTA and Haguy have these points in common. 1) In contrast to the biblical text, the sapiential work makes no mention of the father's annulment. As noted above MTA does mention the father, but only secondarily. 2) While the biblical text does permit the husband and the father to disavow a woman's oath, there is no inkling of female frivolity in it. By contrast, the sapiential text and MTA go out of their way to stress this point. The requirement that the husband can

---

[299] As suggested above, the book of Haguy is a work to which MTA assigns significant importance (4Q415–418).

only annul a vow whose content is exactly certain is not recorded in
Scripture directly, but is stressed here in our text. It goes on to say
that if the wife's vow violates the covenant he is obligated to void it.
This prohibition corresponds to what our author said in CD 16:8b–9,
"But anyone who [obli]gates himself to turn away fr[om the To]rah
shall not fulfill it even at the price of death."

### 3.2.2.9.9.2.3. Gifts and Vows (16:13–22; 9:1)

The list of vows after the heading includes a prohibition against
devoting anything which has been illicitly acquired. Neither may
the priests accept from the public anything taken by force. To what
exactly the third prohibition (lines 14b–15) refers is uncertain. As
we have it, the text reads לעיהו (his neighbor) with the LXX instead
of אחיהו (his brother) as in MT (Mic 7:2). The problem here is the
correspondence between the disallowance of dedicating one's food
to God and its proof text איש את לעיהו יצ[ו]דו חרם (Each together
with his neighbor h[u]nt *ḥerem*). As was noted by Rabin, MTA understands the word חרם not as a trap, but in its more common usage
as a ban, or anathema (Martínez-Tigchelaar).[300] It appears to mean
that food which falls under the category of חרם is, as stated in Lev
27:28, not redeemable. Rather it is totally dedicated to the Lord
and is not even for priestly consumption.

The restoration of the lacuna following אל יקד[ש] אי̇ש מכל א[ in
lines 15–16 of the Genizah text draws on the context combined
with the lettering extant in 4Q271 F4ii:15–16. What follows the א
might have been לה to read מכל א]לה (from all these). But, א[חזה]
(po[ssession]), a word found at the end of the line, is a more likely
reading. The letter ס in the parallel text suggests אנוס (extorted) or as
is more plausible, the active participle אונס (compare 4Q270 F6iii:14).
The line as reconstructed prohibits the dedication of property that
has been purchased from an extorter. Whereas this injunction may
have dealt with what an individual himself bought, what comes next
(lines 16b–17a) appears to deal with land acquired by inheritance,
but which likewise had come into the benefactor's possession illicitly.
If our understanding is correct, CD 16:13–17a concerns itself with
the principle that one may not sanctify anything that is morally
tainted.

---

[300] Rabin, *Zadokite Documents*, 76–77; Martínez and Tigchelaar, *Scrolls Study
Edition*, vol. 1, 565.

The previous theme of dedication continues in CD 16:17b–22 and into the first line of CD 9 which immediately follows. Lines 17b–22 address a case when one has vowed his own personal value where he must add a fifth ([את חמישית כסף ערכו] [ו]נענש הנודר). The use of the word נענש here is puzzling, as the relevant Scripture vocables always use the verb יסף (to add). See for example Lev 27:19. The next extant clause, [לשופט]ים לשפט צדק] (it is the responsibility of the judge[s to judge rightly]), is a wording that is not recorded in Lev 27. However, it is reasonable to suppose that MTA here paraphrases a point made in the Levitical text, that it is incumbent upon the priest to evaluate the produce, whether it is high or low in value (Lev 27:12 and 14). MTA admonishes the *judges* rather than the priests to perform their task fairly. The problem that confronts the reader is determining what preceded the apodosis ". . . it is the responsibility of the judge[s to judge rightly . . . ]" The relevant Levitical passage possibly offers a clue to its protasis. Verses 17–23 begin by stating that if one sanctifies a field in the midst of the jubilee cycle, it belongs to the sanctuary only until the end of that period. It is the priest (in MTA's version, the judges) who is in charge of computing the number of years and the proportion of the produce that is due the sanctuary. We may have a clue as to the wording of this protasis in the remnant ]ה אחר ל[ in 4Q266 F8ii:4, conceivably vestiges whose full text draws on wordage in the biblical verse 18 (עַד שְׁנַת הַיֹּבֵל, "until the year of jubilee"). Qimron reads אחר המודר (after being vowed),[301] a reading which, however, neither makes sense in the context nor does it have a basis in the biblical and Qumran language. What remains of the letters could, perhaps, be read [ע]ד אחר הש[נ]ים הנותרות ביובל] ([un]til after the [remaining] ye[ars in the jubilee]), phraseology which echoes the biblical text. It is reasonable to assume that CD dealt here with the evaluation of one's field at the advent of the jubilee, where the judges must estimate the amount due for the years of sanctification. What is notable is the difference between the rabbinic and MTA traditions in relation to the observance of the jubilee during the Second Temple period. Contrary to our text, the Talmudic sages believed that rules of the jubilee year were discontinued.

Preceding the interjection of the matter of the jubilee year, the author dealt with dedicated property acquired by force (lines 13b–17b).

---

[301] Qimron, "The Text of CDC," 41.

As reconstructed, in lines 20–22 the author addresses the consequences of the actions of an extorter: a) he is to be chastised; b) he must pay the value of the exhorted object plus, as was stated above in line 18, an additional fifth; c) he is required to bring a ram as a guilt offering. The restitution alluded to in what is restored from 4Q266 F8ii:6 and 4Q270 F6iii:14 to the beginning of line 21 draws on Lev 5:16. The reconstruction concerning the guilt offering is based on the broader context of Lev 5. The words כמוה [תו]מבי (from [his] proper[ty] comparable to it), restored from 4Q266 F8ii:7 into the end of line 21, may allude to verse 7 of the biblical text, where if the guilty party cannot afford a ram offering he may substitute it with two turtle doves, as stated also in 4Q266 F6ii:12–13.

Following the requirement to bring a guilt offering for not speaking truthfully, 4Q266 F8ii:8 returns to Lev 27. Paralleling 4Q266 F8ii:8–9 and 4Q270 F6iii:16, CD 9:1 paraphrases elements of verses 28–29 with a probable misreading כל אדם (every man) instead of כל חרם (every devotion), a reading in verse 29 of the biblical text. Likewise CD changes יחרים אדם to יַחֲרָם אִישׁ. Scrollists diverge in the rendition of this line. Some (Ginzberg, Rabin, Cook and Martínez-Tigchelaar) understand that the person who devotes someone should be handed over to pagan law for condemnation.[302] Others (Winter, Lohse and Baumgarten) understand that the sentence is passed by a Jewish court.[303] Since Lev 27:29 ordains death by the Israelite court, it is self evident that our text which paraphrases the Levitical injunction does likewise. Moreover, it is unlikely that the author of MTA would presume to know that this would be a capital offense in pagan jurisprudence, and, if he knew so, would consider it authoritative. This line pertaining to idolatrous vows completes the section dealing with gifts and vows.[304] The term חרם, my reading for אדם of MTA, receives special attention in Lev 27:21 and 28–29. Our text adds to this emphasis by the additional citation of Mic 7:2. Note that the phrase אשר אמר attested in 4Q266 F8ii:8 has not survived at the end of CD 16.

---

[302] Ginzberg, *Unknown Jewish Sect*, 43; Rabin, *Zadokite Documents*, 44; Wise, Abegg and Cook, *Scrolls*, 66; Martínez and Tigchelaar, *Scrolls Study Edition*, vol. 1, 565.

[303] P. Winter, "Ṣadoqite Fragments IX, I," *RevQ* 21 (Feb. 1967): 131–36; Eduard Lohse, *Die Qumran Texte* (München: Kösel-Verlag, 1971), 83; Baumgarten in Charlesworth, ed., *Damascus Document*, 43.

[304] See Hempel, *The Laws of the Damascus Document*, 32, 187.

### 3.2.2.9.10. *Justice (9:2–10:10a)*

CD 9:2 begins a lengthy section of approximately thirty-four lines on the subject of justice. It contains several subthemes: charges pertaining to a capital crime lacking sufficient evidence, theft and misappropriation of lost objects, and issues pertaining to the necessary number of witnesses in capital cases. It concludes with a discussion on the nature of judgeship, the central personnel in the sect's judicial system.

### 3.2.2.9.10.1. Charges of a Capital Crime Without Full Evidence (9:2–10a)

The new topic, as do many other sections in MTA, begins with a citation of a biblical verse, here Lev 19:18, expounding on the difference between legal evidence and gossip. What exactly is meant in the clause לא תקום ולא תטור את בני עמך (Neither avenge nor keep a grudge against your people)? Our text states that, when a person claims without legal proof that his neighbor has done an illicit act, it constitutes gossip, or, speaking biblically, he is a seeker of vengeance or one who keeps a grudge. Line 5 reconciles the wording in Lev 19:18 prohibiting vengeance and holding a grudge, with Nah 1:2 which ascribes such acts to God.[305] The implied answer is that, since God knows the actual events, He may avenge. However, this is forbidden for humans, since any such assertions without factual evidence is sheer insult to the offended (להבזתו).

What follows in lines 6–7 of CD 9 appears to draw on a portion of Deut 19:16, the protasis of a section of legislation pertaining to malicious testimony.

כִּי־יָקוּם עֵד־חָמָס בְּאִישׁ לַעֲנוֹת בּוֹ סָרָה

> When a malicious witness arises against a man to testify against him falsely . . . (Deut 19:16)

The Genizah text is expanded in 4Q267 F9i:1, the several letters that survive in 5Q12 F1:1, as well as in 4Q270 F6iii:20–21. 4Q270 seems to have been approximately a line and a half longer than its parallel in the medieval manuscript. The two versions do not cohere and are problematic in their wording. Modern translations differ as to the antecedents of the phrase ענה בו in CD 9:7. Schechter, followed by

---

[305] Interestingly MTA alters Nah 1:2 from נֹקֵם יְהוָה to נוקם הוא.

Baumgarten, emended עֲנָהּ to read עֲוֺן, making "(his) sin" the subject of the clause and the object the accused, translating "If he held his peace from day to day but in his fierce wrath he spake against him in a matter concerning death *his sin is upon him* because he did not fulfill the commandment of God . . . "[306] Rabin, following more closely the syntax of the biblical text, understood the accuser as the subject of עֲנָהּ and בּוֹ the accused, translating "if he held his peace at him from one day to the next, and spoke about him when he got angry with him, (and) it was in a capital matter *that he testified against him*; because he did not carry out the commandments of God . . . "[307] On the other hand, Martínez-Tigchelaar take the phrase as the accuser testifying against himself and render the sentence "If he kept silent about him from one day to the other, and then, when he was angry, accused him of a capital offense, *he has testified against himself*, for he did not fulfill the commandment of God . . . "[308] In a similar manner, Cook regards the accuser himself as the object of the verb. He differs, however, in interpreting his *transgression* as the subject of the clause, reading the sentence, "If he kept silent day by day and then in anger against his fellow spoke against him in a capital case, *this testifies against him* that he did not fulfill the commandment of God."[309] In spite of these heroic efforts, the Genizah rendition remains problematic. Although only Rabin follows the subject and object identities of the biblical clause cited above, his rendition offers no apodosis.

As was stated, the texts from the caves have readings presumably missing in CD, material drawn from the larger context of the biblical text and which would generate better sense in this section. What appears to emerge from this additional wordage is that the author of MTA presented here a case of what happens if the accuser, being a single witness, charged a capital offense against an individual without bringing legal proof. If the charges were determined to be a falsification manufactured by the accuser, he was to be condemned to death in accordance with Deut 19:18–19. My reconstruction reflects an at-

---

[306] Fitzmyer, ed., *Documents*, (78); Charlesworth, ed., *Damascus Document*, 43. The italics in Schechter's translation are mine.

[307] Rabin, *Zadokite Documents*, 44. The italics in the translation are mine.

[308] Martínez and Tigchelaar, *Scrolls Study Edition*, vol. 1, 567. The italics in the translation are mine.

[309] Wise, Abegg and Cook, *Scrolls*, 67. The italics in the translation are mine.

tempt to make sense of the diverse remains of the Qumran additions in light of the biblical background. The reconstruction וֹהיו [השופטים אמ]ת [להמיתו] ([the judges] shall be [faith]ful [by condemning him to death]) in 4Q270 F6iii:20b–21a draws on the fact that the author presents the judges as governing this entire text, as is evident in CD 16:18–19 and below in CD 9:10 and 9:23b–10:1. Furthermore, the assumption that the accused shall be condemned would logically follow the clause in CD 9:6 דבר בו בדבר מות (he charged him with a capital offense). The author's concern for the integrity of the judges is conceivably a polemic against the sages who would not condemn a single witness, since such testimony in their view would have no legal standing. As to the reconstruction of the fragmentary יהיו נק from 5Q12 F1:1, it appears to parallel the clause "they (those who examine him), will be absolved (נקיאים) if he (the candidate) transgresses" (4Q266 F8i:3–4; CD 15:13). Here too, those who condemn the avenger will not be faulted. The context of the missing words before the reconstruction from 5Q12 F1:1, [ . . . ] יהיו נק[אים כי שקר ענה בו (shall be ab[solved since falsely he has testified against him]), apparently dealt with adjudication of the judges.[310] Evidently what follows in CD 9:7 continues to justify the death sentence for an avenger, "for he has not upheld the commandments of God." The medieval text omits this material and is, as shown, unsatisfactory, since it lacks both the context and the subject that evidently preceded ענה בו. The cave texts, although replete with lacunae, are nevertheless helpful in providing a general theme for the lost material.

Interestingly, this passage contains some unique features. Elsewhere in MTA, a unit either begins or concludes with a citation from Scripture. This pericope both commences and ends with a biblical proof text. It opens with Lev 19:18, going on to reconcile it with Nah 1:2, and comes back to Lev 19, only to verse 17, taking it as an explanation of verse 18 where the passage started.

The author introduces the material which follows with the heading על השבועה (concerning the oath). It links what precedes it with what ensues, going on to cite presumably an authoritative passage, לא תושיעך ידך לך, literally translated "Let your hand not save you," an

---

[310] As for the reconstruction כי שקר ענה בו, see Deut 19:18 (שֶׁקֶר עָנָה בְאָחִיו). See also Exod 20:16.

idiom for "Do not take justice into your own hands." The prefatory
formula אשר אמר, as cited throughout MTA, implies that the author
is quoting a biblical or an authoritative passage which he proceeds
to exegete. However, no such phrase exists either in Scripture or
in the extant Scrolls. Schechter suggested that it is a paraphrase of
וְהוֹשֵׁעַ יָדְךָ לְךָ in 1 Sam 25:26 (and saving yourself with your own hand).
Rabin conjectured that this quote may have come from a sectarian
work. Baumgarten rejects this view, since it is not found in the DSS.
He goes on to say that the sectarian writers used the formula אשר
אמר "for things implied or derived from Scripture as well as what
was explicitly stated."[311] However, this suggestion does not resolve
the problem, since the text goes on to repeat the phrase positively,
that "anyone who makes someone swear in the field concerning a
contention not in the presence of judges or by their command has
acted on his own (הושיע ידו לו)." This exegesis makes no sense if
there had never existed such an injunction. However, Baumgarten's
argument that since no passage has been found thus far in sectarian texts, therefore it never existed, is not cogent. After all, no one
claims that every lost text has been recovered.

Let us take a closer look at the statement that one should not take
justice into his own hand. In the rabbinic tradition, an oath is valid
even if not done in the presence of the court. Our text states that this
would be self executed justice.

### 3.2.2.9.10.2. Misappropriation (9:10b–16a)

The next subject deals with theft and misappropriation of lost objects,
an issue introduced already in 4Q270 F2ii:9b–10a and CD 15:3b–5a.
It draws on Lev 5:20–26 and Deut 22:1–3. These passages require the
finder of an object whose owner is not known to make an endeavor
to identify its owner. If the finder does not do so, Lev 5:24–25 en-
joins him to add a fifth of the value of the object as well as a guilt
offering (אָשָׁם). But, whereas Leviticus prescribes that the fifth should
be added to compensate the loser of the object, MTA, although
ignoring it here, requires the additional fifth in 4Q270 F2ii:9b–10a:
[וכל אשם מושב אשר] אין להשיבה וחוממשה עליה, "[and any guilt restitution
that] cannot be restored (to the owner, which must be given to the

---

[311] Charlesworth, ed., *Damascus Document*, 43.

priest) with an additional fifth (of its value if he knew the owner and didn't return it)." There seems to be no contradiction between the biblical requirement that the fifth be given to the owner, and MTA's apparent injunction that the fifth belongs to the priest. The former refers to a case wherein the owner of the object has been identified, and the latter probably to a situation where the owner remains unknown and the finder kept it for himself rather than as required—handing it over to the priest, with an additional fifth.

While paraphrasing Scripture, our passage greatly amplifies it. The term בעלים in the sense of abstract ownership of property does not appear in Scripture. It is used here four times and occurs frequently in rabbinic literature. In our text, it modifies the formula מאד המחנה (the property of the camp), suggesting that there existed the concept of private property within the community.

Our text goes on to emphasize the next point: that lost objects and the guilt offering be given to the priest(s). It does not specify the priests to whom the lost object is to be entrusted, but it probably was intended for the sacerdote of the camp.

The phrase שבועת האלה (a maledictory oath) recalls the curse of the wayward woman cited in 4Q270 F4:1b–13a, but is a concept amplified above in CD 15:2 as אלות הברית (the curses of the covenant). It is not clear, however, whether שבועת האלה here is identical to or contrasted with אלות הברית. In CD 15, it is said that the tetragrammaton should be used only for the covenantal adjurations at the time of admission into the community, implying perhaps, that it be not employed for any other instances such as in locating lost objects.

### 3.2.2.9.10.3. The Necessity of Two Witnesses (9:16b–10:3)

After dealing with the issue of the lost object, our text treats the biblical injunction requiring two witnesses for substantial accusations. Deut 17:6 and Num 35:30 exclude a single witness from a capital case. Rather, a minimum of two is required. Deut 19:15 amplifies this concept to exclude a single witness from any offense, not just those of homicide. Rabbinics devotes much attention to the evidence of a single witness. Our text does the same, but modifies the rules in the context of the camp and its supervisor. This section begins with the injunction that if there is a single witness to any offense, it cannot be ignored altogether, even though it would not suffice to convict. However, he who saw the misdeed shall report it to the Supervisor who personally is to make a record of it in case the offender repeats it a second time. This ruling diverges from the rabbinic tradition which requires that two witnesses must testify in tandem to be valid. Our text is more lenient. Two consecutive testimonies may be combined for conviction. However, if the testimony of the two witnesses deals with two separate cases of homicide, it suffices to exclude the person from the Purity. The author adds that this is true only if they are trustworthy. In other words, it is not enough that the testimony of a single witness be sufficient to exclude a single member from the community. Rather, the testimony must be weighed for its reliability. See CD 9:2–7a for the case of the unreliable witness. The biblical text does not specify that two witnesses are required. Nevertheless, like the sages, our text necessitates it. CD 9:23b–10:2a further restricts witnesses in capital cases to those who have attained maturity (presumably the age of twenty), been accepted by the community, and are known for their piety. The text concludes by telling that an impious member who has lost his right to serve as a witness in homicidal cases may regain his testimonial rights by meriting restoration to the community. CD 15:7–10a deals with the matter of renewing the trust of the community. The qualifications of witnesses taught in this section bridge to the succeeding subsection, the qualifications of justices.

### 3.2.2.9.10.4. The Nature of Judgeship (10:4–10a)

What follows the section dealing with the necessity of proper witnesses concerns the composition of the community's court and the expertise of the judges. This passage has two other parallels that are, on the one hand, similarly worded, and on the other, contain subtle differences. To facilitate their analysis, I have arranged the three passages in parallel columns. On some points such as the identification of the book of Haguy (Hagi), there exists a vast secondary literature which we can only here summarize. My comments will concentrate on matters rarely discussed in these writings.

## THE BOOK OF HAGUY IN MTA

| CD 10:4–7 | CD 12:22–13:3 | CD 14:3-10 |
|---|---|---|
| 10:4) And this is the rule for the judges of the congregation: a minimum of ten expert men 10:5) from the congregation for the occasion—four from the tribes of Levi and Aaron and six from Israel— 10:6) who are **experts in the book of Hagi** and in the foundations of the covenant, from 10:7) twenty-five to sixty years of age. | Now this is the procedure for the habitation 12:23) of the camps who conduct themselves by these commandments during the epoch of wickedness until the rise of the Messiah of Aaron 13:1) and Israel. (There shall be) a minimum of ten men for the thousands, hundreds, fifties 13:2) and tens. (And where there are ten) there shall not be absent a priest who is **expert in the book of Hagi**. By 13:3) his authority all of them shall be guided. | 14:3) Now for the procedure of the camp sessions. All of them shall be organized by their names: first the priests, 14:4) the Levites second, the Israelites third and proselytes fourth. And they shall be recorded by their names 14:5) one after another: the priests first, the Levites second, the Israelites 14:6) third and the proselytes fourth. And thus they should be seated, and thus should they inquire about any matter. And the priest who will be appointed 14:7) as leader of the Many, shall be between thirty and sixty years of age, **an expert in the book** 14:8) **of Haguy** and in all the injunctions of the Torah to interpret them correctly. And the Supervisor 14:9) of all the camps shall be between thirty and fifty years of age, accomplished in every 14:10) issue of the people of the assembly and in every tongue as (spoken) by their families. |

What is interesting in these comparisons is that, although the description of the book of Haguy is identical in all three, their contexts diverge. In CD 10, MTA is concerned with the number of judges and their divisions by priests, Levites and Israelites. 12–13 deals with the organization of the camps in the Messianic epoch by the thousands, hundreds, fifties and tens (*a la* the divisions of officers appointed by Moses in Exod 18:21). The concern of 14 is the order of the camp headed by the priests and the Supervisor. Other differences are that CD 10 requires that all ten judges be experts in the book of Haguy. 12–13 specifies that the smallest unit of the camp be ten in number.

The text goes on to say that each group must have among it a priest who is an expert in Haguy.[312] In 14, the requirement of being an expert in it is assigned only to the chief priest of the Many, and perhaps to the Supervisor. The book of Haguy, whose importance is so paramount in MTA, is also stressed in 1QSa 1:6–7, which states that one should start training in the book of Hagi as a youth and be instructed in the statutes of the covenant as he matures.

The sapiential work which Strugnell has named מוסר contains two mentions of Haguy—one being, as I suggest, the *Vision* of Haguy and the other a statement that Haguy had not been available to the antediluvian generations. Cited already on page 247, 4Q417 F1i:13b–18a records,

ואתה                                                              13

14 מבין רוש פעלתכה בזכרון הע[ת]ים [בא חרות החוק}כה{ וחקוק כול הפקודה

15 כי חרות מחוקק לאל על כול עתים בני שות וספר זכרון כתוב לפניו

16 לשמרי דברו והואה חזון ההגוי לספר זכרון וינחילונו לאנוש עם עם רוח כ[י·]א

17 כתבנית קדושים יצרו ועוד לוא נתן הגוי לרוח בשר כי לא ידע בין

18 [טו]ב לרע כמשפט [ר]וחו

And you understand the beginning of your (God's) creation in the remembrance of the e[pochs.] In it (the remembrance) the statute is etched, and the entire command is decreed (in it), because it was etched to God's lawgiver (Moses ?) pertaining to all the epochs for the sons of Seth. A memorial volume is written before Him for those who keep His word; and it is the *vision of Haguy* for the memorial volume; and they (the sons of Seth) bequeathed it forthwith to Enosh together with the people of the spirit, be[ca]use he fashioned it as a sacred blueprint. But Haguy had not as yet been given to the spirit of flesh, for it (the spirit of flesh) had as yet not known the difference between [goo]d and evil in accordance with his [spi]ritual nature . . .[313]

The identity of the book of Haguy, so important in MTA, is puzzling. It has aroused a great deal of speculation by scholars of the Damascus Document. Whether or not Haguy in MTA is identical to that of 4Q417 is controversial. I affirmed their interdependence

---

[312] See Baumgarten's restoration in 4Q265 F7:6–7 of a priest being an expert in the book of Hagi; DJD XXXV, 69–70.

[313] See also Ben Zion Wacholder and Martin G. Abegg, *A Preliminary Edition of the Unpublished Dead Sea Scrolls. The Hebrew and Aramaic Texts from Cave Four. Fascicle Two* (Washington, D.C.: Biblical Archaeology Society, 1992), xiii. For a different rendition of these lines, see Strugnell and Harrington in DJD XXXIV, 155.

in our preliminary edition (II, xiii). Strugnell and Harrington argued for the contrary. According to them, their rendition of the clause ועוד לוא נתן הגוי לרוח בשר as "*But* no more *has* meditation been given to *a*(?) fleshly spirit" precludes a reference to that work as "Haguy." However, if these words are taken to mean, as I do, "But Haguy had not as yet been given to the spirit of flesh," their objection is no longer valid. Rather, it suggests that a work such as entitled *Haguy* would yet be given in the future, probably the *Sefer He-Haguy* in the DSS.

As to the identity of Haguy, it seems to be an appellation given to a psalm-like composition. It appears that the author of 4Q417 assumed that the psalter was part of sapiential literature. It is interesting that 4Q491 F11i:21 (4Q War Scroll[a]) contains the hymnic line: ה[שמיעו בהגיא רנה   ], "[P]roclaim joy with Hagi (meditation)." The origin of the name, as frequently noted, comes from Ps 1:2 and Josh 1:8. Such an understanding of the book of Haguy would make sense in CD 10:6 which states, "who are experts in the book of Hagi and in the foundations of the covenant." It also would cohere with the requirement in *Rule of the Community* that this work be assigned for the education of the youth. For the authors of MTA and *Rule of the Community*, the book of Haguy intertwined Torah with psalm-like wisdom. The judges (CD 10:4–10a) could uphold justice only if competent in the books of Haguy and the foundations of the covenant.

### 3.2.2.9.11. *Concerning Bathing (CD 10:10b–13)*

The next three lines have a subtopic concerning bathing in waters insufficient to immerse a person. Lines 12–13 are problematic. One could read them, as does Cook, as a continuous sentence.[314] Or, as done by most scrollists, they could be divided into two sentences. It seems that this passage may correspond to the controversy between the Pharisees and Sadducees in *Yadaim* 4:7 on whether defiled water contaminates other water.

אומרים צדוקין. קובלין אנו עליכם פרושים. (שאתם מטהרים את הנצוק. אמרים הפרושים. קובלין אנו עליכם צדוקים.) שאתם מטהרים את אמת המים הבאה מבית הקברות.

---

[314] "A man may not purify any dish in such water or in any stone cistern that does not have enough water in it to make a ripple and that something unclean has touched, for its water will defile the water of the vessel." (Wise, Abegg and Cook, *Scrolls*, 68)

The Sadducees say: "We complain against you Pharisees, that you declare a steady stream of liquid as clean." The Pharisees say: "We complain against you Sadducees, that you declare as clean the stream of water that passes through a cemetery." (*Yadaim* 4:7)

If our text relates to the Mishnah, וטמא מימיו במימי הכלי (he defiles its waters as if by the waters of a vessel) suggests that an unclean person defiles a body of water in the same manner as do unclean waters contaminate clean waters. Thus, MTA would seem to follow the opinion attributed to the Sadducees.

### 3.2.2.9.12. *Concerning the Sabbath (CD 10:14–11:18a)*

The next major section consists of a compendium of rules concerned with Sabbath observance. Note that the heading not only mentions the main subject, the Sabbath, but includes the injunction to keep it properly, indicating a polemical stance against those who tend to be lax or follow different rules in observing it. It may also echo *Jub.* 2 and 50 which repeatedly reiterate the sanctification of the Sabbath. Interestingly, the Sabbath rules in our text begin with the temporal parameters of the seventh day from its commencement on Friday evening. The list concludes with the prohibition against performing private sacrificial offerings on that day. Thus, the actions prohibited in this compendium tend to be polemical in the sense that these practices were very stringent and must have been neglected by the people in general, as they concerned speech or allusions to weekly labor and movements of objects. Several of them, such as not transporting burdens in or out of a habitation or the tent of meeting, drawing water or fasting, or striking an animal on the Sabbath, also echo *Jubilees*. Note that the last item in this section, that of sanctioning sacrificial offerings on the Sabbath, parallels *Jub.* 50:10.

### 3.2.2.9.12.1. Cessation of Labor on Friday at Sunset (10:14–17a)

From Schechter to Schiffman, scholars have stressed that this text ordains the prohibition of labor on Friday sometime prior to sunset, what is known in rabbinic literature as תוספת שבת (the lengthening of the Sabbath). However, I am not certain that MTA's wording mirrors this Talmudic concept. Note that our text begins with the command that one may not perform labor מן העת (from the moment . . . ) and concludes with the citation from Deut 5:12, שמור (watch), implying the observance of the beginning of the Sabbath. It goes on to define אשר יהיה גלגל השמש רחוק מן השער מלואו as מן העת, literally "when the

disk of the sun is distant from the gate (in) its fullness." The gate here
refers not to the earthly horizon as is commonly understood, the sun's
diameter being some distance from it, but to the astral gates through
which the sun enters and exits in its daily orbit. The term שער, as
Ginzberg notes, alludes to the twelve gates through which the sun
enters and exits the heavens, portals described in *1 En.* 72:2–37. Note
that the author adds the word מלואו (its fullness), apparently stressing the moment when the sun's fullness disappears from the sky.[315]
Thus it suggests that it refers to the very moment of sunset. Had
the author wanted to lengthen the observance of the Sabbath to a
period before the moment of the sun's disappearance from sight, he
would have pointed to more definite temporal dimensions to specify
clearly how long the Sabbath should be extended. In other words,
there is no clear evidence in MTA for the argument that our text
has the concept of extending the Sabbath to Friday prior to sunset.
To the contrary, our passage may reflect an argument against the
positions found in Talmudic literature.

### 3.2.2.9.12.2. Foul Speech (10:17b–18a)
The first prohibition in our list is against profane speech, what is called
in rabbinics נבול פ(ה) (*Leviticus Rabbah* 24:7). It is interesting that the
author begins his list of Sabbatical prohibitions with an injunction
drawn from prophetic literature. Our text exegetes וְדַבֵּר דָּבָר of Isa
58:13 to refer to foul speech. Schiffman, however, citing *Targum Isaiah*
32:9, translates דבר נבל ורק as "a wicked or vain word," and takes it as
prohibited speech concerning business, a subject which the text goes
on to elaborate upon. However, it is unlikely that the speech prohibited here pertains exclusively to business affairs. Rather, as in 4Q266
F10ii:3 (compare also 1QS 7:9) which condemns דבר נבל, followed by
the next injunction which prohibits interrupting the speech of one's
neighbor, the first clause of our text pertains to foul speech in general,
not specifically to that in business. Moreover, note that 4Q266 F10ii:3
prohibits דבר נבל at any time, not just on the Sabbath.

### 3.2.2.9.12.3. Business (10:18b–21)
The first clause pertains to business adjudications. On the basis of Jer
2:35, Ginzberg suggests reading ישפוט as a Nifal, יִשָּׁפֵט (to plead or

---

[315] Ginzberg, *Unknown Jewish Sect*, 55.

dispute about).[316] The wording לעשות את עבודת חפצו (to do his desired work) draws on עֲשׂוֹת חֲפָצֶיךָ (performing your needs) and מֵעֲשׂוֹת דְּרָכֶיךָ מִמְּצוֹא חֶפְצְךָ (neither doing your ways nor fulfilling your needs), clauses from Isa 58:13 which are taken here as a prohibition against transacting business on the seventh day.[317] The radius of a thousand cubits for walking on the Sabbath outside the city draws on Num 35:4. However, CD 11:5b–6a sanctions two thousand cubits for the accompanying of an animal (see section 3.2.2.9.12.8 below).

### 3.2.2.9.12.4. Preparation of Sabbath Needs on Friday (10:22–11:2a)

The first clause prohibits the consumption of anything that has not been prepared on Friday. For the requirement that all foods must be cooked before the Sabbath, see *Jub.* 50:9. The next clause specifies that one may neither eat nor drink anything outside the camp. The question arises as to what one who is *outside* the camp must do on the Sabbath. 11:1–2a states that if one is on a journey and goes down to wash and wishes to drink, he may do so provided he is standing. Not being permitted to draw water into a vessel, he may drink only from the surface of the water without any utensils. A cursory reading of our text suggests that it sanctions washing but not bathing in an immersed position. As Schiffman understands it, לרחוץ "here refers to the ritual cleansing of the hands (and feet?) performed upon rising and before eating."[318] He posits that על עומדו would be an inappropriate posture for one bathing. However, this interprets our text in the light of rabbinic jurisprudence. We do not know that such requirements existed in the sectarian tradition. רחץ frequently means "to bathe." If so, in this instance the text might refer to one standing in water while washing oneself and drinking.

### 3.2.2.9.12.5. Labor by a Proselyte (CD 11:2b)

The clause that one may not authorize a non-Jew to assist him by doing business for him on the Sabbath (CD 11:2) is subject to two interpretations. Rabin understands בן הנכר in light of Isa 56:3–6 to mean a proselyte.[319] Agreeing with the opinions of Yehezkel Kauf-

---

[316] Ginzberg, *Unknown Jewish Sect*, 58.

[317] For a discussion of the rabbinic sources, see Ginzberg, *Unknown Jewish Sect*, 58–59 and Schiffman, *The Halakhah*, 88.

[318] Schiffman, *The Halakhah*, 102.

[319] Rabin, *Zadokite Documents*, 54.

mann and Emil Schürer, that at the time of the composition of MTA
the practice of formal conversion had not as of yet been instituted,
Schiffman concludes that בן הנכר must refer here to a pagan.[320]

In my opinion, the author of MTA does recognize the existence
of the institution of conversion in several passages. CD 12:10–11
prohibits the sale of one's male and female slave "who have entered
with him into the covenant of Abraham." This makes it clear that the
formal conversion of proselytes requiring circumcision was known to
the author of MTA. The author also knows of the requirement to
recognize monotheism, since he tells us in CD 16:6 that "Abraham
was circumcised on the day he came to know (God)." ברית אברהם in
CD 12:11 must include circumcision as well as recognition of monotheism. Moreover, the prohibition of selling one's slave to pagans
takes for granted that converted slaves were fully subject to Jewish
law, a point that is also evident in CD 11:12.

אל ימרא את עבדו ואת אמתו ואת שוכרו ביⁿ⁰⁰ השבת[321]

One shall not command his man servant, his maid servant or his hireling
(to perform tasks) on the Sabbath day.

Returning to CD 11:2, the use of בן הנכר rather than גוי, the standard term for pagans in MTA, favors the view of Rabin, that this
formula refers to one who has converted to Judaism.

3.2.2.9.12.6. Soiled Garments (CD 11:3–4a)

The word זג has given rise to various opinions. Schechter read מובאים
בגו (that were brought by a gentile);[322] Ginzberg emended סואבים
בגל (soiled by excrement).[323] Schiffman and Rabin understand זג as
gazzā, of Persian etymology, and translate it as "put into storage."[324]
My translation "wool shearings" accords with Deut 18:4. Garments
brought into contact with wool would be cleansed with incense.

---

[320] Schiffman, *The Halakhah*, 104–106.
[321] בשבת CD; בֹ]יֹם הֹשֹבֹ[ת 4Q270 F6v:17.
[322] Fitzmyer, ed., *Documents*, 81.
[323] Ginzberg, *Unknown Jewish Sect*, 62.
[324] Schiffman, *The Halakhah*, 107; Rabin, *Zadokite Documents*, 54.

### 3.2.2.9.12.7. Fasting (CD 11:4b–5a)

Early scholars—Schechter, Ginzberg and Rabin—assume a corruption of יתרעב (to hunger) to יתערב (to intermingle).[325] More recently, however, scrollists have insisted on the received reading, paralleled also in 4Q271 F5i:1. Schiffman construes it "to enter partnership";[326] Baumgarten "to intermingle (purities with others)";[327] Cook, "to cross Sabbath borders";[328] Vermes, "to mingle (with others)";[329] Abegg in his computerized morphologically tagged text lists it under the broader glosses, "to mix" or "to interfere."[330] However, in my opinion these translators ignore the import of the word מרצונו (voluntarily), which makes good sense only with the presumption of a metathesis assumed by the early scholars. That one should not go hungry on the Sabbath accords with standard sectarian opinion. *Jubilees* 50:12 and other sectarian writings make fasting on the Sabbath a capital offense.

### 3.2.2.9.12.8.  Pasturing Animals and Moving Objects
###             (CD 11:5b–9a)

What follows are rulings concerning the movement of animals and objects. The proscription limits the pasturing to a maximum of two thousand cubits, diverging from CD 10:21 which specifies the radius of the sabbath walk as one thousand. Drawing on MTA, 4Q265 F7:4–5 limits the accompanying of grazing cattle to a distance of two thousand cubits on the Sabbath.[331]

The basis for both the distance of thousand and the two thousand cubits in MTA draws on Num 35:4–5, which limits the pastureland of the Levites to a thousand cubits and that of the other Israelites to two thousand. Rabbinic exegesis ignores the thousand assigned to the Levites in Scripture, but regards the two thousand cubits as the Sabbatical boundary for both humans and beasts.

Our text goes on to prohibit striking (literally raising the arm

---

[325]  Fitzmyer, ed., *Documents*, 81; Ginzberg, *Unknown Jewish Sect*, 64; Rabin, *Zadokite Documents*, 54.

[326]  Schiffman, *The Halakhah*, 109–111.

[327]  Charlesworth, ed., *Damascus Document*, 47.

[328]  Weis, Abegg and Cook, *Scrolls*, 68.

[329]  Vermes, 140.

[330]  Martin G. Abegg, Jr., *Qumran Sectarian Manuscripts: Qumran text and grammatical tags* (1999–2005), CD 11:4.

[331]  Joshua 3:3–4 stipulates the same length for the distance between the ark and the people who follow it.

to strike) a bovine on the Sabbath. Ginzberg conjectures that this prohibition rests on Exod 20:10, which prohibits animals owned by Israelites from performing labor on the Sabbath. He raises the question whether our text prohibits an owner from inflicting pain upon his beast, or whether the striking refers to directing an animal in its work. According to Ginzberg, the next clause, which says that if the animal be rebellious he may not take it out from its house, suggests the second alternative. *Jubilees* 50:12 makes the striking of an animal a capital offense. Note, however, that according to CD 12:3–4, labor on the Sabbath does not entail the death penalty.

The clause prohibiting bringing objects *from* or *into* a domain draws on Jer 17:21–22, but our text here probably depends on *Jub.* 2:29–30. The proscription restricting carrying anything from a *tent* or *house* on the Sabbath paraphrases *Jub.* 50:8.

### 3.2.2.9.12.9. Opening Sealed Vessels (CD 11:9b)

The word טוח appears in Lev 14:42–43 and 48 in the sense of covering a wall with clay. CD 8:12 employs the phrase טחי התפל (those who plaster with whitewash) metaphorically in the sense of covering up with vain speech. The prohibition against opening sealed vessels diverges from the majority opinion in rabbinics which permits it.[332]

### 3.2.2.9.12.10. Carrying Medications (CD 11:9c–10a)

The sense of סמנים is complicated. Baumgarten, Schechter, Schiffman and Vermes translate it as "spices," Rabin and Cook, "medicine" and Martínez-Tigchelaar, "perfumes."[333] The word סמן could carry the sense of the Aramaic סימנא (gem).[334] According to Schiffman, the sentence refers to women carrying perfume, a notion which diverges from the masculine wording ישא איש עליו.[335] The singling out of carrying סמנים from among all other labors deserves comment. If we posit that it refers to medicines, our text may have a polemical stance, since the rabbis permitted it. See CD 11:16, which prohibits the pulling out of a person who has fallen into water or a pit. Here we

---

[332] See *Tosefta Shabbat* 16(17):13.
[333] Schiffman, *Halakhah*, 116; Rabin, *Zadokite Documents*, 56; Wise, Abegg and Cook, *Scrolls*, 69; Martínez and Tigchelaar, *Scrolls Study Edition*, vol. 1, 569.
[334] Hebrew סמ; cf. *Targum Yerushalmi* Deut 33:19.
[335] Schiffman, *The Halakhah*, 116–17.

find the rejection of the concept known from rabbinics as פקוח נפש דוחה את השבת (a danger to life overrides the Sabbath).

### 3.2.2.9.12.11. Carrying Rock and Earth (11:10b–11a)

These lines prohibit moving rock and soil on the Sabbath, even within a dwelling place (Lev 25:29). Scholars have noted that this corresponds to the Talmudic מוקצה (objects not usable on the Sabbath), which are proscribed by a rabbinic (non-biblical) ordinance. It is, however, doubtful that the sect accepted the concept of מוקצה. Our prohibition, therefore, stems from the exclusion of coming into contact with objects that have not been specifically prepared (מוכן) to be used on the seventh day.

### 3.2.2.9.12.12. Carrying Infants (CD 11:11b)

Our text specifies that a nurse may not take an infant to and from the house. It does not say whether this nurse was Jewish or Gentile. However, the wording "going out or coming in" must refer to the former, as do the other regulations in this section.

### 3.2.2.9.12.13. Requiring a Servant to Work (CD 11:12)

CD reads ימרא איש את, while 4Q271 F5i:7 has ימר את. Our reading ימרא departs from our principle of following the ancient cave texts when there are divergences between the medieval and the Qumran texts. The verb ימרא seems more plausible than ימר. Its root is debated. Rabin understands מרא as cognate to Arabic *mry* (to urge on) and Baumgarten as a jussive form of *mrh* (to resist, provoke).[336] The translation here "command" draws on the Talmudic מר or מרא (Aramaic) meaning "master," but, as a verb, has the sense of "to command." As to the identity of the servant and maid, Schiffman argues that they must be Jewish personnel, since the Essenes did not own slaves.[337] However, CD 12:10–11 which prohibits the sale of one's slave who has entered the covenant of Abraham, suggests that MTA posits the ownership of slaves among the sectarians.

---

[336] Rabin, *Zadokite Documents*, 56; Baumgarten in Charlesworth, ed., *Damascus Document*, 49. Baumgarten translates "Let no man contend (?) with his slave, his maidservant, or his hired man on the Sabbath."

[337] Schiffman, *The Halakhah*, 121.

### 3.2.2.9.12.14. Animal Husbandry (CD 11:13–14a)

Rabin and Schiffman diverge on how to render these two clauses. According to Rabin, they are part of a single injunction.[338] One may not assist an animal, either the mother in giving birth or the young if it is born in a pit. As read by Schiffman, however, the two clauses represent independent ideas—one concerning help for the newborn embryo and the other, if an animal falls into a cistern.[339] Both interpretations can be defended. The first receives support in the CD reading; the second in the cave texts.

### 3.2.2.9.12.15. Socializing with Pagans (CD 11:14b–15a)

The prohibition of camping near pagans draws evidently on Lev 23:3 which commands Israel to keep the Sabbath throughout all their habitations. The implication here is that one could associate with pagans on days other than the seventh day (and festivals). See my comments below on CD 12:6b–11a (section 3.2.2.9.14) pertaining to relations with pagans.

### 3.2.2.9.12.16. Business (CD 11:15b)

For the word יחל see Num 30:3. Ginzberg and Rabin speculate as to the sense of this clause, that it may allude to what is recorded in *Tosefta Eruvin* 3(4):5—that one may not desecrate the Sabbath for the sake of saving property, but may do so to save a life.[340] However, our author is here dependent on Neh 13:15–22 and *Jub.* 50:8.[341] The latter specifically prohibits doing business on the Sabbath and renders buying and selling a capital offense.

### 3.2.2.9.12.17. Assisting a Fallen Person (CD 11:16–17a)

Lines 16–17a tell what to do or not to do (depending on the translation) when one falls into a reservoir of water or a pit. Translators diverge. Schechter, Charles, Baumgarten et al. render, "And if any person falls into a gathering of water or into a place of . . . he shall not bring him up by a ladder or a cord or instrument."[342] Ginzberg and Rabin, regarding it as inconceivable for the sect to have rejected the

---

[338] Rabin, *Zadokite Documents*, 56.
[339] Schiffman, *The Halakhah*, 121–22.
[340] Ginzberg, *Unknown Jewish Sect*, 68; Rabin, *Zadokite Documents*, 57.
[341] See also Schiffman, *The Halakhah*, 125.
[342] Fitzmyer, ed., *Documents*, 81.

rabbinic concept that "saving a life suspends the Sabbath," reconstruct the text to read, "But every living man who falls into a place *full* of water or into a place from which one cannot come up, let *any* man bring him up with a ladder or a rope or *any* instrument."[343] Schiffman accepts Schechter's understanding of the wording of the text, but modifies it to conform in spirit to that proposed by Ginzberg.[344] Thus, according to Schiffman, the sect did believe that saving a life overrides the Sabbath. However, this sanction of violating the seventh day because of a life was restricted only through a case where there was no other means of saving the person (בדיעבד). To begin with (לכתחילה), one should attempt to rescue without violating the Sabbath. In my opinion, however, the author of MTA does not display an awareness of the difference proposed by Schiffman that distinguishes between לכתחילה and בדיעבד. Either way, one may not use an instrument to violate the Sabbath. In fact, as I show in the introduction, a notion that the sectarian writers tended to avoid the imposition of the death penalty cannot be supported by the sources. According to MTA, any violation of biblical proscriptions, except those of the Sabbath and festivals, was subject to capital punishment. Hence, it is not surprising that they prohibit using any instrument for saving the life of one who has fallen into a cistern.

### 3.2.2.9.12.18. Sacrificial Offerings in the Sanctuary (CD 11:17b–18a)

As Baumgarten notes, the verb יעל here bridges with the preceding clause which contains the verb יעלה. Schiffman understands מלבד שבתותיכם to exclude any other offering prescribed in Lev 23 and Num 28, except for the burnt offering.[345] This probably misconstrues the meaning of עולת השבת. First, the word עולה here does not necessarily restrict it to the burnt offerings alone. Rather, it is a collective term summarizing what is itemized in line 19, עולה ומנחה ולבונה ועץ (a burnt, a gift, an incense or a wood offering), bearing a resemblance to those of *Jub.* 50:10 (save burning frankincense and bringing oblations and sacrifices). Moreover, עולת could be read as a חסר form for the plural עולות, meaning here, not the burnt offering exclusively, but all the sacrificial offerings of the Sabbath. The ruling here that only offerings

---

[343] Rabin, *Zadokite Documents*, 56.

[344] Schiffman, *The Halakhah*, 125–27.

[345] Schiffman, *The Halakhah*, 128.

mandated in Scripture may be brought on the Sabbath conforms
to the Talmudic tradition. This injunction is the last clause on the
list of Sabbatical legislation begun in CD 10:14 and as mentioned
earlier, corresponds to the final portion of the Sabbatical commandments found in *Jub.* 50:10. The author of *Jubilees* lists it just prior
to the conclusion of his work.

A word may be said here about Schiffman's summary of the Qumran sabbath code based on our text. It tends to take for granted what
is only conjecture. There is no reason to suppose that the sect had the
concept of מוקצה. What is prohibited is drawn from the biblical passages which include not only the Pentateuchal rules, but also Isa
58:13–14, Jer 17:21–27 and Neh 13:15–22. Partnership is not specified in this sectarian compendium; only fasting on the Sabbath is
prohibited. Of course, it was not necessary for the author to list the
prohibition against establishing a partnership, since it would fall under
the other prohibitions of doing business, such as not adjudicating
concerning matters of property and wealth (CD 10:18). Although
Ginzberg and Rabin agree with Schiffman that the first rule mentioned in this code extends the Sabbath to before the Friday sunset,
thus echoing the view recorded in the Talmudic tradition, a close
analysis of the wording does not affirm this opinion. What the author
of this text insists on is that the observance of the Sabbath begin at
the moment of the astronomical sunset. Schiffman's assertion that
the term סמנים in CD 11:10 refers to perfume carried by women is
unlikely. The vocabulary of this prohibition is masculine, and probably refers to medications. Finally, it is not necessary to maintain, as
Schiffman does, that the author of MTA limited the Sabbatical altar
to the burnt offering alone. The word עולה includes any Sabbatical
offering prescribed in the Torah.

At this point it may be worth mentioning that MTA contains
other allusions to the Sabbath outside this compendium. The author
of MTA tells that God revealed the mysteries of the Sabbath and the
festivals, calendrical observations in which other Israelites have gone
astray (CD 3:12–15). In other words, the sabbath laws in MTA form
part of the polemics embedded in our work. CD 6:17b–19 reinforces
this polemical stance:

6:17 ואת יתומים ירצחו להבדיל בין הטמא לטהור ולהודיע בין
6:18 הקודש לחול ולשמור את יום השבת כפרושה ואת המועדות
6:19 ואת יום התענית כמצאת באי הברית החדשה בארץ דמשק

It is necessary to differentiate between what is defiling and pure and to make known between what is sacred and what is ordinary; and to observe the day of the Sabbath including its elaborations and the festive seasons and the day of fasting (atonement) in accordance with the practice of those who will enter the new covenant in the land of Damascus. (CD 6:17b–19)

CD 12:3b–5a contains one of the most dramatic passages in this work: "However, anyone who strays by profaning the Sabbath and the festivals shall *not be put to death*; rather let the people keep him in custody." These lines appear to nullify the injunctions in Exod 31:14–15, which mandate the death sentence to those who desecrate the Sabbath. It also contradicts both *Jub.* 2 and 50 which constantly reiterate capital punishment for its violators. Reasoning that the text could not have flagrantly diverged from biblical rulings, Schiffman interprets לא יומת in CD 12:4 to refer to accidental transgressions (what the rabbis call בשוגג). However, this view is untenable, since the protasis uses the phrase יתעה לחלל, denoting willful violation.[346]

### 3.2.2.9.13. *The Sanctification of the Temple and the House of Worship (CD 11:18b–12:6)*

The previous section dealt with the keeping of the holy Sabbath. The next ten and one half lines treat the subject of holy places, concluding with the Sabbath and festivals. This pericope pertaining to holy loci links up into a single theme concerning קדושה (holiness). The first clause ordains the community to refrain from sending gifts with a defiled person to the temple, resulting in its contamination. The itemization of the offerings here is interesting. It includes those of burnt, grain, frankincense and wood. The עולה here stands for any sacrificial offering.[347] The grain offering refers to gifts in general. That of wood corresponds to the [קורבן ה]עצים in 11QT 43:4. As is usual, the author of MTA paraphrases the Masoretic text (here Prov 15:8) for his purposes, influenced perhaps by Prov 15:29. It avoids using the tetragrammaton and alters יְשָׁרִים (upright) to צדיקים (righteous). 1QS 9:5 echoes our text. CD 11:21b–12:1a deals with an institution not otherwise attested—the בית ההשתחוות, literally "house of prostration," also characterized as בֵּית קודש (a sacred house). It seems to be related or identical to the traditional synagogue known from

---

[346] Cf. also CD 1:13; 2:15, etc.
[347] See the comments on עולת השבת above.

ancient sources such as Philo, Josephus and the New Testament. Its Hebrew name, בית הכנסת (the house of assembly), goes back to the period of the Second Temple. As described in our passage, this house of worship had features comparable to that of the sanctuary. The service is called עבודה. The author of MTA requires that one may enter it only while washed and that trumpets be employed to assemble and disperse the people. This suggests that it was a large assembly.

The next clause prohibits cohabitation with a woman within the confines of the holy city. The epithet עיר המקדש (city of the Temple), not recorded in the Hebrew Scriptures, occurs in several DSS passages. 11QT 47:3–18 describes its sanctity as being on a higher level than that of any other Israelite city. Sacrificial offerings or any other slaughtered animals and their skins could be neither imported into nor exported from these cities. CD 5:6–7 charges that the opposition defiles the temple by not separating according to the Torah and by sleeping with women during their menses, apparently a reference to actions within the עיר המקדש. 4Q248 F1:6–7 relates the invasion of a king to Egypt, after which he came into the עיר המקדש. Presumably all occurrences of this phrase refer to Jerusalem as a whole, including its borders, not as argued by Schiffman that עיר המקדש was restricted to the הר הבית (the temple mount).[348] If so, the question arises as to why these writers avoided giving its appellation, especially in that the name ירושלם plausibly appears in MTA.[349] Possibly the author intends to emphasize the circumlocution as a polemic against the opinion imbedded in rabbinic tradition which sanctioned cohabitation in Jerusalem.

The key to the understanding of CD 12:2b–3 and the reconstructed parallel in the list of transgressions (4Q270 F2i:9–12) is the contrast between idolatrous practices and the violation of the Sabbath. Whereas breaching the former entails the death penalty (ישפט), the profanation of the latter does not. Hence, the statement in CD 12:3b–4a, וכול אשר יתעה לחלל את השבת (However, anyone who strays by profaning the Sabbath), encompasses the Sabbath regulations from CD 10:14–11:18a as well as the items concerning the Sabbath in the list of transgressions (4Q270 F2i:18b–20).[350] The leniency

[348] See J. Milgrom, "The City of the Temple. A Response to Lawrence H. Schiffman," *JQR* 85 (1994): 125–28.

[349] Cf. ירוש[לי]ם in 4Q267 F5ii:5.

[350] See in particular the clause "One may not profane (יחל) the Sabbath for wealth or business" in CD 11:15 and the reconstruction "or who p[rofanes (יחלל]) the Sabbath day and the festivals" in 4Q270 F2i:19b–20.

concerning the Sabbath may have resulted from its stringent nature, since the legislation embraces speech and movement, actions easy to transgress.

Schechter and others connect the verb ירפא to רפא (to heal), but Ginzberg's rendition that if he "desists" from it (רפה) appears preferable. The rule of keeping one under observance for a period of seven years occurs in 11QT 63:14–15 in connection with a captive woman (Deut 21:11) and in 4Q270 F4:15–16 (paralleled in 4Q266 F12:8), evidently in connection with שופחה החרופה (a betrothed slave).

### 3.2.2.9.14. *Relations with Pagans (CD 12:6b–11a)*

The next five lines concern relations with people who practice idolatry. Lines 6b–7a prohibit anyone from shedding the blood of a pagan for gain. The phrase לשפוך דם could mean either "to slay" or "to injure." Ginzberg understood this clause to refer to receiving money in support of Israelite charities. The text goes on with an interesting conclusion: כי אם בעצת חבור ישראל (unless authorized by the association of Israel). This wording may suggest that there was at this moment enmity between the two groups, denoting that even during hostilities one might not appropriate pagan goods unless explicitly authorized by the association. As to the meaning of חבור, scholars compare it to the rabbinic חבורה (association). This term seems to occur in the Testament of Amram wherein he (Amram) describes, "(when there came) news about a frightening war our [gro]up went ba[ck] to the land of E[gypt]" (שמועת קרב מבהלה תאב[ה חבו]רֹתנא לארעא מן[צרין]).[351] Lines 8b–10a go on to disallow the sale of sacrificial animals, wine or oil to pagans, for they might utilize them for idolatrous purposes. Neither may one sell slaves who have converted to Judaism (CD 12:10b–11a). That the phrase ברית אברהם here refers to circumcision as part of the conversion process becomes apparent from CD 16:6 which affirms that Abraham was circumcised on the day he came to know God. In other words, according to MTA, the institution of conversion goes back to the time of the patriarch. If so, the clause בברית אברהם is conceivably the oldest allusion we have to the institution of גרות.

---

[351]  4Q545 F1a-bii:16. Martínez and Tigchelaar read, however, שמועת קרב מבהלה [האב]ין מן [תנא לארע מן]צרין (rumor of war, frightening those returning [from] here to the land of E[gypt . . .]); Florentino García Martínez and Eibert J. D. Tigchelaar, eds. and translators, *The Dead Sea Scrolls Study Edition, Volume Two: 4Q274–11Q31* (Brill: Leiden, 1998), 1090–91.

### 3.2.2.9.15. *Prohibited Foods (CD 12:11b–18)*

The next eight and one half lines deal with dietary restrictions, another aspect of sanctification. The first phrase, אל ישקץ, appears in CD 7:3, retaining its biblical meaning of detesting. Here שקץ has the sense of not abominating oneself with prohibited foods. The first statement is general and includes any consumption of forbidden creatures or creeping things. According to Ginzberg מעגלי הדבורים refers to the Syriac עגלי דבריתא (little worms). He interpreted thusly because it seemed inconceivable to him that the sect would have prohibited the consumption of honey, since Samson partook of it (Judg 14:8–9).[352] Furthermore its prohibition accords with Lev 11:29. It is more likely, however, that מעגלי הדבורים refers to the larvae of bees and that, contrary to the halakah, the sect considered it prohibited, as did Philo.[353] The דבש in the Hebrew Bible (Exod 3:8 etc.) refers to fruit honey. As to the fish, the sect diverges from the Talmudic halakah. Rabbinic law does not require special ritual for the consumption of fish. Nevertheless, the author of MTA does. Fish are not to be consumed unless they have been sliced open and their blood extracted. As Ginzberg understands lines 14b–15a, the process of eating locusts is by roasting or cooking them. It is, however, more plausible that MTA's concern is their cleansing.

The next two passages, lines 15b–18, are likewise polemical against concepts embedded in the Mishnah and Talmud. According to the latter, defilement is reduced progressively. Thus, items that come into contact with defiled objects contract lower levels of contamination as the process continues from item to item. The author of MTA, however, insists that an object which has touched something defiled becomes itself defiled on the same level as did its source. Thus, our writer was aware of the Talmudic concept of ראשון and שני לטומאה (the first contact and the second contact of contamination), but repudiated it. For the writer, anyone who touches oil that has been contaminated by the presence of a corpse would be likewise defiled.[354]

Translators understand lines 17b–18 as affirming that household items attached to the wall in the proximity of a corpse become defiled

[352] Ginzberg, *Unknown Jewish Sect*, 78–79.

[353] As cited by Rabin, *Zadokite Documents*, 61.

[354] For a discussion of this passage in relation to Josephus' treatment regarding the abstention of the Essenes from oil, see J. Baumgarten, "The Essene Avoidance of Oil and the Laws of Purity," *RevQ* 6 (1976): 183–92.

just as do any implements of standard use. However, this rendition would add little to what has been already stated in lines 15b–17a. Furthermore, this understanding would require a comparative כ before כלי מעשה. As I see it, the central point here is that stationary household items become the source that defiles any manufactured object. Again, the author points out that the level of contamination is continuous and not reduced as argued by the Talmudic sages.

### 3.2.2.10. *The Organizational Structure of the Community (CD 12:19– 14:18a)*

At this point, the author presents two organizational structures within the community: the procedures for the *cities* and the *camps*. Other such headings appear in CD 10:4 dealing with the rules for the justices, in 13:7 pertaining to the role of the Supervisor, in 14:3 concerning the camps, and 14:12 on a tax for the benefit of the needy. A related heading summarizing the procedures for the cities and camps is reiterated in the last lines of the book (4Q266 F11:18–21).

### 3.2.2.10.1. *The Cities (CD 12:19–22a)*

Lines 19–20 highlight the contents of the work, that of separating between the defiled and the pure, and distinguishing what is sacred and what is ordinary. As explained elsewhere, the cities were apparently subject to special rules of purity such as celibacy, a status not practiced in the camps.

The text continues by introducing the משכיל (the sage), a personage already mentioned in 4Q266 F5i:17–18. For the broader implications of the sage, see the comments above. That the statutes pertaining to this leader are sandwiched between the procedures of the cities and those of the camps may accentuate his duties as a spiritual guide for the communities of both. The משכיל is mentioned a third time in CD 13:22, where once again he serves as the spiritual prototype for all Israel to follow.

### 3.2.2.10.2. *The Camps (CD 12:22b–14:18a)*

What follows describes the camps: a classification of their general rank and the intellectual quality of their leadership. It then elaborates at length on the duties of its leader.

### 3.2.2.10.2.1. The Leadership of the Camps (CD 12:22b–13:2a)

This large pericope on the camps begins with the skills required of the leaders of Israel, abilities that should prevail until the community is taken over by the Messiah of Aaron and Israel. What CD 12:22b–13:2a insists is that the organizational structure advocated in MTA not be altered arbitrarily. Only the anointed of Aaron and Israel will establish a new order. The camps of Israel in the messianic age will follow the model recorded in Exod 18: a partition into thousands, hundreds, fifties and tens. The ten, then, is the minimum division. In rabbinic tradition, the reason for the מנין draws on the ten spies dispatched by Moses in Num 13. Our text points to another source alluding to the so-called מנין.

### 3.2.2.10.2.2. The Sacerdote and the Supervisor (13:2b–7a)

CD 13:2b–7a deals with the qualifications of the primary leaders of the camps and exposes us to their hierarchy. This is the second time the author describes the qualifications of the community's leadership. In CD 10 we heard of those of the justices. Here it is those of the priests and evidently their substitutes, the Levites, along with the Supervisor. The sensational qualification required of these leaders is that of being expert in wisdom literature, specifically in the book of Hagi (Haguy), a work that I understand is an amplification of the book of Psalms.[355] The author draws attention to the fact that the priestly office is lineal. Hence, there is no certainty that each successive leader of the decimal subdivision will have mastered the requisite skills. MTA provides that, in the absence of a qualified priest, a trained Levite may assume that office; and, implicitly, if there is no Levite, an ordinary Israelite or proselyte who possesses the necessary expertise may serve. His epithet is the מבקר (Supervisor), a term used in Talmudic literature, but not recorded in the Hebrew Scriptures. It is, nevertheless, derived from the clause in Ezek 34:12 כְּבַקָּרַת רֹעֶה עֶדְרוֹ (as a shepherd cares for his flock). This term is a favorite in MTA, occurring some twenty-one times in the extant text. As are the leaders of each decimal, the מבקר is presumably also an expert in the book of Haguy. Nevertheless, he may not formally do tasks that Scripture assigns to the priests. These responsibilities belong to the leading priests and their descendents. If there is a need for expertise, such as analyzing the state of a leper,

---

[355] See the chart on page 327 for a comparison of the three texts that present leadership responsibilities and qualifications.

and the priest lacks the competence to do so, it is the Supervisor
who instructs the priest in the procedures of the case (CD 13:5).
So far, however, our text has not told us of the precise role of the
מבקר. This is described in CD 13:7–14:18a.

### 3.2.2.10.2.3. The Duties of the Supervisor (13:7b–14:18a)

The author has already introduced his readers to some of the duties
of the camp's Supervisor, namely oversight in the admission process
and instruction of new members. Here he provides more detail on
the responsibilities of this leader, highlighting his directing of spiritual
matters, oversight of the hierarchical system, and his participation in
caring for social needs.

### 3.2.2.10.2.3.1. Spiritual Guidance (CD 13:7b–10)

The text requires the Supervisor to enlighten the many in the acts
of God, explaining what they are. The phrase מעשי אל occurs twice
elsewhere in MTA.[356] Only in this passage, however, does the author
expand on its broader sense. He begins by disclosing the responsibility of the Supervisor to expound upon the mighty wonders of God.
גבורות פלאו is a variant of רזי פלאו.[357] The next clause tells us that
the Supervisor must relate to the community the events of eternity
with their explanations. The exact sense of this clause is obscure.
CD reads בפרתיה (in its details). The reading adopted here follows
4Q267 F9iv:5. This clause apparently refers to the various amplifications found in works such as *Jubilees*, *Enoch* and, perhaps, *Apocryphon of Genesis*, where biblical heroes and events are told in greater
detail. For fatherly compassion toward offspring see Ps 103:13, "as
a father has compassion on (his) children" and 1 John 3:1, "Look at
what kind of love the father has displayed to us, that we be called
the children of God." As to the motif of God shepherding His
people, see my reconstruction of 4Q266 F4:11, apparently alluding
to David. CD 13:10 is unique in ancient literature in that it displays
an awareness for the care of an individual, namely that the leader
of a community must pay attention to the welfare of each person
so that no one be made a scapegoat.

---

[356] CD 1:1–2; 2:14–15. See also my reconstruction [מ̇ע̇שׂי אל] in 4Q266 F1:5.
[357] For other examples of רזי פלא cf. CD 3:18; 1QS 9:18; 11:15; 1QHª 5:8;
9:21; 10:13; 15:27; 19:10; 1Q27 F1i:7; 4Q259 3:17; 4Q417 F1i:2; F1i:13; 4Q418
F219:2; 4Q511 F44-47:6.

3.2.2.10.2.3.2. Supervision of the Hierarchical System (13:11–
                14:12a)

It is the duty of the Supervisor to install each new member into
his appropriate rank within the community hierarchy. 14:3–6 later
divides the community into four classes: priests, Levites, Israelites and
proselytes. The Supervisor places each individual into his appropriate
rank within these classes. He is in charge of analyzing the fitness of
each person along with his material possessions and must record each
sequentially into the membership roll of the children of light.[358]
Thus each member knew who was above or below him in rank.
CD 13:12b–13 reemphasizes the paramount role of the מבקר of
the camp.

Scrollists used to read בני השחת (sons of the Pit) in line 14, but as
noted by Baumgarten, the reading בני השחר is secure. These lines
evidently prohibit all conventional trade using a monetary medium
within the community. Exchanges must be exclusively by barter.
However, the text implicitly allows trading with people outside the
community.[359] Whether exchanges are by barter or through pieces
of silver, they require the authorization of the Supervisor.

CD 13:16b–17a adds that what is true of commercial dealings applies
as well to marriage and divorce. Both require the Supervisor's consent.
The identity of the person who should seek counsel in the clause
וה[ו]א[ ]א[ו]ה יֹעֹשֹה ב[עֵצֹה (And he shall d[o so with] counsel) is uncertain.
It might refer to the one who is taking the wife, stipulating that
he should seek the counsel of the Supervisor. Or, as is more likely,
the clause specifies that the Supervisor not act arbitrarily in matters of marriage, but seek advice from others before issuing decrees
on matrimony. In other words, marriage is not like commerce. In
the former, the Supervisor may act on his own. He may not do so,
however, in anything pertaining to familial issues.

What follows in 13:17b–18a relates to the Supervisor acting as a
disciplinarian of the camps' families. The phrases "humble [spirit]
and gracious love" echo Mic 6:8 ". . . what does the Lord require
of you, except to do justice, to love mercy and to walk humbly with
your God?"[360] It is interesting that MTA itemizes the offspring as

---

[358] That גורל האוֹר refers here to the community of the children of light, see
בֹנֹי[ ב אוֹר in 4Q266 F1:1.
[359] J. Baumgarten, "The 'Sons of Dawn' in *CDC* 13:14–15 and the Ban on
Commerce among the Essenes," *IEJ* 33 (1983): 81–85.
[360] Cf. 1QS 2:24 and 4Q417 F2i:2–3.

sons, (probably) daughters and infants. This makes it clear once again
that the camps were not celibate and that the Supervisor acted as a
disciplinarian, perhaps together with the father. The text continues
in 13:18b–19a by urging the Supervisor not to treat them harshly for
their transgressions (evidently meaning not only those of the children,
but of all the members of the camp). This statement to treat sinners
mildly gives the impression that it is out of line with the general treatment of sin in MTA which requires severe, even capital punishment
for the sinner. The solution may be that פשעים here has a less stringent
sense than elsewhere, as it seems to be explained in the next clause.
Unfortunately the lacunae in 19b–20a deprive us of a clear solution.
If one reads the text with my proposed reconstruction "even (against)
that which is not bound by [the covenantal] oa[th] pertaining to their
disciplinary rules,]" the author himself distinguished between two
types of violations—those that draw on Hebrew Scriptures and form
part of the covenantal oath, and those which are not bound by them
(ואת אשר איננו נקשׁר), rather are part of the discipline imposed independently of sacred writ. The latter conform to the disciplinary
rules in the conclusion to the book (CD 14:18b–23; 4Q266 F10ii;
4Q270 F7i:1–17; 4Q266 F11:1–3a) where the consequences for violation are temporary exclusion and a fine rather than expulsion
from the sect.

CD 13:20b–22a summarizes the preceding material, but how far
back we are not certain. It undoubtedly extends at least to 12:22–23,
introducing the procedures for the camps. However, it may include
the procedures for the cities beginning in 12:19. The phrase
[לֹכֹל זֹ]רַע ישׂראל in 13:20, whose restoration is supported by 4Q266
F9iii:11, tends to favor that the summary applies to both camps and
cities. Aside from the individual consequences for sin, the author prescribes also corporate responsibilities. The failure of the entire community to keep these procedures would have severe results: expulsion
from the holy land and oppression (מצוקות), apparently in exile.

CD 13:22b–14:2 urges the people to live by the precepts of the
משׂכיל. This is the third time MTA deals with this leader. As explained
above, the sage is probably a broader term describing the מבקר,
referring to his place as the spiritual leader of all Israel, both the
communities of the cities and camps. Our text here continues by citing Isa 7:17 in an abbreviated format. This verse was quoted in CD
7:11–12 where the prophetic source is named. There it noted that
Israel would split once again into two parts as it had in the days of
Jeroboam I, one migrating north to Damascus, the other perishing.

The verse has a parallel purpose in our passage, noting that Israel will split again in the messianic age into two parts. One will be saved and the other will vanish. CD 14:1b–2 presages salvation for all those who walk in the way of God because of their trust in the divine covenant which will deliver them from those that are ensnared by the pit. Scholars differ on the reading of the succeeding clause. פתאים, as suggested by Qimron and others, is textually implausible on two grounds. The reading פתאום is secure in CD and not unlikely in 4Q267 F9v:5. Contextually the suggested emendation makes little sense here, for the term פתי in MTA alludes to one who lacks wisdom, not necessarily to a sinner. Thus, CD 13:7 calls the leading priest who is not trained in matters of leprosy a פתי without infringing in any way on his lofty office. In my understanding פתאום עבד[ו] ויענשו would refer to מוקשי שחת "those who are *ensnared by* the pit" in contrast to the righteous who will be delivered in the messianic age.

CD 14:3–12a goes on to relate the order of seating within the camps as administered by the Supervisor. The system follows the four-fold divisions of priests, Levites, Israelites and proselytes. 1QS 6:8–9 alters this formula. It has the priests, followed by the זקנים (the elders) instead of the Levites, then followed by the שאר כול העם (the remainder of all the people). This could be interpreted in one of two ways. *Rule of the Community* does not recognize the existence of proselytes. Indeed, the term גר does not occur in 1QS. Or, it could signify that according to this sectarian text the proselytes were integrated within the remainder of the people.[361] On the other hand, the four-fold division of MTA should be compared to that of *Mishnah Qiddushin* 4:1 where the people are divided into ten classes led by the priests, Levites, Israelites, unfrocked priests, proselytes, and redeemed slaves. It is apparent that our text here assigns a status to the גר not inferior to the preceding groups. It, therefore, seems to draw on Ezek 47:22–23 where the גר has the same status as that of the tribes of Israel. However, it diverges from 4QFlorilegium (4Q174) F1–2i:4 which places the proselyte among the nations with whom intermarriage is forbidden (Deut 23:4).[362]

For the requirement that the chief priest be an expert in the book of Haguy, see our discussion above on the nature of judgeship (CD

---

[361] See Hempel's discussion of the proselytes (*The Laws of the Damascus Document*, 135).

[362] See M. Broshi and A. Yardeni (DJD XIX, 83) on the treatment of the נתינין in 4Q340.

10:4–10a). Note, however, that whereas here the priest must be an expert in the book of Hagi (Haguy) as well as the משפטי התורה, its parallel in CD 10:6 has the variant יסודי הברית (the foundations of the covenant). On the other hand, no other work is mentioned along with the book of Haguy in the second parallel of CD 13:2. Our text makes another point not mentioned in the above parallels, suggesting that the laws of the Torah must be understood in consonance with the book of Haguy.

CD 14:8b–9 limits the age of the מבקר to between thirty and fifty years. This diverges from that of the כוהן who is required to be between thirty and sixty. Does this indicate that the office of the Supervisor cannot be identical to that of the priest? Lines 9b–10a require that the Supervisor must be cognizant of every language found in the community. It follows that the sect was multilingual. That a complainant must bring his legal matter to the Supervisor who evidently assigns it to the justices suggests that this community leader played an important role in settling disputes.

### 3.2.2.10.2.3.3. Social Needs (14:12b–18a)

The role of the Supervisor extends also to his part in regulating the personal needs of each member. The text pays particular attention to the care of the needy: the wounded, the destitute, the debilitated elderly, the leper, he who has been taken captive by foreigners, and maidens and lads who need assistance. The Supervisor together with the judges distribute the withheld wages to the needy, whose combined minimum provision was a distributed income of two days per month of the working days of the community's able, or about 8.3% of their total income. Given this description, depending upon the needs of the community this levy could possibly be increased. As far as I know, this is the oldest record attested in antiquity for the raising of a special tax for the needs of the handicapped. The list evidently reflects the makeup of the association. The last item in this list, ולכול עבודת החבר, which we translated as "all the services provided by the association," literally means "and for all the labor of the association." This wording may imply that the list of the needy given here is not exhaustive. Other categories were also to be supported.

As was mentioned above, CD 12:8 notes the existence of a חבור ישראל (the association of Israel) that was concerned with neighborly relations. A variant חבורה appears to occur also in the Testament of Amram (4Q545) F1a-bii:16 that alludes to the patriarch's group as חבו[רתנא] (our [gro]up). Our text indicates that the בית החבר was apparently a special subgroup which had been designated to deal with social problems. This term might be compared to the phrase בית ההשתחוות in CD 11:22 and בית התורה in CD 20:10. The three refer to institutions dedicated to fulfill tasks such as prayer, study and social services. The concluding words that the association not perish due to a lack of material support of the community may suggest the existence of a social group that collected levies from the people and whose existence was precarious. Lines 17b–18a have two functions. They conclude the section on fulfilling social needs. In a larger sense, they also tell us that the list begun in CD 12:19 which describes the organization of the community ends here.

This section dealing with social wants has, of course, its basis in Scripture containing provisions for the support of the needy. However, whereas the לקט legislation of Lev 19:9–10 and 23:22 served to provide for the needy, nothing in the biblical text indicates an organized system of social care as described here in sectarian literature; nor do other DSS texts, except MTA. Moreover, this section was intended perhaps to serve as a transition to the book's conclusion. What has preceded it contains items drawn from Scripture. However, what follows does not.

### 3.2.2.11. *Discipline within the Community (14:18b–23; 4Q266 F10ii:1–15; 4Q270 F7i:6b–16a; 4Q266 F11:1–3a)*

The last line of CD 14 has been lost, as has what CD contained of MTA's ending. However, most of this material can be confidently restored from the combined parallels in 4Q266 F10ii–F11; 4Q269 F11i:8–ii, F16; 4Q270 F7 as well as 1QS 7:8–21. Together, these manuscripts form most of what is missing following CD 14, the last major section of our work.

The new pericope beginning with CD 14:18b (4Q266 F10i:11) and continuing to the third line of the last page of 4Q266 consists of the disciplinary rules to prevent disorderly conduct. These injunctions have no biblical or even Talmudic parallel, but are unique to the Dead Sea Scrolls, and with his finale in MTA, they serve as the author's ending to the work.

### 3.2.2.11.1. *Introduction to the Disciplinary Injunctions (CD 14:18b–19)*

It is interesting that at this point, what has survived in MTA and its parallel, *Rule of the Community*, contains lists of disciplinary cases which frequently correspond to each other. Indeed, both begin with similar wording as displayed below.

| *MTA (CD 14:18b–19)* | *Community Rule (1QS 6:24a)* |
|---|---|
| And these are the verdicts [by which they shall be judged until the Anoint]ed of Aaron and Israel [arises] and atones for their transgressions by an of[fering, a sin offering or a gift.] | And these are the verdicts by which they shall be judged through the *midrash-Yachad* according to (their) commands. |

A basic difference between the two introductory passages is the term מדרש יחד, present in *Rule of the Community*, but not in MTA. Indeed, the term יחד is ubiquitous in the former, occurring some sixty times in 1QS, but evidently only once in MTA.[363] Thus, the title יחד for the community opens a new chapter in the communal and literary tradition of the Essene movement. As a technical term, יחד was not known to the author of MTA, since it was not mentioned by the authors of *Enoch* and *Jubilees* whose work preceded the composition of our text. Incidentally the word מדרש preceding יחד in 1QS 6:24 may refer to the title of our work, מדרש התורה האחרון, the source from which the משפטים in the יחד were drawn. As was noted elsewhere, MTA and 1QS contain numerous parallel passages. Scrollists have wondered which of the two was the source and which the derivative. If I am correct, the naming of מדרש as the heading for the verdicts in *Rule of the Community* clearly resolves the enigma. *Rule of the Community* followed MTA.

### 3.2.2.11.2. *The Injunctions (CD 14:20–22; 4Q266 F10ii:1–15; 4Q270 F7i:6b–15a)*

Below is a harmonization listing the parallels and divergences between the rules found in MTA and those later incorporated into *Rule of the Community*. I list the verdicts of MTA in their natural sequence. The injunctions found in *Rule of the Community* sometimes deviate, modifying those of MTA. Following this listing the commentary continues, including a brief exposition on the elements of the table.

---

[363] See the composite of 4Q270 F3iii:19 and 4Q271 F2:7 cited above.

## THE DISCIPLINARY RULES OF THE COMMUNITY
## PARALLELS BETWEEN MTA AND RULE OF THE COMMUNITY

### *MTA*

### *1QS*

CD 14:20And any]one w[h]o knowingly speaks falsely in matters of business, [they shall separate from the Purity 14:21afor one year, and] he shall be fined for sixty days.

CD 14:21bAnd he who addre[sses his neighbor haughtily or 14:22holds a grudge against his neighbor] unjustly should be pun[is]hed and [his sentence] shall b[e like that of the preceding case . . . ]

6:24If there be found one who lies 6:25aconcerning property, doing so knowingly, they shall separate him from the Purity of the many one year and they shall withhold a quarter of his ration of bread.

7:5And anyone who addresses his neighbor haughtily or who knowingly practices fraud shall be punished for six months.

6:25bAnd anyone who retorts to 6:26his neighbor with hardness of neck, and speaks with impudence, disregarding the foundation of friendship with him, defying his friend's authority who is listed before him, 6:27[a]cting on his own, shall be fined on[e] year [and separated. And he w]ho makes mention of any matter employing the glorious name (God) above all [ . . . ] 7:1And if he blasphemes or, being frightened by trouble or for any matter with which he is concerned . . . he recites in a book or curses, they shall separate him 7:2and he shall not return to the council of the community. And if he speaks with anger against one of the priests recorded in the book, he shall be fined 7:3for one year and separated into isolation from the Purity of the many. And if he speaks so without intent, he shall be fined for six months. And if he intentionally lies 7:4he shall be fined for six months.

. . . And if 7:6one cheats his neighbor, he shall be fined for three months. And if he cheats regarding communal property, causing a loss, he shall repay it 7:7in full. 7:8aAnd if he cannot afford to compensate him, he shall be fined for sixty days.

*MTA*                                    *1QS*

4Q266 F10ii:1a . . .(and shall be separated) for two [hundred] days and fined for one hundred days.

4Q266 F10ii:1bAnd if he holds a grudge involving a capital offense he [shall] not be permitted to return 2a[[to the Purity).]

7:8bAnd he who holds a grudge against his neighbor unjustly shall be fined for one year.

7:9aAnd the same applies for one who takes vengeance on his own in any matter.

4Q266 F10ii:2bAny]one who [mo]cks his neighbor without authorization of the counsel [shall be sep]arated (from the Purity) for one year and be fi[n]ed 3afor s[ix months.]

7:4bAnd anyone who mocks his neighbor without reason, fully aware that he is doing so, shall be fined for a year 7:5aand be separated.

4Q266 F10ii:3bOne who uses lewd speech shall be fined for t[wen]ty 4a[days and separated] (from the Purity) for three month[s.]

7:9bAnd one who uses lewd speech, three months.

4Q266 F10ii:4b[One who] talk[s] on top of [his neighbor] disruptively 5a[shall be fined ten] days.

7:9cAnd anyone who talks on top of his neighbor, 7:10aten days.

4Q266 F10ii:5b[One who lies dow]n [and] sleeps during the [ses]si[ons of the Many thre]e (times) 6a[shall be separated] (from the Purity) for thirty days [and] fined for ten days.

7:10bAnd anyone who lies down and sleeps during the session of the many, thirty days.

6b[And the same applies to one who lea]ves 7awithout the permission of the M[a]n[y.]

And the same applies to the one who departs in the middle of the session of the many 7:11without permission.

7a [And] he who [dozes off] up to three ti[mes during] one [session] 8shall [be fined] for ten days. And if [when they arise], he leaves [the session (without permission), he shall be fined for thirty] 9ada[ys.]

7:11bAnd he who dozes off364 up to three times at a single session shall be fined for ten days. And if when they arise, 7:12ahe leaves, (without permission), he shall be fined for thirty days.

4Q266 F10ii:9bOne who walks around naked [in the house] in front of [his] neigh[bor or parades naked in the field before] 10ap[e]ople shall be separated (from the Purity) for six [months.]

7:12bOne who walks around naked in the presence of his neighbor, not being compelled to do so, shall be fined for six months.

---

364 The text has הנם (for nothing)

## MTA

4Q266 F10ii:10b[One who spits into the session, or] 11) [draws o]ut his hand from under [his] garment [which has] holes so that [his penis becomes visible, shall be separated (from the Purity) for thir]ty ¹²ᵃ[da]ys and fined for ten.

4Q266 F10ii:12b And anyone who stupid[ly] j[es]ts, [loudly raising his voice, shall be separated (from the Purity) for] ¹³ᵃ[t]hirty <days> and fined for fif[tee]n days.

4Q266 F10ii:13b[One who takes out] his le[ft ha]nd ¹⁴ᵃ[to uri]nate with it shall be fined [for ten days and separated for thirty.]

4Q266 F10ii:14bAnd as for anyone] who goes around [gossiping] ¹⁵[about] his [neigh]bor, [they shall separate him from the Purity for one year and he shall be fined for six months.]

4Q270 F7i:6b[One who goes around] ⁷ᵃ[gossiping about the Many shall be expelled and] shall [not] be r[e]admitted.

4Q270 F7i:7b[And if he complains unjustly against his neighbor, he shall be fined for six] ⁸ᵃ[months.]

4Q270 F7i:8b[And any]one whose [spirit] is vain [before the many by repudiating the Truth and walking in the stubbornness of his heart] ⁹[shall] be se[parated (from the Purity). And if he should be readmitted] he shall be fined for sixty [days. When the sixty days have passed, the Many shall deliberate] ¹⁰concerning [his] statu[s. And if he is to be readmitted, they] should list [him in his rank. Thereafter, he shall inquire into the verdict.]

## 1QS

⁷:¹³He who spits into the habitation of the many shall be fined for thirty days. Also, he who puts out his hand from under his garment, and he is ⁷:¹⁴ᵃnot covered and his penis becomes visible shall be fined for thirty days.

⁷:¹⁴bAnd anyone who stupidly jests, loudly raising his voice shall be fined for thirty ⁷:¹⁵days.

⁷:¹⁵bOne who takes out his left hand to urinate with it shall be fined for ten days.

⁷:¹⁵cAnd as for anyone who goes around gossiping about his neighbor, ⁷:¹⁶ᵃthey shall separate him from the Purity of the many for one year and he shall be fined.

⁷:¹⁶bOne who goes around gossiping about the Many shall be expelled ⁷:¹⁷ᵃand shall not be readmitted.

. . . ⁷:¹⁷cAnd if he complains ⁷:¹⁸ᵃunjustly against his neighbor, he shall be fined for six months.³⁶⁵

. . . ⁷:¹⁷bOne who complains against the foundation of the community shall be expelled and may not be readmitted.

⁷:¹⁸bAnd as for anyone whose spirit is vain before the foundation of the community by repudiating the Truth ⁷:¹⁹and walking in the willfulness of his heart, if he repents he shall be fined for two years. During the first he may not touch the Purity of the many. ⁷:²⁰And during the second he may not touch the drink of the many, and he shall be ranked lower than all the men of the community. When ⁷:²¹two years have passed they shall consult the Many concerning his case. And if he is to be readmitted, he should be listed by his rank. Thereafter, he shall inquire into the verdict.

---

³⁶⁵ *Rule of the Community* proceeds in line 17b with a clause not in MTA, then follows 4Q270 F7i:7b in line 17c.

4Q270 F7i:11a[The man] who despises the
(final) verdict of the many shall exit and
[never again return.]

7:22Anyone who is a member of the
council of the community for a full ten
years, 7:23and his spirit moves him to
become a traitor against the community,
abandoning 7:24the many to follow the
stubbornness of his heart, shall not be
allowed to return again to the council of
the community. And as for anyone from
the people of the commun[ity w]ho
intermingles 7:25with him in his Purity or
his property whi[ch is part of the session
of] the many, his verdict shall be that [he]
be dismis[sed] like that of his associate.

4Q270 F7i:11b One who appropriates]
12afood illicitly shall return it to the man
from [whom] he took it.

4Q270 F7i:12b And one who approa[ch]es
13ahis wife to have sexual relations contrary to the law shall exit and not return.

4Q270 F7i:13b[Any one who rebe]ls against
the fathers 14[should be expelled] from
the community and not return. [But if]
he rebels against the mothers, he shall
be fined for ten days, for mothers do not
have the ornate glory (as do the fathers)
[in] 15a[the community.]

---

### 3.2.2.11.2.1. Business Fraud (CD 14:20–21a)

The first clause, CD 14:20–21a, relates to business fraud, what the
sages of the Talmud call אונאה. Although the text in *Rule of the
Community* resembles that of MTA, interesting differences emerge.
Whereas the former employs the biblical term הון, the latter uses
ממון, a word recorded only in rabbinics and the New Testament. A
more significant distinction is, whereas MTA describes the fine as
sixty days, 1QS specifies את רביעית לחמו (a quarter of his ration).
The change from sixty days in MTA to the bread ration in *Rule of
the Community* may be behind two divergent social structures, the
first penalty developing into the latter during the evolvement of
the sect.

### 3.2.2.11.2.2. Improper Speech (CD 14:21b–22)

The next two clauses in MTA continue to deal with improper
speech—a haughty demeanor and plotting against one's neighbor

(CD 14:21b–22). *Rule of the Community* treats these matters differently, however, scattering them out within a new narrative from 1QS 7:5–8. Moreover, there is a divergence in the verdicts. If we are right, MTA has the verb וֹנֶ[נ]שׁ (he shall be fi[n]ed),[366] without specifying about what his penalty is, except apparently referring to the verdict of the previous clause dealing with business fraud, a fine of sixty days. Furthermore, MTA links haughty speech with plotting against one's neighbor, whereas 1QS 7:5 connects it with the clause או יעשה רמיה במדעו (or who knowingly practices fraud).

What immediately follows CD 14:22 is uncertain. Line 21 restores line 15 of 4Q266 F10i, none of which survives. The lacuna that follows in 4Q266 may have spanned approximately eight lines for a total of twenty-five in fragment 10i. Although we cannot conjecture the text of the lost material, we may nevertheless assume that it continued to deal with the disciplinary injunctions begun in column 1 line 11 (CD 14:18), and virtually paralleled in 1QS 6:24–7:21. It may have contained portions preserved in 1QS 6:25b–7:8a and 7:22–25, material not paralleled in MTA. The last word of 4Q266 F10i probably was והובדל (and shall be separated), to conjoin with [מאת]ים ימים ונענש מאה יום (for two [hundred] days) of line 1 column 2. These missing lines prevent us from guessing the wording of the protasis, whose apodosis concludes with ונענש מאה יום (and fined for one hundred days). At any rate, this verdict has no counterpart in 1QS, which makes no mention of a period of one hundred days.

### 3.2.2.11.2.3. Holding a Grudge Involving a Capital Offense (4Q266 F10ii:1b–2a)

The clause in line 1 of 4Q266 F10ii, ואם בדבר מות ינטור (And if he holds a grudge involving a capital offense), indicates that the preceding injunctions dealt with offenses that did not involve the death penalty. The formula בדבר מות appears above in CD 9:6, likewise concerning keeping a grudge. Capital punishment is a major theme in MTA. CD 9:1 condemns anyone who devotes someone else to idolatry. CD 9:23–10:2 specifies that to adjudicate a capital offense a judge must be a member of the community. CD 12:3–4 asserts that violations of the Sabbath do not warrant a death penalty. Finally, MTA states that anyone whose reading lacks clarity may not par-

---

[366] Literally "he shall be pun[is]hed."

ticipate in public recitation of Scripture, lest he error in a reading
that concerns the death penalty (4Q266 F5ii:1–3).

### 3.2.2.11.2.4. Mocking (4Q266 F10ii:2b–3a)

The next injunction deals with mocking (צחה), a term which some
render as "insult." 1QS 7:4–5 qualifies that punishment be rendered
only if the act was done בדעהא (intentionally). *Rule of the Community*
also diverges in the punishment. Where MTA says that the offender
must be separated for one year and fined for six months, *Rule of
the Community* specifies that he be fined for a year and separated,
without giving the time.

### 3.2.2.11.2.5. Lewd Speech (4Q266 F10ii:3b–4a)

Line 3 contains the second mention of the phrase דבר נבל (lewd
speech) in MTA. CD 10:17b–18a reads דבר נבל ורק (a lewd or empty
word) in the context of unacceptable speech on the Sabbath. The
question is, if lewd speech is prohibited even on weekdays, why
would it be specifically forbidden on the Sabbath? It could be that
the consequence of Sabbath violation would be more stringent. 1QS
7:9 omits the punishment of twenty days.

### 3.2.2.11.2.6. Interrupting Another (4Q266 F10ii:4b–5a)

Lines 4b–14a list clauses which generally concern the decorum required during communal sessions. 4b–5a have their counterpart in
1QS 6:10, altering, however, the ending. Instead of the vague term
פרע (to disturb), *Rule of the Community* amplifies this word with טרם
יכלה אחיהו לדבר (before his friend finishes speaking).

### 3.2.2.11.2.7. Intentionally Sleeping during the Assembly (4Q266 F10ii:5b–6a)

1QS 7:10 does not have the specification that sleeping during the
assembly could occur three times prior to punishment, a requirement
listed in the next injunction of MTA. Likewise *Rule of the Community*
omits the final clause that the offender be fined for ten days.

### 3.2.2.11.2.8. Leaving the Assembly Without Permission (4Q266 F10ii:6b–7a)

Our text and *Rule of the Community* ascribe the punishment of the above
case also to one who leaves the session without its authorization.

### 3.2.2.11.2.9. Dozing Off During the Assembly or Leaving Without Permission (4Q266 F10ii:7b–9a)

For line 7 Baumgarten transcribes [ם]ה[ו], reading וְהֵנָם, "[doing so]" ... (three times).[367] Hempel transcribes [ם]ה[ו] "[with]out [cause]."[368] As noted by Qimron, the second letter of this word in the parallel, 1QS 7:11, was corrected in the manuscript to either ה or ח. For his transcription he chose והנם. Charlesworth on the other hand translates it as if it were והנם (And whoever falls asleep).[369] We read here [ם]ה[ו] ([and] who [dozes off]). Should he who dozes off to sleep also arise and leave the session he shall be fined for an additional thirty days, corresponding to the separation period of the one who deliberately sleeps during the council session.

### 3.2.2.11.2.10. Nakedness (4Q266 F10ii:9b–10a)

The question arises whether lines 9–10a of 4Q266 F10ii form part of a group of rules that relate to decorum during communal sessions. The reference to nakedness in a field could be interpreted in one of several ways in this regard: 1) it is an incidental addition to legislation pertaining otherwise to etiquette in public meetings, complementing the proscription against bodily exposure within a building, or 2) it describes another aspect of the sessions of the community, implying that they were conducted sometimes outside in the open. At any rate, indecent exposure serves to parallel the main concern of this portion of the משפטים—proper conduct during public sessions. Note also the prohibition against exposure of one's genitals described below in line 11. 1QS 7:12a radically alters this injunction against nakedness. It omits the wording בבית או בשדה ע[רום] ה[ל]ך (in the house or pa[rades] n[aked] in the field) preserved in 4Q270 F7i:2 and ה[ר]יאות [לפני] of 4Q266 ([before] p[e]ople), replacing them with ולוא היה אנוש (not under constraint).

---

[367] Baumgarten, DJD XVIII, 75. See also Martínez and Tigchelaar's rendition of אחד [מושב] על מים פע[מים שלוש עד [נם]ה[ו] "[ and that] up to three ti[mes in] one [session]" (Martínez and Tigchelaar, Scrolls Study Edition, vol. 1, 597).

[368] Hempel, The Laws of the Damascus Document, 83, 141–42. Cook similarly translates "for no reason" (Wise, Abegg and Cook, Scrolls, 72).

[369] Charlesworth, ed., Rule of the Community, 30–31.

### 3.2.2.11.2.11. Spitting or Exposing One's Genitals (4Q266 F10ii:10b–12a)

For the filling of the lacuna of line 10, either of two reconstructions is conceivable. The punishment of the previous case relating to nudity could be extended to include another verdict as proposed by Hempel and Martínez-Tigchelaar: "shall be excluded for six [months and punished for thirty days (?).]"[370] A more plausible restoration, however, is to fill the missing words with the protasis of the subsequent case, absent in our text, but preserved in 1QS 7:13. Let us remember that both MTA and *Rule of the Community* frequently omit a second punishment in the משפטים. Conversely, *Rule of the Community* sometimes expands upon the corresponding verdicts of MTA (compare 1QS 7:17–18a and 4Q270 F7i:7b–8a). Moreover, note that the case in *Rule of the Community* on exposure likewise only has a single punishment. Furthermore, if we adopt the alternative reading, an entire parallel apparently preserved in 1QS would not find its place here.[371]

The next case (lines 11–12a) deals with genital exposure. Commenting on its parallel wording in *Rule of the Community*, Qimron argues that יד denotes "penis."[372] I believe this sense is unlikely, since, whatever יד may denote elsewhere in ancient Jewish literature, it does not have directly this sense here. Our text amplifies the word יד with ערותו והואה [פוח ו]נראתה "[which has] holes so that [his penis becomes visible.]"[373] If יד itself means penis, this explanation would be unsatisfactory. If any word in this case has a genital denotation, it is ערוה rather than יד.

### 3.2.2.11.2.12. Loud Jesting (4Q266 F10ii:12b–13a)

Lines 10b–13a condemn loud jesting during public meetings. *Rule of the Community* gives the נענש clause only. On the other hand, MTA contains two punishments. Hence, the reconstruction of והבדל.

---

[370] Hempel, *The Laws of the Damascus Document*, 141–43; Martínez and Tigchelaar, *Scrolls Study Edition*, vol. 1, 597.

[371] The syntax of our reconstruction draws on that of 1QS 7:5. ואשר ידבר את רעהו במרים או יעשה רמיה במדעו ונענש ששה חודשים

[372] Qimron in Charlesworth, ed., *Rule of the Community*, 33, n. 185.

[373] For the sense of "having holes" (פוח) see Charlesworth in Charlesworth, ed., *Rule of the Community*, 33, n. 186.

### 3.2.2.11.2.13. Urinating with the Left Hand (4Q266 F10ii:13b–14a)

The subsequent case in lines 13b–14a addresses an issue whose content is not clear. The infinitive לשׁח, in 1QS 7:15 לשׁוח, corresponds to the biblical hapax legomenon לָשֻׂוחַ in Gen 24:63. Biblical translators diverge as to the meaning of this verb. The Septuagint and the Talmud, following the root שׂיח, take the word to mean "to meditate." The Talmudists claim that Isaac went out to pray the מנחה service, thus the origin of this prayer in Judaism. Some scrollists take this verb as שׁוח, to denote reclining or sinking down, and translate it as "to gesticulate."[374] In my opinion, however, the word לשׁח here means "to urinate." This would explain Isaac's ironic encounter in the field with Rebekah's arriving entourage at this particular time. Moreover, the use of the left hand in our text corresponds to what the rabbis recommend for urination.

### 3.2.2.11.2.14. Gossiping and Unjust Complaints (4Q266 F10ii:14b–15; 4Q270 F7i:6a–8a)

As stated above, the משׁפטים spanning lines 4b–14a of 4Q266 F10ii pertain mostly to proper decorum within the sessions of the community. What follows in lines 14b–15 of this fragment and in 4Q270 F7i:6b–15a concerns decorum in the broader life of the community. The holiness code contains an injunction against gossiping (Lev 19:16), and the Prophets and Proverbs condemn it (Jer 6:28; 9:3; Ezek 22:9; Prov 11:13; 20:19). MTA lists two kinds of gossip (4Q266 F10ii:14b–15; 4Q270 F7i:6b–7a): 1) against a friend for which the punishment is a separation of one year and a fine for six months, and 2) against the entire community, resulting in expulsion. We find the author's concern about gossip early in his introductory prayer: "[ . . . and we will not go around] slandering [those] who seek refuge [in Him (God)], God's commandments [and in His covenant]" (4Q266 F1:16–17).

After listing gossip in the previous two משׁפטים, the text as reconstructed in 4Q270 F7i:7b–8a deals with a related issue: filing a complaint אשׁר לא במשׁפט (unjustly). This conveys attempting to twist the law to one's favor.

---

[374] Martínez-Tigchelaar, *Scrolls Study Edition*, vol. 1, 597; Baumgarten, DJD XVIII, 75; Cook in Wise, Abegg and Cook, *Scrolls*, 73.

### 3.2.2.11.2.15. A Rebel Spirit (4Q270 F7i:8b–10)

The succeeding injunction, 4Q270 F7i:8b–10, is the last case in which
MTA and *Rule of the Community* correspond to each other. Each goes
its own path in the remaining list of injunctions. MTA's wording in
the next two lines is problematic. On the one hand it has a lacuna.
On the other it contains the supralinear letters רש above the presumed ונ[פֿלֿשׁ. On the basis of 1QS 7:19, Baumgarten reconstructs
[ו]הֿוֿ[בדל שתי שנים] ([shall be suspended for two years]) at the beginning
of the apodosis and regards the supralinear lettering as obscure. In my
opinion, רש should be assumed to have been part of the word ופורש
(and he shall be expelled). This would reflect emendation by a later
MTA scribe who felt that the punishment for the offense of acting
treacherously against the people was not stringent enough in this
text. Baumgarten's proposed reading is unlikely in that none of MTA's
listed items contains a separation for two years. Furthermore, *Rule of
the Community*'s amplification of this period of two years (1QS 7:19b–
20) is clearly absent in MTA. We may retrieve the original construction
of this apodosis by combining it with wording found in *Rule of the
Community*, which reads אמ ישוב ונענש שתי שנים (if he returns he shall be
fined for two years). In other words, if he does not repent he is to be
expelled. MTA then may have read [ו]הֿוֿ[בדל ואם ישוב ונ[פֿלֿשׁ ששים יום]
(shall] be se[parated. And if he is readmitted he shall be] fined
sixty [days). Sensing excessive leniency for the offense involved, the
emender interpreted הובדל to mean absolute expulsion, clarifying it
with the supralinear ופו[רש and altering the conditional particle ואם
to a negative ולא. Being less stringent, *Rule of the Community*, then,
allowed for restoration of the apostate member.

Ignoring the supralinear emandation, Baumgarten transcribes much
of the wording found in *Rule of the Community*. According to it, MTA's
apodosis began with the words [ו]הֿוֿ[בדל שתי שנים]. Abbreviating the
wordage of *Rule of the Community*, Baumgarten posits that MTA continued with the injunction that at the end of *two years* the community
should deliberate the case again. If they allow the offender to reenter
the assembly, he shall be reinstated to his position.

As stated above, MTA could not have included the amplification
of the two years found in 1QS 7:19b–20, the first during which the
offender was prohibited from touching the communal purity, and the
second during which he was not to handle its liquid. There is simply not enough space for its inclusion. In our reading, these clauses
would have had no meaning since it is not likely that a period of

*two years* was in the text. Hence, following [יום שֵׁשִׁים שֵׁנֵ[נ]] we read [ובמלאות לו ששים יום ישאלו הרבים] על דֹּבֹּ]רו ([When the *sixty days* have passed, the Many shall deliberate] concerning [his] statu[s]).

### 3.2.2.11.2.16. Despising the Rules (4Q270 F7i:11a)

The next case of MTA and *Rule of the Community* diverge, but with some common ideas.[375] The former has a simple clause—that anyone who despises the rules of the many should be expelled and not allowed to return. The author of *Rule of the Community* perhaps regarded this succinctness with its categorical exclusion from the community as incoherent with the preceding case, which dealt with the matter at length. This perhaps explains its modification in 1QS 7:22–24a, which limits expulsion to a veteran of ten years. In other words, a novice receives more leniency since he may have backslidden unwittingly. Furthermore, it amplifies the nature of the offense to acting treacherously against the יחד, a technical term not used in MTA.

### 3.2.2.11.2.17. Illicitly Appropriating Food (4Q270 F7i:11b–12a)

The succeeding injunction in *Rule of the Community* differs from the contents of the subsequent verdict in MTA. The latter, 4Q270 F7i:11b–12, speaks of taking food outside the camp. 1QS 7:24b–25 on the other hand links the case with its precedent ruling which pertains to a ten year veteran who acts treacherously against his community. It expands upon this by specifying that anyone who shares with this unfaithful member in either purity or property likewise should be expelled.

### 3.2.2.11.2.18. Marital Sex Contrary to Law (4Q270 F7i:12b–13a)

At this point *Rule of the Community*, no longer dealing with the disciplinary injunctions, takes up other matters. MTA, however, has two more משפטים. The first, lines 12b–13a, pertains to one whose sexual relations with his wife are not in accordance with the rules. Unfortunately, the text does not specify the type of violation intended. The verb זנה occurs only here in MTA. However, the noun זנות, used as either sexual violations or evil inclinations, occurs several times. Baumgarten interprets כמשפט as possibly referring to משפטות in 1QSa 1:10–11, which stipulates that a man must be twenty years

---

[375] I place them as parallels in the above comparisons between the משפטים of MTA and those of *Rule of the Community*.

of age before marriage and that "the wife upon her nuptials must promise (תקבל) to admonish (להעיד) her husband about the laws (משפטות התורא) concerning sexual intercourse, with which she is to familiarize herself by learning them (במשמע משפטים) and fulfilling them (ובמלוא בו)."[376] However, this interpretation is implausible. As noted by the editors of 1QSa, the text likely refers to the man who should master the משפטות התורא. Furthermore, as explained in the text, the injunctions of the Torah hardly speak of sexual offenses and therefore, cannot be related to our text as suggested by Baumgarten. S. Talmon posits that MTA's injunction against whoredom refers to those who transgress the community's law of sexual abstinence, albeit limited in time.[377] This understanding is unacceptable, since the very next injunction speaks of the presence of both fathers and mothers in the community. Moreover, the institution of marriage plays a paramount role within MTA.

We must then suppose that לזנות לאשתו אשר לא כמשפט may have two possible interpretations. It might refer to one who does not fulfill the marital rights of his wife (Exod 21:9–10); hence a protection for the woman. Or, perhaps what is meant here is what the rabbis call הבא עליה שלא כדרכה (one who has sexual relations in an un-natural manner), literally "one who has sex not according to her way" (*Rambam Hilchot Isurei Biah* I 9).

### 3.2.2.11.2.19. Rebellion against Parents (4Q270 F7i:13b–15a)

The final case has no exact parallel in *Rule of the Community*. However, 1QS 7:17, dealing with a member's protest against the foundation of the *Yahad*, may have been a variation of this case. If so, the discussion of murmuring against the fathers and mothers has its parallel in grumbling against the יסוד היחד of 1QS. This work tends to transform the injunctions relating to the family in MTA, applying them to the community. The previous case pertaining to illicit sex has no parallel in *Rule of the Community*, perhaps because the injunctions of *Rule of the Community* applied to males only. MTA's statement that mothers have a lower status than that of fathers in the legal structure[378] of

---

[376] Baumgarten, DJD XVIII, 165.

[377] Shemaryahu Talmon, "The Community of the Renewed Covenant: Between Judaism and Christianity," in *The Community of the Renewed Covenant* (ed. E. Ulrich and J. Vanderkam; Notre Dame: University of Notre Dam Press, 1994), 9.

[378] J. Elwolde argues that the term רוקמה (embroidered fabric) in this context serves as a metonymy to signify status, such garments being worn only by people of standing in the community; John F. Elwolde, "*rwqmh* in the *Damascus Document* and Ps

the community is worth noting, since it seems to contravene the argument in CD 5:9–10 that, although Scripture generally addresses itself to males, its legislation applies equally to both genders.

### 3.2.2.11.3. *Conclusion to the Disciplinary Injunctions (4Q270 F7i:15b–16a; 4Q266 F11:1–3a)*

This concludes the injunctions which commenced in CD 14:18 (4Q266 F10i:11). 4Q270 F7i:15–16 and the succeeding 4Q266 F11:1–3a form a summary of and a rationale for these disciplinary rules. All or portions of twenty-six injunctions survive in MTA, each of which has no biblical precedent. The text now addresses the question of who should exact these rules. It responds by asserting that this will be the responsibility of the priest in charge of the camp. MTA goes on to explain that the basis for his authority draws on Levitical texts which require the sinner to submit to priestly jurisdiction (Lev 4:2). Although only four words of this verse (and succeeding verses) are cited, the author presumes that the reader would know the entire passage which states that the anointed priest is in charge of the discipline for any prohibited acts (אֲשֶׁר לֹא תֵעָשֶׂינָה).

Our insertion of the negative in the lacuna at the beginning of line 16 diverges from the reconstruction in the editio princeps. The rationale behind it is twofold. Baumgarten's restoration אשר [יתים]ל is misleading since if one falls under discipline, why should he submit to more discipline (וקבל את משפטו)? Furthermore, the length of the lacuna seems to require additional letters.

### 3.3. *Finale (4Q266 F11:3b–21)*

To understand this concluding section it is necessary to recall the beginning of the work. As reconstructed, lines 1b–2a of MTA ordain that the members of the community separate themselves from the

---

139:15," in *Diggers at the Well: Proceedings of a Third International Symposium on the Hebrew of the Dead Sea Scrolls and Ben Sira* (ed. T. Muraoka and J. F. Elwolde); Vol. XXXVI in *Studies on the Texts of the Desert of Judah* (ed. F. García Martínez and A. S. van der Woude; Leiden: 2000), 65–83. V. Hurowitz suggests alternatively that this word is a phonetic variant of Akkadian *rugummû* (legal claim), signifying that "the mothers have *a priori* no legal claim on one who complains against them, so one who maligns them is punished less severely"; Victor Avigdor Hurowitz, "רוקמה in Damascus Document 4QD$^e$ (4Q270 7 i 14)," *DSD* 9-1 (2002): 35.

way of the wicked and live by the rules of the Torah. The author repeats these themes, admonishing the people to live by all the injunctions of the Torah. This passage recalls that of all nations only Israel was chosen to have the law. Hence, the community should expel anyone who does not follow it, and those who fraternize with the violator must be carefully watched. The book begins and ends with a blessing.

### 3.3.1. *The Convocation of the Camps in the Third Month (4Q266 F11:3b–18a)*

The finale commences with a conflation of phrases from Jer. 5:5 (אֵלְכָה־לִּי), Deut 30:4 (בִּקְצֵה הַשָּׁמָיִם) and Lev. 26:31 (וְלֹא אָרִיחַ בְּרֵיחַ נִיחֹחֲכֶם). These quotations continue with a paraphrase of Joel 2:12–13. Each of these introductory formulas serves to emphasize the author's synopsis of Judaism exposed in the citations of Joel, "to return to God with weeping and fasting . . . rend your hearts and not your garments." Repentance stems from the heart, not from words or superficial acts. Hence, anyone who rejects the law, whether the traditional or eschatological Torah, will be excluded from the community.

Our passage reemphasizes that it is the priest who has the supreme authority over the entire membership. To him is entrusted the benediction of lines 9–14a, a prayer whose vocables are unusual. The noun אוֹן occurs both in Scripture and in the DSS, signifying "strength." However, here it functions adjectivally, modifying the term הו. Baumgarten notes that הו alludes to the divine name, as it does in *Mishnah Sukkah* 4:5.[379] The text continues with phrases glorifying the Lord as the creator of the universe. However, the final clause seems to go back to comment on the clauses preceding the prayer, ordaining that those who despise the Torah be expelled from the community. Preceding this, our text specifies that anyone who associates with these wicked shall be scrutinized.

As to the benediction, it seems to complement two key concepts exposed in MTA's introduction. 4Q266 F1:5b–6a, telling of the glory of the divine acts of creation, parallels line 9a of the concluding prayer to the work. Another element occurring in both the beginning and the end is Israel's commitment to observe the Torah (4Q266 F1:16–18a; F11:9b–14a).

---

[379] Joseph M Baumgarten, "A New Qumran Substitute for the Divine Name and Mishnah Sukkah 4.5." *JQR* 83 (1992): 1–5.

As explained in comments on CD 16:1b–6a, the assembling of the camps on the third month refers to Pentecost, which in *Jubilees* is celebrated on the fifteenth of the month, a festival whose tradition according to CD 16:6 presumably goes back to Abraham. According to *Jub.* 1:1 (4Q216 1:5), on the sixteenth of the month Moses ascended the cloud on Mount Sinai (Exod 24:16) where he stayed for forty days. Perhaps the annual assembly prescribed in our text refers not to the fifteenth, but to the sixteenth day of the third month. 4Q275, a fragmentary text, probably contained details of this annual assembly.[380] Interestingly it is likely that the ceremony described at the beginning of *Rule of the Community*, which goes on to specify that the Levites curse the followers of Belial (1QS 2:4–5), draws on the convocation prescribed in our text. Thus, the author of *Rule of the Community* begins his composition with MTA's finale. 4Q266 F11:17b–18a goes on to recall the introductory lines of our work which contain the assembly's promise not to depart from the commandments of the Torah in any way (4Q266 F1:17–18a), serving to illustrate once more the linkage of the beginning and the ending of MTA.

### 3.3.2. *Epilogue (4Q266 F11:18b–21)*

It is interesting that the manuscripts diverge on the spelling of the first word of the last portion of the book. Whereas 4Q270 F7ii:12 begins the ultimate sentence with זו, 4Q266 lengthens it to והזו, a unicum in both the Hebrew Scriptures and the DSS. If not a grammatical slip, evidently this is an attempt to call attention to the fact that we are approaching the last words of the composition.

The restoration of הפקודה suggested by Baumgarten in line 19 finds support in עד תום מועד הפקודה\הֵ / of line 2 of the work's beginning, serving as one of several common features between the preamble and the finale of the work, among them the title and supplication. The formula קץ הפקודה occurs in CD 7:21 (19:10) and likewise in 19:11 as בקץ פקדת הראשון. Both refer to the redemption from Egypt; that of our passage signifies the messianic era. The text goes on to amplify הפקודה as את אשר יפק]ידו [בכו]ל קצי החרון ([which they shall remem]ber [during al]l the epochs of anger). The repetition here of the root פקד as a noun (הפקודה) and as a verb (יפקידו) reemphasizes the future deliverance. This entire sentence is concerned with the

---

380 See P. Alexander and G. Vermes in DJD XXVI, 209–16.

theme of redemption, an apt prelude to the summary of Israelite tribulations, both past and future, as well as to the title of the composition. The interjectory particle הנה is used here as well as in 4Q266 F5i:16, which likewise mentions MTA. That the author favors this particle in citing an important composition, can be seen also in CD 16:3 where it introduces *Jubilees*. Unfortunately, the first part of line 1 of the book perished. As stated in comments on the preamble, both Stegemann and I have independently advocated the restoration מדרש התורה האחרון. He fronts this formula with the demonstrative זה; I do so with הנה. That the introduction and the finale have common vocabulary and ideas gives additional support to the supposition that this is largely a unitary work, not as has been hitherto supposed, a compilation of extracts from a variety of sources.

# CHAPTER FOUR

# UNINCORPORATED FRAGMENTS

Except for 4Q266 F34, the following list of unincorporated fragments reproduces Joseph Baumgarten's unidentified fragments in DJD
XVIII. Note, however, my additional reconstructions are marked by
superscripted *w*.

## *4.1 – 4Q266*

| | |
|---|---|
| [הקוד'שׁ ] | F13:1 |
| [כמדת ]∘ | F13:2 |
| ואם<sup>w</sup> ר]∘אים עובד א]ת | F13:3 |
| ואם איש אח[ל<sup>w</sup> יעיד את רעה]ו במעשה רע<sup>w</sup> | F13:4 |
| הרם *vacat* הֹר] | F13:5 |
| אשר לא יג]<sup>w</sup>[י]ד[<sup>1</sup> | F13:6 |
| [      ]ל ∘ה[ | F13:7 |
| | |
| [עד אשר לו ] | F14a:1 |
| [ארושים ] | F14a:2 |
| [∘ל∘[ | F14a:3 |
| | |
| [ ]לֹוק[ח | F14b:1 |
| [ים לה] | F14b:2 |
| | |
| [ לֹ לֹ] | F14c:1 |
| | |
| אֹל יקח איש את בת<sup>w</sup> [אֹחותו ] | F14d:1 |
| [מֹה כ] | F14d:2 |
| | |
| [נֹות] | F14e:1 |
| [ֹה לֹו] | F14e:2 |
| | |
| [∘ ∘] | F14:1 |

---

<sup>1</sup> Baumgarten ]∘ֹ

| | |
|---|---|
| תעות[ | F14:2 |
| על[ | F14:3 |
| | |
| מלאכי ה[ן]קודש[ | F15:1 |
| ל[ במה יתה]לכו | F15:2 |
| ל[ קדושי קודש]ים<sup>w</sup> | F15:3 |
| <sup>w</sup>להבי]ט עומק ותחת כב[ודו הוד רקיע<sup>w</sup> | F15:4 |
| ∘ ∘ ∘ לבחירי[ ∘ | F15:5 |
| | |
| כמה מן הדם [ | F16a:1 |
| בה מן איש בר[וש<sup>w</sup> | F16a:2 |
| מקנה באחד] | F16a:3 |
| ל]ם עונם מ[ן | F16a:4 |
| ה אריאל] | F16a:5 |
| | |
| כו]ל ∘ | F16b:1 |
| הוא ה[ [ | F16b:2 |
| ∘ ∘[ | F16b:3 |

| | | |
|---|---|---|
| ד ושובחה[∘ | [ | F17:1 |
| שבע<sup>w</sup> שנים אחר[ ² | [ | F17:2 |
| ע]ליהם | תאכל<sup>w</sup>] | F17:3 |
| ∘[ | [ | F17:4 |

| | |
|---|---|
| ידעו מק[דשי<sup>w</sup>    ∘ב[ | F18:1 |
| ם ביש[ו ע]ליו ישי[שו וישמחו<sup>w</sup> ³ | F18:2 |
| עד עול]ם | F18:3 |
| | |
| א[שר vacat] | F19:1 |
| לגוי[ם<sup>w</sup> בע]בור<sup>w</sup> | F19:2 |
| ל[ | F19:3 |
| | |
| ם[ ] | F20:1 |
| אי[ש א]שר<sup>w</sup> | F20:2 |
| | |
| משפט]∘[ | F21:1 |

---

<sup>2</sup> Perhaps this fragment is a part of 4Q266 F12.
<sup>3</sup> Baumgarten transcribes ]∘ם ביש[ו ישי[.

א[יש א]שר^w     F22:1

]∘ ∘ ∘[     F22:2

[המ]ת[הלכ]ים^b באלה בקץ הרשעה^w     F23:1

]∘ ∘ ∘[     F24:1

אש[ר]^w ה[ו]אה יא[מר]^4 ^w     F24:2

[    ]הש[     F24:3

]∘ שמ ∘[     F25:1

]כֿי[     F26:1

]ת [     F26:2

]כֿו[     F27:1

]ת [     F27:2

]∘ א [     F28:1

]ה [     F28:2

]עֿרי [     F29:1

]ש ול[     F29:2

]כח ∘∘[     F30:1

]∘[     F30:2

]ממ∘[     F31:1

]∘ תֿ∘[     F32:1

]∘∘[     F32:2

[    ]ו[     F33:1

[    ]אֿ[     F33:2

^5F34:1–2

---

4 or יא[כל

5 For Baumgarten's unidentified 4Q266 F34, see its possible parallel in CD 4:17–18.

| | |
|---|---|
| ]שׁ לֹ[ | F35:1 |
| ]∘ ∘ ∘[ | F35:2 |
| | |
| ]∘ ∘[ | F36:1 |
| ]vacat הוא[ | F36:2 |
| ]∘[ | F36:3 |
| | |
| ]∘ ∘ ∘[ | F37:1 |
| ]וע∘ ∘[ | F37:2 |
| ]לֹ[ | F37:3 |
| | |
| י]שׂראא[ל | F38:1 |
| ]vacat ם[ | F38:2 |
| | |
| ]∘ת ה∘[ | F39:1 |
| | |
| ]∘ת̊∘[ | F40:1 |
| [    ]∘[ | F41:1 |
| [    א]שׁר[ | F41:2 |
| | |
| ]וֹכר[ | F42:1 |
| ]שׂא[ | F42:2 |
| | |
| ]שׂ∘[ | F43:1 |
| ]לֹ ∘[ | F43:2 |
| | |
| ]הגן[ | F44:1 |
| | |
| ]ת[ | F45:1 |
| | |
| ]ע ∘[ | F46:1 |
| ]∘ ∘[ | F46:2 |
| | |
| ]ע̊רת[ | F47:1 |
| ]א מ̊ס[ | F47:2 |
| | |
| ]לוֹ לן[ | F48:1 |
| | |
| ]∘ ה̊י[ | F49:1 |

]∘ א∘[   F50:1

]∘[   F51:1
]ל∘[   F51:2

]בׄ[   F52:1
לא[w] ]יׄענה האישׄ] את הגר ואת האלמנה[w]   F52:2
א]ת כולׄ]   F52:3
]∘ נׄיׄ∘[   F52:4

]יׄם∘[   F53:1
]∘ [   F53:2

]טׄ∘[   F54:1
]ה אׄ∘[   F54:2
] אׄ[   F54:3

תש[w]אׄ[ פׄנׄיׄכׄה]   F55:1
כו]לׄ[w] אׄ[יׄ]שׄ יׄ[   F55:2
]לׄ יׄ[ ]∘[   F55:3

∘[   F56:1
נב]ׄיׄאים[6]   F56:2
לׄ[   F56:3

]רׄעׄ[   F57:1
]שׄרׄ[   F57:2
]∘א[   F57:3

]הׄ אׄ[   F58:1
]ׄנים אׄבׄ[   F58:2
]אם ישוׄ]בׄ [w] [7]   F58:3
]רׄת היאׄ[   F58:4
[w] עׄ]שׄרה ∘[   F58:5

]בני הׄ[   F59:1

---

[6] Or יוׄ]צׄאׄים
[7] Baumgarten transcribes ]ׄישׄ.

| | |
|---|---|
| ]הֹן ֯ ֯[ | F60:1 |
| ]֯ ֯ ֯לִ[ | F60:2 |
| ]ה[ | F61:1 |
| ]֯לוֹ֯[ | F62:1 |
| ]מ[ | F63:1 |
| שלו]שׁ[8](8) שָׁנִים[ | F63:2 |
| ]את אל[ | F64:1 |
| שמעו אלי[w](w) ]ואדבר[ן לכם[w](w) | F64:2 |
| ]הֹם והצ[ | F65:1 |
| [w](w)משפ[ט הזֹֹה[ | F65:2 |
| ]הֹ [ | F66:1 |
| ואש]ר [ | F66:2 |
| ]֯ לֹ ֯[ | F66:3 |
| [w](w)מש]פט[ | F67:1 |
| ]ה[ | F67:2 |
| ]֯ ה[ | F68:1 |
| ]שׁ[ | F68:2 |
| ]ז שֹֹמ[ | F69:1 |
| ]֯ י ֯֯[ | F69:2 |
| ]֯ נ[ | F70:1 |
| ]היֹה[ | F70:2 |
| [ ]֯ ֯ ֯[ | F71:1 |
| [ ]לֹ֯ ֯[ | F71:2 |
| ] ח[נם ] | F72:1 |
| ]֯ שֹׁר[ | F72:2 |

---

8 Alternative restorations are שׁ[ש and שׁ[מח.

[ ]° [      F73:1
[    ]רהנֹ[      F73:2

]תֹ ° °[      F74:1
]בֹר[      F74:2

]° °[      F75:1
]תֹ °[      F75:2

*4.2 – 4Q267*

] נֹ[      F10:1
]° הכוהן מ[      F10:2

]°°°[      F11:1
]°ת ויוד[ע$^{\text{w}}$      F11:2
]° ° °[      F11:3

]תֹ וה[      F12:1
]°°[      F12:2

]י[שראלֹ[      F13:1
]פֹ[קֹוד עוון[      F13:2

]מֹשגה[      F14:1
]הֹם אֹת[      F14:2
° ° ° [      F14:3

$^{\text{w}}$ע[לֹיו      F15:1
]לֹם[      F15:2
°[      F15:3
° ° °[      F15:4

אלֹ[ F16:1
לכֹםֹ[ F16:2

]אֹתֹ[      F17:1
]סֹיֹפֹו[      F17:2

]אֹ°[      F18:1

| | |
|---|---|
| ]מ̇ב̇ב̇י̇∘[ | F18:2 |
| ]ה̇ה̇כ̇[ | F18:3 |
| ]∘[ | F18:4 |

## 4.3 – 4Q268

| | |
|---|---|
| ]∘[ | F3:1 |
| ]vacat[ | F3:2 |
| ש]ה את הקוד[ | F3:3 |
| ]∘ ∘ ∘ ∘[ | F3:4 |

## 4.4 – 4Q269

| | |
|---|---|
| ]א̇יש[ | F12:1 |

| | |
|---|---|
| ]ם ויד̇ע̇ו̇[ | F13:1 |
| ]ם̇ לישועתו י̇[ | F13:2 |
| ]ה והמ̇ה̇ [ | F13:3 |
| ]ו̇ג̇ם̇[ | F13:4 |

| | |
|---|---|
| ]לה י̇ם̇[ | F14:1 |
| ]ם ∘ ∘[ | F14:2 |

## 4.5 – 4Q270

| | |
|---|---|
| מוש[ב ונע̇]נש[9] | F8:1 |
| על[w] [כן יקום [האיש על נפשו[w] | F8:2 |
| ∘[ ]∘ל̇[ | F8:3 |

| | |
|---|---|
| ]ט̇מאתם[ | F9:1 |

| | |
|---|---|
| ]ו̇גם אש̇]ר[w] | F10:1 |
| ]ה ואם את ב̇[ | F10:2 |

| | |
|---|---|
| ]∘נ̇∘[ | F11:1 |
| ]∘ לה [ | F11:2 |

---

[9] Baumgarten suggests this fragment was part of the penal code.

]לׄ̇קׄ ̇ל[ F12:1

]∘ ∘ ∘ ∘ ∘[ F12:2

## 4.6 – 4Q272

]מׄ[ F2:1

]הׄואה [ F2:2

]∘ כי כ[ F2:3

]∘ רׄם [ F2:4

]∘ ∘ ∘[ F3:1

]∘∘ א∘[ F3:2

## 4.7 – 4Q273

]ה א[ F7:1

[ ויצ]אwׄ F7:2

]ה אשׄ[ F8:1

]∘ הׄ ∘[ F8:2

]∘ פלא וכ∘ ∘[ F9:1

]הדבר לׄאחׄיׄ[ F9:2

# BIBLIOGRAPHY

Abegg, Martin G., Jr. *Qumran Sectarian Manuscripts: Qumran text and grammatical tags* (1999–2005).

Abegg, Martin G., Jr. and Craig A. Evans. "Messianic Passages in the Dead Sea Scrolls." Pages 191–203 in *Qumran-Messianism. Studies on the Messianic Expectations in the Dead Sea Scrolls*. Edited by James H. Charlesworth, Hermann Lichtenberger and Gerbern S. Oegema. Tübingen: Mohr, 1998.

Allegro, J. M. *Qumran Cave 4.1 (4Q158–4Q186)*. Discoveries in the Judaean Desert V. Oxford: Clarendon, 1968.

Baillet, Maurice. "Fragments du Document de Damas. Qumrân, Grotte 6." *Revue biblique* 63 (1956): 513–23.

———. *Qumrân Grotte 4.III (4Q482–4Q520)*. Discoveries in the Judaean Desert VII. Oxford: Clarendon, 1982.

Baumgarten, Albert. "Pharisees." Pages 657–63 in *Encyclopedia of the Dead Sea Scrolls*. Edited by Lawrence H. Schiffman and James C. VanderKam. 2 vols. Oxford: Oxford University Press, 2000.

———. "The Perception of the Past in the Damascus Document." Pages 1–15 in *The Damascus Document A Centennial of Discovery: Proceedings of the Third International Symposium of the Orion Center for the Study of the Dead Sea Scrolls and Associated Literature, 4–8 February, 1998*. Edited by Joseph M. Baumgarten, Esther G. Chazon and Avital Pinnick. Vol. XXXIV in *Studies on the Texts of the Desert of Judah*. Edited by F. García Martínez and A. S. van der Woude. Leiden: Brill, 2000.

———. "The Zadokite Priests at Qumran: A Reconsideration." *Dead Sea Discoveries* 4-2 (1997): 137–56.

Baumgarten, Joseph M. "A Fragment on Fetal Life and Pregnancy in 4Q270." Pages 445–48 in *Pomegranates and Golden Bells*. Edited by David P. Wright, David Noel Freedman and Avi Hurvitz. Winona Lake, Indiana: Eisenbrauns, 1995.

———. "A New Qumran Substitute for the Divine Name and Mishnah Sukkah 4.5." *Jewish Quarterly Review* 83 (1992): 1–5.

———. "A 'Scriptural' Citation in 4Q Fragments of the Damascus Document." *Journal of Jewish Studies* 43 (1992): 95–98.

———. "Corrigenda to the 4Q MSS of the *Damascus Document*." *Revue de Qumran* 19 (1999): 217–25.

———. "Liquids and the Susceptibility to Defilement in New 4Q Texts." *Jewish Quarterly Review* 85 (1994): 91–101.

———. "Messianic Forgiveness of Sin in CD 14:19 (4Q266 10 i 12–13)." Pages 537–44 in *The Provo International Conference on the Dead Sea Scrolls: Technological Innovations, New Texts, and Reformulated Issues*. Edited by Donald W. Parry and Eugene Ulrich. Vol. XXX in *Studies on the Texts of the Desert of Judah*. Edited by F. García Martínez and A. S. van der Woude. Leiden: Brill, 1999.

———. "Purification after Childbirth and the Sacred Garden in 4Q265 and Jubilees." Pages 3–10 in *New Qumran Texts and Studies. Proceedings of the First Meeting of the International Organization for Qumran Studies, Paris 1992*. Edited by George J. Brooke and F. García Martínez. Vol. XV of *Studies on the Texts of the Desert of Judah*. Edited by F. García Martínez and A. S. van der Woude. Leiden: Brill, 1994.

———. *Qumran Cave 4.XIII: The Damascus Document (4Q266–273)*. Discoveries in the Judaean Desert XVIII. Oxford: Clarendon Press, 1996.

———. *Qumran Cave 4.XXV: Halakhic Texts*. Discoveries in the Judaean Desert XXXV. Oxford: Clarendon Press, 1999.

———. *Studies in Qumran Law.* Vol. 24 in Studies in Judaism in Late Antiquity. Edited by Jacob Neusner. Leiden: Brill, 1977.

———. "The 4Q Zadokite Fragments on Skin Disease." *Journal of Jewish Studies* 41 (1990): 153–65.

———. "The Cave 4 Versions of the Qumran Penal Code." *Journal of Jewish Studies* 43 (1992): 268–76.

———. "The Disqualifications of Priests in 4Q Fragments of the 'Damascus Document,' a Specimen of the Recovery of pre-Rabbinic Halakha." Pages 503–13 in vol. 2 of *The Madrid Qumran Congress: Proceedings of the International Congress on the Dead Sea Scrolls; Madrid 18–21, March, 1991.* Edited by Julio Trebolle Barrera and Luis Vegas Montaner. Vol. XI, 2 in *Studies on the Texts of the Desert of Judah.* Edited by F. García Martínez and A. S. van der Woude. Leiden: Brill, 1992.

———. "The Essene Avoidance of Oil and the Laws of Purity." *Revue de Qumran* 6 (1967): 183–92.

———. "The Essene-Qumran Restraints on Marriage." Pages 13–24 in *Archaeology and History in the Dead Sea Scrolls: The New York University Conference in Memory of Yigael Yadin.* Edited by L. H. Schiffman. Journal for the Study of the Pseudepigrapha: Supplement Series 8. Sheffield: JSOT Press, 1990.

———. "The Laws About Fluxes in 4Q Tohora[a] (4Q274)." Pages 1–8 in *Time to Prepare the Way in the Wilderness. Papers on the Qumran Scrolls by Fellows of the Institute for Advanced Studies of the Hebrew University, Jerusalem, 1989–1990.* Edited by Devorah Dimant and Lawrence H. Schiffman. Vol. XVI in *Studies on the Texts of the Desert of Judah.* Edited by F. García Martínez and A. S. van der Woude. Leiden: Brill, 1995.

———. "The Laws of the Damascus Document - Between Bible and Mishnah." Pages 17–26 in *The Damascus Document A Centennial of Discovery: Proceedings of the Third International Symposium of the Orion Center for the Study of the Dead Sea Scrolls and Associated Literature, 4–8 February, 1998.* Edited by Joseph M. Baumgarten, Esther G. Chazon and Avital Pinnick. Vol. XXXIV in *Studies on the Texts of the Desert of Judah.* Edited by F. García Martínez and A. S. van der Woude. Leiden: Brill, 2000.

———. "The Laws of 'Orlah and First Fruits in the Light of Jubilees, the Qumran Writings, and Targum Ps. Jonathan." *Journal of Jewish Studies* 38 (1987): 195–202.

———. "The Laws of the Damascus Document in Current Research." Pages 51–62 in *The Damascus Document Reconsidered.* Edited by Magen Broshi. Jerusalem: Israel Exploration Society, 1992.

———. "The 'Sons of Dawn' in *CDC* 13: 14–15 and the Ban on Commerce among the Essenes." *Israel Exploration Journal* 33 (1983): 81–85.

———. "Zab Impurity in Qumran and Rabbinic Law." *Journal of Jewish Studies* 45 (1994): 273–77.

Baumgarten, Joseph, and Daniel Schwartz. "Damascus Document (CD)." Pages 4–57 in *Damascus Document, War Scroll, and Related Documents.* Edited by James H. Charlesworth. Vol. 2 of *The Dead Sea Scrolls: Hebrew, Aramaic, and Greek Texts with English Translations.* Edited by James H. Charlesworth. Tübingen/Louisville: J. C. B. Mohr [Siebeck] and Westminster John Knox Press, 1995.

Baumgarten, Joseph, Esther Chazon, and Avital Pinnick, eds. *The Damascus Document A Centennial of Discovery: Proceedings of the Third International Symposium of the Orion Center for the Study of the Dead Sea Scrolls and Associated Literature, 4–8 February, 1998.* Vol. XXXIV of *Studies on the Texts of the Desert of Judah.* Leiden: Brill, 2000.

Betz, O., "The Qumran Halakhah Text Miqsat Ma'ase Ha-Torah (4QMMT) and Sadducean, Essene, and Early Pharisaic Tradition." Pages 176–202 in *The*

*Aramaic Bible. Targums in Their Historical Context.* Edited by D. R. G. Beattie and M. J. McNamara. Sheffield: JSOT Press, 1994.

Bowley, James E. "Prophets and Prophecy at Qumran." Pages 354–78 in vol. 2 of *The Dead Sea Scrolls After Fifty Years: A Comprehensive Assessment.* 2 vols. Edited by Peter W. Flint and James C. VanderKam. Leiden: Brill, 1999.

Boyce, Mark. *The Poetry of the Damascus Document.* Ph.D. diss., Edinburgh, 1988.

―――. "The Poetry of the *Damascus Document* and its Bearing on the Origin of the Qumran Sect." *Revue de Qumran* 14 (1990): 615–28.

Brooke, George J. "The Amos-Numbers Midrash (CD 7:13B–8:1A) and Messianic Expectation." *Zeitschrift für die alttestamentliche Wissenschaft* 92 (1980): 397–404.

―――. "The Messiah of Aaron in the Damascus Document." *Revue de Qumran* 15 (1991): 215–30.

―――. "Book Reviews: *The Use of Scripture in the Damascus Document 1–8, 19–20.*" *Dead Sea Discoveries* 4-1 (1997): 112–16.

―――. "Qumran Pesher: Towards the Redefinition of a Genre." *Revue de Qumran* 10 (1981): 483–503.

Brin, Gershon. "Divorce at Qumran." Pages 231–44 in *Legal Texts and Legal Issues: Proceedings of the Second Meeting of the International Organization for Qumran Studies: Cambridge 1995.* Edited by Moshe Bernstein, Florentino García Martínez, and John Kampen. Leiden: Brill, 1997.

Brownlee, W. H. *The Midrash Pesher of Habakkuk.* Missoula: Scholars Press, 1979.

Büchler, Adolph. "Schechter's 'Jewish Sectaries.'" *Jewish Quarterly Review* 3 (1912/13): 429–85.

Callaway, P. R. "Qumran Origins: From the *Doresh* to the *Moreh.*" *Revue de Qumran* 14 (1990): 637–50.

Campbell, Jonathan. "Essene-Qumran Origins in the Exile: A Scriptural Basis?" *Journal of Jewish Studies* 46 (1995): 143–56.

―――. "Scripture in The Damascus Document 1.1–2.1." *Journal of Jewish Studies* 44 (1993): 83–99.

―――. *The Use of Scripture in the Damascus Document 1–8, 19–20.* New York: Walter de Gruyter, 1995.

Carmignac, Jean. "Comparaison entre les manuscrits "A" et "B" du Document de Damas." *Revue de Qumran* 2 (1959): 53–67.

Charles, R. H., trans. *The Book of Jubilees or the Little Genesis.* London: Adam and Charles Black, 1902.

Charlesworth, James H., ed. *Damascus Document, War Scroll, and Related Documents.* Vol. 2 of *The Dead Sea Scrolls: Hebrew, Aramaic, and Greek Texts with English Translations.* Edited by James H. Charlesworth. Tübingen/Louisville: J. C. B. Mohr [Siebeck] and Westminster John Knox Press, 1995.

―――. *Pesharim, Other Commentaries, and Related Documents.* Vol. 6b of *The Dead Sea Scrolls: Hebrew, Aramaic, and Greek Texts with English Translations.* Edited by James H. Charlesworth. Tübingen/Louisville: J. C. B. Mohr [Siebeck] and Westminster John Knox Press, 1995.

―――. *Rule of the Community and Related Documents.* Vol. 1 of *The Dead Sea Scrolls: Hebrew, Aramaic, and Greek Texts with English Translations.* Edited by James H. Charlesworth. Tübingen/Louisville: J. C. B. Mohr [Siebeck] and Westminster John Knox Press, 1994.

―――. *The Pesharim and Qumran History. Chaos or Consensus?* Grand Rapids: Eerdmans, 2002.

Collins, John J. "Teacher and Messiah? The One Who Will Teach Righteousness at the End of Days." Pages 193–210 in *The Community of the Renewed Covenant: The Notre Dame Symposium on the Dead Sea Scrolls.* Edited by E. Ulrich and J. Vanderkam.

Christianity and Judaism in Antiquity Series 10. Edited by Gregory E. Sterling.
     Notre Dame: University of Notre Dame Press, 1994.
————. *The Scepter and the Star: The Messiahs of the Dead Sea Scrolls and Other Ancient
     Literature*. New York: Doubleday, 1995.
Cothenet, É. "The Document de Damas." Pages 131–204 in *Les Textes de Qumrân:
     traduits et annotés*. Edited by J. Carmignac, É. Cothenet and H. Lignée. Paris:
     Éditions Letouzey et Ané, 1963.
Crawford, Sidnie White. "The Meaning of the Phrase עיר המקדש in the Temple
     Scroll." *Dead Sea Discoveries* 8-3 (2001): 243–54.
Cross, Frank Moore. *The Ancient Library of Qumran*. 3d ed. Minneapolis: Fortress
     Press, 1995.
Davies, Philip R. "Communities at Qumran and the Case of the Missing Teacher."
     *Revue de Qumran* 15 (1991): 275–86.
————. "Halakhah at Qumran." Pages 37–50 in *A Tribute to Geza Vermes: Essays on
     Jewish and Christian Literature and History*. Edited by Philip R. Davies and R. T.
     White. Journal for the Study of the Old Testament: Supplement Series 100. Edited
     by David J. A. Clines and Philip R. Davies. Sheffield: JSOT Press, 1990.
————. "The Birthplace of the Essenes: Where is 'Damascus'?" *Revue de Qumran* 14
     (1990): 503–19.
————. *The Damascus Covenant: An Interpretation of the "Damascus Document."* Journal
     for the Study of the Old Testament: Supplement Series 25. Sheffield: JSOT
     Press, 1983.
————. "The 'Damascus' Sect and Judaism," Pages 70–84 in *Pursuing the Text: Studies
     in Honor of Ben Zion Wacholder on the Occasion of his Seventieth Birthday*. Edited by J.
     C. Reeves and J. Kampen. Sheffield: Sheffield Academic Press, 1994.
————. "The Judaism(s) of the Damascus Document." Pages 27–43 in *The Damascus
     Document A Centennial of Discovery: Proceedings of the Third International Symposium of the
     Orion Center for the Study of the Dead Sea Scrolls and Associated Literature, 4–8 February,
     1998*. Edited by Joseph M. Baumgarten, Esther G. Chazon and Avital Pinnick.
     Vol. XXXIV of *Studies on the Texts of the Desert of Judah*. Edited by F. García
     Martínez and A. S. van der Woude. Leiden: Brill, 2000.
————. "The Ideology of the Temple in the Damascus Document." *Journal of Jewish
     Studies* 33 (1982): 287–301.
————. "The Teacher of Righteousness and the 'End of Days.'" *Revue de Qumran*
     13 (1988): 313–17.
Davies, R. *The History of the Composition of the Damascus Document Statutes (CD 9–16 +
     4QD)*. Ph.D diss., Harvard, 1992.
Denis, A.-M. *Les thèmes de connaissance dans le Document de Damas*. Louvain: Publications
     Universitaires, 1967.
Derrett, J. Duncan M. "'BEHUQEY HAGOYIM': Damascus Document IX,1 Again."
     *Revue de Qumran* 11 (1983): 409–15.
————. "The Reprobate's Peace: 4QD$^a$ (4Q266) (18 V 14–16)." Pages 245–49 in
     *Legal Texts and Legal Issues: Proceedings of the Second Meeting of the International Organi-
     zation for Qumran Studies: Cambridge 1995*. Edited by Moshe Bernstein, Florentino
     García Martínez, and John Kampen. Leiden: Brill, 1997.
Doering, Lutz. "New Aspects of Qumran Sabbath Law from Cave 4 Fragments."
     Pages 251–74 in *Legal Texts and Legal Issues: Proceedings of the Second Meeting of the
     International Organization for Qumran Studies: Cambridge 1995*. Edited by Moshe Ber-
     nstein, Florentino García Martínez, and John Kampen. Leiden: Brill, 1997.
Doudna, Gregory L. *4Q Pesher Nahum: A Critical Edition*. Journal for the Study of
     the Pseudepigrapha Supplement Series 35. Copenhagen International Series

8. Editors Lester L. Grabbe and James H. Charlesworth. Sheffield: Sheffield Academic Press, 2001.

Elwolde, John F. "Distinguishing the Linguistic and the Exegetical: The Biblical Book of Numbers in the Damascus Document." *Dead Sea Discoveries* 7-1 (2000): 1–25.

———. "*rwqmh* in the *Damascus Document* and Ps 139:15." Pages 65–83 in *Diggers at the Well: Proceedings of a Third International Symposium on the Hebrew of the Dead Sea Scrolls and Ben Sira*. Edited by T. Muraoka and J. F. Elwolde. Vol. XXXVI in *Studies on the Texts of the Desert of Judah*. Edited by F. García Martínez and A. S. van der Woude. Leiden: 2000.

———. "The Meaning and Significance of CD 20:13–15." Pages 330–36 in *The Provo International Conference on the Dead Sea Scrolls: Technological Innovations, New Texts, and Reformulated Issues*. Edited by Donald W. Parry and Eugene Ulrich. Vol. XXX in *Studies on the Texts of the Desert of Judah*. Edited by F. García Martínez and A. S. van der Woude. Leiden: Brill, 1999.

Eshel, Hanan. "CD 12:15–17 and the Stone Vessels Found at Qumran." Pages 45–52 in *The Damascus Document A Centennial of Discovery: Proceedings of the Third International Symposium of the Orion Center for the Study of the Dead Sea Scrolls and Associated Literature, 4–8 February, 1998*. Edited by Joseph M. Baumgarten, Esther G. Chazon and Avital Pinnick. Vol. XXXIV of *Studies on the Texts of the Desert of Judah*. Edited by F. García Martínez and A. S. van der Woude. Leiden: Brill, 2000.

Evans, Craig A. "Qumran's Messiah: How Important Is He?" Pages 135–49 in *Religion in the Dead Sea Scrolls*. Studies in the Dead Sea Scrolls and Related Literature. Edited by John J. Collins and Robert A. Kugler. Grand Rapids: Eerdmans, 2000.

Falk, Z. W. "'BEHUQEY HAGOYIM' in Damascus Document IX,1." *Revue de Qumran* 6 (1969): 569.

Fassberg, Steven E. "The Linguistic Study of the Damascus Document: A Historical Perspective." Pages 53–67 in *The Damascus Document A Centennial of Discovery: Proceedings of the Third International Symposium of the Orion Center for the Study of the Dead Sea Scrolls and Associated Literature, 4–8 February, 1998*. Edited by Joseph M. Baumgarten, Esther G. Chazon and Avital Pinnick. Vol. XXXIV of *Studies on the Texts of the Desert of Judah*. Edited by F. García Martínez and A. S. van der Woude. Leiden: Brill, 2000.

Fitzmyer, Joseph A., ed. *Documents of Jewish Sectaries*. New York: Ktav, 1970. Rep., with "Prolegomenon," of Solomon Schechter, *Fragments of a Zadokite Work*. Cambridge: Cambridge University Press, 1910).

Ginzberg, Louis. *An Unknown Jewish Sect*. New York: The Jewish Theological Seminary of America, 1976.

Glessmer, Uwe. "Calendars in the Qumran Scrolls." Pages 213–78 in vol. 2 of *The Dead Sea Scrolls After Fifty Years: A Comprehensive Assessment*. 2 vols. Edited by Peter W. Flint and James C. VanderKam. Leiden: Brill, 1999.

Golb, Norman. "Literary and Doctrinal Aspects of the Damascus Covenant in the Light of Karaite Literature." *Jewish Quarterly Review* 47 (1957): 354–74.

———. "The Dietary Laws of the Damascus Document in Relation to Those of the Karaites." *Journal of Jewish Studies* 8 (1957): 51–69.

Goodman, M. D. "A Note on the Qumran Sectarians, the Essenes and Josephus." *Journal of Jewish Studies* 46 (1995): 161–66.

Greenfield, Jonas C. "The Words of Levi Son of Jacob in Damascus Document IV, 15–19." *Revue de Qumran* 13 (1988): 319–22.

Grossman, Maxine L. *Reading for History in the Damascus Document: A Methodological Study*. Vol. XLV in *Studies on the Texts of the Desert of Judah*. Edited by F. García Martínez and P. W. Flint. Leiden: Brill, 2002.

————. "Reading for Gender in the Damascus Document." *Dead Sea Discoveries* 11-2 (2004): 212–39.

Harkavy, A. "Anan Ben David, Founder of the Karaite Sect." Pages 553–56 in vol. 1 of *The Jewish Encyclopedia*. Edited by Isidore Singer. 12 vols. New York: Funk and Wagnalls Company, 1906.

Hauer, Christian J., Jr. "Who was Zadok?" *Journal of Biblical Literature* 82 (1963): 89–94.

Hempel, Charlotte. "4QOrd[a] (4Q159) and the Laws of the Damascus Document." Pages 372–76 in *The Dead Sea Scrolls Fifty Years After Their Discovery*. Proceedings of the Jerusalem Congress, July 20–25, 1997. Edited by Lawrence H. Schiffman, Emanuel Tov, and James C. VanderKam. Jerusalem: Israel Exploration Society, 2000.

————. "Community Origins in the *Damascus Document* in the Light of Recent Scholarship." Pages 316–29 in *The Provo International Conference on the Dead Sea Scrolls: Technological Innovations, New Texts, and Reformulated Issues*. Edited by Donald W. Parry and Eugene Ulrich. Vol. XXX in *Studies on the Texts of the Desert of Judah*. Edited by F. García Martínez and A. S. van der Woude. Leiden: Brill, 1999.

————. "Community Structures in the Dead Sea Scrolls: Admission, Organization, Disciplinary Procedures." Pages 67–92 in vol. 2 of *The Dead Sea Scrolls After Fifty Years: A Comprehensive Assessment*. 2 vols. Edited by Peter W. Flint and James C. VanderKam. Leiden: Brill, 1999.

————. *The Damascus Texts*. Sheffield: Sheffield Academic Press, 2000.

————. "The Laws of the Damascus Document and 4QMMT." Pages 69–84 in *The Damascus Document A Centennial of Discovery: Proceedings of the Third International Symposium of the Orion Center for the Study of the Dead Sea Scrolls and Associated Literature, 4–8 February, 1998*. Edited by Joseph M. Baumgarten, Esther G. Chazon and Avital Pinnick. Vol. XXXIV of *Studies on the Texts of the Desert of Judah*. Edited by F. García Martínez and A. S. van der Woude. Leiden: Brill, 2000.

————. *The Laws of the Damascus Document: Sources, Tradition and Redaction*. Vol. XXIX in *Studies on the Texts of the Desert of Judah*. Edited by F. García Martínez and P. W. Flint. Leiden: Brill, 1998.

————. "The Penal Code Reconsidered." Pages 337–48 in *Legal Texts and Legal Issues: Proceedings of the Second Meeting of the International Organization for Qumran Studies: Cambridge 1995*. Edited by Moshe Bernstein, Florentino García Martínez, and John Kampen. Leiden: Brill, 1997.

Himmelfarb, Martha. "Impurity and Sin in 4QD, 1QS, and 4Q512." *Dead Sea Discoveries* 8-1 (2001): 9–37.

Horgan, Maurya P. *Pesharim: Qumran Interpretations of Biblical Books*. Catholic Biblical Quarterly Monograph Series 8. Washington, DC: The Catholic Biblical Association of America, 1979.

Hurowitz, Victor Avigdor. "רוקמה in Damascus Document 4QD[e] (4Q270) 7 i 14." *Dead Sea Discoveries* 9-2 (2002): 34–37.

Iwry, Samuel. "Was there a Migration to Damascus? The Problem of שבי ישראל." *Eretz Israel* 9 (1969): 80–88.

Jackson, Bernard S. "Damascus Document IX, 16–23 and Parallels." *Revue de Qumran* 9 (1978): 445–50.

Jastram, Nathan. "Hierarchy at Qumran." Pages 349–76 in *Legal Texts and Legal Issues: Proceedings of the Second Meeting of the International Organization for Qumran Studies: Cambridge 1995*. Edited by Moshe Bernstein, Florentino García Martínez, and John Kampen. Leiden: Brill, 1997.

*Josephus.* Translated by H. St. J. Thackeray et al. 10 vols. Loeb Classical Library. Cambridge: Harvard University Press, 1926–1965.

Kimbrough, S. T, Jr. "The Concept of Sabbath at Qumran." *Revue de Qumran* 5 (1966): 483–502.

Kister, Menahem. "Some Aspects of Qumranic Halakhah," Pages 571–88 in vol. 2 of *The Madrid Qumran Congress: Proceedings of the International Congress on the Dead Sea Scrolls; Madrid 18–21, March, 1991.* Edited by Julio Trebolle Barrera and Luis Vegas Montaner. Vol. XI, 2 in *Studies on the Texts of the Desert of Judah,* Edited by F. García Martínez and A. S. van der Woude. Leiden: Brill, 1992.

Knibb, Michael A. "Eschatology and Messianism in the Dead Sea Scrolls." Pages 379–402 in vol. 2 of *The Dead Sea Scrolls After Fifty Years: A Comprehensive Assessment.* 2 vols. Edited by Peter W. Flint and James C. VanderKam. Leiden: Brill, 1999.

———. "Exile in the Damascus Document." *Journal for the Study of the Old Testament* 25 (1983): 99–117.

———. "Interpreter of the Law." Pages 383–84 in vol. 1 of *The Encyclopaedia of the Dead Sea Scrolls.* Edited by Lawrence H. Schiffman and James C. VanderKam. 2 vols. Oxford: Oxford University Press, 2000.

———. "The Interpretation of Damascus Document VII, 9b–VIII, 2a and XIX, 5b–14." *Revue de Qumran* 15 (1991): 243–51.

———. "Teacher of Righteousness." Pages 918–21 in vol. 2 of *The Encyclopaedia of the Dead Sea Scrolls.* Edited by Lawrence H. Schiffman and James C. VanderKam. 2 vols. Oxford: Oxford University Press, 2000.

———. "The Place of the Damascus Document." Pages 149–62 in *Methods of Investigation of the Dead Sea Scrolls and the Khirbet Qumran Site. Present Realities and Future Prospects.* Edited by Michael O. Wise et al. New York: New York Academy of Sciences, 1994.

———. *The Qumran Community.* Cambridge: Cambridge University Press, 1987.

———. "The Teacher of Righteousness - A Messianic Title?" Pages 51–65 in *A Tribute to Geza Vermes: Essays on Jewish and Christian Literature and History.* Edited by Philip R. Davies and R. T. White. Journal for the Study of the Old Testament: Supplement Series 100. Edited by David J. A. Clines and Philip R. Davies. Sheffield: JSOT Press, 1990.

Krašovec, Jože. "Sources of Confession of Sin in 1QS 1:24–26 and CD 20:28–30." Pages 306–21 in *The Dead Sea Scrolls Fifty Years After Their Discovery.* Proceedings of the Jerusalem Congress, July 20–25, 1997. Edited by Lawrence H. Schiffman, Emanuel Tov, and James C. VanderKam. Jerusalem: Israel Exploration Society, 2000.

Kugler, Robert A. "Priesthood at Qumran." Pages 91–116 in vol. 2 of *The Dead Sea Scrolls After Fifty Years: A Comprehensive Assessment.* 2 vols. Edited by Peter W. Flint and James C. VanderKam. Leiden: Brill, 1999.

———. "The Priesthood at Qumran: The Evidence of References to Levi and the Levites." Pages 465–79 in *The Provo International Conference on the Dead Sea Scrolls: Technological Innovations, New Texts, and Reformulated Issues.* Edited by Donald W. Parry and Eugene Ulrich. Vol. XXX in *Studies on the Texts of the Desert of Judah.* Edited by F. García Martínez and A. S. van der Woude. Leiden: Brill, 1999.

Laato, Antti. "The Chronology in the *Damascus Document* of Qumran." *Revue de Qumran* 15 (1992): 605–07.

———. "The Eschatological Act of *Kipper* in the *Damascus Document.*" Pages 91–107 in *Intertestamental Essays in Honour of Józef Tadeusz Milik.* Qumranica Mogilanensia 6/1. Edited by Zdzislaw J. Kapera. Kraków: Enigma Press, 1992.

Lagrange, J.-J. "La secte juive de la Nouvelle Alliance au pays de Damas." *Revue biblique* 9 (1912): 213–40, 321–60.

Lévi, Israel. "Document relatif a la 'Communaute des fils de Sadoc,'" *Revue des études juives* 65 (1913): 24–31.

Levine, Baruch A. "Damascus Document IX,17–22: A New Translation and Comments." *Revue de Qumran* 8 (1973): 195–96.

Lim, Timothy. "The Wicked Priest or the Liar?" Pages 45–51 in *The Dead Sea Scrolls in their Historical Context*. Edited by Timothy Lim, et al. Edinburgh: T&T Clark, 2000.

Liver, Jacob. "The Sons of Zadok the Priests in the Dead Sea Sect." *Revue de Qumran* 6 (1967): 3–30.

Lohse, Eduard. *Die Texte aus Qumran*. München: Kösel-Verlag, 1971.

Maier, Johann. "Von Eleazar bis Zadok." *Revue de Qumran* 15 (1991): 231–41.

Martínez, Florentino García and Tigchelaar, Eibert J. C., eds. and translators. *The Dead Sea Scrolls Study Edition*. 2 vols. Leiden: Brill, 1997–98.

Mazar, Benjamin. "כתובת רצפת בית־כנסת בעין־גדי." *Tarbiz* 40 (1971): 18–23.

Metso, Sarianna. "The Relationship between the Damascus Document and the Community Rule." Pages 85–93 in *The Damascus Document A Centennial of Discovery: Proceedings of the Third International Symposium of the Orion Center for the Study of the Dead Sea Scrolls and Associated Literature, 4–8 February, 1998*. Edited by Joseph M. Baumgarten, Esther G. Chazon and Avital Pinnick. Vol. XXXIV of *Studies on the Texts of the Desert of Judah*. Edited by F. García Martínez and A. S. van der Woude. Leiden: Brill, 2000.

Meyer, Eduard. *Die Gemeinde des Neuen Bundes im Lande Damaskus: eine jüdische Schrift aus der Seleukidenzeit*. Berlin: Verlag der Akademie der Wissenschaften, 1919.

Milgrom, J. "The City of the Temple. A Response to Lawrence H. Schiffman." *Jewish Quarterly Review* 85 (1994): 125–28.

Milikowski, Chaim. "Again: *Damascus* in Damascus Document and in Rabbinic Literature." *Revue de Qumran* 11 (1982): 97–106.

Muraoka, T and Elwolde, J. F. *The Hebrew of the Dead Sea Scrolls and Ben Sira: Proceedings of a Symposium held at Leiden University 11–14 December 1995*. Edited by T. Muraoka and J. F. Elwolde. Vol XXVI in *Studies on the Texts of the Desert of Judah*, Edited by F. García Martínez and Adam S. van der Woude. Leiden: Brill, 1997.

———. *Sirach, Scrolls, and Sages: Proceedings of a Second International Symposium on the Hebrew of the Dead Sea Scrolls, Ben Sira, and the Mishnah, held at Leiden University, 15–17 December 1997*. Edited by T. Muraoka and J. F. Elwolde. Vol. XXXII in *Studies on the Texts of the Desert of Judah*, Edited by F. García Martínez and Adam S. van der Woude. Leiden: Brill, 1999.

Murphy-O'Connor, Jerome. "An Essene Missionary Document? CD II,14–VI,1." *Revue biblique* 77 (1970): 201–29.

———. "A Literary Analysis of Damascus XIX,33–XX,34." *Revue biblique* 79 (1972): 544–64.

———. "A Literary Analysis of Damascus Document VI,2–VIII,3." *Revue biblique* 78 (1971): 210–32.

———. "The Critique of the Princes of Judah (CD VIII,3–19)." *Revue Biblique* 79 (1972): 200–16.

———. "The Damascus Document Revisited." *Revue biblique* 92 (1985): 223–46.

———. "The Original Text of CD 7:9–8:2 = 19:5–14." *Harvard Theological Review* 64 (1971): 379–86.

Nebe, G. Wilhelm. "Das Sprachvermögen des Mebaqqer in *Damaskusschrift* XIV,10." *Revue de Qumran* 16 (1993): 289–91.

———. "Nocheinmal zu Text und Übersetzung von *CD* VI,11–14." *Revue de Qumran* 16 (1993): 285–87.

Nemoy, Leon. "Al-Qirqisani's Account of the Jewish Sects and Christianity." *HUCA* 7 (1930): 317–97.

———. "Anan Ben David." Pages 919–22 in vol. 2 of *Encyclopedia Judaica*. 2. Edited by Cecil Roth. 16 vols. Jerusalem: The Macmillan Company, 1971.

Neusner, Jacob. "'By the Testimony of Two Witnesses' in the Damascus Document IX,17–22 and in Pharisaic-Rabbinic Law." *Revue de Qumran* 8 (1973): 197–217.

———. "Damascus Document IX,17–22 and Irrelevant Parallels." *Revue de Qumran* 9 (1978): 441–44.

Newsom, Carol. "'Sectually Explicit' Literature from Qumran." Pages 167–87 in *The Hebrew Bible and Its Interpreters*. Edited by W. H. Propp, B. Halpern, and D. N. Freedman. Winona Lake: Eisenbrauns, 1990.

———. "The Sage in the Literature of Qumran: The Functions of the Maskil." Pages 373–82 in *The Sage in Israel and the Ancient Near East*. Edited by J. G. Gammie and L. G. Perdue. Winona Lake: Eisenbrauns, 1990.

Nitzan, Bilhah. *Pesher Habakkuk*. Jerusalem: Bialik Institute, 1986.

———. "Repentance in the Dead Sea Scrolls." Pages 145–70 in vol. 2 of *The Dead Sea Scrolls After Fifty Years: A Comprehensive Assessment*. 2 vols. Edited by Peter W. Flint and James C. VanderKam. Leiden: Brill, 1999.

———. "The Laws of Reproof in *4QBerakhot* (4Q286–290) in Light of their Parallels in the *Damascus Covenant* and Other Texts from Qumran." Pages 149–65 in *Legal Texts and Legal Issues: Proceedings of the Second Meeting of the International Organization for Qumran Studies: Cambridge 1995*. Edited by Moshe Bernstein, Florentino García Martínez, and John Kampen. Leiden: Brill, 1997.

Noack, B. "Qumran and the Book of Jubilees." *Svensk exegetisk årsbok* 22–23 (1958): 191–207.

Olyan, Saul M. "The Exegetical Dimensions of Restrictions on the Blind and the Lame in Texts from Qumran." *Dead Sea Discoveries* 8-1 (2001): 38–50.

Osten-Sacken, Peter. von der. *Gott und Belial. Traditionsgeschichtliche Untersuchungen zum Dualismus in den Texten aus Qumran*. Vol. 6 in Studien zur Umwelt des Neuen Testaments. Edited by Karl Georg Kuhn. Göttingen: Vandenhoeck & Ruprecht, 1969.

Parry, Donald W. "Notes on Divine Name Avoidance in Scriptural Units of the Legal Texts of Qumran." Pages 437–49 in *Legal Texts and Legal Issues: Proceedings of the Second Meeting of the International Organization for Qumran Studies: Cambridge 1995*. Edited by Moshe Bernstein, Florentino García Martínez, and John Kampen. Leiden: Brill, 1997.

Parry, Donald, and Eugene Ulrich, eds. *The Provo International Conference on the Dead Sea Scrolls: Technological Innovations, New Texts, and Reformulated Issues*. Vol. XXX in *Studies on the Texts of the Desert of Judah*. Edited by F. García Martínez and A. S. van der Woude. Leiden: Brill, 1999.

Parry, Donald, and Emanuel Tov. *The Dea Sea Scrolss Reader*. 6 vols. Leiden: Brill, 2004–05.

Pfann, Stephen. "4Q298: The Maskil's Address to All Sons of Dawn." *Jewish Quarterly Review* 85 (1994): 203–35.

Porton, G. "Midrash." Page 818–22 in vol. 4 of *Anchor Bible Dictionary*. Edited by David Noel Freedman. 6 vols. New York: Doubleday, 1992.

Qimron, Elisha. "שבועת הבנים in the Damascus Covenant 15.1–2." *Jewish Quarterly Review* 81 (1990): 115–18.

———. "Celibacy in the Dead Sea Scrolls and the Two Kinds of Sectarians." Pages 287–94 in vol. 1 of *Proceedings of the International Congress on the Dead Sea Scrolls Madrid 18–21 March, 1991*. Edited by Julio Trebolle Barrera and Luis Vegas

Montaner. Vol. XI, 1 in *Studies on the Texts of the Desert of Judah.* Edited by F. García Martínez and A. S. van der Woude. Leiden: E. J. Brill, 1992.

———. "Further Observations on the Laws of Oaths in the Damascus Document 15." *Jewish Quarterly Review* 85 (1994): 251–57.

———. "Notes on the 4Q Zadokite Fragments on Skin Disease." *Journal of Jewish Studies* 42 (1991): 256–59.

———. *The Hebrew of the Dead Sea Scrolls.* Atlanta: Scholars Press, 1986.

———. "The Text of CDC." Pages 9–49 in *The Damascus Document Reconsidered.* Edited by Magen Broshi, Jerusalem: The Israel Exploration Society, 1992.

Rabin, Chaim. *The Zadokite Documents.* 2d rev. ed. Oxford: Clarendon, 1958.

Rabinovitch, N. L. "Damascus Document IX,17–22 and Rabbinic Parallels." *Revue de Qumran* 9 (1977): 113–16.

Rabinowitz, Isaac. "A Note on Damascus Document IX,7." *Revue de Qumran* 9 (1977): 237–40.

———. "A Reconsideration of 'Damascus' and '390 Years' in the 'Damascus' ('Zadokite') Fragments." *Journal of Biblical Literature* 73 (1954): 11–35.

———. "The Meaning and Date of 'Damascus' Document IX,1." *Revue de Qumran* 6 (1968): 433–35.

Rainbow, Paul. "The Last Oniad and the Teacher of Righteousness." *Journal of Jewish Studies* 48 (1997): 30–52.

Regev, Eyal. "Yose Ben Yoezer and the Qumran Sectarians on Purity Laws: Agreement and Controversy." Pages 95–107 in *The Damascus Document A Centennial of Discovery: Proceedings of the Third International Symposium of the Orion Center for the Study of the Dead Sea Scrolls and Associated Literature, 4–8 February, 1998.* Edited by Joseph M. Baumgarten, Esther G. Chazon and Avital Pinnick. Vol. XXXIV of *Studies on the Texts of the Desert of Judah.* Edited by F. García Martínez and A. S. van der Woude. Leiden: Brill, 2000.

Reif, Stefan C. "The Damascus Document from the Cairo Genizah: Its Discovery, Early Study and Historical Significance." Pages 109–31 in *The Damascus Document A Centennial of Discovery: Proceedings of the Third International Symposium of the Orion Center for the Study of the Dead Sea Scrolls and Associated Literature, 4–8 February, 1998.* Edited by Joseph M. Baumgarten, Esther G. Chazon and Avital Pinnick. Vol. XXXIV of *Studies on the Texts of the Desert of Judah.* Edited by F. García Martínez and A. S. van der Woude. Leiden: Brill, 2000.

de Roo, Jacqueline C. R. "David's Deeds in the Dead Sea Scrolls," *Dead Sea Discoveries* 6-1 (1999): 44–65.

Rowley, H. H. "The 390 Years of the Zadokite Work," Pages 341–47 in *Melanges bibliques rédigés en l'honneur de Andre Robert.* Paris: Bloud and Gay, 1957.

Rubinstein, Arie. "Urban Halakhah and Camp Rules in the 'Cairo Fragments of a Damascene Covenant.'" *Sefarad* 12 (1952): 283–96.

Sanders, J. A. *The Psalms Scroll of Qumran Cave 11 (11QPs^a).* Discoveries in the Judaean Desert IV. Oxford: Clarendon, 1965, 92.

Schechter, Solomon. "Reply to Dr. Büchler's Review of Schechter's 'Jewish Sectaries.'" *Jewish Quarterly Review* 4 (1913/14): 449–74.

Schiffman, Lawrence H. "Exclusion from the Sanctuary and the City of the Sanctuary in the Temple Scroll." *Hebrew Annual Review* 9 (1985): 301–20.

———. "Legislation Concerning Relations with Non-Jews in the *Zadokite Fragments* and in Tannaitic Literature." *Revue de Qumran* 11 (1983): 379–89.

———. *The Halakhah at Qumran.* Leiden: E. J. Brill, 1975.

———. "The Law of Vows and Oaths (*Num.* 30,3–16) in the *Zadokite Fragments* and the *Temple Scroll.*" *Revue de Qumran* 15 (1991): 199–214.

———. "The Relationship of the Zadokite Fragments to the Temple Scroll." Pages

133–45 in *The Damascus Document A Centennial of Discovery: Proceedings of the Third International Symposium of the Orion Center for the Study of the Dead Sea Scrolls and Associated Literature, 4–8 February, 1998.* Edited by Joseph M. Baumgarten, Esther G. Chazon and Avital Pinnick. Vol. XXXIV of *Studies on the Texts of the Desert of Judah.* Edited by F. García Martínez and A. S. van der Woude. Leiden: Brill, 2000.

Schniedewind, William M. "Structural Aspects of Qumran Messianism in the *Damascus Document.*" Pages 523–36 in *The Provo International Conference on the Dead Sea Scrolls: Technological Innovations, New Texts, and Reformulated Issues.* Edited by Donald W. Parry and Eugene Ulrich. Vol. XXX in *Studies on the Texts of the Desert of Judah.* Edited by F. García Martínez and A. S. van der Woude. Leiden: Brill, 1999.

Schremer, Adiel. "Qumran Polemic on Marital Law: CD 4:20–5:11 and Its Social Background." Pages 147–60 in *The Damascus Document A Centennial of Discovery: Proceedings of the Third International Symposium of the Orion Center for the Study of the Dead Sea Scrolls and Associated Literature, 4–8 February, 1998.* Edited by Joseph M. Baumgarten, Esther G. Chazon and Avital Pinnick. Vol. XXXIV of *Studies on the Texts of the Desert of Judah.* Edited by F. García Martínez and A. S. van der Woude. Leiden: Brill, 2000.

Schuller, Eileen. "Women in the Dead Sea Scrolls." Pages 117–44 in vol. 2 of *The Dead Sea Scrolls After Fifty Years: A Comprehensive Assessment.* 2 vols. Edited by Peter W. Flint and James C. VanderKam. Leiden: Brill, 1999.

Schwartz, Daniel R. "'To Join Oneself to the House of Judah': Damascus Document IV,11." *Revue de Qumran* 10 (1981): 435–46.

Schwarz, Ottilie. *Der erste Teil der Damaskusschrift und das Alte Testament.* Lichtland/ Diest, 1965.

Segal, M. H. "Additional Notes on 'Fragments of a Zadokite Work.'" *Jewish Quarterly Review* 3 (1912/13): 301–11.

Shemesh, Aharon. "Scriptural Interpretations in the Damascus Document and Their Parallels in Rabbinic Midrash." Pages 161–75 in *The Damascus Document A Centennial of Discovery: Proceedings of the Third International Symposium of the Orion Center for the Study of the Dead Sea Scrolls and Associated Literature, 4–8 February, 1998.* Edited by Joseph M. Baumgarten, Esther G. Chazon and Avital Pinnick. Vol. XXXIV of *Studies on the Texts of the Desert of Judah.* Edited by F. García Martínez and A. S. van der Woude. Leiden: Brill, 2000.

———. "'The Holy Angels Are in Their Council': The Exclusion of Deformed Persons from Holy Places in Qumranicand Rabbinic Literature." *Dead Sea Discoveries* 4-2 (1997): 179–206.

Soloff, R. A. "Toward Uncovering Original Texts in the Zadokite Documents." *New Testament Studies* 5 (1958): 62–67.

Solomon, Avi. "The Prohibition Against Ṭevul Yom and Defilement of the Daily Whole Offering in the Jerusalem Temple in CD 11:21–21:1: A New Understanding." *Dead Sea Discoveries* 4-1 (1997): 1–20.

Stegemann, Hartmut. "4QDamascus Document[d] frgs. 10, 11 (Re-edition), 15, 16." Pages 201–11 in *Qumran Cave 4.XXVI: Cryptic Texts and Miscellanea, Part 1.* Discoveries in the Judaean Desert XXXVI. Oxford: Clarendon, 2000.

———. "Das Gesetzeskorpus der 'Damaskusschchrift' (CD IX-XVI)." *Revue de Qumran* 14 (1990): 409–34.

———. "Towards Physical Reconstructions of the Qumran Damascus Document Scrolls." Pages 177–200 in *The Damascus Document A Centennial of Discovery: Proceedings of the Third International Symposium of the Orion Center for the Study of the Dead Sea Scrolls and Associated Literature, 4–8 February, 1998.* Edited by Joseph M. Baumgarten, Esther G. Chazon and Avital Pinnick. Vol. XXXIV of *Studies on the Texts of the Desert of Judah*. Edited by F. García Martínez and A. S. van der Woude. Leiden: Brill, 2000.

Steudel, Annette. "אחרית הימים‎ in the Texts from Qumran." *Revue de Qumran* 16 (1993): 225–46.

———. "The Houses of Prostration CD XI,21–XII,1—Duplicates of the Temple." *Revue de Qumran* 16 (1993): 49–68.

Strickert, Frederick. "Damascus Document VII, 10–20 and Qumran Messianic Expectation." *Revue de Qumran* 12 (1986): 327–49.

Strugnell, J, Harrington, D. J., and Elgvin, T. in consultation with J. A. Fitzmyer, *Sapiential Texts, Part 2: Cave 4.XXIV*. Discoveries in the Judaean Desert XXXIV. Oxford: Clarendon, 1999.

Talmon, Shemaryahu. "The Community of the Renewed Covenant: Between Judaism and Christianity." Pages 3–24 in *The Community of the Renewed Covenant: The Notre Dame Symposium on the Dead Sea Scrolls*. Edited by E. Ulrich and J. Vanderkam. Volume 10 in Christianity and Judaism in Antiquity Series. Notre Dame: University of Notre Dame Press, 1994.

———. "The 'Manual of Benedictions' of the Sect of the Judaean Desert." *Revue de Qumran* 2 (1960): 475–500.

Thorion-Vardi, Talia. "The Use of the Tenses in the Zadokite Documents." *Revue de Qumran* 12 (1985): 65–88.

VanderKam, James. "Jubilees and the Priestly Messiah of Qumran." *Revue de Qumran* 13 (1988): 353–65.

———. "Messianism in the Scrolls." Pages 211–34 in *The Community of the Renewed Covenant: The Notre Dame Symposium on the Dead Sea Scrolls*. Edited by E. Ulrich and J. Vanderkam. Volume 10 in Christianity and Judaism in Antiquity Series. Edited by Gregory E. Sterling. Notre Dame: University of Notre Dame Press, 1994.

———. *The Book of Jubilees*. 2 Vols. Louvain: Peeters, 1989.

———. *The Dead Sea Scrolls Today*. Grand Rapids: Wm. B. Eerdmans Publishing Co., 1994.

———. "Zadok and the SPR HTWRH HHTWM in Dam. Doc. V, 2–5." *Revue de Qumran* 11 (1984): 561–70.

Vermes, Geza. *The Complete Dead Sea Scrolls in English*. New York: Penguin Press, 1997.

Wacholder, Ben Zion. "A Qumran Attack on the Oral Exegesis? The Phrase *'šr btlmwd šqrm* in 4Q Pesher Nahum." *Revue de Qumran* 5 (1966): 575–78.

———. "Calendar Wars Between the 364 and the 365-Day Year." *Revue de Qumran* 20 (2001): 207–22.

———. "Deutero-Ezekiel and Jeremiah (4Q384–4Q391)." Pages 445–61 in *The Dead Sea Scrolls Fifty Years After Their Discovery. Proceedings of the Jerusalem Congress, July 20–25, 1997*. Edited by Lawrence H. Schiffman, Emanuel Tov, and James C. VanderKam. Jerusalem: Israel Exploration Society, 2000.

———. "Does Qumran Record the Death of the *Moreh*? The Meaning of *he'aseph* in *Damascus Covenant* XIX, 35, XX, 14." *Revue de Qumran* 13 (1988): 323–30.

———. "Historiography of Qumran: The Sons of Zadok and their Enemies," Pages 347–77 in *Qumran Between the Old and the New Testaments*. Edited by Frederick H. Cryer and Thomas L. Thompson. Journal for the Study of the Old Testament: Supplement Series 290. Sheffield: Sheffield Academic Press, 1998.

———. "*Jubilees* as the Super Canon: Torah-Admonition versus Torah-Commandment." Pages 195–211 in *Legal Texts and Legal Issues: Proceedings of the Second Meeting of the International Organization for Qumran Studies: Cambridge 1995*. Edited by Moshe Bernstein, Florentino García Martínez, and John Kampen. Leiden: Brill, 1997.

————. "Rules of Testimony in Qumranic Jurisprudence: CD 9 and 11Q Torah 64." *Journal of Jewish Studies* 40 (1989): 163–74.

————. *The Dawn of Qumran.* Cincinnati: Hebrew Union College Press, 1983.

————. "The Omer Polemics in 4Q513 Fragments 3–4: Is Ananni Their Author?" *Revue de Qumran* 20 (2001): 93–108.

————. "The Righteous Teacher in the Pesherite Commentaries." *HUCA* 73 (2002): 1–27.

————. "The 'Sealed' Torah versus the 'Revealed' Torah: an exegesis of Damascus Covenant V 1–6 and Jeremiah 32:10–14." *Revue de Qumran* 12 (1986): 351–68.

————. "The Teacher of Righteousness is Alive, Awaiting the Messiah: האסף in CD as Allusion to the Siniatic and Damascene Covenants." *HUCA* 70-71 (1999–2000): 75–93.

————. "The 'Torah of Moses' in the Dead Sea Scrolls: An Allusion to the Book of Jubilees" in *Proceedings of the Thirteenth World Congress of Jewish Studies.* Jerusalem, 2001.

Wacholder, Ben Zion and Martin G. Abegg, Jr, reconstructors and eds. *A Preliminary Edition of the Unpublished Dead Sea Scrolls. The Hebrew and Aramaic Texts from Cave Four. Fascicles One–Four.* Washington, D.C.: Biblical Archaeology Society, 1991–96.

Werman, Cana. "Apart from Your Sabbaths." Pages 201–12 in *The Damascus Document A Centennial of Discovery: Proceedings of the Third International Symposium of the Orion Center for the Study of the Dead Sea Scrolls and Associated Literature, 4–8 February, 1998.* Edited by Joseph M. Baumgarten, Esther G. Chazon and Avital Pinnick. Vol. XXXIV of *Studies on the Texts of the Desert of Judah.* Edited by F. García Martínez and A. S. van der Woude. Leiden: Brill, 2000.

————. "The Sons of Zadok." Pages 623–30 in *The Dead Sea Scrolls Fifty Years After Their Discovery.* Proceedings of the Jerusalem Congress, July 20–25, 1997. Edited by Lawrence H. Schiffman, Emanuel Tov, and James C. VanderKam. Jerusalem: Israel Exploration Society, 2000.

Wernberg-Moller, Preben. "צדק, צדיק and צדוק in the Zadokite Fragments (CDC), the Manual of Discipline (DSD) and the Habakkuk-Commentary (DSH)." *Vetus Testamentum* 3 (1953): 310–15.

White, Sidnie Ann. "A Comparison of the 'A' and 'B' Manuscripts of the Damascus Document." *Revue de Qumran* 12 (1987): 537–53.

Wieder, N. "The 'Law-Interpreter' of the Sect of the Dead Sea Scrolls: The Second Moses." *Journal of Jewish Studies* 4 (1953): 158–75.

Winter, P. "Sadoqite Fragments IX, I." *Revue de Qumran* 6 (1967): 131–36.

Wise, Michael O. "Dating the Teacher of Righteousness and the *Flouruit* of his Movement." *Journal of Biblical Literature* 122/1 (2003): 53–87.

————. "The Teacher of Righteousness and the High Priest of the Intersacerdotium." *Revue de Qumran* 14 (1990): 587–613.

Wise, Michael O., Martin G. Abegg, Jr., and Edward M. Cook. *The Dead Sea Scrolls: A New Translation.* San Francisco: Harper Collins, 1996).

van der Woude, Adam S. "Once Again: The Wicked Priests in the Habakkuk Pesher from Cave 1 of Qumran." *Revue de Qumran* 17 (1996): 375–84.

Zahavy, T. "The Sabbath Code of Damascus Document X,14–XI,18: Form Analytical and Redaction Critical Observations." *Revue de Qumran* 10 (1981): 589–91.

# INDEX OF MODERN AUTHORS

Abegg, M.G., Jr. xix, 22, 23, 25, 50, 72, 80, 115, 134, 198, 282, 309, 320, 322, 328-29, 334-35, 359, 361

Allegro, J.M. 168-69

Baillet, M. 179

Barrera, J.T. 203, 280

Baumgarten, A. 120

Baumgarten, J.M. xvii, xx, 9, 12, 22-6, 29-30, 38, 42-3, 48, 50-2, 54, 56, 58-9, 61-2, 64, 66, 68, 70, 72-4, 78, 80, 90, 94, 96-8, 100, 102, 104, 106, 109-15, 118-20, 123, 125, 128, 132-36, 138, 144, 149, 190, 197, 199, 206, 250, 252-53, 258-62, 264, 267-68, 270, 273-75, 277-79, 281-83, 285, 287-88, 290, 293, 295-99, 301-03, 306, 309, 314, 320, 322, 324, 328, 334-38, 343, 347, 359, 361-67, 369-71, 373, 376

Bernstein, M. 135

Broshi, M. 30, 214, 349

Brownlee, W.H. 153-56, 158-59, 167

Campbell, J. xx

Charles, R.H. 11, 126, 136, 278-79, 292, 337

Charlesworth, J.H. 48, 78, 80, 90, 94, 96-8, 111, 113-14, 135, 147, 153, 194, 198, 210, 223, 251, 270, 309, 314, 322, 334, 336, 359-60

Chazon, E. 22, 110

Cross, F.M. 220, 240

Cryer, F.H. 6

Davies, P.R. 116, 193, 198, 219-20, 223, 227, 236

Elgvin, T. 133

Elwolde, J.F. 364-65

Fitzmyer, J.A. 6-7, 111-12, 133, 195, 219, 248, 307, 322, 333, 334, 337

Flint, P.W. 50

Freedman, D.N. 298

Ginzberg, L. 98, 135, 172, 194-95, 201, 203, 207, 212, 219, 228, 243, 306-07, 314, 320, 331-5, 337-9, 342-3

Harrington, D.J. 133, 247, 328-9

Hempel, C. 112, 264, 288, 320, 349, 359-60

Horgan, M.P. 153, 155

Hurowitz, V.A. 104, 365

Hurvitz, A. 298

Kampen, J. 135

Kister, M. 280

Lévi, I. 6

Lim, T. 155-56

Lohse, E. 146, 150, 320

Martínez, F.G. xvii, 22, 50, 96, 110, 112, 115, 133, 164, 166, 169, 182, 198, 203, 219, 223, 227, 251, 276, 279-80, 282, 307, 309, 318, 320, 322, 335, 342, 359, 360-61, 365

Mazar, B. 296

Milgrom, J. 278, 341

Milik, J.T. 128, 131-2, 162, 252, 264, 274, 287, 301, 316

Mohr, J.C.B. 48, 111, 113, 153

Montaner, L.V. 203, 280

Muraoka, T. 365

Nemoy, L. 5, 8, 112, 206, 229, 294

Nitzan, B. 153

Pinnick, A. 22, 110

Porton, G. 115

Qimron, E. xvii, 30, 36, 43-4, 48, 78, 80, 82, 88, 90, 96, 98, 203, 214, 228, 239, 248, 280, 297, 306-07, 319, 349, 359-60

Rabin, C. xvii, 36, 40, 46, 48, 78, 80, 82, 89, 94, 96, 98, 111, 114, 135, 144, 179, 193, 195, 198, 210, 214, 219, 223, 227, 243, 248, 251, 306-07, 309, 318, 320, 322, 324, 332-39, 343

Rabinowitz, I. 159

de Roo, J.C.R. 198

Sanders, J.A. 199

Schechter, S. xx, xxi, 1, 7, 9, 12, 14, 111-12, 144, 194-5, 212, 219, 243, 248, 306, 321-22, 324, 330, 333-35, 337-38, 342

Schiffman, L.H. 174, 194-95, 255, 310, 331-41

Schwartz, D.R. xvii, 48, 114, 144, 147, 194, 198, 210, 219, 223, 227, 251

Solomon, A. 111, 179-81, 183, 196
Stegemann, H. xvii, 22-3, 96, 109-11, 113, 115, 118-20, 126, 128, 149, 252-53, 274, 368
Strugnell, J. 133, 239, 247, 328-29
Talmon, S. 364
Thackeray, H.St.J. 135, 240
Thompson, T.L. 6
Tigchelaar, E.J.C. xvii, 96, 115, 133, 164, 182, 219, 223, 227, 251, 276, 279, 282, 307, 309, 318, 320, 322, 335, 342, 359-61

Ulrich, E. 364
VanderKam, J.C. 147, 149, 192, 255, 278, 315, 364
Wacholder, B.Z. xvii, xix, xxi, 9, 12, 17, 22-6, 50, 115, 134, 142, 154, 158, 165, 196-97, 241, 328
White, S.A. 335
Winter, P. 320
Wise, M.O. 115, 198, 282, 309, 320, 322, 335, 359, 361
Wright, D.P. 298
van der Woude, A.S. 22, 110, 280

# SUBJECT INDEX

Aaron 211, 212, 219, 254, 267, 269, 283, 295, 327, 345, 352
Abiathar 178, 183
Abijah 115
Abraham 122, 126, 139, 176, 190-91, 211, 231, 243, 256, 260, 305, 312, 315-16, 333, 336, 342, 367
Absolom 153-54, 167, 249
acts of God xix, 124, 142, 176, 211, 298-99
Adam 125, 185, 190, 199, 207, 234
admonition 12, 117-18, 131-2, 135, 168, 201, 223, 251, 285, 287-88
adultery 198, 210, 260-61, 301-03
agadah 189-90
Ahaz 115
Akko 171
Alexander 220, 242-43, 367
al-Qirqisani, Jacob xx, 4-6, 8, 112, 114, 196-97, 206-07, 213, 215, 229, 294
altar 7, 162, 222, 271, 339
Amram 342, 350
Anani 197
ancestor/ancestral 126, 144-45, 148, 173, 177, 211, 213, 231, 237, 242-43, 251-52
antediluvian 5, 176, 215, 312-13, 328
Antigonus of Socho xx, 5, 197
Antiochan (Syrian) persecution 3, 120
Antiochus 3, 170
apocalypse/apocalyptic 163, 184, 154, 213, 262
apocrypha/apocryphal 243, 246
apostate 223, 309, 362
Aramaic 183, 335-36
Aramaicism 160
Asaph 270
Assembly (Great) 116, 119, 121, 130, 151, 189, 217, 241, 244-46, 268, 327, 341, 358-59, 362, 367

Baal 144
Babylon 144, 222, 237
Baruch 243-4
bathing 329, 332

Bathsheba 198-9
Belial 145, 164, 186-89, 191, 200, 211-12, 214, 228, 238, 295, 315, 367
- see Mastema/Satan
biblical text 166, 176, 181, 195, 199, 206, 209, 218, 234-35, 241, 273, 275, 281, 284-85, 287, 290, 301, 304, 308, 316-17, 319-20, 322, 326, 351
blood 157, 159-61, 175, 181, 197-98, 267, 270, 297, 342-43
- of menstruation 272, 297, 301-02
Boethus xx, 5, 8, 112, 114, 197, 229
business 259-60, 283, 287, 308, 331-32, 337, 339, 341, 353, 356-57

Cairo Genizah text xix, 1, 3, 6, 15-16, 18, 109, 120, 230, 236, 241, 269
calendar 3, 5-6, 8, 129, 136-37, 158, 161, 177-79 183, 197, 227, 229, 314-15
calendric 130, 136, 177-78, 229, 339
Canaan 144, 213-14, 241
capital offense 13, 227, 261, 273, 289-92, 303, 316, 320, 322-23, 334-35, 337, 354, 357
- non-capital offense 288-89
celibacy 203, 237, 240, 273, 344
Chaldeans 152
childbearing 269, 272-73, 315
Christianity 3, 16-17,
- pre-Christian 3, 266
chronology 137, 164, 176, 186, 244, 246, 270, 315
chronological 119, 145, 147, 176, 244
chrono-messianism/messianic 9, 146, 185
commandment 12-13
commerce 252, 260, 280
composite xix-xxi, 1, 9, 12, 14-15, 109-10, 128, 132, 168, 188, 213, 232, 237, 242, 256, 262, 280, 283, 294, 297, 299, 311, 313, 352
confess /confession 145, 169, 246, 249-50, 291
congregation 7, 113, 149, 153, 155, 164, 166-67, 200, 228, 234, 339, 241, 308, 311-12, 327

covenant 116, 123-24, 128, 130, 142-45, 148-49, 151, 156, 164, 172-74, 177, 184, 194-95, 209, 211, 215-18, 222-25, 229, 231, 233-34, 237, 241, 242, 244, 246, 249, 250-52, 255, 260, 267, 291, 301, 305-09, 312-13, 315-16, 318, 325, 327-29, 333, 336, 340, 348-50
creation 118-19, 124-25, 129, 134, 137-38, 173, 180, 199, 202, 204, 211, 247, 273, 297, 299, 328, 366
crop 146, 280, 294

Damascus 9-10, 116, 146, 158, 160-61, 164-65, 173, 181, 186, 216-17, 222, 229, 237, 240, 244, 246, 248, 250, 263
date/dating 3-4, 142-43, 163, 173, 185-86, 206, 211, 215, 315
David 117, 130, 153-4, 163, 171-72, 179, 180, 183, 191-92, 196-200, 220, 238-39, 254-5, 262, 346
Day of Atonement 154, 158, 161, 163-64, 227-28
death penalty 13, 273, 289-92, 335, 338, 341, 357-58
debt 257-59
  -indebtedness 257
debtor 256, 258-59
defile/defiled/defiling 114, 160, 187-88, 200-04, 208-09, 222-26, 232, 238, 249, 269, 271, 273, 278, 283-5, 295, 303, 329-30, 340-41, 343-44
defilement 189, 201, 203-04, 204, 208, 222-23, 225, 233, 248-49, 269, 272-73, 284-85, 295, 311, 343
Demetrius 3, 170
destitute 13, 159-60, 164, 166, 226, 230-31, 251, 256, 176, 306, 350
divine
  - acts 119, 130, 366
  - anger/wrath 141, 185, 205, 308
  - covenant 172, 234, 349
  - law/legislation 136, 214, 218-19, 298,
  - name 183, 308, 366
  - other 121, 174, 176, 185, 193, 217, 243, 246, 258, 298
Divisions of the Times 109-10, 117, 134
Divisions of the Epochs 140, 186

Egypt 9, 31, 43, 51, 122, 158, 165, 184, 212, 241, 244, 267, 341, 367

elders/elderly 13-14, 121-22, 127, 165, 174, 192-93, 231, 276, 349-50
Eleazar 127, 192-94, 262
Elijah 143-44, 151, 172
Elisha 144, 203, 235, 243-44, 271
emissions
  - bodily 230, 270, 272
  - seminal 270, 272
  - sexual 269
End of Days xxi, 12, 152, 156-7, 179, 182, 215, 217, 220-1
Endzeit 9, 118, 175, 243, 245, 299, 313
En-gedi 146
Ein Gedi 295
Enoch 5, 139
Ephraimites 170
Esau 200, 296
eschatological 7, 112, 115-16, 126-27, 134, 139, 147-48, 150-53, 155, 157-62, 164, 166-72, 175, 177, 182, 185, 187, 193, 209, 216, 238, 245, 249, 256, 263, 275, 293, 298, 310, 314-15
eschatology 11, 16, 138, 141, 262
eschaton 137-40, 143, 151, 158, 172, 184-86, 200, 241, 143, 245, 247, 253, 298-99
Essenes 6, 8, 14, 16, 114, 135, 142, 156, 172, 174, 180, 197, 224, 237, 241, 255, 270, 295, 336, 343, 347, 352
Essenism 139
Ethiopic 110, 183, 279
etiology 171, 237

fasting 154, 158, 161, 164, 228, 330, 334, 339-40, 366
fertility 146, 215, 254, 263, 275
festivals 13, 129, 136-37, 164, 227-30, 273, 275, 314-15, 337-41, 367
first fruits 275, 278-80, 294
Flavius Josephus 174
flood 126, 133-34, 137, 176, 190, 199, 204, 207, 211, 215, 312-13
food 233, 261, 266-7, 280, 293, 303, 318, 332, 343, 356, 363
fructification 146, 214

Gamul 178
garment 204, 259, 282-3, 333, 355, 364, 366
generation 9, 125, 140, 144, 147-53, 156-57, 173, 176-77, 184-85, 193, 201, 213, 221, 227, 230, 234, 241, 248, 299, 328

genitals 359-60
geographic 160, 229
gift 244, 278, 306, 318, 320, 338, 340, 352
gleaning 277
Gog and Magog 152
gossiping 296, 321, 355, 361
grammar 2, 17, 135
Great Assembly
- see Assembly
Greek texts 8, 187
Gregorian 136-7

Hagiographa 239
Haguy (Hagi) 9, 131, 133-34, 247, 255, 271, 299, 317, 326-9, 345, 349-50
halakah 172, 189-90, 343
haplography 43, 260
harmonization 110, 352
Hasmonean 3-4, 154, 189, 220
Hebrew (language) 17, 111, 275, 335,
- name 117, 341
- Scripture 1, 10, 227, 239, 250, 272, 309, 341, 343, 345, 348, 367
- slave 257, 304
- Text xix, 1, 14-15, 17-18, 235
hierarchy 282, 345-47
Hilkiah 195
Hillel 206-07
Hippocrates 270
historiography 174, 176
Hodayot 127, 170
holidays 161, 178
Holy Land 9, 146, 211, 222, 275, 348
house of worship      249, 340
human/humanity/mankind 13, 125-27, 133-34, 137, 140, 148, 173-74, 177, 180, 211, 290, 311-13, 321, 334
husband 261, 301-02, 306, 317, 364
husbandry 337

Iddo 115
ideological 2, 140, 142
ideologue 172
ideology 140
idolatrous 284, 293, 295, 308, 316, 320, 341-42
idolatry 271, 285, 291, 342, 357
illicit
- mixtures 260, 282-83
- sexual relations 261-62, 268, 282-83, 293, 297, 364
- other 223, 225, 297, 321

indebtedness
- see debt
institute/institution 143, 153, 177, 333, 340, 342, 351, 364
interpreter of the Torah 116, 220, 238
Isaac 122, 176, 243, 256, 316, 361
Israel 10, 116, 121-22, 131, 134, 136, 139, 142-50, 152, 156, 165, 173-75, 177, 179, 181-2, 184-85, 187, 189, 192-94, 200-01, 212-17, 219, 222, 224-25, 237-38, 240-41, 243-44, 246, 248, 250, 253-56, 266, 280, 307, 309, 313, 337, 344-45, 348-49, 352, 366
Israelites 9, 138, 144, 158, 165, 205, 213-14, 216-17, 225, 231, 244, 246, 256, 284, 327, 334-35, 339, 347, 349

Jacob 9, 116, 122, 162, 176, 183, 187, 191, 200, 238, 243, 256, 296, 312
Jerusalem 10, 119, 144, 152-53, 158, 160-62, 185-86, 189, 201-03, 213-14, 220, 222-24, 236, 242-43, 248-50, 263, 279-80, 294, 341
Jonathan (high priest) 154
Joshua 121, 127, 192-94, 214, 234, 275
Jubilee Year (Year of Jubilee) 256-58, 275-76, 319
Judaism 12-13, 117, 206, 250, 333, 342, 361, 364, 366
Judas (high priest) 242
Judea 4, 6, 10, 16, 154, 236, 263
justice 113, 139, 143, 151, 161, 167, 188, 209, 225-56, 254, 303, 321, 324, 326, 329, 344-45, 347, 350

Kadesh Barnea 9, 165, 184, 213, 267
Karaite xx, 5-6, 8
Khirbet Qumran 4, 229, 236
Kittim 152, 254, 170-71

law 7, 11-13, 109-117, 121, 125-26, 131-32, 136, 138, 140, 149, 162, 166-67, 185, 189, 192, 194-95, 201, 205, 210-11, 214, 216, 218-23, 227, 233, 237-38, 241, 247, 249-53, 256-57, 260, 262, 264, 267, 271, 273-74, 276, 284, 287-88, 290-92, 297-98, 302, 304, 309-10, 314-15, 320, 328, 333, 339, 341, 343, 349-50, 356, 359-61, 363-64, 366
Lebanon 159
legal 5, 12-13, 117-18, 131-32, 135, 138, 140-41, 171-72, 189, 207, 210, 212,

224, 229-30, 237, 241, 250, 252, 256,
262, 264-65, 267-68, 287, 291-92, 299,
301, 321-23, 350, 364-65
leprosy 117, 138, 202, 204, 230, 269-71,
285, 295, 302, 349
Levi 187-88, 238, 327
Levites 181-82, 193-94, 231, 256, 271,
327, 334-35, 347, 349, 367
lex talionis 290
Liar xxi, 156
- see Scoffer/Wicked Priest
liberation 165, 220
literacy 265-66
literary
- aspect 200
- composition 111, 170
- inclusio 140
- style 11
- title 111
- tradition xx, 352
- unity 140
- work 111
liturgical (liturgy) 130, 265

Macedonians 242
Maimonides 8, 193, 265-66, 278, 291
Man of Lies 151, 153-55, 165, 167, 172
mankind
- see humanity
marital relations/practices 139, 191, 199,
252, 300, 303, 305, 363-64
marriage 117, 132, 191, 202-03, 205,
207-08, 252, 260-61, 268, 282, 287,
292-93, 297, 303-05, 347, 349, 364
Masoretic Text 2, 150, 340
Mastema 211-12, 315
- see Satan/Belial
medication 335, 339
Mediterranean 146
Menasseh 170
menstruation 202, 270, 272, 304
Messiah xxi, 7, 9-10, 112, 120, 140, 144-
45, 148, 165, 214, 217, 240, 244, 247,
249, 253, 255-56, 282, 293, 298
Messiah of Aaron 10, 116, 185, 213-15,
222, 241, 244, 327, 345
messianic
- age/epoch 138-39, 152, 173, 185,
230, 234, 246-47, 249, 256, 299,
312-13, 327, 345, 349
- other 196, 200, 255, 367
messianism 11, 216

methodology 1, 4, 199, 209
Methuselah 313
Middle Ages xx, 3, 6, 8, 269
midrash xx, 110, 111-13, 115-117, 139,
149-50, 160, 186, 188-90, 199, 217,
219, 238-39, 352
midrash-agadah 189
midrash-halakah 189
migrate/migration 9-10, 158, 216-18,
223, 234, 236-37, 248, 267
misappropriation 271, 321, 324
Moab 138
Molech 205, 291, 308
monogamy 192, 196
Moses (Mosaic) 13, 111, 116-17, 119,
121, 125, 127, 130-32, 135, 140, 143,
148, 151, 156, 165, 169, 173, 181, 184,
192-97, 199-200, 205, 209, 211-19,
221, 239, 241, 245, 247, 264, 266-
67, 271, 306-07, 310, 313-15, 327-28,
345, 367
mysteries 109, 118, 122, 124-25, 127,
137, 140, 142, 177, 193, 226, 339

Naaman 244, 271
naked/nakedness 205, 304, 354, 359
Nazirite 12, 14, 113-14, 200-01, 225
Nebuchadnezzar 144, 148, 173, 185-86
New Testament 3-4, 6, 165, 209, 341,
356
Nineveh 170
Noah 137, 176, 190, 199, 276, 311

oath 156-57, 194, 225, 234, 285, 288,
291, 300-02, 306-09, 316-17, 323-5,
348
offering 129-30, 143, 205, 223-24, 278,
280-81, 302-03, 305, 308, 316, 320,
324, 330, 338-41, 352
omer 197, 274-75, 281
oppression 122, 153, 158, 160, 165,
348
oral/orality xx, 122, 170, 209, 266
Oral Torah 8, 209
orlah 230, 278, 281, 293-94
orthography 4, 15, 120, 134

pagan 163, 171, 205, 225, 243, 266-
67, 284, 293, 295, 304-05, 320, 333,
337, 342
paleography 2, 50-51, 78, 80, 118, 120,
252, 264, 275, 307

patriarch/patriarchal 8, 16, 127, 139, 143-44, 176, 184-85, 187, 190, 199, 216, 243, 251, 315-16, 342, 350
Paul/Pauline 13, 212, 260
Peleg (house of) 170, 248-9
Pentateuch 13, 117, 125, 127, 138, 141, 148, 168, 181, 194, 199, 218, 239, 246, 250, 309-10, 314, 339
Pentecost 130, 275, 316, 367
Persian 242, 333
Pharisees (Pharisaic) 9, 120-22, 136-37, 172, 174, 189, 209-10, 213, 215-17, 226, 233, 243, 266, 288, 294, 329-30
Philistine 171, 192
Philo of Alexandria 174, 341, 343
Pliny the Elder 174
polemic 5, 12, 18, 120-21, 132-33, 136, 140, 170, 197, 204, 209, 228, 233, 243, 281, 288, 293, 323, 330, 335, 339, 341, 343
polygamy (or bigamy) 13, 190-92, 196, 198-99, 204, 207-08, 262, 304
poor 13, 160, 225-26, 230-32, 251, 256, 266, 276-78
prayer 109, 119, 128-30, 133-34, 140, 264-65, 271, 276, 351, 361, 366
preamble (or prologue) 12, 109, 114, 139-42, 149, 173, 176, 188, 199, 201, 212, 215, 224, 228, 250, 256, 367-68
promise 109, 122, 124, 126, 130, 141, 143, 146, 230, 237, 243, 254, 275, 316, 364, 367
prophet 115, 117, 121, 127, 133, 143, 146, 151-52, 163, 181, 186-87, 189, 195, 222, 229, 237, 239, 244, 253, 255, 277, 290, 299, 313, 361
prophecy 157, 172, 189, 248
proselyte 115, 146, 226, 230-31, 256, 327, 332-33, 345, 347, 349
pseudepigraphic 2, 174, 314
Ptolemaic 216
public recitation/reading 264-65, 358
purity 7, 117, 138, 203, 253, 269, 285, 288, 305, 326, 344, 353-56, 362-63
 - impurity 7, 179, 209, 227, 269

Rabbi Ishmael 206-07
Rabbi Judah ben Betherah 316
Rabbi Judah Ha-Nasi 170
rabbinic
 - Judaism 250

 - exegesis 261, 270, 334
 - law 273, 292, 343
 - literature/sources xx, 5, 19, 89, 115, 165, 183, 186, 197, 205, 207, 211-12, 227, 231, 260, 268, 276, 278, 284, 293, 307, 325, 330-2, 335-36, 356
 - midrash xx
 - scholars 189
 - terminology 207
 - tradition xx, 13, 212, 261, 295-96, 319, 324, 326, 341, 345
 - other 207, 209, 257, 285, 336, 338
rebel/rebellion 121, 150, 165, 176, 185, 213-15, 245, 289, 293, 296, 335, 356, 362, 364
reconstruction 2, 22-3, 25, 32, 48, 56, 66, 68, 73, 76, 80, 96, 102, 110, 113, 118-20, 125, 128, 132-33, 140, 153, 155, 166-69, 171, 185, 193, 206, 252-54, 256-57, 262-63, 265, 267-68, 274-75, 277-82, 284, 286-87, 289-90, 295, 297-99, 301, 320, 322-23, 341, 346, 348, 360, 365, 369
redemption 9, 122, 141, 143, 145-46, 206, 214, 240, 367-68
religious 3, 139, 201, 208, 223
remnant
 - of Israel 118, 121, 133-34, 141, 143-44, 174, 177, 179, 215, 233
 - of texts 58, 82, 100, 135, 258, 289, 319
renew/renewal 126, 129, 313, 315-16, 326, 364
repent/repentance 132, 147, 185, 218, 242, 245-46, 309-10, 313, 355, 362, 366
restoration
 - of Israel 242, 257-58, 326, 362
 - of texts 2, 29, 62, 80, 94, 96, 110, 113, 118-19, 126, 131, 134, 136, 147, 169, 283, 290, 293, 312, 318, 348, 360, 365, 367-68, 374
retribution 157, 178, 215, 290
revelation 137, 142, 177, 193
righteous/righteousness xix, xxi, 3, 9, 17, 120, 122-24, 126, 139, 142-45, 150-55, 163, 165-67, 169, 173-77, 179, 182, 185, 187, 199-201, 213, 217, 221, 225-26, 233, 243, 246, 247-51, 253, 260, 264, 287, 299, 340, 349
 - unrighteous 186-87, 189, 226, 238

Sabbath 13, 154, 158, 161, 164, 177-78, 207-08, 227-30, 265, 268, 273, 292, 294, 305, 315, 330-42, 357-58
sacerdos 266, 295, 325, 345
sacrifice 130, 296, 338
sacrificial 330, 338, 340-42
salvation 163, 217, 246, 248, 251, 253, 315, 349
Samaria 162
Samaritan text 278
sanctity 203, 223, 293, 341
sanctify/sanctification 7, 10, 202, 208, 261, 279-80, 294, 318-19, 330, 340
sanctuary 146, 160, 178-82, 187-88, 200-01, 211, 222-26, 238, 263, 272-73, 319, 338, 341
sapiential 131, 133, 175-76, 212, 299, 317, 328-29
Satan 212
Scoffer xxi, 17, 150, 154-55, 162, 171, 223, 263
- see Liar/Wicked Priest
scriptorium 4, 274
Second Temple xx, 1, 4, 6, 15, 196, 319, 341
sectarian
- calendar 5, 129, 137, 164, 178-79, 197
- movement/community xx, 114, 117, 137-38, 202-03, 231, 238-39, 315, 336
- texts xx, 6, 19, 112, 203, 209, 221, 228, 274, 304, 315, 349, 351
- Torah 117, 194, 216, 224
- other 163, 177, 194-95, 197, 210, 226, 229, 231, 237, 288, 292, 310, 324, 332, 334, 338-39
Sefer He-Haguy 329
Seleucid 170, 220
Septuagint 1, 42
sexual relations 139, 201-02, 227, 261-62, 293-94, 297, 305, 356, 363-4
Shaphan 195
Shifters of the Boundary 8, 118, 120-21, 177, 188, 212-13, 215, 242-43, 254
Shiloh 221
Shulchan Aruch 226
Sinai 121, 143, 194, 199, 211, 218, 221-22, 245-46, 367
sobriquet 116, 149, 151, 155-56, 160-61, 163, 166, 170-72, 174, 178, 181-82, 188, 213, 215, 220, 229, 248, 254, 300

Solomon 179, 180, 183, 196
Solomonic sanctuary 179, 181
sons of darkness (children of) 113-14, 138, 200, 224
sons of light (children of) 113-14, 118, 225, 347
speech 13, 264, 330-31, 335, 342, 354, 356-58
Spewer of Lies 155, 161-63, 243
spirit/spiritual 118-19, 126, 130, 188, 195, 201, 208-09, 214, 233, 247, 249, 263, 270-71, 273, 295, 299, 328-29, 338, 344, 346-48, 355-56, 362
spit/spitting 14, 287, 322, 355, 360
straying wife 230, 300-01, 304
Super Canon 135, 138
Supervisor 13-14, 202-03, 231-32, 253, 263, 271, 285-86, 288, 309-10, 325-28, 344-50
supplication 119, 128-30, 132, 134, 140, 367
Syria 3, 158, 237, 271
Syriac texts 8, 343

Talmud /Talmudic xx, 2, 13, 18, 115, 162, 170, 172, 178, 197-98, 207, 209, 212, 227, 250, 257, 260-61, 265-66, 271, 284, 288, 291-92, 294, 296, 304, 316, 319, 330-31, 336, 339, 343-45, 351, 356, 361
Tanakh 1, 117
Teacher 148, 151, 155, 160, 165, 168, 172, 241, 168, 171-72, 241, 245-46, 251
- Just xxi, 9-10, 16-17, 116, 141, 144, 147, 150-51, 153-58, 160-63, 165-69, 171-72, 185, 216, 220, 241, 243, 248, 250-51, 254
- of Righteousness 116, 145, 155, 169, 196
- Unique 116, 164, 241, 244
Temple 6, 120-21, 143-44, 147, 173-74, 178-80, 185, 201-05, 211, 213, 215, 222-25, 229, 266, 273, 340, 341
tetragrammaton 306, 308, 340
- sage 6, 8, 13-14, 109, 113, 115, 121, 123, 133, 138, 171-72, 179, 182, 197, 206, 216, 233, 237, 243, 250, 258, 263-64, 266, 278, 285, 290-91, 294, 296, 304-05, 316, 319, 323, 326, 344, 348
theology 8, 11-12, 199, 200

tithing 117, 230, 276-79, 281
transgression 114, 143, 145, 162, 175, 179, 188, 199, 204-05, 210-11, 225, 232, 246, 252-53, 258, 268, 271, 288, 293-94, 298, 322, 340-41, 348, 352
transgressors 205-06, 287, 298
True Lawgiver 220-21

unify/unification xx, 4, 9, 11, 14-15, 112, 139, 163, 201
Uriah 197-98
Urim (Thummim) 212, 267
urinate/urination 355, 361
Urzeit 9, 118, 175, 243, 245, 299, 313
Uzziah 271

vessel 302, 329-30, 332, 335
vocabulary 10-11, 131-32, 134, 140, 151, 183, 203, 232, 305, 339, 368
vow 114, 139, 200, 225, 287, 306-07, 316-20

wealth (or exploitation) 114, 152, 156, 187, 200, 222-23, 225, 238, 245, 265, 339, 341
whore/whoredom 132, 175, 187, 189-90, 201, 209, 211, 225, 238, 271-72, 283, 364
Wicked Priest 17, 154-60, 166-68, 172, 222
  - see Liar
wilderness 9, 121, 138, 142, 151, 162, 165, 195, 203, 211, 213-14, 216-17, 236-37, 240-41, 245, 254, 267, 274
wine 14, 200, 342
wisdom 17, 126-27, 131-32, 134, 140, 167, 175-76, 212, 329, 345, 349

Zadok xx, 5-9, 111-12, 114, 127, 174, 178, 180-81, 183-84, 194-7, 199, 206-07, 229, 262, 294,
  - sons of 174, 176-78, 181-84, 193, 195, 218, 263
Zadokite 5-9, 174, 184, 197, 209, 229

# INDEX OF ANCIENT SOURCES

## Hebrew Bible

| | | | |
|---|---|---|---|
| Genesis | 138, 190 | 12:5 | 63 |
| 1:27 | 35, 190 | 12:8 | 63 |
| 6-8 | 133 | 13-14 | 269 |
| 6:1-7 | 312 | 13:2 | 59, 269 |
| 7:2 | 190 | 13:4 | 59 |
| 7:9 | 190 | 13:29-37 | 269 |
| 10:5 | 98 | 13:31 | 59 |
| 14:10 | 255 | 13:33 | 61 |
| 18:27 | 132 | 13:54 | 61 |
| 24:63 | 361 | 14:42-43 | 335 |
| 32:12 | 296 | 14:48 | 335 |
| 41:40 | 95 | 15 | 273 |
| 46:34 | 49 | 15:2-18 | 272 |
| 47:3 | 49 | 15:11 | 75, 295 |
| 48:19 | 130 | 15:19 | 62 |
| 49:10 | 221, 238 | 15:25 | 272 |
| | | 16:13-17 | 319 |
| Exodus | 143, 261, 304, | 16:18 | 320 |
| | 313 | 16:20-22 | 320 |
| 35:2 | 13 | 16:21 | 320 |
| | | 17:4 | 267 |
| Leviticus | 143, 205, 269, | 17-22 | 278 |
| | 272-73, 275, | 18 | 207 |
| | 278-79, 324 | 18:5 | 33 |
| 2:4 | 278 | 18:13 | 37 |
| 2:9 | 281 | 18:18 | 75, 304 |
| 2:14 | 280 | 18:21 | 205, 308 |
| 4:2 | 105, 365 | 19 | 304, 323 |
| 4:2-3 | 134 | 19:9-10 | 277, 351 |
| 5 | 320 | 19:12 | 291, 291, 308 |
| 5:7 | 320 | 19:16 | 361 |
| 5:15-18 | 134 | 19:17 | 85, 287, 232 |
| 5:16 | 320 | 19:17-18 | 232, 286 |
| 5:20-26 | 324 | 19:18 | 85, 230, 321 |
| 5:21-26 | 295 | 19:18-19 | 257 |
| 5:23 | 308 | 19:19 | 53 |
| 5:24-25 | 308, 324 | 19:20 | 304 |
| 5:25 | 83 | 19:20-22 | 304 |
| 7:12-13 | 278 | 19:23 | 279 |
| 8:26 | 278 | 19:23-25 | 278, 294 |
| 11:29 | 343 | 19:24 | 67 |
| 12 | 273 | 19:25 | 67, 279-80 |
| 12:2-4 | 63, 273 | 19:33-34 | 51, 256 |
| 12:4 | 62-3, 272 | 20 | 207 |

| | | | |
|---|---|---|---|
| 20:3 | 291, 308 | 19:20 | 273 |
| 20:6 | 291 | 21:17 | 217 |
| 20:18 | 75, 293 | 21:18 | 39, 217-19, 222, 237 |
| 20:27 | 291 | | |
| 22:4 | 75, 295 | 24:17 | 43, 237-38 |
| 22:10-11 | 304-05 | 28 | 338 |
| 22:14-16 | 134 | 30:3 | 337 |
| 22:28 | 296 | 30:4-5 | 307 |
| 23 | 338 | 30:4-17 | 317 |
| 23:3 | 337 | 30:9 | 83 |
| 23:22 | 277, 351 | 30:17 | 41 |
| 23:38 | 91 | 31:18-24 | 285 |
| 24:5 | 278 | 31:20 | 284 |
| 24:17 | 290 | 32:23 | 298 |
| 24:19 | 290 | 35:4 | 332 |
| 24:21 | 290 | 35:4-5 | 334 |
| 25 | 275 | 35:30 | 325 |
| 25:5 | 276 | | |
| 25:10 | 51, 257-58 | Deuteronomy | 138, 191, 195-96, 234, 260, 301 |
| 25:11 | 276 | | |
| 25:14 | 53, 259 | 2:14 | 165 |
| 25:29 | 336 | 4:30-31 | 313 |
| 26:25 | 29 | 5:12 | 87, 208, 330 |
| 26:31 | 105, 366 | 6:5 | 316 |
| 27 | 319-20 | 6:6-9 | 217 |
| 27:12 | 319 | 7:8 | 45, 243 |
| 27:14 | 319 | 7:9 | 41, 49, 224, 248 |
| 27:17-23 | 319 | 9:5 | 45, 243 |
| 27:18 | 319 | 9:7 | 234 |
| 27:19 | 319 | 9:23 | 32-3 |
| 27:21 | 320 | 11:7-17 | 254 |
| 27:28 | 83, 318 | 12:1 | 51, 257 |
| 27:28-29 | 320 | 16:9 | 275 |
| 27:29 | 83, 320 | 17:6 | 325 |
| 28-29 | 320 | 17:15 | 191 |
| | | 17:173 | 35, 190-92, 196, 199, 207, 262 |
| Numbers | 317 | | |
| 5:7-8 | 75 | 18:4 | 333 |
| 5:12-31 | 301 | 19:14 | 213 |
| 5:13 | 301 | 19:15 | 325 |
| 5:18 | 77, 302 | 19:16 | 321 |
| 5:21 | 77, 302 | 19:18 | 323 |
| 5:24 | 77, 302 | 19:18-19 | 322 |
| 5:25 | 302 | 21 | 304 |
| 5:27 | 77 | 21:10-14 | 304 |
| 5:27-28 | 303 | 21:11 | 342 |
| 6:3 | 14 | 21:15 | 191, 199 |
| 12:1-15 | 271 | 22:1-3 | 295, 324 |
| 13 | 213, 345 | 22:5 | 51, 259 |
| 13:26 | 32 | 22:9 | 53 |
| 19 | 284 | 22:13-21 | 301 |
| 19:18-19 | 285 | 23:2-9 | 312 |

| | | | |
|---|---|---|---|
| 23:4 | 349 | 26:16-21 | 271 |
| 23:24 | 81 | 30 | 136, 230 |
| 24:19 | 277 | 31:5 | 281 |
| 27 | 288 | 34 | 195 |
| 27:13-26 | 308 | 35 | 230 |
| 27:18 | 53, 260 | | |
| 28 | 306 | Ezra | 220 |
| 28:1-18 | 254 | 3:12 | 180 |
| 29:20 | 308 | 7:10 | 117 |
| 30:4 | 105, 366 | | |
| 31:9 | 192-93 | Nehemiah | 220 |
| 31:19 | 192 | 8:8 | 227 |
| 31:22 | 192 | 9:27 | 33 |
| 31:22-26 | 192-93 | 11 | 195 |
| 31:25 | 194 | 13:15-22 | 337, 339 |
| 31:26 | 192 | | |
| 32:28 | 37 | Job | |
| 32:33 | 45 | 2:7 | 270 |
| 33:8 | 212 | 4:15 | 270 |
| 33:8-10 | 267 | 12:24 | 29 |
| 33:19 | 335 | 30:19 | 132 |
| | | 30:20 | 131 |
| Joshua | | 37:14 | 131 |
| 1:8 | 266, 329 | | |
| 3:3-4 | 334 | Psalms | 151, 160, 163-64, |
| 9:15 | 234 | | 172, 233, 239, |
| | | | 345 |
| Judges | | 1 | 233 |
| 14:8-9 | 343 | 1:1 | 233 |
| | | 1:2 | 329 |
| 1 Samuel | | 1:4-5 | 200 |
| 2:35 | 179 | 2:10 | 77 |
| 5-6 | 192 | 2:12 | 130 |
| 25:26 | 324 | 29:11 | 7 |
| | | 37 | 163, 228 |
| 1 Kings | | 37:7 | 165-6 |
| 19 | 143 | 37:10 | 164, 244-45 |
| 19:15 | 41 | 37:11 | 164 |
| | | 37:23-24 | 166 |
| 2 Kings | | 37:23-26 | 166 |
| 5:20-27 | 271 | 37:25-26 | 166 |
| 15:3-5 | 271 | 37:32-33 | 167-68 |
| 22 195 | | 37:35-36 | 168 |
| | | 45 | 163 |
| 1 Chronicles | | 45:2 | 168-69 |
| 9 | 195 | 56:6 | 169 |
| 16:15 | 234 | 60 | 163 |
| 24 | 178, 183, 229 | 72:19 | 307 |
| | | 90:9-11 | 312 |
| 2 Chronicles | | 90:10 | 125, 312 |
| 24:20 | 298 | 94:6 | 226 |
| 24:27 | 115 | 94:21 | 29 |

| | | | |
|---|---|---|---|
| 96:2 | 307 | 6:28 | 361 |
| 99:8 | 37 | 9:3 | 361 |
| 103:13 | 346 | 11:9-10 | 50, 55 |
| 105:8 | 234 | 13:21 | 219 |
| 107:40 | 29 | 17:21-22 | 335 |
| 111:9 | 133 | 17:21-27 | 339 |
| 115:17 | 286 | 31:31 | 81 |
| 118 | 163 | 31:31-34 | 313 |
| 119:97 | 130 | 34:8 | 258 |
| 127 | 163 | 34:15 | 258 |
| 127:2 | 169 | 34:17 | 258 |
| 129 | 163 | 45:4-5 | 243 |
| | | | |
| Proverbs | 361 | Ezekiel | 3, 143, 146, 152, 173, 78, 254, 263, 276, 281-82, 290-91 |
| 3:11 | 167 | | |
| 5:7 | 175 | | |
| 6 | 210 | | |
| 6:26 | 175 | 1:2 | 173 |
| 6:26-29 | 210 | 9:4 | 43, 235 |
| 7:10 | 175 | 13:1-16 | 188-89 |
| 7:24 | 175 | 13:3 | 32 |
| 7:26 | 175 | 13:10 | 243 |
| 8:32 | 175 | 18 | 289 |
| 11:13 | 361 | 18:8 | 290 |
| 15:8 | 91, 340 | 18:13 | 290 |
| 15:29 | 340 | 18:17 | 290 |
| 17:18 | 290 | 22:1-17 | 289 |
| 28:8 | 290 | 22:2 | 290 |
| | | 22:7 | 290 |
| Isaiah | 171, 172, 181, 186-88, 226, 235 | 22:9 | 361 |
| | | 22:11 | 290 |
| 7:17 | 41, 97, 235, 348 | 22:12 | 290 |
| 10:2 | 39, 226 | 22:15 | 290 |
| 10-11 | 171 | 22:21 | 47 |
| 11:1-5 | 171 | 31:12 | 219 |
| 20:5 | 219 | 34 | 253-54 |
| 24:17 | 35, 186-88 | 34:12 | 263, 345 |
| 27:11 | 37 | 34:13-24 | 254 |
| 28:9-14 | 188-89 | 34:23 | 51 |
| 40:3 | 195 | 34:23-24 | 253 |
| 40:26 | 262 | 37 | 270 |
| 50:11 | 37, 210 | 37:10 | 270 |
| 51 | 122 | 39:23 | 148 |
| 54:16 | 39, 221 | 39:23-24 | 143 |
| 56:3-6 | 332 | 39:25-29 | 143 |
| 58:13 | 331-2 | 40-48 | 174 |
| 58:13-14 | 339 | 40:46 | 181 |
| 59:5 | 37, 210 | 43:19 | 181 |
| | | 44:15 | 33, 177-78, 180-81, 186, 263 |
| Jeremiah | 235, 243-44, 313, 390 | 45-46 | 281 |
| 2:35 | 331 | 45:11 | 69, 281 |

| | |
|---|---|
| 45:13 | 69, 276 |
| 45:15 | 281 |
| 47 | 146, 275 |
| 47:7-12 | 254 |
| 47:13-23 | 146 |
| 47:22 | 256 |
| 47:22-23 | 349 |
| 48 | 231, 275 |
| 48:11 | 181 |

| | |
|---|---|
| Daniel | 16 |
| 1:1-2 | 173 |
| 5:28 | 278 |
| 9:15 | 49, 250 |
| 11 | 180 |

| | |
|---|---|
| Hosea | 150, 181 |
| 3:4 | 47, 246 |
| 4:16 | 29, 150 |
| 5:8 | 168, 246 |
| 5:10 | 43, 188, 235, 241 |
| 5:10-11 | 188 |
| 5:11 | 188 |
| 10:12 | 147, 149-50, 221 |

| | |
|---|---|
| Amos | 181, 237 |
| 5:26 | 42, 238 |
| 5:27 | 10, 43, 229, 235 |
| 9:11 | 42-3, 229, 235, 238-39 |

| | |
|---|---|
| Micah | 151, 172 |
| 1:5 | 162 |
| 1:6 | 162 |
| 2:6 | 35 |
| 6:8 | 347 |

| | |
|---|---|
| 7:11 | 35, 185 |
| 7:2 | 83, 318, 320 |

| | |
|---|---|
| Nahum | |
| 1:2 | 85, 232, 321, 323 |
| 3:4 | 115, 170, 209 |
| 3:9 | 248 |
| 3:10 | 248 |

| | |
|---|---|
| Habakkuk | 151-52, 154, 156, 160-61, 167, 171 |
| 1:1-2 | 153 |
| 1:4 | 155 |
| 1:13 | 153-54, 163 |
| 2:5-8 | 156 |
| 2:8 | 157, 160 |
| 2:12-13 | 161 |
| 2:15 | 158 |
| 2:17 | 159-60 |

| | |
|---|---|
| Haggai | 277 |
| 2:3 | 180 |

| | |
|---|---|
| Zechariah | 235, 277 |
| 2:16 | 275 |
| 7:9 | 254 |
| 7:10 | 226 |
| 11:7 | 41, 254 |
| 13:7 | 41, 235, 254 |

| | |
|---|---|
| Malachi | 222, 277 |
| 1:10 | 38-9, 222 |
| 3:16 | 49, 247 |
| 3:18 | 49, 248 |
| 3:23 | 144 |

*Qumran*

| | |
|---|---|
| CD-A | |
| (*Damascus Document*) | |
| 1 | 140 |
| 1:1 | 123, 173, 175, 256, 298, 299 |
| 1:1-2 | 123, 130, 142, 176, 346 |
| 1:1-7 | 141 |
| 1:1-2:1 | 141, 173, 26 |
| 1:1-7:5 | 141 |
| 1:1-8:21 | 141, 224 |
| 1:3 | 231 |

| | |
|---|---|
| 1:4 | 141, 144, 188, 252 |
| 1:4-5 | 215 |
| 1:4-7 | 143, 146 |
| 1:5 | 146, 159, 173, 185 |
| 1:5-6 | 119, 244 |
| 1:7-8 | 146, 254, 275 |
| 1:7-12 | 173 |
| 1:8-9 | 120 |
| 1:8-10 | 146 |
| 1:10 | 150 |

| | | | |
|---|---|---|---|
| 1:10-12 | 144, 147 | 3:13 | 181 |
| 1:10-2:1 | 163 | 3:13-15 | 228 |
| 1:11 | 148, 220, 245, | 3:14-16 | 179 |
| | 254 | 3:18 | 179, 346 |
| 1:12 | 148 | 3:18-20 | 179 |
| 1:13 | 340 | 3:19 | 180 |
| 1:13-2:1 | 150, 174, 246 | 3:19-20 | 211 |
| 1:14-15 | 161-2 | 3:20 | 177, 180 |
| 1:15 | 170, 218 | 3:20-21 | 181 |
| 1:15-19 | 151 | 3:20-4:2 | 180-81 |
| 1:16 | 28 | 3:21-4:2 | 178, 180, 291 |
| 1:17 | 308 | 4-7 | 289 |
| 1:18 | 170, 288 | 4 | 184 |
| 1:20 | 16, 177 | 4:1 | 178 |
| 1:20-21 | 177 | 4:1-10 | 263 |
| 2 | 141 | 4:2-3 | 185 |
| 2:2 | 142, 298 | 4:2-7 | 181-82 |
| 2:2-3 | 123 | 4:3 | 182 |
| 2:2-13 | 173-74 | 4:4 | 182 |
| 2:2-3:12 | 173 | 4:4-5 | 183 |
| 2:2-4:18 | 28 | 4:5-6 | 183 |
| 2:3 | 15 | 4:6 | 183-84 |
| 2:4 | 128, 131 | 4:6-7 | 184 |
| 2:6-7 | 28, 120 | 4:7-10 | 184 |
| 2:7 | 211 | 4:9 | 253 |
| 2:7-8 | 175 | 4:10 | 184 |
| 2:9-10 | 175 | 4:10-12 | 185 |
| 2:11-13 | 233 | 4:10-6:2 | 184 |
| 2:12 | 214 | 4:12 | 186, 211 |
| 2:12-13 | 296 | 4:12-13 | 211 |
| 2:13 | 214 | 4:12-19 | 186 |
| 2:14 | 8, 123, 142, 175, | 4:12-5:19 | 186 |
| | 298-99 | 4:19-20 | 188 |
| 2:14-15 | 124, 130, 176, | 4:19-5:19 | 188 |
| | 346 | 4:20-5:6 | 189 |
| 2:14-17 | 211 | 4:2-3 | 248 |
| 2:14-21 | 133 | 4:3 | 182 |
| 2:15 | 340 | 4:3-4 | 195 |
| 2:16 | 175 | 4:4-5 | 110, 179 |
| 2:16-17 | 175 | 4:7-13 | 145 |
| 2:17 | 211 | 4:8-10 | 146 |
| 2:18 | 212 | 4:9 | 181 |
| 3:2-3 | 256 | 4:9-10 | 251-52 |
| 3:4-12 | 122 | 4:10 | 231 |
| 3:5-7 | 267 | 4:12-19 | 187 |
| 3:6 | 175 | 4:12-5:19 | 117 |
| 3:7 | 9 | 4:14 | 151 |
| 3:8 | 15 | 4:14-18 | 238 |
| 3:12 | 176 | 4:14-19 | 189 |
| 3:12-15 | 339 | 4:15-5:10 | 132 |
| 3:12-4:7 | 177 | 4:16-18 | 226 |
| 3:12-4:10 | 176 | 4:17 | 225 |

| | | | |
|---|---|---|---|
| 4:17-18 | 371 | 6:3 | 217 |
| 4:19 | 243 | 6:4 | 218 |
| 4:19-7:5 | 34 | 6:4-8 | 116 |
| 4:20-22 | 289 | 6:4-11 | 238 |
| 4:20-5:2 | 76, 304 | 6:5 | 10, 182, 219, 248 |
| 4:21-5:1 | 204 | 6:6 | 219 |
| 5 | 209, 288 | 6:6-11 | 220 |
| 5:1-2 | 190-1 | 6:7 | 116 |
| 5:2 | 112 | 6:7-11 | 221, 238 |
| 5:2-4 | 192 | 6:9 | 218 |
| 5:2-5 | 127 | 6:11 | 215, 224 |
| 5:4-5 | 193, 262, 310 | 6:11-13 | 38 |
| 5:5 | 195, 310 | 6:11-14 | 222 |
| 5:5-6 | 197-98 | 6:13-14 | 222 |
| 5:6-7 | 201, 341 | 6:15 | 225 |
| 5:6-11 | 201 | 6:14 | 38, 223-24 |
| 5:7 | 203, 268 | 6:14-15 | 114, 139, 232 |
| 5:7-8 | 268 | 6:14-16 | 200 |
| 5:7-10 | 294, 297 | 6:14-7:5 | 224 |
| 5:7-11 | 205-06 | 6:16 | 225 |
| 5:9-10 | 206, 365 | 6:16-17 | 226 |
| 5:9-11 | 207 | 6:17-18 | 226 |
| 5:11-19 | 208 | 6:17-19 | 339-40 |
| 5:12 | 209 | 6:18 | 227, 268, 339 |
| 5:12-13 | 210 | 6:19 | 224, 229, 313 |
| 5:15 | 211 | 6:20 | 230, 293 |
| 5:15-19 | 211 | 6:20-21 | 256 |
| 5:16-17 | 212 | 6:21 | 230-31 |
| 5:18-19 | 212 | 6:21-22 | 232 |
| 5:20 | 212 | 6:21-7:2 | 289 |
| 5:20-6:2 | 212 | 7 | 229, 239 |
| 5:2-6 | 198 | 7:1 | 256 |
| 5:4-5 | 193-94 | 7:2 | 286, 289 |
| 5:6-19 | 189, 201 | 7:3 | 232, 343 |
| 5:9 | 195 | 7:4 | 233 |
| 5:11-13 | 208 | 7:4-6 | 172 |
| 5:13-15 | 210, 289 | 7:5 | 40, 233 |
| 5:15-16 | 22, 120 | 7:5-6 | 40, 217 |
| 5:16 | 36 | 7:5-8:21 | 141, 216 |
| 5:17-6:2 | 289 | 7:6 | 40, 213, 230, |
| 5:18 | 212 | | 234, 236 |
| 5:20 | 188, 211, 213, | 7:6-8 | 235 |
| | 215 | 7:6-9 | 202-03, 236 |
| 5:20-21 | 254 | 7:6-8:1 | 234, 236 |
| 5:20-6:2 | 120-21 | 7:6-8:21 | 40, 234 |
| 5:21 | 216, 296 | 7:7 | 16, 119, 235 |
| 5:21-6:1 | 213 | 7:9-10 | 40 |
| 6 | 239 | 7:9-8:1 | 237 |
| 6:1 | 255 | 7:11-12 | 348 |
| 6:2 | 213, 231, 252 | 7:13 | 177 |
| 6:2-11 | 215, 217, 237 | 7:13-14 | 237, 237 |
| 6:2-7:5 | 216-17 | 7:13-15 | 229 |

| | |
|---|---|
| 7:14-21 | 237, 237 |
| 7:15 | 239, 246 |
| 7:15-16 | 238 |
| 7:18-20 | 116 |
| 7:18-21 | 238 |
| 7:20 | 238 |
| 7:21 | 16, 42, 235, 367 |
| 8 | 243 |
| 8:1 | 16, 42 |
| 8:1-21 | 151, 240 |
| 8:2 | 42, 159 |
| 8:3 | 42, 241-43 |
| 8:4 | 43, 313 |
| 8:4-5 | 242 |
| 8:5-6 | 286 |
| 8:8 | 44 |
| 8:9 | 242 |
| 8:12 | 335 |
| 8:13 | 44, 151 |
| 8:14 | 44, 243 |
| 8:14-18 | 243 |
| 8:15 | 44 |
| 8:16-21 | 185 |
| 8:17 | 44 |
| 8:18 | 44 |
| 8:18-19 | 243 |
| 8:20-21 | 271 |
| 8:21 | 224, 244, 313 |
| 9-12:18 | 268 |
| 9 | 232, 295, 319, 321 |
| 9:1 | 225, 273, 300-01, 316, 318, 320, 357 |
| 9:1-11:2 | 82 |
| 9:1-14:17 | 141, 255 |
| 9:2 | 321 |
| 9:2-5 | 286 |
| 9:2-7 | 326 |
| 9:2-8 | 232 |
| 9:2-10 | 321 |
| 9:2-10:10 | 321 |
| 9:5 | 321 |
| 9:6 | 273, 323, 357 |
| 9:7 | 321, 323 |
| 9:7-8 | 232 |
| 9:10 | 323 |
| 9:10-16 | 227, 295, 324 |
| 9:13 | 308 |
| 9:13-14 | 75 |
| 9:13-16 | 295 |
| 9:14 | 308 |

| | |
|---|---|
| 9:16-10:3 | 325 |
| 9:23-10:1 | 323 |
| 9:23-10:2 | 326, 357 |
| 10-11 | 227 |
| 10 | 327, 345 |
| 10:2-3 | 17 |
| 10:4 | 268, 344 |
| 10:4-7 | 327 |
| 10:4-10 | 329, 326, 350 |
| 10:6 | 9, 255, 317, 329, 350 |
| 10:7-10 | 125, 312 |
| 10:10-13 | 329 |
| 10:12-13 | 327, 329 |
| 10:14 | 327-08, 339 |
| 10:14-17 | 207-08, 330 |
| 10:14-11:18 | 13, 230, 292, 330, 341 |
| 10:14-12:5 | 268 |
| 10:17-18 | 331, 358 |
| 10:18 | 339 |
| 10:18-21 | 331 |
| 10:21 | 334 |
| 10:22-11:2 | 332 |
| 10:22-13:2 | 237 |
| 11:2 | 332-33 |
| 11:3-4 | 333 |
| 11:3-11 | 88 |
| 11:4 | 334 |
| 11:4-5 | 334 |
| 11:5-6 | 332 |
| 11:5-9 | 334 |
| 11:9 | 335 |
| 11:9-10 | 335 |
| 11:10 | 339 |
| 11:10-11 | 336 |
| 11:11 | 336 |
| 11:12 | 305, 333, 336 |
| 11:12-18 | 90 |
| 11:13-14 | 337 |
| 11:14-15 | 337 |
| 11:15 | 337, 341 |
| 11:16 | 335 |
| 11:16-17 | 13, 337 |
| 11:17-18 | 338 |
| 11:18-12:6 | 340 |
| 11:19-14:2 | 90 |
| 11:19 | 338 |
| 11:21-12:1 | 340 |
| 11:22 | 218, 351 |
| 12 | 233 |
| 12:1 | 112, 201, 227 |

| | | | |
|---|---|---|---|
| 12:1-2 | 201 | 13:18-19 | 348 |
| 12:2 | 268, 295 | 13:19-20 | 348 |
| 12:2-3 | 290-92, 341 | 13:20-22 | 348 |
| 12:3-4 | 335, 341, 357 | 13:22 | 344 |
| 12:3-5 | 227-28, 273, | 13:22-23 | 263 |
| | 292, 340 | 13:22-14:2 | 348 |
| 12:4 | 13, 273, 340 | 14 | 351 |
| 12:6-11 | 337, 342 | 14:1-2 | 349 |
| 12:8 | 350 | 14:2 | 40, 234 |
| 12:8-10 | 342 | 14:3 | 344 |
| 12:8-11 | 284 | 14:3-7 | 231 |
| 12:10-11 | 231, 305, 333, | 14:3-10 | 327 |
| | 336, 342 | 14:3-12 | 349 |
| 12:11 | 233, 260, 333 | 14:3-21 | 96 |
| 12:11-18 | 343 | 14:4 | 295 |
| 12:15-17 | 344 | 14:7-8 | 9, 317 |
| 12:15-18 | 284 | 14:8-9 | 350 |
| 12:17-18 | 343 | 14:12 | 268, 344 |
| 12:19 | 351 | 14:12-14 | 276 |
| 12:19-20 | 203 | 14:12-17 | 13, 230-32 |
| 12:19-22 | 344 | 14:15 | 266 |
| 12:19-13:4 | 202 | 14:17 | 287 |
| 12:19-14:18 | 344 | 14:18 | 252, 286-87, |
| 12:20-21 | 263 | | 351, 357, 365 |
| 12:22 | 264, 268 | 14:18-19 | 98, 102, 109, |
| 12:22-13:2 | 345 | | 351, 352 |
| 12:22-13:3 | 327 | 14:18-23 | 141, 255, 348 |
| 12:22-14:18 | 344 | 14:19 | 10, 214, 255 |
| 12:23 | 111, 119 | 14:20 | 353 |
| 12:23-24 | 214 | 14:20-21 | 356 |
| 12:23-13:1 | 10, 255 | 14:20-22 | 352 |
| 12:23-13:7 | 271 | 14:21 | 353 |
| 13:2 | 9, 317, 350 | 14:21-22 | 356-57 |
| 13:2-7 | 345 | 14:22 | 357 |
| 13:7 | 344 | 15 | 78-9, 141, 168, |
| 13:7-10 | 346 | | 253, 255-56, |
| 13:7-14:18 | 346 | | 285, 287-88, |
| 13:3-6 | 285 | | 300-01, 306, |
| 13:3-7 | 271 | | 308, 313 |
| 13:4-7 | 302 | 15-16 | 141, 255, 268, |
| 13:5 | 346 | | 300 |
| 13:7 | 263, 268, 349 | 15:1 | 306 |
| 13:7-10 | 346 | 15:1-2 | 156 |
| 13:7-14:18 | 346 | 15:1-5 | 306 |
| 13:8 | 125 | 15:1-8 | 306 |
| 13:9 | 176, 256 | 15:1-16:6 | 306 |
| 13:10 | 346 | 15:1-16:22 | 225, 301, 306 |
| 13:11-14:12 | 347 | 15:2 | 183, 306-07, 325 |
| 13:12 | 114 | 15:2-3 | 306 |
| 13:14-15 | 347 | 15:3 | 291, 308 |
| 13:16-17 | 202-03, 347 | 15:3-5 | 227, 291, 324 |
| 13:17-18 | 130, 347 | 15:4 | 308 |

| | | | |
|---|---|---|---|
| 15:4-5 | 273 | CD-B | |
| 15:5 | 306 | *(Damascus Document)* | |
| 15:5-6 | 17, 307-08 | 19 40, 245 | |
| 15:5-16:6 | 316 | 19:1 | 234 |
| 15:7 | 119 | 19:1-2 | 217, 224, 234 |
| 15:7-10 | 309, 326 | 19:1-34 | 40, 141, 216 |
| 15:7-13 | 309 | 19:1-19:34 | 234 |
| 15:9 | 169 | 19:1-20:34 | 224 |
| 15:10-11 | 309 | 19:2 | 234, 236 |
| 15:11 | 286 | 19:2-4 | 235 |
| 15:12-13 | 310 | 19:2-5 | 203, 236 |
| 15:13 | 323 | 19:2-13 | 234 |
| 15:13-14 | 17, 195 | 19:3 | 211, 237 |
| 15:13-16:6 | 310 | 19:4 | 40, 119, 159, 235 |
| 15:15 | 80, 311 | 19:5-13 | 237 |
| 15:15-17 | 265 | 19:7 | 41 |
| 15:15-16:1 | 311 | 19:7-9 | 254 |
| 15:16-17 | 311 | 19:10 | 16, 235, 263, 367 |
| 15:18 | 312-3 | 19:10-11 | 10, 214, 255 |
| 15:19 | 312 | 19:13 | 54 |
| 15:19-20 | 313 | 19:13-33 | 151, 240 |
| 15:21 | 308 | 19:14 | 42 |
| 15:21-22 | 313 | 19:15-16 | 215, 242-3 |
| 16 | 80, 111, 316, 320 | 19:16 | 313 |
| 16:1-3 | 111, 168 | 19:16-17 | 43, 242 |
| 16:1-6 | 125, 313, 315, 367 | 19:18 | 44, 286 |
| | | 19:20 | 44 |
| 16:2-3 | 135, 149, 199, 228, 239, 310 | 19:22-20:1 | 116 |
| | | 19:23 | 44 |
| 16:2-4 | 292 | 19:26-31 | 243 |
| 16:3 | 135, 368 | 19:28-20:1 | 185 |
| 16:3-4 | 275 | 19:30 | 44 |
| 16:4 | 81 | 19:31-33 | 243 |
| 16:4-5 | 169 | 19:33 | 244 |
| 16:4-6 | 315-16 | 19:33-34 | 174, 313 |
| 16:6 | 256, 333, 342, 367 | 19:33-35 | 267 |
| | | 19:33-20:1 | 116 |
| 16:6-9 | 316 | 19:33-20:17 | 151, 240 |
| 16:6-22 | 316 | 19:34 | 224 |
| 16:8-9 | 273, 318 | 19:34-20:32 | 216 |
| 16:10-12 | 307, 317 | 19:34-20:34 | 46 |
| 16:13 | 98 | 19:35 | 165, 241, 245 |
| 16:13-17 | 318 | 19:35-20:1 | 241, 251 |
| 16:13-22 | 318 | 20 | 141, 252-53, 255-56, 285, 287-88 |
| 16:14-15 | 318 | | |
| 16:15-16 | 318 | | |
| 16:16-17 | 318 | 20:1 | 10, 214, 313 |
| 16:16-18 | 17 | 20:1-17 | 185, 245 |
| 16:17-22 | 319 | 20:1-32 | 141 |
| 16:18 | 308 | 20:2 | 268 |
| 16:18-19 | 323 | 20:3-6 | 245 |
| | | 20:5 | 268 |

| | | | |
|---|---|---|---|
| 20:6 | 110, 112 | 7:10-11 | 113 |
| 20:7 | 268 | 8:8-11 | 156 |
| 20:8-9 | 245 | 9:4-7 | 152, 222 |
| 20:8-10 | 149 | 9:8-12 | 157 |
| 20:10 | 351 | 10:5-13 | 161 |
| 20:12-15 | 241 | 10:9 | 152, 162 |
| 20:13-15 | 151, 164, 246 | 11:2-8 | 158 |
| 20:14 | 165, 245 | 11:5 | 154 |
| 20:14-15 | 244 | 11:6-8 | 154, 161 |
| 20:17 | 246 | 11:17-12:6 | 159 |
| 20:17-18 | 247 | 12:6-10 | 160 |
| 20:17-20 | 247 | 12:7-9 | 223 |
| 20:17-34 | 246 | | |
| 20:23 | 248-9 | | |
| 20:24 | 248 | 1Q27 | |
| 20:25 | 248 | (*Mysteries*) | |
| 20:28 | 245 | F1i:10-12 | 226 |
| 20:31 | 245 | F1i:7 | 346 |
| 20:33 | 251 | | |
| 20:20 | 307 | 1QS | |
| 20:20-22 | 248 | (*Rule of the Community*) | 2, 4, 10, 19, 102, |
| 20:22-27 | 248 | | 159, 308, 349, |
| 20:25-26 | 154, 313 | | 352-57, 360, 364 |
| 20:26-27 | 249 | 1:8 | 30 |
| 20:27 | 177, 249 | 1:9-10 | 113-14 |
| 20:27-28 | 249 | 2:4-5 | 367 |
| 20:27-32 | 249 | 2:11 | 288 |
| 20:32-33 | 72, 251-52 | 2:24 | 347 |
| 20:33 | 252 | 3:18 | 22 |
| 20:33-34 | 141, 251-52 | 3:20 | 212 |
| 20:34 | 291, 307 | 3:21 | 218 |
| | | 4:9 | 209 |
| | | 4:9-11 | 209 |
| 1Q14 | | 4:10 | 209 |
| (*Micah Pesher*) | | 4:11 | 209 |
| F8-10:8 | 163 | 4:12 | 28 |
| | | 5:1 | 218 |
| 1QpHab | | 5:1-3 | 218 |
| (*Habakkuk Pesher*) | 151, 152-56, | 5:2 | 155 |
| | 161, 163, 168, | 5:3 | 218 |
| | 170-72, 222, | 5:7 | 241 |
| | 229, 244 | 5:8 | 194 |
| 1:2-3 | 153 | 5:8-10 | 195 |
| 1:10-13 | 155 | 5:9 | 155, 194 |
| 1:11 | 161 | 5:10 | 194 |
| 2:1-2 | 152 | 6:4-6 | 282 |
| 2:5-10 | 157 | 6:8-9 | 349 |
| 2:7 | 152 | 6:10 | 358 |
| 5:8-12 | 152-53, 167 | 6:16-17 | 311 |
| 5:9 | 249 | 6:24 | 102, 110-11, 352 |
| 5:11 | 152 | 6:24-25 | 96 |
| 5:11-12 | 155 | 6:24-7:22 | 353-56 |
| 7:2 | 152 | 6:25 | 286 |

| | | | |
|---|---|---|---|
| 6:25-7:8 | 357 | 1:24 | 155 |
| 6:26 | 296 | 2:3 | 155, 311 |
| 6:27 | 291, 307 | 2:3-9 | 311 |
| 7:1-2 | 102 | 2:4 | 311 |
| 7:4 | 286 | 2:5 | 311 |
| 7:4-5 | 358 | 2:6 | 311 |
| 7:5 | 357, 360 | 2:7 | 311 |
| 7:5-6 | 102 | 2:8 | 311 |
| 7:5-8 | 357 | 2:8-9 | 80 |
| 7:8 | 286 | 2:9 | 311 |
| 7:8-16 | 100 | 2:17-22 | 282 |
| 7:8-21 | 351 | 2:18-19 | 278 |
| 7:9 | 331, 358 | 3:22 | 155 |
| 7:10 | 358 | | |
| 7:11 | 359 | **1QSb** | |
| 7:12 | 359 | 1:2 | 177 |
| 7:13 | 100, 360 | 5:27-29 | 251 |
| 7:14 | 56, 100 | | |
| 7:14-15 | 268 | **1QM** | |
| 7:15 | 286, 361 | (*War Scroll*) | 163 |
| 7:16 | 102 | 2:2-6 | 178 |
| 7:16-21 | 102 | 5:5-14 | 104 |
| 7:17 | 286, 364 | 11:7 | 255 |
| 7:17-18 | 360 | | |
| 7:18 | 102, 284, 286 | **1QHa** | |
| 7:19 | 103, 362 | (*Hodayot*[a]) | 127, 170 |
| 7:19-20 | 102, 362 | 1:2-3 | 153 |
| 7:22 | 102 | 5:8 | 346 |
| 7:22-24 | 363 | 7:19 | 30 |
| 7:22-25 | 357 | 9:21 | 346 |
| 7:24-25 | 363 | 10:13 | 346 |
| 7:17-18 | 102 | 10:14 | 218 |
| 7:19-20 | 102 | 12:12 | 218 |
| 8:14 | 195 | 12:16 | 218 |
| 8:14-16 | 195 | 12:20 | 218 |
| 8:15 | 195 | 15:27 | 346 |
| 8:16 | 195 | 18:5 | 132 |
| 9:5 | 340 | 18:18 | 218 |
| 9:11 | 255 | 19:10 | 346 |
| 9:18 | 346 | 20:8 | 136 |
| 9:26-10:6 | 129 | 21:12-13 | 127 |
| 10:2 | 130 | 26:1 | 177 |
| 10:6 | 136 | | |
| 10:8-9 | 276 | | |
| 11:15 | 346 | **4Q159** | |
| 11:18-19 | 127 | (*Ordinances*[a]) | 259, 261 |
| | | | |
| **1QSa** | 241, 289, 363 | **4Q161-165** | |
| 1:1 | 241 | (*Isaiah Pesher*[a-e]) | 10, 171 |
| 1:2 | 155 | | |
| 1:6-7 | 328 | **4Q161** | |
| 1:10-11 | 363 | (*Isaiah Pesher*[a]) | |
| 1:19-20 | 289 | F5-6:11 | 171 |

| | | | |
|---|---|---|---|
| F8-10:19 | 104 | 4Q177 | |
| F8-10:17-18 | 171-72 | (*Catena*ᵃ) | 168, 170, 246 |
| | | F1-4:12 | 111 |
| 4Q162 | | F1-4:13-14 | 168, 246 |
| (*Isaiah Pesher*ᵇ) | | | |
| F2:6-10 | 223 | 4Q249 | |
| F2:6-7 | 263 | (*Midrash Sefer Moshe*) | 116 |
| 4Q163 | | 4Q251 | |
| (*Isaiah Pesher*ᶜ) | | (*Halakha A*) | |
| F23ii:10 | 288 | F16 | 305 |
| | | F17:2-3 | 206 |
| 4Q164 | | | |
| (*Isaiah Pesher*ᵈ) | | 4Q252 | |
| F1:4-5 | 212 | F2:2-30 | 311 |
| 4Q165 | | 4Q258 | |
| (*Isaiah Pesher*ᵉ) | | (*Rule of the Community*ᵈ) | |
| F1-2:3 | 171 | F1:1-2 | 113 |
| | | F9:3 | 129 |
| 4Q169 | | | |
| (*Nahum Pesher*) | 3, 170-71, 209, | 4Q266-273 | |
| | 223, 248, 288 | (*Damascus Document*ᵃ⁻ʰ) | xix, xx, 12, 22, |
| F3-4i:2 | 288 | | 118, 252 |
| F3-4i:7 | 288 | | |
| F3-4i:11-12 | 223 | 4Q266 | |
| F3-4ii:2 | 288 | (*Damascus Document*ᵃ) | 15, 22, 38, 56, |
| F3-4ii:4 | 288 | | 104, 109, 120, |
| F3-4ii:8 | 162, 170, 209 | | 35, 138, 236, |
| F3-4ii:8-10 | 115 | | 269, 351, 367 |
| F3-4iii:3 | 173, 288 | F1(a-b) | 128, 132 |
| F3-4iv:1 | 249 | F1(a-b):20 | 128 |
| | | F1(a-b):25 | 128 |
| 4Q171 | | F1(c-f) | 128, 132 |
| (*Psalms Pesher*ᵃ) | 163 | F1(c-f):3-4 | 132 |
| F1-2i:17-ii:1 | 166 | F1(c-f):5 | 133 |
| F1-2ii:5-8 | 164, 244-45 | F1-2i:1 | 23 |
| F1:2ii:6-8 | 165 | F1 | 22, 109, 134 |
| F1-2ii:8-10 | 228 | F1:1 | 113, 136, 138, |
| F1-2ii:8-11 | 164 | | 200, 347 |
| F1-2ii:9 | 166 | F1:1-2 | 11, 139, 199- |
| F1+3-4iii:10 | 166 | | 201, 224, 232 |
| F1+3-4iii:14-19 | 166 | F1:1-3 | 109 |
| F3-10iv | 168 | F1:1-5 | 122 |
| F3-10iv:7-10 | 167 | F1:2 | 119, 136, 140, |
| F3-10iv:13-14 | 168 | | 367 |
| F3-10iv:26-27 | 169 | F1:2-3 | 139 |
| F11:1 | 169 | F1:3 | 119-20, 140, 159 |
| | | F1:3-5 | 119-20, 139 |
| 4Q173 | | F1:4 | 120, 159, 188, |
| (*Psalms Pesher*ᵇ) | 163 | | 215, 288 |
| F1:2-5 | 169 | F1:4-5 | 136 |
| F2:2 | 169 | | |

| | | | |
|---|---|---|---|
| F1:5 | 120, 122, 127, 130, 298, 346 | F2ii:14 | 30 |
| | | F2ii:15 | 30 |
| F1:5-6 | 119, 142, 176, 366 | F2ii:20 | 30 |
| | | F2ii:21 | 30 |
| F1:5-7 | 123, 140 142 | F2iii | 184 |
| F1:5-9 | 122 | F3i:3 | 145 |
| F1:6 | 177 | F3ii | 34 |
| F1:6-7 | 125, 126, 137 | F3ii:3 | 36 |
| F1:7 | 140 | F3ii:7 | 36 |
| F1:7-8 | 128, 131 | F3ii:7-9 | 120 |
| F1:7-9 | 140 | F3ii:8 | 36 |
| F1:8 | 128, 137 | F3ii:18 | 38 |
| F1:8-9 | 126-7, 193 | F3ii:21 | 224 |
| F1:9 | 122, 128 | F3iii:4-6 | 34 |
| F1:9-13 | 128 | F3iii:17 | 42 |
| F1:9-14 | 128 | F3iii:18-25 | 40 |
| F1:10-14 | 128-29 | F3iii:21 | 42 |
| F1:10-15 | 122 | F3iii:23 | 42 |
| F1:14 | 129 | F3iii:24 | 42 |
| F1:14-25 | 129 | F3iii:25-3iv:1 | 42 |
| F1:15-18 | 130 | F3iii:25-iv:1 | 241-42 |
| F1:16-17 | 361 | F3iv:1 | 43 |
| F1:16-18 | 119, 366 | F3iv:2 | 43 |
| F1:17-18 | 12, 131, 140 | F4 | 141, 216, 224, 246, 249, 252-53 |
| F1:18-25 | 130 | | |
| F1:19 | 130-31 | F4:7 | 252 |
| F1:19-25 | 119 | F4:7-8 | 50 |
| F1:20 | 130, 134 | F4:9 | 251 |
| F1:21 | 131-32 | F4:9-13 | 49, 252 |
| F1:22 | 132 | F4:10-13 | 253-54, 256 |
| F1:23 | 132, 159 | F4:11 | 346 |
| F1:24 | 133 | F5i(c-d) | 54-55, 263-64 |
| F1:25 | 133-34 | F5i | 52-3, 252, 262 |
| F2 | 134 | F5i:1 | 261, 301 |
| F2:6 | 141 | F5i:1-2 | 260 |
| F2i:1 | 135, 22, 25 | F5i:5 | 262 |
| F2i:1-6 | 24, 109, 234 | F5i:5-17 | 262 |
| F2i:2 | 15, 26 | F5i:8 | 262, 310 |
| F2i:3 | 26, 298 | F5i:8-9 | 195 |
| F2i:5 | 137 | F5i:9 | 291, 307 |
| F2i:6-25 | 26 | F5i:11-12 | 262 |
| F2i:18-20 | 150 | F5i:13 | 263 |
| F2i:19 | 150 | F5i:13-14 | 285 |
| F2i:22 | 28 | F5i:14-17 | 110 |
| F2i:24 | 177 | F5i:15-16 | 248 |
| F2ii:1-2 | 26 | F5i:15-17 | 182, 263 |
| F2ii:2-24 | 28 | F5i:16 | 155, 368 |
| F2ii:4 | 28 | F5i:16-17 | 110, 262 |
| F2ii:5-6 | 28 | F5i:17 | 110, 262-63 |
| F2ii:6 | 28 | F5i:17-18 | 344 |
| F2ii:11 | 233 | F5i:17-19 | 263 |
| F2ii:13 | 30 | F5i:18 | 264 |

| | | | |
|---|---|---|---|
| F5ii | 54-5 | F6iii:3-7 | 277 |
| F5ii:1-4 | 264 | F6iii:3-10 | 276 |
| F5ii:1-3 | 358 | F6iii:4 | 274 |
| F5ii:2-3 | 264 | F6iii:4-5 | 277 |
| F5ii:3 | 56, 273 | F6iii:6-7 | 277 |
| F5ii:3-4 | 265 | F6iii:7-8 | 277 |
| F5ii:5-7 | 266 | F6iii:7-10 | 230, 277 |
| F5ii:5-14 | 266 | F6iii:8 | 278 |
| F5ii:5-16 | 264 | F6iii:10 | 66 |
| F5ii:9-11 | 267 | F6iv(a) | 278 |
| F5ii:11-14 | 267 | F6iv(a):1-2 | 280 |
| F5ii:14 | 268 | F6iv(a):1-3 | 12 |
| F5ii:14-15 | 268 | F6iv(a):2 | 281 |
| F5ii:14-17 | 268 | F6iv | 66, 230, 274, |
| F5ii:16-17 | 268 | | 278, 293 |
| F6i(a-e) | 60-1, 272 | F6iv:1-3 | 279 |
| F6i(c) | 272 | F6iv:2 | 279, 294 |
| F6i | 58, 295 | F6iv:3 | 275, 279 |
| F6i:1-5 | 270 | F6iv:3-8 | 279 |
| F6i:1-13 | 230 | F6iv:4 | 279 |
| F6i:1-ii:13 | 269-70 | F6iv:4-5 | 279 |
| F6i:2 | 58 | F6iv:5-6 | 280 |
| F6i:3 | 58 | F6iv:7 | 279 |
| F6i:5-13 | 269-70 | F6iv:7-8 | 280 |
| F6i:6-7 | 58 | F6iv:8 | 279, 281 |
| F6i:8 | 59 | F7 | 71, 253, 285 |
| F6i:9 | 60 | F7i-iii | 70 |
| F6i:11 | 60 | F7i:3-4 | 287 |
| F6i:12 | 60 | F7i:4-5 | 286 |
| F6i:14-15 | 203, 230, 270, | F7i:4-14 | 360 |
| | 272 | F7i:14-15 | 361 |
| F6i:15 | 203 | F7ii | 70, 286 |
| F6ii(a):1 | 62 | F7ii:7 | 286 |
| F6ii | 58, 63, 274 | F7ii:9 | 286 |
| F6ii:1-2 | 272 | F7ii:10 | 286 |
| F6ii:1-4 | 268, 270, 272 | F7iii:1 | 286 |
| F6ii:3-4 | 273 | F7iii:3-4 | 287 |
| F6ii:5-9 | 273 | F7iii:5 | 287 |
| F6ii:5-13 | 270, 273 | F8i | 78, 265 |
| F6ii:6 | 315 | F8i:2 | 78 |
| F6ii:9-10 | 273 | F8i:3-4 | 323 |
| F6ii:10 | 273 | F8i:7 | 311 |
| F6ii:11 | 273 | F8i:8-9 | 311 |
| F6ii:12-13 | 320 | F8i:9 | 80 |
| F6iii(a-b) | 274 | F8ii:1-8 | 80 |
| F6iii(a-b)-iii:3 | 275 | F8ii:4 | 319 |
| F6iii(a) | 274 | F8ii:6 | 320 |
| F6iii(a):2 | 275 | F8ii:7 | 320 |
| F6iii(b) | 274 | F8ii:8 | 320 |
| F6iii-iv | 67 | F8ii:8-9 | 320 |
| F6iii | 64-5, 274, 276, | F8ii:8-iii:10 | 80 |
| | 278 | F8iii:8 | 125 |

| | |
|---|---|
| F9i:1-4 | 90 |
| F9i:16-17 | 90 |
| F9ii | 90 |
| F9ii:14 | 94 |
| F9iii | 90 |
| F9iii:4 | 98 |
| F9iii:5 | 94 |
| F9iii:6 | 94, 98 |
| F9iii:11 | 96, 98, 348 |
| F9iii:12 | 96 |
| F9iii:18 | 96 |
| F10:9-10 | 359 |
| F10i | 90, 96, 230, 357 |
| F10i:3 | 98 |
| F10i:11 | 286, 365 |
| F10i:12 | 98, 112 |
| F10i:18-25 | 99 |
| F10i:25 | 100-01 |
| F10ii | 100-01, 348, 357, 359, 361 |
| F10ii-11 | 351 |
| F10ii:1-2 | 273, 357 |
| F10ii:1-8 | 141, 255 |
| F10ii:1-15 | 298, 351-52, 354-55 |
| F10ii:2-3 | 102, 358 |
| F10ii:3 | 331 |
| F10ii:3-4 | 358 |
| F10ii:4 | 100 |
| F10ii:4-5 | 358 |
| F10ii:5-6 | 358 |
| F10ii:6-7 | 358 |
| F10ii:7 | 359 |
| F10ii:7-9 | 359 |
| F10ii:8-15 | 141, 255 |
| F10ii:10 | 355, 360 |
| F10ii:10-12 | 360 |
| F10ii:11-12 | 360 |
| F10ii:12 | 56, 100, 355 |
| F10ii:12-12 | 268 |
| F10ii:12-13 | 360 |
| F10ii:13 | 355 |
| F10ii:13-14 | 361 |
| F10ii:14 | 355 |
| F10ii:14-15 | 361 |
| F11 | 104-05, 240 |
| F11:1-3 | 141, 255, 298, 348, 365 |
| F11:3 | 286 |
| F11:3-18 | 366 |
| F11:3-21 | 365 |
| F11:5-6 | 119 |

| | |
|---|---|
| F11:9 | 119, 366 |
| F11:9-14 | 119, 130, 366 |
| F11:16-18 | 119, 130 |
| F11:16-21 | 240 |
| F11:17-18 | 263, 315-16, 367 |
| F11:18 | 252, 287 |
| F11:18-19 | 109 |
| F11:18-21 | 344, 367 |
| F11:19 | 367 |
| F11:20-21 | 11, 110 |
| F12 | 76, 141, 255, 285, 300, 370 |
| F12:1-2 | 303 |
| F12:1-4 | 301 |
| F12:4 | 76 |
| F12:5-6 | 76 |
| F12:5-9 | 304 |
| F12:8 | 342 |
| F13-75 | 369-75 |
| F14d:1 | 206 |
| F34 | 34, 369, 371 |
| | |
| 4Q267 | |
| (*Damascus Document^b*) | 56, 109, 138, 258 |
| F1 | 130 |
| F1-4 | 289 |
| F1:1-8 | 22 |
| F1:4 | 132 |
| F1:5 | 132 |
| F1:6 | 133 |
| F1:7 | 25, 133-34 |
| F1:8 | 134 |
| F2 | 34, 134 |
| F2:4-7 | 120 |
| F2:5 | 120, 216 |
| F2:6 | 214, 255 |
| F2:7 | 213 |
| F2:12 | 38 |
| F3 | 249 |
| F3:2 | 81 |
| F4 | 72-3, 287-89 |
| F4:2-15 | 72 |
| F4:4 | 72 |
| F4:9-11 | 289 |
| F4:10 | 290 |
| F4:10-11 | 290 |
| F4:11 | 290 |
| F4:11-12 | 73, 289 |
| F4:11-15 | 205, 289 |
| F5ii | 52 |
| F5ii:5 | 341 |

| | | | |
|---|---|---|---|
| F5iii | 54 | F2:2 | 97 |
| F5iii:1-2 | 54-5, 264 | F3 | 376 |
| F5iii:2 | 264 | | |
| F5iii:5-6 | 56 | 4Q269 | |
| F5iii:6 | 56 | (*Damascus Document*ᵈ) | 58, 104, 376 |
| F6:1-6 | 64 | F1-2 | 28 |
| F6:2 | 277 | F2:1-2 | 32 |
| F6:7 | 66 | F2:2 | 15 |
| F7 | 50, 255-56 | F3-4 | 34 |
| F7:1-2 | 141, 224 | F4ii:3 | 38 |
| F7:1-3 | 50-1 | F5 | 40 |
| F7:3 | 141, 252, 257 | F6 | 40 |
| F7:4-14 | 50 | F7 | 58, 295 |
| F7:6 | 258 | F8:3 | 283 |
| F8 | 70 | F8i-ii | 68 |
| F8:1-2 | 286 | F9 | 50 |
| F8:2 | 286 | F9:1-2 | 259 |
| F9i | 82 | F9:5 | 226 |
| F9i:1 | 321 | F10i-ii:8 | 90 |
| F9ii:2-3 | 88 | F10ii:4 | 96 |
| F9ii:8 | 90 | F10ii:9-12 | 96 |
| F9iii | 90 | F11i:7 | 100 |
| F9iv | 90 | F11i:8 | 102 |
| F9iv:5 | 346 | F11i:8-ii | 351 |
| F9v:1-6 | 90 | F11i:8-ii:2 | 100 |
| F9v:2 | 234 | F11ii | 56, 100 |
| F9v:4 | 40, 96 | F12-14 | 376 |
| F9v:5 | 96, 349 | F15:1 | 56, 100 |
| F9v:6-14 | 96 | F16 | 104 |
| F9v:12 | 86, 97 | F16:16-19 | 110 |
| F9vi | 102 | | |
| F10-18 | 375-6 | 4Q270 | |
| | | (*Damascus Document*ᵉ) | 104, 274, 299, |
| 4Q268 | | | 303, 321, 376 |
| (*Damascus Document*ᶜ) | 15, 25, 109, 135, | F1i | 28 |
| | 138, 144, 376 | F1i:2-3 | 30 |
| F1 | 25, 131, 134 | F1ii(a) | 28 |
| F1:1 | 133, 135 | F1ii(b) | 28 |
| F1:1-3 | 314 | F2 | 253, 287, 289, |
| F1:1-8 | 24, 134, 140 | | 298-99 |
| F1:2-3 | 144, 148-9, 175 | F2i-ii | 72-3, 252 |
| F1:3 | 135, 147 | F2i | 253, 288-89 |
| F1:3-5 | 137 | F2i:1-3 | 252 |
| F1:4 | 15, 135, 177 | F2i:1-14 | 287 |
| F1:4-5 | 228 | F2i:6 | 252 |
| F1:5 | 298 | F2i:7 | 289 |
| F1:5-8 | 137 | F2i:7-20 | 205, 289 |
| F1:8 | 30, 137, 256 | F2i:8 | 290 |
| F1:9 | 123-4, 127 | F2i:9-12 | 341 |
| F1:9-17 | 26 | F2i:9-ii:18 | 290 |
| F1:12 | 16, 148 | F2i:10 | 289-91 |
| F2 | 96 | F2i:11 | 291, 307-08 |

| | | | |
|---|---|---|---|
| F2i:12 | 290 | F3i:20 | 275 |
| F2i:13 | 273 | F3i:21 | 274 |
| F2i:13-16 | 291 | F3ii(a) | 66-7, 274, 276- |
| F2i:15-21 | 287 | | 77 |
| F2i:16-17 | 292 | F3ii:1 | 64, 277 |
| F2i:17 | 290 | F3ii:12 | 274 |
| F2i:18-20 | 292, 341 | F3ii:12-16 | 64 |
| F2i:19-20 | 341 | F3ii:15 | 277 |
| F2ii | 132, 293 | F3ii:17-19 | 278 |
| F2ii:1-14 | 293 | F3ii:17-21 | 65-6, 274, 276- |
| F2ii:1-21 | 287 | | 77 |
| F2ii:2-3 | 293 | F3ii:17-3ii(a) | 230 |
| F2ii:5-6 | 293 | F3ii:19 | 278 |
| F2ii:5-10 | 293-94 | F3ii:19-21 | 278 |
| F2ii:7 | 294 | F3iii | 66, 281 |
| F2ii:9-10 | 295 | F3iii:12-13 | 69 |
| F2ii:10 | 295 | F3iii:13 | 68, 281 |
| F2ii:10-11 | 271, 293 | F3iii:13-21 | 68 |
| F2ii:11-12 | 293 | F3iii:14 | 181 |
| F2ii:12 | 295 | F3iii:19 | 102, 283, 352 |
| F2ii:13 | 293 | F4 | 76-7, 141, 255, |
| F2ii:13-15 | 293 | | 285, 300, 306 |
| F2ii:15 | 293-94 | F4:1 | 302, 306 |
| F2ii:15-16 | 294 | F4:1-2 | 303 |
| F2ii:15-17 | 293 | F4:1-13 | 230, 300, 301, |
| F2ii:18 | 295 | | 306, 325 |
| F2ii:5-10 | 293 | F4:2 | 301 |
| F2ii:9-10 | 227, 271, 308, | F4:3-4 | 301 |
| | 324 | F4:4 | 302 |
| F2ii:10 | 295 | F4:4-5 | 301 |
| F2ii:10-11 | 295 | F4:5 | 302 |
| F2ii:12 | 271 | F4:6 | 306 |
| F2ii:13 | 295 | F4:9-11 | 303 |
| F2ii:13-15 | 296 | F4:12 | 303 |
| F2ii:14 | 214 | F4:13 | 76 |
| F2ii:15 | 296 | F4:13-21 | 300, 303-04 |
| F2ii:15-16 | 204 | F4:15 | 305 |
| F2ii:15-17 | 297 | F4:15-16 | 342 |
| F2ii:15-19 | 289 | F4:16-18 | 261, 305 |
| F2ii:15-21 | 293 | F4:20 | 305 |
| F2ii:16-18 | 206 | F4:20-21 | 305 |
| F2ii:16 | 206, 268 | F4:21 | 268, 305 |
| F2ii:17 | 206 | F5 | 50 |
| F2ii:17-18 | 205, 298 | F5:14-17 | 259 |
| F2ii:18 | 206 | F5:19 | 226 |
| F2ii:19 | 142, 287, 289 | F6i:20-ii:10 | 78 |
| F2ii:19-20 | 124, 142 | F6ii:9 | 311 |
| F2ii:19-21 | 298, 301 | F6ii:9-10 | 80 |
| F3i | 275 | F6ii:17-21 | 80 |
| F3i:17-21 | 64-5, 274 | F6iii:14 | 318, 320 |
| F3i:19 | 275 | F6iii:16 | 320 |
| F3i:19-21 | 274 | F6iii:20-21 | 321, 323 |
| | | F6iv:17 | 86 |

| | | | |
|---|---|---|---|
| F6iv:18 | 86 | F2:2-3 | 281 |
| F6iv:19 | 125 | F2:3 | 281 |
| F6v:12-16 | 86 | F2:10 | 284 |
| F6v:16-21 | 90 | F2:10-11 | 284 |
| F6v:17 | 333 | F2:11-13 | 285 |
| F6v:18 | 90 | F2:4-5 | 282 |
| F6v:20 | 90 | F2:6-7 | 260, 282 |
| F7 | 351 | F2:7 | 102, 283, 352 |
| F7:11-12 | 363 | F2:8-14 | 284 |
| F7i:1-6 | 100, 141, 255 | F2:13 | 281 |
| F7i:1-17 | 348 | F3 | 50-1, 255, 257, |
| F7i:2 | 359 | | 259, 261 |
| F7i:4 | 100 | F3:1 | 257 |
| F7i:6 | 355 | F3:1-3 | 257 |
| F7i:6-7 | 361 | F3:3 | 258 |
| F7i:6-8 | 361 | F3:3-4 | 259 |
| F7i:6-15 | 352, 354-55, 361 | F3:4-10 | 259 |
| F7i:6-16 | 102, 298, 351 | F3:5 | 252, 259 |
| F7i:6-17 | 141, 255 | F3:6-7 | 259 |
| F7i:7 | 355 | F3:7 | 259 |
| F7i:7-8 | 360-1 | F3:9 | 259-60 |
| F7i:8 | 102, 284, 355 | F3:9-10 | 282 |
| F7i:8-10 | 362 | F3:10 | 260 |
| F7i:6-16 | 103 | F3:10-16 | 260 |
| F7i:11 | 356, 363 | F3:11-13 | 292 |
| F7i:11-15 | 102 | F3:12 | 226 |
| F7i:12 | 356 | F3:15 | 261, 305 |
| F7i:12-13 | 363 | F4i:4 | 78 |
| F7i:13 | 356 | F4i:4-ii:3 | 78 |
| F7i:13-15 | 364 | F4ii:1 | 313 |
| F7i:15-16 | 365 | F4ii:1-3 | 313 |
| F7i:16 | 365 | F4ii:2 | 313 |
| F7i:16-21 | 104 | F4ii:3-17 | 80 |
| F7i:18 | 104 | F4ii:4 | 81 |
| F7i:19 | 104 | F4ii:6 | 81 |
| F7ii | 240 | F4ii:8 | 81 |
| F7ii:12 | 252, 287, 367 | F4ii:9-10 | 82 |
| F7ii:12-13 | 109 | F4ii:12 | 82 |
| F7ii:14-15 | 11, 106 | F4ii:15-16 | 318 |
| F7ii:15 | 110 | F5i:1 | 334 |
| F8-12 | 376-77 | F5i:1-7 | 88 |
| | | F5i:7 | 90, 336 |
| 4Q271 | | F5i:7-12 | 90 |
| (*Damascus Document*ᶠ) | 292 | F5i:13-21 | 90 |
| F1 | 34 | | |
| F1:2 | 36 | 4Q272 | |
| F2 | 68, 69, 281 | (*Damascus Document*ᵍ) | 269, 377 |
| F2:1 | 281 | F1 | 295 |
| F2:1-3 | 277, 281 | F1i-ii | 58-9, 269-70 |
| F2:1-5 | 276 | F1i:1-13 | 270 |
| F2:1-7 | 274 | F1i:1-ii:2 | 230, 269 |
| F2:2 | 181, 281 | F1ii:3-7 | 270, 272 |

F1ii:3-18          230, 268, 272
F1ii:4-5           271
F1ii:5             272-73
F1ii:7             272
F1ii:7-8           62
F1ii:7-18          270, 272
F1i:14-ii:2        269-70
F1i:16             59
F2-3               377

4Q273
(*papDamascus Document*[h]) 58, 300, 377
F1                 52, 262
F1:1               262
F2                 54
F2:1               264
F3                 54
F3:1               273
F4i                54
F4i:9              56, 268
F4ii               58, 295
F5                 76, 77, 300, 303-
                   04
F5:2-4             300-01, 303, 306
F5:2-5             303
F5:3-4             303
F5:4               304
F5:4-5             300
F5:5               304
F7-9               377

4Q287
F2:5               104
F2:8               218
F10:13             255

4Q298              122
F1-2i:1            94

4Q301
F4:3               132

4Q317-334          3

4Q320-330          178

4Q390
(*Apocryphon of Jeremiah
C*[e])
F1:7               227
F1:7-8             227
F1:8               227

4Q394-399
(4QMMT[a-f])       280, 293, 294

4Q394
(4QMMT[a])
F8iii:7-9          297
F8iv:9-10          203
F8iv:12-13         280, 294

4Q396
(4QMMT[c])
F1-2i:3-4          297
F1-2iii:2-3        280, 294
F1-2iv:5-11        283

4Q397
(4QMMT[d])         239
F4:2               297
F6-13:4-5          280, 294
F14-21:10          239
F14-21:11          299

4Q400-407
(*Songs of the Sabbath
Sacrifice*[a-h])    130

4Q400
(*Songs of the Sabbath
Sacrifice*[a])
F1:2               218

4Q403
(*Songs of the Sabbath
Sacrifice*[d])
F1i:33             218
F1ii:1             104

4Q405
(*Songs of the Sabbath
Sacrifice*[f])
F14-15i:3-6        104
F19:5              104
F20ii-22:11        104
F23ii:7            104

4Q415-418          133-34, 317

4Q416
F2:4-5             148
F2iv:6-9           317

| | | | |
|---|---|---|---|
| 4Q417 | 328-29 | 4Q545 | |
| F1i:2 | 346 | (*Testament of Amram*) | |
| F1i:13 | 346 | F1(a-b)ii:16 | 342, 350 |
| F1i:13-18 | 247 | | |
| F1i:16-17:52 | 133 | 5Q12 | |
| F1i:17-18 | 299 | (*Damascus Document*) | xix, 19 |
| F2i:2-3 | 347 | F1 82 | |
| | | F1:1 | 321, 323 |
| 4Q418 | | | |
| F43-45i:13 | 86 | 6Q15 | |
| F81+81a:17 | 133 | (*Damascus Document*) | xix, 19 |
| F81:2 | 200 | F1-4 | 34 |
| F103ii:6-9 | 282-83 | F3:4 | 214, 255 |
| F218:2 | 346 | F3:5 | 213 |
| | | F5 | 72, 287, 289, 293 |
| 4Q427 | | F5:4 | 74, 289 |
| (*Hodayot*[a]) | | F5:5 | 74, 289 |
| F7i:18-19 | 127 | | |
| F8ii:14 | 136 | 11Q5 | |
| | | (11QPs[a]) | |
| 4Q491 | | 22:3-6 | 299 |
| (*War Scroll*[a]) | | 27:2-10 | 130 |
| F11i:11 | 163 | 27:10 | 199 |
| F11i:21 | 329 | 27:11 | 239 |
| | | | |
| 4Q504 | | 11Q13 | |
| Fragments | | (*Melchizedek*) | 258 |
| F1-2 recto v:4 | 32 | 2:2-6 | 51 |
| | | 2:5-6 | 258 |
| 4Q508 | | 2:6257 | |
| F2:3 | 228 | | |
| | | 11QT | |
| 4Q509 | | (*Temple Scroll*) | 110, 138-39, |
| F16:3 | 228 | | 142-43, 174, |
| | | | 184, 191, 196- |
| 4Q510 | | | 97, 199, 201-04, |
| F1:7-8 | 228 | | 225, 229, 246, |
| | | | 262, 264, 269- |
| 4Q511 | | | 70, 272, 296, |
| F8:5 | 228 | | 305, 314 |
| F10:4 | 228 | 48:15 | 269 |
| F10:6 | 228 | 53:16-54:5 | 317 |
| F44-47:6 | 346 | 56-57 | 196 |
| F121:2 | 228 | 63:14-15 | 305 |
| F126:2 | 132 | | |
| | | PAM | |
| 4Q513 | | 42:398 | 100, 274 |
| F3-4:5 | 197 | 43:692 F80:1 | 218 |
| | | 43:295 | 274 |

## Pseudepigrapha

| *Jubilees* | xix, 4, 11-12, | 23:26 | 126 |
| | 13, 109-11, 115, | 23:26-27 | 126 |
| | 117-18, 126-27, | 50 | 330, 340 |
| | 134-39, 42-43, | 50:1-13 | 227 |
| | 148-49, 168, | 50:5 | 227 |
| | 174, 176, 178, | 50:8 | 13, 227, 292, |
| | 183-84, 194, | | 335, 337 |
| | 196, 199, 209- | 50:9 | 332 |
| | 10, 218, 227-29, | 50:10 | 330, 338-39 |
| | 239, 246, 255, | 50:12 | 334-5 |
| | 262, 264, 270, | 50:13 | 11, 110 |
| | 275-76, 278-78, | | |
| | 310, 313-16, | *Enoch* | 4-5, 13, 126, |
| | 330, 339, 346, | | 139, 174, 176, |
| | 352, 367-68 | | 178, 183, 229, |
| 1 | 149 | | 346, 352 |
| 1-6 | 125 | | |
| 1:1 | 148, 367 | *1 Enoch* | 207 |
| 1:4 | 11, 110, 136, | 72 | 208 |
| | 148 | 72:2-37 | 331 |
| 1:10 | 227 | 72:4 | 207 |
| 1:12-13 | 148-9 | 76 | 271 |
| 1:26 | 136, 144, 148 | 91:13 | 179 |
| 2 | 124, 299, 330, | | |
| | 340 | *2 Baruch* | |
| 2:29-30 | 335 | 84:5 | 243 |
| 2:31-33 | 227 | | |
| 6 | 129 | *Ben Sira* | |
| 6:32 | 136 | 51:12 | 8 |
| 6:38 | 175, 267 | | |
| 7:35-37 | 278 | *Book of the Giants* | 176 |
| 7:36 | 279-80 | | |
| 15 | 315-16 | *Genesis Apocryphon* | 176 |
| 15:1 | 315 | | |
| 22:24 | 179 | *Testament of Levi* | 186-87, 238 |
| 23 | 125-6 | | |
| 23:8-9 | 126, 313 | *The Testaments of the* | |
| 23:12 | 312 | *Twelve Patriarchs* | 187 |

## Mishnah

| *Sukkah* | | *Avot* | 189 |
| 4:5 | 366 | 1:1 | 121 |
| | | | |
| *Qiddushin* | | *Yadaim* | |
| 4:1 | 349 | 4:7 | 329-30 |

## Talmud

*Bavli Hullin*
78:2                    296
137                     277

*Bavli Shebu'ot*
27                      316

*Bavli Menahot*
85                      212

## Other Ancient Sources

*Avot d'Rabbi Natan*    197
5                       5, 197

*Bava Metzi'a*
4:1-2                   260
4:3-12                  259

*Derekh Eretz Zuta*     268

Maimonides
*Gifts for the Poor*
7:5                     278

*Hilchot Teshuvah*
3:8                     8

Josephus
*Jewish War*
2:120                   14

2:159                   135
2:160                   240
3:142                   295

*pergCfr*
1-7                     6

*Rambam Hilchot Isurei Biah*
I 9                     364

*Talmud Torah*
1:8-9                   265-66

*Tosefta Eruvin*
3(4):5                  337

*Tosefta Shabbat*
16(17):13               335

## New Testament

Matthew
5:22                    89
23                      209

Romans
9:19                    219

2 Corinthians
6:14                    260

2 Timothy
3:8                     212

1 John
3:1                     346